AMERICAN NATIONS

AMERICAN NATIONS

ENCOUNTERS IN
INDIAN COUNTRY,
1850 TO THE PRESENT

Edited by FREDERICK E. HOXIE, PETER C. MANCALL,
and JAMES H. MERRELL

Routledge
New York and London

Published in 2001 by
Routledge
29 West 35th Street
New York, NY 10001

Published in Great Britain by
Routledge
11 New Fetter Lane
London EC4P 4EE

Routledge is an imprint of the Taylor & Francis Group.

Copyright © 2001 by Routledge

Printed in the United States of America on acid-free paper.

10   9   8   7   6   5   4   3   2   1

Library of Congress Cataloging-in-Publication Data

American Nations : encounters in Indian country, 1850 to the present / [collected by] Frederick E. Hoxie, Peter C. Mancall, and James H. Merrell.
     p. cm.
    Includes bibliographical references and index.
    ISBN   0-415-92749-8 — ISBN 0-415-92750-1 (pbk : alk. paper)
    1. Indians of North America—History. I. Hoxie, Frederick E. 1947–   II. Mancall, Peter C. III. Merrell, James Hart, 1953–

E77.2 A.476 2001
970.004'97—dc21   00-068420

To our students—past, present, and future

Contents

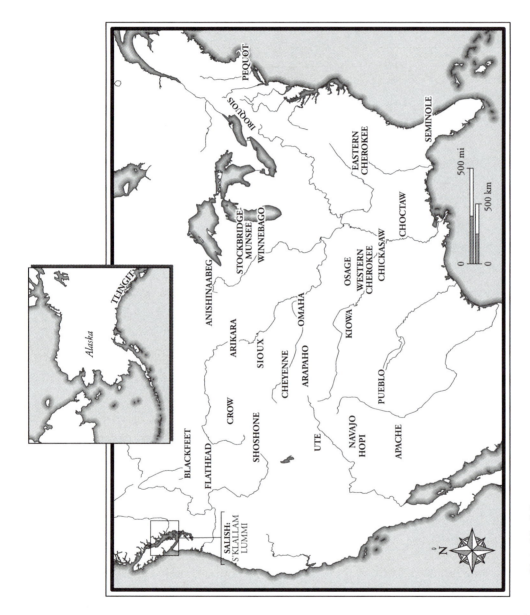

Native North America

Introduction

In a world where popular music divides the public into smaller and smaller communities of like-minded listeners, where "basic" cable service beams fifty television channels into our living rooms, where nonstop global markets offer daily measurements of wealth and poverty in every corner of creation, it is hard to imagine a uniform outlook on any single subject. Nevertheless, when it comes to modern American Indian history—the history of Native peoples in the United States from the "winning of the West" to the present—it is not difficult to identify a single core narrative. For most people the story goes something like this:

> After the Mexican War and the California gold rush extended America's borders to the Pacific Ocean, hordes of United States citizens rushed across the Mississippi River to settle the new territories. As they blazed trails westward, these hardy pioneers fought and overwhelmed the Indians who stood in their way. Despite occasional setbacks such as the defeat of the Seventh Cavalry at the Little Big Horn, U.S. troops bested the Indian tribes in battle and then herded them onto bleak reservations, where the pathetic remnants of once-proud peoples suffered silently in poverty and isolation. During the twentieth century, Native Americans gradually lost touch with their old cultures and adopted the trappings of civilization. Sadly, however, these peoples never fully embraced white ways; they remained caught between the past and the present. In recent years, political activists have tried to revive tribal communities with radical slogans, media stunts, confrontations with authorities, and legal schemes, but Indians remain mired in poverty and hopelessness.

This tale about the triumph of civilization has played a central role in shaping the American national identity. It casts the United States as an agent of advancement, moving westward to develop the continent's resources through industrialization and commercial agriculture and in the process displacing the prehistoric peoples already there. In this narrative, Americans—those citizens of the United States who tended not to apply this name to the indigenous peoples who resided within the boundaries of the United States—are progressive. Americans are builders. Americans are teachers who bring democracy, Christianity, and literacy. In essence Americans are tamers of a wild land. If the Indians' defeat and displacement is regrettable, as it is to some, it was also inevitable and necessary for the greater good of the American nation.

Now that the century has turned, we can reflect on a hundred-year period that began when this tale of conquest and decline was an article of national faith. In 1900 the U.S. Census Bureau reported that the Indian population was less than 300,000; the downward trend of the previous century appeared fixed, the Indians' disappearance seemed inevitable. Ten decades later we have reports that there are approximately 3 million Native Americans within our borders. With the indigenous population arguably having returned to its pre-1492 level, and with Indian concerns leaping off the front pages of newspapers in every region of the country, it would seem that the old story is in need of some serious revision. Past generations may have accepted a history of dispossession and conquest, but today (and tomorrow) people need something else in order to understand this dynamic, multicultural world. Recent events, summarized by one recent observer as "the reconquest of America," have set scholars to looking again at old assumptions about cultural decline and to exploring new themes in their research: cultural persistence, adaptation, struggle, and community survival. *American Nations: Encounters in Indian Country, 1850 to the Present* presents the best products of this recent process of historical reexamination.

Taken together, the essays collected in *American Nations* challenge the substance of the time-worn nationalist narrative. They offer images of Indians that will be unfamiliar to most readers: Indians who plot precisely how and when to surrender to American troops; Indians who start new religions; Indians who talk back to missionaries, government officials, and others bent on telling them how to live; Indians who go to court and win; and Indians who insist on being recognized before the United Nations as representatives of sovereign peoples. These essays also introduce some startling characters to the American pageant: Indian people who do not wear feathered headdresses and have never ridden a horse; Indian farmers in Oklahoma and Minnesota; Indian healers at work in Buffalo, New York; Indian politicians who fought segregation in Alaska ten years before Martin Luther King, Jr. led bus boycotts in the South; and a whole host of others, from Indian dancers and Indian ministers to Indian physicians and Indian lobbyists.

But the significance of these unexpected actors on the American stage goes well beyond their novelty. Together, these essays depict contacts between the United States and Native Americans not as simple tales of conquest and civilization, but as a series of encounters between peoples belonging to rapidly changing cultural traditions. These encounters involved more than a brief battle or an exchange of trade goods. Encounters involved strategy, conversation, and a search for common ground as well as warfare, retreat, and mistreatment. Encounters are three-dimensional human interactions, not the cartoon meetings of mounted warriors and cavalrymen. By viewing the interaction of Indians and non-Indians as encounters, the authors of these essays replace the popular plot of victory and defeat (and their aftermath of despair and hopelessness) with a wonderfully colorful, variegated tapestry in which people negotiate, adjust, debate, resist—and struggle onward. In this telling, American history becomes more complicated—and more interesting—than the story of a foreordained triumph.

The seven sections in *American Nations* isolate times and themes that help trace the encounters between Indians and other Americans over the past 150 years. The articles cover an array of topics ranging widely across the land from Mississippi to Alaska and many points between, across time from 1850 to the present, and across tribes from the more famous (Navajo, Sioux, Iroquois) to the more obscure (Stockbridge-Munsee, S'Klallam). Beginning with the era of military confrontation and its aftermath (Part I) and the development of reservation life (Part II), the volume pauses to focus on gender issues (Part III) before going on to explore matters of faith (Part IV) and the quieter but crucial first decades of the twentieth century (Part V). Studies focused on the resurgence of Indian activism in the 1960s and 1970s (Part VI) precede a concluding cluster of essays (Part VII) examining Indian Country today. Many of the authors in this final section also use the vantage point of the 500th anniversary of the first of Columbus's voyages to reflect on the present, and future, of Native America.

For all the variety here, readers will notice certain continuities, certain central themes, that stretch across the sections. The impact of historical events on gender relations and religious life appears in many essays, as do shifting ideas about effective resistance strategies and an evolving sense of what reservation communities mean and can accomplish for their residents. The U.S. government is also a steady presence; in war as well as in peace, government programs have had a profound effect on Indian life. No less constant, though, has been Indian resistance to the efforts of outsiders. Depending on the setting, tribal leaders have often been able to ignore, blunt, undermine, and even reshape governmental authority in ways that suited them and their communities.

For almost a century, scholarship on Indian history focused on the federal side of the equation; the Indian Agency and the Indian agent dominated the stories being told. By thinking of Natives not as victims but as actors, the essays in *American Nations,* all but one written within the last ten years, give a whole new meaning to the term "Indian agency." Just as powerfully, these essays collectively demonstrate the extraordinary complexity of the relationship between Indians and the United States. No longer separated physically from non-Indians and now bound to their white neighbors by laws, language, economic enterprise, and even ancestry, Native Americans continue to seek a distinctive place for themselves and their communities on the continent that has always been their home.

A generation ago the ethnohistorical approach displayed by the authors in *American Nations* would not have been so prominent. Until recently American Indians, if studied at all, were within the academic realm of anthropologists, or historians who limited themselves to studies of government policy. That division of labor no longer holds; many scholars begin their projects to look beneath the surface of government reports or conventional definitions of culture. Historians and anthropologists generally pursue different goals—the latter focusing on the nature of culture, the former tracing change over time—but rarely do they stay consistently on their own side of the street. Readers will notice that many of the essays reprinted here begin with an examination of culture and end by shedding light on a particular moment. Others, taking the opposite tack, start by studying a cultural phenomenon and go on to demonstrate the impact of events on community values and practices.

As editors, we hope that the twenty-three chapters in this collection, by challenging conventional historical narratives and demonstrating the power of interdisciplinary scholarship, will inspire reflection and discussion, raising difficult questions about both the Indian and non-Indian past. What has been the nature of American expansion? Has history been a one-way street, with the majority culture dictating the course of events to the minority? If not, to what extent and in what ways have Indians been masters of their own fate? Is it true that for Native peoples the colonial period of American history has yet to end? How can scholars create an intellectual framework for understanding the distinctiveness—and the interconnectedness—of Indian and non-Indian history?

Our enthusiasm for this book does not diminish our regret that we could not include more essays between its covers. We organized the volume to engage major themes in Native American history and to bring together the most interesting and provocative scholarship available on the subject. Scouring academic journals and recent monographs, we sought out work that challenged accepted narratives, shifted the focus from institutions to Native people, and drew upon insights from a variety of disciplines. We looked for originality and historical imagination, sacrificing coverage in a few of our decisions in our desire to include challenging and creative work. While some significant topics such as World War II are not addressed directly, most are discussed within the essays we selected. Our search for the best scholarship occasionally weighed as well against considerations of geographical breadth and thematic coherence; while *American Nations* contains essays on nearly every major region, the diversity of the Native American cultural landscape ensured that we would slight some areas. While we are excited by our final selections, we urge readers to examine the section entitled "Further Reading," at the end of the volume, to learn more about the rich and rapidly expanding body of scholarly literature from which the selections reprinted here were drawn.

Any book—even one with three editors—draws on many more people than are listed on the title page. This work is no exception. Deirdre Mullane's enthusiasm for the project got it off the ground quickly and helped guide it to completion with a speed that has surprised (and delighted) all three of us. Derek Krissof and Vikram Mukhija at Routledge did a splendid job tracking down permissions for the articles and illustrations that grace these pages and making excellent editorial suggestions. Frank Rzeczkowski at Northwestern University was a model research assistant, locating and retrieving essays for consideration with speed and good humor. The computer staff at the University of Kansas—Paula Courtney, Pam LeRow, and Lynn Porter—did wonders of technological transformation in scanning the articles selected, then Matthew Jennings at the University of Illinois painstakingly checked the computer's work. We are grateful to all these people for their assistance but we remain responsible for whatever flaws may appear in the finished product.

FEH

PCM

JHM

Chronology

1851   Fort Laramie Treaty establishes peace between the Plains tribes and the United States.

Lewis Henry Morgan publishes *League of the Ho-dé-no-sau-nee or Iroquois*, considered the foundation of modern anthropology, making Native Americans the subject of scholarly inquiry.

1853   Gadsden Purchase acquires southern Arizona for the United States.

1854   Twenty-nine U.S. soldiers killed near Fort Laramie, Wyoming, in "Grattan Massacre," an attack initiated by the Americans in retaliation for the "theft" of an abandoned, diseased cow.

1862   Sioux Indians attack Santee agency and the town of Mankato, Minnesota. Thirty-eight leaders of the uprising are later hanged, the largest mass execution in American history.

1863   U.S. Army forces 8,000 Navajos to complete the "Long Walk" from their homeland to Fort Sumner, New Mexico, 350 miles away.

1864   Sand Creek Massacre. Colorado volunteers attack Black Kettle's peaceful band of Cheyennes. Estimates of Indian dead range from 200 to 500.

1867   United States purchases Alaska Territory from Russia.

Southern Plains tribes gather at Medicine Lodge, Kansas, to conclude peace treaty with the United States, ending fighting along the Red River in Oklahoma.

1868   Northern Plains tribes gather at Fort Laramie, Wyoming, to end fighting along the Bozeman Trail and establish permanent reservations in Dakota and Montana Territories.

Navajos sign treaty with United States at Fort Sumner and begin returning to their homeland.

Colonel George Armstrong Custer attacks Black Kettle's band of peaceful Cheyennes along Washita River in Oklahoma, killing Black Kettle and approximately 100 other Indians.

1869   Seneca leader, Colonel Ely S. Parker, appointed Commissioner of Indian Affairs by President Ulysses Grant.

1871   Congress adopts a resolution declaring an end to further treaty making with Indian tribes. Previously negotiated treaties remain in effect.

1873   Modoc leader Kintpuash (Captain Jack) surrenders near Tule Lake, California, after resisting U.S. Army efforts to return him to the Klamath reservation in Oregon. Kintpuash is hanged by the United States government.

1876   Colonel Custer and the Seventh Cavalry defeated by Sioux and Cheyenne forces at Little Big Horn, Montana.

1877   Chief Joseph and several bands of Nez Perces flee from U.S. Army forces, traveling 1,700 miles from Oregon to the Bear Paw Mountains in Montana Territory.

1879   Captain Richard H. Pratt opens Carlisle Industrial Training School for Indians in Carlisle, Pennsylvania.

1881   Sitting Bull returns from Canada and surrenders to U.S. authorities at Fort Buford, Dakota Territory.

1882   U.S. Navy shells Tlingit village of Angoon, Alaska, following reports of an Indian uprising.

1883   William F. Cody organizes the first of his "Wild West" shows.

1886   Geronimo surrenders to General Nelson Miles at Skeleton Canyon, Arizona Territory.

1887   President Grover Cleveland signs General Allotment (Dawes) Act, establishing a process for dividing reservations into individual homesteads and selling off "surplus" lands.

1889   Portion of Indian Territory opened to homesteading in the first Oklahoma "land rush."

1890   Ghost Dance spreads from Nevada to the Plains; Sitting Bull killed amid growing tension surrounding the new ritual; Seventh Cavalry attacks Big Foot's band of Minneconjous along Wounded Knee Creek on the Pine Ridge Sioux Reservation.

1903   "Chief" Charles Bender (Ojibwe) begins illustrious professional baseball career with the Philadelphia Athletics.

1908   U.S. Supreme Court announces its decision in *U.S. v. Winters,* giving Indian tribes priority in claims to water in the arid West.

1911   Ishi, the only survivor of the Yahi tribe, walks into Oroville, California, looking for food and shelter.
Society of American Indians founded in Columbus, Ohio.

1912   Jim Thorpe (Sauk and Fox) wins gold medals in the decathlon and pentathlon at the Olympic Games in Stockholm, Sweden.

1918   Native American Church incorporated in Oklahoma.

1924   Congress approves a measure granting citizenship to all American Indians.

1928   Institute for Government Research issues Meriam Report on conditions among American Indians.

1934   Franklin Roosevelt signs the Indian Reorganization (Wheeler-Howard) Act into law, permitting Native American communities to form tribal governments and corporations.

1944   National Congress of American Indians founded in Denver, Colorado.

1946   Congress approves a law establishing an Indian Claims Commission to hear complaints against the United States for unfair dealings and treaty fraud.

1948   Supreme Courts of Arizona and New Mexico uphold the right of Indians to vote.

1953   House Concurrent Resolution 108 approved by Congress, calling on the U.S. government to work toward the termination of federal responsibility for Indian Affairs.

1961   American Indian Chicago Conference held on the campus of the University of Chicago. Conference adopts a "Declaration of Indian Purpose" calling for greater self-determination and an end to the policy of termination.

1962   Institute for American Indian Art opens in Santa Fe, New Mexico.

1968   American Indian Movement (AIM) founded in Minneapolis, Minnesota.

1969   N. Scott Momaday (Kiowa) wins the Pulitzer Prize for his novel, *House Made of Dawn.*

       Indians of All Tribes occupy an abandoned federal prison on Alcatraz Island in San Francisco Bay and demand that the facility be turned over to them for use as a cultural center. Occupation continues until June 1971.

       Navajo Community College (now Diné College) opens its doors. First of more than twenty tribally chartered institutions to open over the next two decades.

1971   Alaska Native Claims Settlement Act becomes law, settling land titles in Alaska and establishing twelve native corporations to manage Indian assets.

1972   Group led by the American Indian Movement occupies the Bureau of Indian Affairs building in Washington, D.C.

1973   AIM members and Pine Ridge residents occupy village of Wounded Knee on the Pine Ridge reservation for more than two months. Those holding the village declare themselves the founders of an "Independent Oglala Nation."

       Federal District Court in Tacoma, Washington, declares Puget Sound tribes are entitled by treaty right to 50 percent of the area's fish harvest. U.S. Supreme Court later upholds this decision.

1975   American Indian Educational Assistance and Self-Determination Act approved by Congress. Establishes policy whereby tribes can contract with the Bureau of Indian Affairs to provide educational, health, and other social services.

       Two FBI agents and one Indian person killed in a shootout with activists on the Pine Ridge reservation in South Dakota. Leonard Peltier, an AIM member, was later convicted for the murders on evidence many consider questionable. Peltier was sentenced to life imprisonment.

1978   Congress approves the American Indian Religious Freedom Act, intended to protect Native American religious life, and the American Indian Child Welfare Act, which gives tribes jurisdiction over adoptions involving tribal members.

1980   Maine tribes settle dispute over illegal seizure of tribal lands in the early nineteenth century by accepting $81.5 million from the United States.

1986   Ben Nighthorse Campbell (Northern Cheyenne) elected to the U.S. Congress from Colorado.

1988   Congress approves American Indian Gaming Regulatory Act. The law, which regulates casino gambling on Indian reservations, was passed in the wake of a 1987 U.S. Supreme Court decision upholding the right of a California tribe to conduct bingo games on its reservation.

1990   Native American Graves Protection and Repatriation Act signed into law by President George Bush.

1991   Custer Battlefield in Montana renamed Little Bighorn Battlefield National Monument.

1992   Mashantucket Pequots open Foxwoods Casino on their Connecticut reservation.

Native American leaders oppose the celebration of the 500th anniversary of the Columbus voyages. As a result, commemorations across the U.S. stress the "encounter" of two worlds rather than European "discovery."

Ben Nighthorse Campbell elected to the U.S. Senate from Colorado.

1994   President Clinton holds an unprecedented meeting at the White House with representatives of all federally recognized tribes.

1998   *Smoke Signals,* a feature film written, directed, and coproduced by Native Americans, receives the Audience Award for Dramatic Films at the Sundance Film Festival.

2000   Assistant Secretary of the Interior for Indian Affairs, Kevin Gover (Pawnee), offers a public apology that the Bureau of Indian Affairs has "at various times profoundly harmed the communities it was meant to serve."

Leonard Peltier's appeal for a pardon for health reasons is denied by the pardon board at Leavenworth.

I

Agency amid Conquest, 1850–1900

Reel upon reel of Hollywood movies offer a powerful, almost indelible image of the West during the era of the "Indian wars," an image of warriors and bluecoats, buffalos and battles, defeat and death. The three chapters in this section examine this place and time in a different light. Visiting the Navajos in the Southwest, the Sioux and their allies on the northern Plains, and Indians living near Puget Sound in Washington, the authors explore how Natives coped with conquest. Each story is different, but several themes run through all of them. One theme is cultural continuity; as they came to terms with American power, Indian people abandoned neither their loyalties nor their traditions. A second theme is modes of combat; there were many sorts of battlefields in these years, and not all of them looked like Little Big Horn. On reservations and in courtrooms, it turns out, Indians found ways to resist without firing a shot. A third, more implicit message broadcast by this section is that there were, as historians such as Patricia Nelson Limerick and Richard White have pointed out, many "Wests," and most of them bore no resemblance to Hollywood's.

1

While Abraham Lincoln's administration was committing the Union's resources to conquering the Confederacy, one part of the federal government was fighting a different sort of war. Brigadier General James H. Carleton, the commander of the military department of New Mexico (lands that became part of the United States in 1848 when the Treaty of Guadalupe Hidalgo ended the war with Mexico), decided that the time had come to make the Navajos and Mescalero Apaches live according to the rules of the American nation. Since these peoples had been defeated on the field of battle, Carleton assumed that the government would encounter no resistance to its plans to change their ways. He thus ordered the Indians moved to a reservation known as Bosque Redondo in southeastern New Mexico, a place he thought suitable for the Natives' reeducation.

Once they arrived there, the Indians discovered that Bosque Redondo was hardly an ideal place to live. The harsh environment made it difficult to grow enough food, yet the government routinely provided inadequate rations. The water supply was so alkaline that dysentery, a potentially lethal intestinal illness, was constant, and other diseases in the area, including malaria and measles, took a terrible toll. Small wonder, then, that Navajos who relocated to Bosque Redondo found life difficult.

Small wonder, too, that they resisted any government official trying to tell them how to live. As Katherine M. B. Osburn notes in this article which combines government reports and oral traditions, Navajos refused to follow every order that Carleton and his subordinates issued. While many were interested in learning a trade, few wanted to go to school. And though many did work hard at farming, as the government wanted, they still could not grow enough food. In order to get by, some Navajo women became prostitutes, though this violated both Navajo precepts and reservation rules. Other Navajos responded in more traditional fashion, finding solace and sustenance in Native ceremonies. They adopted the Chiricahua Windway, an Apache curative ritual; they also practiced their own customary rites, including the Squaw Dance and the Coyote Way. Through such means, Navajos managed to maintain some control over their lives even amid the reservation's squalor and desperation. Still, given the terrible circumstances (which included rape as well as forced relocation and starvation), this early experiment in reservation life held powerful lessons for Natives, whose future demanded adapting to the government and its plans for Indian Country. It also contained instructive lessons for those federal policymakers. Later chapters in this volume will reveal whether those officials had learned from the mistakes at Bosque Redondo.

The Navajo at Bosque Redondo: Cooperation, Resistance, and Initiative, 1864–1868

Katherine M. B. Osburn

DESPITE THE TRAUMATIC EXPERIENCE of military defeat and incarceration in a strange and hostile environment, the Navajo at the Bosque Redondo, 1864–68, did not respond passively to the reservation experience. Rather, they devised active adaptive strategies using a pattern of cooperation, resistance, and initiative. While Navajo religion furnished the Indians with a means of devising their own responses to many problems they faced, it also acted as a basis for solidarity in an experience potentially devastating to the Navajo's cultural survival. Since Indian behavior worked against the military's purposes and functioning at the Bosque Redondo, Indians were a variable in the reservation's demise, actively participating in its failure—not merely observing its collapse. Thus, while administrative and military aspects of the Bosque are important, the Navajo's behavior warrants equal consideration.

As a result of the Kit Carson campaign of 1863–64, Brig. Gen. James H. Carleton, commander of the military department of New Mexico, moved the Navajo to a plot in southeastern New Mexico known as Bosque Redondo.[1] There he had established a military post, Fort Sumner, and a reservation, where he planned to transform the Mescalero Apache and the Navajo into peaceful, Christian Americans.[2] The Navajo who arrived at the Bosque Redondo were starving and impoverished, and over the next four years, their miserable condition did not improve greatly. Shortages of food and fuel were continual, and the alkaline water caused dysentery. Other illnesses at the reservation included malaria, pneumonia, rheumatic fever, measles, and venereal disease. The Indians reported that sometimes military personnel beat them and that Navajo women were raped. Further, the Navajo were raided by other Indian tribes.[3]

Despite this evidence, Carleton interpreted the Navajo's degraded condition as an indication that they were now passive and dependent. "It is a mockery," he wrote, "to hold councils with a people who . . . have only to await our decisions. [We should] care for them as children until they can care for themselves."[4] In his view, the Navajo were his to transform. The Indians initially proved cooperative. As a condition of their surrender, the Indians agreed, as former Indian Superintendent James L. Collins noted in 1864, "to abandon their nomadic, marauding way of life, to settle on

SOURCE: *New Mexico Historical Review*, v. 60, n. 4 (October 1985), pp. 399–413.

a reservation away from their cherished mountain homes, and to devote themselves to the pursuit of industry as their means of support."[5]

Observers at the Bosque Redondo generally commented on how industriously the Indians worked. In 1865, the Indians testified before the Doolittle Commission, a Senate investigative committee, that they were more than willing to farm despite the problems involved. In addition, Michael Steck, superintendent of Indian Affairs in 1864, commented that "the tribe has for three centuries been engaged in planting and they are also far in advance of all other wild tribes in various fabricks such as blankets, baskets, ropes, saddles and bridle bits."[6] Thus it appeared, to individuals who visited the reservation in the early years, that the experiment had tremendous potential and that the Indians were hard-working and cooperative.

Indian cooperation was, however, more complex than it first appeared. Although the Navajo recognized that farming was a necessity—because the rations provided by the United States government were inadequate—the Indians had more choice in this area than is initially apparent. In 1868, for instance, they staunchly refused to plant any crops, explaining, "We have done all that we could possibly do, but we found it to be labor in vain and have therefore quit it; for this reason we have not planted or tried to do anything this year."[7] Thus, cooperation, though mandated by hunger, was also a choice, for the Indians did refuse to farm. In this act they demonstrated their ability to decide for or against cooperation, regardless of the circumstances.

Similarly, the Navajo considered the benefits of the education programs at the Bosque and chose to accept training in carpentry, leatherworking, and black-smithing. Delgadito, the Navajo headman, realized his people's need to repair their newly acquired farm implements and also concluded that they would now have to learn how to make a living. The Navajo also perceived that the trades provided them with such an opportunity.[8] Accommodation in this realm, then, was a strategy born of immediate needs and of an understanding of the new economic realities facing the Indians.

While the Navajo appreciated instruction in the trades, they were much more reticent about the benefits of other types of education. For example, although General Carleton established a school at the Bosque Redondo in 1865, the Indians rarely utilized it.[9] Apparently, they were more interested in receiving the ration coupons that the school distributed than in procuring an education for their children. As post surgeon Dr. George Gwynther noted: "I do not think that the juvenile savages shared either love of or aptitude for the alphabet, nor rightly appreciated the treasure to which it was the key; inasmuch as they often stipulated for additional bread rations as a condition of longer attendance at school."[10]

The Navajo's resistance to the reservation school was a serious blow to Carleton's plans for acculturation. Yet the Indians claimed they were not opposed to education; they were simply more absorbed with the immediate concerns of daily survival and considered the benefits of education to be peripheral to more urgent matters such as obtaining enough food to fend off starvation.[11] Their attempt to procure money and extra ration coupons for sending their children to school demonstrates the Indians' shrewd survival strategy.

Navajos receiving ration tickets, Fort Sumner, N. Mex. Courtesy National Archives, photo no. 111-SC-87966.

The Navajo gave top priority to procuring more food. They often tried pleading for larger rations. While officers struggled to find a solution, sometimes increasing the size of the ration, other times shifting its frequency, the Indians acted to meet their needs by their own methods. They stole any available food and also produced some three thousand extra ration coupons.[12] By forging metal coupons, the Navajos were utilizing an old skill to meet a new need. In addition, since the number of forged tickets increased from January to May of 1865, the number of Indians who benefitted from this practice probably increased.[13] Apparently, however, this strategy profited some Indians at the expense of others.

Another method of obtaining extra food was prostitution, which was not a standard practice under less stressful conditions. Navajo women were generally considered to be modest and decent, before and after the Bosque Redondo years. Indeed, the Navajo moral code discourages promiscuity, and Navajo religion had a ritual designed for "the removal of prostitution or mania," called The Prostitution Way.[14] While the Navajo recognized the degradation of prostitution at Fort Sumner, they also indicated that the women were compelled to set aside their moral prescriptions because of poverty and hunger.[15]

Although some Navajo disregarded the moral injunctions of their culture against prostitution, the taboos governing residence were generally upheld. Carleton had originally planned to house the Navajo in neatly ordered barracks similar to the type of housing found in Pueblo villages.[16] The Navajo, however, found this scheme unacceptable because their traditional housing was widely dispersed. Furthermore, they rejected the notion of permanent homes because of their beliefs about departed souls. "The custom of our tribe," the chiefs claimed, "is never to enter a house where a person has died, but abandon it." Consequently, they settled "in scattered and extended camps, unorganized by bands or otherwise."[17]

The Navajo's refusal to adhere to Carleton's plans for their housing represents another assertion of their autonomy. Instead of conforming to the military's plans, the Navajo forced the military to restructure their administration procedures. As Nelson H. Davis complained, the dispersed Indians were difficult to control, and his troops were severely taxed in their efforts to round up Indians for work.[18] Thus, the defiance of the Indians allowed them to continue their traditional settlement patterns in spite of their captivity and to exert some control over the decisions that affected their lives.

For similar reasons, the Navajo refused medical treatment at the post hospital. The Indians explained that they shunned the hospital because "all that have reported there have died." Because of this belief, Dr. Gwynther insisted on removing from the hospital all patients who were near death.[19] Thus the Indians' behavior helped to dictate hospital policy.

Resistance to the hospital can also be traced to the Navajo's preference for their native medicine men. Dr. Gwynther complained that "the relations of the sick person have [occasionally] carried the patient off clandestinely, to get such benefits as may accrue from the practice of their native medicine-men."[20] The Indians admitted that the medicine men were often ineffectual in combatting diseases on the reservation, but explained that they lacked the plants necessary for native cures.[21]

Army doctors viewed illness as a natural occurrence treatable with scientific methods, but the Navajo had a different interpretation. In the Navajo world view, illness is an example of disharmony in the cosmic order that the performance of a religious ceremony can correct. During the ceremony, the Navajo invoke their Holy People to rectify the disturbance of order. If the ritual is correctly carried out, the deities are obligated to grant the mortal's requests, for a principle of reciprocity governs the exchange.[22] In this regard, Navajo oral tradition emphasizes the importance of healing ritual at the Bosque. Charlie Mitchell, a Navajo who had been a child at the reservation, explained that ceremonies were performed to prevent the Navajo from dying in captivity.[23]

In seeking solutions to disease, the Navajo rejected Anglo cures but embraced some from other Indians. They borrowed, for instance, the Chiricahua Windway from the Apache at the fort. This ritual cures a variety of sicknesses such as those caused by the winds (being knocked over by wind, cooking with a tree felled by wind, or sleeping in a place hollowed out by winds); those caused by snakes (eating food touched by a snake, injury to a snake, or snake bites); those from a cactus (because of cooking with tree cactus); or those caused by flooding. Another Navajo explanation for sickness at the Bosque Redondo was witchcraft. To help combat illness resulting from witchcraft, the Navajo also adopted the Apache's Suckingway ritual technique for curing a witchcraft victim: sucking out the witch's darts.[24]

To bring about other cures, the Navajo also performed many of their own ceremonies. For instance, the Squaw Dance, a ritual of the Navajo Evilway, which purifies an individual from disease-inducing contacts with foreigners, was used at the Bosque.[25] According to this ceremony some sicknesses are the result of the ghosts of aliens, either those whom a Navajo warrior has killed, or those who died from other causes and with whom the Navajo may have had contact, sexual or otherwise. Touching the corpse or stepping on the grave of an "outsider" may also cause alien ghosts to torment a Navajo with sickness.[26] Because the Navajo were in close contact with Apache and Anglos who died, they no doubt felt that at least some of their sicknesses necessitated the performance of the Squaw Dance.

Other reasons for enacting the Squaw Dance were probably connected with Navajo raids from the Bosque reservation. Since Navajo warriors were killing enemies during this time, they required a Squaw Dance to prevent or cure a retaliating illness. In March of 1866, as an example, seven Navajo went on a foray against the Utes who had killed one of their children. The Navajo pursued their enemies for approximately twelve or thirteen days and then attacked them, killing five and capturing a ten-year-old Ute boy, twenty-four horses, and saddles and guns.[27] Another account of a Navajo campaign from Fort Sumner does not end so happily. While on a raid in the Comanche country, the Navajo lost four of their war party. The raid had been doomed, the raiders concluded, when a coyote appeared one night in the warrior's camp. In October of 1867, a contingent of Navajo retaliated against the Comanches for a raid on 9 September. The Navajo had pursued their attackers and killed twelve.[28]

In addition to retaliatory raids, the Indians also committed offensive raids aimed at obtaining more stock. In this regard, settlers in eastern new Mexico claimed that Navajo from Fort Sumner attacked their homes and stole their livestock. Yet while some Navajo did engage in such activities, it is important to note that a large number of the complaints were probably exaggerated and that the Navajo were often blamed for depredations that other Indians committed.[29] Regardless of blame, warfare conducted at the Bosque Redondo required ceremony to counteract the disturbance it wrought in the natural order.

The Navajo also performed the Fire Dance, a ritual of the nine-night Mountainway or Nightway ceremonies that restore harmony. The Fire Dance combines, in a single ceremony, the abbreviated forms of many ceremonials. Dancers representing a variety of other Holyway ceremonies, such as Beautyway, Windway, or Waterway, perform a portion of their chant. The patient receives the specific benefits of each without undergoing the entire ceremony. Thus the Fire Dance saves time and expense and would serve the Navajos by adapting their more elaborate ceremonies to the limited resources of the reservation.[30]

The Fire Dance was also possibly connected with the food problems at the Bosque. Certainly, corn-growing rites and the ritualistic treatment of food employed

Barboncito, Navajo leader designated head chief of the Navajos by Gen. Sherman in 1868. From *The Army and the Navajo* by Gerald Thompson. Courtesy, National Museum of the American Indian Smithsonian Institution.

in the dance were relevant to experiences of the Navajo on the reservation. According to their eschatology, an individual who has eaten another person's food without ritualistic preparation may be in danger of being transformed into that person. Therefore, the Navajo may have performed Fire Dances as protection from being "transformed" by the white person's food. The recitation of rituals concerned with agriculture suggests that, although the Navajos utilized the American's technology, they were convinced that their success in farming was contingent upon their controlling the forces of nature that were responsible for the harvest.[31]

While the Navajo employed a variety of responses in order to survive at the Bosque, their ultimate goal was to return to their homeland. From April to August of 1865, approximately 1,300 Navajo left the reservation, hoping to return to their old country where roughly 1,000 to 2,000 Navajo remained, having escaped the roundup. General Carleton dealt sternly with the runaway problem, telling his newly appointed post commander Maj. William McCleave that he would kill every Indian found off the reservation without a passport. Despite this threat, Indians continued to leave the reservation over the next several years. In 1868, for example, 250 to 300 more Navajo escaped.[32]

The majority of Navajo, however, remained at the Bosque Redondo and attempted to obtain their liberty through pleading and ceremony. As early as 1865, the Indians begged for their release, warning that if they were forced to remain upon the reservation they would "all die very soon." They explained that they had been instructed by their Holy People to remain within the boundaries of three rivers, the Rio Grande, the Rio San Juan, and the Rio Colorado, and their violation of this restriction was responsible for their current suffering. They extolled the productivity of their old country where they had enough food and firewood and were safe from their enemies.[33]

According to Navajo oral tradition, it was not pleading alone that secured the Navajo's release, but also the performance of the Coyote Way ritual. Although some informants claimed that the ritual was divinatory, indicating that the government was now ready to free the Navajo, other Navajo attributed their freedom to this ceremony. The years of pleading had been unsuccessful, they claimed, until the performance of the Coyote ritual, "during which our leader was blessed with Coyote power." Because of this ceremony, the next request to leave was approved.[34]

Moreover, the Navajo called on their religious ritual to aid them in interaction with the reservation personnel. Recognizing that Anglos controlled the reservation, the Navajo attempted, at the same time, to circumvent government officials and to procure release by petitioning their Holy People. To this day, some Navajo believe that, ultimately, their Holy People, not the United States government, returned them to their current reservation. Whatever the cause of release, on 1 July 1868, the Navajo signed a treaty with the U.S. government allowing them to return to their traditional homeland.[35]

An examination of the Navajo's behavior at the Bosque Redondo reveals that the Indians worked toward two primary goals, survival and release, by using a pattern of cooperation, resistance, and initiative. Cooperation meant farming and learning the trades, while resistance was manifested in refusing formal education, barracks housing, and Anglo medical treatment. In addition, prostitution, forgery, raiding, fleeing, and ceremony represented Indian initiative. These varied activities indicate that the Navajo had no single survival strategy. In fact, solutions that individuals employed sometimes clashed with the interests of the tribe as a whole. For example, when Navajo leaders promised to curtail raiding, while other Navajo raided, the Indians were factionalized, increasing the potential for cultural disintegration.[36]

Navajo religion, however, was an important element in avoiding this fate. Oral histories recount how special the ceremonies were to the Indians during captivity and indicate their belief that their Holy People sustained the tribe at the bosque.[37] In addition to providing comfort, religion was also a source of social cohesion. Navajo ceremonies require large gatherings of people, some of whom are involved with the ceremony while others come to meet friends and family.[38] The largest number of spectators gather during the final day and night of a sing, and the patient's kinsmen are expected to feed them. Consequently, there is social pressure on all nearby relatives to contribute time and labor to help defray the costs of a ritual. Thus, kinsmen and neighbors are bound together by reciprocal obligations governing the ceremony.[39]

Ceremony also functions ideally as a means of reducing intergroup tensions by redistributing wealth. The singer is expected to give a large portion of his fee to friends and relatives. Navajos who stint on ceremonies risk accusations of witchcraft, and prosperous Navajos must sponsor elaborate ceremonies to avoid similar suspicions.[40] In a situation such as that at the Bosque Redondo, where resources were limited and tensions great, ceremony would have provided a means of reducing stress the uneven distribution of resources generated. Religion, then, was the key to the Navajo's survival as a cultural unit during their stay near Fort Sumner.

The Bosque Redondo experiment failed for a number of reasons, most of which historians have discussed. The reservation was not economically feasible because of environmental and administrative problems, yet the failure of the Bosque Redondo cannot be understood without discussing Navajo activities. Clearly, their behavior taxed the labors of the military in administering them, because of their dispersed settlement pattern, and in containing them, because they left the post without the proper papers. Their refusal to accept the Bosque Redondo, seen in their nearly constant begging to go home, also contributed to the realization that Carleton's plan was not workable. The Navajo at the Bosque Redondo were not passive observers of the reservation's rise and fall, but were, instead, active participants in the successes and failures of the experiment.[41]

NOTES

1. Lawrence C. Kelly, *Navajo Roundup* (Boulder, Colo.: Pruett Publishing Company, 1970).
2. Gen. James H. Carleton to Adj. Gen. Lorenzo Thomas, Santa Fe, 6 September 1863, Letters Received by the Adjutant General's Office (LRAGO), Albert H. Schroeder Collection, State Records Center and Archives (SRCA), Santa Fe.
3. George Gwynther, "An Indian Reservation," *Overland Monthly* 10 (February 1873): 126; Theodore H. Dodd to A. Baldwin Norton, 7 December 1867, 29 September 1867, Letters Received by the New Mexico Superintendency (LRNMS), Microscopy 234, rolls (R) 554, 555, box 13, National Archives (NA), 1956; Charles L. Werner, testimony before the Doolittle Commission, U.S. Congress, Joint Special Committee on Indian Affairs, *Condition of the Indian Tribes,* S. Doc. 148 (Serial 1279), 39th Cong., 2d sess., 1867; Testimony of the Navajo Chiefs before the Doolittle Commission, in *Condition,* pp. 307–11, 353.
4. Carleton to Thomas, Santa Fe, 12, 19 March 1864, LRAGO, Schroeder Collections, SRCA.
5. James L. Collins to Carleton, 18 July 1864, LRNMS, roll 552.
6. Annual Report of Michael Steck, Territorial Indian Superintendent, 10 October 1864, Papers of Michael Steck, folder number 2, Schroeder Collection, SRCA.
7. "A Council with the Navajos," *Window Rock Navajo Times,* 28 May 1868, Navajo Tourist Guide, July 1966.
8. Capt. Henry Bristol, testimony, *Condition,* p. 344; Delgadito, testimony, *Condition,* p. 335.
9. Carleton to Secretary of the Interior John P. Usher, *Condition,* pp. 310–11.
10. Gwynther, "An Indian Reservation," pp. 127–28.
11. Testimony of the Navajo chiefs, *Condition,* p. 335.
12. Carleton to Capt. William H. Bell, chief commissary, Santa Fe, 10 December 1864, *Condition,* p. 412; Nelson H. Davis to Ben Cutler, 25 March 1865, LRAGO, Schroeder Collection, SRCA.
13. Arthur Woodward, *A Brief History of Navajo Silversmithing* (Flagstaff: Northern Arizona Society of Science and Art, 1938), 14–15, 60; 2d Lt. George W. Arnold to Brig. Gen. Marcellus M. Crocker, 1 January 1865, Abstract, Fort Sumner: Rations, Bosque Redondo File, box 3, Frank McNitt Collection, SRCA, Santa Fe.
14. Donald E. Worcester, "The Navaho during the Spanish Regime in New Mexico," *New Mexico Historical Review* 26 (April 1951): 101–18; Aleš Hrdlička, *Physiological and Medical Observations among the Indians of the Southwestern United States and Northern Mexico,* Bureau of American Ethnology, Bulletin 34 (Washington, D.C.: Government Printing Office, 1908), 33; John Ladd, *The Structure of a Moral Code, a Philosophical Analysis of Ethical Discourse Applied to the Ethics of the Navaho Indians* (Cambridge, Mass.: Harvard University Press, 1957): 243–44; Leland C. Wyman and Clyde Kluckhohn, *Navajo Classification of Their Song Ceremonials* (Menasha, Wis.: American Anthropological Association, 1938), Memoir 53, 25–27.
15. Delgadito, testimony, *Condition,* p. 357.
16. Carleton to Maj. Henry D. Wallen, Santa Fe, 28 February 1863, *Condition,* p. 161.
17. "Report of a Council with the Navajos," Indian Agent A. Baldwin Norton to Nathaniel G. Taylor, 15 September 1867, LRNMS, roll 554; Delgadito, in *Condition,* p. 356. See Gladys Reichard, *Navajo Religion: A Study of Symbolism,* 2 vols. (New York: Pantheon Books, 1950): 40–45, for an explanation of Navajo beliefs concerning departed souls. Leland C. Wyman also notes that homes in which an individual died of old age need not, because of the prayers of Blessingway, be destroyed upon the elderly person's death (Leland C. Wyman, *Blessingway* [Tucson: University of Arizona Press, 1970], p. 10); Davis to Cutler, 25 March 1865, LRAGO, Schroeder Collection, SRCA.
18. Davis to Cutler, 25 March 1865, LRAGO, Schroeder Collection, SRCA.
19. John Brooke to Mason Howard, 19 December 1867, LRNMS, roll 554; Testimony of the Indian chiefs, in *Condition,* p. 334; Gwynther, testimony, *Condition,* p. 334.
20. Gwynther, testimony, *Condition,* 334.
21. Testimony of the Navajo chiefs, *Condition,* p. 356; testimony of John Bowman before the Indian Claims Commission, 16, 17 January 1951, Window Rock, Ariz., Schroeder Collection, SRCA; *Navajo Stories of the Long Walk Period,* Ruth Roessel, ed. (Tsaile, Ariz.: Navajo Community College Press, 1973), 260.

22. Leland C. Wyman, in *The Mountainway of the Navajo* (Tucson: University of Arizona Press, 1970), 4, calls Navajo religion "medical theory and practice," but Reichard, *Navajo Religion,* 1:11, argues that the curing of disease is not the sole purpose of a chant, and "affinity with our medical terms, if there is any, is fortuitous." Thus, while Navajo religious rites may be performed for a number of reasons, the curing of disease is usually central to their performances.

23. Wyman, *The Windways of the Navajo* (Colorado Springs: The Taylor Museum, 1962), 20–21, 21; Karl W. Luckert, "Toward a Historical Perspective on Navajo Religion," in *Navajo Religion and Culture: Selected Views,* eds. David M. Brugge and Charlotte Frisbee (Santa Fe: Museum of New Mexico Press, 1982), 190; Jesus Arvisio, a Mexican interpreter, told Captain Bristol that witchcraft was a common explanation for illness and had a host of "charms" and ceremonies to combat it (Bristol, testimony, *Condition,* p. 358).

24. David Aberle, *Peyote Religion among the Navajo* (Chicago: Aldine Publishing Company, 1966), 49–50.

25. *Navajo Stories,* pp. 215, 227, 264; Gladys Reichard, *Navajo Medicine Man: Sandpaintings and Legends of Miguelito* (New York: Dover Publications, 1939), 19; Bernard Haile, *The Navajo War Dance* (Saint Michaels, Ariz.: Saint Michaels Press, 1946), 4.

26. W. W. Hill, "Navajo Warfare," in *Yale University Publications in Anthropology,* no. 5 (New Haven, Conn.: Yale University Press, 1936), 14–18; Haile, *War Dance,* pp. 4–6.

27. David M. Brugge, "A Navajo Campaign from Fort Sumner," *Window Rock, Ariz., Navajo Times,* Centennial Edition, 14 July 1968.

28. Hill, "Navajo Warfare," p. 18; Dodd to Norton, 11 September 1867, LRNMS, roll 554.

29. The National Archive records contain innumerable references to Navajo depredations during the Fort Sumner years. For examples of such complaints, see Cutler to Crocker, 9 November 1864; Lorenzo Labadie to Steck, 22 October 1864, 3 November 1865; Steck Papers; and LRNMS, roll 555, especially settlement of claims against Navajo raiders, 20 February 1867. At one point, Carleton himself encouraged the Navajo to raid the Comanches to supplement their herds; see Carleton to Crocker, 31 October 1864, in *Condition,* p. 211. Upon several occasions, however, Navajo were falsely blamed for raids. See Carleton to Usher, 27 August 1864, in *Condition,* pp. 192–93; and Brugge, "A Navajo Campaign."

30. *Navajo Stories,* pp. 215, 264; Wyman, *Mountainway,* p. 28.

31. Reichard, *Navajo Religion,* pp. 114–15, 265. For a comprehensive discussion of the role of religion in Navajo agriculture, see W. W. Hill, *The Agricultural and Hunting Methods of the Navajo Indians* (New Haven, Conn.: Yale University Press, 1938).

32. The exact number of Navajo who escaped the roundup is not known. Robert A. Roessel, Jr., in "Navajo History, 1850–1923," pp. 513–14, sets the estimate at around 1–2,000. A fascinating account of a family of Navajos who hid for four years before finally going to the Bosque is found in *Museum Notes of The Museum of Northern Arizona,* 9 (May 1937). See Abstract no. 6, "Exodus: 1865," Frank McNitt's personal notes, McNitt Collection, SRCA, Santa Fe, for a summary of Navajos' escape activity. Carleton's threat is found in his letter of 9 August 1865, Carleton to Maj. William McCleave, in "Exodus: 1865." Dodd to Norton, 7 December 1867, LRNMS, roll 555; A. Rosenthall to Davis, 1 February 1868, LRNMS, roll 555.

33. "A Council with the Navajo," 28 May 1868, *Navajo Times,* Report of Indian Agent Edmund A. Graves, December 1865; Navajo Chief Manuelito in *Condition,* p. 222. For a comprehensive discussion of the geographical elements in Navajo religion, see Richard V. VanValkenburgh and Clyde Kluckhohn, "Navajo Sacred Places" in *Navajo Indians III,* David Agee Horr, ed. (New York: Garland Publishing Co., 1974).

34. Testimony of informants who claimed that the Coyote Way was divinatory is found in *Navajo Stories,* pp. 85, 136–37, 224, while reports of persons believing that the Coyote Way was compulsory are found on pp. 179, 212, 238, 270.

35. U.S., Cong., Senate, Indian Affairs, Laws and Treaties, "A Treaty with the Navajo Indians," S. Doc. 452 (Serial 4254), 57th Cong., 1st sess., 1901–1902, pp. 82–85.

36. The factionalization of the Navajo over raiding practices is well documented. For example, in the period following the relocation at Fort Sumner, the Navajo chief Manuelito executed forty Indians as witches. These men were raiders and warriors who advocated armed resistance against the

Anglos. See Kluckhohn, *Navajo Witchcraft* (Boston: Beacon Press, 1967), Papers of the Peabody Museum of American Archeology and Ethnology, Harvard University, 1944, Paper 22, No. 2, pp. 63–64. Evon Vogt describes the tension between rich Navajo who opposed raiding and poor Navajo who wanted to continue the practice in "The Navajos," in *Perspectives in Indian Culture Change,* Edward H. Spicer, ed. (Chicago: University of Chicago Press, 1961), 306. Many Navajo also discuss the problem of raiding in *Navajo Stories.*

37. *Navajo Stories,* pp. xi, 264; Robert J. Roessel, *Pictorial History of the Navajo from 1860–1910* (Rough Rock, Ariz.: Navajo Curriculum Center of the Rough Rock Demonstration School, 1980), 20.

38. Reichard, *Navajo Religion,* xxxiii; Wyman, *Mountainway,* pp. 6–7.

39. Clyde Kluckhohn, "Some Personal and Social Aspects of Navajo Ceremonial Practice," *Harvard Theological Review* 32 (January 1939): 78–79.

40. Kluckhohn, "Personal Aspects," pp. 80–81.

41. The importance of religion in sustaining other relocated peoples is examined in Elizabeth Colson, *The Social Consequences of Resettlement: The Impact of the Kariba Resettlement upon the Gwembe Tonga* (Manchester, Eng.: University of Manchester Press, 1971).

2

Everyone has heard of Little Bighorn, the battle where legendary Native leaders Sitting Bull and Crazy Horse defeated the no less legendary Lt. Col. George Armstrong Custer and his men. But few remember that this clash was only one chapter in a larger war story, now known as the Great Sioux War, which lasted from early 1876 until the late spring of 1877. And fewer still, before Kingsley M. Bray, have untangled the Native politics and diplomacy that brought to a close this conflict, the most decisive military contest on the Great Plains in the nineteenth century.

This war story actually begins some two generations before 1876, when the three Sioux nations—the Tetons (comprised of the Hunkpapa, Miniconjou, Oglala, Brulé, Two Kettles, Sihaspas, and Sans Arc), Yanktons, and Yanktonais—gained control over much of the plains in the early nineteenth century. By learning how to take advantage of changing circumstances (such as the growing availability of horses), they had, as the historian Richard White put it, won the West. No group could rival their power, as federal troops learned in June 1876 when the Sioux defeated not only Custer and his troops but also forces under the command of General George Crook at the Battle of the Rosebud. A mere decade after Union soldiers had prevailed over the South, the might of the United States could do little to extinguish Sioux power in the West.

Yet, as Bray makes clear, the Sioux found it impossible to keep control over the plains. Drawing on oral accounts and a fragmentary set of records left by Native Americans, Bray has reconstructed, in rich detail, the troubles that the Sioux faced. During the conflict of 1876–1877, the stresses of war and the debate over the very wisdom of that war broke the Sioux apart. The charismatic religious and political figure Sitting Bull led many Sioux across the 49th Parallel—which Indians called the "medicine line"—and into exodus in Canada, beyond the reach of United States troops. Meanwhile Crazy Horse, a firm opponent of negotiations, fought on. However, with the number of Sioux under his influence steadily falling, this powerful Native leader eventually surrendered, thereby bringing an end to the military conflict.

Bray's account is notable for its painstaking reconstruction of Indians' negotiations, and for uncovering the logic that compelled Crazy Horse first to cling to authority during a long, harsh winter and then to relinquish it the following spring. Yet this essay is significant for more than illustrating how, far from backward and bloodthirsty warriors determined to fight to the death, Indians were savvy politicians and diplomats, navigating treacherous historical terrain. It also introduces a new source for exploring the Indian experience. Like the Civil War, the Great Sioux War drew photographers to record key participants. Several pieces appear here, suggesting the new medium's rich promise, and its genuine problems.

CRAZY HORSE AND THE END OF THE GREAT SIOUX WAR

Kingsley M. Bray

AS NEW GRASS GREENED THE NORTHERN Plains in the first week of May 1877, events signaled the end of Indian resistance in the Great Sioux War. On May 7, Col. Nelson A. Miles dealt a decisive blow against Lame Deer's village, the last group of Sioux to try to maintain the old nomadic life in the Lakota hunting grounds of the Powder River Country. Two hundred and fifty miles northward, where the invisible medicine line of the Forty-ninth Parallel offered a haven from U.S. military pursuit, a larger body of Sioux followed Sitting Bull into exile in Canada. And far to the south, thousands more Sioux and Cheyennes succumbed to the inevitable and surrendered at the garrisons of the Sioux Reservation. The mass capitulations climaxed on Sunday, May 6, when Crazy Horse, the greatest Lakota war leader of his generation, led his village into Red Cloud Agency and symbolically surrendered three Winchester rifles. The Sioux War was over.[1]

A wealth of Indian testimony exists that enables us to understand the Great Sioux War from Indian perspectives. Sioux and Cheyenne combatants, and their relatives who served as army scouts or acted as peace negotiators, have left a vast body of source material from which we can reconstruct Indian motivations. Some of these accounts are the result of military debriefings within weeks of the events which they describe; others are recollections recorded by the pioneer historians of the Indian wars early in the twentieth century. Like all historical sources they need rigorous evaluation and careful weighing to detect bias and inconsistency. The special problems posed by translation must always be borne in mind in Indian history.

I shall attempt to formulate an Indian perspective on the last stages of the Sioux War, and in particular to trace the processes and events that led to the surrender of Crazy Horse on that distant spring afternoon. Other authors have addressed the late phases of the Sioux War from a military perspective, or attempted to understand something of the complexities of Indian politics in both the agency and non-agency camps.[2] Here the use of previously untapped documents, viewed through the prism of Lakota political organization and kinship networks, aims to create a perspective from within the Crazy Horse village, and to map more closely than ever before the sequence of events as they unfolded week by week until surrender became inevitable.

The Sioux War of 1876–77 grew out of years of mounting frustration between

SOURCE: *Nebraska History* 79 (Fall 1998), pp. 94–115.

the United States and the hunting bands of Sioux and Northern Cheyennes, who roamed the Powder River Country between the Black Hills and the Big Horn Mountains. The discovery of gold in the Black Hills powered high command voices that wished a military solution to the "Sioux Problem." After the hunting bands declined to report to the agencies of the Great Sioux Reservation, where a majority of the Sioux already lived, the army was turned loose in spring 1876.

To a centennial nation's bewilderment, the coalition of Sioux and Cheyennes responded by defeating the forces of Gen. George Crook at the Battle of the Rosebud on June 17, and barely one week later, annihilating the immediate command of Lt. Col. George A. Custer on the Little Bighorn River. For several critical weeks the stunned columns of Crook and of Custer's superior, Gen. Alfred H. Terry, lay becalmed at base camps, freeing the Indian coalition to move off after buffalo.

By midsummer that coalition numbered upwards of one thousand lodges, housing six thousand people and at least 1,500 adult males. About one half of this number, the "winter roamers," lived in the hunting grounds year-round, shunning the reservation and its culture of dependence. Each spring they were strengthened by the arrival of the "summer roamers," bands that spent the cold months at the agencies, drawing rations with their reservation kin. At the head of the coalition stood two leaders of outstanding character and ability, with keen strategic insight and total commitment to the hunting life: Sitting Bull, holy man of the Hunkpapa division of Sioux; and Crazy Horse, war chief of the Oglalas. Together these two leaders had worked hard to foster a spirit of solidarity in total rejection of reservation life, and to forge an autonomous tribal identity for the disparate hunting bands as a new Sioux division, the Northern Nation.[3]

By fall the Northern Nation could no longer remain united, however. Typically this was a season of dispersal, as game became scattered. Summer roaming bands usually drifted in to the agencies ahead of cold weather. And with the regrouping of the demoralized columns of Crook and Terry, the coalition finally faced a slow, dogged pursuit. Faced with these realities, the coalition gradually broke up into four blocs. By late November these blocs were occupying distinct districts and pursuing different strategies regarding the war. Farthest south was the main Cheyenne village, at least 183 lodges. Having made fall buffalo hunts in the upper Bighorn Valley, it had retired to winter quarters in the southern reaches of the Bighorn Mountains, probably hoping to sit out further military operations.

Farthest north, Sitting Bull's Hunkpapas and their associates, aggregating about 230 lodges, had gravitated beyond the Missouri to attempt trade both at Fork Peck and with the Canadian Métis. Although no Hunkpapas approved peace negotiations with the Americans, a minority favored a complete withdrawal from the war zone. Fifty-seven lodges, led by headmen Iron Dog, Long Dog, Little Knife, and Lodge Pole, had crossed into Grandmother's Land—the British possessions of Queen Victoria—early in November. There they could make fall hunts without further interference and plan cold-weather operations secure from pursuit.[4]

Largest of the blocs was that of the Miniconjous and Sans Arcs. Even after a modest surrender at Cheyenne River Agency following negotiations and hostage

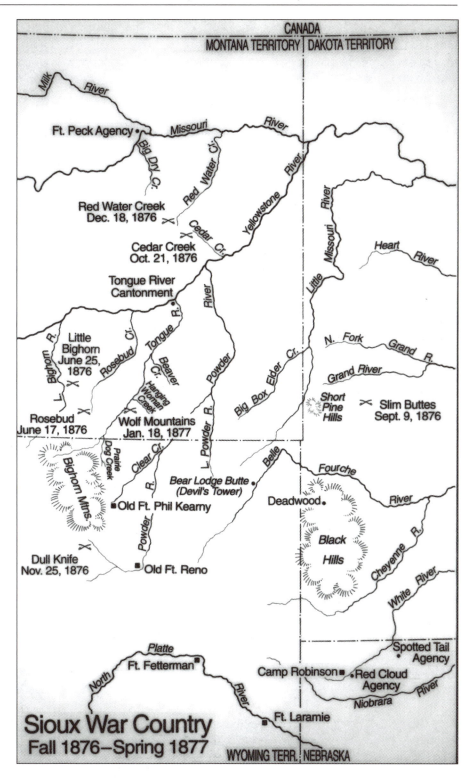

Sioux War Country: Fall 1876–Spring 1877

taking by Col. Nelson A. Miles, this village counted perhaps 380 lodges. It also remained deepest divided over the issue of war. Although its leadership forbade further surrender at the agencies, by early December a strong peace movement favored reopening talks with Miles, possibly to explore his floating the idea of relocating their home agency from the mouth to the forks of Cheyenne River, nearer the hunting grounds and the Black Hills. Locating close to Miles's headquarters at the junction of the Yellowstone and Tongue rivers, this village was attracting moderates from Crazy Horse's Oglalas.[5]

The Crazy Horse village, comprising about 250 lodges of Oglalas, Brulés, straggling Cheyennes, and others, was located in the middle Tongue River valley. Crazy Horse, thirty-six years old and utterly fearless, was the inspiration of the battlefield. His bravery in the Custer battle was already legendary; his generosity, mysticism, and normal peacetime reserve lent him the charisma of enigma. As Oglala war chief, Crazy Horse was in tight control of his village through the *akicita* police, which enforced council decisions. During the fall, as news from the agencies dwelled on pony and arms confiscations, the arrest of incoming "hostiles," and the surrender of Lakota rights to the Black Hills and the Powder River Country, Crazy Horse's rhetoric had hardened against capitulation to the Americans. The council passed a ruling that no movement be permitted to the agencies. *Akicita* leaders were entrusted with punitive powers to enforce the order, empowered to beat offenders, destroy their property, and kill their horses.

Concerned at the potential fragmentation of the coalition, Crazy Horse sent runners to arrange talks with Sitting Bull, but the first big army victory of the war forced a new process of reconsolidation. On November 25 Col. Ranald S. Mackenzie's command surprised the Cheyenne village in the Big Horns, killing over forty people and driving the half-clothed survivors into the frozen Wyoming mountains. The Cheyennes, suffering terrible hardships, moved north to contact Crazy Horse's village. On December 6 the ragged vanguard of Cheyennes found the Oglalas encamped high up Beaver Creek, an east tributary of Tongue River barely sixty miles from Miles's Tongue River Cantonment.

The Oglala reception of the defeated Cheyennes was controversial. According to Wooden Leg:

> The Oglala Sioux received us hospitably. They had not been disturbed by soldiers, so they had good lodges and plenty of meat and robes. They first assembled us in a great body and fed us all we wanted to eat. To all of the women who needed other food they gave a supply. They gave us robes and blankets. They shared with us their tobacco. Gift horses came to us. Every married woman got skins enough to make some kind of lodge for her household.[6]

Wooden Leg's account typifies one pole of Cheyenne opinion. Significantly, he belonged to the winter roamer Cheyennes and lived in a small kindred that had spent all fall with Crazy Horse. Young Two Moons, another warrior belonging to the non-agency Cheyennes, also remembered that the Oglalas fitted out the refugees with "lodges, robes, and pack saddles—and fitted them out well."[7]

On the other hand, Cheyennes with stronger ties to the agencies told a less favorable story. Crazy Horse "received them with very slight manifestations of pity," reported Cheyennes surrendering the following spring, "and made them feel that their presence in his camp was only tolerated and not desired."[8] Arapaho Chief recalled that the Sioux "gave [the Cheyennes] nothing," forcing them to trade for the "few small lodges" they received. And Little Wolf, a principal chief of the Cheyennes, singled out Crazy Horse himself as without "compassion" for the refugees.[9]

A rather complex process was clearly at work. After initial feasting in Crazy Horse's village, Oglala compassion quickly became selective, targeted at non-agency Cheyennes. Black Elk's recollection, that Oglala men "went from camp to camp to collect clothes and tipis for the Cheyennes," indicates that the *akicita* became the main channel of redistribution. *Akicita* donors would seek to bind Cheyenne recipients to agreeing to the no-surrender line. Indeed, in intertribal councils the Sioux recognized Black Moccasin and his nephew Ice as principal Cheyenne leaders, marginalizing the position of such moderate leaders as Dull Knife and Standing Elk.[10]

Crazy Horse seized upon the Cheyenne disaster to reinforce his anti-agency ideology. One hundred and fifty Indian scouts enlisted at Red Cloud Agency had led Mackenzie to the Cheyenne village, a point not lost on hardliners. Moreover, the reinforcements brought by the Cheyennes encouraged Crazy Horse in a growing conviction that he need not sit out the war. The war chief had already sent runners to invite Sitting Bull back to the hunting grounds south of the Yellowstone. Alone among the Northern Nation leaders, Sitting Bull and Crazy Horse grasped the strategic challenge posed by Miles. Miles's plan was to isolate the Sitting Bull and Crazy Horse groups, then break them piecemeal. Both chiefs sought to keep the two wings of the Northern Nation close enough for ready communication. The Hunkpapa chief had spent a few days of intensive trading with the Métis, but on December 7 he crossed to the south side of the frozen Missouri, heading toward a new rendezvous with Crazy Horse. With his column was a train of mules packing fifty boxes of fixed ammunition, the fruit of the Métis trade.

Nevertheless, Sitting Bull could not dictate to his followers, and even as he turned southward, a further fifty-two lodges, led by Black Moon, White Guts, and Crawler, opted for refuge in Canada. The 109 lodges now in Grandmother's Land constituted almost half of the non-agency Hunkpapas. Sitting Bull remained in control of the main Hunkpapa village, 122 lodges, but on December 18 Lt. Frank D. Baldwin caught Sitting Bull unaware near the head of Redwater Creek. The Hunkpapas scattered over the frozen plains between the Missouri and the Yellowstone. Although he captured the camp and seized the supplies, Baldwin failed to inflict casualties or to capture the ammunition pack train. By the last days of December the Sitting Bull village was regrouping on the lower Powder, but the time lost in refitting prevented the rapid journey to Crazy Horse that the Hunkpapa chief had planned.[11]

The Crazy Horse village had by this time received other reinforcements. On December 16 five headmen from the Miniconjou-Sans Arc village were shot down by Crow army scouts as they approached Tongue River Cantonment to reopen talks with Miles. The peace movement was immediately discredited, and the village leadership resumed total control. This leadership was vested in four chiefs known as

Deciders (*wakicunze*), who were granted temporary control of the village. Spotted Eagle, of the Sans Arcs, was the principal chief; his fellow Deciders were Red Bear, another Sans Arc, and the Miniconjous Lame Deer and Black Shield—four of the most vehement opponents of agency life. Ignoring placatory messages from Miles, the Deciders ordered the village to leave the Yellowstone Valley immediately. They hurried southwest to join Crazy Horse, finding the Oglalas and Cheyennes in a new wintering site just below where Hanging Woman Creek joins the Tongue.[12]

By about December 20 four villages, roughly equal in size, were established at Hanging Woman: Oglala, Cheyenne, Miniconjou, and Sans Arc. Numbering over eight hundred standard lodges, this massive winter gathering included most of the summer strength of the Northern Nation, since significant defections had been prevented by the soldiers' lodge. White Eagle, a headman related to one of Miles's hostages, had made several attempts to leave the Sans Arc village with his four lodges of kin, but each time *akicita* drove him back.[13]

Crazy Horse again seized upon the killing of the peace talkers to swing moderate opinion behind his war front. Vowing revenge upon the Crows, he personally scouted Tongue River Cantonment, but found Miles had dismissed the offending scouts. He returned to Hanging Woman to plan a more ambitious campaign. He proposed to take the offensive, crush Miles, and win back the hunting grounds of the Northern Nation. By the last week of December the strategy had taken shape. Fifty Oglala and Cheyenne warriors were sent to harry the cantonment and draw Miles up the Tongue into a massive ambush to be staged somewhere in the upper valley.[14]

Always a precarious tactic, the decoy plan depended on careful coordination. To ensure surprise, the soldiers' lodge even tried to keep the plan secret from the women. The last thing Crazy Horse needed was village dissension. When a new peace movement emerged in the Miniconjou and Sans Arc villages, he moved swiftly to nip it in the bud. The peace party grew in response to the arrival, about December 23, of two delegates from Cheyenne River Agency. The envoys were Important Man, a Miniconjou headman and brother to hostage Bull Eagle, and Fool Bear, a Sans Arc. They carried tobacco from Lt. Col. George P. Buell, commanding the post overseeing Cheyenne River, but his terms were flatly unconditional: Surrendering parties must give up all horses and arms. The delegates' candid account of the military takeover on the reservation caused much unease, some listeners declaring "they never would submit [on such terms] . . . as long as they lived."[15]

At councils and feasts held throughout the villages, the delegates found that the "Sans Arcs and Minneconjoux were disposed to listen to a little kind talk from us, but the Cheyennes and Ogallalas would not listen, and abused us very much."[16] Red Bear, the Sans Arc Decider, chided them with American bad faith: "'My Friend, we sent a man, your own brother, to the whites, to see on what terms they would let us come in, but they have kept [the hostages] in prison and sent you here, and want us to come in and deliver ourselves up to release them.'" The delegates also spoke to Yellow Grass, a holy man who claimed to be in "constant communion with the spirit of General Custer," even taking his Lakota name of Long Hair. Yellow Grass had access to sources of ammunition, for he was conjuring cases of the stuff at night feasts. Speaking as a former moderate converted to the war faction, he said that he had been "a great friend of the whites, living around the traders a great deal, in the old times ... but now I see they are determined to destroy all our peace and happiness, and my advice will be to my people, as long as I live, never submit to the whites."[17]

As this council closed, Important Man and Fool Bear went to visit the families of the hostages. Suddenly Crazy Horse appeared. Without constituted authority, in a private lodge outside his own village, the war chief warned the delegates they "would never be allowed to take anyone from that camp. If any left they would be followed and killed."[18] His willingness to claim authority beyond the Oglala village demonstrated his determination to preserve the war front at all costs. The decoy party was now en route to Tongue River Cantonment, and Crazy Horse would not tolerate desertions.

Nevertheless the delegates continued to whittle at Miniconjou-Sans Arc solidarity. About December 25 they slipped out of the village after nightfall with thirteen lodges: "We got quite a ways, supposing we had got away, when all at once 'Crazy Horse['] appeared with a good many warriors, who shot all our horses, took our arms and knives, and all our plunder, and then told us if we wanted to go to the whites to go on, but the snow was so deep we could not travel without horses, and we had to return to the hostile camp."[19]

The following day, undaunted, the delegates sought to secure village consensus for a daylight departure. At least 150 lodges, almost one-half the strength of the combined Miniconjous and Sans Arcs, were now willing to leave for Cheyenne River, perhaps alienated by the highhanded manner adopted by Crazy Horse. But when the *akicita* deployed in force, "and told us no Indians could leave that camp alive," the movement petered out. *Akicita* speakers ordered Important Man and Fool Bear to leave the village. They departed, but returned singly by night to toll away four lodges, close relatives of the hostages. As an indicator of the way the wind sat in the Miniconjou village, headman Spotted Elk sent word by the delegates "that he would like to come in if his horses and arms would not be taken from him."[20]

Meanwhile the decoy party had reached Miles's post. On December 26 they drove off 150 head from the beef contractor's herd. Miles was quite as determined as Crazy Horse to end the war swiftly. His column of over four hundred infantry began the march up the Tongue River on December 29, exchanging gunfire with the decoys on January 1 and 3, 1877. On January 6, as the column approached Hanging Woman Creek, it passed the just deserted village sites. The ambush plan called for the villages to move higher up the Tongue toward the Big Horn foothills, where a surprise attack would be easier.

The fragmentary Indian reports and oral histories indicate that dissension continued to threaten the unity of the war front. Upon striking the lodges, part of the Indians headed up the Tongue River, part ascended Hanging Woman. Crazy Horse's Oglalas and most of the Cheyennes, including war leaders Ice and Two Moons, were with the Tongue River group, clearly the core of the war faction. Smaller numbers of Cheyennes and other Sioux took the eastern trail. When Miles's scouts captured a small party of Cheyenne women and children on January 7, however, the two groups

The Battle of Wolf Mountains. *Army and Navy Journal*, May 5, 1877.

hurried to reunite on the Tongue. Disagreement continued on how to free the captives. The Cheyenne White Frog recalled that a party of Sioux "went back to meet Miles and [to] fight or make peace," perhaps reflecting an uneasy compromise between war leaders and moderates.[21]

The party attempted no negotiations; however, over two hundred warriors engaged in a spirited skirmish at dusk until darkness and several artillery rounds dispersed them. That night *akicita* meetings backed Crazy Horse's demand for a full-scale assault on Miles. But disagreement continued. Some argued that the decoys should continue their operations until Miles entered the broken country. Others urged an immediate ambush between Miles's present camp at Belly Butte and the breaks of Wall Creek. Crazy Horse clearly favored the latter option, and early on January 8 he led out some five hundred warriors, about half the total force, identified as Oglalas and Cheyennes. The rest, evidently the majority of the Miniconjous and the Sans Arcs, stayed behind. Perhaps angrily, Crazy Horse "directed the Indians to go down and meet [Miles] . . . or else move camp."[22]

The Battle of Wolf Mountains opened as war party organization collapsed and a rush of warriors alerted Miles that he was under serious attack. Crazy Horse and the other leaders—fellow Oglala Little Big Man, Hump (a Miniconjou *akicita* leader strongly identified with the Oglala war front), and the Cheyennes Ice and Two Moons—sought to control the assault by dividing the force. Oglala warriors took the west side of Tongue River, and Cheyennes attacked from the east. Crazy Horse had his pony shot from under him in one charge. The leaders signaled maneuvers on shrill eagle bone whistles, but despite a spirited attack the warriors could not dislodge Miles from his defensive positions, especially when his artillery began to find the range. As afternoon drew on a blizzard arose, forcing the Indians to disengage and withdraw upstream. Four warriors, including Crazy Horse himself, performed as rearguards while the main party retreated.[23]

As the warriors engaged Miles the villages pressed on up the Tongue, marching through the night and the next day before relocating in a strong defensive position late on January 9. Here at the junction of the Tongue and Prairie Dog Creek (near the modern Montana-Wyoming boundary) the rearguard returned on January 10 to report that Miles had turned back to the cantonment. Miles's withdrawal gave the villages time to regroup and muster resources. Scouts brought still more good news: Buffalo were plentiful "some miles below" the new site, and the jubilant hunters were able to concentrate on making surrounds to replace depleted stores and horsemeat rations.[24]

The presence of game relieved the pressure on the war front, temporarily silencing voices that urged negotiation and surrender. The villages were now grouped in two equal-sized clusters: probably one of Oglalas and Cheyennes, and one of Miniconjous and Sans Arcs. One week after Wolf Mountains the war front received another fillip. Sitting Bull made his delayed arrival on January 15 with about one hundred Hunkpapa lodges, the ammunition pack train, and a fund of scare stories from the agencies. Immediately morale was revived in a flurry of feasts, dances, and councils. "The Heralds harangued through the camp, directing all the Indians to get themselves in good condition for fighting, saying: 'You see, by going to the whites, you will be put in the guard house and held as prisoners.'"[25]

Sitting Bull presided over the distribution of the ammunition, as well as blankets, beads, and tobacco, at village giveaways. "I got some of the cartridges and also some tobacco," reported Eagle Shield. "I got about thirty [needle gun cartridges]. Others got more than I did." Eagle Shield's grandfather, Miniconjou Decider Black Shield, was glad of the revival of the war spirit, stating "he wants to fight—he wants war."[26] Others were able to use Sitting Bull's ammunition to further the war front's aims. The holy man Yellow Grass revived his night rituals, conjuring up no less than ten boxes of cartridges at one meeting.[27]

Yet Sitting Bull's arrival posed new questions for the Northern Nation. What was the coalition's long term strategy? Did it intend to try to remain in the Lakota hunting grounds this year, despite the certainty of renewed campaigning in spring? At inter-village councils Sitting Bull declared his intention to return north of the Missouri, to trade again with the Canadian Métis, and to "induce the Red River Indians [Assiniboins and Crees] to join the hostiles."[28] Carefully worded, this plan left open his subsequent intentions—a return to the war zone, or regrouping in Canada. Although Sitting Bull remained committed to maintaining the coalition, many Hunkpapa headmen were becoming convinced they should join their relatives in Grandmother's Land. Four Horns, Hunkpapa peace chief and Sitting Bull's uncle, most clearly articulated this view.

However nuanced, Hunkpapa opinion was united on a bottom line: no negotiations with Americans, no surrenders at the agencies. Contrasting with Hunkpapa unity, the Miniconjous and Sans Arcs remained deeply polarized over these issues. The village leadership was committed to keeping up the war, but of the Deciders only the Sans Arc Spotted Eagle supported a move to Canada. A number of lesser headmen and war leaders—notably the Miniconjous Flying By and Red Thunder and the Sans Arc Turning Bear—drew closer to Spotted Eagle over the issue. Still other headmen favored peace talks. Eagle Shield, who deserted the village about January 17, summed up their mood after he arrived at Cheyenne River Agency: "Many would come in now if the Indian soldiers would not prevent them." Like him, they "do not want to fight, do not want to see any more war. . . . I heard that [they were] . . . willing to make a treaty provided they can retain all their country and the whites will move out of it."[29]

One of the key players in the reemerging peace party was Miniconjou headman Red Horse, a brother-in-law of Crazy Horse himself. Recalling a visit to Cheyenne River, with its regular rations and security, Red Horse spoke up in open council and "told Crazy Horse in presence of his soldiers" that he recognized the U.S. President as his Great Father—conceding the U.S. government a kinship status denied by hardliners. In his experience, he continued, the whites were "ready to feed the hungry and clothe the naked."[30] Other peace proponents were leaders who had fled Cheyenne River Agency after the military takeover to preserve their pony herds from confiscation. They included Miniconjous Spotted Elk, his brother Touch the Clouds, and their relative Roman Nose; and White Eagle of the San Arcs. All feared pony and arms confiscations, but all agreed that Canada held no attractions. Their stipulation that peace must entail American withdrawal from the hunting grounds was unrealistic, but may have been floated to bring on board hardliners who supported the war, but did not seriously consider exile in Canada.

The peace party had numbered 150 lodges of Miniconjous and Sans Arcs in late December. Regrouping after Wolf Mountains, it was finding new support in the hitherto united Oglala village. On January 16 two Brulés, Charging Horse and Make Them Stand Up, were sent to Spotted Tail Agency "to get the news" and to ask that Brulé head chief Spotted Tail "go there to them with tobacco." They were to state that Spotted Tail's people and theirs were "one and the same," and assure agency chiefs and army officers that a peace embassy would net large-scale surrenders.[31]

Just what body authorized these messengers is unclear. Since it was clearly not any of the hardline village organizations, they were probably deputed at a feast of moderate headmen held in a private lodge. Brulés were certainly present; the later actions of Touch the Clouds and Roman Nose suggest that they also may have sponsored the message. Spider, an Oglala headman and half-brother to agency head chief Red Cloud, may also have been represented in the talks.[32]

Thus by late January two opposing strategies were cohering: One rejected all U.S. dialogue and favored regrouping in the safety of the British possessions; the other urged peace talks through reservation intermediaries. Together, the two factions probably accounted for only half the total strength of the Sioux in the Tongue River villages. Crazy Horse himself, together with almost all Oglalas and Cheyennes, plus significant numbers of Miniconjous and Sans Arcs, belonged in neither faction. For them, continued occupation of the Powder River hunting grounds remained the prime objective.

Crazy Horse had never visited the agencies, rejecting all invitations to counsel with reservation leaders. He realized that surrender would constitute a political minefield for any Northern leader committed to maintaining a position independent of the agency hierarchy. Canada, however, offered no solutions. The country north of the Missouri had been opened to Sioux expansion by the Hunkpapas: Sitting Bull's people could claim primacy in dealing with Canadian officials, marginalizing Oglala leaders. Hence Crazy Horse's determination to maintain the Northern Nation in its traditional hunting grounds.

Despite enjoying greater initial support than the other factions, Crazy Horse's position gradually became untenable. Serious cracks were now appearing in the Oglala front. On January 24 a minor headman named Red Sack unexpectedly found himself invited to the Oglala council tipi. The councilors formally deputed him to go immediately to Red Cloud Agency—hitherto entirely off limits—"to ascertain how matters were and to return and let them know as soon as possible."[33] Red Sack's mission represented a radical departure. Unlike the two Brulé messengers, Red Sack formally represented the Oglala village organization. It is impossible that the mission had the backing of Crazy Horse, but elders and moderate leaders such as No Water may have pressed the issue until the war chief withdrew opposition to preserve solidarity.[34]

About the same time as Red Sack's departure, one even more controversial took place. Some fifteen lodges of Brulés, Oglalas, and Miniconjous slipped away to surrender at Spotted Tail Agency. Led by Eagle Pipe, a Brulé, and the Oglala Spider, they had made an earlier attempt to leave, but had their arms and ponies confiscated by the *akicita*. Relatives secretly outfitted the party with fifty-four horses and a handful of guns. After eluding detection they headed east, their tiny procession floundering through deep snows.[35]

Within a day or so further defections revealed the depth of the crisis faced by the war front. At a soldiers' lodge feast Red Horse told Crazy Horse to his face, "I was going where the whites lived and [would] give myself up to them. I told him he must not send his soldiers to intercept me, better for his cause if he did not for . . . there are many of his own people who [are] like me."[36] Crazy Horse offered no immediate objection, but Red Horse and his supporters had learned the lessons of December and laid careful plans. Both Red Horse and White Eagle visited the tipis of their personal followings, advising them to steal away at night and to rendezvous on Powder River.

A few lodges slipped away, evidently including the kindred of Spotted Elk. Red Horse was successful in invoking his relationship as brother-in-law to Crazy Horse, meeting no resistance as he departed about January 28. But as White Eagle's womenfolk completed their packing, Crazy Horse led "about a hundred of his soldiers, [and] surrounded my camp. Some of them dismounted, entered our lodges and took our guns. . . . I was very angry then at the soldiers, and pulled down my lodge and started right in the face of them. They shot down two of my horses, but I moved on." Altogether some thirty-nine lodges, 229 people, left with the three headmen for Cheyenne River Agency.[37]

So far the desertions were small-scale, but stark realities meant that the massive winter gathering on Tongue River would have to break up. Even in bountiful summer such a huge camp could not remain together long; in winter the scattering of game dictated dispersal. The Hunkpapas were keen to move north, and about January 25 Sitting Bull led some fifty lodges out of the camp. Although many Hunkpapas continued to press for immediate retreat into Canada, Sitting Bull did his best to maintain coalition solidarity. He announced that he would camp at the forks of Powder River; and he and Crazy Horse agreed on a later rendezvous at Blue Earth Creek, an east tributary of the lower Powder. Final decisions about the increasingly divisive issue of Canada could wait till then.[38]

The breakup only encouraged more waverers in the Oglala village. White Eagle Bull, with another man and a woman, left on January 26; five lodges of Brulés left on January 29, both parties bound for Spotted Tail Agency. In a final attempt at enforcing martial law, Crazy Horse's police deployed on February 1 to prevent the departure of leading Cheyenne chief Little Wolf. In an angry scene Little Wolf defied the *akicita*, who confiscated or killed eleven of the Cheyenne ponies, and pressed on with his four lodges for Red Cloud Agency, swearing vengeance on the Oglala war chief.[39]

The policy of "soldiering" that had effectively controlled the Crazy Horse village for almost six months was clearly breaking down. In the face of a growing peace party that tacitly favored opening negotiations, continued soldiering could only rupture what remained of village solidarity. Crazy Horse's actions after February 1 show that he understood this, and moderated his opposition to the peace party. His decision reflected political realities, but it is tempting to speculate that Crazy Horse had reached a critical point in his life. By nature reserved, even diffident, the soldiering may have become an intolerable burden to the war chief: initially necessary to maintain unity, but increasingly coercive and resented by the ordinary people. Faced with soldiers' lodge rhetoric about punitive surrender terms, waverers could point to the pony and arms confiscations carried out by their own *akicita* as scarcely less harsh.

As Northern Nation unity cracked, Crazy Horse became increasingly confused over mapping a concerted strategy. Within a few days of Sitting Bull's departure, another 150 lodges of Hunkpapas, Sans Arcs, and Miniconjous started to join him at Powder River forks, following Spotted Eagle. Early in February most of the remaining Miniconjous and Sans Arcs, about two hundred lodges, drifted uncertainly in their wake. The Oglalas and Cheyennes remained together, but now scouts reported buffalo herds in the Bighorn Valley. A move west after game would compromise Crazy Horse's ability to reunite with Sitting Bull: precisely the opportunity Miles would exploit in breaking the coalition. Crazy Horse continued to favor a move east to counsel with the Hunkpapas at Blue Earth Creek, perhaps citing reports of buffalo even farther east on the upper Little Missouri.[40]

All other Oglala and Cheyenne leaders urged the Bighorn option, and Crazy Horse found himself without support. About February 3 the main village moved west into the Bighorn Valley, about 350 lodges strong. Their number included perhaps thirty lodges of Miniconjous and Sans Arcs, following Hump, who chose to stay with the Oglalas. Only a small cluster of lodges remained on the Tongue. The majority of these—about twenty lodges of Oglalas and Brulés led by No Water, and thirty of Cheyennes following headmen American Horse, Red Owl, Tangle Hair, and Plenty Camps—evidently turned south toward the upper Powder, ultimately bound for surrender at Red Cloud.[41]

Crazy Horse was left with only his own *tiyospaye* or kindred group, some ten lodges strong, composed of his closest relatives. This kindred was one of three that composed the *Hunkpatila* band of Oglalas. The dissolution of the Hunkpatila illustrates well the divisive situation facing Crazy Horse. A second kindred led by his father's brother Little Hawk remained with the main Oglala village, while the third *tiyospaye*, led by his uncles Iron Crow and Running Horse, perhaps followed Spotted Eagle to seek refuge in Canada.[42]

No acrimony seems to have been involved in the division of the village. Soon Crazy Horse's tiny camp moved east across the snowy ridges into the middle Powder valley. His objective thus remained rendezvous with Sitting Bull, but now alarming news arrived from that quarter too. On February 7 the Hunkpapas broke camp at Powder River forks, bound for immediate refuge in Canada. Perhaps Sitting Bull left only after learning of the Oglala move west, thinking Crazy Horse had given up the rendezvous plan. Once beyond the Yellowstone, other Hunkpapa leaders forced the pace, crossing the frozen Missouri on February 15 twenty miles above Fort Peck. But, in a mirror image of Crazy Horse's actions, Sitting Bull himself budded off the main village with ten lodges, stalling on the headwaters of Big Dry Creek.[43] There Sitting Bull monitored the back trail, still seeking to maintain a chain of camps linking his followers with Crazy Horse. But his position was plain: regrouping of the coalition in Canada and only an indefinite return to the homeland.

Crazy Horse must have been bitterly disillusioned when Sitting Bull's runner found him. As the unity of the Northern Nation irretrievably broke down, it seemed that the homeland was now his sole burden. With a divided people, and a dual threat from military action and the subtler compromises of negotiation, Crazy Horse was unsure how to formulate a new strategy for preserving the hunting grounds. Such a strategy would have to encompass the previously unthinkable: that the remnant Northern Nation could no longer resist the bluecoated troops it had so comprehensively defeated not one year before. Psychologically, Crazy Horse seemed unable to summon the reserves of willpower that had driven him through the winter to maintain the war front at all costs. He drew back from the spiral of punishment imposed upon his own people and withdrew into a caricature of his normal peacetime diffidence. As the late winter wore on, Crazy Horse turned increasingly for guidance to the holy men of his band, preparing himself to undergo the *hanbleceya* or vision quest, that he might beg the powers of the universe for guidance in this deepest crisis of his life, of his people.

Meanwhile at base camps becalmed by winter, army commanders prepared a new diplomatic offensive against the Northern Nation. From Tongue River Cantonment Colonel Miles dispatched his half-Sioux scout Johnny Bruguier and Sweet Taste Woman, one of the Cheyenne captives, on February 1. Three hundred miles southeast, the White River agencies were the scene of intense talks between General

Crook's subordinates and the reservation chiefs. Courted by Crook, Spotted Tail declined to lead an embassy north until unconditional surrender terms were relaxed, but at Red Cloud Agency Crook's proposals met with a warmer response. The Oglala agency had long been perceived as a trouble spot, but a younger generation of Oglala leaders were determined to improve its image and to forestall government proposals to remove the reservation Sioux to Indian Territory. Many had already served as scouts in Mackenzie's winter campaign. When Maj. Julius W. Mason, commanding Camp Robinson, asked for delegates to go north, thirty men volunteered. Representing all the agency Oglala bands, their leader was Hunts the Enemy, a nephew of Red Cloud himself and an *akicita* leader in his Bad Face band.[44]

Equipped with tobacco packages and presents for the Northern chiefs, Hunts the Enemy's party set out on January 16. They were beset by Cheyenne horse thieves and morale problems, and made slow progress until they crossed the Belle Fourche on February 8. There they met Red Sack's small party bound for the agency. Red Sack's report seems to have galvanized the delegates, for they now made good progress through worsening conditions. Passing down the thickly snowed valley of the Little Powder, the party cut the trail of forty lodges heading east. These were the tracks of the camp of Red Horse, Spotted Elk, and White Eagle. These people had met as planned on Powder River. Detailing one man to follow up the trail, Hunts the Enemy continued down the Little Powder. As they neared its mouth they "met three Indians who told them that Crazy Horse was encamped some little distance above on Powder River and that Sitting Bull was just below the mouth of Little Powder."[45] Deciding that their Oglala relatives were the priority, the delegation swung up the valley of Powder River. About February 11, as they approached the mouth of Clear Creek, the delegates made out through the thick bottomland timber a small cluster of ten tipis, Crazy Horse's camp.

The delegates were "kindly received," they later reported, in deep contrast to Crazy Horse's reception of earlier envoys. Many people in the camp were their relatives, and the thirty-man party numbered about twice the strength of the tiny camp. After a feast of welcome a herald called a formal council. There, Hunts the Enemy and other speakers presented the army's terms of surrender at the agencies. "Their speeches," the delegates reported, "were not [immediately] responded to."[46] Etiquette prescribed that messengers sleep at the host village after making their proposal, leaving the camp council to debate the issues and reach a decision. In a small camp and on such a matter, all adult males with a war record would participate in the council. Red Feather, Crazy Horse's young brother-in-law and comrade, remembered clearly his kinsman's mood. "Crazy Horse didn't want to go to the agency. He didn't answer them for a long time."[47]

Indeed, the second council called the following day was an exercise in stalling. Crazy Horse was surprisingly gracious, saying that the delegates "were relations and should be friends."[48] After the pipe had circulated, he said,

> the smoke was good. He did not commence the war. His relations were at the Agencies; he could send for all the [Northern Nation] Indians and let them decide

what they could do; that if he told them to stay they would do so, even if they were to die, but he would let them say.[49]

Politely, Crazy Horse declined to open the delegates' tobacco. He told Hunts the Enemy to take it to the main Oglala village in the Bighorn Valley. Whatever their decision, he reiterated, he would "do the same as the others did."[50]

After a couple of days of talks, the delegates divided. Some, including Crazy Horse's relative Tall Man, stayed in the war chief's camp. Others started for the agency. Only four pressed on to the main Oglala village: Hunts the Enemy himself; Running Hawk (a brother of agency Oglala chief Young Man Afraid of His Horses); Long Whirlwind (formerly an *akicita* leader in the Oyuhpe band with relatives in the Northern Oglala village); and the Cheyenne-Sioux Fire Crow. Although mounted on fresh horses from Crazy Horse's own herd, the going was bad, and the delegates took three days to reach Tongue River. Finally they located the Oglala-Cheyenne village on Rotten Grass Creek in the foothills of the Big Horn Mountains. Uproar seized the village and warriors raced out to meet the four delegates, leading them to the council tipi.[51]

After a brief talk the delegates were dismissed to private lodges. They learned that Miles's envoys had already opened negotiations. A deputation of twenty-nine men, chiefly Cheyennes but including the Miniconjou Hump and three other Sioux, had left for Tongue River Cantonment with Bruguier and Sweet Taste Woman five nights before. Little else reassured the four delegates, and they spent an anxious night. So fearful were Long Whirlwind and Fire Crow that they decided not to attend the big council called the next day.

Only Hunts the Enemy and Running Hawk entered the great council tipi and sat before the circle of Oglala and Cheyenne leaders. After the pipe had passed, an Oglala *akicita* arose and ordered Hunts the Enemy to speak. The delegate stood and addressed the council, stating that he was sent by General Crook himself. Crook's message was that the Great Father in Washington wished all wars between Indians and whites to end. All the Oglalas should live, like the agency bands, in peace. The Northern bands should come to Red Cloud Agency, where "there shall be nothing untoward done to them."[52]

The *Akicita* now ordered Oglala elder Iron Hawk to respond, "but speak as we said to speak, only." An accomplished orator and camp herald, Iron Hawk ordered Hunts the Enemy to "carefully hearken as you sit." He reviewed the intrusion of Americans into the Lakota hunting grounds and the resulting war. If, however, the Great Father was serious in wishing peace,

he shall have it . . . [for] I am the very one who, when someone tries to outdo me in being agreeable, I always win. So I shall move camp and approach [Red Cloud Agency], but I am burdened down with much meat; I am heavy; there is much snow; all the rivers lie across my road; and they are deep. I must travel slowly, so [Hunts the Enemy], before I arrive, you shall come to me again, or else send your men to me.[53]

Iron Hawk concluded by saying that he spoke for the Oglalas and Cheyennes. The Miniconjous and Hunkpapas were in the country "below," and would have to be consulted separately.

An undertaking had been made. The Oglalas and Cheyennes would visit Red Cloud Agency in the spring and make peace with General Crook. More problematic issues, such as pony and arms confiscations, were passed over for the present, perhaps for debate with the later delegates requested by Iron Hawk. The decision had been made without consulting Crazy Horse. Although no formal break had occurred with the nominal war chief, and both delegates and councilors were at pains to cite Crazy Horse's amenability to village consensus, the Northern Oglala council was now acting independently of him.

The delegates remained in the village for several days, observing developments and awaiting news from Miles and Crazy Horse. Soon after the big council, runners from Crazy Horse arrived to invite all bands "to meet him on little Powder river."[54] Crazy Horse had now heard reports of an embassy led by Spotted Tail, and wished to finally decide the issue of peace or war at a full gathering of the Northern Nation.[55] During the last week of February Crazy Horse moved his ten lodges east across the bleak divide into the upper valley of the Little Powder, camping amidst deep snows. As they traveled they were joined by people from the main village, responding to Crazy Horse's invitation. By February 26, when five more of Major Mason's delegates departed for the agency, a total of 120 lodges, chiefly Oglalas and Cheyennes, had gathered on the Little Powder.[56]

Near the forks of Powder River was the main village of Miniconjous and Sans Arcs, while Spotted Eagle's village was somewhere on the east side of the lower Powder—a total of about three hundred lodges or more. Crazy Horse may briefly have believed that he could recombine the majority of the Northern Nation, but late in February new discouragements multiplied. Sitting Bull's response to the Oglala invitation to a new rendezvous was flat: "He was going north to the British Possessions," and was unequivocally abandoning the hunting grounds.[57] Faced with Sitting Bull's imminent departure, the Spotted Eagle village hurried across the frozen Yellowstone on February 26–27, ascending Cedar Creek to join the Hunkpapa war chief in the upper Missouri valley.[58] About the same time the main Miniconjou-Sans Arc village moved east to the upper Little Missouri. Its intentions were unclear, but constituted a rejection of any grand council with Crazy Horse.[59]

Closer to home, the 110 lodges of Oglalas and Cheyennes camped near Crazy Horse declined to form a united village with his tiny camp. As February turned into March they organized for buffalo hunting, making two successful surrounds, but maintained their distance from the war chief. When delegate Tall Man left for the agency on March 4, he observed only that "quite a number of Indians were camped within about a days march" of Crazy Horse.[60] Thus even those Oglalas who had responded to Crazy Horse's invitation were careful not to recharter a village in which he could reassert martial law through the *akicita*. It seems likely these people were already committed to surrender ahead of any council. Perhaps in an effort to mollify them, Crazy Horse made a reluctant undertaking to the delegates to "come in [to Red Cloud Agency] and hold a council" during the spring.[61]

Even more discouraging, Crazy Horse's own kindred was beginning to fragment by the beginning of March. Four lodges, evidently including that of his own father, Worm, left on a hunt for small game down the Little Powder. Most demoralizing of all, another four lodges turned south to join No Water in immediate surrender, arriving at Red Cloud Agency on March 14.[62] This left Crazy Horse, the greatest Lakota war leader of the day, with a following of two lodges in the snow drifts of the Little Powder. Every day brought news of fresh defections. On March 3 Four Horns crossed into Canada with fifty-seven lodges of Hunkpapas, bringing the total in exile to 166 lodges. On March 4 the deputation sent to Tongue River Cantonment arrived home in the main Cheyenne-Oglala village on the Little Bighorn. Miles had offered them a home at Tongue River if they surrendered and agreed to enlist as scouts against hostile Indians. Leaving that question open, the council was satisfied enough to call a formal end to hostilities, and had it "cried through the camps that the war was over, and that no more hostile expeditions would be allowed against the white man."[63]

A further arrival from the reservation brought significant news. Red Sack had reached Red Cloud Agency on February 23 and had been permitted to return north, his fact-finding mission complete. He confirmed that Spotted Tail was mounting the biggest diplomatic initiative yet.[64] The two Brulé messengers from the north had arrived at his agency on February 10 with the news that an embassy led by Spotted Tail would net at least one hundred surrendering lodges. Immediately the Brulé head chief went into intensive talks with Crook and won crucial (if off-the-record) concessions. The thorny topic of pony confiscations was finessed when Crook agreed that stock be surrendered to enlisted Sioux army scouts, who would be free to redistribute them to their Northern relatives. Most significantly, he promised to recommend to the President in Washington that the Northern Nation be assigned a separate reservation in the hunting grounds, once all hostile bands had surrendered.[65]

Armed with these concessions Spotted Tail had departed his agency on February 13, taking the trail along the east edge of the Black Hills. With him were 250 Brulé headmen, including band chiefs Swift Bear, Two Strike, and Iron Shell, a mule train of presents, and interpreters José Merrivale, Frank C. Boucher, and Tom Dorion. Crazy Horse was evidently apprehensive at the news. His father, Worm, was married to two sisters of Spotted Tail, women the war chief called "mother." In Lakota society an uncle had compelling influence over his nephew. As the non-treaty coalition dissolved, an able politician like Spotted Tail might assimilate surrendering Indians into his own agency bands, marginalizing Northern leaders. Aware of his own precarious position, and unprepared to negotiate with his Brulé uncle, Crazy Horse at last decided to set out on a vision quest, to implore the cosmic powers for guidance for himself and his people. "There were things that he had to figure out," recalled his cousin Nicholas Black Elk in 1931, "and he was wanting the spirits to guide him. He would then go back to his people and tell them what he had learned."[66]

About March 5 Crazy Horse and his wife, Black Shawl, packed their tipi and struck into the snowy hills between the forks of Powder River. Black Shawl was probably already sick with a serious respiratory illness, so although childless, the couple was not alone. Also living in their tipi was Tall Bull (possibly a Miniconjou relative) and two women and two boys—useful to Black Shawl in running the lodge in her husband's absence. A second tipi of relatives accompanied them, all that was left of the ten lodges that had followed the war chief from Tongue River.[67]

For almost three weeks Crazy Horse disappeared among the snowy ridges between the Powder and Little Powder. Only one eyewitness account exists from those missing weeks. The Black Elk family was pressing on to surrender when, recalled Nicholas Black Elk:

> We found Crazy Horse all alone on a creek with just his wife. He was a queer man. He had been queer all of this winter. Crazy Horse said to my father: "Uncle, you might have noticed me, how I act, but it is for the good of my people that I am out alone. Out there I am making plans—nothing but good plans—for the good of my people. I don't care where the people go. They can go where they wish. There are lots of caves and this shows that I cannot be harmed. . . . This country is ours, therefore I am doing this."[68]

For days at a time, carrying only a pipe and tobacco bag, Crazy Horse left his tipi to seek the vision of guidance. Sheltering in caves only when late winter storms blasted the Plains, he fasted and prayed, wept and begged the powers for the vision that could show him how best to preserve his people's lands. Still the vision eluded him. He was an experienced quester, having dreamed of such powerful healers as Thunder and Rock, and Horse and the Shadow, but this desperate effort yielded nothing. At endurance's end he would return home and make purifying sweat baths, talking over his experiences with his relatives, before leaving once more for the wilderness.

As this private drama unfolded, pivotal public events centered on Spotted Tail's peace mission. On February 20 the delegation met Eagle Pipe's fifteen lodges at Box Elder Creek. Eagle Pipe told the Brulé chief that he had left the camp of Red Horse, Spotted Elk, and White Eagle on the Little Missouri, en route for surrender at Cheyenne River Agency. Spotted Tail hurried Eagle Pipe southward while the delegation pressed north of the Black Hills. Near Where-the-Crows-Were-Killed Butte, a landmark commanding the trail to Cheyenne River Agency, a base camp was established. Spotted Tail sent runners to all villages, scheduling a grand council on Little Powder River late in March. In doing this he was adopting as his own Crazy Horse's aborted plan for a Northern Nation council.[69]

In setting up his base camp Spotted Tail also hoped to open early negotiations with the Miniconjous and Sans Arcs. By the first days of March their main village, 136 lodges, had located on the Little Missouri River within thirty miles of Spotted Tail's camp. The village remained deeply divided over the issue of war. A part, cohering about the leadership of Roman Nose, was clearly keen to parley with the Brulé delegation. Another faction, associated with Touch the Clouds, was perhaps awaiting word of the reception accorded to Spotted Elk upon surrender at Cheyenne River. A significant faction remained committed to war, however, and had unleashed a new offensive against the Black Hills miners. Beginning the second week of February, a thirty-man war party struck panic into the mining settlements of the northern Black Hills, stealing horses and hundreds of cattle and sheep.[70]

Divided and hungry, the village continued to fragment in search of game, but one hundred lodges moved near Spotted Tail's base camp and opened tentative negotiations by March 5. Lame Deer's son, the *akicita* leader Fast Bull, acted as spokesman. He said that the rest of the scattered village "had been sent for[,] and when they came back they would then have a grand council" with Spotted Tail on the Little Missouri. Although Fast Bull assured the Brule chief that "they would then take tobacco and make peace.... [He] would not take the tobacco until they had the council."[71]

The Miniconjous and Sans Arcs remained divided, however, and by the second week of march a majority were gravitating back westward into the Powder River valley perhaps to await the grand council at Little Powder, some perhaps to monitor the continuing negotiations with Miles. Growing impatient, Spotted Tail himself struck west to reach the Little Missouri some ten miles above the Short Pine Hills about March 13. There he found thirty crowded lodges. Nearby was a second hunting camp of forty lodges. After the arrival of Spotted Tail the two camps reunited in a single village. Comprising Miniconjous, Sans Arcs, and a few Oglalas, the village nominated Touch the Clouds as its speaker. This son of late Miniconjou head chief Lone Horn was a regular visitor at the White River agencies. Probably by now aware that his brother Spotted Elk had been forced to surrender all his stock upon capitulation at Cheyenne River, Touch the Clouds was glad to hear Spotted Tail's assurances about his ponies and the qualified promise of a reservation in the north. After five days of talks held during fierce storms, Touch the Clouds "promised to return" with Spotted Tail to the Brulé agency.[72]

With the storm blown out, the Brulé delegation pressed westward to rejoin the main Miniconjou-Sans Arc village, now located on the Little Powder about fifteen miles above its mouth. Spotted Tail arrived there on March 20, finding one hundred crowded lodges, including a few Oglala and Cheyenne visitors. The village had reorganized itself again, and appointed as Deciders Lame Deer, his son Fast Bull, Black Shield, and Roman Nose. This leadership was still polarized, and Spotted Tail had to deploy all his powers of persuasion in six days of intense debate. Both Lame Deer and Fast Bull insisted that peace was impossible as long as miners remained in the Black Hills and Miles's troops occupied the Lakota hunting grounds. To this point Spotted Tail may have intimated that Miles's garrison would be closed once hostilities ended. Of the other Deciders, Roman Nose was "specially anxious for peace," according to interpreter Frank Boucher. Roman Nose had strong Brulé connections. Clearly influenced by the presence of his close associates Iron Shell and Swift Bear, Roman Nose favored immediate surrender at Spotted Tail Agency.[73]

Black Shield, the remaining Decider, was the key to village consensus. Long opposed to reservations, and a staunch supporter of the war, just what persuaded Black Shield to finally swing his support behind Roman Nose is unclear. Spotted Tail's promise of a new reservation in the hunting grounds, and the assurances of nominal surrenders of stock coupled with the deepening poverty of his people, must have borne out the arguments of the peace party. By March 25 a clear majority of people favored surrender at Spotted Tail, formalized in a consensus statement by the Deciders. Roman Nose and Black Shield accepted Spotted Tail's tobacco and smoked the pipe of agreement. Lame Deer and Fast Bull declined to smoke, but chose not to force the issue, stating only that they wished to remain and "collect more [Miniconjous] . . . who were scattered."[74]

There remained the unresolved issue of Crazy Horse and the Oglalas. The largest Cheyenne and Oglala village was still on Tongue River, awaiting the return of a second delegation to Miles. Six Oglalas from that village were visiting the Miniconjous and San Arcs as delegates to the grand council. Their leader, Black Twin's Son, advised Spotted Tail that a new Oglala rendezvous had been arranged at Bear Lodge Butte (modern Devil's Tower), near the northwest edge of the Black Hills. Those Oglalas that had been on the Little Powder near Crazy Horse early in March had already moved to Bear Lodge; the village now on Tongue River would soon join them. Black Twin's Son assured Spotted Tail that "so soon as he got to his people, he was going to move in [to Red Cloud Agency] with his family."[75]

Spotted Tail remained unconvinced. The Bear Lodge rendezvous constituted a rejection of his own grand council. Other reports indicate that the Oglalas intended leaving their village at Bear Lodge, while the men alone traveled to Spotted Tail Agency to parley and "trade their robes & furs"—a traditional courtesy visit only.[76] Mindful of Crook's stipulation that all Northern Indians must surrender, Spotted Tail sent his last package of tobacco to Bear Lodge, warning the Oglalas "not to come in unless they brought their women and children—that they must bring their wives and children with them."[77]

On Crazy Horse, above all, the Brulé chief remained unsure. No satisfactory news had been heard from the war chief since he departed on his vision quest. Spotted Tail's own runners could not locate him. His father, Worm, had arrived in the Little Powder village with his four lodges. Worm told his brother-in-law that Crazy Horse "was out hunting by himself," but insisted that he would make peace, "and shakes hands through his father the same as if he himself did it." Worm presented a pony to José Merrivale "as a token that Crazy Horse makes peace."[78]

Still concerned that Crazy Horse was deliberately avoiding him, Spotted Tail detailed one Brulé warrior and an agency Oglala to take tobacco and search for the war chief. Then, on March 26, Spotted Tail turned eastward. Up to ninety lodges followed him. As well as the Miniconjous and Sans Arcs, Worm's small party of Oglalas opted for surrender. Only ten or fifteen lodges chose to remain with Lame Deer and Fast Bull. Despite wretched trails, swollen streams, and the exhausted stock, Spotted Tail forced the pace to cover seventy miles in two days, reuniting with Touch the Clouds's camp late on March 27. Here a single village organization was re-established, seating Miniconjous Touch the Clouds and Roman Nose, with the Sans Arcs High Bear and Red Bear, as Deciders. The village then started south at a more leisurely pace. After crossing the Belle Fourche on April 2, Spotted Tail felt confident enough to leave the village and hurried in to his agency with the news of the imminent surrender.[79]

Even as Spotted Tail turned east from the Powder River drainage, Oglalas and Cheyennes from the main village were approaching the valley from the west. Dissatisfied at reports of the second delegation to Miles, they were heading for the

"Delegation of Sioux Indians who made the treaty whereby the Black Hills were surrendered to the U.S. Government." Seated: (l. to r.) Yellow Bear, Interpreter José Merrivale, Interpreter Billy Garnett, Interpreter Leon Pallardy, Three Bears. Standing: (l. to r.) He Dog, Little Wound, American Horse, Little Big Man, Young Man Afraid of His Horses, Hunts the Enemy (George Sword). NSHS-RG2095-78

new rendezvous at Bear Lodge. Probably on March 2 they arrived on Powder River some twenty miles above the Little Powder. Awaiting them at the campground was a familiar tipi: Crazy Horse had at last returned from his vision quest and, with Spotted Tail's departure, seemed ready to resume his role as war chief.[80]

An Oglala council was called. The delegates to Miles had left Tongue River Cantonment on the twenty-third, and were doubtless present. Little Hawk, Worm's brother, was the ranking Oglala delegate, with Hard to Kill (another relation of Crazy Horse's) representing the Hunkpatila band *akicita*. Four Crows, an *akicita* in the Sore-Backs band, had also visited Miles. They reported that both Hump and his brother, the Miniconjou headman Horse Road, with seven Cheyennes, had remained at Tongue River Cantonment as hostages guaranteeing the surrender of their relatives. Nevertheless, their report discouraged any Oglala capitulation to Miles. A clear consensus prevailed for negotiations at Red Cloud Agency, but expectations were high that Crazy Horse would have a significant contribution to make to the council. Instead, the war chief sat quietly through the debate. It was left to Iron Hawk to once more crystalize the consensus position: "You see all the people here are in rags, they all need clothing, we might as well go in." Crazy Horse indicated his weary, tacit approval, and the council closed.[81]

Crazy Horse's silence actually betrayed his continued indecision. The three weeks of his vision quest had left him gaunt but unenlightened. If the powers had granted him any vision, its significance was unclear, committing him to no definite course of action. That was demonstrated immediately after the council, when messengers arrived at his tipi with the astonishing news that Lame Deer had remained on the Little Powder that morning, rejecting Spotted Tail's tobacco and planning to leave on a buffalo hunt on Tongue River the following day. Instantly galvanized, Crazy Horse determined to join the Miniconjou chief. That evening he confided in his old comrade He Dog, who unsuccessfully tried to talk him out of the plan. On the morning of March 27, as the Oglala village prepared to press on to Bear Lodge, Crazy Horse departed to join Lame Deer.[82]

Crazy Horse clearly felt that Lame Deer's stance was nearest to his own. He still wished to keep the Northern coalition alive, and retain Lakota hunting grounds in the Powder River Country. Lame Deer's hunt offered the last opportunity for that course of action. Crazy Horse may have calculated that his dramatic departure would cause a break in the Oglala village, with the core winter roamers choosing to follow their war chief. If so, his hopes were cruelly dashed. Only one other Oglala lodge, that of the eternally defiant Low Dog, decided to join Lame Deer. About ten lodges of Hump's Miniconjous, flouting their chief's order to surrender to Miles, may have followed Crazy Horse down the Powder.[83]

Once united with Lame Deer, the reality of the situation soon became plain to Crazy Horse. Lame Deer had no strategic aim, stating simply that he wished to make one more buffalo hunt; then he might turn in his camp at Cheyenne River. A few more irreconcilables gravitated toward Lame Deer's camp. At Bear Butte thirty lodges of disillusioned Miniconjous and Sans Arcs broke away from the village bound for Spotted Tail. Several lodges of Hunkpapas appeared from Sitting Bull with more depressing news. Camped in the Missouri River bottoms forty-five miles above Fort Peck, Sitting Bull's village had been caught by a sudden thaw on the morning of March 17. His camp destroyed, the Hunkpapa leader had finally withdrawn toward the Canadian border.[84]

Peaking at only sixty-three lodges, wavering between defiance and the nostalgic wish for one last hunt before surrender, the Lame Deer camp offered no military solution to Crazy Horse's quandary. In despair, perhaps concerned by his wife's weakening condition, Crazy Horse finally turned back to rejoin the Oglalas. Chastened, with no announcement, he rode quietly into the Oglala village at Bear Lodge about April 3. His dream of a revived coalition to hold the Powder River Country was over.

After the frantic activity of March, the pace of Crazy Horse's life slowed abruptly. The village took time to regroup, resting and recouping stock. After two months of dispersal, it reorganized in a single camp circle of up to 155 lodges, mostly Oglalas but including about twenty-five lodges of Brulés, ten of Miniconjous, and five of Sans Arcs. Four new Deciders were seated to administer affairs: Little Hawk, Little Big Man, Old Hawk, and Big Road. They selected He Dog to act as head *akicita*. Hunting parties departed, small family groups scattering to forage in a terrain still blasted by storms and mired by thaw.[85]

At first Crazy Horse seemed listless, despairing. "This country is ours, therefore I am doing this," he had told the Black Elk family a month before. Now he seemed to believe that "[a]ll is lost anyway . . . the country is lost."[86] News continued to confirm his despair. The main Miniconjou-Sans Arc village surrendered at Spotted Tail Agency on April 14. Reports from the north located Sitting Bull's village in the Milk River valley within fifty minutes of the Canadian line. Numbering 135 lodges of Hunkpapas, Sans Arcs, Miniconjous, and a few Oglalas, they would finally cross the medicine line into Grandmother's Land during the first week of May, bringing the total of refugee Lakotas in Canada to about three hundred lodges.

Closer to home the Cheyenne resistance had finally collapsed. When the Oglalas pressed on to Bear Lodge the Cheyennes had remained in camp on Powder River for an intense round of councils. The delegates from Miles prevailed upon some three hundred people, including forty-three lodges of Cheyennes (and four lodges of Hump's closest Miniconjou relatives) to surrender at Tongue River Cantonment. These Cheyennes, including war-leaders like Ice and Two Moons, had been the core of Crazy Horse's Cheyenne supporters during the winter soldiering regime. A contingent of sixty Southern Cheyennes rode through the village and announced that they would turn themselves in at their own agency in Indian Territory (modern Oklahoma). Most, however, were swayed by the arrival of seven Cheyenne messengers from Red Cloud and their assurance of good treatment. When the chiefs' council announced that every Cheyenne could choose his place of surrender, the majority—almost six hundred people—opted for Red Cloud. Two small parties decided to stay out, one joining Lame Deer, but for the Cheyennes the war was over. The main village, following chiefs Dull Knife and Standing Elk, hurried on past Bear Lodge early in April. Living in wretched tents made from gunny sacks and old blankets, horse-poor and hungry, many Cheyennes still nursed their grievance against Crazy Horse. They made no secret that upon surrender many warriors would volunteer as army scouts for a spring campaign against the Oglala war chief.[87]

Yet as the days passed, Crazy Horse seems to have undergone a change of heart. In private talks with agency envoys and Oglala headmen, he mulled over Crook's plan to seek a separate reservation for the Northern Indians. Little Big Man, Big Road, and the other headmen had heard that the presidential election of 1876 had placed a new Great Father, Republican Rutherford B. Hayes, in Washington. Crazy Horse had always rejected the kinship status of the president, but word that Hayes was an old Civil War comrade of Crook's boosted confidence that the general could deliver on his promises.

Slowly, Crazy Horse began to formulate a more measured response to the offer of peace. One development that may have clinched his decision was that agency Oglala chiefs Young Man Afraid of His Horses, American Horse, and Yellow Bear had opened a dialogue with Colonel Mackenzie at Camp Robinson. In return for locating their three bands, over two hundred lodges, at a new reserve on Tongue River, they promised to make peace with neighboring tribes and work as scouts against hostile Indians. Mackenzie undertook to report favorably up the chain of command.[88] The assurance that agency and Northern Oglalas could cooperate in seeking a reserve in the hunting grounds may have gone far to convince Crazy Horse that an honorable peace could be won for his people. In a momentous private decision, the war chief decided he would gamble upon Crook's promise and go to Red Cloud

Agency. And in a startling shift towards pragmatism, he even approved a provisional agency site high up Tongue River, near the site of modern Sheridan, Wyoming.[89]

Finally, at a big council held in his honor, Crazy Horse delivered his considered response to the latest round of agency delegates. Rising briefly from his seat, Crazy Horse spoke tersely and simply: "This day I have untied my horse's tail and layed [*sic*] my gun aside and I have sat down." The envoys pressed him to order the camp moved, but the war chief demurred: "Not until I rest, then I will be willing to go. But before I go, give lots of ammunition to my people. I have set a place for my people that will be the reservation."[90]

At this, or another council held within a few days, Crazy Horse expanded on his change of heart. He cited the new Great Father in Washington, "who was a very good man, and [who] would probably do more for the Indians than any who had proceeded him." The very fact that Crazy Horse conceded kinship status to the president was a radical departure. The decision had at last been made. Six Northern messengers were sent to Red Cloud with positive word. The village would leave Bear Lodge and cross the Belle Fourche River on April 16, hoping to arrive at the Red Cloud Agency by April 28.[91]

Meanwhile at Camp Robinson the army had continued to monitor ambivalent reports about Crazy Horse's intentions. From statements by agency Oglalas, Mackenzie concluded that Crazy Horse was unlikely to surrender, and that the winter roaming segments of the Oglalas and Cheyennes "will almost certainly stay out."[92] Such an eventuality would require a spring campaign, for which Crook and Mackenzie must implement immediate plans. Anxious to confirm Crazy Horse's intentions, Crook conferred with Red Cloud himself about April 10. The Oglala agency head chief had been out of favor with Crook since the previous fall, when the general deposed him and appointed Spotted Tail nominal chief of both White River agencies. Both Crook and, subsequently, his chief of Indian Scouts, Lt. William P. Clark, played on Red Cloud's insecurity. After three days of talks, in which Clark tacitly promised Red Cloud's restoration by appointing him first sergeant of scouts, the Oglala chief formed an eighty-man Oglala delegation to meet Crazy Horse. Led by Red Cloud and band chiefs Yellow Bear, Slow Bull, and the lately surrendered No Water, accompanied by interpreters Antoine Ladeau, Antoine Janis, and José Merrivale, the party struck north on April 13, leading the obligatory pack train of rations and presents.[93]

Within three days of Red Cloud's departure, the runners from the Northern village began to appear at the agency with the positive news that the army had awaited so long: Crazy Horse was coming in. Up the trail Red Cloud's party also fielded encouraging news. The village indeed broke camp on April 16, making its first overnight stop on Bear Lodge Creek, on the south side of the Belle Fourche. With *akicita* restrictions lifted, three lodges of Brulés immediately departed for Spotted Tail Agency, traveling much faster than the main village, which was delayed in awaiting the return of hunting parties. Its schedule further slowed by "very rainy weather" and the rail-thin stock, the village made slow progress. But about April 20 the van met Red Cloud's party. Red Cloud's heralds had a simple message: "All is well; have no fear; come on in."[94]

Nervousness was inevitable as agency leaders and Northern Oglalas met, but Red Cloud handled the amenities well. He succeeded in assuring Crazy Horse and the other leaders that no punishment would follow their surrender—no academic issue, for Kiowa, Comanche, and Southern Cheyenne leaders in the Red River War had been sent to imprisonment in Florida only two years before. He carefully explained the procedure of surrendering stock: It would all be given up to the agency Oglala scouts, and later redistributed among the Northern village. The village herd, although in poor shape, was exceptionally large at 2,200 head. Keen to reaffirm their kinship status with agency relatives, five hundred head were given as presents by the Northern people during the march south. On firearms, Red Cloud could offer no good news: All would have to be given up, he explained, perhaps sniping at Spotted Tail, who seems to have claimed the army would demand only captured weapons. Here was a flashpoint for trouble, but Crazy Horse merely remarked: "All right, let them have them."[95]

If any leader ever needed careful handling, it was Crazy Horse, but the diplomatic Red Cloud was equal to the occasion. "We all went in to the agency in good spirits," recalled Short Bull; there "was no bad feeling among the chiefs or anybody."[96] Crazy Horse's surprising tractability can only be explained by his new commitment to a negotiated solution to his people's predicament. Red Cloud explained that a delegation of Oglala leaders would be invited to counsel with the president in Washington about Crook's scheme for a reservation in the hunting grounds. Although he had refused to represent the Northern Oglalas on a similar delegation prior to the war, Crazy Horse now immediately agreed to go to Washington. Welcoming the opportunity to lay the Northern Nation's case before the new Great Father, he questioned Red Cloud and his comrades closely about the protocol and practicalities of such trips.[97]

The difficult details of surrender worked out, it remained only for a full-dress feast and council to make a public announcement to the village of what lay ahead. Hosted by Crazy Horse and the Northern leadership, Red Cloud and the agency delegates were formally invited to the council tipi. Rising from his seat, Crazy Horse personally spread a buffalo robe for Red Cloud to sit upon. Then, in the most conciliatory gesture yet, he removed his own hair-fringed war shirt, symbolic of his status as principal war chief of the Oglalas, and placed it over Red Cloud's shoulders.[98]

Crazy Horse thus transferred symbolic supremacy in the village to Red Cloud, and tacitly accepted the primacy of the agency Oglalas' tribal organization over that of the Northern village. It was a startling gesture of conciliation at the end of this winter of unprecedented polarization and hardship, when Crazy Horse had taken the coercive potential of Lakota society further than any leader in history. Through an effort of extraordinary will, he had sought to maintain the Northern coalition as a military force all winter, keeping up village strengths that were unmatched even for summer operations. Repeatedly he had tightened the bonds of *akicita* control, normally relaxed after each major hunt or war party, over a people increasingly war weary. In unprecedented fashion he had sought to impose his personal control even beyond his own Oglala camp circle, marching boldly into other villages—even into private lodges—to persuade, to cajole, or even to inflict punishment, whatever was necessary to maintain the war front and save the hunting grounds of his people.

Now it was over. With military options used up and exile in Canada unacceptable, only diplomacy remained. Warily, Crazy Horse accepted the inevitable and agreed to surrender and then open negotiations with military and civil authorities over a reservation in the hunting grounds. As the Deciders issued their orders to strike the tipis and start the final march to Red Cloud Agency, Crazy Horse was determined to pursue that negotiated solution. With newfound confidence in his agency peers and trust in the promises made by General Crook, he rode to the head of the column and started it southward, out of the hunting grounds.

NOTES

1. The best modern overviews of the Great Sioux War are John S. Gray, *Centennial Campaign: The Sioux War of 1876* (Fort Collins: Old Army Press 1976), and Jerome A. Greene, *Yellowstone Command: Colonel Nelson A. Miles and the Great Sioux War* (Lincoln: University of Nebraska Press, 1991). An excellent outline of events is supplied in Robert M. Utley, *Frontier Regulars: The United States Army and the Indian, 1866–1891* (Lincoln: University of Nebraska Press, rpt. 1984), chaps. 14–15.

2. Jerome A. Greene, ed., *Lakota and Cheyenne Indian Views of the Great Sioux War, 1876–1877* (Norman: University of Oklahoma Press, 1994). The introduction provides a valuable insight into assessing Indian testimony in the context of the Sioux War. Two important articles that address the surrender process are Harry H. Anderson, "Peace-Talkers and the Conclusion of the Sioux War of 1876," *Nebraska History* 44 (Dec. 1963): 233–54, and Oliver Knight, "War or Peace: The Anxious Wait for Crazy Horse," *Nebraska History* 45 (Winter 1973): 520–44. The single most important source on Lakota social and political organization is James R. Walker, *Lakota Society*, ed. Raymond J. DeMallie (Lincoln: University of Nebraska Press, 1982).

3. On the Northern Nation, see Lakota texts collected in Eugene Buechel, S.J., *Lakota Tales and Texts*, ed. Paul Manhart, S.J. (Pine Ridge, S. Dak.: 1978), especially Thunder Tail's account of Crazy Horse, 363ff. Gray, *Centennial Campaign*, chap. 29, suggests a figure of one thousand lodges for the Indian coalition as of June 25, 1876. I differ somewhat from Gray's ratio of persons to lodges, but his lodge estimate squares well with what we can reconstruct from surrender tallies, 1877–81. See also Kingsley M. Bray, "Teton Sioux Population History, 1655–1881," *Nebraska History* 75 (Summer 1994): 165–88. Robert M. Utley, *The Lance and the Shield: The Life and Times of Sitting Bull* (New York: Henry Holt & Co., 1993), supersedes all biographies of Sitting Bull. Mari Sandoz, *Crazy Horse, the Strange Man of the Oglalas* (Lincoln: University of Nebraska Press, rpt. 1961), is a hagiographical historical novel. Crazy Horse awaits a definitive biography.

4. Greene, *Yellowstone Command*, chaps. 4–5, is the best overview of this phase of the war. On Hunkpapa movements to Canada, see "Papers relating to the Sioux Indians of the United States who have taken refuge in Canadian Territory. Printed Confidentially for the use of the Ministers of the Crown" (Ottawa, 1879), 9ff. (hereafter cited as Canadian Papers); also Lt. R. H. Day to post adjutant, Ft. Buford, Feb. 10, 1877, in Papers Relating to Military Operations in the Departments of the Platte and Dakota Against the Sioux Indians, 1876–96 ("Sioux War Papers") (National Archives Microfilm Publication M666, rolls 272–92), Letters Received by the Office of the Adjutant General (Main Series), 1871–80, Record Group 94, National Archives and Records Administration (hereafter cited as Sioux War Papers).

5. See especially Spotted Elk statement in Col. W. W. Wood to assistant adjutant general, Dept. of Dakota, Mar. 1, 1877, Sioux War Papers.

6. Thomas B. Marquis, *Wooden Leg, A Warrior Who Fought Custer* (Lincoln: University of Nebraska Press, rpt. 1962), 287–88.

7. Young Two Moons to George Bird Grinnell, Sept. 20, 1908, in Peter Powell, *People of the Sacred Mountain: A History of the Northern Cheyenne Chiefs and Warrior Societies*, 2 vols. (San Francisco: Harper and Row), 2: 1071.

8. John Gregory Bourke, "Diary," vol. 24, 12, U.S. Military Academy, West Point, N.Y.

9. Arapaho Chief to George Bird Grinnell, Sept. 16, 1906, in Powell, *People of the Sacred Mountain* 2:1378 n.76; Bourke, "Diary," vol. 19, 1854.

10. Black Elk statement, in Raymond J. DeMallie, *The Sixth Grandfather: Black Elk's Teachings Given to John G. Neihardt* (Lincoln: University of Nebraska Press, 1984), 201; statements of Fool Bear and Important Man, in Col. W. W. Wood to assistant adjutant general, Dept. of Dakota, Jan. 24, 1877, Sioux War Papers. Black Moccasin and Ice were leaders of the ten lodges of Cheyennes that had stayed with the Oglalas throughout fall 1876.

11. On Hunkpapa movements to Canada, see sources in note 4. Baldwin's pursuit and flight are detailed in Greene, *Yellowstone Command*, chap. 6, and Utley, *The Lance and the Shield*, 177–79. Sitting Bull's subsequent movements are traceable from Lt. R. H. Day to post adjutant, Ft. Buford, Jan. 26, 1877, Sioux War Papers.

12. Fool Bear and Important Man statements; Eagle Shield statement, in Col. W. W. Wood to assistant adjutant general, Dept. of Dakota, Feb. 16, 1877, Sioux War Papers.

13. Fool Bear and Important Man statements.

14. Black Elk statement, in DeMallie, *Sixth Grandfather*, 199–200; Greene, *Yellowstone Command*, 157; Harry H. Anderson, "Nelson A. Miles and the Sioux War of 1876–77," Chicago Westerners' *Brand Book* 16 (1959): 25–27, 32.

15. Fool Bear and Important Man statements.

16. Ibid.

17. Ibid.

18. Ibid.

19. Ibid.

20. Ibid.

21. White Frog to George Bird Grinnell, Aug. 17, 1913, in Powell, *People of the Sacred Mountain*, 2:1380 n. 18.

22. Swelled Face statement, in Col. W. W. Wood to assistant adjutant general, Dept. of Dakota, Feb. 21, 1877, Sioux War Papers.

23. The Battle of Wolf Mountains is well described in Greene, *Yellowstone Command*, 163–76. Cheyenne accounts are synthesized in Powell, *People of the Sacred Mountain*, 2:1072–78; see also Marquis, *Wooden Leg*, 289–93. An Oglala perspective is provided by Black Elk in DeMallie, *Sixth Grandfather*, 201–2. Short Bull's 1930 recollection is in "Oglala Sources on the Life of Crazy Horse. Interviews given to Eleanor H. Hinman," *Nebraska History* 57 (Spring 1976): 1–52. See also Col. Nelson A. Miles to assistant adjutant general, Dept. of Dakota, Jan. 23, 1877, Sioux War Papers.

24. Eagle Shield statement.

25. Ibid.

26. Ibid.

27. Ibid.

28. Swelled Face statement.

29. Eagle Shield statement. Assessments of the attitudes of Spotted Eagle and other pro-Canada leaders, and subsequently of surrender advocates, are based on their later actions.

30. Red Horse statement, in Col. W. W. Wood to assistant adjutant general, Dept. of Dakota, Feb. 27, 1877, Sioux War Papers.

31. Charging Horse and Make Them Stand Up statements, in Lt. Horace Neide to Lt. John G. Bourke, Feb. 10, 1877, Sioux War Papers.

32. Shortly afterwards, Spider left the village to surrender at Spotted Tail Agency (see below).

33. Red Sack statement in Lt. William P. Clark to Lt. John G. Bourke, Feb. 24, 1877, Sioux War Papers.

34. As an intriguing possibility, could these headmen have enlisted the support of Little Big Man, a prominent *akicita* leader? Little Big Man was a pragmatic politician with a keen grasp of the realities of the Northern Nation's predicament. As early as 1873 Little Big Man conceded to Red Cloud Agent Jared W. Daniels that "I should want a country," i.e. the Powder River hunting grounds, no longer than thirty-five years, presumably because he knew that the game would not last and his people would have to take up farming on the reservation. Daniels to commissioner of Indian affairs,

Apr. 15, 1873, Letters Received by Office of Indian Affairs, 1824–81, Red Cloud Agency (National Archives Microfilm Publication M234, roll 717), Records of the Bureau of Indian Affairs, Record Group 75, National Archives and Records Administration. After surrender Little Big Man notoriously deserted Crazy Horse. Perhaps his shift in allegiance began late in the winter, just when an ambitious leader might seek to embody an emerging consensus for negotiation.

35. Eagle Pipe statement, in Lt. Jesse M. Lee to Lt. John G. Bourke, Mar. 6, 1877, Sioux War Papers.

36. Red Horse statement.

37. Ibid., and White Eagle statement in Col. W. W. Wood to assistant adjutant general, Dept. of Dakota, Feb. 27, 1877, Sioux War Papers. For a tally of surrendering people at Cheyenne River Agency, see "Register of Whites, Indians, and Indian Bands at Cheyenne River Agency, 1876–1877," Post at Cheyenne River Agency, vol. 54, 146–47, 152–53, 166–67, Records of United States Army Continental Commands, Record Group 98, National Archives and Records Administration.

38. This is my interpretation of White Eagle Bull statement, in Lt. Horace Neide to Lt. John G. Bourke, Feb. 16, 1877, Sioux War Papers. On Sitting Bull's movements see also Lt. William P. Clark to adjutant general, Dept. of the Platte, Sept. 14, 1877, Sioux War Papers. This is Clark's invaluable report on the Sioux War, based on Indian statements collected after surrender. It is printed, with valuable contextual material and notes, in Thomas R. Buecker, "Lt. William Philo Clark's Sioux War Report and Little Big Horn Map," *Greasy Grass* 7 (1991): 11–21.

39. White Eagle Bull statement; Lt. Jesse M. Lee to acting adjutant general, Dist. of the Black Hills, Mar. 19, 1877; Little Wolf statement in Clark to Bourke, Feb. 24, 1877, both Sioux War Papers.

40. Clark to adjutant general, Dept. of the Platte, Sept. 14, 1877, records the movement of Spotted Eagle's 150 lodges to join Sitting Bull. The main Miniconjou-Sans Arc village seems to have moved slowly after Spotted Eagle. Swelled Face (as n. 22) seems to indicate their arrival on Powder River about the second week of February. This must be at a point below the forks of the Powders, since Hunts the Enemy's agency deputation did not meet them when in the vicinity of the forks, about February 10. White Eagle Bull (as n. 39) reported buffalo at the head of the Little Missouri, significantly near the proposed rendezvous.

41. Village movements and fissions are now extremely complex. Three hundred and fifty lodges is a best guess figure based on a standard six persons: one lodge ration. However, by late winter, many people were living in cramped privation conditions. (This seems particularly true of the Miniconjous and Sans Arcs.) Actual privation lodges in the main village of Oglalas and Cheyennes in early February may be reconstructed at about 310 lodges, since Oglala agency delegates who left the village on February 22 estimated it at two hundred lodges, after the departure of 110 lodges to rejoin Crazy Horse. See delegates' statements in Lt. William P. Clark to Lt. John G. Bourke, Mar. 3 and 8, 1877, Sioux War Papers. The surrendering followers of No Water, American Horse (Cheyenne), et al., are listed in the "Report of Arrivals of Indians from the North," in the Red Cloud Agency register. See Thomas R. Buecker and R. Eli Paul, eds., *The Crazy Horse Surrender Ledger* (Lincoln: Nebraska State Historical Society, 1994), 101–4.

42. Hunkpatila organization is based on detailed band reconstructions that I have assembled for a history of the Oglalas in progress. The Iron Crow kindred probably represents a mixing of Hunkpatila and Oyuhlpe band elements. The Oyuhpe may be defined as a kind of "floating" band between the Oglalas and Miniconjous. Iron Crow's kindred in 1881 is listed in the "Big Road Roster" of Northern Oglalas then held at Standing Rock Agency after returning from Canada. (See Garrick Mallery, "Pictographs of the North American Indians: A Preliminary Paper," *Annual Report of the Bureau of American Ethnology* IV [1882–83], 174.) Unlike other kindreds in the "Roster," there seems virtually no overlap with people surrendering at Red Cloud and Spotted Tail agencies in 1877, outside of Iron Crow himself and Human Finger. My belief is that the kindred followed Spotted Eagle to Canada in spring 1877, led by Iron Crow's brother, the *akicita* Running Horse; but Iron Crow himself took a few lodges to surrender at Spotted Tail Agency with Touch the Cloud's Miniconjous. Iron Crow (a.k.a. Jumping Shield) seems to have moved unofficially to Red Cloud Agency during May 1877, where he seems to replace Old Hawk as one of the four Deciders in the Crazy Horse village. Human Finger perhaps surrendered at Spotted Tail Agency as one of the four lodge heads following Worm, Crazy Horse's father. He transferred to Red Cloud in May also, perhaps later joining

Iron Crow in flight to Canada in January 1878. For the flights of surrendered Sioux to Canada, see Kingsley M. Bray, "'We Belong to the North': The Flights of the Northern Sioux from the White River Agencies, 1877–78," *Montana, The Magazine of Western History*, in press.

43. Hunkpapa movements are based on "Canadian Papers," 12–13; Lt. R. H. Day to post adjutant, Ft. Buford, Feb. 19, 1877, Sioux War Papers.

44. *Army and Navy Journal*, Feb. 3, 1877, notes the departure of Mason's Oglala delegates. See also William Garnett, Interview No. 2, 1907, in Eli S. Ricker Collection, MS8 (microfilm), Nebraska State Historical Society, Lincoln. Hunts the Enemy, who took the name of George Sword later in 1877, gave his own account to Pine Ridge physician James R. Walker. I have used the translation by Ella Deloria, "Sword's Acts Related," in typescript at the Colorado State Historical Society, Denver.

45. Delegates' statement, in Clark to Bourke, Mar. 3, 1877. This intelligence was a little outdated: Sitting Bull's village had probably left Powder River two or three days before. Conceivably the reference is to the Spotted Eagle village.

46. Ibid.

47. Red Feather statement to Eleanor Hinman, July 8, 1930, in "Oglala Sources on the Life of Crazy Horse."

48. Tall Man statement, in Clark to Bourke, Mar. 8, 1877.

49. Delegates' statement, in Clark to Bourke, Mar. 3, 1877.

50. Red Feather statement.

51. Deloria (trans.), "Sword's Acts Related."

52. Ibid. See also Running Hawk statement, in Lt. William P. Clark to Lt. John G. Bourke, Mar. 9, 1877, Sioux War Papers; Short Bull statement to Hinman, "Oglala Sources on the Life of Crazy Horse."

53. "Sword's acts Related." Iron Hawk (born 1833) was a son of Oglala Chief Old Smoke, met by Francis Parkman in 1846, and a headman in the Sore-Backs kindred of the Bad Face band of Oglalas.

54. Tall Man statement.

55. *Omaha Daily Bee*, Mar. 14, 1877, embodying delegates' information. See also n. 64.

56. Delegates' statement, in Clark to Bourke, Mar. 3, 1877.

57. Ibid.

58. Miles's scout reports noted: "A considerable body, estimated variously from fifty to one hundred and fifty lodges, crossed the Yellowstone and went up Cedar creek Feb. 26 or 27." Miles to assistant adjutant general, Dept. of Dakota, Mar. 24, 1877, reproduced as undated *Chicago Times* clipping in Bourke "Diary," vol. 19, 1902–3. This must be the Spotted Eagle village, which I reconstruct as: forty-five lodges Sans Arcs; thirty-five lodges Miniconjous; fifteen lodges Oglalas, total ninety-five lodges.

59. The Miniconjou-Sans Arc main village, reported at 136 (privation) lodges, was on the Little Missouri fifty miles north of the mining settlement of Spearfish, early in March. See Col. Ranald S. Mackenzie to Lt. John G. Bourke, Mar. 17, 1877, Sioux War Papers. From later reports, it seems that up to thirty lodges may have stayed in the Powder River valley.

60. Tall Man statement.

61. *Omaha Daily Bee*, Apr. 17, 1877.

62. Tall Man statement.

63. "Canadian Papers," 12–13; Miles to assistant adjutant general, Dept. of Dakota, Mar. 24, 1877.

64. Tall Man statement; Clark to Bourke, Feb. 24, 1877. Uncertainty exists as to when Crazy Horse first received word of Spotted Tail's embassy. One newspaper report claims that six runners were sent up the west side of the Black Hills to carry news of Spotted Tail's departure. *Omaha Daily Bee*, Mar. 14, 1877. These delegates could have reached Crazy Horse during the third week of February, resulting, as the report states, in his summoning all Northern Indians to a grand council. Although this fits well with the course of events, delegate Tall Man was unequivocal that, when he left Crazy Horse for Red Cloud Agency on March 4, "Spotted Tail had not been heard from, except through the information given them by Red Sack." Tall Man statement. Red Sack could hardly have arrived with Crazy Horse much before March 1. Perhaps Tall Man meant that Red Sack's was the first intelligence received after the formal announcement of Spotted Tails' departure from his agency.

65. Neide to Bourke, Feb. 10, 1877; Lt. Jesse M. Lee to commissioner of Indian affairs, Mar. 20, 1877. Letters Received by the Office of Indian Affairs, 1824–81, Spotted Tail Agency (National Archives Microfilm Publication M234, roll 841). Records of the Bureau of Indian Affairs, Record Group 75, National Archives and Records Administration; Bourke "Diary," vol. 19, 1835 (on pony surrenders), 1901, 1903–1905 (outlines proposed Northern Sioux reservation in southeastern Montana, bounded on west and north by Little Bighorn, Bighorn and Yellowstone rivers). On Crook's arrangements about surrendering stock, see also Lee to Bourke, Mar. 6, 1877.

66. Black Elk statement, in DeMallie, *Sixth Grandfather*, 202.

67. F. C. Boucher, Spotted Tail's son-in-law, stated that Crazy Horse "went out by himself" about three weeks before Spotted Tail reached the Little Powder (March 20). Boucher statement, in Lt. Jesse M. Lee to assistant adjutant general, Dist. of Black Hills, Apr. 8, 1877, Spotted Tail Agency; Letters Sent, vol. 1, 667–70, Field Records, National Archives Central Plains Region, Kansas City. But Crazy Horse was still in camp when Tall Man left for the agency on March 4. I therefore assume that Crazy Horse left on his vision quest soon after Tall Man's departure. Boucher also states that Crazy Horse had only his own lodge with him, but Indians arriving at Spotted Tail Agency told Lt. Clark that Crazy Horse "was out hunting with . . . two lodges." Lt. William P. Clark to Lt. John G. Bourke, Apr. 2, 1877, Sioux War Papers. On the composition of Crazy Horse's household at surrender see Buecker and Paul, eds., *The Crazy Horse Surrender Ledger*, 162. On Black Shawl's illness, diagnosed as tuberculosis by surgeon V. T. McGillycuddy on May 7, see Julie B. McGillycuddy, *McGillycuddy Agent: A Biography of Valentine T. McGillycuddy* (Stanford: Stanford University Press, 1941), 75.

68. Black Elk statement, in DeMallie, *Sixth Grandfather*, 202.

69. Lee to Bourke, Mar. 6, 1877, incorporating Spotted Tail and F.C. Boucher to [Spotted Tail Agent], Feb. 20, 1877; Gen. George Crook to Lt. Gen. P. H. Sheridan, Mar. 25, 1877; Good Breast statement, in Lt. Jesse M. Lee to Lt. John G. Bourke, Mar. 10, 1877, all in Sioux War Papers.

70. For a detailed account of the Black Hills raids from a military perspective, see Thomas R. Buecker, "'Can You Send Us Immediate Relief?': Army Expeditions to the Northern Black Hills, 1876–1878," *South Dakota History* 25 (1995): 95–115.

71. Good Breast statement.

72. F. C. Boucher statement; also anonymous Sioux statement in Clark to Bourke, Apr. 2, 1877.

73. Ibid.; also Lone Bear statement, in Col. Ranald S. Mackenzie to Lt. John G. Bourke, Apr. 1, 1877; Turning Bear statement, in Lee to assistant adjutant general, Dist. of the Black Hills, Apr. 2, 1877, all in Sioux War Papers. For Miles's jaundiced view of Spotted Tail's negotiations, see Miles to assistant adjutant general, Dept. of Dakota, Mar. 24, 1877.

74. F. C. Boucher statement; Turning Bear statement; Lone Bear statement (including quotation).

75. Lone Bear statement.

76. Ibid.; F. C. Boucher to "Major Neide," Mar. 25 [error for 27?], 1877, copy enclosed with Lee to assistant adjutant general, Dist. of the Black Hills, Apr. 2, 1877 (includes quotation), Sioux War Papers.

77. Spotted Tail statement, in Lt. Jesse M. Lee to assistant adjutant general, Dist. of the Black Hills, Apr. 5, 1877, Sioux War Papers.

78. Ibid.

79. Lone Bear statement; Boucher statement; Turning Bear statement.

80. Red Feather to Hinman, July 8, 1930, states: "The Indians who were in the Big Horn Mountains [i.e. the main Oglala-Cheyenne village] started for the agency. *They found Crazy Horse waiting on the Powder River*" (my italics). "Oglala Sources on the Life of Crazy Horse," 26. The March 26 dating seems definite because of the tight chronological coordinates governing the movements of Spotted Tail and Lame Deer. See also Marquis, *Wooden Leg*, 297f.

81. Red Feather to Hinman (includes quotation). On the second deputation to Miles, see Miles to assistant adjutant general, Dept. of Dakota, Mar. 24, 1877.

82. He Dog, "History of Chief Crazy Horse (as written down by his son, Rev. Eagle Hawk)," in Robert A. Clark, ed., *The Killing of Chief Crazy Horse* (Lincoln: University of Nebraska Press, rpt. 1988), 53–54. This is a late and difficult text, taken down long after the event. However, it is emphatic that Crazy Horse left the Oglala village to join Lame Deer. My chronology is derived from the tight dating of the contemporary documents, which do not mention this important incident.

83. Low Dog was the *kola* or comrade of Lame Deer's nephew, Iron Star, killed in the fight with Miles on May 7, 1877. Low Dog enrolled at the Spotted Tail Agency with the surrendering Lame Deer village on Sept. 4, 1877, "Census Roll of Indians at Spotted Tail Agency, 1877," G4 Rosebud Indian Agency File, National Archives Central Plains Region, Kansas City. He then played a leading part in the November 17 flight to Canada. See Bray, "We Belong to the North."

84. Clark to adjutant general, Dept. of the Platte, Sept. 14, 1877; Gen. George Crook to Lt. Gen. P. H. Sheridan, Apr. 27 and May 30, 1877 (telegrams). On Sitting Bull, see also Utley, *The Lance and the Shield*, 181.

85. Intelligence that Crazy Horse had recently arrived at Bear Lodge was received by Capt. Peter D. Vroom, in camp near Crook City, from José Merrivale on April 5. Vroom to Gen. George Crook, Apr. 5, 1877 (telegram), transmitted in Crook to Sheridan, Apr. 7, 1877 (telegram), Sioux War Papers. Oglala village strength is based on surrender statistics in Buecker and Paul, eds., *The Crazy Horse Surrender Ledger*, 114, 157–64. Leadership is reconstructed from *Army and Navy Journal*, May 12, 1877; and cf. Bourke, "Diary," vol. 20, 1984–85; also John G. Bourke, *On the Border with Crook* (Lincoln: University of Nebraska Press, rpt. 1971), 412.

86. "Life of Crazy Horse and Fast Thunder," traditional statement by Matthew H. King to E. Kadlecek, Mar. 12, 1967, in Edward and Mabell Kadlecek, *To Kill an Eagle: Indian Views on the Last Days of Crazy Horse* (Boulder: Johnson Books, 1981), 125.

87. Marquis, *Wooden Leg*, 197–300; Powell, *People of the Sacred Mountain*, 2:1124–28. See also Lt. William P. Clark to headquarters, Dept. of the Platte, May 4, 1877 (telegram), transmitted in R. Williams to assistant adjutant general, Div. of the Missouri, May 5, 1877 (telegram); Col. Nelson A. Miles to assistant adjutant general, Dept. of Dakota, Apr. 22, 1877, Sioux War Papers.

88. Col. Ranald S. Mackenzie to commissioner of Indian affairs, Mar. 19, 1877, Sioux War Papers.

89. Short Bull to Hinman, July 13, 1930; Little Killer to Hinman, July 12, 1930, in "Oglala Sources on the Life of Crazy Horse," 40, 44.

90. Black Elk statement, in DeMallie, *Sixth Grandfather*, 203.

91. *New York Tribune*, Apr. 28, 1877 (includes quotation); Bourke "Diary," vol. 19, 1884; vol. 20, 1977.

92. Mackenzie to Bourke, Apr. 1, 1877.

93. Bourke "Diary," vol. 19, 1885–86; Garnett Interview No. 2, tablet 2, Ricker Collection. A valuable group of documents, including a list of all delegates in the Red Cloud party, is collected in "Red Cloud's Mission to Crazy Horse, 1877: Source Material," *Museum of the Fur Trade Quarterly* 22 (1986): 9–13.

94. *New York Herald*, May 11, 1877; *New York Tribune*, Apr. 28, 1877 (incorporating Red Cloud to [Lt. William P. Clark], Apr. 16, 1877); Short Bull to Hinman.

95. *Chicago Tribune*, May 8, 1877; Little Killer to Hinman.

96. Short Bull to Hinman.

97. Garnett Interview, tablet 2, Ricker Collection.

98. *Chicago Tribune*, May 8, 1877.

3

A year after the end of the Great Sioux War and a thousand miles to the west, a S'Klallam woman named Xwelas shot and killed her husband, a Welsh immigrant. According to our assumptions about the American West in the late nineteenth century, her fate was predictable; she either would have been lynched, as were some Indians of murdering whites, or she would have stood trial, during which her defense would have been perfunctory and her death sentence certain.

But Xwelas (pronounced hweh-LASS) suffered no such fate. The jury of white men found her innocent of murder; finding her guilty only of manslaughter, they sentenced her to just two years in prison. Since her husband, George Phillips, was a known abuser of both alcohol and his spouse, we might conclude that the verdict was an early example of sympathy for an abused wife who acted in self-defense. But that was not the case. Xwelas was also known to drink heavily, and observers noted that she fought her husband long before she killed him; in their eyes, she seemed to have given as good as she got. The truth of what lay behind the murder, and the community's response to it, tells us much about the nature of relations between the Northwest's indigenous peoples and the Europeans who settled among them.

As Coll-Peter Thrush and Robert H. Keller, Jr., point out in this riveting narrative, George Phillips was Xwelas's third white husband. That fact was not too surprising. With white women then scarce in the Northwest, local Indians and newly arrived Euro-Americans alike recognized the benefits of forming alliances, cemented through marriage, just as different Native groups in the region had customarily done.

As Thrush and Keller demonstrate, the story of Xwelas cannot be understood apart from its social setting, and that setting was complicated indeed. While Indians of the Northwest had had limited contact with European colonizers before the nineteenth century, by the time of Xwelas the familiar litany of problems, ranging from epidemic disease to alcohol abuse to land loss, plagued the S'Klallams and nearby Indians. Still, as this hitherto obscure woman's life reveals, the tale was not all about death and destruction. Understanding her life and her fate can help us trace how relations in that multicultural world unfolded. Only this knowledge can explain why a native woman who murdered her white husband could receive such a light sentence. Even though the local context is crucial, the story has wider implications and connections, as later chapters on gender (Part III) and Sidney Harring's study of another court case suggest.

"I See What I Have Done": The Life and Murder Trial of Xwelas, a S'Klallam Woman

Coll-Peter Thrush and Robert H. Keller, Jr.

> *Bones scatter like the hand of winter,*
> *ghost that comes back for the marrow,*
> *or evidence.*
>
> —Gloria Bird, Spokane Nation,
> "Bare Bone Winter"

CHRISTMAS DAY, 1878. GEORGE PHILLIPS, a Welsh immigrant cooper at the Langdon Lime Works on Orcas Island in Washington Territory, trudges along a forest trail with his teenage stepson, Mason Fitzhugh. Suddenly a gun explodes, lead shot ripping through underbrush beside the path and tearing into Phillips, who staggers backwards and cries to Fitzhugh for help. The boy eases his stepfather to the ground, but within moments Phillips is dead. As Mason Fitzhugh runs for help, he sees the killer standing in the brush along the trail. Shotgun in hand, a baby strapped to her back, the assailant is his mother and Phillips's wife, a woman known as Mary, but whose true name is Xwelas. She had fired the gun; she would be indicted for murder and she would eventually be tried and convicted by a court of white men.

As a nineteenth-century native woman, her life was both common and exceptional, and it offers insight into ethnic, gender, and legal relations in the Pacific Northwest.

Only select histories survive intact. Frequently, these are the histories of war and diplomacy, of the great movers and shakers. In seeking out the other voices—those of mothers, slaves, laborers, natives, and others—we often confront the silence and darkness of historical anonymity. When a voice can be traced through echoes reverberating in the records of those around it, that voice can reveal a darker side of our cultural myths. Such is the case in revisionist histories of the American West, in which an emphasis on Indians, women, Asian immigrants, and other "peripheral" voices has challenged and reshaped conventional popular images of the frontier, exposing new stories of accomplishment and survival, exploitation and oppression.[1]

SOURCE: *Western Historical Quarterly*, v. 26, n. 2 (Summer 1995), pp. 168–183.

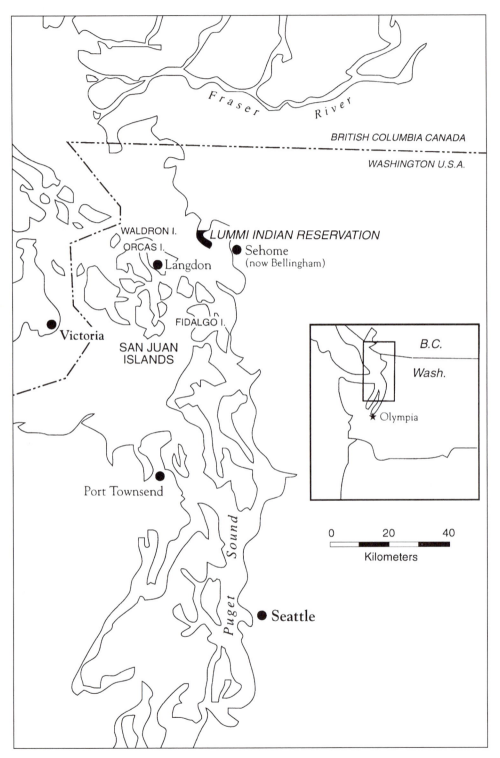

Map: Courtesy of David Denton, Western Washington University Media Services.

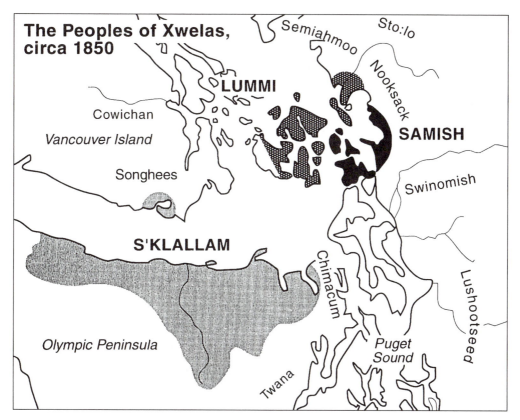

The Peoples of Xwelas, circa 1850

Map: Courtesy of David Denton, Western Washington University Media Services.

When Xwelas (pronounced hweh-LASS) was born in the 1830s, her people faced hidden and profound changes. She belonged to the S'Klallam, who lived along the northern coast of Washington's Olympic Peninsula, to the southwest of the San Juan Islands. Speakers of the Lkungen dialect of Straits Salish, and relatives of the nearby Lummi and Samish, the S'Klallam in the 1830s were only a few years away from meeting the first large waves of Euro-American settlers. The S'Klallam had first encountered white explorers in July of 1788, when British officer Robert Duffin and his crew explored south from Vancouver Island. Duffin reached the site of today's Port Townsend before being driven away by canoes manned by S'Klallam warriors. Spanish visitors were equally unwelcome during this early period of contact, but when George Vancouver sailed into S'Klallam territory in 1792, the tribe decided to ignore the whites altogether. Vancouver recorded in May of 1790 that the villagers showed "the utmost indifference and unconcern . . . as if such vessels had been familiar to them, and unworthy of their attention."[2] A half-century later, new forces gave the S'Klallam, and surrounding native communities, little choice but to pay attention. Diseases such as smallpox began to ravage the coastal peoples, and deadly epidemics—along with a new economy, European trade goods that included alcohol, and massive immigration of white settlers—eroded the North Coast's traditional lifeways.

Thus, Xwelas reached adulthood in a period of rapid social change and emotional turmoil. Not only were the S'Klallam forced to contend with the Euro-American settlers, but intertribal raiding and violence in the region may have also increased during the first half of the nineteenth century. Attacks by Vancouver Island tribes and bands from the south, together with the threat of slavery, depopulation due to disease, and the breakdown of traditional ways, could have encouraged a young Indian woman to seek relative refuge in marriage with a white man, miles from her home.[3]

Xwelas's marriage reveals an important dynamic. Her people and other Northwest native communities did not simply drown under a flood tide of immigrants, merchants, and missionaries. Rather, for several generations after Euro-American settlement, we find extensive cultural interdependence. Newcomers, whether British, Russian, Spanish, American, Hawaiian, or Asian, depended upon native knowledge for survival and for access to resources that fueled the new economies. Likewise, Indians came to depend upon immigrants for trade and protection. Alliances between Indians and whites proved necessary for both parties, one form of alliance being marriage. Before contact with Euro-Americans, different native communities had traditionally intermarried to strengthen bonds and prevent conflict; that practice soon extended to European and American male settlers after 1840.

One such marriage took place in the 1850s between E-yow-alth and Edmund Clare Fitzhugh. E-yow-alth was herself the daughter of a marriage of alliance between Xwelas's S'Klallam brother S'ya-whom, and Tsi-swat-oblitsa, a Samish noblewoman. White settlers knew S'ya-whom well enough to apply his anglicized name, Sehome, to a small town on the shores of Bellingham Bay, east of the San Juan Islands. E. C. Fitzhugh resided in Sehome.[4]

Fitzhugh, a native of Virginia's Stafford County, had served in the Virginia legislature in 1846 and 1847 and had practiced law in California before coming to the Pacific Northwest in the early 1850s.[5] Although there is no evidence that he was involved in any skirmishes—or that any skirmishes took place at all—Fitzhugh participated as a colonel in the coordination of American troops during the Pig War of 1859, a dispute between Britain and the United States over title to the San Juans.[6] Lottie Roeder Roth, an early popular chronicler of northwest Washington history, described Fitzhugh's years in Sehome as those of the archetypal frontier hero as:

> . . . a born fighter, quick to take offense, absolutely without fear, something of a roisterer, imperious and self-willed, following his code of honor without thought of consequences, but withal a man of superior intellect and many kindly impulses. Generous, hospitable, impulsive, self-indulgent, honest and brave; Virginia never sent a more typical example of its chivalry into the Northwest than Edmund Clare Fitzhugh.[7]

Roth's hyperbole aside, Fitzhugh nonetheless was an influential figure during the early years of Sehome. He became, among other things, superintendent of the Bellingham Bay Coal Company, Indian agent, county auditor, customs inspector, military aide to Governor Isaac I. Stevens, and territorial supreme court justice under President James Buchanan.[8] His busy career did not escape scandal, however.

According to one settler's diary, during Fitzhugh's tenure as judge, he allegedly shot and killed a man after a gambling dispute, then promptly tried and acquitted himself of the murder charge.[9]

But perhaps Fitzhugh's most glaring escapades involved his relations with women. Whenever Xwelas or other Indians visited the new white settlements around Bellingham Bay, they did not encounter neatly kept and morally upright communities following an ideal New England or midwestern model. In 1876, Phares B. Harrison, a "home missionary" to Sehome and its sister settlement of New Whatcom, found just the opposite and reacted with revulsion:

> We have confronting us here heathenism—enlightened and benighted, civilized and legalized—in its most repulsive forms. . . . Drunkenness with its bloated impurities and crime, is not the most corrupting form of vice among us. Adultery, open, unconcealed, bold, and unblushing, in the cabins of the miners, and in *higher places*, in the Chinese quarters, resists the pure gospel of the Son of God.[10]

Part of this debauchery, in Christian missionary eyes, involved white man's liaisons with native women. In the early Northwest, eligible white brides were few and far between, encouraging the common practice of Caucasian men marrying Indian women, a pact often made for both sexual and economic reasons.[11] In Sehome and surrounding Whatcom County, the Lummi Indians had provided so many brides or "kloochman" to white settlers that by the time E. C. Fitzhugh sought a partner, Lummi leader Chowitzit protested that too many young women had already married outside the tribe. Chowitzit referred Fitzhugh to the nearby Samish people to the south of Bellingham Bay. There, the Lummi presided over negotiations between Fitzhugh, "the tyee [chief] of Whatcom Falls," and S'ya-whom, the Samish headman. Following the traditions of his culture, in which romantic love played a lesser part in marriage than political diplomacy or social mobility, Chowitzit pointed out the advantages of a marriage alliance, while Fitzhugh spoke of his own wealth and how well he would be able to provide for a wife. In the end, S'ya-whom gave his sixteen-year-old daughter E-yow-alth to Fitzhugh, a man more than twenty years her senior. Throughout the nuptial negotiations, E-yow-alth's aunt, Xwelas, watched from the sidelines.[12]

Years later, Xwelas would remember traveling to visit her married niece on Bellingham Bay. The trip required five or six hours by canoe, following the shoreline below the storm-sculpted sandstone cliffs of the Chuckanut Mountains. On arriving for a visit not long after E-wow-alth's wedding, Xwelas learned that all was not well in the white man's household. Fitzhugh had become discontented with E-yow-alth, who had borne him a daughter they named Julia, and now began to entice his young wife's aunt. Eventually, Fitzhugh took Xwelas as his second wife. While multiple marriages would not have raised eyebrows among the Indian population, one might expect it to have done so among white society, particularly when involving a figure as public as Fitzhugh. Surprisingly, however, no recorded condemnation of his bigamy exists. And so Fitzhugh—the "example of chivalry"—took both E-yow-alth and

Xwelas, now christened respectively as Julie and Mary, to form a single family. Xwelas soon gave birth to two sons named Mason and Julius.[13]

Over time, even with two wives, Fitzhugh found that the appeal of domestic life waned. Sometime in the late 1850s, he suddenly left Sehome for Seattle, taking daughter Julia with him. She disappears from the historical record, but Fitzhugh reappears from time to time. We find him fighting as a confederate major in the Civil War, representing his home state of Virginia. He formed another family after the war and apparently abandoned them as well, as he would yet a third family in Iowa. Fitzhugh returned briefly to Bellingham Bay in 1875, seeking out his son Mason, now seventeen. Mason, however, gave his father a cold shoulder, and the elder Fitzhugh soon left for San Francisco. On 24 November 1883, his body was found on the floor of a room in that city's What Cheer Hotel.[14] Edmund Clare Fitzhugh's life and death in many ways typify the schism between frontier myth and historical reality: fondly remembered as a brave pioneer and community leader, he was also an irresponsible, transient womanizer.

While Fitzhugh roamed, E-yow-alth and Xwelas rebuilt their lives. For E-yow-alth, that meant starting again, her daughter having disappeared with Fitzhugh. Eventually, she would marry Henry Barkhousen, yet another county auditor, and would raise a new family on Fidalgo Island.[15] Xwelas also would marry again, this time to a man with a colorful name, but about whom the historical record reveals little: William King Lear.

Lear, an immigrant from Alabama who had profited from the Fraser River gold rush of 1858, settled among the few houses and shops clinging to a spit called Semiahmoo, twenty miles to the north of Bellingham Bay. A land speculator, Lear dispensed titles to lots on the spit and also served his clients as a storekeeper.[16] In the mid-1860s, he married Xwelas, now in her thirties. No details remain of their union, but sometime around 1866, Xwelas gave birth to William Jr., or "Billy." Not long after Billy's arrival, Lear abandoned his family and rushed back to Alabama where he learned that a relative had died. He next appears in 1878, on Wrangell Island in Alaska, where he petitioned to purchase another tract of land.[17] William King Lear did not return to Bellingham Bay for more than twenty years, finally attracted by the 1889 boom in Sehome and surrounding towns. Whether or not he then made any contact with Xwelas or his son is unknown. Lear's later life is a mystery, but legend has it that he went down with his ship sometime around the turn of the century on another profit-driven passage to Alaska.[18] So, by her early thirties, Xwelas had been twice abandoned by white husbands who pursued their dreams—and their deaths—elsewhere.

According to one report, Xwelas returned to her people near Port Townsend after King Lear left for the East. A single woman with children required support that the extended kinship systems of the S'Klallam community could provide. That she would marry yet a third time came as no surprise; the S'Klallam allowed and even encouraged individuals to remarry, especially to continue useful alliances.[19] The social standing of Xwelas's third spouse, however, does come as a surprise. Rather than choosing a prominent figure in politics or business such as Fitzhugh or King

Lear, she wedded a common laborer. Why? Perhaps, as a forty-year-old woman with three children fathered by two different men, Xwelas may have been considered "used merchandise" by potential white suitors and by tribal leaders looking for strategic marriage alliances. Or perhaps there may have been a romantic attraction between Xwelas and the Welsh cooper. For whatever reasons, Xwelas married George Phillips on 9 February 1873.[20]

As a poor immigrant barrel-maker at a lime kiln in the rough-and-ready Orcas Island outpost of Langdon, George Phillips lacked any political or economic standing. Local histories cast him in a much less beneficent light than Xwelas's first two husbands, and by any standard, her life as Mary Phillips seems to have been the worst of the three marriages. Virtually every account of George Phillips mentions his alcoholism and his penchant for violent rages. His beating of Xwelas often drew the attention of neighbors, although she was not incapable of defending herself. One account describes an argument between the couple in a canoe, in which Phillips hit Xwelas with a paddle. After a moment of silence, she asked if she could take over the rowing, and after a few strokes hit him with the same paddle. Such violence appears to have been a staple of their relationship.[21]

Again, there were children. Two toddlers, young enough to remain unnamed in the records, were playing at the lime works in 1877, when one dropped a lighted match into an open powder keg. The resulting explosion, fire, and deaths may have struck a crippling blow to the already unhealthy marriage of George and Mary Phillips, even though another child named Maggie followed, and Xwelas was pregnant once again on Christmas, 1878.[22]

What exactly provoked the yuletide killing of George Phillips? Some reports claimed that the family—George, the pregnant Xwelas, the infant Maggie, and Xwelas's eldest son Mason Fitzhugh—had attended a "squaw dance," where Phillips's flirtations with another Indian woman provoked Xwelas's anger. According to this theory, she later ambushed and shot her husband out of jealousy.[23]

Xwelas herself described the events of that day during her trial. She and Phillips had gone to the house of a neighbor, William Shattuck, to drink and gamble. She recalled that both she and her husband drank considerably, with Phillips "in very high spirits, laughing & singing songs." Eventually, he became so intoxicated that she asked for help escorting him home after finally persuading him to leave the party:

> After we had gone some distance George said, "where were you last night, you old whore you, when I was hunting for you?" After some quarreling I called him a dog & he struck me with the oar on the cheek, then everything became dark and I fell forward. I then rose up & picked up the child when he punched me in the side with the oar. I then called him a dog & said, "don't you know I've got a child in my bowels?" He said he didn't care if he killed me; he'd get another woman, that I was whoring with Siwashes.[24]

According to Xwelas's testimony, her husband repeatedly threatened to kill her after they reached the Langdon settlement and their house in the late afternoon.

"George told me to get my things and leave, calling me a slut. He demanded the key to the house & ere I could give it to him, he took the axe & broke open the door." Phillips then grabbed two guns from above the mantle and began loading them. Although Mason Fitzhugh assured her that George would sober up, Xwelas decided to spend the night in the woods. Putting baby Maggie on her back, she took a double-barreled shotgun and walked to a neighbor's root house. As her husband and Mason approached the building along the trail a short time later, Xwelas hid in the nearby brush. Then Maggie cried out "Papa," alerting Phillips:

> I raised up from behind the brush. George then rushed forward & grasped the gun by the middle of the barrel. We each tried to pull the gun from the other, & while we were thus struggling the gun went off shooting George. He staggered back calling for Mason.... Mason came [and] said to me, "Do you see what you have done?" I answered, "I see what I have done."[25]

The testimony of other witnesses quoted Xwelas as saying that she had feared for her life, but they contradicted her account of self-defense. Especially damaging were descriptions of how buckshot had ripped leaves and branches from the brush along the trail and how no one could have reached the point of firing from the path. To compound the issue, Phillips's body showed no powder burns, alerting jurors to the fact that he was killed from a distance.

Immediately after Phillips was killed, Mason Fitzhugh, who was near enough that wadding from the shotgun blast flew past him, dragged his stepfather's body into a barnyard and enlisted neighbors to keep the hogs away from the corpse.[26] After a hasty coroner's inquest, the next day Xwelas was indicted for murder. The Orcas Island sheriff immediately took her by boat across the water to Port Townsend, where she awaited a trial that would bring together the two driving personalities in Orcas Island politics and society—Colonel Enoch May and James Francis Tulloch.

Enoch May was no real colonel. The title served merely as a poker-table epithet for this Massachusetts immigrant who led a rough life on Orcas and who had also been present at the Shattuck Christmas party prior to Phillips's death. Although he had been sheriff in Sehome for a few months at the end of the 1850s, locals knew Enoch May better for his criminal exploits in the San Juans, where he smuggled opium, Chinese laborers, and Canadian wool. He once made a bid for the Waldron Island postmaster's job by drafting cronies to sign up as that island's residents when most of them lived elsewhere. May was the San Juan correspondent for at least one newspaper; his letter to the *Puget Sound Argus* first broke the story of George Phillips's death at the hands of Xwelas, whom the editor named "A Disciple of Lucretia Borgia." May used connections with the media to his advantage, once fabricating the story of "Lucy Bean," a bogus orphan supposedly living with a missionary family who desperately needed funds to set up schools for Indian children. Thousands of dollars poured in from eastern cities before locals exposed May's scam.[27]

Enoch May had complex relations with the Lummi and other original inhabitants of Orcas. He lived at North Beach where, according to his archrival, James Tulloch,

[May] had a band of the worst Indian characters always camped under the leadership of an outlaw Indian known as Old Tom to whose credit more than one murder was attributed. Here May posed as King of the Squaw Men, declaring that it was their last ditch [stand] and that he would fight to prevent settlement of the island by white families.[28]

Despite an apparent commitment to maintain Native American dominance on Orcas, May in fact brokered Indian brides to white men. In exchange for fees ranging from twenty-five to fifty dollars depending on age, appearance, health, and social status, May provided women of the Lummi, S'Klallam, Songhees, and other tribal communities to Euro-American settlers. It is quite possible that he sold Xwelas to George Phillips. Men who acquired women through May's service rarely married their mates. In fact, when Superior Court Judge Lewis decreed that white men must either marry their Indian women and assign them one third of their property or face punishment, a mob of May's men burned the judge in effigy.[29] One wonders at May's motives in preventing white families from settling on Orcas. Was he really an advocate of native control of the island, or was he merely seeking to maintain a clientele of single white men?[30]

Enoch May's role in race relations on Orcas brought him into direct conflict with the island's other major figure who would also testify at Xwelas's trial: James Francis Tulloch. A Methodist preacher's son and a neighbor of George and Mary Phillips, Tulloch had moved to Orcas in 1875 to work at the lime kilns and to farm. He founded and directed the Orcas Island Improvement Association to promote settlement of the island by white Christian families, placing him in direct opposition to May. "[T]he fact was," Tulloch remarked in his diary, "that the half-breed element had always held a grudge against me because they knew I was opposed to miscegenation and had worked hard to get in the white families."[31] May's retinue consisted of Indians, outlaws, miscegenators, and smugglers, while Tulloch enlisted preachers, merchants, and families. Black hat collided with white hat; chaos and debauchery confronted order and purity.

Orcas Island was no simple spaghetti western, however, and the hats worn by May and Tulloch were of a more mixed fabric than is at first apparent. On the surface, Tulloch represented an ideal of the pious settler paving the road for civilized progress. At the same time, however, he represented a drive for white racial supremacy in the Northwest. In addition to his negative views of Indians, Tulloch clearly promoted social order exclusive of other races as well. He founded the Orcas Island Anti-Chinese Association in the 1880s, drafting a constitution and bylaws that would become the model used by similar groups in Sehome, Tacoma, and Olympia.[32]

Despite their personal and political disagreements, testimony from Tulloch and

May differed little regarding the death of George Phillips. Both men recalled Phillips drinking, the fights between him and Xwelas, and the events of Christmas Day. Neighbors Henry Stone and William Shattuck, stepson Mason Fitzhugh, and other witnesses offered only slight variations on the same theme. The major contradiction in testimonies regarded Xwelas's claim that she and Phillips had struggled over the gun; witnesses reported that she had indeed fired from behind a screen of underbrush.[33]

Most of Xwelas's neighbors seemed sympathetic, inclined toward what modern courts would call an insanity defense. Henry Stone, like several other Orcas residents, recalled that:

> George has at often times told me that the prisoner was not in her right mind. He has often come to my house and told me and my wife that his wife is crazy, and getting worse every day; and he has told that he was afraid of her. I have seen indications of insanity in her, for instance, she publicly expresses her belief that the death of her two children [at the lime works] was a plot.[34]

Even Xwelas's son, Mason Fitzhugh, testified that she would at times act "as if she were not in her right mind and at other times she is all right."[35]

Judge Roger Greene had instructed the jurors to weigh whether or not Xwelas understood the consequences of her action, and whether or not the action was justified in the light of her husband's violence. Judge Greene also reminded jurors to consider Phillips's character and that he had attacked Xwelas with "the intention of destroying her unborn child."

By common notions of frontier justice, Xwelas should have hung. The jury might have doubted whether she was sane or whether her actions were justified, but that she had in fact killed George Phillips was never in question. During this period in the American West, no legal precedents existed that took into account as justification for homicide domestic violence against women.[36] Moreover, one would have expected the bias of white male jurisprudence to prevail over the interests of an Indian woman.

But Xwelas did not hang. When the two-day trial ended on 16 September 1879—almost ten months after the shooting—foreman Rufus Calhoun read the verdict: "We find the defendant guilty of manslaughter and not guilty of murder." The jury recommended Xwelas to the mercy of Judge Green, who sentenced her to two years in prison, less the ten months spent awaiting trail. In the case of *Washington Territory v. Mary Phillips*, the territorial justice system and Xwelas's neighbors had spent over $1600 to maintain due process of law, to bond witnesses, and to care for Xwelas's children, including the infant Tom, born while she was in Port Townsend jail.[37] Finally, Xwelas herself was allowed to testify, as was her mixed-blood son Mason. Our conventional wisdom about intercultural relations, about the status of women, about the low value placed on Indian opinion, and about the whimsy of nineteenth-century justice tells us that a jury of white men should have been less forgiving in a case such as this. So why the lenient treatment?

One explanation of the verdict may have been pangs of conscience over convicting a mother with five surviving children, including an infant born in prison. A burgeoning Northwest town with eager boosters, prolific newspapers, and a concern for its own image may have found a harsh sentence and the ensuing publicity to its detriment. But other factors emerge as well.

First, many local white men, perhaps even a majority at the time, had married or enjoyed liaisons with Indian women. Even Xwelas's defense attorney had once been a "squaw man."[38] Very possibly some of the jurors had been as well. Thus, while notions of racial and cultural superiority were central to territorial society, white male familiarity with native women could have favored Xwelas in the eyes of the jury.

Second, the presence of Xwelas's S'Klallam kin in the community could have influenced the jury's decision. During the 1870s, Native Americans of the Chimacum, S'Klallam, Lushootseed, Twana, and other tribal groups remained a familiar sight in Port Townsend and other Northwest communities. Just as interracial marriages could provide alliances between racial groups, a fair trial and positive outcome for Xwelas could have been important in maintaining stable relations between whites and S'Klallams.[39]

Third, George Phillips's reputation could have prejudiced the jury. Had Xwelas killed Edmund Clare Fitzhugh, William King Lear, or another prominent civic figure, she more likely would have suffered a harsher sentence. But to ambush Phillips, a poor, alcoholic, abusive Welsh laborer, signified no great loss. Social class and national standing could be at least as important as race and gender in ordaining the relative value of human life in the West.

Ultimately, the legal decision probably rested on whether or not Xwelas understood her actions. Unfortunately, the most important psychological evidence, the opinions of doctors called to testify at her trial, has been lost. The foreman's note says nothing on this matter, but it may have been easier to dismiss Xwelas as a crazy Indian woman and to mete out a lesser sentence than to deal with the personal and political consequences of a more severe judgment.

Finally, the murder trial of Xwelas took place during a period in which legal and judicial standards, as they applied to Native Americans, were ill-defined and in a constant state of flux. For example, five years previously in 1874, a mixed-blood Indian named Henry, or Harry, Fisk stood trial in Olympia for the murder of a Squaxin Indian shaman called Doctor Jackson. Fisk's primary defense for killing Jackson was that the shaman had caused Fisk's wife to become ill, and that only Jackson's death could reverse the illness. While nineteenth-century American jurisprudence was not known for allowing shamanic self-defense as a justification for murder, the trial proceedings were marked by an attempt to understand native concepts of justice, and the all-white jury acquitted Fisk after only eight minutes of deliberation.[40] Five years after Xwelas's trial, in 1884, the Sto:lo youth Louie Sam was abducted and lynched by a white mob near Sumas on the Canadian border for the murder of a prominent local shopkeeper named James Bell. According to at least one historian, another white settler named William Osterman was the more likely culprit. Nevertheless, local white thirst for vengeance was slaked when a mob strung up Louie Sam.[41] Considered alongside the trail of Xwelas, in which an Indian woman ironically benefited from a legal system largely created by and for white men, these cases illustrate the kaleidoscopic morass that was the legal status of nineteenth-century Native Americans.

After her conviction, Xwelas virtually disappears from the historical record. Her later life seems to have been removed from crisis or controversy, living with sons Billy Lear and Tom Phillips on the Lummi Reservation. She did not marry again, nor did she bear more children, and she seems to have withdrawn from the white world altogether. Sometime near the end of World War I, Mary Sehome Fitzhugh Lear Phillips—Xwelas—died in her tiny home on the reservation.[42]

Xwelas was buried in an unmarked grave at the old Lummi cemetery. Mason Fitzhugh and his family lie in a plot on Orcas Island a few miles from Madrona Point, the traditional Lummi burial ground where the two children killed at the lime works are most likely interred. Other descendants of Xwelas are buried on San Juan Island and near Bellingham Bay. A number of families of the modern Lummi, Samish, Swinomish, and S'Klallam nations are part of her extended lineage.[43]

In his home near the new Lummi cemetery, Gordon Charles keeps a file of yellowed clippings about his ancestors, including Xwelas. One of Charles's grandfathers was Billy Lear and the other Julius Fitzhugh, making him Xwelas's great-grandson on both sides. He brings out photos of William King Lear and family trees penciled on restaurant placemats. He can tell the stories of Xwelas's marriage to E. C. Fitzhugh, of E-yow-alth, and the negotiations with S'ya-whom. He knows the tale of the murder trial, and of King Lear going down with his ship.

Gordon Charles also possesses a photograph of Xwelas. Taken sometime after 1900, it shows a small woman in a gingham dress, her face nearly hidden in shadow by the wide brim of a straw hat. In the background squats the dark, square bulk of a fish cannery; further in the distance are the islands where she spent her years with George Phillips.

Away from Lummi, Xwelas is less well-known. On Orcas, only a few people have heard hints of her story; none know her name. Today, the abandoned lime kiln where Xwelas killed her husband is hidden by tangles of bindweed and alder, and the little community called Langdon has disappeared into the forest. Only sixty years after her death, Xwelas is barely a ghost, her voice but a whisper. The evidence of her life is scattered, like the hand of winter.

The story of Xwelas sheds light on the realities of frontier experience in the Northwest, laying bare several assumptions about the region, its history, and its cultural legacy.

First, Xwelas's tribal affiliations reveal the fluid nature of Native American societies on the Northwest Coast. Born among the S'Klallam, she lived with the Samish and with whites, returned for a time to the S'Klallam, and then died among the Lummi. In light of her life, we must question the concept of geographically and culturally distinct native tribes existing separate from each other. Instead, complex ties of kinship, political interdependence, and economic alliance wove the native communities together into a regional fabric.[44]

Second, the interdependence of white settlers and Indian residents also becomes clear through her story. Rather than a tide of immigrants erasing the native presence on many levels—sexual, financial, political—Xwelas's life illustrates the continuing importance of Native Americans long after initial contact. In fact, it may have been the influential political and social presence of her S'Klallam kin that saved Xwelas from a murder conviction.

Finally, Xwelas's relationship to white men helps to shatter the myth of Christian pioneers such as Henry Spalding, Marcus and Narcissa Whitman, Cushing Eels, and Jason Lee bringing civilization and morality to a savage frontier. In many ways, the deserter Edmund Clare Fitzhugh, the profiteer William King Lear, the abusive George Phillips, the criminal Enoch May, and the supremacist James Francis Tulloch *were* the savage frontier.

NOTES

1. Leading examples of such history include Patricia Nelson Limerick's *The Legacy of Conquest: The Unbroken Past of the American West* (New York, 1987); and Richard White's *"It's Your Misfortune and None of My Own": A History of the American West* (Norman, 1991). A superb book using a single life as a window to the past is Laurel Thatcher Ulrich's *A Midwife's Tale: The Life of Martha Ballard, Based on Her Diary, 1785–1812* (New York, 1990). For methodological difficulties in studying the lives of nineteenth-century native women, see Rosemary and Joseph Agonito, "Resurrecting History's Forgotten Women: A Case from the Cheyenne Indians," *Frontiers* 6, no. 3 (1982): 8–16.

2. Edmund S. Meany, ed., *Vancouver's Discovery of Puget Sound* (Portland, 1957), 85.

3. The best ethnography of the region is Wayne Suttles, *Coast Salish Essays* (Seattle, 1987). On the S'Klallam specifically, consult Erna Gunther, *Klallam Folk Tales*, University of Washington Publications in Anthropology, vol. 1, no. 4 (Seattle, 1925) and *Klallam Ethnography*, University of Washington Publications in Anthropology, vol. 1, no. 5 (Seattle, 1927). For inter-tribal raiding and violence during this era, see Robert H. Ruby and John A. Brown, *Indian Slavery in the Pacific Northwest* (Spokane, 1993), chap. 6. For Indian-White relations in the region, see Jerry Gorsline, ed., *Shadows of Our Ancestors: Reading in the History of Klallam-White Relations* (Port Townsend, 1992). Robin Fisher's *Contact and Conflict: Indian-European Relations in British Columbia, 1774–1890* (1977; 2d ed., rev., Vancouver, 1992) concerns British Columbia but is relevant to the interaction of cultures. Also see Fisher's "Indian Warfare and Two Frontiers: A Comparison of British Columbia and Washington Territory during the Early Years of Settlement," *Pacific Historical Review* 50 (February 1981); 31–51. Also refer to Robert H. Keller, Jr., "A Missionary Tour of Washington Territory: T. Dwight Hunt's 1855 Report," *Pacific Northwest Quarterly* 76 (October 1985): 148–55; and Daniel L. Boxberger, *To Fish in Common: The Ethnohistory of Lummi Indian Salmon Fishing* (Lincoln, 1989).

4. Percival Jeffcoat, "Samish Chief Negotiates with Fitzhugh for Princess," *Bellingham (WA) Herald*, 13 October 1968. Although Jeffcoat was a respected local historian, we realize that relying on his undocumented newspaper accounts raises legitimate doubts.

5. *The Virginia General Assembly, July 30 1619 to January 11 1978: A Bicentennial Registry of Members*, comp. Cynthia Miller Leonard (Richmond, 1978).

6. See David Richardson, *The Pig War Islands* (Eastsound, Wash., 1971) and Keith A. Murray, *The Pig War*, Pacific Northwest Historical Pamphlet No. 6 (Tacoma, Wash., 1968).

7. Lottie Roeder Roth, *History of Whatcom County* (Seattle, 1926), 1: 38.

8. Roth, *History*, 38, 45–46; Percival R. Jeffcoat, "Why Samish Chief's Name Became Sehome," *Bellingham Herald*, 20 October 1968. Fitzhugh's alarm over the plight of the Samish Indians may be found in the Commissioner of Indian Affairs's *Annual Reports, 1856–58*, and in the records of the Bureau of Indian Affairs, Washington Superintendency, for the same years.

9. James F. Tulloch, *The James Francis Tulloch Diary, 1875–1910*, ed. Gordon Keith (Portland, 1978), 11.

10. From Harrison's November 1876 correspondence with the American Home Mission Society. Correspondence held in the Amistad Research Center, Old U.S. Mint, New Orleans. Quoted in Robert H. Keller, Jr., "The Gospel Comes to Northwest Washington," *Pacific Northwest Forum* 10 (Winter 1986): 4. (Emphasis in text.)

11. Gender relations and mores on the frontier were extremely fluid throughout the American and Canadian Wests, continually changing with time and place. Social, economic, political, and personal motives seem to have been as compelling as libido, whether we examine the experiences of the Lewis and Clark expedition or alliances *à la façon du pays* at Fort George, Fort Vancouver, Spokane House, Victoria, or Fort Colville. The life of Xwelas becomes more understandable when we realize that modern categories about racial mixing and generalizations about "marginal people" and "contrived opposites," about public and private spheres, and about personal, ethnic, and social identity do not necessarily hold up in the context of her life. The authors in the anthology edited by James A. Clifton debunk many of these concepts in *Being and Becoming Indian: Biographical Studies of North American Frontiers* (Chicago, 1989), 1–37. Richard White drives home the same point in *The Middle Ground: Indians, Empires, and Republics in the Great Lakes Region, 1650–1815* (Cambridge, Eng., 1991). For the mixing of trade and personal life as well as the active economic role of native women in the early Northwest, see Sylvia Van Kirk, *Many Tender Ties: Women in Fur-Trade Society, 1670–1870* (Norman, 1980); and James P. Ronda, *Lewis and Clark among the Indians* (Lincoln, 1984). For specific insights into the lives of Xwelas's peers, including her granddaughter Maggie Tom, consult Karen Jones-Lamb, *Native American Wives of San Juan Settlers* (Bryn Tirion Publishing, 1994, place of publication unknown). For discussion of mixed-blood identity, see Jacqueline Peterson and Jennifer S. H. Brown, eds., *The New Peoples: Being and Becoming Métis in North America* (Lincoln, 1985), especially the contributions of Olive Patricia Dickason and John E. Foster. William E. Unrau examines the issue in *Mixed-Bloods and Tribal Dissolution: Charles Curtis and the Quest for Indian Identity* (Lawrence, Kan., 1989), 1–21.

12. Jeffcoat, "Samish Chief Negotiates." For more information on S'Klallam and Lummi marriage traditions, see Wayne Suttles, "Central Coast Salish," in *Northwest Coast*, ed. Wayne Suttles, vol. 7 of *Handbook of North American Indians*, ed. William C. Sturtevant (Washington, DC, 1990), 453–75.

13. Jeffcoat, "Why Samish Chief's Name."

14. Jeffcoat, "Why Samish Chief's Name"; and Roth, *History*, 38.

15. Percival R. Jeffcoat, "The Last Days of Chief Sehome," *Bellingham Herald*, 3 November 1968.

16. Roth, *History*, 107–8.

17. U. S. Senate, 45th Cong., 3d Session, *Report of the Committee on Private Land Claims* (S. Rpt. 764), Washington, DC: Government Printing Office, 1879 (*Serial Set* 1838).

18. Jeffcoat, "Last Days"; Roth, *History*, 798; and Gordon Charles, informal interview conducted by Coll-Peter Thrush, Lummi Reservation, 18 May 1993, notes of interview in authors' possession.

19. Suttles, "Central Coast Salish."

20. John D. Carter, ed., *Washington's First Marriages of the 39 Counties* (Spokane, 1980).

21. Pre-trial affidavits in Washington Territory v. Mary Phillips File, Case no. 1070, Series 1, Box 21, Washington Territorial Case Files, Third Judicial District, Jefferson County, Washington Territory, Washington State Archives: Northwest Region, Western Washington University, Bellingham (hereafter Wash. Terr. v. Phillips File, Case no. 1070). We are grateful to Jim Moore, director of the archives, for bringing these records to our attention.

22. Tulloch, *Diary*, 32.

23. *Seattle Weekly Intelligencer*, 4 January 1879.

24. Affidavit of Mary Phillips, Orcas Island, 26 December 1878, Wash. Terr. v. Phillips File, Case no. 1070.

25. Testimony of Mary Phillips, Wash. Terr. v. Phillips File, Case no. 1070.

26. Pigs are voracious omnivores.

27. Roth, *History*, 35; *Puget Sound Argus* (Port Townsend), 2 January 1879; and Tulloch, *Diary*, 39–40.

28. Tulloch, *Diary*, 11.

29. Ibid., 11–12.

30. May's position regarding race relations was apparently neutral enough that he was allowed to serve during Xwelas's trial as her interpreter, since she seems to have spoken little, or at best, broken English.
31. Tulloch, *Diary*, 72.
32. Ibid., 71.
33. Testimonies in Wash. Terr. v. Phillips File, Case no. 1070.
34. Stone testimony in Wash. Terr. v. Phillips File, Case no. 1070.
35. Fitzhugh testimony in Wash. Terr. v. Phillips File, Case no. 1070.
36. See Cynthia K. Gillespie, *Justifiable Homicide: Battered Women, Self-Defense, and the Law* (Columbus, Ohio, 1989), 45.
37. To put this monetary figure in context, consider that in 1880 streetcar operators in New York City earned less than twenty cents an hour, while coal miners earned approximately $500 a year for working twelve hours a day, six days a week.
38. Tulloch, *Diary*, 36.
39. For an account of nineteenth-century Port Townsend, see Ivan Doig's *Winter Brothers: A Season at the Edge of America* (New York, 1980).
40. Brad Asher, "The Shaman-Killing Case on Puget Sound, 1873: American Law and Salish Culture," paper presented at the Pacific Northwest History Conference at Western Washington University in Bellingham, 25 March 1994, copy in authors' possession. It is interesting to note that Judge Roger Greene, who presided over Xwelas's trial, also was the judge in the trial of Henry or Harry Fisk.
41. Keith Thor Carlson, "The Lynching of Louis Sam: A Story of Cross-Cultural Confusion, Tri-National Relations, and Murder," paper presented at the Pacific Northwest History Conference at Western Washington University in Bellingham, 25 March 1994, copy in authors' possession.
42. Gordon Charles interview.
43. Ibid., and Jones Lamb, *Native American Wives*.
44. Wayne Suttles further explores this theme in his essay entitled "The Persistence of Intervillage Ties among the Coast Salish," chap. in *Coast Salish Essays*, 209–30.

II

RESERVATION CULTURES, 1880–1930

THIS CLUSTER OF ESSAYS TAKES A close look at life on the newly created reservations. None of the three authors denies the federal government's power to defeat, and then to confine, Native peoples. But each author here, following the lead of Katherine Osburn studying Navajo life a generation before, paints a portrait of reservation life in which Indians were far from passive victims. In these articles, reservations become not physical or cultural wastelands but communities, places where groups of Natives gathered to construct common lifeways. These people struggle over the meaning of their new homelands, they seek out new ways to make a living (and to make a life), they try to cope with changes that inevitably overtake them. But they engage in these pursuits as people who still think of themselves as distinctive. They were, as Oglala author Luther Standing Bear (quoted in Thomas Biolsi's essay) put it, still deeply attached to *wouncage,* "our way of doing." Building on that abiding attachment, Native people gradually made reservations part of "Indian Country."

4

Indian immigrants, to most people, is a contradiction in terms. Native peoples have been in the Americas for untold millennia; according to conventional wisdom, then, everyone now here, *except* the Indian, is an immigrant. Yet as Melissa L. Meyer demonstrates in this account of life on the White Earth Reservation in Minnesota, careful attention to the rhythms of reservation life yields a story full of surprises. Not only does Meyer's tale include Indian immigrants, it also explores Indian capitalists, and (along with David Rich Lewis and other authors in this volume) even casts doubt on such common terms as "progressive" and "traditional," "mixed blood" and "full blood."

Meyer begins in 1867, when the United States government created the White Earth Reservation. Unlike the bleak Bosque Redondo, set up a few years earlier for Navajos, this land in the new state of Minnesota seemed to offer a cornucopia: endless forests for harvesting lumber and maple sugar, lakes and rivers teeming with fish, a climate and soil suitable for farming. So desirable was this spot that other Indians, inhabiting lands less blessed, wanted to move there. For these Indian immigrants, White Earth became something of a promised land.

A promised land, perhaps even a land of opportunity, but no melting pot. Indeed, as Meyer delineates so clearly, questions of culture and ethnicity became pressing issues to reservation residents. Though whites at the time (and since) were prone to lump all Indians together in one undifferentiated mass, the White Earth Reservation failed to reflect that homogenization. Like groups of Native peoples across the Americas, many at White Earth had either converted to Christianity or adopted elements of that faith into their own religious beliefs. As they did elsewhere in those years, government agents and missionaries ran boarding schools and used them to inculcate Anglo-American habits, further dividing groups one from another. Residents of White Earth began to pay ever greater attention to appearance, drawing lines between "full blood" and "mixed blood." In a superb piece of detective work, Meyer has discovered changes in naming patterns that point to an ongoing challenge to Anishinaabe culture over time. Yet despite a decline in traditional names, her research suggests that various cultural patterns, old and new, endured at White Earth. This sure sign of Indian Country's continuing complexity bears comparison not only with the Navajo and Lakota experiences in this section but also with David Lewis's treatment of developments among the Northern Utes and Benjamin Kracht's study of the Kiowas.

Signatures and Thumbprints: Ethnicity among the White Earth Anishinaabeg, 1889–1920

Melissa L. Meyer

HISTORIANS HAVE OFTEN PORTRAYED American Indian populations as relatively homogeneous. Notorious in this regard is the genre of formulaic tribal histories, in which individuals or subgroups are scarcely seen and amorphous tribes merely react to U.S. policy directives and agents' actions.[1] When internal differences are noted, they tend to be lumped into dichotomized categories, with little attention given to their composition or to the historical processes from which they arose. Hence the literature is replete with references to traditionalists and progressives, Christians and pagans, and mixed bloods and full bloods, to name only a few. But history does not unfold in fixed oppositional stages, and dichotomizing these terms, even if they were employed by historical participants themselves, reveals little about social processes. They indicate, instead, a recognition that intratribal heterogeneity was increasing, perhaps in patterned ways.[2]

Native people of the Americas share a common fate in that the expansion of Europe, beginning in the fifteenth century, set in motion processes that reverberated through their cultures. Whether Native Americans persisted or adapted, they did so within the broad parameters of Euro-American colonization. Structures of numerous state governments engaged in colonization changed over time, as did their positions within the world economy. Resources that they coveted varied with market demands and determined the manner in which they hoped to interact with native people.[3]

For their part, indigenous peoples who survived initial epidemics and population declines were continually presented with altered conditions brought about both directly and indirectly by the expanding Euro-American presence. Incorporation of native groups into the world economic system was not a uniform process. The nature and impact of incorporation depended on the structure of the native group, the resources and technologies it utilized, its own position in the world economy, the timing of incorporation attempts, its relations with each specific state government, and the resources being sought after.[4]

Although native peoples suffered much as a result of colonization, they also confronted new opportunities. One of the most significant was the opportunity to become actively involved in the market economy to some degree. Native responses to

SOURCE: *Social Science History,* v. 14, n. 3 (Fall 1990), pp. 305–345. Copyright © 1990, Social Science History Association.

market opportunities varied greatly but frequently included outright resistance to a process that threatened their notions of equity and concern for the collective welfare of the group. If recent scholarship has demonstrated anything, it is that native cultures, their values, ethics, and worldviews, shaped Indians' involvement with Euroamericans and their responses to market opportunities.[5]

Nonetheless, some took advantage of opportunities for market participation. Whether through trade mediation, cash-crop agriculture, or some other means, certain individuals within native societies eventually learned to function within market constraints and integrated basic capitalistic values into their decision making. Some members of native societies gradually became more individualistic and acquisitive in outlook. Increasingly, they began to accumulate wealth and distribute it more narrowly to benefit their close families. The term *capitalistic* in this sense refers more to a basic value orientation than to the practice of reinvesting capital into business enterprises to generate ever greater profits.

Ubiquitous dichotomous labels reflect the uneven and often conflict-ridden ways in which capitalistic values entered native societies. Avenues were numerous—intermarriage, education, and religion, for example—and varied considerably across time and space. Equally diverse were the particular members of a society who were most receptive to these new values. A great deal of variance in local case studies must be anticipated even as the expansion of market capitalism determined the overall trend.[6] Even though polarized terms used to describe internal differences changed from reservation to reservation, parallels between groups suggest that their symbolic content may have been largely the same.[7] The intrusion of market capitalism and the opportunities it presented to native peoples may bear primary responsibility for increasing social heterogeneity among reservation populations, especially in the nineteenth and twentieth centuries.

In the western Great Lakes area during the mid-nineteenth century, nearly two centuries of interaction between Euroamerican fur traders and native peoples had produced an economic and social subgroup composed of members who specialized in mediating between the two cultures. Their economic activities required that they participate in the market economy more fully than their Indian kin, even as they evolved a syncretic culture that reflected their understanding of both cultures. Many reservation populations throughout this region would come to comprise individuals descended both from Indian cultures and from the bicultural occupational subgroup created by the demands of the North American fur trade.[8] That these two cultural groups might come to disagree over management of reservation resources might be anticipated.

Robert Berkhofer observed that historians knew relatively little about the cultural bases of political factions on reservations—whether they broke down according to "old politics of ins and outs, patronage distribution, and family affiliation."[9] Over a decade later, his appraisal still applies not only to political factions but to social and ethnic cleavages. By and large, social history has not taken hold among those who study American Indian history despite an abundance of both narrative and quantifiable source material upon which such research might rest.[10]

An analysis of social relationships that evolved at the White Earth Reservation can help to account for the heterogeneity evident within the population between 1889 and 1920. Ethnic divisions characterized the White Earth Indian population as more market-oriented families descended from Great Lakes fur trade society joined more conservative Indians from interior Minnesota bands. These ethnic differences marked the genesis of community relationships at White Earth. Settlement patterns, social and religious affiliations, household sizes, and surname frequencies all reflect a spectrum of intra-reservation band differences. The terms *mixed blood* and *full blood* were used to distinguish ethnic groups and become politicized as disagreement over the inequitable distribution of resources escalated. Recognizing dichotomous labels as symbols for patterned cultural differences can move scholars closer to discovering the origins of heterogeneity within reservation populations in the nineteenth and early twentieth centuries.

White Earth Reservation was created in 1867 amidst high expectations. Straddling Minnesota's prairie-forest transition zone, it contained diverse and abundant resources and water and was located close to markets. Agriculture would thrive on the western prairies, and the sale of timber from the eastern forests would fuel U.S. government assimilation programs, or so the logic went. Forests, streams, lakes, and marshes ensured that Indians could continue their seasonal harvesting of fish, game, wild rice, and maple sugar as they had in the past. At first White Earth's ecozones supported diverse options for securing a livelihood.[11]

Both the 1867 treaty and the 1889 Nelson Act furthered the U.S. government's agrarian assimilation plans for the Anishinaabeg. In keeping with national policy, both documents prominently featured allotment of the reservation land base. U.S. Indian policy intended nothing less than the wholesale replacement of Indian cultures with a romantic version of the American agrarian ideal, the small-scale, independent yeoman farmer. Policymakers reasoned that allotment of the land base and education in American mores and the principles of market behavior would foster an appreciation of private property among Indians with collective values. Treaties and legislation provided for agricultural implements, houses, schools, and periodic distributions of tribal funds to transform Indian values. The U.S. government would hold allotted lands in trust for 25 years to protect naive Indians from unscrupulous corporations and settlers. If U.S. assimilation policy had a chance to succeed anywhere, White Earth should have become a showcase.[12]

Three major chain migrations brought various aggregations of Anishinaabe families and bands together at White Earth in the late nineteenth century. The Gull Lake Mississippi band and mixed-blood ex-traders and merchants and their offspring from the Crow Wing trade entrepôt migrated following creation of the reservation in 1867. By 1875, 800 had migrated. In 1876, two bands, the Otter Tail Pillagers and members of the Pembina band, also relocated to White Earth, raising the total population to 1,427. Each of these bands settled in an area of the reservation suited to its cultural orientation.[13] The lack of serial documents or censuses makes it difficult to determine much social detail before 1885, when the Indian Office began producing annual censuses.[14]

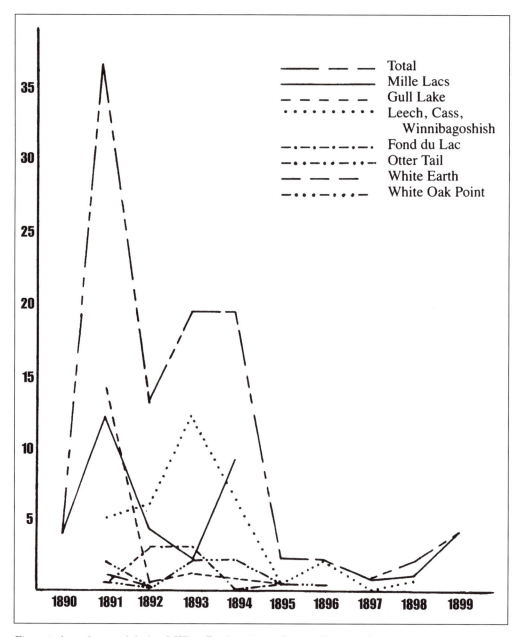

Figure 1. Annual removals by band, White Earth, 1890–99. Source: Chippewa Commission 1890–99.

The third major migration began after passage of the 1889 Nelson Act, which implemented the 1887 General Allotment Act among the "Chippewa Indians of Minnesota." Through the Nelson Act, policymakers attempted to concentrate all of the various Anishinaabe bands in Minnesota at White Earth. Removal provisions, however, were made voluntary, producing migrations from northern Minnesota reservations that spanned a 15-year period. Increasingly after 1890, emigrants from the interior Minnesota reservations of Mille Lacs, Leech Lake, Lake Winnibago-shish, Cass Lake, Fond du Lac, and Gull Lake joined resident White Earth Indians who had migrated earlier (Figure 1).[15]

Over the years, opportunities available at White Earth enticed diverse immigrants. Some Indian immigrants had faced decreasing game populations and sought to integrate subsistence farming into their seasonal round by moving to White Earth's relatively abundant prairie-forest transition zone. Due to the reservation's location in an old buffer zone between the Dakota and Anishnaabeg, extensive human habitation had not exhausted White Earth's resources as it had around forested areas of Leech Lake and Gull Lake. By selling both native and cultivated produce and working for wages, the White Earth Anishinaabeg replaced the fur trade connection through which they had received manufactured goods without severe social or economic dislocation.[16]

Provisions for land and services also attracted mixed-blood individuals scattered throughout northern Minnesota, who faced diminishing economic opportunities. Great Lakes fur trade/métis society spawned this class of bilingual, bicultural brokers who relied on their genetic ties to the Anishinaabeg to gain recognition for their claims to benefits at White Earth. The denouement of the western Great Lakes fur trade displaced these individuals, who brought their market behavior with them to White Earth in search of a renewed economic niche. A few tried the agricultural option—a difficult venture in the northern climate. Others adapted their entrepreneurial skills to the reservation environment, becoming merchant-traders, real estate agents, and newspaper publishers and filling positions associated with the operation of the Indian Agency. They perpetuated their roles as cultural brokers, mediating between more conservative Indians and the dominant society.[17]

The diversity of this entirely immigrant population meant that community genesis and intrareservation differences would characterize the reservation's social structure. Early on, community relationships developed in local, geographical settlements reflecting previous band ties. Indians intent on pursuing the seasonal round settled in the eastern forest and lake country. The midsection and western prairies were better situated for market agriculture and entrepreneurial activities. However, band members did not all settle together, which fostered a commingling of those who shared similar lifeways. Although band ties influenced settlement patterns, cultural or ethnic differences were the most significant divisions on the reservation.

Immigrants who came in response to the Nelson Act perpetuated the east-west settlement pattern, with most joining relatives in the eastern forests.[18] Two distinctive cultural patterns emerged, and their adherents interacted largely within their own group. Literary sources clearly suggest that residential, marital, religious, and educational choices acted as boundary-maintaining mechanisms reinforcing these ethnic divisions.[19] As the twentieth century wore on, these basic ethnic differences would come to eclipse band ties as primary determinants of reservation residents' social affiliations.[20]

The Midewiwin or Grand Medicine Society represented the most hierarchical, organized expression of Anishinaabe spirituality. Adherents had transferred this religious complex and healing society to the White Earth Reservation during the earliest migrations, and it persisted into the twentieth century. The Anishinaabeg attached great importance to dreams. Visions experienced during youth revealed a guardian spirit that provided guidance throughout life and reinforced the individual's role in the circle of life. This cosmogony emphasized "being" and "right living." "Good" behavior ensured individual control and harmony with Kitchi-Manido, the dominant spiritual force, and many lesser spirits. "Wrong" behavior brought recrimination in the form of sickness. The Anishinaabeg interpreted illness as a sign of spirits' displeasure. Disease, then, served as a check on social deviance.[21]

Mide priests and priestesses, having learned their calling through special dreams, intervened to mediate between individuals and spirits. Once admitted, lodge initiates elected to work their way through an internal hierarchy of four ranks. Many failed to attain the uppermost ranks due to the expense involved in amassing the necessary presents and in preparing feasts. A potential member paid fees for the privilege of spending years learning the "secrets." When the period of preliminary instruction ended, initiates hosted a feast and distributed presents that they had worked for years to accumulate. Mide specialists possessed healing powers and a knowledge of medicinal properties of herbs and plants and served the community by performing healing ceremonies when so called upon. Mide members also preserved their traditions by recording them on birchbark scrolls in hieroglyphs that typically recounted the genesis and migrations of the Anishinaabeg, the organization of the Midewiwin, and the proper course for initiates to follow to achieve each successive level. Spiritual leaders convened the Mide membership periodically and kept its rituals and traditions in the deepest secrecy.

Those who believed in and practiced Mide rituals faced a period of transition. U.S. assimilation programs worked to undermine native religious practices and to align individuals with a Christian denomination.[22] Administrators made special efforts to win schoolchildren to the Christian faith, requiring that they attend church services on Sunday. Most predicted the demise of the Midewiwin through "the death of their aged predecessors" and "the adoption of new religions,"[23] but its practitioners continued to offer their services in the first two decades of the twentieth century.[24]

Many White Earth residents practiced some form of Christianity. Once early interdenominational conflicts dissolved into a peaceful, harmonious relationship after 1889, Catholic and Episcopal missionaries ministered to congregations that were largely segregated. Their missions' geographical locations reflected their clienteles' differential ethnic composition. The main Episcopal mission was located at White Earth Village, and there were other churches farther east, where more conservative Indians resided. Even though Episcopals had attracted only about 300 adherents by 1894, they had succeeded in establishing an institutional infrastructure that blended better with Anishinaabe religious practices. In fact, some suggested that the hybrid Episcopal congregations evolved in areas where no Mide priests or priestesses were located, filling a need felt by more conservative people. In 1894, eight of nine Episcopal clergymen were of Indian descent, and "every Sunday services [were] conducted in both English and Chippewa."[25] Episcopal parishioners learned to sing standard Christian hymns in the Anishinaabe language. Even though their membership totals remained low in relation to the overall population, Episcopal methods reflected tolerance, flexibility, and use of the Anishinaabe language and native personnel. Episcopals had greater success in blending elements of new and old ways to produce a syncretic religion that proved more attractive to conservative Indian people who were inclined to sample Christianity.[26]

Referring to Catholic personnel as "missionaries" belies the fact that they were greeted by a substantial Catholic population upon arriving at the reservation. French-Canadian and métis descendants of fur trade society who came to White Earth during the earliest migrations in 1868 brought a heritage of Catholicism with them. Thereupon they beseeched the church to provide them with resident parish priests and nuns. In 1894, Catholics outnumbered Episcopals four to one. Most parishes were located in the western and central parts of the reservation, reflecting the settlement preferences of their ethnically homogeneous congregations. Catholic priests and nuns ministered to the resident population, kept proselytizing to a minimum, and seldom extended their religious pursuits beyond the missions' doors, urging residents "but very little to come to the Catholic church."[27]

Members of White Earth's two ethnic groups made decisions concerning their children's education that were based on their different cultural orientations. Prior to sustained interaction with Euroamericans, Anishinaabe children had received training in appropriate gender roles through their families and bands. Attending school daily, especially at distant boarding schools, disrupted this pattern. People of dual heritage who were descended from fur trade society were more likely to have attended school themselves and to seek the opportunity for their children. These different choices reflected and perpetuated ethnic divisions at the reservation.

Several educational options were directed toward different constituencies. Boarding schools, both on- and off-reservation, were intended to serve children who lived farther away. Instruction emphasized basic competence in reading, writing, and arithmetic, along with chores designed to instill habits needed for an agrarian lifestyle. Boys tended gardens and livestock, chopped and fetched firewood, carried water, and otherwise assisted in heavier manual labor. Girls learned the domestic skills of cooking, cleaning, laundering, and sewing.[28] Besides lessons and chores, Indian students were subjected to heavy doses of U.S. patriotism and the "habits of industry."[29] School personnel emphasized order, neatness, and punctuality, training children to answer to bells and march in step, "even to the smallest mite."[30]

The changes involved with attending boarding school could be wrenching, especially for Indian children with minimal exposure to Euroamerican culture. Besides the trial of leaving their close-knit family group for the first time, Anishinaabe children from more conservative families encountered an all-out cultural assault. Authorities cut boys' hair, assigned them English names, and punished children for speaking their native language;[31] those whose cultural practices already more closely resembled those of Euroamerican society fared better.

In the early 1890s, some parents from the eastern forests did "all they [could] to keep their children away" from the boarding schools and took "great satisfaction" in hiding those who ran away.[32] Long absences from the family, sometimes amounting to years, disrupted the seasonal round, when children were a "great help to their parents."[33] It would take time for them to regard formal education as an asset.

However, inadequate school facilities made it impractical for authorities to enforce attendance stringently. Superintendents complained of their inability to accommodate all children of school age.[34] The schools were "always crowded," which fostered the spread of disease,[35] and administrators routinely had to "refuse places to many."[36] Establishing day schools on the reservation for children who lived close by should have opened more space for Indian children from isolated areas, but the schools still failed to meet the demands of all who sought admission. Coercion served no purpose; runaways and delinquents simply created spaces that others quickly filled.[37]

Both choice and circumstance excluded more conservative Indian children from school. Since the ricing season overlapped with the start of the school year, Indian children from the eastern forests were almost sure to arrive too late to find vacancies. The parents who least understood the institutions of the dominant society were the slowest to apply for admission, so that "the ones most needy [were] the ones left out."[38]

White Earth Indians reacted to the prospect of sending their children to U.S. boarding and day schools in patterned ways determined by their ethnic affiliations. Those who regarded this form of education as a priority, particularly descendants of the bicultural ethnic group, applied promptly and sent their children to school regularly. They supported establishing day schools and later championed the integration of Indian children into predominantly white public schools, where the curriculum afforded a better education. Others who objected to the prospect, often more conservative Indians, either stayed away or were refused admittance. Once they came to approve of formal education, they more often supported the "Indian schools," despite the poorer quality of education, as places where their presence was not greeted with scorn and derision. In this fashion, experiences with institutionalized schooling reinforced the separation of ethnic groups at White Earth.

Socially, members of each ethnic group affiliated largely with themselves. Most social occasions therefore were essentially segregated.

The seasonal round offered countless opportunities for socializing. Larger social groupings that gathered for weeks at a time for sugaring in the spring and ricing in the fall made these especially festive occasions, where social ties were reinforced. Besides these regular seasonal events, conservative Indians also participated in a complex of visiting and dancing both within the reservation and throughout northern Minnesota and the eastern Dakotas, traveling "a hundred miles or more to visit another band of Chippewas or ... to visit the Sioux two or three hundred miles away."[39] Gambling and giveaways were also prominent activities at dances. Skilled Anishinaabe gamblers sometimes spent the entire summer seeking out opportunities to try their skills. The moccasin game, a sleight-of-hand game, went on "day and night for three or four days."[40] Giveaways enhanced the reputation of givers, served as occasions for redistributing material possessions, and were accompanied by socializing with family and friends. Dancing, visiting, and gambling formed important elements of a social complex that persisted among more conservative White Earth residents.

Cultural brokers of mixed descent who opted for a lifestyle more closely tied to the market economy were also involved in a visiting complex. Some socialized with relatives on nearby reservations, but they also journeyed more frequently to larger towns and cities, sometimes purely for social reasons but just as often to take care of business interests.[41]

Those who lived at White Earth Village, where the agency was located, tended to affiliate more often with themselves due both to proximity and to their overall cultural orientation. They included Euroamerican agency employees among their friends and held their dances, characterized by more formal "bowery" dancing to music provided by a local band, at the White Earth Hall. White Earth Villagers hosted parties for each other at private homes, where they played cards and "games, music and refreshments were the order of the evening."[42] Agency employees happily participated in these social activities, noting with approval that mixed bloods were the "better class" of Indians on the reservation. Oscar Lipps, newly appointed superintendent of the White Earth School and fresh from a reservation in the Dakotas, found that White Earth Villagers resembled those in any average white community: "To one whose work has been among the 'wild' Indians, it is very difficult to realize that this is actually an Indian reservation."[43] Social activities among cultural brokers of mixed descent bore little resemblance to the social complex of more conservative Anishinaabeg. Separate social activities helped to maintain cultural boundaries that distinguished ethnic groups on the reservation.

Although separated by many cultural facets, members of the two ethnic groups were drawn together by two annual events. The annuity payment served as a magnet for most of the reservation's population. Also, the June 14 Celebration of White Earth's creation in 1867 played an integrating role. However, each cultural group left its distinctive stamp on these interethnic social events.

Every year, federal agents distributed money and goods due to the Anishinaabeg through treaty rights. Payment usually occurred in October, barring unforeseen delays caused by inclement weather or congressional failure to appropriate funds. More Indians assembled for festivities associated with the annuity payment than at any other time of year. Drums associated with traditional singing and dancing could be heard from a distance, and participants visited stores, gambling places, and the dance all in turn.[44]

Merchant-traders of mixed descent frequented the paying places, waiting outside for those to whom they had extended credit; the annuity payment was an obvious occasion when the merchants' presence might remind native peoples of their debts before other attractions lured them to spend their newly acquired cash.[45] Merchants also displayed their wares at the annuity payment, which conveniently took place near their establishments. What better time for Indians who had just received a sizable amount of money to purchase a sewing machine, a horse, yard goods, or groceries? In fact, the annuity payment was ripe for any cash transaction; saloons and gambling houses also profited.

The June 14 Celebration of White Earth's founding drew people from all over northern Minnesota and the Dakotas in addition to White Earth residents. The White Earth Anishinaabeg looked forward to the annual visit of the Dakota and Nakota and made preparations to host them; they organized planning meetings and solicited donations for the feast, encouraging Indians to assume financial responsibility for the festivities themselves.[46] U.S. policymakers supported the event, hoping that it would instill pride in the reservation among its diverse residents.

Before the appointed day, 150 to 200 visiting Dakota and Nakota assembled in encampments at the celebration grounds in White Earth Village. At dawn, the "Grand Celebration began with the firing of the federal salute, signalling the onset of the festivities." The parade that followed symbolically recounted the most significant happenings that had contributed to the establishment and prosperity of the reservation. Representing Indians of the past, riders in warrior costumes, astride brightly decorated ponies, pranced past the crowd of spectators, keeping time to beating drums in the "Grand Aboriginal Parade." They reminded onlookers of a time when the Anishinaabeg had been in more direct control of their political lives and diplomatic relationships. (By the twentieth century, threats of war had all but disappeared, but Indians fondly remembered their more autonomous past.)

Next, participants staged a "PEACE MEETING between the SIOUX AND CHIPPEWA," bringing to a symbolic end the generations-old conflict that had by then attained almost mythic proportions in the folklore of the Anishinaabeg, the Dakota, and Minnesota society at large. Although conflict between the two nations was never as all-encompassing as folklore had it, the presence of Dakota friends and relations underscored the significance that mending their differences had for them.

Following the reenactment of the peace meeting, "survivors of the first arrivals" in 1868 filed past and were honored by the crowd. Having persevered through the difficult early years, these "old settlers" were accorded the status of veterans who had endured weighty sacrifices on behalf of generations to come. The parade concluded with White Earth residents representing "Indians of today." Their promenade was accompanied by the White Earth School Band and the White Earth Cornet Band. People in this group wore Euro-American–style clothing and celebrated the transformation of Anishinaabe culture.

The "Grand Parade" had something for everyone, and members of both ethnic groups could find an acceptable niche. Events of the previous 50 years that retained prominence in the collective Anishinaabe memory found a place in the pageantry of the June 14 Celebration. Those who orchestrated the parade shared the evolutionary, progressive interpretation of history popular among U.S. policymakers. The parade symbolically represented the demise of a "traditional" way of life and the ushering in of a new, "modern" order. There is no doubt that U.S. policymakers viewed changes in Anishinaabe culture in this way, but whether all celebration participants shared this perspective is open to question.

Social activities familiar to each ethnic group filled the afternoon. Those skilled at lacrosse, pony races, and foot races were given a chance to compete. Spectators watched Indian men perform "war, scalp, skull and pipe dances" and the shawano-gah dance, where women joined in. Also, "bowery dances were scheduled all after-noon and evening," with a local band providing tunes to which dancers kept time. Indian "chiefs" presided, and sometimes even the governor of the state of Minnesota made an appearance.[47]

The event truly offered an opportunity for members of both ethnic groups to come together. Everyone participated in a celebration replete with pageantry, contests, and revelry. Period photographs reflect the interethnic nature of the celebration. Men in derbies and women with parasols stood in their store-bought finery next to their horseless carriages, while Indians bedecked in feathers and beaded buckskin danced around center drummers, their wigwams, tipis, and tents in the background.[48]

While interethnic celebrations drew people together in a physical sense, familiar divisions were yet apparent. Perceptions of ethnic differences that the Indians observed among themselves were encapsulated in the terms *mixed blood* and *full blood*. Hairstyle, clothing style, type of house, cultural practices, and, most impor-tantly, economic ethics all contributed to the cultural or ethnic symbols that reserva-tion residents used to describe themselves. Participants and observers alike consistently described full bloods as "poor" Indians, concerned only with their subsis-tence and the equitable distribution of resources. Mixed bloods were "shrewd," understood how the market economy operated, and accumulated material wealth. Prior to the involvement of key mixed-blood leaders in land fraud, the term *mixed blood* carried few of the pejorative connotations that it later came to bear. Only U.S. policymakers interpreted the terms genetically; Indian definitions revolved around cultural characteristics that eventually came to include a political dimension.[49]

When asked to define *mixed blood* and *full blood* precisely, Indian informants often had difficulty responding. Rules for determining descent were not concrete. The common denominator in all definitions of *mixed blood* was some admixture of white blood. An individual could be a "little mixed-blood" or "nearly white." Generally, informants agreed that *half-breed* signified equal parts of white and Indian blood. As such, half-breeds were a subclass of mixed bloods that had been more numerous during the fur trade era. Aside from these commonalities, an individual's identity rested on the interpretation of the observer.

Many informants cited some genetic characteristics in their attempts to describe mixed bloods and full bloods. For some, physical features were the most distinguish-ing characteristics. Full bloods were more darkly complected and had straight black hair, dark brown eyes, and no body hair. Mixed bloods had lighter skin, brown, some-times curly hair, and lighter eyes; men grew facial hair. However, Anishinaabe informants understood that these general characteristics served only as guidelines, since some genetic variation occurred naturally. Mezhucegeshig observed that "some Indians are blacker than others, and some are lighter."[50] Mah-do-say-quay con-curred: "Sometimes there is one lighter. . . . It just happens."[51] These informants objected to establishing fixed physical standards by which to differentiate among Indians because of variations they observed among themselves.[52]

Informants most often relied on cultural characteristics to distinguish between mixed bloods and full bloods. Clothing was a telltale attribute. When asked if an acquaintance was a mixed blood, Ke-che-mah-quah thought, "He would have looked that way if he had pants on, but . . . he wrote [a] breech cloth clear up to his death."[53] Similarly, Wah-way-zho-o-quay identified a group of men as full bloods, saying "They would have had hats if they were white." Another clue for her was that "they would wear pants; and white collars" if they were mixed bloods.[54]

Other distinguishing cultural features surfaced as well. When asked whether he had ever lived at his grandfather's house, Ay-dow-ah-cumig-o-quay protested that "he did not have any house—he was an Indian."[55] Me-zhuc-e-ge-shig's explanation of his friend's religious conversion illustrates how one's status as mixed blood or full blood could change with cultural preferences: "He was a very old Indian. He was a full-blood Indian but when he adopted the church, why he felt as though he was a Frenchman. He acted as one."[56] Most agreed that mixed bloods with white fathers possessed no dodaim (totem or clan affiliation), because dodaims were inherited through the paternal line. Bay-ba-daung-ay-yaush fastened on this attribute to describe a woman she knew, saying, "I believe that she was an Indian because she had a dodaim. Indians have dodaims."[57] Atypical marriage patterns might produce mixed bloods with dodaims, but these were exceptions. Confronting such a case confused Gah-mah-nah-che-wah-nay. He claimed that these people were not "regular Indians." "They didn't look like it, but the only peculiar thing about them, they had a dodaim."[58] Through comments such as these, the cultural or ethnic content of the mixed-blood and full-blood symbols emerged.

As White Earth residents made clear, the cultural content of these ethnic symbols revolved around differences in lifestyle. George Morrison explained that those who wore breechcloths and blankets, lived in wigwams, and associated primarily with Indians were considered to be full bloods, "not on account of their blood . . . it was their way of living that regulated that."[59] Cultural affiliations and way of life made all the difference. Bay-bah-daung-ay-aush was asked if a person with only a small amount of white blood who lived as an Indian would be called a mixed blood. He answered, "No, because he would be poor, and he just would look after what he wants to eat . . . to subsist."[60] Residents had evolved a mélange of cultural characteristics to differentiate between ethnic groups on the reservation.

Marital preferences also reflected marked ethnic differences between mixed bloods and full bloods. Genealogical research into the backgrounds of several prominent mixed-blood families revealed very few marriages between mixed bloods descended from Lake Superior bands and Mississippi band members.[61] When asked if his former father-in-law had been white, Me-zhuc-e-ge-shig quickly dismissed the idea, saying, "If he had white blood his daughter would have had white blood and she wouldn't have liked me, and she wouldn't have married me."[62] These patterns arose during the fur trade era, when intermarriage between Euroamerican fur traders and native women produced a large population of individuals of mixed descent. These mixed bloods then evolved into a unique society throughout the Great Lakes fur trade network, maintaining their distinctive cultural attributes through marriage with people like themselves. White Earth residents described marital preferences as endogamous boundary-maintaining mechanisms, reinforcing ethnic differences.

Me-zhuc-e-ge-shig denied that mixed bloods who lived at La Pointe married Indian women: "They didn't marry Indian women. They married mixed bloods."[63] Marital patterns reinforced and maintained social and cultural differences among the White Earth Anishinaabeg that were recognized by natives themselves. Mah-do-say-quay reflected on the ethnic characteristics of mixed bloods recognized by many: "They were Indians, but they were different . . . a different class of people."[64]

Older White Earth residents remembered the days of their youth when blood status meant little. Many Indians from interior Minnesota bands firmly believed that earlier in the century, they had never seen a mixed blood—only people like themselves. They realized that mixed bloods had proliferated throughout the north country because of their trading ties. Mah-do-say-quay could tell a mixed blood from a full blood by sight when she "saw them at Crow Wing."[65]

The Crow Wing connection, where many ex-traders and their offspring developed close relationships with Mississippi bands, remained prominent in people's minds. They identified Crow Wing as the point from which mixed bloods had entered the population and continued to grow in numbers. Like many others, Ke-zhe-wash testified that mixed bloods had not lived among Indians when she was a young woman: "They came around when they began to have annuity payments."[66]

Anishinaabe use of the term *mixed blood* suggests that its meaning was evolving as Indians adapted to the increased presence of mixed bloods and to changes in their lifeways. Mixed-blood chiefs were included among signers of several treaties. Proliferation of clans and chiefs indicates a changing social structure. Some suggest that the appearance of the eagle clan for those of British descent and the maple leaf clan for those of French descent represented attempts to accommodate dodaim-less mixed bloods with clans of their own. Along social and demographic lines, the Anishinaabeg faced a time of transition.[67]

If the labels *mixed blood* and *full blood* accurately identify basic cultural differences between White Earth residents, the behavior of individuals ought to reflect this. The relative proportion of French or English surnames as opposed to Anishinaabe names can serve as a very rough indicator of the cultural orientation of each band (Table 1).[68] Anglicized names in this context indicate a more innovative choice of names, while Indian names reflect more conservative ones. They also reflect the degree of intermarriage with Euroamericans.[69]

Names listed on Bureau of Indian Affairs censuses do not necessarily reflect individuals' choices. Anishinaabe names could change during individuals' lifetimes. Initially, children might be named after a peculiar incident at their birth or some special power possessed by another Indian. As they grew, names might be added or completely changed.[70] Furthermore, the anglicization process was not uniform: some translated their Indian names into English and added an English first name; some took their clan name as a family name; nicknames stuck; lumber company employees and school officials assigned names arbitrarily; and names were misspelled and mistranslated phonetically.[71] In addition, names recorded in censuses often are nothing more than Anishinaabe words meaning, for example, "old woman" or "little girl." Individuals might possess both an English name and an Anishinaabe name, which

TABLE 1   ANISHINAABE VS. ENGLISH NAMES, 1890–1920

	FdL	P	M	GL	WOP	C&W	OT	ML	LL
1890									
% Anishinaabe	—	30	25	—	—	—	84	—	—
% English	—	70	75	—	—	—	16	—	—
N	—	218	1,107	—	—	—	652	—	—
1900									
% Anishinaabe	3	11	14	28	72	57	70	50	75
% Both	3	—	0.7	0.3	3	6	—	—	2
% English	93	89	86	71	25	37	30	50	23
N	91	318	1,539	336	88	51	741	323	310
1910									
% Anishinaabe	2	5	5	12	30	16	42	45	43
% Both	—	0.3	3	3	9	6	10	8	15
% English	98	95	92	85	61	78	48	47	42
N	111	361	1,995	401	259	63	744	990	277
1920									
% Anishinaabe	0.9	2	2	6	13	16	16	24	19
% Both	0.9	3	3	7	13	18	22	19	29
% English	98	95	95	88	74	66	62	57	52
N	113	472	2,764	469	315	61	886	1,308	281

Source: Bureau of Indian Affairs 1889–1920.

Note: *Anishinaabe* refers to names recorded in the native language without surnames. FdL = Fond du Lac band; P = Pembina band; M = Mississippi band; GL = Gull Lake band; WOP = White Oak Point band; C&W = Cass Lake & Lake Winnibagoshish bands; OT = Otter Trail Pillager band; ML = Mille Lacs band; LL = Leech Lake band.

could be used interchangeably. Many factors combined to create the census listings. But any problems with the censuses apply equally to all bands. Resulting surname patterns complement other social and demographic patterns that differentiated bands at White Earth.

The breakdown of bands at White Earth by surname frequency reflects differences in the duration and intensity of those bands' involvement in Great Lakes fur trade/métis society. Centered at a long-established fur trade depot on the St. Louis River, the Fond du Lac band stood at one end of a spectrum of surname frequencies. The Pembina band, an offshoot of the métis population of the Turtle Mountain Reservation in North Dakota and closely affiliated with the Red River Colony in Canada, exhibited characteristics similar to the Fond du Lac band. The White Earth Mississippi band regularly placed third after these two bands in proportion of anglicized surnames. The Mississippi band at White Earth consisted of an amalgamation of social groups. In the earliest migrations to White Earth, a large number of mixed-blood descendants of fur traders from Crow Wing and Lake Superior and Wisconsin bands at Anishinaabeg joined the more conservative Mississippi band centered at Gull Lake. Both patterns were reflected in the White Earth Mississippi band. However, the mixed bloods predominated, causing characteristics of the Mississippi band to resemble more closely those of the Pembina and Fond du Lac bands; they shared common origins in fur trade society.[72] The Fond du Lac, Pembina, and Mississippi bands continually exhibited higher proportions of French and English surnames.

Conservative Anishinaabe bands from more isolated locations in Minnesota's interior retained their Indian names longer. Despite the overall trend toward increasing anglicization of names, the Leech Lake, Otter Tail, and Mille Lacs bands maintained higher proportions of Anishinaabe names. In the past, their seasonal existence at interior Minnesota lakes circumscribed their interaction within Great Lakes fur trade society. While they engaged in trade, intermarriage occurred on a more limited scale among them than among bands located near major trade entrepôts like Crow Wing, La Pointe, and the Red River Colony.[73]

The patterning of bands within this spectrum of surname frequencies does not represent a hard-and-fast categorization of bands by cultural characteristics. Several bands lie in a middle zone and exhibit some individual variation. However, it is clear that specific bands continually occupied upper and lower limits, establishing the pattern. It is therefore correct to say that naming patterns at White Earth reflected cultural differences between bands.[74]

Age pyramids showing the distribution of names illustrate the anglicization process (Figures 2-5). In 1890, the White Earth Mississippi band showed a 75% majority of French and English surnames. Only a small, shrinking core of Indian names remained. By 1920, Anishinaabe names had all but disappeared. Some older residents took their Indian names to the grave; fewer children were identified officially

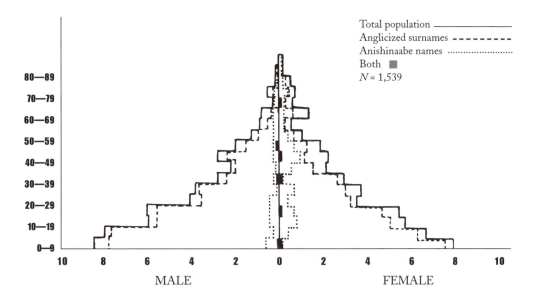

Figure 2. Age Structure and Patterns of Names: Mississippi Band, 1900.
Source: Bureau of Indian Affairs 1900.

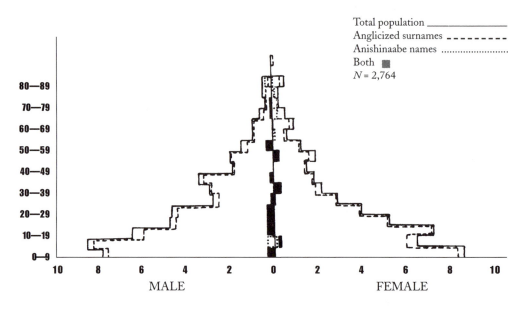

Figure 3. Age Structure and Patterns of Names: Mississippi Band, 1920.
Source: Bureau of Indian Affairs 1920.

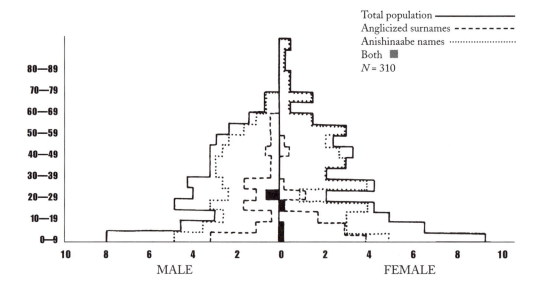

Figure 4. Age Structure and Patterns of Names: Leech Lake Removals, 1900.
Source: Bureau of Indian Affairs 1900.

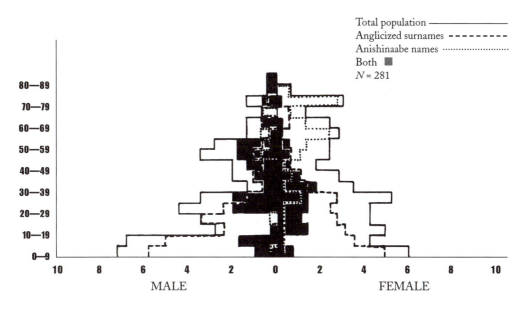

Figure 5. Age Structure and Patterns of Names: Leech Lake Removals, 1920.
Source: Bureau of Indian Affairs 1920.

by their Anishinaabe names. The pattern of names in the Otter Tail band replicates this larger trend but reveals an earlier stage of the process: 84% Anishinaabe names in 1890, 38% by 1920. When members of interior bands did adopt surnames, they were more likely to use Anishinaabe ones, like Wadena or Gahbow, or to anglicize Anishinaabe names, producing family names like Rock, Squirrel, Skip-in-the-Day, or Skinaway. The anglicization process reflected ethnic differences at White Earth.

The average size of households also varied among bands at White Earth. A spectrum of household sizes at White Earth corresponds in its basic configurations to the spectrum of surname frequencies (Table 2). With some annual variation, diagnostic bands at the upper and lower ends of the spectrum remain the same. Bands with a longer history of participation in Great Lakes fur trade/métis society tended to have smaller households. Cultural differences between bands were reflected in the reservation's social structure.

None of these rough measures alone can be considered conclusive. However, recurrence of established patterns through several measures enhances their reliability. Bureau of Indian Affairs censuses for White Earth cannot be used to construct reliable age structures in the years after about 1910, when out-migration escalated, but they can help establish patterned interband differences. When information derived in this fashion complements interpretations drawn from literary sources, the reliability of both is strengthened.

As might be expected, such pronounced ethnic differences influenced political formation on the reservation, especially as competition over the management and

TABLE 2   MEAN HOUSEHOLD SIZE, BY BAND, WHITE EARTH
RESERVATION, 1890–1920

Band	1890	1900	1910	1920
Fond du Lac	—	5.3	5.3	7.5
Pembina	4.9	5.7	6.0	7.0
White Earth Mississippi	3.8	5.0	5.0	5.0
Gull Lake	—	5.1	4.6	5.3
White Oak Point	—	4.6	4.5	5.4
Cass and Winnibagoshish	—	4.6	6.3	7.6
Otter Tail Pillagers	4.2	4.4	4.2	4.8
Mille Lacs	—	5.1	4.4	4.7
Leech Lake	—	4.4	3.7	4.9

Source: Bureau of Indian Affairs 1809–1920.
Note Solitary individuals have been omitted.

distribution of resources escalated. After initial migrations in the 1860s and 1870s, various band leaders continued to perform roles to which they had become accustomed. Earlier treaty provisions entitled each band to certain rights and benefits from the U.S. government. Band leaders and member of their constituencies continued to safeguard these rights by petitioning various U.S. government officials. Prior to 1907, the band remained the primary unit of political identity. While all band leaders made reference to White Earth as their reservation, a reservation-based political consciousness had yet to supplant earlier band ties.[75]

The political involvement of individuals of mixed descent complicated matters. Though blood distinctions meant little to earlier generations of Anishinaabeg, women who married Euroamerican men broke the patrilineal clan line. Patrilineal descent systems meant that children without Anishinaabe fathers had no institutionalized role within the clan structure. Because the clan system was flexible, native communities easily accommodated these children, but their parents were also likely to send them away from the reservation to acquire a better formal education. When they returned to the Anishinaabeg, they found that their training had prepared them to mediate between the two cultures, much as their fathers and mothers had done before them.

Some individuals found power in this role. They were often present as interpreters at political and diplomatic gatherings and, through their linguistic skills, controlled the exchange of ideas and information. Their experience enabled them to understand treaty and legislative negotiations, the intentions of the U.S. government, and the likely consequences of policies. Together with band leaders, they sought to safeguard their tribal and economic interests. Often their services were indispensable in the struggle to preserve Anishinaabe resources.

Moreover, their greater wealth and close associations with both reservation and state political leaders increased their visibility and power. The merchants and mediators among them enjoyed patron-client relationships with Indian people and received not only payment but, sometimes, political support in exchange for their credit and services. Their leadership style reflected their ethnic heritage of brokerage, rooted in Great Lakes fur trade society, and their stronger adherence to market values.[76]

Since the inception of the reservation in 1867, powerful patron-traders of mixed descent, such as Clement and Gus Beaulieu and Benjamin L. Fairbanks, had managed to exert a great deal of political influence on the reservation. The "Beaulieu-Fairbanks gang," as some called them, dominated self-proclaimed "elective" council meetings at White Earth from the 1890s to about 1910, when the factional dispute escalated.

Privatization of collectively owned resources by the 1889 Nelson Act created new opportunities for those with a capitalist ethic. Their understanding of surveyors' marks and the value of land as real estate allowed those of mixed descent to acquire the most valuable resources at the expense of their less savvy neighbors. When restrictions on allotted land and timber were removed between 1904 and 1907, the most prominent mixed-blood mediators aided lumber companies, banks, and speculators in victimizing those who did not understand mortgages and real-estate transactions.[77]

These same individuals also turned their attention to the "Chippewa in Minnesota Fund," which was held in common by Anishinaabeg on all northern Minnesota reservations. Increasingly, they focused their domineering political activities on gaining access to this fund. They scheduled councils for their own convenience, always at White Earth Village, and publicized them only through their newspaper, the *Tomahawk*, without regard for the extent of its circulation. Sometimes "the tribal councils were not in fact held"; instead, "a small party of Beaulieu's friends and followers went from place to place," counted those to whom they spoke, and tried to pass off their opinion as a council resolution.[78] When a majority threatened to vote independently, reservation "bosses" used wagons and drivers to round up eligible voters from around town to stack the deck in their favor. Ringleaders bullied speakers at council meetings and, through manipulations of parliamentary procedure and rules of order, refused to recognize those whose opinions ran counter to their own.[79] Ben Fairbanks was not above coercing "Indians of the various reservations to the support of their designs" by withholding credit from those who were not forthcoming with political support at election time.[80]

Through strong-arm tactics of this nature, highly visible cultural brokers of mixed descent selected themselves and their supporters as reservation representatives and widely claimed that their views reflected majority opinion. They achieved success through a shrewd blend of personal charisma, expertise in the methods of boss politics, and pressuring of their clients.[81] However, their complicity in land frauds, in conjunction with their acquisition of wealth and domineering behavior, irreparably damaged their reputations.

Patterns of fraud in the allocation and transfer of allotted land and timber were not immediately apparent. Although many people recited instances of fraud and misrepresentation, they failed to see the general pattern in their stories. Testimony taken and reports filed by government investigators between 1909 and 1913 drew these facts to their attention, and a clearer picture began to emerge. "Assimilation" for the White Earth Anishinaabeg had meant the passing of over 90 percent of the reservation land base from Indian ownership![82]

The obvious involvement of key individuals of mixed descent in land fraud claims, in addition to their continued efforts to monopolize political power both at White Earth and among all the Anishinaabe of northern Minnesota, prompted a fundamental political realignment among more conservative band leaders. Styling themselves the "Full Blood Faction," they united across band lines and began a counteroffensive to halt the inequitable dissipation of reservation resources and to undermine the political power of those whom they called "mixed bloods." In this way, land fraud claims contributed to the development of a true interband, reservation-based political consciousness.[83]

Contestants in the ensuing factional struggle transformed mixed-blood and full-blood ethnic symbols to include a political dimension. In reality, political leaders recognized that each faction contained both genetic mixed bloods and genetic full bloods. Use of these symbolic terms masks the fact that culturally determined values, especially economic ones, were of greatest importance in establishing factional affiliations. Full-blood leaders complained that mixed bloods were "shrewd" men who cared only for self-gain.[84] They accused them of having grown wealthy from "cheating their people"[85] and held up their own leaders as "conservative men, safeguarding the interest of the tribe as a whole without any regard to personal interest or private gain."[86] Leaders of mixed descent espoused a capitalist ethic and charged full bloods with being "lazy," "idle," and "indolent" men who received undue welfare gratuities from tribal funds.[87] They recommended that they be "turned loose to fend for themselves,"[88] as they had successfully done.

Members of both factions evaluated each other on the basis of ethical criteria that transcended family, community, and band relationships. Although all of these considerations influenced alliances that individuals formed with each other and with organized factions, participants in the factional struggle cited economic indicators as determinants of one's political identity as a mixed blood or a full blood. The ethnic divisions that characterized the White Earth populace reverberated through the political realm as well.

Marked ethnic boundaries characterized the social order at the White Earth Reservation between 1889 and 1920. One group consisted of conservative Anishinaabeg from north-central Minnesota, still organized along band lines. The other group was composed of members of a long-standing, bicultural, occupational subgroup accustomed to mediating exchanges between Indians and U.S. society. Neither group was "traditional" in the static, aboriginal sense. Both groups had grown accustomed to adapting to altered conditions from a foundation of continuity with past cultural constructs. Members of both ethnic groups saw that White Earth offered them an opportunity to relocate and prosper.

For a time, both groups coexisted in relative harmony. However, U.S. policymakers intensified their emphasis on privatizing and alienating reservation resources. At times they deemed it more important that Indians learn individualistic values than that policymakers implement directives according to the letter of the law. These policy shifts allowed those with acquisitive values to take advantage of their unsuspecting neighbors. Nothing offended conservative Anishinaabeg more than the inequitable accumulation by a few of what had been collective resources. The ascendance of capitalist values disrupted and nearly destroyed the entire social and economic fabric of the reservation.

The White Earth case represents but one example of the ways in which capitalistic values entered native societies. It may stand as an extreme along a spectrum of possible local configurations. Intermarriage and education figured prominently in the social dynamics of White Earth, as at other reservations, but many other factors existed as well. Disruption of economic subsistence systems has sometimes prompted efforts at market agriculture.[89] Members of prominent families might have gained privileged access to resources or lines of power and developed increasingly acquisitive values.[90] These new tensions between individualism and collectivism may have played off older divisions within a culture, which then formed a unique response to those tensions and divisions.[91] The paths by which individualistic values gained prominence were numerous and need to be researched more fully.

In some cases, Indian societies managed to adapt older patterns to defuse individualism and acquisitiveness. Many Pueblo groups, as veritable theocracies, relied on traditional deference to fused religious and political institutions to maintain their collective cohesiveness.[92] The Arapaho upheld a long-standing practice of determining political leaders through age grading as a means of ensuring conservatism in decision making, thus holding individualism in check.[93] In the early twentieth century, the Red Lake Anishinaabeg, having observed firsthand the White Earth fiasco, put in place a governing structure composed of seven conservative appointed leaders to thwart the designs of capitalistic businessmen among them.[94] These are only a few suggestive examples. The ingenious accomplishments of these groups attest to their convictions, but they also affirm the importance of the more general intrusion of capitalist values.

Ever-present dichotomous labels give the impression that some Indians embraced U.S. assimilation programs more readily than others. In some cases this was true, but it fails to capture the full picture. Acquisition of capitalist values formed the very backbone of assimilation as policymakers construed it. However, some individuals had adapted to market conditions long before the United States had enough power to force cultural changes. Once U.S. Indian policy *did* take on a coercive cast, native peoples approached assimilationist directives with their own objectives in mind, creating complex syncretic adaptations that policymakers had never dreamed of. Native people adjusted their behavior to circumstances they faced, as they had for centuries. U.S. assimilation policy was just one arena of change. The major process with which they had to contend was the expansion of market capitalism.

Social heterogeneity never broke down into neatly polarized contingents. The divisions separating the two ethnic groups at White Earth were not hard-and-fast, and individuals frequently crossed boundaries to create unique adaptations.[95] An individual might simultaneously exhibit both "traditional" and "progressive" traits, especially if these terms are defined in rigid, categorical ways that fail to allow for change over time.[96] But regardless of how they entered or through which members, it is likely that capitalist values will emerge to bear primary responsibility for increasing heterogeneity within reservation societies in the nineteenth and early twentieth centuries.

NOTES

1. J. A. Clifton, "The Tribal History: An Obsolete Paradigm," *American Indian Culture and Research Journal* 3 (1979): 81–100; P. Iverson, "Indian Tribal Histories," in W. Swagerty, ed., *Scholars and the Indian Experience* (Bloomington: Indiana University Press, 1984), 223–58.

2. J. A. Clifton, "Alternate Identities and Cultural Frontiers," in J. A. Clifton, ed., *Being and Becoming Indian: Biographical Studies of North American Frontiers* (Chicago: Dorsey, 1989), 1–37.

3. I. Wallerstein, *The Modern World System: Capitalist Agriculture and the Origins of European World-Economy in the Sixteenth Century* (New York: Academic, 1974); Wallerstein, *The Capitalist World Economy* (Cambridge: Cambridge University Press, 1979); C. Chase-Dunn, "Core-Periphery Relations: The Effects of Core Capitalism," in B. H. Kaplan, ed., *Social Change in the Capitalist World Economy* (Beverly Hills: Sage, 1978), 159–175; Chase-Dunn, "The Development of Core Capitalism in the Antebellum United States: Tariff Politics in an Upwardly Mobile Semiperiphery," in A. Bergesen, ed., *Studies of the World System* (New York: Academic, 1980), 89–230; R. H. Chilcote and D. L. Johnson, *Theories of Development: Modes of Production or Dependency?* (Beverly Hills: Sage, 1983); D. Chirot and T. D. Hall, "World System Theory," in *Annual Review of Sociology* 8 (1982): 81–106; A. G. Frank, *Capitalism and Underdevelopment in Latin America: Historical Studies of Chile and Brazil* (New York: Monthly Review, 1969); Frank, *Latin America: Underdevelopment or Revolution* (New York: Monthly Review, 1969); J. G. Jorgensen, "Indians and the Metropolis," in J. O. Waddell and O. M. Watson, eds., *The American Indian in Urban Society* (Boston: Little, Brown, 1971), 67–113; and Jorgensen, "A Century of Political and Economic Effects on American Indian Society, 1880–1980," *Journal of Ethnic Studies* 6 (1978): 1–82. World systems and dependency theories have only touched on the experiences of indigenous Americans without giving much attention to the internal structures and dynamics of their social and economic systems.

4. T. D. Hall, "Peripheries, Regions of Refuge and Nonstate Societies: Toward a Theory of Reactive Social Change," *Social Science Quarterly* 64 (1983): 582–97; Hall, "Change and Assimilation: Native Americans Under Spain and the United States," *Free Inquiry* 13 (1985): 173–77; Hall, "Incorporation in the World System: Toward a Critique," *American Sociological Review* 51 (1986): 390–402; Hall, "Patterns of Native American Incorporation into State Societies," in C. M. Snipp, ed., *Public Policy Impacts on American Indian Economic Development* (Albuquerque: University of New Mexico, Native American Studies, 1988), 23–38; Hall, *Social Change in the Southwest, 1350–1880* (Lawrence: University Press of Kansas, 1988); C. M. Snipp, "The Changing Political and Economic Status of American Indians: From Captive Nations to Internal Colonies," *American Journal of Economics and Sociology* 45 (1986): 145–57; Snipp, "Old and New Views of Economic Development in Indian Country," in *Overcoming Economic Dependency: Papers and Comments from the First Newberry Library Conference on Themes in American Indian History, 1988* (Occasional Paper Series, No. 9); G. C. Anders, "The Internal Colonization of Cherokee Native Americans," in *Development and Change* 10 (1977): 41–55; Anders, "The Reduction of a Self-Sufficient People to Poverty and Welfare Dependence: An Analysis of the Causes of Cherokee Indian Underdevelopment," in *American Journal of Economics and Sociology* 40 (1981): 225–38; and Hall, "Theories of Underdevelopment and the American Indian," in *Journal of Economic Issues* 14 (1985): 681–702. Scholars who have attempted to explicate the processes by which American Indians were incorporated into world systems are few. Sociologists have taken the lead, and the work of Thomas D. Hall is exemplary among them.

5. R. White, *The Roots of Dependency: Subsistence, Environment, and Social Change among the Choctaw, Pawnee, and Navajo* (Lincoln: University of Nebraska Press, 1984).

6. Hall, *Social Change in the Southwest*. Hall offers a useful comparative framework for local case studies. Hall's model, however, places heavier emphasis on the nature of states and the world economy than it does on the nature of Indian cultures. Ideally, aspects of Indian cultures in addition to social organization should be included. Native economic systems, political structures, ideologies, and the resources that they themselves exploited all influenced the outcome of their interaction with Euroamericans. Integration of these cultural facets into the model would introduce a corrective holistic perspective.

7. L. Fowler, *Arapaho Politics, 1851–1978: Symbols in Crises of Authority* (Lincoln: University of Nebraska Press, 1982); and Fowler, *Shared Symbols, Contested Meanings: Alternate Views of Culture and History in an American Indian Society: The Gros Ventres, 1778–1984* (Ithaca: Cornell University Press, 1987). For example, Loretta Fowler discusses the symbolic cultural meanings behind the terms *mixed blood* and *full blood* as employed by the Gros Ventres and Arapaho. The type of research necessary to unearth the specific symbolic content of the dichotomous terms used and the composition of factional groups in each local situation is extremely detailed and time-consuming. In some cases, it may not be possible at all. Further research along these lines is necessary to determine whether apparent parallels are real.

8. Clifton, *The Prairie People: Continuity and Change in Potawatomi Culture, 1665–1965* (Lawrence: Regents Press of Kansas, 1977).

9. R. F. Berkhofer, Jr., "Native Americans," in J. Higham, ed., *Ethnic Leadership in America* (Baltimore: Johns Hopkins University Press, 1978), 128.

10. M. L. Meyer and R. Thornton, "Indians and the Numbers Game: Quantitative Methods in American Indian History," in C. Calloway, ed., *New Directions in American Indian History* (Norman: University of Oklahoma Press, 1988), 5–29.

11. H. E. Wright, Jr., "Late Quaternary Vegetational History of North America," in K. K. Turekian, ed., *The Late Cenozoic Glacial Ages* (New Haven: Yale University Press, 1971), 425–64; P. K. Simms and G. B. Morey, eds., *Geology of Minnesota: A Centennial Volume* (St. Paul: Minnesota Geological Survey, 1972); J. R. Borchert, *Minnesota's Changing Geography* (Minneapolis: University of Minnesota Press, 1959); H. Hickerson, "The Virginia Deer and Intertribal Buffer Zones in the Upper Mississippi Valley," in A. Leeds and A. P. Vayda, eds., *Man, Culture, and Animals: The Role of Animals in Human Ecological Adjustments*, Publication No. 78 (Washington, D.C. : American Association for the Advancement of Science, 1965), 43–65; and A. M. Davis, "The Prairie-Deciduous Forest Ecozone in the Upper Middle West," *Annals of the Association of American Geographers* 67 (1977): 204–213.

12. F. E. Hoxie, *A Final Promise: The Campaign to Assimilate the Indians, 1880–1920* (Lincoln: University of Nebraska Press, 1984); L. Carlson, *Indians, Bureaucrats, and Land: The Dawes Act and the Decline of Indian Farming* (Westport, Conn.: Greenwood Press, 1981); R. D. Hurt, *Indian Agriculture in America: Prehistory to the Present* (Lawrence: University Press of Kansas, 1987); D. S. Otis, *The Dawes Act and the Allotment of Indian Land* (Norman: University of Oklahoma Press, 1973); and H. C. Miner, *The Corporation and the Indian: Tribal Sovereignty and Industrial Civilization in Indian Territory, 1865–1907* (Columbia: University of Missouri Press, 1976).

13. Commissioner of Indian Affairs, *Annual Reports, 1850–1940*, U.S. Congressional Serial Set (Washington, D.C.: U.S. Government Printing Office), 1867: 397; 1868: 301; 1870: 305; 1871: 588, 592; 1872: 210; 1874: 195; 1875: 53, 298; 1876: 84; 1877: 129; 1878: 81; and U.S. Statutes at Large, 1887–1920 (Washington, D.C : U.S. Government Printing Office), 17: 189, 534; 18, pt. 3: 173–74.

14. The National Archives catalogues the annual censuses of reservation populations as "Bureau of Indian Affairs' censuses." However, the term *Indian Office* was used in the late nineteenth and early twentieth centuries. In this essay, the label *BIA censuses* will be used to describe the censuses to avoid confusion about archival sources. However, *Indian Office* will be used to refer to the institution that later became the Bureau of Indian Affairs.

15. U. S. Congress, "Chippewa Indians in Minnesota," 51st Congress, 1st Session, H. Exec. Doc. 2747, No. 247; Bureau of Indian Affairs, Censuses, 1889–1907 (National Archives and Records Service, Washington, D.C.); and Chippewa Commission, Register of Arrivals, 1890–99, Bureau of Indian

Affairs, Record Group 75, Entry 1305, National Archives and Records Service, Washington, D.C. Chippewa Commission 1890–99 lists removals by band for each consecutive year. Furthermore, it records the timing of migrations by day, month, and year, the chief of the band of origin, and the destination at White Earth of each household. As such, it represents the best source of statistics regarding migrations during these years. No other source, published or in manuscript, records this detail in serial fashion.

The reporting of removal statistics by various representatives of the U. S. government was uneven at best. Irregular methods resulted in overlapping estimates, gaps in reporting, and contradictory figures. Sources must be cross-checked to detect these variances and determine the most reliable figures.

16. Meyer, "Tradition and the Market: The Social Relations of the White Earth Anishinaabeg, 1889–1920," Ph.D. diss., University of Minnesota, 1985; P. A. Shifferd, "A Study in Economic Change: The Chippewa of Northern Wisconsin, 1854–1900," *Western Canadian Journal of Anthropology* 6 (1976): 16–41; and J. Kay, "Native Americans in the Fur Trade and Wildlife Depletion," *Environmental Review* 9 (1985): 118–130.

17. The historical literature dealing with community and society in the North American fur trade is vast and growing. Of greatest importance to the history of the White Earth Reservation are works that focus on the genesis of mixed-blood or métis peoples in the Great Lakes area. J. Peterson, "Prelude to Red River: A Social Portrait of the Great Lakes Metis," *Ethnohistory* 25 (1978): 41–67; Peterson, "The People in Between: Indian-White Marriage and the Genesis of a Métis Society and Culture in the Great Lakes Region, 1702–1815," Ph.D. diss., University of Illinois, Chicago Circle, 1981; Peterson, "Ethnogenesis: The Settlement and Growth of a 'New People' in the Great Lakes Region, 1702–1815," *American Indian Culture and Research Journal* 6 (1982): 23–64; J. S. H. Brown, *Strangers in Blood: Fur Trade Company Families in Indian Country* (Vancouver: University of British Columbia Press, 1980); S. Van Kirk, *"Many Tender Ties": Women in Fur Trade Society, 1670–1870* (Winnipeg: Watson and Dwyer, 1980); H. H. Tanner, "The Glaize in 1792: A Composite Indian Community," *Ethnohistory* 25 (1978): 15–39; and O. P. Dickason, "From 'One Nation' in the Northeast to 'New Nation' in the Northwest: A Look at the Emergence of the Metis," *American Indian Culture and Research Journal* 6 (1982): 1–21.

18. Chippewa Commission, 1890–99.

19. Thomas Shearman conducted genealogical research as part of his effort to determine whether certain individuals had legal rights to reside on the White Earth Reservation. Shearman Report, 6 May 1913, White Earth Agency (1889–1918), Bureau of Indian Affairs, Record Group 75, National Archive and Records Service, Washington, D.C., CF 150; Shearman Report, 11 December 1913, White Earth Agency, CF 211; F. Barth, "Introduction," in F. Barth, ed., *Ethnic Groups and Boundaries: The Social Organization of Culture Difference* (London: George Allen and Unwin, 1969), 9–38; and R. L. Trosper, "Native American Boundary Maintenance: The Flathead Indian Reservation, Montana, 1860–1970," *Ethnicity* 3 (1976): 256–74.

20. Many sources support this discussion of ethnic divisions among the White Earth Anishinaabeg. Reservation residents and outside observers alike noted these differences. Agents' reports, congressional testimony, missionaries' accounts, newspapers, maps, and oral tradition all reinforce this interpretation.

21. Variations in Anishinaabe culture necessitate a general description of over-arching commonalities regarding worldview. Sources that have a direct bearing on the White Earth Reservation are the most relevant. W. W. Warren, *History of the Ojibwa Nation* (Minneapolis: Ross and Haines, 1957); R. Landes, *Ojibwa Religion and the Midewiwin* (Madison: University of Wisconsin Press, 1968); Warren, *The Ojibwa Woman* (New York: Columbia University Press, 1969), 5; A. I. Hallowell, "Ojibway Ontology, Behavior, and World View," in S. Diamond, ed., *Culture in History: Essays in Honor of Paul Radin* (New York: Columbia University Press for Brandeis University, 1960); Hallowell, *Culture and Experience* (New York: Schocken Books, 1967); Hallowell, *Contributions to Anthropology* (Chicago: University of Chicago Press, 1976); F. Densmore, *Chippewa Customs*, Bureau of American Ethnology, Bulletin 86 (Washington, D.C.: U.S. Government Printing Office, 1929), 44–48, 78–97, 175–76; J. A. Grim, *The Shaman: Patterns of Siberian and Ojibway Healing* (Norman: University of Oklahoma Press, 1983); C. Vecsey, *Traditional Ojibwa Religion and its*

Historical Changes (Philadelphia: American Philosophical Society, 1983); and W. J. Hoffman, "The Midewiwin or Grand Medicine Society of the Ojibway," Bureau of American Ethnology, Seventh Annual Report (Washington, D.C.: U.S. Government Printing Office, 1891).

22. Commissioner of Indian Affairs, 1899: 216.

23. Hoffman, "The Midewiwin or Grand Medicine Society of the Ojibway," 167.

24. The anthropologist Walter J. Hoffman studied the Midewiwin as it was practiced at White Earth in some detail. The four levels of hierarchy he discussed represent a specialized adaptation at White Earth. Sources for other groups of Anishinaabeg discuss more degrees. Hoffman's study provides details of this religious complex at White Earth in the early years, 1887–89. Information beyond this basic source is limited. Missionaries and educators who would have preferred to see it disappear verified its existence with their complaints. However, it is impossible to ascertain the extent or com-position of its membership. Frances Densmore also studied the Midewiwin at White Earth, but her discussion is far less involved. Hoffman, "The Midewiwin or Grand Medicine Society of the Ojibway"; Densmore, *Chippewa Customs*, 44–48, 78–97, 175–76.

25. Commissioner of Indian Affairs, 1894: 152.

26. M. N. Zanger, "'Straight Tongue's Heathen Wards': Bishop Whipple and the Episcopal Mission to the Chippewas," in C. A. Miller II and F. A. O'Neil, eds., *Churchmen and the Western Indians, 1820–1920* (Norman: University of Oklahoma Press, 1985), 177–214.

27. U.S. Congress, Senate Committee on Indian Affairs, "An Investigation of Affairs at White Earth Reservation to Investigate the Conduct of Agents and their Subordinates" (Washington, D.C.: U.S. Government Printing Office, 1887), 45, 64–65, 127, 176, 220, 225–226, 229–230; C. J. Berg, "Agents of Cultural Change: The Benedictines at White Earth," *Minnesota History* 48 (1982): 158–70; Berg, "Climbing Learners' Hill: Benedictines at White Earth, 1878–1945," Ph.D. diss., University of Minnesota, 1983, 46, 63; J. C. Scott, "'To Do Some Good Among the Indians': Nineteenth-Century Benedictine Missions," *Journal of the West* 23 (1984): 26–36; and Commissioner of Indian Affairs, 1887: 210; 1888: 147; 1894: 152.

28. Commissioner of Indian Affairs, 1890; 1892: 151; 1895: 175; and 1905: 235–36.

29. Each annual report of the commissioner of Indian affairs contains reports by the various schools on the White Earth Reservation, except for the Catholic orphanage. The nature of the educational experience students received at White Earth can be discerned through these reports. General com-ments about national policy toward Indian education can also be found.

30. Commissioner of Indian Affairs, 1893: 171; and F. P. Prucha, *The Churches and the Indian Schools* (Lincoln: University of Nebraska Press, 1979).

31. J. Rogers, *Red World and White: Memories of a Chippewa Boyhood* (Norman: University of Oklahoma Press, 1974 [orig. pub. 1957]).

32. Rogers, *Red World and White*, 170.

33. Hurr to Michelet, 21 March 1904, White Earth Agency, LR 1904.

34. Commissioner of Indian Affairs, 1896: 170; 1897: 158; and 1899: 215.

35. D. T. Putney, "Fighting the Scourge: American Indian Morbidity and Federal Policy," Ph. D. diss., Marquette University, 1980, 78–109; and R. Thornton, *American Indian Holocaust and Survival: A Population History Since 1492* (Norman: University of Oklahoma Press, 1988).

36. Commissioner of Indian Affairs, 1897: 160.

37. Commissioner of Indian Affairs, 1900: 262.

38. Commissioner of Indian Affairs, 1896: 172; and 1901: 255.

39. J. A. Gilfillan, "The Ojibways in Minnesota," *Minnesota Historical Society Collections* 9 (1898): 82.

40. Rogers, *Red World and White*, 130.

41. *Tomahawk,* 9 April 1903–1 September 1904: 4. Comments about such travels were regularly reported in the "Local and Personal" column.

42. *Tomahawk,* 23 April 1904: 4.

43. Commissioner of Indian Affairs, 1901: 225.

44. Gilfillan, "The Ojibways in Minnesota," 122.

45. The system of credit operated rather informally. Most Indian clients regularly carried a debt load, making an occasional payment to ensure that they would continue to receive credit. This system, which was partially of the Indians' own making, served their needs, allowing them to acquire credit

while they met their obligations gradually. Merchant-traders benefitted by keeping their clients beholden to them.

46. *Tomahawk*, 21 May 1903: 4; 28 May 1903: 1; and 4 June 1903: 4.

47. *Tomahawk*, 11 June 1903: 1; 14 June 1903: 1; and 15 June 1903: 1.

48. For historical photographs of the June 1 Celebration, contact the Audio-Visual Division of the Minnesota Historical Society, St. Paul.

49. This discussion of Anishinaabe understandings of the terms *mixed blood* and *full blood* draws heavily on testimony taken by Ransom J. Powell in connection with his work on the 1920 blood roll. The Ransom J. Powell Papers (RJP) are housed in the Minnesota Historical Society Archives, St. Paul.

50. Mezhucegeshig, 14 April 1914, RJP, Box 5, Folder 29,

51. Mah-do-say-quay, 9 March 1914, RJP, Box 5, Folder 28.

52. The spelling of some American Indian names varies considerably in the sources. The variations are preserved below so that the documents cited might be easily and accurately retrieved.

53. Ke-che-mah-quah, September 1914, RJP, Box 6, Folder 34.

54. Wah-way-zho-o-quay, 15 January 1914, RJP, Box 5, Folder 21.

55. Ay-dow-ah-cumig-o-quay, 15 January 1914, RJP, Box 5, Folder 21.

56. Me-zhuc-e-ge-shig, 14 April 1914, RJP, Box 5, Folder 29.

57. Bay-bah-daung-ay-yaush, 15 January 1914, RJP, Box 5, Folder 21.

58. Gah-mah-nah-che-wah-nay, 4 February 1914, RJP, Box 5, Folder 26.

59. Morrison, September 1914, RJP, Box 6, Folder 24.

60. Bay-bah-daung-ay-aush, 27 July 1914, RJP, Box 6, Folder 32.

61. The families of Beaulieu, Fairbanks, and Bellefeuille were targeted in a petition as having no rights to enrollment as "Chippewa in Minnesota. " As part of an investigation of these charges, Thomas J. Shearman submitted the results of a genealogical inquiry into the marital relationships of these three families. Shearman Report, 6 May 1913, White Earth Agency, CF 150; and Shearman Report, 11 December 1913, White Earth Agency, CF 211.

62. Me-zhuc-e-ge-shig, 14 April 1914, RJP, Box 5, Folder 29.

63. Me-zhuc-e-ge-shig, 14 April 1914, RJP, Box 5, Folder 29.

64. Mah-do-say-quay, 9 March 1914, RJP, Box 5, Folder 28.

65. Mah-do-say-quay, 9 March 1914, RJP, Box 5, Folder 28.

66. Ke-zhe-wash, 15 January 1914, RJP, Box 5, Folder 21; see also Shin-ow-aince, 15 January 1914, RJP, Box 5, Folder 21.

67. C. J. Kappler, comp., *Indian Affairs: Laws and Treaties,* vol. 2 (Washington, D.C.: U.S. Government Printing Office, 1904), 2: 491–93, 567–69; F. Weaver, Interview with Winona LaDuke, White Earth Oral History Project, American Indian Studies Program, Bemidji State University, Tape, c. 1982; M. Bellanger, Interview with Unknown Interviewer, Minnesota Chippewa Tribe Reservation History Project, Minnesota Chippewa Tribe, Cass Lake, Handwritten Transcription, c. 1982; F. Keahna, Interview with Unknown Interviewer, Minnesota Chippewa Tribe Reservation History Project, Minnesota Chippewa Tribe, Cass Lake, Handwritten Transcription, c. 1982.

68. Bureau of Indian Affairs censuses for White Earth have special utility for these issues because they are organized by band and enumerate individuals, ages, genders, modified households, and the relationships of each individual to the head of household. No other form of serial documentation records band differences, making these censuses crucial for exploring social relationships.

   However, closer evaluation reveals that the "censuses" are actually enrollment lists that record those entitled to rights as White Earth band members, not actual reservation residents. Strange enumeration procedures initially caused me to question the composition of these censuses. Unusual strings of solitary individuals skewed measures of average households, producing a mean of 1. Many examples of single parents labeled "wife" or "husband," with no spouse listed, led me to believe that the documents record band enrollment. Marriages across band lines probably produced this listing of odd households. When I encountered the names of individuals I knew lived off-reservation, I began to take my hunch more seriously.

   No instructions explain these censuses, and no correspondence explains the enumeration procedure. There are no reports of visits to Indian homes and no directives issued by the commissioner of Indian affairs to commence the compilations. Considering the voluminous documentation relating to the White Earth Reservation, this lack of bureaucratic attention seems doubly strange.

I suspect that the agent compiled the listing in the agency office annually from cards that he periodically updated. Several Indian Office inspectors referred to such cards. Marriages, births, and deaths required changes in the original numbers assigned to individuals and were recorded at the end of each band listing. Off-reservation residents appeared as strings of individuals who presumably would serve as the stem for a new family grouping of off-reservation enrollees. Criteria for enrollment changed over time. These enumeration patterns help to account for the skewed mean household size of 1. Rather than list reservation residents, the BIA censuses actually enumerate all those officially recognized by the federal government as members of the "White Earth Band" of the "Chippewa Indians of Minnesota."

The implications of this discovery for aggregate populations totals change over time; the censuses are more reliable earlier as they recorded immigrants and less reliable later as out-migration increased. The enrollment lists cannot produce reliable aggregate statistics with comparative, cross-cultural value, but they can still illuminate intra-reservation band differences, because the problems affected all bands alike. If solitary individuals are omitted from the sample, a predictable spectrum of ethnic band differences emerges. Of course, some individuals actually lived alone. However, this approach is profitable despite the inherent inaccuracies.

69. Densmore, *Chippewa Customs*, 52–53; and R. Ritzenthaler, "Acquisition of Surnames by the Chippewa Indians," *American Anthropologist* 47(1945): 175–77.

70. Densmore, *Chippewa Customs*, 52–53.

71. Ritzenthaler, "Acquisition of Surnames by the Chippewa Indians."

72. B. Coleman, *Where the Water Stops: Fond du Lac Reservation* (Superior, Wisc.: Arrowhead Printing, 1967); Hickerson, "The Genesis of a Trading Post Band: The Pembina Chippewa," *Ethnohistory* 3 (1956): 289–345; A. Ross, *The Red River Settlement: Its Rise, Progress, and Present State, with Some Account of the Native Races and Its General History to the Present Day* (London, 1856); Peterson, "Prelude to Red River"; Peterson, "The People in Between"; Peterson, "Ethnogenesis"; W. Babcock, "With Ramsey to Pembina: A Treaty-Making Trip in 1851," *Minnesota History* 38 (1962): 1–10; E. Hawkinson, "The Old Crossing Chippewa Treaty and Its Sequel," *Minnesota History* 15 (1934): 282–300; R. R. Gilman et al., *The Red River Trails: Oxcart Routes between St. Paul and the Selkirk Settlement, 1820–1870* (St. Paul: Minnesota Historical Society Press, 1979); Coleman et al., *Old Crow Wing: History of a Village* (Duluth: College of St. Scholastica, 1967); and E. Danziger, *The Chippewa of Lake Superior* (Norman: University of Oklahoma Press, 1979).

73. Studies of interior Minnesota reservations are more limited. However, those studies that do exist emphasize the greater isolation of interior bands and hypothesize greater endogamy. Government investigators conducted genealogical inquiries into the backgrounds of the 86 individuals accused of having no rights at White Earth. Their efforts revealed very few marriages between these individuals with Lake Superior band origins and Mississippi band members. H. Hickerson, "The Southwestern Chippewa: An Ethnohistorical Study," *American Anthropological Association*, 92 (1962); Hickerson, *The Chippewa and Their Neighbors: An Ethnohistorical Study* (New York: Holt, Rinehart, and Winston, 1970); Warren, *History of the Ojibwa Nation*; R. Buffalohead and P. Buffalohead, *Against the Tide of American History: The Story of the Mille Lacs Anishinabe* (Cass Lake: Minnesota Chippewa Tribe, 1985); R. Kugel, "Factional Alignment among the Minnesota Ojibwe, 1850–1880," *American Indian Culture and Research Journal* 9 (1985): 23–47; Kugel, "'To Go About on the Earth': An Ethnohistory of the Minnesota Ojibwe," Ph.D. diss., University of California, Los Angeles, 1986; Shearman Report, 6 May 1913, White Earth Agency, CF 150; and Shearman Report, 11 December 1913, White Earth Agency, CF 211.

74. BIA censuses reveal that surnames of Anishinaabe origins increased within particular bands after 1910. This timing and the differential patterning of surnames support the notion that Indians from more conservative bands retained Anishinaabe names longer and more often chose to anglicize them instead of adopting new English or French names.

75. J. G. E. Smith, *Leadership among the Southwestern Ojibwa*, Publications in Ethnology, No. 7 (Ottawa: National Museums of Canada, 1973); Kugel, "Factional Alignment among the Minnesota Ojibwe," and "'To Go About on the Earth'"; Densmore, *Chippewa Customs*; Gilfillan, "The Ojibways in Minnesota"; U.S. Congress, "Chippewa Indians in Minnesota"; Morgan to Shuler, 12 October 1889, OIA LR; and Me-zhuc-e-ge-shig, 14 April 1914, RJP, Box 5, Folder 29.

76. U. S. Congress, "Chippewa Indians in Minnesota," 105, 108; Me-zhuc-e-ge-shig, 14 April 1914,

RJP, Box 5, Folder 29; Shearman Report, 6 May 1913; Shearman Report, 11 December 1913; Daniels Report, n.d., White Earth Agency, CF 150; Moorehead Report, 9 August 1909, White Earth Agency, CF 150; Pine Point Proceedings, 20–22 January 1915, White Earth Agency, CF 054; Pay kin ah waush et al. to Commissioner of Indian Affairs, 2 March 1889, WEA, LR 1889; Weaver, Interview with Winona LaDuke; Vizenor, *Escorts to White Earth, 1868–1968: 100 Year Reservation* (Minneapolis: Four Winds, 1968), 213–218; and Vizenor, *The People Named the Chippewa: Narrative Histories* (Minneapolis: University of Minnesota Press, 1984).

77. U.S. Congress, 1913, "Report in the Matter of the Investigation of the White Earth Reservation," 62nd Congress, 3rd Session, H. Rept. 6336, No. 1336; Meyer, "Warehousers and Sharks: Chippewa Leadership and Political Factionalism on the White Earth Agency, 1907–1920," *Journal of the West* 23 (1985): 32–46; and Meyer, "Tradition and the Market."

78. Ah bow ege shig to Linnen, 31 January 1918, White Earth Agency, CF 056; Bassett to Linnen, 1 February 1918, White Earth Agency, CF 056; Linnen to Commissioner of Indian Affairs, 14 February 1918, White Earth Agency, CF 056; Chief Mah een gaunce et al. to Hinton, 5 February 1918, White Earth Agency, CF 056; Nay tah waush Petition, 21 February 1918, White Earth Agency, CF 056; Coffey to CIA, 14 February 1918, White Earth Agency, CF 056; Hinton to Moorehead, 23 February 1918, White Earth Agency, CF 056; Wakefield to Warren, 23 February 1918, White Earth Agency, CF 054; Ball Club Proceedings, 25 April 1918, White Earth Agency, CF 054.

79. Wakefield to Warren, 23 February 1918, White Earth Agency, CF 054; memorandum, c. 9 July 1918, White Earth Agency, CF 155; memorandum, c. 9 July 1918, White Earth Agency, CF 150; Linnen and Elis to Sells, 20 September 1918, White Earth Agency, CF 054; Walters and Chief Way-ya-gua-gi-shig to Commissioner of Indian Affairs, 3 June 1918, White Earth Agency, CF 150; Wakefield to Coffey, 5 June 1918, White Earth Agency, CF 054; Hinton to CIA, 15 June 1918, White Earth Agency, CF 150; Sells to Walters and Chief Way-ya-gua-gi-shig et al., 27 June 1918, White Earth Agency, CF 150; Elko Theatre Proceedings, 9 July 1918, White Earth Agency, CF 054; City Hall Delegates, 9 July 1918, White Earth Agency, CF 054; Coffey to CIA, 11 July 1918, White Earth Agency, CF 054; Coffey to Linnen, 25 July 1918, White Earth Agency, CF 054.

80. U.S. Congress, "Chippewas of Minnesota," Hearings Before the Committee on Indian Affairs, 21 January to 22 March (Washington, D.C.: U.S. Government Printing Office, 1920).

81. Elko Theatre Proceedings, 9 July 1918, White Earth Agency, CF 054.

82. Moorehead Report, 9 August 1909, White Earth Agency, CF 150; U.S. Congress, "Report in the Matter of the Investigation of the White Earth Reservation."

83. Folstrum to Department of the Interior, 18 February 1902, White Earth Agency, LR 1902; Wright to Commissioner of Indian Affairs, 28 February 1905, White Earth Agency, LR 1904; Wright and Walters to Sherman, 7 February 1908, White Earth Agency, CF 056; May zhuc ke ge shig to CIA, 10 May 1909, White Earth Agency, CF 050; May zhak ke ge shig et al. to CIA, 5 April 1909, White Earth Agency, CF 050; Schneider to Howard, 17 March 1909, White Earth Agency, CF 050; Wah-we-yea-cumig to Leupp, 24 January 1909, White Earth Agency; Beaulieu to Moorehead, 17 February 1910, White Earth Agency, CF 056; Pine Point Petition, 10 March 1910, White Earth Agency, CF 056; Schneider to Attorney General, 13 December 1910, White Earth Agency, CF 050; Ga je-ge-zhick and Skippingday to Long, 1 February 1911, White Earth Agency, CF 056; "Full Blood" Report, 8 February 1911, White Earth Agency, CF 056; statements of Indians, 17 June 1911, White Earth Agency, CF 056; Star Bad Boy to CIA, 22 December 1911, White Earth Agency, CF 050; Beaulieu to Moorehead, 15 April 1911, White Earth Agency, CF 424; May-chuz-ke-ge-shig to CIA, 3 October 1912, White Earth Agency, CF 056; Oge-mah-woub to CIA, 28 October 1912, White Earth Agency, CF 056. By linking names attached to council proceedings and petitions with BIA censuses for White Earth, the band affiliations of Indian leaders can be determined. Names of "chiefs" and "headmen" are the most diagnostic, and they tend to represent band constituencies. Not all names can be linked, but enough linkages can be made to reveal changing political affiliations.

84. "Full-Blood Faction" Proceedings, 21 May 1913, White Earth Agency, CF 156.

85. May-chuc-ke-ge-shig to CIA, 10 May 1909, White Earth Agency, CF 050.

86. "Full-Blood Faction" Proceedings, 21 May 1913, White Earth Agency, CF 156.
87. Legislative Committee to Hopkins, 18 February 1918, White Earth Agency, CF 211.
88. *Tomahawk,* 20 July 1916: 1. Publishers of the *Tomahawk* used the term *warehousers* to describe the Indians of Pine Point, implying that the full bloods are dependent on welfare gratuities from the Chippewa tribe. However, Indian Office officials maintained that those who received such assistance were either old, sick, or indigent and were therefore entitled to it.
89. R. Meyer, *History of the Santee Sioux: United States Indian Policy on Trial* (Lincoln: University of Nebraska Press, 1968); and G. C. Anderson, *Kinsmen of Another Kind: Dakota-White Relations in the Upper Mississippi Valley, 1650–1862* (Lincoln: University of Nebraska Press, 1984).
90. T. Wilson, *The Underground Reservation: Osage Oil* (Lincoln: University of Nebraska Press, 1985); and W. Unrau, *Mixed Bloods and Tribal Dissolution: Charles Curtis and the Quest for Indian Identity* (Lawrence: University Press of Kansas, 1989).
91. L. Fowler, *Shared Symbols, Contested Meanings.*
92. P. Whiteley, *Deliberate Acts: Changing Hopi Culture through the Oraibi Split* (Tucson: University of Arizona Press, 1988); E. C. Parsons, *Pueblo Indian Religion* (Chicago: University of Chicago Press, 1939); F. Eggan, *Social Organization of the Western Pueblos* (Chicago: University of Chicago Press, 1950); and A. Ortiz, *The Tewa World: Space, Time, Being, and Becoming in a Pueblo Society* (Chicago: University of Chicago Press, 1969).
93. Fowler, *Arapaho Politics.*
94. M. Meyer, "The Ojibwe of the Red Lake Peatland Area," in H. E. Wright et al., eds., *The Patterned Peatlands of Minnesota* (Minneapolis: University of Minnesota Press, 1992); and E. F. Mittelholz, "Historical Review of the Red Lake Indian Reservation, Redlake, Minnesota: A History of Its People and Progress," *Beltrami County Historical Collections* 2 (1957).
95. F. Barth, "Introduction"; Trosper, "Native American Boundary Maintenance"; and K. I. Blu, *The Lumbee Problem: The Making of an American Indian People* (Cambridge: Cambridge University Press, 1980).
96. M. McFee, "The 150% Man: A Product of Blackfeet Acculturation," *American Anthropologist* 70 (1968): 1096–1107.

5

At least since the legendary sale of Manhattan Island to the Dutch, Europeans in the Americas have believed that Natives lacked any understanding of economics. Indians were, many colonizers claimed, too primitive to comprehend the workings of the market. Though the historical record is full of examples of Indians grasping intricate elements of the European colonial economy, the stereotype has nonetheless persisted. Even Indians (such as Cherokees in the early nineteenth century) who embraced many elements of Anglo-American culture still seemed, to non-Indians, commercially backward.

Robert S. McPherson's study of Navajo trading houses belies such notions. Far from dupes of foreign traders, Navajos quickly picked up the tricks of the trade and got non-Navajo merchants to offer the best terms. Such commerce offered substantial dividends. Navajo blankets, for example, which brought Indians $50,000 in 1899, earned them $700,000 by 1914; these items found a national market so well that they were even offered for sale in the Sears catalog.

But such commercial success did not mean immediate or wholesale embrace of a capitalist economy and ethos. Like Navajos in the 1860s that Katherine Osburn studied, Navajo traders a generation later remained rooted in customary ways, adopting only those foreign elements—whether goods or practices—that suited them. As McPherson's close attention to songs, stories, handshakes, "idle" chat, and other trade customs reveals, the exchange of goods was but one strand in a larger, enduring cultural fabric. Did these Navajo traders resemble the Indian entrepreneurs on the White Earth Reservation?

Naalyéhé Bá-Hooghan—"House of Merchandise": The Navajo Trading Post as an Institution of Cultural Change, 1900–1930

Robert S. McPherson

WITHIN THE NEXT WEEK, MOST OF YOU will enter a supermarket that has electric-eye doors for convenience, plays soothing Muzak, and presents its produce in a display worthy of *Better Homes and Gardens*. Oranges treated with chemicals to make them turn the desired color, apples coated with wax, and glistening fruits and vegetables sprayed with water are placed beside brightly colored packaging that screams "one-third off," or "fewer calories," or "organically grown, natural food." As you speed through the express lane checkout and glance at your watch, you select the shortest distance to sprint to your car, located near the handicap parking stall. Weaving between the parked cars, you manage to hit the main flow of traffic, never giving a second thought to the series of choices you have just made, many of which were influenced by the environment and the store manager as much as by you. In short, many of those value-laden decisions derived, whether consciously or subconsciously, from the culture in which you operate. So it is with all people.

The purpose of this paper is to examine a similar transaction at another time, another place, in a different cultural setting. The Navajo trading post started as an institution in 1868, reached its height between 1900 and the 1930s, then declined. Recognized by many as the focal point where two cultures came together on equal terms, the post served as a vehicle for both change and preservation.[1] Most historians, however, look only at the economic transactions—the exchange of rugs, wool, and silver across the counter—rather than at the role of the post as a vehicle of acculturation. The following brief analysis examines the posts of the northern part of the reservation for their importance in facilitating change in a people noted for adaptability. The Navajo accepted alterations selectively, as a means of enriching their lives without sacrificing cultural integrity. Only later, after the disastrous livestock reduction of the mid to late 1930s, did their culture experience a rate and direction of change totally foreign to previous traditional practices and patterns.

Between 1900 and 1930, there were basically two types of posts that serviced the Navajo. The first belonged to licensed traders, approved by the Bureau of Indian Affairs, which gave operating instructions for a post at a specific location. The store and inventory may have belonged to the trader, but the land surrounding it was the tribe's, and the license was the government's.[2] Federal regulation dictated the screening of traders, limited the locations of posts, and controlled certain sale items.

SOURCE: *With the Land: Navajo Economic and Cultural Change in the Twentieth Century.*

95

According to the BIA, a "proper person" to be involved in the business had to be of good moral standing, honest in his dealings, fair in establishing prices, concerned about his customers, and opposed to the sale and use of alcohol by the Indians.

Anyone caught trading on the reservation without a license forfeited all of his merchandise and paid a fine of up to five hundred dollars. How much money would actually be lost in such an incident varied from post to post, but one trader estimated that his store cost him five thousand dollars, with two thousand down and a 6 percent mortgage, along with an inventory of fifteen hundred dollars. On the other hand, a person with a license was never guaranteed that it would be renewed at the end of his tenure, which could last from one to five years.[3] The adage of "damned if you do and damned if you don't" in a sense applied to the trader, who theoretically was at the mercy of everyone from the local agent to the Washington bureaucrat on one side, and the Navajo customer on the other.

Although the real may be far from the ideal, the general impression of the traders of this era is that they were basically honest, moral people who worked hard. Those who were not honest did not last long, forced out of the market by competitors who were. Most of the traders were white men, although a handful were Navajo. An Indian had an advantage in that he could establish a post anywhere, whereas an Anglo had to go to a previously specified location. For example, John Wetherill opened a store in Oljato in 1906 after receiving approval to locate on an abandoned mining claim that was surrounded by, but not part of, reservation lands. By 1910, he, his wife Louisa, and his partner Clyde Colville decided that Kayenta, twenty-six miles away, would be a better site because of the traffic that flowed through Marsh Pass. The Wetherills again had to submit to the application process, with accompanying character references, in order to be approved.

The second type of post avoided many government regulations by locating off the reservation. Generally found on the San Juan River, these posts were strung along the northern boundary of Navajo land extending from Farmington, New Mexico, to Aneth, Bluff, and Mexican Hat, Utah, to the western boundary and settlements along the Colorado and Little Colorado rivers. Before the 1890s, these posts flourished as a never-ending source of aggravation to the agents, who watched their charges get siphoned off the reservation, only to be cheated and sent home impoverished.[4] The national depression of the 1890s generally wiped the slate clean, so that with the establishment of the northern and western agencies in the early 1900s, closer surveillance of border activities was possible. Again, the general impression of trading in these establishments is that, with a few exceptions, those who sold to the Indians were honest and concerned.

Over a thirty-year period, the number of posts fluctuated. A military expedition led by Lieutenant Colonel George Hunter in 1908 provides an educated estimate.[5] Hunter identified posts at Oljato, Round Rock, Bluff, Tuba City, Teec Nos Pos, and Red Lake as those visited by the Navajo from that region. There were also stores in the Farmington/Shiprock area, although he did not mention them. One of Hunter's captains visited the Bluff post and reported that 950 adult Navajo had traded there within the past year, but only half of them had homes within a sixty-mile radius. Hunter, basing his population figures on traders' statements, concluded that from

Navajo Mountain to the Carrizo Mountains there was a total population of men, women, children, and slaves of 1,512. Even as a rough estimate, these figures are a strong indicator of Navajo mobility for trade relations.

By 1930, there were additional posts located at Ismay, Aneth, Mexican Hat, Monument Valley, Kayenta, Chinle, Red Mesa, Shonto, Inscription House, and Navajo Mountain, just to name the most prominent. To chronicle the rise and fall of all of these posts is not my intent here, but only to indicate how prolific they were during this period.

In general, the Navajo welcomed the posts to their area for two reasons: The closer they were, the more convenient; and having more options available provided an opportunity to play one store against another for better prices. In either instance, travel was involved, and for the Navajo, unlike the whites, setting out on a journey could hold serious implications. Supernatural beings populated the Navajo world, beings who could be either benevolent or vengeful, depending on the ceremonial precautions taken by the traveler. Many people, before setting out, wrapped themselves in a protective shield of good thoughts, prayers, and songs of the Mountainway and Blessingway.[6] Just as in the myths and legends from which these songs came, the traveler identified with a supernatural hero who had also journeyed far and been protected. The Navajo felt impelled to invoke supernatural aid, especially when posts were located in distant areas or across mythological boundaries that separated safe refuge from the lands of the enemy.

For example, the San Juan River was established by the gods as the northern boundary of safety. Known by various names such as Old Age River, Male Water, and One With a Long Body, this powerful force is also described as a snake wriggling through the desert, a flash of lightning, and a black club of protection to keep invaders from Navajo land. These elements serve as protective symbols to separate realms of safety and danger. Even today, when older people cross the river, they sprinkle corn pollen to the holy being within, to ask for help. When questioned about going to a post on the other side, the Navajo expressed how frightened they were as they loaded their sacks of wool and goat skins into a wooden boat, then watched a young man row them through the sand waves and across the San Juan to the Bluff Co-op.[7]

Fear was not only associated with crossing water. Navajo Oshley, a longtime resident of southeastern Utah, told of the time he traveled to the unfamiliar post of Chilchinbii'to. As darkness fell, he approached an abandoned corral and heard soft singing and what he thought was a ceremony. His horse became skittish, and a feeling of foreboding overwhelmed him. He hurried on and finally arrived at his destination, where he spent the night, but the next day, curiosity got the best of him and he returned to the spot. There was no hogan and no ceremony, only a set of human tracks that changed into coyote prints that headed for the trading post. Oshley was convinced that he had had a close encounter with a skinwalker, an evil personification created through witchcraft.[8]

In addition to danger, however, travel to a post also brought opportunity for riches. The Navajo sang songs to beguile the trader into giving a good deal. To the Navajo, thought is as important as action, so good thoughts and wishes needed to precede what occurred at the store. Prayers and songs could work wonders on the traders, one of them wishing "the white man will be generous with his money as well as with his food."[9] An excerpt from a trading song says,

> Hard good of all sorts are attached to it as it becomes mine.
> Soft goods of all sorts are attached to it as it becomes mine.
> It shall be beautiful behind it as it becomes mine.
> It shall be beautiful in front of it as it becomes mine.
> Good and everlasting one am I, as it becomes mine.[10]

Once the people arrived at the post, a new set of concerns arose. The stores, constructed of rock, adobe, or wood, followed a basic pattern, with a large front room called the bullpen. This room held a wood-burning stove and plenty of space for customers to gather and visit. On the outskirts of the room, in an L or U configuration, were wide wooden counters worn smooth by the blankets, wool, and merchandise that flowed back and forth. Some posts had a six-inch elevation behind the counters, allowing the trader to look out into the bullpen over the heads of his customers, while also appearing larger in size, a slight psychological advantage. One trader also put wire mesh eighteen inches above the counter to prevent being lassoed and dragged over the top, although this fencing does not appear to be a common practice.

All goods were stored well out of the reach of customers, who identified articles by pictures and colors instead of by reading labels. A disadvantage of this physical layout was that in the winter, heat radiated from the stove into the bullpen but rarely made it over the counter to the feet and legs of the trader. Locks on the doors, a pistol or rifle nearby, and the trader's wits were the main means of safeguarding his establishment in times of trouble. Service for the customer and security for the owner divided the two worlds.[11]

The trader usually lived in a back room that served as both a kitchen and a bedroom. Outside the typical post was a well, a corral for livestock, a guest hogan stocked with wood and some cooking utensils for long-distance visitors, and perhaps a storage shed for the ten- to twelve-foot long sacks of wool. Most of the items taken in trade or pawn remained in the post.

When people entered the bullpen, they saw brightly colored shirts and hats, bolts of cloth, cans of peaches, tomatoes, and milk, candy, and hardware items, but the staples of the trade were sacks of flour, Arbuckle coffee—either whole or ground—sugar, and baking powder. Packing crates served as shelves, seats, and storage bins and were also sold to the Navajo for similar uses in their hogan.[12] Anything that enhanced life on the reservation and could be freighted in a wagon or, later, by motor vehicle went to the trading post for sale.

The entire experience of buying and selling was laced with cultural values. When the Navajo entered the store, a lengthy process started in motion. The first thing one did was nothing—just come in, look around, sit down, and later greet other Navajos in the bullpen. Personal relations and trade were not rushed. Eventually, the customer approached the counter and started a light conversation with the owner, telling where dances and ceremonies were going to be held, where he had come from, and what he had been doing. Most traders and their wives spoke Navajo; only a few depended on interpreters.

Evolving from this commerce came a linguistic variation called "trader Navajo," a communication that emphasized the economic side of post life but missed the subtleties of more sophisticated speech. Some traders like Louisa Wetherill, Ray Hunt, and Stokes Carson became so expert that the Navajo detected few flaws in their speech. Regardless of linguistic ability, the universal sign of recognition was the handshake, a warm, slight touch rather than a vigorous, tooth-jarring pump. To the Navajo, one held the hand briefly and did not grip it tightly, since to do so boasted of one's physical strength and belittled that of the recipient.[13]

The Navajo expected the traders to show some type of special kindness to each of the customers. For instance, there might be a box for tobacco and cigarette papers nailed down to the counter, or a plug of tobacco from which the trader cut a five-, ten-, or twenty-five-cent slice. A little hard candy, a can of tomatoes, some coffee and bread, or popcorn induced the customer to feel relaxed and welcomed. A coffeepot, matches, and blankets might be borrowed for the night, while occasionally a child might be given a shirt or some other article of clothing. A 103-year-old woman claimed that she never feared the trader, because he gave her food, gave clothing to her brother, and called them his children.[14]

This last point is important. The Navajo language has titles that indicate kinship relations, such as sister, mother, father, grandmother, grandfather, son. These same names can be used to indicate respect and social status for a person who is not related by blood but is only an acquaintance. Owners and customers used these terms freely as they bartered over the counters, but underneath the chatter were implied responsibilities and relationships. The Navajo naturally placed the trader in the position of a parent who needed to provide for his or her children because of a sense of obligation. Hilda Wetherill Faunce, as a new trader, illustrates her feeling of frustration by describing a monologue she heard many times. The customer starts by saying,

My dear grandmother, come into this corner with me. We will speak slowly and not get mad. The children at my house who call you mother are hungry. They cry and call for candy and bread. One has a [bad] stomach. He said his mother would send medicine and apples and candy to him by me. Your children need shoes. In six months I shall sell my wool. Allow me, my mother, my sister, my pretty younger sister, to owe you twenty dollars until I shear my sheep. This will make all your children who live at my house warm. . . . See, my coat is worn out and no good. Let me have a new coat. Let me owe you four dollars for a new coat. Is this four dollars? It is very thin and ugly for four dollars. But I am poor, so I will take it. I tell all Navajos how nice you are, how you feed anyone who asks, and give apples and candy to all the children who come to your store. The Indians all say you are good. It's a long way to my house, and my horse is tired. While he rests I have time to eat. Give me a can of pears and a box of crackers, because I live a long way off and come all this distance in the cold to trade . . . with you because I know you are good and we are friends. That's right, that's good. This is for friendship. Thanks my mother. Good, good. Now I go.[15]

Although to a twentieth-century Anglo used to a system of impersonal economic transactions this speech lies somewhere between wheedling and begging, in reality it shows the sense of responsibility and obligation emphasized in relations. Inherent in Navajo culture is the desire for cooperation and sharing fostered in a land that could be harsh and pitiless. The trading post was one more resource for survival, although to many whites with ethnocentric biases, this fact at times was hard to accept.

The trader also received a name that, unlike kinship terms, described a prominent physical or social characteristic. However, a previously existing pattern taught that a person is not called by this name face-to-face, because it could embarrass him or her by calling attention to a noticeable characteristic.[16] Examples of names emphasizing physical qualities are Curly Head, Big White Man, Slender Woman, Red Beard, Swinging Arm, Skinny Hand, Hairy, Little Man with Big Ears, Looks Like a Mouth, and Rough Hands. Those centering on personality traits include Big Boss, One That Jokes Around, One Who Is Hungry, Lady Who Lies Around, and The Poor One, given to O. J. Carson, because he often said, "I can't lend you any money; I haven't any."[17]

The wide acceptance of women as traders also tied in with Navajo values. In a culture that was strongly matrilineal, Navajo women not only held the most important role in descent lines but also controlled substantial property and prestige. Both sexes accepted white women as competent traders, and an impression exists that in some cases they were preferred.

Louisa Wetherill provides the most prominent example. She spoke Navajo better than her husband John, did the trading while he was off exploring, was adopted by the most prominent leader in the Oljato/Kayenta region, acted as lawyer and judge in local disputes, was given access to ceremonial knowledge, and received all the property of her adopted father when he died. One Navajo described her by saying, "Asdzaan Tsosie is like a Navajo herself. Even when she speaks English, she speaks with the tone of a Navajo."[18] Hilda Faunce of Covered Water, Mary Jones of Bluff, Elizabeth Hegemann in Shonto, Mildred Heflin in Oljato, and "Mike" Goulding in Monument Valley all had positive interaction with Navajo clients and earned respect as knowledgeable and sharp bargainers.

The daily life of the trader is so well documented that only a brief sketch is necessary here.[19] The implied theme that courses through all of these accounts is the importance of understanding the culture. For example, many have written about the Navajo fear of the dead and how the traders were often called in to bury a body as a service to the family. However, one trader earned the hostility of the community when he buried an important medicine man facing the wrong direction.[20] Jot Stiles, in a Tuba City trading post, watched a Navajo consumed with epileptic seizures. Realizing that his store and its inventory would be supernaturally defiled if the man died inside, Stiles vaulted over the counter and dragged him outside before it was too late. This action would hardly be expected in an establishment serving Anglo customers, but it met with strong Navajo approval. Stiles also trooped the streets of Tuba during a parade or gathering to identify those who owed him money. Other traders watched to see who came into their posts wearing new clothes purchased elsewhere. If that person already had a lot of pawn hanging on the wall or under the counter, the trader was alerted as to how much additional credit should be allowed.[21]

Those not wise to the ways of the world became the butt of Navajo humor. Catherine and Frank Moore were living near the Oljato trading post doing some surveying, when the store owner died. His wife and daughter put the corpse in a box and asked the Moores to manage the business while they went to Cortez to make funeral arrangements. The temporary traders opened the doors of the store the next day, hoping their slim Navajo vocabulary would get them through. There were in the neighborhood a number of children who had been to school and spoke fairly good English, but the Moores did not know this. Some of them marched into the store and asked for everything in Navajo. After removing many items from the shelves, the traders finally brought down a box of shells, only to receive the reply, "Yes. Twenty-two shells; that is what we want." The pranksters and the heretofore silent Navajo adults in the store broke into grins and laughter at the Anglos' consternation.[22]

Between 1900 and the 1930s, the trading post fostered a variety of changes. As the Navajo people grew increasingly desirous of and dependent on the products of the posts, they increased the economic activity that allowed them to trade there. I am not suggesting that this was the only force moving them towards acculturation; it was one of many. Anthropologists and historians generally agree that societies are constantly changing. The main questions therefore become, In what direction, at what rate, and to what extent does the change occur? For the Navajo, the posts provided an introduction to white culture ranging from ruins to roads, from dollars to dyes, and from country fairs to current events.

TRADERS AND ARCHEOLOGISTS

Anasazi ruins provide a good example of the introduction of white culture. In traditional society, the Navajo generally avoided these sites because of their association with the dead. Traders, however, often were an effective force in decreasing the amount of fear connected with the Anasazi. There are numerous accounts that indicate that both men and women operating trading posts encouraged the Navajo to set aside their anxiety and guide people to the ruins, assist in the digging of artifacts, and locate objects on their own. Indeed, the traffic became so intense that in the *Report of the Commissioner of Indian Affairs* in 1905, traders were warned that the artifacts from Anasazi sites were "not private property to be disposed of at will." The report continued,

> It is well known that for some years past, Indian traders have greatly encouraged the despoliation of ruins by purchasing from the Indians the relics secured by them from the ruined villages, cliff houses, and cemeteries. . . . Much of the sale of such articles is made through licensed Indian traders, to whom the Indians bring their "finds." It seems necessary, therefore, to curtail such traffic upon the reservation [Navajo, Southern Ute, and Zuni] and you will please inform all the traders under your jurisdiction that thirty days after your notice to them, traffic in such articles will be considered contraband. . . . A failure to comply with these instructions will be considered sufficient ground for revocation of license.[23]

This decree apparently had little effect on most traders, since the traffic continued unabated.

The tenor of these transactions varied in scope, some of the traders being less zealous than others. A man in Shonto reported that after extended windstorms in the spring or intense cloudbursts in the summer, Navajo shepherds brought in pots, ladles, and bowls exposed by the storms. In exchange, the seller received five cents worth of hard candy in a brown paper sack. Two Navajos took this same trader to a site where they had been digging, only to find that the huge pot located at the corner of the ruin had burst into three pieces, the sand inside shattering the jar outward.[24]

Louisa Wetherill received a basket that had been discovered twenty-five years previously by a person who, until that time, did not want to touch a thing that belonged to the Ananazi. With the trader present, his attitude changed.[25] Another man sold a circular piece of sandstone, one foot in diameter, that was etched with an Anasazi petroglyph. He had used the rock for its healing power by rubbing sand off its edges and giving it to his patients. The cure was said to be effective against almost any disease.[26]

Wives were as active as their husbands in collecting artifacts. A Navajo woman led Hilda Faunce from her post at Covered Water to a mound filled with shards. Seizing a piece of broken bone, Faunce unearthed a skull and some vertebrae. Her Navajo guide herded her children away, fearing that a "devil" might be present, while an old man warned Faunce to get the skull out of sight. She later found a bowl in the grave and proudly displayed it on her mantle.[27]

Navajos also entered the excavating business, some with excessive zeal. In 1906, one man took a plow and scraper and leveled a mound for a few pieces of pottery to sell at a post. He apparently destroyed much more than he saved.[28]

In addition to the purchase of artifacts, traders also encouraged the Navajo to enter the ruins by enlisting them to work for archeologists as laborers around the sites. The degree of willingness varied with each individual, but many sought employment simply because of economic pressures. How daring they became once they were hired was another story. Responses varied considerably. For instance, Bill Lippincott, a trader at Wide Ruin, employed Navajos to help dig a ditch for a pipeline to his store. As the men labored with their shovels, they uncovered pottery, mortars, and beads. The Indians refused to dig until the entire pipe system was rerouted. The rerouting of the pipeline ensured not only their immediate help but future business at the post as well.[29]

The trader Richard Wetherill hired Navajos to dig in the Chaco ruins, which they did until they found an Anasazi corpse and promptly quit. Eventually, others came looking for work, and the number of Navajos reached a high of twenty employed in 1897. One of the problems Wetherill faced was that his Navajo workers took objects like arrowheads, figurines, and turquoise found during the excavation. Part of his solution lay in putting more than one workman in a room, hoping that the rivalry would cause one person to report the other's action. This was not totally successful. One frog figurine made of jet with jeweled eyes disappeared, only to turn up at a trading post in Farmington; it required fifty dollars to get it back. Wetherill also sent his wife among the Navajo to purchase any arrowheads they happened to have.[30]

Trading posts provided other forms of employment, including herding the trader's livestock, hauling supplies to railhead towns, doing odd jobs at the post, and serving as guides. The net effect of many of these activities was to encourage the men to leave home. Navajo Oshley tells how a trader hired him for fifty dollars a month to herd sheep. His wife remained at Dennehotso, a hundred miles away, while he earned some money, much of which went for a saddle and food he obtained from the post.[31] This in-house sale and trade was a common practice among traders, who wanted to keep the cash flowing back over the same counter.

Another man, Old Mexican from Aneth, hauled hay for the trader, traveled to Cortez, Mancos, and Durango to obtain supplies and drop off goods, and became so proficient at it that he decided not only to deliver the products from the trader but to sell and buy his own wares at a better price.[32] For a six-day round-trip to Mancos he received twelve dollars, and when he returned he was warmly welcomed. Old Mexican said, "When I got back to Aneth a crowd was there waiting for me to pull in. They were expecting quilts and blankets on this wagon. They bought up nearly all I brought." Although he was a trusted worker, the trader sent him home, admonishing him that he needed to go back and care for his wife and children: "They want you to support them and not leave them. Some day one of your children might starve to death or freeze to death and you would get in trouble."[33]

Home industries were the heart of the economy, the most famous of all being the rugs and saddle blankets woven in the hogans of the people. There are a number of very good studies about the rise of the weaving industry, the role of the trader in encouraging a better product, the movement from utilitarian to artistic creations, the struggle to introduce better qualities of wool, and the attempt to keep vegetable-dyed designs a part of the Navajo heritage. In *A History of the Navajos*, Garrick and Roberta Bailey give an excellent summary of the economic impact of this industry. Starting in the late 1890s, real commercialization of the craft began, as Navajo weavers grew desirous of entering the Anglo-American marketplace. Part of this shift occurred because of a recent economic depression, part because of the abandonment of older, heavier blankets for lighter, machine-woven Pendleton blankets for personal use, and partly because of a craze for Indian decorations in Anglo homes. Traders welcomed the demand head-on, encouraging Navajos to weave for the tourist industry and for export to outlets as far away as New York and Los Angeles. Their impact was obvious. In 1899, the weaving trade amounted to only $50,000 reservation-wide; fifteen years later it had sky rocketed to $700,000, and, by 1923, a variety of blankets were available from the Sears and Roebuck catalog.

The trade had its ups and downs as demand fluctuated. For instance, a decline in weaving occurred as World War I markets gobbled up wool for military purposes. The general pattern existing up through the early 1930s, however, was that when wool was available and cheap, the rug industry prospered, but when it became scarce, weaving slowed down appreciably. Before and after World War I, when wool was plentiful and the price low, the rug industry reached its height.[34]

Weaving varied from region to region, family to family, and person to person, some individuals commanding better prices at the post than others. Blankets called "quickies" or "bread and coffee rugs" were loosely woven, poorly designed, and bought according to weight, varying anywhere from fifty cents to a dollar a pound. A well-woven 3 x 5-foot rug, on the other hand, might command up to eight dollars and a 9 x 12 not more than twenty dollars.[35]

As with most things in Navajo culture, weaving was not solely a matter of economics. The knowledge associated with it originated in the time of the myths, when Spiderwoman taught the first Navajo this trade. Songs and prayers accompany the creative process, but there is also danger involved. Improper use or a mistake in the songs can offend the holy beings and, instead of helping the weaver, can cause harm or spoil the product. When asked if she used songs when weaving, one woman replied that it was too dangerous and that, although her weaving would probably be much improved, she preferred not to get involved but just take her chances in the market. Another suggested that she never let children touch any of her blankets before trading, because they would handle them playfully and so the trader might not want them. She associated playing with poverty.[36]

The traders helped to nurture the industry along. While they shipped large amounts of raw wool to the railheads, they also kept enough at the posts to sell back to the Indians in the winter. This maintained steady employment and flow of cash. By 1914, the traders in the northern and western agencies were placing linen tags and lead seals on rugs to guarantee Navajo genuineness to the buyer.[37]

Another part of this protection and improvement process included the purchase of raw wool. Agents and traders realized that the Navajo sheared their sheep under primitive conditions. They used the same old corrals, because there were only a limited number of places for watering. Vermin and disease infected the animals at these sites. Herders sheared the animals in the spring and early fall and often got sticks, sand, manure, burrs, and briars mixed in with the clippings. Agents sent out directives, urging the traders to protect both themselves and their clients by purchasing only clean wool. Post owners realized that when the product reached the buying markets in Kansas City or further east, if the wool was found dirty, the purchaser would either refuse it or subtract a substantial amount that more than covered the cost of cleaning it.

In 1922, raw Navajo wool, characterized as "coarse in quality and light in quantity," sold for forty cents per pound with a three- to six-cent margin on market prices. By the time it was transported to the buyer's building and cleaned, some clippings were reduced to fifty percent of their original weight. Two traders reported that between dirty wool and fluctuations in market prices, they suffered disastrous financial problems. They had purchased the wool in 1920 at thirty-five cents a pound, stored it for a year-and-a-half because of poor market conditions, freighted it at one-and-a-half cents per pound, then sold it at nine cents per pound with an estimated loss of $38,000.[38] The accuracy of these figures is difficult to determine, but they do dramatize a very real problem.

A final set of figures summarizes the importance of raw wool and rugs. In 1922 in the western agency, 23,080 pounds of rugs sold for roughly $41,000; raw wool for $22,000, comprising 78 percent of all the commerce for that year to include the sale of sheep, cattle, pelts, silver, and miscellaneous items.[39] Little surprise that the traders and agents did all they could to improve upon the breeding stock, the shearing practices, and the control of disease among sheep.

In 1909, a new incentive for improving crafts and production helped the trader instill the Anglo-American value of competition. The Shiprock agency, founded in 1903 by William T. Shelton, sponsored a regional fair. Trading posts from different areas had booths that competed in all types of industries. Shelton's reputation for carrying out the ethnocentric process of "civilizing" the Navajo was abundantly clear in some of the categories of exhibits at the fair. In addition to prizes for the best general display of Indian products and vegetables and the best team of work horses and mules, there were also entries such as "prettiest Navajo baby" and "cleanest Navajo baby." He awarded a cook stove as first prize for the best wool blanket, a wash tub for the best Germantown blanket, and a handsaw for the best wool.

The fair drew Navajo contestants from over a hundred miles away and was so successful that it became an annual event. The traders and their clients took the cue, starting preparations months in advance. Specialty rugs declaring the name of the post and products from that area fostered regional pride and competition. Shelton invited tourists to attend, encouraged the Navajo to sell traditional artifacts such as bows and arrows and silver work, and even allowed some Indian dances. By 1914, seven hundred blankets graced the traders' booths, five of which were purchased and sent to the Panama-Pacific Exposition.[40]

Although silversmithing did not become an important commercial industry in the northern part of the reservation until the early 1930s, silver bracelets, necklaces, brooches, and bridles still served as pawn. One problem confronting the trader was the Navajos' love for silver coins, used as buttons and decorations on clothing. The federal criminal code clearly stated that anyone who "fraudulently defaced, mutilated, . . . or lightened" United States currency could be fined two thousand dollars and imprisoned for up to five years. Agents contacted traders, requesting that they discourage the Navajo from drilling holes in coins and putting loops of copper through them to fasten them to their shirts. The traders did not like the practice any more than the government did, since banks would not accept mutilated currency because of decreased value and because it did not stack well.

Yet the traders had little choice but to accept it when Navajos in need cut dimes, quarters, half dollars, and dollars off their clothing. The only solution was to circulate this money among their clients, since few people accepted it off the reservation. Some posts even created their own money stamped with a unique design, and used these tokens in place of regular United States currency, another practice frowned upon by the government.[41]

As the outside world became increasingly aware of Navajo crafts and as trading posts became more numerous, a natural outgrowth occurred: roads. One of the keys to any economic system is transportation, and the isolated posts dotting reservation lands were no exception. The development of roads is a story for another time, another place, but their importance as a promoter of commerce cannot be doubted. Dirt preceded macadam; the network stretching across reservation lands sprang from the posts located where water and traffic flowed.

In the early part of this century, traders willingly worked to build roads into their isolated locales, improving routes to encourage customers. John Wetherill and Clyde Colville smoothed and widened the road through Marsh Pass that tied in with Flagstaff, 160 miles away. Elizabeth Hegemann tells of working with her husband to blast away dirt and sandstone for safe passage to Shonto, while Hubert Richardson headed a survey party over an old Ute war trail to the site of Rainbow Lodge. Traders from Kayenta, fearing competition, opposed the creation of this latter road, and a confrontation resulted, with the surveyors throwing sticks of dynamite to disperse their assailants.[42]

Rain, drifting sand, and snow could present huge problems to the wagons, and later to automobiles, that traversed mile after mile of sand, rock, and canyon. Navajos served as pathbreakers when the track was obliterated or temporary bridges were needed to span washouts. By 1916, the Denver and Rio Grande Railroad served as a magnet to the northern end of the reservation, drawing traffic to Thompson, Utah; Dolores, Mancos, and Durango, Colorado; and Farmington, New Mexico. The *Cortez Herald* applauded efforts to extend paved roads, especially the one from Gallup in the south to Shiprock in the northern part of the reservation. Articles claimed, "This road would be of material advantage to the Navajo Indians who do practically all of the freighting for different traders on the reservation. . . . With a good road, the Indians can haul [more], save much wear and tear on their wagons, and keep their teams in better condition."[43]

While some people argued vociferously that these improvements would benefit the traders and the Navajo, their real goal often was to encourage tourist traffic. BIA money supported many of the paving projects on the reservation, but, for many whites, it was more important that the Gallup-Shiprock road, completed in the early 1930s, terminated near Mesa Verde National Park. One Indian agent, H. E. Williams, boldly declared "that the tourists, the Indians, and the government have the same common interest and purpose," suggesting that roads would "facilitate the necessary mingling with a reasonably good class of whites, to the end that the Indians will be better prepared for citizenship . . . [and] a new life different to that of the reservation and the trading post."[44]

By 1930, good oil and dirt roads extended from Flagstaff to Tuba City, opening up the Grand Canyon to an increasing tourist trade, with a lateral east-west artery extending from Tuba City to Kayenta, then on to the north-south Shiprock-Gallup thoroughfare. Spur roads opened Natural Bridges, Rainbow Bridge, Inscription House Ruins, Keetseel Ruins, and Monument Valley to the tourist trade.[45] Little wonder that when two cars passed through Kayenta on the same day, John Wetherill quipped, à la Daniel Boone 150 years previous, that "the country's getting crowded."[46]

Bridges were an integral part of this burgeoning network. Starting in 1909, the government made preparations for bridges to span the San Juan River at Shiprock and Mexican Hat and a year later at Tanner's Crossing on the Little Colorado.[47]

Part of the justification for the Tanner's Crossing bridge was that traders and the western Navajo agency were shipping across the river over a million pounds of merchandise per year, most of which was hauled by Indians at $1.25 per hundred pounds. "Goods damaged or washed away and the value of time lost at this crossing" required that a structure be built.[48]

As with the roads, however, this cry at times was only a camouflage for other purposes. The Lee's Ferry bridge, for instance, had an initial estimated cost of $200,000, half of which was to be paid by the Navajo tribe. Proclaimed as an "outlet for the Indians . . . [to assist] them toward a more advanced situation," the bridge spanned the Colorado River in a section of country that was sparsely inhabited by trader and Navajo alike.[49] The $100,000 debt placed around the neck of the tribe became a topic of congressional investigation that eventually led to revocation of the debt. Acrimonious testimony sprang from the reports of this incident, some people claiming that no Navajo lived within fifty miles of the bridge, that the tribe had opposed its construction from the beginning, and that the Navajo believed this to be an attempt to obtain oil royalty money. Other critics called the political maneuvering "highway robbery" in its purest form. Even the name was unsatisfactory: President Heber J. Grant of the Church of Jesus Christ of the Latter-day Saints, who was averse to honoring John D. Lee of Mountain Meadow Massacre fame, made a special trip to the Arizona legislature in Phoenix to request a name change from the Lee's Ferry bridge to the Grand Canyon bridge. However, the name of Lee's Ferry has remained to this day.[50]

CONCLUSION

In summarizing the role of trading posts on the Navajo Reservation between 1900 and 1930, one quickly realizes what an influential position they held between the two cultures. Each post had its own personality, its own economic emphasis, yet all shared the common goal of commercial exchange in a foreign cultural setting. As agents of change, the traders provided desirable goods, but the Navajo purchased only what they wanted. In a free market economy where competition exists, the buyer has as much influence as the seller in determining rate and flow of exchange. The question of whether the trader cheated the Navajo is not the issue here but, rather, whether the trader encouraged change. The answer, obviously, is yes. The location and organization of the post, the traffic in prehistoric artifacts, the marketing of wool and rugs, the establishment of the Shiprock Fair, the construction of roads, and the employment of Navajos in a mixed barter and wage economy all emphasized white values in an Indian world. They encouraged the Navajo towards the "civilizing" process so important to the Indian agents.

However, to look at the post solely as a tool of white imperialism is to suggest that the Navajo were helpless pawns. This is far from the truth. The Navajo were sharp bargainers who knew what they wanted and worked towards the means to obtain it. Traders stocked only those goods that would sell and charged prices that were competitive with other posts. While long-distance travel might be an inconvenience, the evidence indicates that Navajos were not averse to traveling to posts that offered the best prices. And as soon as a customer entered the store, the trader was obliged to operate substantially on Navajo terms. The giving of initial presents, the use of kinship terms, the bestowal of trader names, the speaking of a "foreign" language, the dependence on pawn, and the social obligations placed upon the trader indicate anything but a passive acceptance of white imperialism on the part of the Navajo.

The Navajo accepted and rejected according to their own cultural dictates, but they were also moving inexorably towards greater acculturation. In general, they were in the driver's seat but did not, could not, realize where the future would take them. Until the 1930s, they selectively chose those things that fit into traditional cultural patterns. With enforced livestock reduction and John Collier's BIA programs, the government catapulted the Navajo into the wage economy of twentieth-century Anglo-America. When the government removed the basis of their economy—livestock—the Navajo increased mobility, and their growing dependence on roads, railroads, and consumer goods pushed them into the Depression of the 1930s and the New Deal programs of Franklin Delano Roosevelt.

The trader, economically crippled but surviving, watched many of his customers turn first to him for help, then look elsewhere for employment and products. Other elements such as service in World War II, attendance at boarding and day schools, access to the media, purchase of trucks and cars, and participation in the Federal Trade Commission hearings of the early 1970s affected both the Navajo and the trading post as economic partners. The golden days of the trading post were over; the days of plastic, tin, and Saran Wrap had arrived.

NOTES

1. For examples that stress the importance of trading posts in bringing about change, see Garrick Bailey and Roberta Bailey, *A History of the Navajos: The Reservation Years* (Santa Fe: School of American Research, 1986); Frank McNitt, *The Indian Traders* (Norman: University of Oklahoma Press, 1962); and H. Baxter Liebler, "The Social and Cultural Patterns of the Navajo Indians," *Utah Historical Quarterly* 30 (Fall 1962).

2. Elizabeth C. Hegemann, *Navaho Trading Days* (Albuquerque: University of New Mexico Press, 1963), 267–68.

3. "Indian Traders," *Report of the Commissioner of Indian Affairs, 1903* (Washington, D.C.: U.S. Department of the Interior), 34; E. B. Meritt to William T. Sullivan, 26 March 1914, Record Group 75, Bureau of Indian Affairs, Western Navajo, National Archives, Washington, D.C.; Hegemann, *Navaho Trading Days*, 267–68.

4. See Robert S. McPherson, *The Northern Navajo Frontier, 1860–1900, Expansion through Adversity* (Albuquerque: University of New Mexico Press, 1988), 63–78.

5. LTC George Hunter to Adjutant General-Colorado, 26 August 1908, Record Group 393, U.S. Army Continental Command, 1821–1920, National Archives, Washington, D.C.

6. Fred Yazzie interviewed by author, 5 November 1987; Charlie Blueeyes interviewed by author, 7 June 1988.

7. J. M. Sherwood, "Notes Regarding Charles E. Walton," Utah Historical Society, Salt Lake City, Utah, 3; Yazzie interview; Martha Nez interviewed by author, 10 August 1988.

8. Navajo Oshley interviewed by Winston Hurst and Wesley Oshley, January 1978 (multiple interviews).

9. Rose Begay interviewed by Bertha Parrish, 17 June 1987.

10. W. W. Hill, "Navaho Trading and Trading Ritual: A Study of Cultural Dynamics," *Southwestern Journal of Anthropology* (Autumn 1948): 385.

11. Hegemann, *Navaho Trading Days*, 345; Arthur L. Chaffin interviewed by P. T. Reilly, 24 December 1966, Utah State Historical Society, Salt Lake City, Utah.

12. Blueeyes interview; Martha Nez interview; Slim Benally interviewed by author, 8 July 1988; Hegemann, *Navaho Trading Days*, 272.

13. Cecil Richardson, "The Navajo Way," *Arizona Highways* (July 1948): 22.

14. Hegemann, *Navaho Trading Days*, 342; Blueeyes interview; Nez interview.

15. Hilda Wetherill, "The Trading Post: Letters from a Primitive Land," *The Atlantic Monthly* 142 (September 1928): 289–90.

16. Richardson, "The Navajo Way," 24.

17. Kitty At'iinii interviewed by Fern Charley and Dean Sunberg, 13 July 1972, California State University, Southern Utah Oral History Project.

18. Genevieve Herrick, "Women in the News," *Country Gentlemen* 46 (October 1939): 46.

19. For examples of daily life in a post, see Frances Gillmor and Louisa Wade Wetherill, *Traders to the Navajos* (Albuquerque: University of New Mexico Press, 1934); Hegemann, *Navaho Trading Days*;

Hilda Faunce, *Desert Wife* (Lincoln: University of Nebraska Press, 1928); Willow Roberts, *Stokes Carson: Twentieth Century Trading on the Navajo Reservation* (Albuquerque: University of New Mexico Press, 1987); and Gladwell Richardson, *Navaho Trader* (Tucson: University of Arizona Press, 1986).

20. Mary Shepardson and Blodwen Hammond, *The Navajo Mountain Community* (Berkeley: University of California Press, 1970), 203.
21. Hegemann, *Navaho Trading Days*, 58–59.
22. Catherine Moore interviewed by Jessie Embry, 23 April 1979, Charles Redd Center, Brigham Young University, Provo, Utah.
23. "Traffic in Relics from Indian Ruins," *Report of the Commissioner of Indian Affairs* (Washington, D.C.: U.S. Government Printing Office, 1905): 29–30.
24. Hegemann, *Navaho Trading Days*, 366–68.
25. Gillmor and Wetherill, *Traders to the Navajos*, 130.
26. David M. Brugge, *A History of the Chaco Navajos* (Albuquerque: National Park Service, 1980), 166.
27. Faunce, *Desert Wife*, 238–40.
28. T. Mitchell Prudden, *On the Great American Plateau* (New York: G. P. Putnam's Sons, 1906), 172–74.
29. Alberta Hannum, *Spin a Silver Dollar* (New York: Ballantine Books, 1944), 24–26.
30. Ann Axtell Morris, *Digging the Southwest* (Chicago: Cadmus Books, 1933), 167; Frank McNitt, *Richard Wetherill: Anasazi* (Albuquerque: University of New Mexico Press, 1957): 143, 165–68; see also Brugge, *Chaco Navajos*, 155, 159–60.
31. Oshley interview.
32. Walter Dyk, *A Navaho Autobiography* (New York: Viking Fund, Inc., 1947), 87.
33. Ibid., 95.
34. Bailey and Bailey, *A History of the Navajos*, 150–52.
35. Hegemann, *Navaho Trading Days*, 299.
36. Daisy Buck, conversation with author, 18 August 1989; Begay interview.
37. G. W. Hayzlett to commissioner of Indian affairs, 18 September 1902, Record Group 75, Bureau of Indian Affairs, National Archives, Washington, D.C.; "Navajo Blankets," *Report of the Commissioner of Indian Affairs*, vol. 2 (Washington, D.C.: U.S. Department of the Interior, 1914): 36.
38. F. E. Brandon, "Wool," Western Navajo, 28 November 1922, Record Group 75, Bureau of Indian Affairs, National Archives, Washington, D.C.
39. Sharp to commissioner of Indian affairs, 1 March 1923, Record Group 75, Bureau of Indian Affairs, National Archives, Washington, D.C.
40. "Shiprock Has First Navajo Indian Fair," *Farmington Enterprise*, 29 October 1909; Dyk, 143; "Navajo Blankets," 36.
41. Bailey and Bailey, *A History of the Navajos*, 191; Hegemann, *Navaho Trading Days*, 274; Richardson, *Navajo Trader*, 49–57.
42. Gillmor and Wetherill, *Traders to the Navajos*, 191; Hegemann, *Navaho Trading Days*, 274; Richardson, *Navajo Trader*, 49–57.
43. "Latest on Gallup Road," *The Cortez Herald*, 28 October 1915.
44. H. E. Williams, "Report on the Western Navajo Indian Reservation," 31 July 1929, Record Group 75, Bureau of Indian Affairs, National Archives, Washington, D.C.
45. C. L. Walker to commissioner of Indian affairs, 8 August 1927, Record Group 75, Bureau of Indian Affairs, National Archives, Washington, D.C.
46. Gillmor and Wetherill, *Traders to the Navajos*, 255.
47. Charles J. Kappler, *Indian Affairs, Laws and Treaties*, vol. 3 (Washington, D.C.: U.S. Government Printing Office, 1913): 407, 433, 491, 575.
48. U.S. Senate, "Report on the Necessity of a Bridge Near Tanner's Crossing, Navajo Indian Reservation, Arizona," S. Ex. Doc. 684, 61st Cong. 3d sess., 1910, 1–2.
49. U.S. Senate, "Bridge Across the Colorado River Near Lee's Ferry, Ariz.," S. Rpt. No. 111, 68th Cong. 2d sess., 1925, 1–2.
50. U.S. Senate, "Hearings Before a Subcommittee on Indian Affairs," *Survey of Conditions of the Indians in the United States*, part 6, 70th Cong. 2d sess., 1930, 2205–2206; U.S. Senate, "The Navajo Indians of New Mexico," *Senate Congressional Record*, vol. 71, part 4, 71st Cong. 1st sess., 1929, 4484–4485; C. L. Walker to commissioner of Indian affairs, 6 July 1929, Record Group 75, Bureau of Indian Affairs, National Archives, Washington, D.C.

6

As we know from Katherine Osburn's work on Navajos and Melissa Meyers's exploration of the White Earth Reservation, reformers and United States officials during the late nineteenth century sought ways to change Native Americans. This was nothing new. These were only the latest in a long line of colonizers, starting with Europeans who arrived in the sixteenth century, determined to convert the indigenous peoples of North America to Christianity and "civility." But this time, people thought, the situation was different. With its victory over the Sioux in the 1870s, the federal government knew it would encounter no more serious military threats from Indians. At last troops, so authorities hoped, could give way to teachers and missionaries. The Dawes Severalty Act of 1887, which called for the dismantling of Natives' communal properties, became the cornerstone of federal programs in this latest attempt to bring the alleged benefits of civilization to Native peoples, peoples that had so far managed to resist generations of would-be saviors.

Officials believed Lakotas were finally ready for the conversion program. For that program to go forward, however, the government had to convince Indians that they, like other Americans, must see themselves first as individuals, not as members of some corporate entity. This philosophy was the foundation of the Dawes Act, which gave to every Indian over the age of 18 a parcel of 160 acres of land (or 320 acres if it was used only for pasture). The civilization mission fell under the control of the Office of Indian Affairs (OIA), whose agents were to find ways to persuade Lakotas to accept the new order.

Using a method of analysis pioneered by the French theoretician Michel Foucault, Thomas Biolsi here reconstructs the program, "the four modes of subjection," through which the OIA tried to guide Lakotas into their government-ordained future. As Biolsi makes clear, the OIA needed to do more than break up communal holdings and instruct Lakotas in the workings of a market economy; it had, to use the words that John Adams had used a century earlier in referring to the essence of the American Revolution, to alter Lakotas' very "hearts and minds." This proved no easy task, especially when Lakotas devised subversive strategies. In 1885, for example, flustered census workers had to figure out who "Dirty Prick" and "Shit Head" (names that appeared in their records) actually were. Like those Navajos at Bosque Redondo forging extra ration coupons, Lakotas were padding the census lists with fictitious (and scornful) names in order to get more food from the government.

Nonetheless, Biolsi argues, subjection did indeed occur. The government's allotments and character appraisals, the development of blood quantums and genealogies as markers—these and other tools had a profound effect on Lakota life. Even as scholars have highlighted Indian forms of resistance and cultural persistence, they have not forgotten the genuine and pervasive power the victorious United States could wield in Indian Country. Do Biolsi's conclusions about that power correspond with, or contradict, the conclusions drawn from Bosque Redondo and White Earth?

THE BIRTH OF THE RESERVATION: MAKING THE MODERN INDIVIDUAL AMONG THE LAKOTA

Thomas Biolsi

*The individual is no doubt the fictitious atom of an "ideological"
representation of society; but he is also a reality....*

—Michel Foucault[1]

BY 1885, THE AMERICAN WEST HAD BEEN WON, and the Lakota had been militarily pacified. The Lakota bands no longer roamed the Plains, but had been sequestered on the Great Sioux Reservation, comprising the western half of what is now South Dakota. There were no more Indian wars, intertribal war parties, buffalo hunts, or sun dances. The United States government had embarked on a policy of *civilizing* the Lakota and other western Indian peoples, and schools and even family gardens appeared on the reservation. Although the Lakota had formerly been recognized by the United States in treaties as a "nation," the government no longer made treaties with Indians, and the internal sovereignty of native polities had been denied by extending federal jurisdiction over crimes in Indian country. Political sovereignty now resided with the local agent of the Office of Indian Affairs (OIA), whose material sources of power included the paramilitary Indian force that he paid and commanded, and the rations he dispensed on which the Lakota had come to depend for subsistence with the destruction of the prereservation mode of production.

But just how completely had the Lakota been politically subdued by 1885? In that year, the agents on the Great Sioux Reservation lined up their charges to take the annual census in order to establish the size of the populations for the purpose of issuing rations. At the Rosebud Agency, the OIA office established on the Great Sioux Reservation to administer the Sicangu (or Brule) Lakota, the 1885 census takers recorded some remarkable English translations of Lakota names. Peppered throughout the census, in between names such as "Black Elk," "Walking Bull," and "Dull Knife," were names such as "Bad Cunt," "Dirty Prick," and "Shit Head."[2] What happened is not difficult to unravel: Lakota people were filing past the census enumerator, and then getting back in line—or lending their babies to people in line—to be enumerated a second time using fictitious and rather imaginative names. The intention was to pad the census lists in order to receive more rations. The

Source: *American Ethnologist*, v. 22, n. 1 (1995), pp. 28–53.

Lakota people at the neighboring Pine Ridge Agency had, by such subterfuge, inflated their census list by 70 percent according to later censuses taken under guard. From the point of view of the colonial administrators, all the Lakota looked alike—they had no individual identities in any practical administrative sense—and the OIA had no idea how many Lakota there were.[3] If colonialism is about making the colonized "legible," "readable," and "available to political and economic calculation,"[4] the Lakota were yet to be colonized.

The Lakota were on the reservation and were under the formal authority of the United States government. They were even subject to the formidable power of the police and to coercion through the withholding of rations. They had been militarily pacified, but not internally pacified, that is, under predictable, bureaucratic control.[5] All of that was to change, however, over the next several decades as a series of administrative techniques was deployed that constructed new subjects among the Lakota—new kinds of individuals with specific practical, recordable, and predictable identities and self-interests. In this article I describe the process on the Pine Ridge and Rosebud Reservations in South Dakota,[6] from the 1880s to the 1930s.

INTRODUCTION

There were, of course, "individuals" among the Lakota in prereservation times. In fact, the Lakota in particular and Plains Indians in general have been recognized in the anthropological literature as particularly "individualistic" societies in which political power was not centralized but tended to cohere around self-made leaders, and individuals competed for wealth, prestige, and power.[7] But this form of individuality emerged in the context of social relations profoundly different from those of the industrial capitalism of late nineteenth century America. The Lakota were not "modern" individuals. In the third quarter of the nineteenth century, they were an equestrian, bison-hunting, warring, "stateless," social form in which the primary sociopolitical units were kinship-based, leader-centered bands (*tiošpaye*) and larger intermittent, ecologically and militarily strategic political clusters.[8] This social form is perhaps best characterized as a kind of kin-ordered mode of production,[9] with communal access to strategic resources (food, shelter, clothing, basic instruments of production), but with more privatized ownership of buffalo robes, which were exchanged with traders in the American fur trade.[10]

The problem for the state apparatus, when it finally sought to regulate the Lakota on the reservations in the last quarter of the nineteenth century, was that the kind of "individual" prevalent among them could not easily be fitted into either the government's jural and administrative schemata or the market economy in which land and labor were commodities. It was not that the Lakota had not already been influenced by "civilization" or had not already experienced significant "acculturation." Indeed, their entire way of life in the nineteenth century was made possible by the Indian trade niche generated by European and American merchant capital. Rather, what occurred in the late nineteenth century is that the Lakota and other western Indian peoples were being integrated into global processes—not for the first time, but in new ways—on reservations. These reservations were playing an increasingly crucial, historical role as western Native Americans were displaced in order to vacate the American West and make the lands available for mining, commercial agriculture, and railroads. In the process, the Lakota were being transformed from a people with a specialized role at the periphery of society to a people—albeit a disempowered people—in the core.

The civilization program of the OIA is most usefully viewed not as a process of "culture change," "directed acculturation," or "ethnocide." Whatever the public statements of OIA officials about fostering civilization and eradicating barbarism, OIA policy in fact has generated and sustained much of the social and cultural distinctiveness of the Lakota. The degree of control necessary to secure the internal pacification of the Lakota under the changed circumstances of reservation life was much less ambitious than "civilization." The Lakota had to be forced to conform to a certain minimum definition of modern individuality. In this way, they would be constituted as social persons who could fit into the American nation-state and the market system of metropolitan capitalism. Without this political groundwork, any attempt to deal with the Lakota directly would—as the census results indicate—be like trying to force round pegs into square holes.

This article is a history of the making of reservation individuals among the Lakota. It is not an ethnohistory (understood as the "history of an ethnic group") of the Lakota during this period, nor is it a study of federal Indian policy during the "assimilation period"[11] or an institutional study of the Indian assimilation period.[12] Nor is it a study of "acculturation" or "culture change," as these processes are usually understood. Rather, this article traces the history among the Lakota of what Foucault calls "subjection."[13] Subjection is the construction by the powerful of spaces in which human beings are enabled to participate in the social life of public institutions, in the economy, and in the body politic of the nation. It involves the official promulgation of fundamental social classifications through which individuals are to be *known* (by themselves, by other individuals, and by the officials) and allowed to act. Subjection also involves the linkage of these social classifications to power, both negative and positive: not only can individuals be punished by the officials for violating the social classifications, they quickly come to find that abiding by them opens up avenues of enablement. Thus, subjection is not absolutely imposed from above; it also seduces the subaltern to live by its rules, and thereby shapes new and predictable self-interests, outlooks, and behavior patterns.[14]

Subjection can be seen as the creation of a "matrix of individualization,"[15] the axes of which constitute modes of subjection. During the period under consideration, four modes of subjection operated in the internal pacification of the Lakota by the state apparatus. Lakota people experienced the first mode, empropertiment, as did other populations in metropolitan capitalist society. The Lakota shared the application of the second mode, "competence," with wards and inmates in "total institutions."[16] The third mode of subjection, "degree of Indian blood," was uniquely applied to Indian people in the United States. The fourth mode, registration of genealogy, was shared with others in the United States, but it was applied more oppressively to Indian people. Together, these modes of subjection facilitated the penetration of the subjectivities of Lakota by the state and by capitalism, and determined the channels through which the Lakota people would be known by the state and allowed to act as individuals. Ultimately, the processes of subjection largely determined how Lakota people thought—and, to some extent, still think—about themselves and "society" and how they perceived and acted in their own self-interest. This does not mean that an autonomous Lakota culture was obliterated by subjection or that there was no resistance to subjection, but the new forms of individuality, even where resisted, could not be ignored.[17]

PROPERTY OWNERSHIP

One of the most important and well-known elements of the civilization program of the OIA was the allotment of Indian lands in severalty. OIA officials and eastern "friends of the Indians" recognized that empropertying individuals would reduce the problems inherent in civilizing a population. The commissioner of Indian Affairs, for example, wrote in a report:

> The allotment system tends to break up tribal relations. It has the effect of creating individuality, responsibility, and a desire to accumulate property. It teaches the Indians habits of industry and frugality, and stimulates them to look forward to a better and more useful life, and, in the end, it will relieve the government of large annual appropriations.[18]

Allotment is now widely understood in American Indian studies to have been a project that did *not* result in the elusive civilization of Indians, but that did effectively help to transfer Indian property to non-Indians.[19] In terms of *civilizing* effect, allotment is considered by some contemporary scholars to have been a fanciful figment of the Victorian colonial mind and a self-referential discourse without basis in practical reality: "Some reformers of the late nineteenth century had as much faith in the magical effects of property and laissez-faire in transforming the Indians as some missionaries of the early decades of the century had in the miraculous influence of the Bible and the institution of the Sabbath."[20] But empropertying Indians *did* have consequences that were phantasmic, to use Marx's term, if not magical; beyond drawing Indian land into the market, it helped to secure a new sovereignty on the reservations. This was because private property under capitalism—instituted in the Native American case by the allotment of Indian lands in severalty—presupposes the state as a protector of the common interests of individual property owners.

In 1889 a U.S. commission traveled to Pine Ridge Agency in Dakota Territory to negotiate with the Oglala Lakota for the sale of lands on the Great Sioux Reservation to the federal government and for the allotment in severalty of the remaining reservation lands. Before the commission arrived, Red Cloud and other chiefs had organized the majority of the men at the agency to stand firm against the proposal and to refuse to sell any land. During the proceedings, one Oglala related to the commissioners, through an interpreter, a now well-know indigenous discourse on land:

I am an Indian and the Great Spirit has made me, and this land is the Great Spirit's wife, and I am born from there, and my heart comes from there, and I am an Indian and I am standing on my own land. . . . I went with Red Cloud. We belong to his band, and we will not sell the land.[21]

This pronouncement was unmistakably clear on the moral attachment of people to land, with obvious implications not only for the sale of land, but also for the privatization of land.

Both the cession and allotment eventually took place, however, under the provisions of the Great Sioux Agreement, which became law in 1889.[22] Allotment in severalty began on Rosebud Reservation in 1894 and on Pine Ridge Reservation in 1904. Under the original formula, each family head received 320 acres,[23] each single person over 18 years received 160 acres, and each child under 18 received 80 acres; acreages were doubled in the case of lands usable only for grazing purposes.[24] Allotments were originally held in trust status and could not be sold or leased without the permission or supervision of the OIA (legislation enacted in 1906 authorized the Interior Department to remove from trust status allotments of individuals deemed competent [see below]).

The Lakota people on both reservations were divided on the matter of accepting allotments. Some people were eager for allotment. Some "scrambled to get lands where they wanted them."[25] Other Lakota were apparently less interested in land than they were in the annuities, called Sioux benefits, which allottees received. Under the provisions of the Great Sioux Agreement, each adult allottee was to receive two milch cows, one pair of oxen with yoke and chain, or two mares and one harness set, one plow, one wagon, one harrow, one hoe, one axe, one pitchfork, and $50 cash.[26] Given a primary motivation of obtaining goods and cash, many allottees understandably did not give much consideration to the agricultural value of the allotments they chose. The allotting agent on Rosebud reported to the commissioner in 1905: "The bulk of the allotments do not constitute, by any means, the best land on the reservation. They have apparently selected them on account of their nearness to the Agency, to some principal stream . . . or to some favorite camping ground instead of selecting them with regard to the character of the surface soil."[27] Another agent reported that families chose allotments so as to be near "friends"—probably band members.[28] Many Lakota were quite lackadaisical about the business of allotment. One agent complained about the sudden departure for a dance of Indians whom he had expected to come to his office for allotments: "With a dance in prospect, allotments are of no importance."[29]

Some Lakota people were opposed to allotment in principle—perhaps because they were perceptive enough to suspect that it would transform social relations in profound ways. On Rosebud Reservation, a man who had been active in the Ghost Dance movement in 1890 organized a group of "kickers" (OIA slang for troublemakers) in resistance to allotment. The allotting agent reported in 1903: "finally this [resistance] developed [into] open opposition, culminating one day in the approach of a war party in war paint, dress, mounted and armed of some sixty or ninety young braves, and ordering the party [the allotment survey crew] to quit work and clear out or we should all be killed."[30] On Pine Ridge Reservation, the Oglala Council, composed of "the older and nonprogressive Indians," opposed the presidential order to allot the reservation.[31]

Despite their resistance, the Lakota people were eventually allotted, and allotments quickly became important resources as the reservation lands began to be drawn into the broader agricultural economy of the West. Although allotments were initially chosen to receive Sioux benefits, so that almost any piece of land would suffice, the Lakota soon began to recognize the value of land in the market economy: as a means of commercial production or, more commonly, as a marketable commodity itself. The Rosebud allotting agent reported in 1902 that "many younger persons [whose allotments were injudiciously chose for them by their parents] have grown up and see the necessity of better land."[32] These people sought to exchange their poor land for more valuable allotments. In 1904, "surplus" Rosebud Reservation lands were opened by the federal government for sale by lottery to non-Indian homesteaders. Over one hundred thousand people registered for the 2,412 homesteads available from the government for prices ranging from $400–$640—44 competitors for each available homestead.[33] The effect of this intense demand on land prices in South Dakota was, predictably, profound. One former homestead just off the reservation had sold, with improvements, for $5,000—ten times the price at which the government was selling comparable Rosebud lands. The appreciation of the value of land had the effect of "radically changing the idea of the Indians as to what constitutes good land." Many people who had poor allotments now wanted to exchange them for the remaining valuable farm land on the reservation.[34] The "great demand for lands in that neighborhood and the high price at which farming lands are held" were "well known to the Indians," an OIA official reported.[35] By the second decade of this century, there were many white settlers in and about the reservations, and when the prices of agricultural commodities began to appreciate with the start of World War I in 1914, Lakota land came into demand for sale and rent to non-Indian farmers and ranchers. Income from land leases and sales was critical to Lakota subsistence during this period.

Leasing and sale of lands that attended allotment had the effect of making Indian lands available for use by non-Indians in the agricultural economy, and allotment is a well-recognized mechanism in the economic underdevelopment of the reservations.[36] But how did allotment affect the process that is the focus of this article—the subjection of the Lakota? How did the privatization of land help to reconstitute Lakota political subjectivities? Recalling the Lakota references to "mother earth" and land in 1889, it is noteworthy that less than a decade later the Rosebud agent reported that some Lakota were beginning to refer to their allotments as "my land."[37] By the 1930s, ownership of an allotment in trust status was an important symbol of being a traditional Lakota.[38] Some Lakota protested OIA policies regarding trust lands during the New Deal as "un-American" because they interfered with what they saw as their right of private property. An Oglala complainant submitted a written statement to the Investigating Subcommittee of the Senate Committee on Indian Affairs in 1938 that said, among other things, that certain "Russian ideas are creeping in" on the reservation:

The Constitution of the United States says that no land shall be taken away without due process of law and that there shall be no servitude. From what I learned about Abraham Lincoln, after the Emancipation Act was passed, slavery was abolished in the United States. But under the Wheeler-Howard Act [the Indian Reorganization Act, 1934], it seems the Bureau [OIA] is handling the Indian lands in the way that will fit in with their program whether the Indians like it or not. The superintendent [OIA agents were called superintendents after 1908] says the Indian can lease this piece of land but some other land is set aside and they cannot lease that. And it seems that the programs are all made and they are forced upon the Indians and the Indians do not have anything to say. Now we want to continue under the Constitution of the United States. That is, we would like to remain Americans. We want to be governed by the Constitution of the United States, and not be governed by policies which are entirely un-American. If the Commissioner [of Indian Affairs], John Collier, cannot respect the Constitution of the United States and the policies which are American, he should be removed and not allowed to continue in office.[39]

There is good reason to believe that few Lakota knew what the phrase "Russian ideas" meant in the popular media and political images of the 1930s and 1940s. This written statement may have been translated or even drafted by someone else. Whether or not the Lakota were worried about communism, their strong sentiments regarding private property rights have been amply documented. In 1940 the Lakota Treaty Council (an unofficial, traditionalist resistance body)[40] adopted a resolution "that the theories of a German Karl Marz [*sic*], expounded in the last centuries, 'That all men are created equal, that there will be no poor people and no rich people, advocating an abolition of private properties, and controlling of everything by the masses and all will be under one master,' cannot be attained among the Sioux Nation, the honest Americans."[41] As early as 1887, the commissioner of Indian Affairs had identified private property as one of "the great conservative forces" that would help pacify Indians.[42]

Clearly something unprecedented had happened in the Lakota situation with the acceptance of allotments. The significance of property ownership as a form of modern subjectivity lies in its implications for political sovereignty, specifically for the state: privatization of the means of production/subsistence creates fundamentally new subjects with radically new interests and social and political relations to each other. It reconfigures social life and creates "a new human nature,"[43] "economic man," which in turn presupposes the state as a sovereign entity that "stands above" and represents the parallel interests of self-interested, atomized property owners in the marketplace. The moment of the creation of civil society, a social world of private property owners, is simultaneously the moment of the creation of the bourgeois state and its sovereignty.[44] Within the context of private property relations, social interaction of the more peaceful variety as opposed to Hobbesian chaos cannot take place without the emergence of a fundamentally new kind of "imagined community."[45] This "community" is vital even if it is in fact a "community" of alienated individuals[46]—and by this I mean a community that is built upon, and exists to protect, the interests of individuals against violations of basic property rights by other individuals, blocs, classes, and class fractions, and even by elements of the state apparatus itself. This is the *rational* and *consensual* basis of the state—from the standpoint of the propertied—as John Locke recognized.[47] The state as a "social contract" among property owners, and between property owners and the government, like the atomized individual, is both ideological representation and social reality. Theorists of differing conceptual vantage points may characterize the modern nation-state as a "monopoly on violence," a form of "organized terror," a "class weapon," or the "executive committee of the ruling class"—in short, an *imposition*. For social life to flow relatively smoothly under capitalism, however, government must in part be a genuine social contract between property owners—even *petty* property owners[48] such as the Lakota—and between each individual and "the constituted authorities."[49]

Of course, the Lakota were enmeshed in property relations in fundamentally different ways than were their non-Indian neighbors on the plains, and it would be a grave error to assume that allotment simply reconstituted the Lakota individual as an "economic man." For most Lakota people, property and its proceeds (money, livestock, crops) necessarily served different social ends from those found among non-Indian farmers. The local logic of social reproduction and of accumulation on the reservation was distinct and was a perennial concern of the colonizers. The Pine Ridge agent complained in 1896:

> A serious drawback in the work of civilizing these or any Indians . . . is found in the universal custom of relatives and connections by marriage considering that what one has belongs to all. As such relations are usually very numerous and for the most part idle and improvident, no one family can accumulate anything. Let a man be in receipt of a salary, no matter how large, or let him by industry raise a crop, and he gets no real benefit from it. His own relations and those of his wife swarm down upon him and consume everything, so that he has nothing for his industry. This not only discourages any attempt to be industrious and to accumulate property, especially things that can be used for food, but it puts a premium on idleness and unthrift, for he who idles not only saves his muscle, but fares as well as does he who works.[50]

The Rosebud superintendent wrote to his district "farmers"[51] in 1922:

> It is . . . conceded by all who know Indians, that they are the most liberal people in the world so far as feeding each other is concerned. . . . They have not only been liberal in feeding the hungry but have been liberal in giving away horses, blankets, shawls, money, and other valuable property.
>
> The give-away spirit has been prominent among the Sioux for a number of years and is still practiced to some extent. I believe that time has come when this matter should be brought to the attention of the Indians and have them discuss it in a friendly way, and have them to understand that we are not criticizing their old customs but that the time has come when their own comfort and the comfort of their families depends upon a change of this old time custom.[52]

But this social use of wealth, which the anthropologist Haviland Scudder Mekeel described as "virtually . . . a state of socialism,"[53] did not detract from the fact that the

Lakota were empropertied as individuals and depended upon the state apparatus for the security of their property. People may have given away, but what they gave away was theirs to give. Once the Lakota had been empropertied as individuals, each man, woman, and child had a material stake in the protection of private property relations (even if the property was not fully private because it was held in trust) and in a social apparatus—the state—that could claim to "stand above" and, in so doing, represent their "common interest" and guarantee protection. Lakota individuals owned land that generated income. As petty property owners, they had a clear interest in "petty property rights"[54]—despite their social use of wealth—and it was the government that could guarantee those rights: protection against violation of leases, trespass of livestock on allotments, and protection against other infringements by non-Indians, by other Lakota people, and even by government agencies. In 1907, for example, one Oglala sued another Oglala in the OIA agency court. The defendant was instructed by the Indian judges:

> _____ wants to build a fence around his land that was reserved for his allotment by the Allotting Agent but your house is on the land and desires that you remove your house on to your land that was reserved for your allotment. He has given you ample time in which to remove your house. It is time that you attend to your own affairs and let other people alone. We wrote you once before but you did not heed us. We advise you again to remove your house on to your own land, so that he can fix his fence and other improvements on his land.[55]

In 1916, Oglalas were sued by other Oglalas in the agency court for cattle that trespassed and destroyed a garden and hay.[56] Recognition of this obligation of government to "stand above" disputes and protect property was obviously behind the Lakota reference to the U.S. Constitution and their rights as property owners. Although it may not have "civilized" them as was the stated intention, empropertying the Lakota certainly opened up their subjectivities to the penetration of the state, its sovereignty, and its law. The Lakota may have been "virtually socialists," but they had also been made into "Red Lockeans."[57]

COMPETENCE

The reservation system of the late nineteenth and early twentieth centuries was based on the congressionally authorized and judicially sanctioned status of wardship applied with considerable administrative discretion. Wardship was founded on the assumption of Indian incompetence to function effectively in the market economy of the wider American society.[58] As a 1928 report on the OIA, known as the Meriam Report and commissioned by the secretary of the interior, explained: "Indian guardianship was assumed when the Indians as a race were unquestionably incompetent. Relinquishment of this trust cannot lightly be made. The Indian, therefore, is assumed to be incompetent until formally declared to be competent."[59] What was termed incompetence was rooted in the essentialized characteristics of most Indians presumed in the colonial gaze. "[T]heir instincts are purely nomadic," the Pine Ridge superintendent insisted in 1922, which constituted one of the main problems of inducing Indians to become farmers: they preferred to travel to dances and fairs rather than tend their crops and stock.[60] "[T]hese Indians are not far enough away from the old buffalo days to succeed as Cattle growers," the Rosebud superintendent reported.[61] Still hunters at heart, the Lakota could not be trusted to arrive at "the proper viewpoint with respect to their live stock. Nine out of ten Indians look upon cattle as to their meat value only," the Pine Ridge superintendent complained in 1922.[62] The commissioner of Indian Affairs in 1881 found the Lakota to be "proverbially improvident,"[63] and though the Lakota people undoubtedly changed over the ensuing years, government assessments of their competency changed little. Fifty years later, in 1931, the Rosebud superintendent dismissed the Lakota as "notoriously improvident." Moreover, he reported that the Lakota people have "little conception of how money is obtained or how it should be invested."[64] They did not understand financial transactions of more than $100, and "their interests and thoughts are in other directions than business or economic problems"—directions such as feasts, giveaways, showing generosity toward friends and relatives, dancing, and traveling. "[T]here can be no question about Indian incompetence to manage much of a business enterprise," the Rosebud superintendent wrote in 1933, as "the Indian at heart is rather shiftless in matters of industry." Progress was being made under his tutelage, the superintendent reported to his superiors in Washington, but he believed it "pertinent to add here that because of racial factors and characteristics the process of self-support and full ability to make the best of things will come rather slow—a little progress each year."[65] The Meriam Report summarized the situation for Indians generally: "With respect to knowledge and experience in the use of property, many of them are still children and must be given training in the use of property and its value before they are declared competent to handle it independently."[66] In the opinion of some OIA personnel, the Lakota were simply "shiftless, lazy and irresponsible,"[67] and their homes and farms were "slovenly."[68]

Given all this essentializing of the Lakota (whether based on a colonial theory of "racial characteristics" or on the premise that the Lakota were simply "not far enough away from the old buffalo days"),[69] they could hardly be considered sufficiently responsible to manage their resources—any more than could a mental incompetent, a spendthrift,[70] or a juvenile. Consequently, the government concluded that the Lakota had to be closely supervised and, ideally, trained. Allotment, substantial sums of money, and some personal property were held in trust for individual Indians unless or until they were deemed competent. This wardship system was ultimately rooted in law enacted by Congress. Under an administrative procedure known as Individual Indian Money (IIM) accounts, expenditure of income accruing to individuals from federal annuities (from tribal land sales) or sales or leases of allotments was supervised by the agency bureaucracy. Farm equipment or livestock purchased with IIM funds was also regulated,[71] and cattle were branded "ID" (Indian Department). Sale or lease of allotments was also supervised by the OIA.[72]

At least officially, OIA policy sought a solution "at the earliest time possible, when the Indian will not need supervision but will take his place in the community where he lives."[73] According to the officials, developing the competence of the Lakota required a delicate and judicious balance of supervision, training, and gradual exposure to free market forces. There was some sentiment in the OIA that a sink-or-swim approach would be in the best interests of Indian people. The Rosebud agent suggested in 1889, the year before the Wounded Knee massacre:

> The time has arrived when it is absolutely cruel to treat the Sioux as children or wards. Public sentiment is restive under the [budgetary] strain and will not long permit them to retain their present status; they must become individualized and acquire the rights of citizenship. The strain of civilization will deplete their numbers, as in the case of the Omahas, Winnebagos, and other semi-civilized tribes, but the principle of the survival of the fittest will apply, and such may acquire a reasonable degree of independence.[74]

Most OIA personnel, however, believed that such an abrupt policy shift—essentially cutting Lakota loose—would be cruel. True, the "process of assimilation and enlightenment will be held in check by too much restraint."[75] In 1929 the commissioner of Indian Affairs authorized the annual dispensation of $500 to "reasonably competent" adults from their IIM accounts for unsupervised use, "that they may be encouraged to assume personal responsibility and to acquire that self-reliance and practical business experience which will enable them to become independent and progressive members of the community."[76] Happily for the administrators, however, wardship status would still be necessary for many Lakota in most areas of personal business for some time to come.

Wardship entailed a complex set of formal and informal character appraisals that were applied to Lakota persons, on the basis of which administrative decisions on individual cases were made. In 1923 the OIA began conducting an "Industrial Survey" of all families on reservations in the United States. The intent of the survey was to collect data on the relative standing of families in "the march of progress"—to evaluate OIA programs and individual families' advancement.[77] A page was allocated to each family, with a photograph of the members, their home, and farm (see Figures 1 and 2). Detailed if not systematic data were recorded on the size and legal status of lands, blood quanta, the ages, wardship status, health status, and mental competence of family members, and on crops and livestock, and sources of income. In addition, discursive comments on the character of the head of household were included in many entries. Most of these character appraisals concerned the extent to which the individual behaved in conformity with the OIA's ideal of self-support.

Thus, one Rosebud man was described in the survey as "white . . . to all intents and purposes," no doubt because he "supports himself by his own efforts."[78] Another family was described thus: "They live like white people in every way."[79] It was noted of another Rosebud man that he was a "good farmer."[80] One Pine Ridge man was listed as "industrious . . . and doing well," while another was described as "inclined [at least] to be progressive."[81] Another Pine Ridge man was described as "doing much more and better than the average Indian."[82] Others did not fare as well in OIA evaluation. One Rosebud man was described as making "only a feeble attempt at

Figure 1. Photograph from the Industrial Survey, Rosebud Reservation, 1923. Washington, D.C.: National Archives and Records and Administration.

Figure 2. Photograph from the Industrial Survey, Pine Ridge Reservation, 1925. Washington, D.C.: National Archives and Records and Administration.

farming," and his home was described as showing "no thrift or progress."[83] The Pine Ridge survey included this dire note on one man: "[A local OIA employee] reports that he is practically a total failure;"[84] another man was simply dismissed thus: "Amos is nil."[85] Amos's father was described in this way: "The old man is interested in the past and cares little about the present and future."[86] Other men were described as "not industrious,"[87] "not reliable,"[88] and "N.G." (no good).[89]

The same normalizing gaze is apparent in the "honor roll" maintained in each of the outlying districts on Pine Ridge in 1927. Men were grouped on the roll on the basis of their "efforts." One OIA district farmer maintained a list of "coffee coolers" who not only "loafed" but visited and consumed the food of others. As a positive example, the superintendent also installed an exhibit in the agency office of the garden products of one determined Oglala farmer.[90] In 1927 the Rosebud superintendent wrote to a Lakota housewife:

> Dear Madam: In looking over the reports submitted by the various employees on inspection of Indian homes on clean-up day, I wish to advise you that [the field matron] says you had your house in excellent condition, clean and everything properly arranged. . . . The condition of your house will be pointed out as an example or model for the other Indians to be guided by. I was in your house one time and everything indicated that you were a first class housekeeper.

This letter appeared on the front page of the local newspaper on the reservation.[91]

The authorities' record keeping and their self-righteous, patronizing, racist, and invidious character appraisals of individual Lakota were not just matters of "discourse" understood as purely representational. As Corrigan and Sayer insist,[92] one must also consider the materiality of the state's actual and fictive creation of individuals. The files and appraisals had serious, practical consequences for people. Because Lakota individuals were wards unless declared otherwise, they were supervised in everything from their expenditure of cash to their public assemblies, and the files and character appraisals (both formal and informal) had a significant impact on official decisions in individual cases.

For example, in 1906 the Rosebud agency had drawn up a "roll of honor" on which were listed those individuals who were deemed "temperate, prudent, honest and otherwise fitted to take charge of the [IIM] money of their children."[93] This money included substantial sums from tribal land sales that could make a great difference in the day-to-day lives of families on the reservations, in terms of subsistence level, dependence on intermittent labor for subsistence, and surplus for social and ceremonial funds. Access to this money depended on how one's character was perceived by the bureaucrats.

The work of the "competency commission" that visited Pine Ridge in 1917 provides another example of the serious consequences of OIA knowledge and appraisals. The commission "interrogated"[94] applicants for fee patents; these patents, if granted, would essentially remove restrictions on the sale and lease of allotments owned by the patentees.[95] Simultaneously, the land became subject to state and local property taxes, and the patentees became U.S. citizens (all Indian people were made citizens by Congress in 1924)[96] and subject to the jurisdiction of state law even while residing on the reservation.[97] The competency commissioners referred to fee-patented Indians as having been "turned loose." For each application recommended for approval, the commission provided detailed information—similar to that included in the Industrial Surveys—on age, degree of blood, marital status, health status, land assets, crops and livestock, sources of income, education, and fluency in English. The reports authorized by "competency commissions" justified the approval of a fee patent with general appraisals of the applicant's competence and related characteristics.

Many people were simply described as "capable of transacting business affairs intelligently," without government "supervision." Some were said to have a "reputation for industry" and to be "well spoken of by the Agency Employees." Some of the commissions' recommendations for fee patents were justified by pointing out that the applicants were "strong," "robust," and in "the prime of life" or of "the desirable age to be turned loose."[98] These appraisals meant only that the applicants were young and were likely to survive the difficult times involved in trying to keep their land or were capable of sustaining themselves despite the probable loss of their land. The commission was also concerned with the intelligence of patentees: was the individual "bright," "above the ordinary Sioux Indian in intelligence," or "of more than ordinary intelligence"? In a capitalist context, competency was often gauged through material accumulation. In one case a commission report observed that a couple owned a Dodge, in another that the couple was "well to do" and "prosperous." One man's competence was argued in this way: "Is said by his neighbors to be very penurious and always has money for his needs." Other cases were argued on the basis of presentability to non-Indians: "A very nice appearing woman"; "He is a nice appearing and modest young man"; "Is a very self-possessed and nice appearing women"; "She with her husband are one of the most intelligent and nice appearing families we met on this reservation." The commission went on at length about one man's appearance: "He is a splendid specimen of manhood, 6 feet, 4 inches in height, weighs 230 pounds, and perfect physique, and being quite intelligent."[99] There were also occasional individuals who clearly evinced competency because they could be assessed as "in every respect a white man, other than his Indian blood," "in every respect an educated white woman other than her degree of Indian blood," or one who "[r]eads, writes and speaks English like a white society girl."[100] The commission recommended the fee patenting of 370 individuals on Pine Ridge Reservation.[101]

Later the same year, the commissioner of Indian Affairs looked critically on existing procedures for declaring competency and ordered that allottees must genuinely demonstrate "a business capacity equal to the average white man in order to receive a patent."[102] In 1929, the commissioner advised field personnel that fee patenting procedures must be more "conservative" and that real evidence of competency must be demonstrated.[103] Most Lakota patentees had quickly sold their land or mortgaged and subsequently lost it.[104] According to administrators, rapid land loss was due to the fact that "incompetent" Indians had been mistakenly declared competent and had been turned loose.[105] This explanation indicates an important point about the administrators' gaze and their "knowledge" of the colonized subjects: it was essentially arbitrary with reference to any hard reality locatable in the characters of individual Lakota people. The knowledge of administrators can be characterized as both interested and self-referential. Their "interested knowledge" is visible in that fee patenting was a project conditioned by administrative and political concerns to reduce the number of wards and consequent administrative costs, and to convey Indian lands into the market and onto state tax rolls. The "self-referential knowledge" of administrators is reflected in the discursive world they constructed and in which they trafficked in essentializing theories of Indian incompetence and resultant codings of individuals. This world was occupied with administrative fictions rather than with objective, measurable, or fixed qualities in the subjects.[106] Much of the administrative "knowledge" of Lakota individuals circulated among OIA employees as reputations. Many of the appraisals in the Industrial Surveys, for example, were based on summary opinions drawn from local agency personnel. Thus, among the Lakota, as James Scott tells us generally,[107] the subaltern had much at stake in how they were seen by the powerful.

The question of the extent to which the Lakota "internalized" the colonial discourse of "competence" is, of course, complex. Certainly, the Lakota developed their own "readings" of, and their own strategies for, manipulating their new legal statuses. In the eyes of the Lakota people, special arrangements the OIA termed wardship (for example, tax exemption, exemption from state jurisdiction, the issuance of rations) had more to do with treaty rights than with "incompetence."[108] Indeed, the idea of "guardianship" seemed pointedly ironic to some Lakota. In 1909 an Oglala told an OIA official in an open council that the ideal that Congress was the Indians' guardian was "laughable." It was Native Americans who were the guardians, who had been relinquishing land ever since the whites had crossed the ocean to provide the whites with a place to live.[109] But if Lakota people could live against the new administrative codings of degrees of "competence," they also had to live within them. They could not live as if the codings did not matter in their lives because they were obligatory in everyday life on the reservations. The new gaze mattered too much to ignore when one dealt with the OIA, and there was a great deal to be gained in going along with the official interpretation, at least within earshot of officials. Being seen both as competent and as incompetent by the bureaucrats had distinct advantages (more potential freedom in the case of the former, exemption from state taxation and legal jurisdiction in the latter), and individual Lakota people calculated their interests in terms of this prevailing political-economic situation. In 1991 an elderly Lakota man told me that the Lakota were not truly a "sovereign nation," as the younger people and tribal attorneys were insisting, but that they were "captives" or "wards" of the United States—with attendant legitimate claims on the federal government, notwithstanding the obvious disadvantages and humiliations of wardship.[110]

DEGREE OF INDIAN BLOOD

The blood quantum has long been recognized by scholars as an important ascriptive status and social and cultural fracture line among the Lakota, and the administrative use of blood quanta began in the period under consideration.[111] By the second decade of the twentieth century, the OIA registered the blood quanta of all people living on the reservation, calculating degree of Indian blood to sixteenths.[112] By this time, even the federal courts had delved into the question of what degree of "white blood" an Indian needed to be considered legally a "mixed blood" (*First National Bank of Detroit v. United States*, 1913; *United States v. First National Bank of Detroit*, 1914), and physical anthropologists Arles Hrdlicka and Albert Ernest Jenks had worked out anthropometric methods for determining the "blood status" of hybrid individuals when genealogies were not reliable.[113] The registration of blood quanta was connected to the eventual resolution of "the Indian problem" envisioned—at least officially—by the central office of the OIA in Washington: the elimination of discrete Indian tribes and of the protected legal status of Indian individuals. This involved the eventual division and distribution, or liquidation, of all tribal lands, the division and subtraction of tribal trust funds into pro rata shares, the removal of the trust protections on individual allotments and bank accounts, the termination of special federal services to Indians (such as law and order, education, health care, rations, and federal employment), and the graduation of Indian people into United States citizenship and the extension of state and local jurisdiction over erstwhile reservations. Such was the stated goal of federal Indian policy. The existence of tribes as political and legal entities and of federal trust authority over individual Indian wards was seen as a temporary state that would gradually wither away.[114]

Blood quantum registration was an administrative technique that anticipated, measured, and even facilitated this process. The special significance of racial registration for Indian assimilation becomes clear when contrasted with racialization under the "one drop rule" or "hypodescent" for African Americans.[115] The latter entails rigid social and legal boundaries between discrete and clearly demarcated races. Blood quantum registration, on the other hand, was a matter of a *gradient*; inevitably, it generated the interpenetration of "races"—both conceptually and practically. It was useful to the powerful, not for defending discrete boundaries— although racial privilege can, and did, exist without such boundaries—but rather for blurring racial boundaries. Blood quantum was associated not with the separation of the races, but with assimilation. The Pine Ridge superintendent put it this way in 1922: "It is without question, advisable, in the matter of the bringing the Indians to a reasonable standard of competency, to provide for *an inter-mingling of the races*," facilitated by allowing white settlers to purchase Indian land from which trust status had been removed.[116] "The real progress of the Indian," he pointed out, "lies in his *contact with white neighbors*."[117] Of course, such intermingling would result in intermarriages and sexual contacts and, thus, children with higher degrees of non-Lakota "blood." The OIA agencies maintained statistics on intermarriage during this period, presumably because intermingling was seen as a step toward assimilation.

Degree of blood was both a measure of individual assimilation and an active tactic for reducing the size of tribes and ending trust authority over individuals.[118] There was a general and official assumption within the OIA that competence was correlated with degree of blood. The "full-blood class of Indian, which of course includes the less intelligent Indian," was commonly juxtaposed in OIA discourse with the class of "intelligent Indians, which of course includes the younger gen-eration as well as the mixed-bloods."[119] In 1917 the OIA unilaterally removed trust authority over (fee patented) all Indians of less than one-half Indian blood and declared them U.S. citizens, no longer wards of the government. By this act, their allotments were fully commoditized and made subject to state taxes, and they received "unrestricted control" of monies to their credit in IIM accounts. The commissioner of Indian Affairs declared that the "time has come for discontin-uing guardianship of all competent Indians and giving ever closer attention to the incompetent that they may more speedily achieve competency." This policy meant, according to the commissioner, the "ultimate absorption of the Indian race into the body politic of the Nation. It means, in short, the beginning of the end of the Indian problem."[120] The justification for the criterion of discrimination between who would be turned loose and who would remain a ward was put this way by the commissioner:

> While ethnologically a preponderance of white blood has not heretofore been a criterion of competency, nor even now is it always a safe standard, it is almost an axiom that an Indian who has a larger proportion of white blood than Indian partakes more of the characteristics of the former than of the latter. In thought and action, so far as the business world is concerned, he approximates more closely the white blood ancestry.[121]

In conformity with this policy, 319 fee patents were issued on Rosebud and 463 on Pine Ridge. Most of this land was rapidly lost.[122]

Thus, one's blood quantum had material consequences for the individual and served to differentiate interests—for example, between those of Lakota with land and those of Lakota who lacked it. Furthermore, in the face of extremely limited reservation resources dependent upon federal funding, Lakota people quickly came to recognize that standard of living was directly connected to the number of tribal members competing for resources. The political economy of the reservation has thus fostered an "image of limited good"[123]—through the actual scarcity of limited resources—in which any criterion for expanding or contracting trial enrollment and claims on reservation resources was inescapably politicized. Degree of blood is one such basis for delineating trial enrollment and has been used by the OIA and, since 1936, by the Oglala and Rosebud Sioux tribal governments.[124]

Given both the differentiation of interests between those who were fee patented and those who were not, and the use of blood quantum minima for defining trial enrollment, it is not surprising that Lakota people internalized blood quantum as part of the way they saw themselves in the world or that they perceived full bloods and mixed bloods as being different, even mutually antagonistic, social groups. "Only full bloods shall have the power to participate in all tribal matters being conducted in Council," the Oglala Council resolved in 1926.[125] On the other hand, one Oglala mixed blood explained why a council controlled by full bloods could not complete any business in 1921: "The principal reason for the failure was that the council was composed of too many of the aged full-blooded men, who are very particular that a council should be managed in the old traditional way."[126] In 1930 the "enrolled mixed bloods" on Pine Ridge sought to organize a separate council as a counterpart to the full bloods' Oglala Council.[127] When Lakota on Rosebud executed applications for marriage licenses in Todd and Tripp counties during the late 1920s, they listed their blood quanta under the heading of "nationality."[128] Although they probably did not believe that blood quantum was equivalent to nationality, they obviously saw blood quanta as an essential element of identity—essential enough to require knowledge of one's blood quantum when filling out the application.[129]

The degree to which the blood quantum has persisted as part of a person's internalized individuality among the Lakota is reflected in the remarks of one of my contemporary (1991) Lakota consultants, who happens to have a greater degree of Indian blood than his father:

My dad . . . lives out in Antelope [an Indian community], and I live in [Mission, a mixed Indian-White] town, and he says, "Well, you're just another White boy like the guys in town." "Hey, Dad," I say, "well let's go to the enrollment office and see who's more Indian. You know, I'll show you my [tribal identity] card, and you show me yours." And that kind of settles that.

In the fall of 1992, a Rosebud full blood wrote to the editor of the local paper in opposition to a proposed tribal ordinance to lower the "Sioux blood" quantum required for enrollment:

Here on the Rosebud reservation, we see most of the good-paying jobs going to people with one-quarter blood quantum. The 1/2 and 4/4 Lakotas rarely get the good paying jobs and may have to remain on welfare and other government programs. This is the way it goes. People of only one-quarter blood, many with wasicu [white] values and thinking, are the ones with the good jobs and in positions to govern our Lakota people. But, there are many young, well-educated full bloods here who do not get the opportunities to work with and lead our people. Is this the way it should be? If we, the Sicangu Lakota people, lower the tribe's blood quantum requirement to one-sixteenth, who will be getting the good jobs and be in positions of governing our people in the future? Will these one-sixteenth "Indian" people really be able to understand the thoughts and feelings of our Lakota people? If we began enrolling people of only one-sixteenth blood quantum, what will the other fifteen-sixteenths be, wasicu or some other blood that is not Lakota? Do we want to remain a proud Lakota people, or do we we want to become absorbed into a dominant, different culture and totally lose our identity?[130]

As in the case of property ownership, degrees of blood quickly became a *fact*—in this case based on the "indisputable" evidence of ancestry—that entered into the commonsense ways Lakota individuals thought and think about themselves.

GENEALOGY

Closely connected to the status of the blood quantum in the construction of the new individual was the administrative establishment and recording of an individual's genealogy. Family relationships—which quickly became *nuclear* family relationships listed under a male head and a patronymic family name, whether or not the actual domestic unit looked like this[131]—were recorded in the OIA censuses from 1885. By the turn of the century, it was apparent that registration of genealogy would be necessary in order for the OIA to carry out one of its most important functions, the probating of allotments (or proceeds from the sale of allotments). Estates of allottees were probated according to the laws of the State of South Dakota, and the Interior Department had legal jurisdiction over, and administrative responsibility for, probating estates held in trust. Accurate records of genealogy were essential for determining heirs. Thus, in 1901, the commissioner issued a circular to the agencies, explaining that reliable and permanent records of marriage and family relationships were necessary, and agents were instructed to keep such records.[132] The agencies soon developed a system of family history files to meet this need: on each form were recorded the names and allotment numbers of the husband, wife, their parents, and their children (separate forms were filled out for "additional" wives in the case of polygynous marriages).[133]

Upon the death of an allottee, the agency was responsible for executing a Report on Heirship, based upon a search of the agency records and an official hearing to determine heirs.[134] The report included a complex legal form on which were identified the decedent's spouse(s) and former spouse(s), indicating whether marriage and divorce had been by Indian custom or legal ceremony; children, indicating whether legitimate, illegitimate, or adopted; as well as other lineal and collateral relatives. Testimony from relatives and friends of the decedent was taken under oath, transcribed, and signed by the witnesses.[135] At one heirship hearing on Rosebud in 1918, the widow of the decedent was sworn in and questioned about her grandchildren (who stood to inherit shares in the estate) and deceased son by the examiner through an interpreter:

> *Q.* Is Seth the only child that John . . . ever had?
> *A.* There is another daughter of his living, Lucy. . . .
> *Q.* Who was the mother of Lucy?
> *A.* Ida. . . .
> . . .
> *Q.* Were she and John married?
> *A.* No.
> *Q.* Was Ida a single woman at the time this child was born?
> *A.* Yes.
> *Q.* Did John . . . marry Ida after the child was born?
> *A.* No.

Q. Did he ever in writing or the in presence of witnesses, acknowledge that he was the father of this child, Lucy?

A. John acknowledged that the child was his—he told me that.

Q. Have the other members of your family recognized this Lucy as being John's child?

A. Yes.

Q. Where these the only children that John ever had?

A. Yes.[136]

But in order to record the (putatively) precise genealogy of individual allottees and heirs, the OIA went much further than keeping files and interviewing witnesses under oath. The officials attempted to bring Indian domestic relations into conformity with legal marriage, and they used force to do it. By 1901, because of "general moral laxity" (marriages being "broken off and resumed at will," wives being "thrown away," children being "abandoned," all problems leaning to "uncertainties, disputes, and suits in court over the inheritance" of estates)[137] the OIA issued instructions that marriage licenses would henceforth be issued by the agencies and rations could be withheld from people who refused to obtain licenses.[138] The OIA agency courts established on the reservation in the 1880s also had authority to incarcerate Indian people for misdemeanors, under which illicit relationships were categorized. The Rosebud superintendent reported in 1917 that adultery was "the most serious offense committed by the Indians of this jurisdiction."[139] Throughout the period, cases concerning sexual immorality and domestic arrangements predominated on the dockets of the agency courts on the reservations.[140] In 1935 the Pine Ridge superintendent lamented that "a few weeks in the Agency jail or guardhouse" was all the punishment that his court could mete out in order to enforce legal marriage.[141]

CONCLUSION

In this article I have explored the modes by which particular kinds of individuals were constructed among the Lakota by the discourse and practices of the OIA. These individuals were bound to the state and civil society through various cultural and material means: as property owners, as wards of various degrees of competency, as bearers of blood quanta, and as kin in officially recognized genealogical grids. Because subjection was linked to both negative and positive power, the Lakota people, by necessity, learned to view their own self-interests in terms of these forms of subjectivity and also learned to shape their thoughts and actions in these terms.

My examination of the processes of subjection is not meant to imply that a distinct Lakota culture was erased, nor do I wish to imply that the administrators truly intended to erase native custom during the "civilization" period. Although there was clearly "culture change" during this period—change that entailed both new identities and some "deculturation"—an autonomous Lakota culture survived and even thrived: the language, a rich social and ceremonial life, a native kinship system entailing rights and obligations, and an indigenous form of political process.[142] But the state apparatus and the capitalist social formation could live with this native cultural persistence—as long as the Lakota were subjected to the new definitions of the individual.[143]

The Oglala writer Luther Standing Bear once described the nineteenth-century Lakota people as "self-governors" who were guided by *wouncage*, custom, "our way of doing," a way that "it was hard for a person to get away from."[144] By "civilizing" the Lakota, the OIA made them into a *new kind* of self-governors, with a new way of doing things that would be just as difficult to escape. That is the essence of subjection.

NOTES

1. Michel Foucault, *Discipline and Punish: The Birth of the Prison*, trans. Alan Sheridan (New York: Vintage Books, 1979), 194.
2. Rosebud Agency 1885 Census, Record Group 75, Kansas City, Mo., National Archives.
3. Commissioner of Indian Affairs, *Annual Report, 1886* (Washington, D.C.: Government Printing Office, 1886), 294.
4. Timothy Mitchell, *Colonising Egypt* (Berkeley: University of California Press, 1988), 33.
5. Anthony Giddens, *The Nation-State and Violence* 2: *A Contemporary Critique of Historical Materialism* (Berkeley: University of California Press, 1987), 172–97.
6. The Pine Ridge and Rosebud Reservations were carved out of the Great Sioux Reservation in 1889.
7. Esther Goldfrank, "Historic Change and Social Character: A Study of the Teton Dakota," *American Anthropologist* 45 (1973): 67–83; Goldfrank, *Changing Configurations in the Social Organization of the Blackfoot Tribe during the Reserve Period* (New York: J.J. Augustin, 1945); Oscar Lewis, *The Effects of White Contact upon Blackfoot Culture, with Special Reference to the Role of the Fur Trade* (New York: J.J. Augustin, 1942); Bernard Mishkin, *Rank and Warfare among the Plains Indians* (New York: J.J. Augustin, 1940).
8. On Lakota sociopolitical organization, see Ella Deloria, *Speaking of Indians* (Vermilion, S.D.: State Publishing, 1983 [orig. pub. 1944]), 27–28; Raymond Demallie, "Sioux Ethnohistory: A Methodological Critique," *Journal of Ethnic Studies* 4:3 (1976): 80–82; Demallie, "Pine Ridge Economy: Cultural and Historical Perspectives," in *American Indian Economic Development,* ed. Sam Stanley (The Hague: Mouton, 1978), 240–248; Stephen E. Feraca, *The History and Development of the Oglala Sioux Tribal Government* (Washington, D.C.: Office of Tribal Operations, Bureau of Indian Affairs, 1964); Stephen E. Feraca, "The Political Status of the Early Bands and Modern Communities of the Oglala Dakota," *Museum News* 27 (1966): 1–19; Royal B. Hassrick, "Teton Dakota Kinship System," *American Anthropologist* 46 (1944): 38–47; Hassrick, *The Sioux: Life and Customs of a Warrior Society* (Norman: University of Oklahoma Press, 1964); James H. Howard, "The Teton or Western Dakota," *Museum News* 27 (1966): 3; Alan M. Klein, "The Plains Truth: The Impact of Colonialism on Indian Women," *Dialectical Anthropology* 7:4 (1983): 299–313; Jeannette Mirsky, "The Dakota," in *Cooperation and Competition among Primitive Peoples,* ed. Margaret Mead (Boston: Beacon Press, 1966 [orig. pub. 1937]), 390–392; William K. Powers, *Oglala Religion* (Lincoln: University of Nebraska Press, 1975), 25–42; Ernest L. Schusky, *The Forgotten Sioux: An Ethnohistory of the Lower Brule Reservation* (Chicago: Nelson Hall, 1975), 23–26; Schusky, "The Evolution of Indian Leadership on the Great Plains," *American Indian Quarterly* 10:1 (1986): 65–82; Luther Standing Bear, *Land of the Spotted Eagle* (New York and Boston: Houghton Mifflin, 1933), 12–147; James R. Walker, "Oglala Kinship Terms," *American Anthropologist* 16 (1914): 96–109; J. Walker, *Lakota Society,* ed. Raymond Demallie (Lincoln: University of Nebraska Press, 1982); and Clark Wissler, "Societies and Ceremonial Divisions in the Oglala Division of the Teton Dakota," *Anthropological Papers* (American Museum of Natural History) 11:1 (1912): 7–11.

9. Eric R. Wolf, *Europe and the People Without History* (Berkeley: University of California Press, 1982).

10. For an analysis of "individuals" among the similar Blackfeet, see David Nugent, "Property Relations, Production Relations, and Inequality: Anthropology, Political Economy, and the Blackfeet," *American Ethnologist* 20:2 (1993): 336–62.

11. See Frederick E. Hoxie, *A Final Promise: The Campaign to Assimilate the Indians, 1880–1920* (Lincoln: University of Nebraska Press, 1984); Janet A. McDonnell, *The Dispossession of the American Indian, 1887–1934* (Bloomington: Indiana University Press, 1991); D.S. Otis, *The Dawes Act and the Allotment of Indian Lands,* ed. Francis Prucha (Norman: University of Oklahoma Press, 1973).

12. On Indian police and courts, see William T. Hagan, *Indian Police and Judges: Experiments in Acculturation and Control* (New Haven: Yale University Press, 1966). On Indian schools, see Alice Littlefield, "The B.I.A. Boarding School: Theories of Resistance and Social Reproduction," *Humanity and Society* 13 (1989): 428–441; Alice Littlefield, "Learning to Labor: Native American Education in the United States, 1880–1930," in *The Political Economy of North American Indians,* ed. John H. Moore (Norman: University of Oklahoma Press, 1993), 43–59; K. Tsianina Lomawaima, "Domesticity in Federal Indian Schools: The Power of Authority over Mind and Body," *American Ethnologist* 20:2 (1993): 227–240; Lowawaima, *They Called It Prairie Light: The Story of the Chilocco Indian School* (Lincoln: University of Nebraska Press, 1994); Sally McBeth, *Ethnic Identity and the Boarding School Experience of West-Central Oklahoma Indians* (Washington, D.C.: University Press of America, 1983); Robert A. Trennert, *The Phoenix Indian School: Forced Assimilation in Arizona, 1891–1935* (Norman: University of Oklahoma Press, 1988).

13. Foucault, "The Subject and Power," in *Michel Foucault: Beyond Structuralism and Hermeneutics,* ed. Hubert L. Dreyfus and Paul Rabinow (Chicago: University of Chicago Press, 1983), 208–226; Philip Corrigan and Derek Sayer, "How the Law Rules: Variations on Some Themes in Karl Marx," in *Law, State, and Society,* Bob Fryer et al., eds. (London: Croom Helm, 1981), 21–53.

14. Foucault, *Discipline and Punish*; Foucault, *The History of Sexuality,* trans. Robert Hurley (New York: Vintage Books, 1980).

15. Foucault, "The Subject and Power," 215.

16. Erving Goffman, *Asylums: Essays on the Social Situation of Mental Patients and Other Inmates* (Garden City, NY: Doubleday, 1961); David J. Rothman, *The Discovery of the Asylum: Social Order and Disorder in the New Republic.* Rev. ed. (Boston: Little, Brown, 1990).

17. The absence of gender making in this analysis of the modes of subjection is not an inadvertent omission. Obviously, gender was and is a part of one's fundamental social being for Native Americans in the context of the reservation. In this context, however, gender was constituted at levels of social activity very different from those under examination here—namely, in a new reservation economy based on OIA-issued rations, intermittent male wage work, and male petty commodity production; in subtle (and not-so-subtle) biases in the daily activities of OIA officials; in the disciplines and curricula of the government and religious schools; in the tutelage of OIA "field matrons" who instructed women in domestic science while their husbands received instruction from OIA extension agents in farming (see Board of Indian Commissioners, *Twenty-Fourth Annual Report* [Washington, D.C.: Government Printing Office, 1892], 60–62; *Twenty-Seventh Annual Report* [Washington, D.C.: Government Printing Office, 1895], 100–102, and *Fifty-Sixth Annual Report* [Washington, D.C.: Government Printing Office, 1925], 10–11; Commissioner of Indian Affairs, *Annual Report, 1893* [Washington, D.C. Government Printing Office, 1893], 54–57; Lewis Meriam, *The Problem of Indian Administration* [New York: Johnson Reprint Corporation, 1971 (1928)], 591–598; and in the teaching of Protestant and Jesuit missionaries (for analyses of gender differentiation among the Lakota and other plains peoples, see Patricia Albers and Beatrice Medicine, eds., *The Hidden Half: Studies of Plains Indian Women* [Washington, D.C.: University Press of America, 1983]; Klein, "Plains Economic Analysis: The Marxist Complement" in *Anthropology on the Great Plains,* ed. Raymond Wood and Margot Liberty [Lincoln: University of Nebraska Press, 1980], 129–140; Klein, "The Plains Truth"; Marla Powers, *Oglala Women: Myth, Ritual, and Reality* [Chicago: University of Chicago Press, 1986]; see also Lomawaima, "Domesticity in Federal Indian Schools"; Meriam, *The Problem of Indian Administration*; and Trennert, "Victorian Morality and the Supervision of Indian Women Working

in Phoenix, 1906–1930," *The Journal of Social History* 22:1 (1988): 113–128, on the construction of gender in OIA policy).

Subjection through the administrative tactics described in this article was not the *only kind* of domination faced by the Lakota people; in addition to subjection, they faced a "conjugated oppression" (see Philippe Bourgois, "Conjugated Oppression: Class and Ethnicity among the Guyami and Kuna Banana Workers," *American Ethnologist* 15:2 [1988]: 328–348) that included gender, racial, and class domination, each with its own logic (see Stanley Aronowitz, *The Crisis in Historical Materialism: Class, Politics and Culture in Marxist Theory*, 2nd edition [Minneapolis: University of Minnesota Press, 1990], 73–112; Foucault, "The Subject and Power"; Michael Omi and Howard Winant, *Racial Formation in the United States: From the 1960s to the 1980s* [New York: Routledge, 1986]; Cornel West, "Marxist Theory and the Specificity of Afro-American Oppression," in *Marxism and the Interpretation of Culture*, eds. Cary Nelson and Lawrence Grossberg [Urbana: University of Illinois Press, 1988]). This does not by any means suggest that these different sites of oppression were irreducible structures, or that they cannot be grasped with a single, "unified theory" (A. Belden Fields, "In Defense of Political Economy and Systemic Analysis: A Critique of Prevailing Theoretical Approaches to the New Social Movements," in *Marxism and the Interpretation of Culture*; Karen Sacks, "Review Article: Toward a Unified Theory of Class, Race, and Gender," *American Ethnologist* 16:3 [1989], 534–540; Iris Young, "Beyond the Unhappy Marriage: a Critique of Dual Systems Theory," in *Women and Revolution: A Discussion of the Unhappy Marriage of Marxism and Feminism*, ed. Lydia Sargent [Boston: South End Press, 1981], 43–69). It is unnecessary to adopt a "post-Marxist" stance to understand the domination of the Lakota. The analytic isolation of the modes of subjection from the other forms of domination that I create in this article is only for the purpose of highlighting this previously unrecognized form of domination in the history of Native Americans.

18. Commissioner of Indian Affairs, *Annual Report, 1881* (Washington, D.C.: Government Printing Office, 1881), 17.

19. Hagan, "The Reservation Policy: Too Little and Too Late," in *Indian-White Relations: A Persistent Paradox*, ed. Jane F. Smith and Robert M. Kvasnicka (Washington, D.C.: Howard University Press, 1976), 157–169; Hoxie, *A Final Promise*; McDonnell, *The Dispossession of the American Indian*; Otis, *The Dawes Act and the Allotment of Indian Lands*.

20. Robert F. Berkhofer, Jr., *The White Man's Indian: Images of the American Indian from Columbus to the Present* (New York: Vintage Books, 1978), 172; see also Meriam, *The Problem of Indian Administration*, 7.

21. United States Senate, *Report and Proceedings of the Sioux Commission*, Senate Document 51, Serial 2682, 1890, 106.

22. United States Congress, *United States Statutes at Large, 1899*, 890.

23. Widows, "subsequent" wives in polygynous marriages, and Indian women married to white men were considered heads of families for allotment purposes.

24. United States Congress, *United States Statutes at Large, 1899*, 890. The law was later modified to grant women full allotments on Pine Ridge Reservation and to grant each married woman half of her husband's allotment on Rosebud (U.S. Congress, *U.S. Statutes at Large, 1899*, 1365, U.S. Congress, *U.S. Statutes at Large, 1907*, 1049).

25. Special Alotting Agent, Letter to Commissioner dated February 13, 1911. Allotment Folder No. 1646. Mission, S.D.: Rosebud Agency.

26. U.S. Congress, *U.S. Statutes at Large, 1889*, 895. Many adults quickly chose allotments for themselves in order to receive goods and cash, but were less diligent about selecting allotments for their children because only adults received Sioux benefits. Land, in other words, was clearly not the motivation prompting Lakota people to seek allotments. See Allotting Agent, letter to Commissioner, dated November 7, 1900. File 147, Rosebud. Special Cases. Record Group 75. Washington, D.C.: National Archives.

27. Allotting Agent, letter to Commissioner dated October 1, 1905. File 147, Rosebud. Special Cases. Record Group 75. Washington, D.C.: National Archives.

28. Allotting Agent, letter to Commissioner dated May 22, 1902. File 147, Rosebud. Special Cases. Record Group 75. Washington, D.C.: National Archives.

29. Allotting Agent, letter to Commissioner dated July 22, 1901. File 147, Rosebud. Special Cases. Record Group 75. Washington, D.C.: National Archives.

30. Allotting Agent, letter to Commissioner dated March 1, 1903. File 147, Rosebud. Special Cases. Record Group 75. Washington, D.C.: National Archives.

31. Pine Ridge Agent, letter to Commissioner dated March 28, 1907. File 48952–1909–054, Pine Ridge. Central Classified Files. Record Group 75. Washington, D.C.: National Archives.

32. Allotting Agent, letter to Commissioner dated May 22, 1902.

33. Herbert Schell, *History of South Dakota,* 3rd edition (Lincoln: University of Nebraska Press, 1975), 254.

34. Allotting Agent, letter to Commissioner dated October 1, 1905.

35. James McLaughlin, letter to Secretary of the Interior dated August 31, 1903. Major James McLaughlin Papers. Richardson, N.D.: Assumption Abbey Archives. Microfilm.

36. Joseph G. Jorgensen, "Indians and the Metropolis," in *The American Indian in Urban Society,* ed. Jack O. Waddell and O. Michael Watson (Boston: Little, Brown, 1971), 67–113; Jorgensen, *The Sundance Religion: Power for the Powerless* (Chicago: University of Chicago Press, 1972); Jorgensen, "A Century of Political Economic Effects on American Indian Society," *Journal of Ethnic Studies* 6:3 (1978): 1–82.

37. Commissioner of Indian Affairs, *Annual Report, 1897* (Washington, D.C.: Government Printing Office, 1897), 275.

38. See Biolsi, *Organizing the Lakota: The Political Economy of the New Deal on Pine Ridge and Rosebud Reservations* (Tucson: University of Arizona Press, 1992), 170.

39. United States Senate, *Survey of the Conditions of the Indians of the United States,* Hearings before a subcommittee of the Committee on Indian Affairs, 1940, 21462–63.

40. Biolsi, *Organizing the Lakota,* 151–171.

41. Eight Reservations Treaty and Claims Council, "Resolutions," April 6, 1940. South Dakota File, Box 126, Records of the Investigating Subcommittee of the Senate Indian Committee. Record Group 46. Washington, D.C.: National Archives. In this resolution, the Treaty Council was motivated by concern with the possible OIA infringement upon their property rights. Indeed, during the New Deal period, certain Department of the Interior functionaries were prepared to sacrifice the vested private property rights of individual Indian allottees for their social engineering project. In 1933, for example, the assistant solicitors in the Department of the Interior drafted a confidential memo on proposed legislation that would eventually become the Indian Reorganization Act of 1934. The memo, which concerned the unequal land holdings among individuals on the reservations, read, in part: "Plainly, such inequality must be eliminated as quickly as possible, if every member of the [tribal] community is to be granted some opportunity to wrest a livelihood from the limited resources of the community." This could be accomplished through a non-stock membership corporation "from which members of the community will be entitled to receive a *fair* share of community income and the use of a *fair* share of the community assets." This plan was not to have been included in the bill because the memo concluded that "[t]o state these objectives in statutory terms is perhaps politically inadvisable" (Assistant Solicitors, Memo to Commissioner dated December 29, 1933, File 3395–1934–066, General Service, Central Classified Files, Record Group 75, Washington, D.C.: National Archives; emphasis added). Indeed it would have scandalized not only Congress but also the Lakota.

42. Quoted in William T. Hagan, "Property, the Indian's Door to Civilization," *Ethnohistory* 3:2 (1956): 131.

43. E. P. Thompson, "Time, Work, and Discipline in Industrial Capitalism," *Past and Present* 38 (1967): 56–97.

44. See Philip Corrigan and Derek Sayer, "How the Law Rules"; Peter Gabel, "The Phenomenology of Rights-Consciousness and the Pact of the Withdrawn Selves," *Texas Law Review* 62 (1984): 1563–1599; Karl Marx, "On the Jewish Question," in *Karl Marx: Early Writings,* trans. Rodney Livingstone and Gregor Benton (New York: Vintage Books, 1975), 211–241.

45. Benedict Anderson, *Imagined Communities: Reflections on the Origins and Spread of Nationalism* (New York: Verso, 1983), 15.

46. Bertell Ollman, *Alienation,* 2nd edition (Cambridge: Cambridge University Press, 1976). This kind

of imagined community corresponds to what Sartre (Jean-Paul Sartre, *Critique of Dialectical Reason,* trans. Alan Sheridan Smith [London: Verso, 1976]) called a "collective," as distinguished from a "group."

47. John Locke, *Second Treatise of Government,* ed. C.B. Macpherson (Indianapolis: Hackett, 1980), 65–68. Locke's error was not in arguing that the propertied have an interest in the state apparatus— Marx was in agreement with this generalization—but in assuming that property *preceded* the state in history. As Marx clearly saw, however, the state was already there and deeply involved in "primitive accumulation" (Karl Marx, *Capital,* trans. Ben Fowkes [New York: Vintage Books, 1977]).

48. E. P. Thompson, *Whigs and Hunters: The Origin of the Black Act* (New York: Pantheon, 1975), 264.

49. "The state" is an extremely complex, multilayered phenomenon. If we are to bring the state back in to our analysis (Evans et al., *Bringing the State Back In* [Cambridge, Eng.: Cambridge University Press, 1985], we need to avoid hypostatizing, conflating, essentializing, and turning the state into a black box (see Nugent, "Building the State, Making the Nation: The Bases and Limits of State Centralization in 'Modern' Peru," *American Anthropologist* 96:2 [1994]: 336–362). For example, it is clear that some manifestations of "the state" may be oppressive from the standpoint of the particular constituency resisting them, while other manifestations may be empowering and actively welcomed by the same constituency. This is no less true of the Lakota than it is of black civil rights activists in the South who found some utility in the courts, Congress, and even the FBI, or of middle-class whites who derive a wide variety of benefits from the government.

50. Commissioner on Indian Affairs, *Annual Report, 1896* (Washington, D.C.: Government Printing Office, 1896), 291.

51. Farmers were agency officials who lived and maintained subagency offices in the reservation districts.

52. Rosebud Superintendent, Letter to District Farmers dated December 9, 1922. Letters to Farmers File, Box A-402. Rosebud Agency Records, Record Group 75. Kansas City, Mo.: National Archives.

53. Haviland Scudder Mekeel, *The Economy of a Modern Teton Dakota Community* (New Haven: Yale University Press, Yale University Publications in Anthropology No. 6, 1936), 11.

54. Thompson, *Whigs and Hunters,* 264.

55. OIA Judges, Letter to Defendant dated April 4, 1907. Civil Cases, 1907 File, Box 217, Pine Ridge Agency Records, Record Group 75, Kansas City, Mo.: National Archives.

56. Pine Ridge Agency, Civil Case. Civil Cases, 1907 File, File 173, Box 217, Pine Ridge Agency Records, Record Group 75, Kansas City, Mo.: National Archives; Pine Ridge Agency, Civil Case. Civil Cases, 1907 File, Box 217, Pine Ridge Agency Records, Record Group 75, Kansas City, Mo.: National Archives.

57. Ronald Takaki, *Iron Cages: Race and Culture in 19th Century America* (Seattle: University of Washington Press).

58. For legal analyses, see Nancy Carol Carter, "Race and Power Politics as Aspects of Federal Guardianship over American Indians: Land-Related Cases, 1887–1924," *American Indian Law Review* 4:2 (1977): 197–248; Felix Cohen, *Handbook of Federal Indian Law* (Washington, D.C.: Government Printing Office, 1942), 167–173.

59. Meriam, *The Problem of Indian Administration,* 101.

60. Pine Ridge Superintendent, *Annual Report, 1922,* Superintendents' Annual Statistical and Narrative Reports (Washington, D.C.: National Archives), microfilm.

61. Rosebud Superintendent, *Annual Report, 1916,* Superintendents' Annual Statistical and Narrative Reports (Washington, D.C.: National Archives), microfilm.

62. Pine Ridge Superintendent, *Annual Report, 1922.*

63. Commissioner of Indian Affairs, *Annual Report, 1881* (Washington, D.C.: Government Printing Office, 1881), 110.

64. Rosebud Superintendent, *Annual Report, 1931,* Superintendents' Annual Statistical and Narrative Reports (Washington, D.C.: National Archives), microfilm.

65. The introduction of "racial characteristics" into the discourse should not be at all surprising given the popular appropriation of "scientific" racism during the period (see Thomas F. Gossett, *Race: The History of an Idea in America* [New York: Schocken Books, 1965]; Audrey Smedley, *Race in North*

America: Origin and Evolution of a Worldview [Boulder, Co.: Westview Press, 1993]). It was at about the same time that an OIA consultant was "scientifically" ascertaining the "blood quanta" of Lumbee individuals—for the purpose of federal recognition as Indians—on the basis of anthropometric measurements (Gerald Sider, *Lumbee Indian Histories: Race, Ethnicity, and Indian Identity in the Southern United States* [New York: Cambridge University Press, 1993], 136–137; see also David L. Beaulieu, "Curly Hair and Big Feet: Physical Anthropology and the Implementation of Land Allotment on the White Earth Chippewa Reservation," *American Indian Quarterly* 8 [1984]: 281–314).

66. Meriam, *The Problem of Indian Administration*, 101.

67. Commissioner of Indian Affairs, *Annual Report, 1894*, 288.

68. Rosebud Superintendent, *Annual Report, 1933*. The moralizing tone of much of the colonial discourse on American Indians is noteworthy. It is, in fact, a perennial pattern in the representation of Indian people by non-Indians (see Berkhofer, *White Man's Indian*, 26), and it is no historical accident, at least as far as the OIA is concerned. Although there were impersonal, deterministic theories about why Indians behaved as they did—because they were savages, because of their race—day-to-day control on the reservations required that individuals be given *moral, voluntaristic responsibility* for their actions. As Erving Goffman points out, pragmatic control in "total institutions"—and the reservation was not far from a total institution—requires that "both desired and undesired conduct . . . be defined as springing from the personal will and character of the individual inmate himself, and defined as something he can do something about. In short, each institutional perspective contains a personal morality" (Goffman, *Asylums*, 86). Thus, Lakota individuals who did not measure up were not so much "a product of their environment" or "racially inferior" as they were, in the final analysis, "shiftless, lazy and irresponsible."

69. Some OIA officials clearly did not see the problem as a *racial* one, but rather a matter of "habitus" (Pierre Bourdieu, *Outline of a Theory of Practice*, trans. Richard Nice [Cambridge: Cambridge University Press, 1977], 72). It was a common, official belief that progress would be made as the older generation, which had lived in the buffalo days, passed away, and was replaced by the younger generation, which had grown up on the reservation and had been educated in OIA or mission schools (Commissioner of Indian Affairs, *Annual Report, 1897*, 270; Pine Ridge Superintendent, *Annual Report, 1915*; see also Meriam, *The Problem of Indian Administration*, 102).

70. Richard V. Mackay, *Guardianship Law: The Law of Guardian and Ward Simplified* (New York: Oceana Publications), 52–3; J.G. Woerner, *A Treatise on the American Law of Guardianship of Minors and Persons of Unsound Mind* (Boston: Little, Brown, and Company, 1897), 379.

71. Biolsi, *Organizing the Lakota*, 16–17.

72. Biolsi, *Organizing the Lakota*, 11–15.

73. Pine Ridge Superintendent, Letter to the Commissioner dated September 13, 1921, File 062, Main Decimal File, Pine Ridge Agency Records, Record Group 75. Kansas City, Mo.: National Archives.

74. Commissioner of Indian Affairs, *Annual Report, 1899*, 1591.

75. Pine Ridge Superintendent, *Annual Report, 1923*.

76. Office of Indian Affairs, Circular 2725, Procedural Issuances: Orders and Circulars, Washington, D.C.: National Archives, microfilm, 1930.

77. Office of Indian Affairs, Circular, March 17, Reports of Industrial Surveys, Rosebud, Record Group 75, Washington D.C.: National Archives, 1923.

78. Rosebud Agency, Reports of Industrial Surveys, Record Group 75, Washington, D.C.: National Archives, 1923.

79. Rosebud Agency, Reports of Industrial Surveys, 1923.

80. Rosebud Agency, Reports of Industrial Surveys, 1923.

81. Pine Ridge Agency, Reports of Industrial Surveys, Record Group 75, Washington, D.C.: National Archives, 1924.

82. Pine Ridge Agency, Reports of Industrial Surveys, 1924.

83. Rosebud Agency, Reports of Industrial Surveys, 1923.

84. Pine Ridge Agency, Reports of Industrial Surveys, 1924.

85. Pine Ridge Agency, Reports of Industrial Surveys, 1924.

86. Rosebud Agency, Reports of Industrial Surveys, 1923.

87. Rosebud Agency, Reports of Industrial Surveys, 1923.

88. Pine Ridge Agency, Reports of Industrial Surveys, 1924.

89. Pine Ridge Agency, Reports of Industrial Surveys, 1924.

90. Pine Ridge Superintendent, *Annual Report, 1927*. The fact that the man was a full-blood and 52 years of age was mentioned by the superintendent, probably because he hoped to convey to his wards that *even older full-bloods* were capable of productive labor and self-support.

91. "Good Indian Housekeepers," *Todd County Tribune* 23 June 1921: 1. South Dakota State Historical Society, microfilm. Clearly, "competence" was gendered.

92. Corrigan and Sayer, *The Great Arch: English State Formation as Cultural Revolution* (Oxford: Basil Blackwell, 1985), 196.

93. James McLaughlin, "Proceedings of a Meeting Held at Rosebud Agency, December 15, 1906," Major James McLaughlin Papers, Richardton, N.D.: Assumption Abbey Archives, microfilm.

94. James McLaughlin, Letter to Correspondent, dated July 31, 1920, Major James McLaughlin Papers.

95. The Burke Act in 1906 authorized fee patenting for allottees deemed competent by the Secretary of the Interior was enabled by (U.S. Congress, *United States Statutes at Large, 1906*, 182).

96. The federal courts held, however, that citizenship was not necessarily inconsistent with wardship: an Indian could still be considered incompetent and supervised by the OIA if Congress so chose (*United States v. Nice*, 1916; *United States v. Sherburne Mercantile*, 1933).

97. Attorney General of South Dakota, *Biannual Report, 1939–1940* (Pierre: State of South Dakota, 1939–40), 212; *Louie v. United States*, 1921; *State v. Big Sheep*, 1926; *State v. Monroe*, 1929.

98. Pine Ridge Competency Commission, Reports, 1920, Major James McLaughlin Papers.

99. This concern with "appearance" was no doubt generated by the question of how individual Indians would fare in a wider society in which racist stereotypes of Indians and other people of color abounded. I know of at least one case in which a Lakota man who left the reservation in the 1920s to attend South Dakota State College in Brookings changed his name from an English translation of a Lakota name (such as "Crazy Horse") to a "white" name—and apparently tried to "pass" as a white man.

100. All quotations from Pine Ridge Competency Commission Reports, 1920, Major James McLaughlin Papers.

101. James McLaughlin, Letter to the Secretary of the Interior dated September 11, 1920, Major James McLaughlin Papers.

102. Pine Ridge Superintendent, *Annual Report, 1920*.

103. Office of Indian Affairs, Circular 2553, Procedural Issuances: Orders and Circulars, Washington, D.C.: National Archives, microfilm, 1929.

104. Department of Indian Studies, University of South Dakota, *A Report on the Bureau of Indian Affairs Fee Patenting and Canceling Policies, 1900–1942* (Aberdeen, S.D.: Bureau of Indian Affairs, 1981).

105. Meriam, *The Problem of Indian Administration*, 100–105; Laurence F. Schmeckebier, *The Office of Indian Affairs: Its History, Activities and Organization* (New York: AMS Press, 1972[1927]), 148–165. It is more reasonable to assume that individuals who "squandered" their resources from the point of view of the OIA were, in fact, behaving "rationally" in the context of the political economy of the reservation. "Investing" resources in commercial production made little sense for most Lakota families, while "giving away" surpluses reproduced kinship and friendship ties and buffered families against the extremely unpredictable economic times.

106. One of Foucault's main arguments is that "discursive formations" exist more to ensure the power of some over others than to get closer to an absolute truth (on self-referentiality, see also Mark Poster, *The Mode of Information: Poststructuralism and Social Context* [Chicago: University of Chicago Press, 1990]).

107. James Scott, *Weapons of the Weak: Everyday Forms of Peasant Resistance* (New Haven: Yale University Press, 1985); Scott, *Domination and the Arts of Resistance: Hidden Transcripts* (New Haven: Yale University Press, 1990).

108. Biolsi, "The Political Economy of Lakota Consciousness," in John H. Moore, ed., *The Political Economy of North American Indians*.

109. James McLaughlin, Proceedings of a Council Held at Pine Ridge Agency, September 1, 1909, Major James McLaughlin Papers.

110. He was concerned that the more Indian people are perceived as sovereign nations, the less they are perceived as wards of the government, and greater will be the threat of "termination"—the loss of the protected legal status of, and federal fiscal support for, Indian people and their communities.

111. On blood quantum among the Lakota, see Robert E. Daniels, "Cultural Identities among the Oglala Sioux," in Ethel Nurge, ed., *The Modern Sioux: Social Systems and Reservation Culture* (Lincoln: University of Nebraska Press, 1970), 198–245; Gordon Macgregor, *Warriors Without Weapons: A Study of the Society and Personality Development of the Pine Ridge Sioux* (Chicago: University of Chicago Press, 1946), 25; Marla Powers, *Oglala Women,* 144; William Powers, *Oglala Religion,* 117–119; Ruth Hill Useem, *The Aftermath of Defeat: A Study of Acculturation among the Rosebud Sioux,* Ph.D. dissertation, University of Wisconsin, 1947; Murrary Wax, *American Indians: Unity and Diversity* (Englewood Cliffs, N.J.: Prentice-Hall, 1971), 75–77; Wax et al., "Formal Education in an American Indian Community," *Social Problems* 11:4 (1975, supplement): 29–41. For a nonscholarly treatment, see Iktomi, *America Needs Indians* (Denver: Bradford-Robinson, 1937). For examples from other tribes, see Beaulieu, "Curly Hair and Big Feet," and Deward Walker, "Measures of Nez Perce Outbreeding and the Analysis of Culture Change," *Southwestern Journal of Anthropology* 23 (1967): 141–158.

112. Calculation of degree of blood was already well established in the antebellum South for the determination of the legal boundary between the white and negro races. See John Codman Hurd, *The Law of Freedom and Bondage in the United States* (New York: Negro University Press, 1968), vol. 2: 4, 19, 86, 340; Gilbert T. Stephenson, *Race Distinctions in American Law* (New York: AMS Press, 1969[1910]), 12–25.

113. Beaulieu, "Curly Hair and Big Feet"; Albert Ernest Jenks, *Indian-White Amalgamation: An Anthropometric Study* (Minneapolis: Bulletin of the University of Minnesota, Studies in the Social Sciences No. 6, 1916).

114. Of course, OIA officials may not have actively wished to bring about their obsolescence, but this was the stated long-term goal of federal Indian policy.

115. See F. James Davis, *Who Is Black? One Nation's Definition* (University Park: Pennsylvania State University Press, 1991); Virginia Dominguez, *White by Definition: Social Classification in Creole Louisiana* (New Brunswick, N.J.: Rutgers University Press, 1986); Marvin Harris, *Patterns of Race in the Americas* (New York: W.W. Norton, 1964); Winthrop Jordan, *White over Black: American Attitudes Toward the Negro, 1550–1812* (New York: Penguin Books, 1969); Smedley, *Race in North America*; Takaki, *Iron Cages*.

116. Pine Ridge Superintendent, *Annual Report, 1922,* emphasis added.

117. Pine Ridge Superintendent, *Annual Report, 1932,* emphasis added.

118. M. Annette Jaimes, "Federal Indian Identification Policy: A Usurpation of Indigenous Sovereignty in North America," in Jaimes, ed., *The State of Native America: Genocide, Colonization, and Resistance* (Boston: South End Press, 1992), 123–138; Patricia Nelson Limerick, *The Legacy of Conquest: The Unbroken Past of the American West* (New York: W.W. Norton, 1988), 338; Lenore A. Stiffarm and Phil Lane, Jr., "The Demography of Native North America: A Question of American Indian Survival," in Jaimes, ed., *The State of Native America,* 23–53.

119. Pine Ridge Superintendent, Letter to Commissioner dated September 13, 1921.

120. All quotations from the commissioner of Indian Affairs, "Declaration of Policy," April 17, 1917, Ordinances and Resolutions, Rosebud Agency Records, Record Group 75, Kansas City, Mo.: National Archives. It also meant substantial reduction of federal expenditures for the administration of Indian allotments, an increase in property tax revenues, and the flow of Indian lands into the control of non-Indian farmers and ranchers as restrictions on leasing and sale of land disappeared.

121. Commissioner of Indian Affairs, *Annual Report, 1917,* 3.

122. Department of Indian Studies, University of South Dakota, "A Report on the Bureau of Indian Affairs Fee Patenting and Canceling Policies."

123. George M. Foster, *Tzintzuntzan: Mexican Peasants in a Changing World* (Boston: Little, Brown, 1967), 123.

124. Oglala Sioux Tribe, Constitution and By-Laws, article 2 (Pine Ridge: Oglala Sioux Tribal Office, n.d.). For a Flathead example, see Ronald L. Trosper, "Native American Boundary Maintenance; The Flathead Indian Reservation, Montana, 1860–1970," *Ethnicity* 3 (1976): 256–274.

125. Oglala Council, Proceedings, January 21–23, 1926, File 064, Main Decimal File, Pine Ridge Agency Records, Record Group 75, Kansas City, Mo.: National Archives.

126. Lakota Correspondent, Letter to Commissioner dated September 2, 1921, File 062, Main Decimal File, Pine Ridge Agency Records, Record Group 75, Kansas City, Mo.: National Archives. Lakota individuals who authored documents referenced in this article are not identified by name but are instead listed in the references as "Lakota Correspondents" in order to protect the privacy of Lakota families.

127. Lakota Correspondent, Letter to Superintendent dated May 29, 1930, File 1131–1924–054, Pt. 1, Pine Ridge, Central Classified Files, Record Group 75, Washington, D.C.: National Archives.

128. Todd and Tripp Counties, Marriage Record (Winner, S.D.: Tripp County Court House, n.d.).

129. It is not possible to know whether they were prompted to do this by the clerk in the county courthouse, or if they volunteered their blood quanta.

130. *Todd County Tribune*, 18 November 1992, "Letter to the Editor," 4. This is an old and recurrent discourse on Lakota reservations (see Biolsi, *Organizing the Lakota*, 151–171).

131. See Nancy Shoemaker, "The Census as Civilizer: American Indian Household Structure in the 1900 and 1910 U.S. Censuses," *Historical Methods* 25:1 (1992): 4–11.

132. Office of Indian Affairs, Circular, April 5, 1901, Procedural Issuances: Orders and Circulars, 1854–1955, Washington, D.C.: National Archives, microfilm.

133. Office of Indian Affairs, n.d. Family History Forms, Allotment Folders, Mission, S.D.: Rosebud Agency.

134. This procedure was devised by the Secretary of the Interior under legislative authorization enacted in 1906 and 1910 (U.S. Congress, *United States Statutes at Large, 1906*, 182; U.S. Congress, *United States Statues at Large, 1910*, 855).

135. Office of Indian Affairs, n.d. Report on Heirship Forms, Allotment Folders, Mission, S.D.: Rosebud Agency.

136. Rosebud Agency, Report on Heirship, 1919, Allotment Folder No. 1646, Mission, S.D.: Rosebud Agency.

137. Commissioner of Indian Affairs, *Annual Report, 1901*, 42.

138. Office of Indian Affairs, Circular, April 5, 1901. Regulation of Lakota domestic relations had actually begun much earlier and was probably associated with the official intent to establish paternity in order to assign responsibility for child support. In 1883, the agent at Pine Ridge reported that he had built a guardhouse for incarcerating any Oglala in his charge who might require disciplinary action. Apparently, (sexual) "immorality" was the crime with which he was most concerned. He punished "immorality of any kind," and he boasted to the commissioner that he was not only the first agent to confine errant Oglala to the agency guardhouse but was also the first to correct their immoral acts. The Lakota marriage tie, it seems, was "very loose," and did not entail a license or solemnization by clerical or civil authorities. During his campaign against Indian immorality, he was told by the Oglala that fluid conjugal arrangements were "Indian custom with which [he] had no right to interfere," but he pledged to continue to "interfere" and "correct" the situation (Commissioner of Indian Affairs, *Annual Report, 1883*, 99). He reported that he had trouble finding Oglalas to sit as judges in the court of Indian offenses at the agency, because "from [an] Indian stand point [*sic*] the offenses set forth, and for which punishment is provided, are no offenses at all, and I doubt if one could be found willing to punish another for the offenses" (Commission of Indian Affairs, *Annual Report, 1883*, 100).

139. Rosebud Superintendent, Letter to Commissioner dated January 25, 1917, File 2043–1917–155, Rosebud, Central Classified Files, Record Group 75, Washington, D.C.: National Archives.

140. Biolsi, *Organizing the Lakota*, 10–12.

141. Pine Ridge Superintendent, *Annual Report, 1935*. The Supreme Court had held (*United States v. Quiver* 1916) that the federal courts did *not* have jurisdiction to try an Indian for adultery; domestic relations were *tribal* matters subject to *tribal* jurisdiction. The administrative procedures of OIA agency courts, however, were not legally the same as the jurisdiction of the federal courts, and there was no procedure to review agency court decisions, except by the local superintendent (Commissioner of Indian Affairs, *Annual Report, 1888*, 29, *Annual Report, 1892*, 27; Meriam, *The Problem of Indian Administration*, 17; Office of Indian Affairs, "Regulations of the Indian Office," Washington D.C., 1904, 101–105; see also Hagan, *Indian Police and Judges*). It is not clear what

the Supreme Court would have decided regarding the jurisdiction of OIA courts over domestic relations, had that question been entertained.

142. This "traditional" Lakota culture was not necessarily inherited from a primordial past, or even from the more recent buffalo days. Much of the Lakota culture was produced and reproduced by the reservation situation itself.

143. The federal government experienced consistent problems with this autonomous Lakota culture because Lakota "traditionalism" has been the source of recurrent resistance to domination—from the time of the Ghost Dance in 1890 to the occupation of Wounded Knee in 1973. Neither the state apparatus nor the capitalist system is, nor can be, omnipotent. Each, instead, generates its own peculiar contradictions.

144. Standing Bear, *Land of the Spotted Eagle*, 124.

III

GENDER AND CULTURE CHANGE

The historian Kathleen M. Brown, pondering relations between Natives and new-comers in early Virginia, has concluded that besides the various frontiers customarily studied—military, economic, diplomatic, and so on—scholars must add another, a "gender frontier," for gender, she argues, was a crucial variable in the equation of encounter. Earlier chapters on the Navajos, which discussed women as prostitutes and as traders, confirm Brown's insight. This section follows that line of thinking more closely, tracing the role of gender in relations between Indian communities and the United States during the late nineteenth and early twentieth centuries. Samples of a fascinating and rapidly growing field of scholarship, these four essays show how the desire to alter Indian gender categories fueled a number of the government's "civilization" programs. They also demonstrate that gender roles became yet another battleground between Indians and whites. Finally, the chapters underscore the fluidity of gender concepts in both the Native and non-Native worlds, as Indian women and white women alike disagreed among themselves about women's appropriate roles and responsibilities.

7

While Cherokee leaders, white missionaries, and federal officials hoped that boarding schools would win the hearts and minds of Native American children, agents in the Office of Indian Affairs (OIA) devised a second strategy for educating Indians—place female role models into indigenous communities to work among those who did not go off to school. On paper, the program certainly made sense. For one thing, it was cheaper to station field matrons on reservations than to build and staff an entire school. For another, teachers in the field could reach a large number of Native women. How better to implant Victorian values?

In her study of one group of these field matrons, Lisa E. Emmerich examines the candidates best suited to this task—Native American women who had already adopted Anglo-American ways and could therefore serve as role models as well as teachers and health-care workers. Yet though the number of acculturated women must have been growing from the 1890s to the 1930s when the field matron program was in place, OIA officials relied on them far less than might be expected. Only from 1895 to 1905 did Native women constitute a sizable percentage of field matrons; thereafter the OIA, suspicious about the loyalties and effectiveness of these women, hired fewer of them.

Ironically, it might have been the very success of Native field matrons that made federal officials suspicious. These Indian women, with a deeper understanding of tribal culture than their white counterparts, knew from personal experience how hard it was to venture down the "White Woman's Road." Hence they handed out praise more readily than their white counterparts, a tactic that they hoped would further encourage their charges. Yet to the OIA such support for Native women, along with the Indian field matrons' failure to condemn traditional tribal healers, smacked of laziness or complicity. The OIA then decided that indigenous women were not sufficiently imbued with the logic of the program. Emmerich shows how, once again, dreams of non-Native reformers faded when those who sought change could not understand how best to make change happen. In addition, her research brings to light, in rich and human detail, the difficult personal and professional path Native field matrons had to negotiate.

"Right in the Midst of My Own People": Native American Women and the Field Matron Program

Lisa E. Emmerich

In January 1892 Indian agent Major George LeR. Brown asked the Office of Indian Affairs (OIA) for assistance with the Pine Ridge reservation population. Little more than a year after Sioux attempts to reclaim a fading tribal past ended tragically at Wounded Knee, he found precious little evidence of individual or community progress toward "civilization." The agent, arguing that "the pressing need [here] is for better homes and better cooking," requested the appointment of a field matron.[1]

Implementing an innovative Indian Service program begun in 1890, field matrons promoted assimilation through intensive domestic work with Indian women. Brown believed that Julia Kocer was an ideal candidate for the post. Interested in introducing tribal women to the "ways of White Women," she appeared to personify the "certified civilizer" reformers and OIA policy makers hoped to attract to the program.

Major Brown saw Kocer as a potential catalyst for change at Pine Ridge. The OIA, however, did not share his enthusiasm.[2] Neither impeccable qualifications nor genuine interest could alter the fact that Julia Kocer differed from other prospective field matrons. They were all Anglo-Americans. Educated, competent, and respectable, she was a mixed-blood Arikara Indian.

The first Native American field matron might have been Julia Kocer. Assimilated and concerned with the welfare of her Arikara peers, she clearly represented the "new" Indian woman the OIA hoped to create.[3] Nonetheless, the field matron corps remained closed to women like her until 1895. Then, Indian women could join Anglo-American women in helping their tribal peers accept the "White Woman's [sic] road." From 1895 to 1905, they played an active and occasionally prominent role in civilization work. Neither their participation nor their visibility, though, could guarantee a permanent place in the program. While field matrons continued their work on reservations until the 1930s, Native American involvement declined rapidly after 1905.

The story of Native American field matrons is a special, albeit abbreviated, chapter in the larger history of the field matron program. Their experiences as members of the Indian Service revealed the public and private worlds of women whose positions compelled them to create identities consistent with the demands of

Source: *American Indian Quarterly*, v. 15 (Spring 1991), pp. 201–216.

professional duties, traditional heritage, and adopted culture. Examining their work as role models in this program makes these long invisible women full participants in this story.

These women and their experiences also offer students of the assimilationist era of Indian policy a window into the world of Native Americans who incorporated Anglo-American culture into their lives. Scholars have concentrated on identifying the "friends of the Indian" and delineating their programs for Indian advancement.[4] The shadows cast by this historical spotlight have somewhat obscured those tribal people who became partners with the Anglo-Americans. Cases like the Native American field matrons reveal the practical, and personal, ramifications of assimilationist rhetoric and policies.

Julia Kocer sought entry to a program established at a moment when many Anglo-Americans believed the struggle to end tribalism had begun in earnest. Education and land in severalty could erase some, but not all, remnants of Native American traditionalism. Ethnocentric reformers, profoundly influenced by contemporary Victorian reverence for domesticity and the "woman's sphere," concluded that Indian home life exerted a powerful conservative force. Within the homes, they regarded Indian women as degraded captives of ignorance, custom, and superstition.[5] Congress created the field matron program in 1890 to bring both the women and their domestic world the benefits of modernity and Anglo-American culture.[6]

Field matrons, boasted one OIA official, stimulated "a contagion of homemaking on the reservations."[7] This process incorporated lessons in cooking, cleaning, sewing, basic carpentry, animal husbandry, and health care. The women were also directed to lead religious activities and sponsor social events that would further the cause of assimilation. Few skills or tasks, in short, did not fall under the rubric of the field matron's job.[8]

Cooking classes, religious services, and child care seminars all offered tribal women much more than practical help in adapting to sedentary reservation life. The agenda of these activities grew out of the field matron program's mission: helping Native American women adopt Victorian Anglo-American standards of womanhood. Field matrons used their lessons to establish cross-cultural personal bonds and to emphasize the superiority of Anglo-American models of femininity, wifehood, and motherhood.

While the official version of this program remained relatively static, a number of factors acted in concert to alter the composition of the field matron corps and shift the focus of their duties. The domestic ideology of "true womanhood" may have helped to create the field matrons, but health care rapidly took precedence over domesticity. Simultaneously, an increasing number of Anglo-American women who would never have identified themselves as "certified civilizers" found the program an attractive employment opportunity. Four decades of substantial change separated the field matrons of the 1890s and the 1930s.

Ethnocentrism, gender role redefinition, redirection of duties, and changes in Anglo-American personnel made up the backdrop to Native American participation in the field matron program. From 1895 to 1927, 34 Indian women representing a wide range of tribes and levels of assimilation worked as field matrons.[9] Proximity to reservation communities and familiarity with conditions there probably, as in the case of Julia Kocer, accounted for the appointment of some women. But the absence of any discernible hiring pattern suggests that the OIA gave no preference to any one tribal group over another.[10]

Native American women constituted roughly 13 percent of the total field matron corps and 8 percent of those employed between 1895 and 1927. Slightly more than half, some 52 percent of the 34 Indian women, participated in the program between 1895 and 1905. For five years during the peak period, they formed a significant minority within the total corps. In 1897, for example, Indian women made up 31 percent of the field matrons corps; that figure increased to 33 percent in 1899. The remaining 16 who entered and left the Indian Service before 1927 never regained that statistical parity. In 1910, the next highest year, Native American field matrons comprised only 12 percent of the total corps (Figures 1 and 2).[11]

The OIA hoped to attract young, well-educated, single women to the field matron program. Both Anglo-American and Native American appointees usually deviated from this personnel profile. Indian field matrons ranged in age from 20 to 67. The median age for this group was 42. Sixteen were the products of one branch of the OIA's assimilation framework, the Indian School system. Twelve attended institutions like the Haskell Institute, the Phoenix Indian School, and the Albuquerque Indian School. Four more matriculated at the more elite institutions, the Carlisle School and the Hampton Institute. About half of the 16 women whose marital status can be determined were single; three were widows. At least one married while a field matron, helping set a precedent for her peers.[12]

It is hardly surprising that racial differences superseded whatever commonalities these women shared with their Anglo-American peers. Yet, within the Native American group, there were also racial divisions. Blood quantum further segmented the group between full and mixed bloods. The total group was about evenly split between full and mixed bloods, the participation of the former women almost evenly matched by that of the latter.[13] This factor was not initially an important consideration for tribal women interested in these positions. After 1897, though, mixed-blood women played an increasingly visible role in the program.

Native American women combined altruism and pragmatism in the field matron program by teaching skills defined as "civilized" to other Indian women in return for wages. Application letters sent to the Indian Office usually stressed the correspondent's desire to help other tribal women adjust to the new ways of life. Julia DeCora, a full-blood Winnebago graduate of the Hampton Institute, emphasized this theme in an 1899 letter. She explained her interest in the position by noting that "as a member of that tribe [Winnebago] I feel very anxious to do whatever is in my power [to help] . . . ."[14] Mary Rice, a mixed-blood Pawnee woman looking for a position in 1903, echoed DeCora's letter. She felt the OIA should know that she was "very anxious to see advancement among my people."[15] Anna R. Dawson's plea in 1895 was heartfelt. The field matron position offered her a chance to work "right in the midst of my own people . . . [teaching] them all I have been able to learn from the white[s]. . . ."[16]

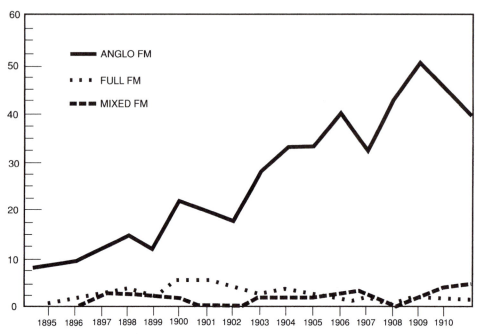

Figure 1. Field Matron Corps, 1895–1910. Sources: Annual Report of the Commissioner of Indian Affairs, Miscellaneous Salary Records, Employee Records, Efficiency Reports, and General Correspondence Files, RG75, BIA.

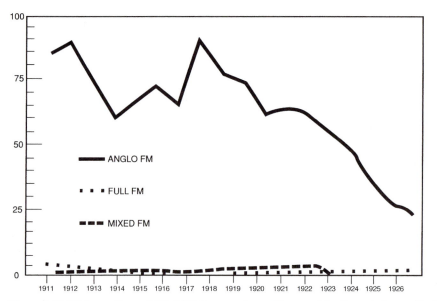

Figure 2. Field Matron Corps, 1911–1927. Sources: Annual Report of the Commissioner of Indian Affairs, Miscellaneous Salary Records, Employee Records, Efficiency Reports, and General Correspondence Files, RG75, BIA.

These women rarely mentioned salary as a factor motivating their employment search. This self-imposed reticence was in spite of the fact that the wages for a field matron, $600 to $720 per year, and a $300 per year salary for assistant field matrons, were quite high by Indian Office standards.[17] When it seemed clear that salary, not civilization, lay behind the interest in the job, women carefully couched that admission in language acceptable to OIA policy makers. Sadie Warren, a mixed-blood Ojibwa woman, tied her request for an appointment to salary because she was a widow. Emphasizing her wish to be self-supporting and help others, she explained "I am left a widow with two small children. . . . I will in a very short time be in need."[18]

Whatever their reasons for seeking employment, Indian field matrons shared with their Anglo-American counterparts the challenge of transforming the field matron position into a job that met the needs of the reservation population. This usually meant that immediately relevant lessons in sewing "citizens" dress or home sanitation took precedence over instruction in beekeeping or sidewalk construction. Field matrons spent much of their time working with tribal women on cooking, sewing, and housekeeping skills. These three subjects were the most useful and afforded the Native American field matrons their best chance for successful cultural transmission.

Pursuing this objective, many Indian women quickly became valued members of the OIA civilization team. In 1901, Omaha and Winnebago agent Charles P. Mathewson commended Maude Holt for her devotion and efficiency during four years of field matron work. He described Holt, a full-blood Winnebago herself, as an "exceptionally good employee."[19] R. C. Preston, agent at the Seger Colony, was so impressed with the work of Mary C. Gillette, a full-blood Arikara, that he asked the OIA for additional field matrons. Two years of her work persuaded him that employees like her "might do much toward advancing these Indian women in the ways of civilization."[20]

Native American field matrons clearly equalled the efforts of their Anglo-American peers in the domestic education sphere. Yet, it was there that some subtle differences between these two groups became apparent. As a group, field matrons wanted to see tribal women adopt as many "civilized" skills as possible under their tutelage. Undoubtedly sensitized by their own experiences to the amount of effort this involved, the Indian field matrons seemed willing to take a longer view of change than their non-Indian peers.

In a variety of domestic areas where Anglo-American women would have criticized the practices of tribal women, Native American matrons often accepted and praised whatever degree of progress had been made. Maude Holt reported that the women of her tribe had great difficulty in adopting civilized domestic practices like canning and sanitary food storage. Yet, she applauded them for their ready acceptance of "citizens" dress and their sewing skills.[21] Marie McLaughlin, a mixed-blood Sioux woman stationed at Standing Rock, found much to criticize about tribal life but still saw noteworthy progress in the fact that "men are doing more of the chores."[22] Howyer Senoia, a mixed-blood Pueblos woman working at Paguate, went so far as to append to her description of cooking lessons that the women there did well with traditional culinary techniques because "they are not so bad after all."[23]

While this willingness to concede some value to traditional culture may initially seem rather innocuous, other Indian Service personnel may very well have interpreted it as damaging to assimilation efforts. Acceptance and praise of domestic traditions had especially frightening implications for this program when they came from women whose education supposedly freed them from that same world. Those Native American field matrons who, along with some of their Anglo-American counterparts, accorded a positive value to "uncivilized" domesticity challenged the very foundations of their position and duties. The great difference between the two groups was that there was no danger of Anglo-American field matrons "going back to the blanket." That was not the case for the Indian women.

Health care was a second area where these field matrons and the Indian Office seemed at odds. Part of a field matron's job was to campaign aggressively for better community sanitation and the prevention of the spread of disease. Women coming into the program, though, were not required to have any formal medical or public health training. Apparently relying on Florence Nightingale's assertion ("every woman is a nurse") that nursing and other skills are learned through life experience, the OIA assigned them a demanding round of duties.

Education and individualized nursing formed the core of this attempt to make the Native American population less vulnerable to illness. Though health work did not start out at the center of the field matrons' activities, the appalling consequences of rampant tuberculosis and trachoma, high infant mortality, and a host of other diseases brought about a shift in priorities. Independent of the OIA, most field matrons took on greater responsibility for tribal health.[24]

Native American field matrons generally responded to the demand for increased health care. They treated colds, nursed the critically ill, and delivered babies as part of their regular work. Yet their involvement in medical affairs rarely ever reached the level that it did among the Anglo-American field matrons. These women left few reports or letters that directly address this issue. But some may have inadvertently spoken for the large group in reports that consistently ignored or under-emphasized health care. Marie L. Van Solen, a mixed-blood Sioux stationed at Standing Rock, summed up the attitude apparently shared by many Indian peers when she noted only that health and medical aid "was given where it was possible to do so."[25] Kiowa field matron Laura D. Pedrick echoed this sentiment in her reports when she stated that "I have taught and helped how they should care for their sick more properly."[26] While assessing lack of interest from medical reports is problematic, available information suggests that this may not have been one of the Indian field matrons' strong points. Perhaps here, more than in the realm of housework, they struggled to reconcile the conflicting demands of assimilation and traditional culture.

The reticence of Native American field matrons sometimes exhibited in connection with their health work was pronounced in their dealings with traditional healers and healing arts. Shamans, herbalists, sing doctors, and medicine men and women flourished on many reservations while the field matrons were trying to promote "civilized" medicine. Anglo-American field matrons regularly railed at the native healers for undercutting their efforts and allegedly endangering patients' lives. With two striking exceptions, Indian field matrons remained silent on this subject.

Mary C. Gillette and Anna Dawson Wilde were apparently the only Native American field matrons who directly challenged the authority and power of traditional healers in their respective communities. Gillette, assigned to the Cheyenne and Arapaho agency in 1909, reported a long siege of springtime illnesses. Exacerbating tribal bouts with the measles and influenza were the problems associated with the work of the native healers who, she believed, impeded her work. In an otherwise calm report, she confessed heatedly that "if the Indians are ever taught to care for the sick, the sick must be taken from the tent . . . and placed in a house near the school where the Indian medicine men would not be allowed to practice."[27] Wilde, a full-blooded Arikara from Fort Berthold in 1908, concurred with Gillette. Yet she found some reason for optimism after confronting a local healer and discovering that "some of the most conservative class, even, have turned to us for succor when they have found their [the traditional healers'] ways inadequate. . . ."[28]

The cumulative effect of the Native American field matrons' seeming indifference to health care work was not good. As the OIA became more involved in promoting tribal health care after 1900, the agency demanded more from its field employees. Elsie E. Newton, Superintendent for Field Matrons, addressed this point directly in 1915 while assessing the efficiency of Ada Rice, a mixed-blood Kiowa woman stationed at the Klamath agency. Newton characterized Rice as only a "fair" matron and advocated her dismissal. An ardent supporter of professionalization within the field matron corps, the superintendent based her recommendation on Rice's "perfunctory" care of the sick. Newton's evaluation implied that Rice's failure to take on more health duties somehow suggested a faulty commitment to assimilation.[29]

Tribal heritage sometimes played an important role for the Indian field matrons in a third area, where their relationships with the larger Native American community and the Anglo-American community intersected. Perhaps because of their genuinely sympathetic bonds with the other Indians they sought to serve, or perhaps because their authority as OIA employees carried with it the suggestion that the same power to help could be used for other, less beneficial purposes, few incidents of friction involving these women are documented. It was obviously to their advantage to disguise any unusual tensions that may have developed as they pursued their work. Nonetheless, the Indian Service informal network was usually quick to report any discord where field personnel, especially Native American employees, played a role.

Occasionally, these women did become entangled in tribal or community disputes. Factors like intraband factionalism, intergroup rivalry over land bases or Indian Office services, and intraband conflict over "conservative behavior" or religious rituals, either individually or in tandem, sometimes left them vulnerable to challenges from individuals and entire communities. These problems were not unusual in reservation settings; field service personnel sometimes found themselves involved in controversies whether or not they wished to be. These episodes were not happy events for any OIA employee; they proved especially dangerous for Native American field matrons. Such conflicts made it easier to single out these women, label them unreliable, and curtail their employment.

Conflict with an Indian group sometimes stemmed from factionalism born out of competition between family or clan members, or assimilated and traditional tribal segments. In 1905 Anna Dawson Wilde found herself at the center of a controversy that generated charges of dereliction of duty and land fraud. Married to one of the leading progressive men at Fort Berthold, Wilde aligned herself solidly alongside the other like-minded Indian residents. Because of the political affiliation, she found herself caught in a dispute that began with criticism of her treatment of a paralyzed woman who later died. Wilde was accused of deliberately neglecting the terminally ill woman, hastening her death through the resulting onset of gangrene. Agent Amzi Thomas reported the accusations to Washington, D.C., and agreed with Wilde's accuser that it was a "pitiful case." Next, the Indian field matron faced charges that she falsified her field matron reports and involved herself in a land fraud scheme.[30]

As the accusations flew, the other Arikara field matron at Fort Berthold spoke out to defend her colleague. Mary W. Howard attested to the quality of Wilde's work and dismissed the charges by explaining that "she [the accuser] has hated Mrs. Wilde . . . because she advised her to stop flirting with a certain married employee." Agent Thomas, apparently trying to keep his distance from the women involved to preserve his authority among the reservation residents, seemed unimpressed with Wilde's self-defense and Howard's corroboration. Reporting the details of the situation to the OIA, he alleged that the Native American woman who originally brought the charges against Wilde "is likely to prove her case if given the opportunity."[31] Though Dawson retained her position, the intraband animosity created by the quarrel made her work very difficult. Moreover, it tainted her relationship with the Anglo-American OIA personnel at Fort Berthold.

This same kind of tension was very much in evidence in a case involving Laura D. Pedrick, a full-blood Kiowa. In 1898 members of the Kiowa, Comanche, and Apache tribes living in Oklahoma petitioned the OIA for her appointment as field matron. More than two hundred signatures attested to her qualifications and their wish for her assistance as they learned "the white man's road."[32] In early 1899 she received her assignment.

Pedrick proved to be an energetic and competent field matron who pursued the standard housekeeping and health activities successfully. She also chastised members of the tribe who lived "like the Lilies of the Valley or as if each day was to be their last." She criticized those who kept "useless" pony herds instead of raising cattle, pigs, and sheep. Participants in Ghost Dances and mescal feasts found themselves singled out in reports that alerted local OIA officials to those activities. This condemnation, it is worth noting, was not forthcoming from Anglo-American field matrons who probably did not have the language skills or the personal connections to learn about the dances and the feasts.[33] Pedrick could, and apparently did, use her Kiowa heritage and personal ties to gather information possibly inaccessible to Anglo-American personnel.

Those same relationships proved problematic in 1900, when the opening of the Kiowa, Comanche, and Apache reservation looked imminent. Because her brother Apiatan opposed fellow Kiowa Delos Lone Wolf's attempt to keep the land base intact, Pedrick found her position in jeopardy. Ostensibly, her remarks about stock-raising and her exposure of the Ghost Dances and mescal feasts were to blame for the erosion of support that brought her to the field in 1899. In fact, tribal politics and family ties very nearly caused her downfall.[34]

In 1901 the Anadarko area agent tersely informed the Indian Office that "the Kiowa and Comanche Indians . . . have requested me to inform you that Mrs. Laura Padrick [*sic*] . . . is objectionable."[35] Members of the three groups who originally called for her appointment, apparently angered by her brother's position on the issue of tribal lands, asked that a special investigator examine her work and evaluate her conduct. Though Pedrick remained in her position, the incident irrevocably changed her relationship with the reservation population.

Intertribal hostility and animosity were clearly forces, as Pedrick's case illustrates, that proved dangerous to the Native American field matrons. Such tension frequently caught them between Anglo-American Indian Service personnel and other tribal people in an unenviable tug of war. Assistant field matrons Rosalie M. Nejo and Juanita LaChappa found themselves in such a situation in 1909 while they worked with some of the Mission Indians of California. Members of the Guyapipa and Mesa Grande bands respectively, these young mixed-blood women entered the Indian Service in 1904 after graduation from the Sherman Institute.[36] Nejo and LaChappa quickly won the affection and respect of Indian Service personnel and tribal people through their hard work and compassion.[37] Less than a year after their arrival in the field, Superintendent Charles Shell informed Mamie Robinson, the field matron supervising their work, that he was more than pleased with their efforts. Sending his regards to Nejo and LaChappa, he noted "each . . . fill[s] a different niche. If I should say what I real [*sic*] think, I fear each of you would think I was flattering and you know I am not given to that."[38]

Five years after Nejo and LaChappa began their work they found themselves involved in an intertribal dispute that threatened their positions as it escalated. Tension between the Campo, Mesa Grande, Posta, and Guyapipa bands in 1909 resulted in complaints about their work habits and willingness to assist Indians outside their own groups.[39] Controversies among tribal people were not rare, and Nejo and LaChappa were not the first field matrons criticized for alleged favoritism. Anglo-American field matrons usually survived such episodes unscathed; the two mixed-blood women did not. Superintendent Philip Lonergan used the problems among the Indians to call for the replacement of the field matrons. Foreseeing a future challenge to OIA authority if the conflict continued with Nejo and LaChappa near the center, he informed Washington, D.C., that "what the Campo situation requires more than a Field Matron is a good Farmer and teacher."[40] Shortly thereafter, the positions were abolished.

For field matrons who needed the trust and respect of the tribal people and Indian Service personnel they worked among, confrontations like these could prove devastating. Heightened visibility made them vulnerable to challenges that did not go unnoticed by the OIA hierarchy. Conflict inspired lasting animosity in Indian communities, rendering subsequent efforts at health care and domestic civilization all but useless. Such disputes also damaged professional reputations by creating a context for suspicions that these field matrons used their language skills and family ties to undermine Indian Service authority. Any one of those results could have been enough to justify the dismissal of a Native American woman from her post as "certified civilizer."

Studying the experiences of Native American field matrons allows us to assess the history of assimilation policy in the late nineteenth century. From Julia Kocer onward, Indian women presented themselves to the OIA as success stories anxious to impart their knowledge of Anglo-American culture to tribal peers. Their reports and correspondence reveal a number of important details about work within an environment that daily tested their commitment to assimilation.

Indian field matrons entered the program in 1895 confident of their ability to assist other tribal women in the assimilation process. Overcoming initial bureaucratic resistance, most pursued their work with competence and compassion. By offering other Native American women accessible role models, they materially contributed to the OIA's effort to end tribalism and replace traditional culture with Anglo-American culture. For this, their efforts frequently won them praise from the Indian Service hierarchy.

The assimilated personas these women projected in their work were not, however, totally seamless. In several areas, their experiences differed from those of their Anglo-American peers. Because they understood that the process of adopting civilized domestic techniques was a long one, they sometimes chose to be more tolerant of the habits Indian women had and were more willing to praise those adaptations already made. Native American field matrons did not always engage as fully as some Anglo-American peers in health care. They particularly did not try to challenge the status of native health care practitioners or ridicule those who accepted their help. And, the Indian field matrons sometimes became more visible than they might have wished because of involvement in tribal disputes. These field matrons often found that their personal identity gave them a political identity that could not be escaped on the reservation or in the Indian Service. Education and assimilation notwithstanding, the Native American field matrons were always Native Americans first, OIA employees second. The uncertainty perceived by Anglo-Americans to be inherent in that first identity ultimately helped curtail opportunities to adopt the second.

Stella Bear learned this in 1911. One of four Native Americans in the program that year, she asked the OIA for reassignment to Fort Berthold. A mixed-blood Arikara woman, Bear echoed many of the Indian field matrons employed before her in her hope to live and work with members of her own tribe. The OIA rejected her request for a transfer, not because of funding or staffing problems, or Bear's lack of qualifications. Stella Bear could not go home to live and work with other Arikara women because "it is not the policy of this Office [OIA] to appoint Indians to positions of this character among their own people."[41]

APPENDIX 1

FIELD MATRON CORPS, 1895-1927

Year	Total N=	Full Blood N=	Mixed Blood N=	Percent
1895	10	1		10.00
1896	12	2		16.60
1987	19	3	3	31.57
1898	22	4	3	31.81
1899	18	3	3	33.33
1900	30	6	2	26.66
1901	26	6		23.07
1902	22	4		18.18
1903	34	3	2	14.70
1904	39	4	2	15.38
1905	38	3	2	13.15
1906	45	2	3	11.11
1907	37	2	3	13.51
1908	43	1		2.32
1909	53	2	1	5.66
1910	50	2	4	12.00
1911	89	3	1	4.49
1912	92	1	2	3.26
1913	77	1	1	2.59
1914	62	1	1	3.22
1915	69	1	2	4.34
1916	74		2	2.77
1917	66		1	1.51
1918	90		1	1.11
1919	78		1	1.28
1920	76	1	1	2.63
1921	63	1	2	4.76
1922	65	1	1	3.07
1923	63	1	1	3.17
1924	55	1		1.81
1925	49	1		2.04
1926	35	1		2.85
1927	29	1		3.44

Sources: Annual Reports of the Commissioner of Indian Affairs, Miscellaneous Salary Records, Employee Records, Efficiency Reports, and General Correspondence Files, 1975, BIA

NOTES

1. Major George LeR. Brown to Thomas J. Morgan, January 1, 1892, Letters Received 1892/3289, Record Group 75, Records of the Bureau of Indian Affairs, National Archives, Washington, D.C. (Hereafter cited as LR, RG 75, BIA, NA.)
2. Thomas J. Morgan to Major George LeR. Brown, August 24, 1892, Letters Sent 1892/301731A, RG 75, BIA, NA (hereafter cited as LS). See also Herbert Welsh to Thomas J. Morgan, October 12, 1892, LR 1892/37179, RG 75, BIA, NA; Herbert Welsh, "Civilization among the Sioux Indians," Pamphlet No. 7 (Philadelphia: Indian Rights Association, 1893), p. 43; and Julia Kocer to George LeR. Brown, August 17, 1895, Box 30, Miscellaneous Correspondence Received, 1891–1895, Records of the Pine Ridge Agency, RG 75, BIA, National Archives-Kansas City (hereafter cited as NA-City).
3. Theodore Roosevelt, following a visit to Pine Ridge, described Kocer as "one of the most intelligent, capable, and generally philanthropic women I have ever met." He believed that "it would be impossible to get a woman better qualified for the duties of field matron among these women." See Theodore Roosevelt, "Report of the Honorable Theodore Roosevelt Made to the United States Civil Service Commission upon a Visit to Certain Indian Reservations and Indian Schools in South Dakota, Nebraska, and Kansas" (Philadelphia: Indian Rights Association, 1893), p. 10.
4. More space than this essay contains would be needed to fully enumerate the articles and books dealing with the subject of Indian assimilation. See especially Frederick E. Hoxie, *A Final Promise: The Campaign to Assimilate the Indian, 1880–1920* (Lincoln: University of Nebraska Press, 1984); Francis Paul Prucha, *The Churches and the Indian Schools, 1888–1912* (Lincoln: University of Nebraska Press, 1979); Henry E. Fritz, *The Movement for Indian Assimilation, 1860–1890* (Philadelphia: University of Pennsylvania Press, 1963); and William T. Hagan, *The Indian Rights Association: The Herbert Welsh Years* (Tucson: University of Arizona Press, 1985).
5. The Lake Mohonk conference records for this period reveal the views most Anglo-Americans had of Native American home life. See especially *Proceedings of the Seventh Annual Meeting of the Lake Mohonk Conference of Friends of the Indian, 1886* (Washington, D.C.: Government Printing Office, 1887), pp. 2 and 19 (hereafter cited as *LMC*). An excellent discussion of the evolution of the "squaw drudge" myth can be found in David Smits, "The 'Squaw Drudge': A Prime Index of Savagism," *Ethnohistory* 29 (Fall 1982): 281–306.
6. For a more fully developed discussion of this topic, see Chapters 1 and 2 in Lisa E. Emmerich, "'To Respect and Love and Seek the Ways of White Women': Field Matrons, the Office of Indian Affairs, and Civilization Policy, 1890–1938" (Ph.D. dissertation, University of Maryland, 1987).
7. Emily S. Cook, "The Field Matron," in *LMC*, 1892, pp. 58–59.
8. Circular 1269, Miscellaneous Correspondence, Box 17, Records of the White Earth Agency, RG 75, BIA, NA-Chicago.
9. Native American field matrons examined in this paper represent the group of women whose employment could be traced through OIA and United States Office of Personnel Management files. The size of the pool does have an impact on this paper; but to ignore these women and their experiences within the field matron program would be a mistake.
10. The OIA drew field matrons from Arikara, Kiowa, Mesa Grande, Guyapipa, Ojibwa, Shoshone, Pima, San Idelfonso, Mescalero Apache, Omaha, Seneca, Pawnee, and Winnebago tribes.
11. See Appendix 1 for a complete statistical breakdown of the field matron corps during the period covered by this paper.
12. Personal information on the Native American field matrons was drawn from the following sources: *Annual Reports of the Commissioner of Indian Affairs*; Personnel Files; Agency Employee Rosters; Miscellaneous Salary Lists; Efficiency Reports; and Miscellaneous Correspondence Files, RG 75, BIA, NA. Additional information came from selected Personnel Files, United States Office of Personnel Management.
13. See Appendix 1 for a complete breakdown between full- and mixed-blood field matrons.
14. Julia DeCora to William A. Jones, February 4, 1899, LR 1899/6984, RG 75, BIA, NA.
15. Mrs. Mary Rice to W. A. Jones, March 12, 1903, LR 1903/17563, RG 75, BIA, NA.

16. Anna R. Dawson to Commissioner of Indian Affairs, January 1895, LR 1895/8170, RG 75, BIA, NA.
17. Until 1912, field matrons earned more than any other female field service employees.
18. Sadie Warren to Honorable Commissioner of Indian Affair, December 30, 1899, LR 1900/514, RG 75, BIA, NA.
19. Charles P. Mathewson to Honorable Commissioner of Indian Affairs, June 25, 1901, LR 1901/34998, RG 75, BIA, NA.
20. R. C. Preston to Commissioner of Indian Affairs, January 2, 1906, LR 1906/1465, RG 75, BIA, NA.
21. Quarterly report of Maude Holt, July-October 1898, LR 1898/49238, RG 75, BIA, NA.
22. Quarterly report of Marie L. McLaughlin, April-June 1900, LR 1900/35322, RG 75, BIA, NA.
23. Quarterly report of Howyer Senoia, January-March 1906, LR 1906/36813, RG 75, BIA, NA.
24. This shift is discussed in Chapters 5 and 6 of Emmerich, "'To Respect and Love and Seek the Ways of White Women.'"
25. Monthly report of Marie L. Van Solen, August 1906, LR 1906/98637, RG 75, BIA, NA.
26. Monthly report of Laura D. Pedrick, April 1901, Field Matron Files, Records of the Kiowa Agency, Oklahoma Historical Society, Oklahoma City, Oklahoma (hereafter cited as OHS).
27. Quarterly report of Mary C. Gillette, April–June 1909, Field Matron Files, Records of the Cheyenne and Arapaho Agency, OHS.
28. Anna Dawson Wilde and Adelina P. Beauchamp to Honorable Commissioner of Indian Affairs, August 15, 1908, File 61102–1908–150, Central Classified Files, Records of the Fort Berthold Agency, RG 75, BIA, NA.
29. Elsie E. Newton to Commissioner of Indian Affairs, September 27, 1915, File 107473–15–917.1, Records of the Klamath Agency, RG 75, BIA, NA.
30. Amzi Thomas to Honorable Commissioner of Indian Affairs, October 26, 1905, and Ella Rickert Ripley to Honorable Commissioner of Indian Affairs, August 28, 1905 (enclosure 1), LR 1905/87626, RG 75, BIA, NA.
31. Ibid.
32. Petition to W. A. Jones, November 5, 1898, LR 1898/54860, RG 75, BIA, NA.
33. Monthly report of Laura D. Pedrick, August 1899, and Quarterly report, January-March 1900, Field Matron Files, Records of the Kiowa Agency, OHS.
34. William T. Hagan, *United States-Comanche Relations* (New Haven: Yale University Press, 1976), pp. 262–265.
35. William M. Springer to Honorable William A. Jones, June 28, 1901, LR 1901/34365, RG 75, BIA, NA.
36. J. S. Lockwood to Honorable William A. Jones, October 10, 1904, LR 1904/72459, RG 75, BIA, NA.
37. Superintendent Charles Shell to Honorable Commissioner of Indian Affairs, September 23, 1904, LR 1904/67400, and Mary B. Watkins to Miss F. Sparhawk, September 29, 1904, LR 1904/68001 (enclosure 1), RG 75, BIA, NA.
38. Superintendent to Mamie Robinson, April 21, 1905, Box 180C, Miscellaneous Letters Sent, Records of the Pala Superintendency, RG 75, BIA, NA-Laguna Niguel.
39. J. H. Dortch to Philip T. Lonergan, May 15, 1909, Box 4, Letters Received, 1903–1921, Records of the Pala Superintendency, RG 75, BIA, NA-Laguna Niguel.
40. Philip T. Lonergan to Honorable Commissioner of Indian Affairs, May 24, 1909, Box 188A, Letters Sent to the Office of Indian Affairs, January 1908–August 1914, Records of the Pala Superintendency, RG 75, BIA, NA-Laguna Niguel.
41. C. F. Hauke to Miss Stella Bear, March 17, 1911, Field Matron Files, Records of the Cheyenne and Arapaho Agency, OHS.

8

Missionaries tried many techniques to win Indians to Christ, and to "civilization." Some ventured, alone, into the remote reaches of Indian Country in order to win the trust of prospective converts. Others enticed entire villages close to colonial settlements, then encouraged Indians to build clapboard houses, erect fences, don European clothes, go to church, and otherwise conform to colonial modes of belief and behavior. Increasingly, however, missionaries came to feel that the adult Indian was too steeped in the old ways to change. Indian children, not yet so thoroughly indoctrinated into savagery, then became the target. The goal was to take control of these youngsters, secure them in a safe place, and then inculcate in them the values of Anglo-American society. To us, this might seem like nothing more than kidnapping and brainwashing; to the devout Christian, however, it was saving souls from pagan darkness and eternal damnation. As Carol Devens points out in this perceptive inquiry, to missionaries "the abandonment of native ways for Western ones was a creative rather than a destructive process."

By 1850, Devens argues, many missionaries came to believe that conversion would be most successful if they focused their energies on Indian girls. The shift reflected prevailing notions in Anglo-American society about the power women had to reform society by teaching their children how to be moral agents in a sinful world.

But a focus on female students did not guarantee success. Though teachers in mission schools often attempted to instruct their charges about the values of domesticity and purity, so vital in Victorian America, they often found girls unwilling to accept their lessons, or unable even to understand the worth of such values at all. Teachers might have wanted to be role models, but many failed to grasp that their school often represented a threat, not an opportunity, to Native girls. Since indigenous families commonly refused to support schools—some even likened a child's departure for school to a death in the family—missionaries faced a difficult task. That task was all the more difficult because education was not, and could not be, confined to the classroom. As the historian Bernard Bailyn made clear forty years ago, education—in its truest, fullest sense—means the transmission of culture from one generation to the next. From such a perspective, Native mothers and grandmothers had more to do with the education of Indian girls than did missionary schools. In such a situation, it seems reasonable to ask if schools ever could have succeeded—indeed, to ask how one might define "success." While raising these questions, Devens's article also joins with the chapters by Melissa Meyer, Margaret Jacobs, and others to show how the classroom was yet another battleground in the ongoing contest between Indians and whites.

"If We Get the Girls, We Get the Race": Missionary Education of Native American Girls

Carol Devens

> *When I saw the lonely figure of my mother vanish in the distance, a sense of regret settled heavily upon me. I felt suddenly weak, as if I might fall limp to the ground. I was in the hands of strangers whom my mother did not fully trust. I no longer felt free to be myself, or to voice my own feelings. The tears trickled down my cheeks, and I buried my face in the folds of my blanket. Now the first step, parting me from my mother, was taken, and all my belated tears availed nothing.*
>
> Zitkala-Sa

MISSION SCHOOL EDUCATION, WITH ITS wrenching separation from family, had a profound impact on Native American girls and on their female kin. Zitkala-Sa's description of her departure for boarding school in 1884 characterized the experience of thousands of young girls in the nineteenth century.[1] Most left no written record of their years in school; Zitkala-Sa (Gertrude Bonnin), a Dakota (Sioux) writer and activist on Native American issues, was unusual in that respect. She recorded both her own memories of her school years and her mother's reaction to the Western education of her daughter.

Zitkala-Sa's mother, heartbroken by the child's departure, was convinced that someone had "filled [her daughter's] ears with the white man's lies" to persuade her to leave for school. What else would induce an eight-year-old to quit her mother for the company of strangers? "Stay with me, my little one!" she futilely implored the child, overwhelmed by anxiety about her safety among white people.[2] The woman's fears were not unfounded. Her child's well-being at school was by no means assured, as an examination of the experiences of Ojibwa and Dakota girls suggests.[3] A girl's exposure to Anglo-American religious, economic, and gender values often had a permanent effect on her, whether or not she accepted them. Moreover, the time in school deprived her of the continuing tutelage of her mother and other female relatives—instruction that was key to assuming her place as a woman within her own cultural tradition.

SOURCE: *Journal of World History*, v. 3, n. 2 (1992), pp. 219–237.

The history of mission schools is a troubling one in which stories of benevolent, self-sacrificing missionaries contend with accounts of relentlessly rigid discipline, ethnocentrism, and desperately unhappy children.[4] Native Americans received their introduction to Anglo-American education at the hands of British missionaries in 1617, following King James's advocacy of schooling Indians to promote "civilization" and Christianity. Dartmouth College soon was established to teach young Indian men, and both Harvard College and William and Mary College incorporated the education of native youth into their missions. The Church of England's Society for the Propagation of the Gospel in Foreign Parts also regularly instructed Indians until the American Revolution. Following independence, a host of missionary societies was organized with the stated intent of evangelizing native peoples, among them the American Society for Propagating the Gospel among the Indians and Others in North America (1787) and the New York Missionary Society (1796).[5]

The founding of the interdenominational American Board of Commissioners of Foreign Missions (ABCFM) in 1810 ushered in a new era of missionary endeavor. The combined influences of the religious revival known a the Second Great Awakening and heightened nationalism following the War of 1812 added a further goal to the missionary effort: rescuing Indians from destruction by the inexorable march of Anglo-American progress. Numerous denominational organizations were formed, such as the Missionary Society of the American Methodist Episcopal Church in 1820 and the Presbyterian Board of Foreign Missions (BFM) in 1837.[6]

Nineteenth-century missionaries and their sponsors firmly believed in the linear progression of history and in their own elevated place on the ladder of civilization. They clearly understood their charge to be the transformation of native peoples into Christian citizens. Admittedly, it was a monumental undertaking. "We cannot be too grateful that God did not make us heathens," observed Sherman Hall, of ABCFM's La Pointe mission in Wisconsin, in 1833. "It is an awful calamity to be born in the midst of heathen darkness."[7] Heathenism seemed a surmountable obstacle, however, if children could be brought into the fold at a tender age and raised as Christians. As one missionary put it: "This can only be effectually accomplished by taking them away from the demoralizing & enervating atmosphere of camp life & Res[ervation] surroundings & Concomitants."[8] Although bringing adults to knowledge of gospel truths was important, it was "the rising generation" who provided hope for the salvation of the native population.

Schooling became the primary means of enticing young Native Americans to reject tradition and seek conversion. To missionaries, the abandonment of native ways for Western ones was a creative rather than destructive process that made new Christian citizens out of savages. School, missionaries hoped, was a way to change Indians from "others" to dusky versions of themselves. Rayna Green, a Native American scholar, has offered this observation of a photograph of pupils at the Hampton Institute, a nineteenth-century boarding school in Virginia for African-American and Native American pupils: "School put them into drawing classes, where young Indian ladies in long dresses made charcoal portraits of a boy dressed in his Plains warrior best. These Victorian Indians look toward the camera from painting class, their eyes turned away from their buckskinned model."[9]

Missionaries worked diligently to gather girls and boys of all ages into day and boarding schools near villages and reservations, as well as at distant Indian schools such as the Hampton Institute or the Carlisle School in Pennsylvania (founded in 1879 to prove to the public that Native Americans were educable). Because missionary teachers could not forcibly round up and remove Native American children to schools as their government counterparts often did, it was a real challenge to enroll them. Zitkala-Sa was lured to the Quakers' Indiana Manual Labor Institute in Wabash by tales of lush, rich land bursting with sweet fruits for the child's taking.[10] Charles Hall, a minister at the ABCFM's Fort Berthold mission in North Dakota (which served mostly Mandan, Hidatsa, and Arikara rather than Dakota) in the late nineteenth and early twentieth centuries, reported that "getting the children to go to school was as delicate and cautious work as catching trout. To send a child to school meant, to the Indian, the giving up of all his distinctive tribal life, his ancestral customs, his religious beliefs, and sinking himself into the vast unknown, the way of the white man."[11] After several years, Hall developed a recruitment strategy that he later explained in a section of his memoirs entitled "Capturing Children":

> How to reach the children was a problem. They were told by shrewd parents that owls and bears and white men would harm them, so naturally they ran and hid when we approached. . . . White Shield, the old Ree [Arikara] chief, said in regard to our problem, "If you feed the children, they will come to school like flies to syrup." His advice was taken, and a Friday dinner, in the manner of the white man, was provided. This was as attractive as ice cream and lollipops. The school became a popular institution, especially on Friday.[12]

Other missionaries reported similar use of food and other enticements, such as singing, to get the children into the classroom.[13]

Initially, mission schools concentrated on teaching boys and men, with little emphasis on female schooling. By mid century, however, they had shifted their approach in response to the growing belief among Americans that women, as mothers, must be educated in order to raise virtuous male citizens.[14] According to Isaac Baird, who served at the Presbyterian BFM Odanah mission in Wisconsin, "The girls will need the training more than the boys & they will wield a greater influence in the future. If we get the girls, we get the race."[15] ABCFM's Santee Normal Training School in Nebraska, founded in 1870, exemplified this position in its annual bulletin, which stated that the school's purpose was the "raising up [of] preachers, teachers, interpreters, business men, and model mothers for the Dakota Nation."[16]

Once the commitment to female education had been made, however, missionaries faced low enrollments and high dropout rates. Presbyterian and ABCFM missions to the Ojibwa and Dakota suffered a shortage of schoolgirls and, moreover, were dissatisfied with the performance of the female pupils they did have. William

Boutwell, ABCFM missionary at Leech Lake, Minnesota, reported in the 1830s that girls avoided him and refused to come to school; he was uncertain whether fear or shame motivated their response.[17] At the Presbyterian BFM mission in Omena, Michigan, Peter Dougherty thought he could not go wrong with his female school; he had provided women teachers to instruct girls in domesticity and Christianity as well as some academic subjects. When the school opened in 1848, it had a fine enrollment of twenty-two, but this quickly dwindled, and by 1850 Dougherty was forced to close the school. The boys' school, however, flourished as fathers sent their sons to acquire reading and ciphering skills that allowed them to deal with Anglo-Americans on their own terms.[18] The manual labor boarding school Dougherty opened in 1853 had similar problems, attracting only five girls out of twenty-seven students. The Presbyterians were even more discouraged by the situation at Middle Village, a satellite mission of Omena, where women refused to send any children to school. Their action led to the school's closing in 1858, despite the village men's petition to the BFM to keep it open.[19]

At Sisseton agency in the Dakota Territory, the local U.S. Indian agent, J. G. Hamilton, was shocked by how tenaciously Dakota women clung to their old ways. He urged the Women's Board of Missions (affiliated with the ABCFM) to send a lady to teach the native women. "I was struck, upon my arrival here some two months ago," he wrote to the Women's Board in 1875, "with the vast difference in the general appearance of the men & women. Contrary to the usual rule, the men of this tribe have made far greater progress & have yielded more readily to civilizing forces than the women have."[20] He hoped that female teachers might be able to reach them. His comment suggests that, like the Ojibwa, Dakota women sought to keep distance between themselves and whites and were reluctant to adapt to Anglo-American customs or values. Susan Webb, a missionary teacher at Santee, reported that "the older women could not read and the younger women would not."[21] The female aversion to interaction included an unwillingness to have their daughters involved in mission schooling. When Captain Richard H. Pratt, founder of the Carlisle School, visited Fort Berthold in 1878 to recruit Dakota children for the Hampton Institute, he had a difficult time securing students, especially girls. "The people feared to give up their girls," Charles Hall explained, "not trusting the white people."[22]

One teacher contemplating the enrollment problem suggested that the Ojibwa, at least, saw no point in educating girls. Revealing his poor understanding of Ojibwa gender roles and cultural values, he explained that women were destined for a life of servitude. A more likely explanation, however, came from a perceptive missionary who suggested that close ties between mothers and daughters were to blame—that women who maintained a traditional way of life were loath to relinquish control of their daughters' upbringing. It was with tremendous reluctance, for example, that Zitkala-Sa's mother allowed her to go to school. She eventually consented only after concluding that Western education would provide her daughter greater protection against the growing number of Anglo-Americans settling on Dakota lands than traditional training could.[23]

Much like their Ojibwa counterparts, those Dakota girls who did enroll seldom seemed to conform to the missionaries' expectations. Susan Webb commented that her female students always seemed the opposite of what she hoped they would be. She saw her work with them as a lesson in the depths of the human condition: "I think as I work for these girls I am learning the weakness and depravity of our own human natures."[24]

Despite women's traditionalism and their suspicion of missionaries, many girls did end up attending school for at least short periods of time.[25] Once there, they immediately began the physical transformation that missionaries hoped would be a catalyst for their intellectual and spiritual metamorphosis into Christian citizens. A young girl, whether faced with the total immersion of boarding school or the less comprehensive (but nonetheless thorough) indoctrination attempted by day schools, was presented with an alien world view, behavior code, and language to which she was quickly expected to adhere. It was a confusing and frightening whirlwind of strangers, journeys, haircuts, and loneliness. Zitkala-Sa again provides a window on the experience of starting school: "My long travel and the bewildering sights had exhausted me. I fell asleep, heaving deep, tired sobs. My tears were left to dry themselves in streaks, because neither my aunt nor my mother was near to wipe them away."[26] She recalled how humiliating the mandatory haircuts were for Native American children. "Our mothers had taught us that only unskilled warriors who were captured had their hair shingled by the enemy. Among our people, short hair was worn by mourners, and shingled hair by cowards!" She had to be dragged out from under a bed before she submitted to having her long braids snipped off. Charles Hall remembered the children's horror of losing their long hair at his school, and the Indian agent, J. C. McGillycuddy, reported that when new Lakota students at Pine Ridge reservation caught a glimpse of teachers giving haircuts, they feared that he intended to disgrace them, and all fled in alarm.[27]

The school world was tough and confusing. Mission schools' programs for girls were intended to indoctrinate them with the ideals of Christian womanhood—piety, domesticity, submissiveness, and purity. By the missionaries' Victorian standards, Native American women were careless, dirty, and unfamiliar with the concept of hard work. Indian girls, they complained, were woefully unfamiliar with the lore, paraphernalia, and routines of female domesticity.[28] Schools therefore trained girls in sewing, knitting, cooking, and other domestic skills and tasks, as well as in academic subjects, such as history, natural sciences, arithmetic, and spelling.[29] The content of the curriculum bore no relationship to the intellectual, social, or philosophical constructs in which the girls had been raised. Indeed, the schools' underlying principle was that Anglo-American history, morality, and health were inherently superior to and should replace those of their students' cultures.

This perspective was reinforced by typical textbooks, such as Webb's *Readers*, Webster's *Spelling Book*, Greenleaf's *Intellectual Arithmetic*, and Colbun's *Mental Arithmetic*, used by Ojibwa children in the 1860s at ABCFM's Odanah Manual Labor Boarding School.[30] These books unabashedly proclaimed the Anglo-American vision of progress and morality subscribed to by the missionaries. Even texts written specifically for Native American pupils (ABCFM teachers usually taught in their students' language) tended to be literal translations of standard classroom lessons that teachers applied to their pupils with little or no regard for context and appropriateness. The sailboats depicted in Stephen Rigg's *Model First Reader* (1873), for example, were a world away from the experiences of the Dakota children learning to read out of this book at the Santee Normal Training School.[31]

The curriculum often placed an even heavier emphasis on vocational instruction for girls than for boys. The thirty-six girls at the Shawnee Quaker School, for example, in 1827 alone produced 400 pieces of student clothing, 50 sets of sheets and towels, and 80 pairs of socks. They also spun and wove 100 pounds of wool and 40 yards of rag carpet, churned 800 pounds of butter, made 600 pounds of cheese, 2½ barrels of soap, and 100 pounds of candles. In addition, they did daily housekeeping, laundry, cooking, and cleaning. The girls worked in groups, rotating jobs every two weeks in order to learn all aspects of housekeeping.[32] Martha Riggs Morris at ABCFM's Sisseton (Dakota) mission, explained the rationale for this approach, which still held sway in 1881: "The book learning is after all not so important for them, at least after they have learned to read and write fairly well. But to take care of themselves—to learn to keep body and mind pure and clean, to learn to keep house comfortably— these are most important for the advancement of the people."[33]

Ideally, the missions' female teachers were to be role models for appropriate gender activities, values, and work, showing Native American girls through daily example both the techniques of household economy and a womanly demeanor. In reality, however, the teachers were overworked and often ill. Furthermore, rigid schedules and overcrowding often made the situation impersonal and miserable. At the Wesleyan Methodist Missionary Society's Aldersville School in Ontario, Canada, a report of the girls' schedule in 1841 indicated their rigorous life. The children (mostly Ojibwa) arose at 4:30 a.m. in summer, a lazy 5 a.m. in winter. Between rising and 9 a.m., the girls did the milking, prepared the school breakfast, attended prayers and a lecture, made cheese, and did housework. They then spent six hours in the classroom, with a break for lunch, followed by needlework, supper, evening milking, prayers at 8 p.m. and bed at 8:30.[34]

Throughout the 1880s, Martha Riggs Morris complained that her twenty-eight Dakota students were crowded into two tiny buildings measuring 10 x 24 feet and 17 x 24 feet. At the Santee Normal Training School, the Bird's Nest, a boarding home for small girls, was more spacious, having two kitchens, a dining room, teachers' sitting room and bedrooms, sick bay, laundry room, and three dormitories for the girls. Still, both teachers and students felt cramped and hurried.[35] Zitkala-Sa's account of the Wabash school once again personalizes the depressing impact of frantic school regimes on pupils and teachers alike:

> A loud-clamoring bell awakened us at half-past six in the cold winter mornings. . . .
> There were too many drowsy children and too numerous orders for the day to waste a
> moment in any apology to nature for giving her children such a shock in the early

morning.... A paleface woman, with a yellow-covered roll book open on her arm and a gnawed pencil in her hand, appeared at the door. Her small, tired face was coldly lighted with a pair of large gray eyes. She stood still in a halo of authority.... It was next to impossible to leave the iron routine after the civilizing machine had once begun its day's buzzing.[36]

Susan Webb's comments about her pupils indicate that the schooling process alienated and confused the girls. "When I look about me," Webb wrote in 1881, "and see how helpless and indifferent apparently are the young women I long to help arouse them to a sense that there is something for them to be doing. I cannot endure the thought that our girls will leave us to settle down with no weight of responsibility."[37] Zitkala-Ša's experience confirmed this: "The melancholy of those black days has left so long a shadow that it darkens the path of years that have since gone by. These sad memories rise above those of smoothly grinding school days."[38]

Stories of her grandmother's experiences in a turn-of-the-century mission school prompted Mary Crow Dog (Lakota Sioux) to write: "It is almost impossible to explain to a sympathetic white person what a typical old Indian boarding school was like; how it affected the Indian child suddenly dumped into it like a small creature from another world, helpless, defenseless, bewildered, trying desperately and instinctively to survive at all."[39] Some young girls at the school killed themselves or attempted suicide to escape an unhappy situation beyond their control.

The demoralizing effect of school programs was often rivaled by their futility. Most of the domestic instruction that girls received was virtually useless when their schooling ended and they returned to the village or reservation. Only if a family had made the transition from tipi or lodge to frame house, as Zitkala-Ša's had, were the girl's Western housekeeping skills applicable—unless she worked as a domestic servant for local Anglo-Americans or at the mission itself. Native American girls' servitude filled a perceived need for trained household help; girls at the government's Phoenix Indian School were pressured to become servants, and this may have been the case at mission schools as well.[40]

The conditions that children reported enduring in school led many Native American parents to become firmly entrenched in their opposition to Anglo-American education. Other factors influenced them as well. The loss of the children to school was, in a way, like death in the family and community. "Since you have been here with your writing ... the place has become full of ghosts," one person told Charles Hall. In fact, schooling often did end in death, as Hall observed, especially for children at boarding schools, where infectious diseases took a high toll.[41]

The schools' threat to family well-being was heightened for mothers and grandmothers. A girl's participation in mission school undermined the women's ability to oversee her upbringing and to assure that she would take her place as a woman within the tribal tradition. "The grandmothers and many of the parents," reported Eda Ward, a teacher at Fort Berthold, "wish their children to be wholly Indian."[42] Female kin were responsible for instructing the child in both the practical and ritual activities that would shape her life as an adult within the community. Schooling removed a girl from the warmth of her kin's care, left her with no one to teach, comfort, or guide her as they would at home. Zitkala-Sa's mother had warned her departing child that "you will cry for me, but they will not even soothe you."[43]

Overworked, ill, and ethnocentric teachers were no substitute for the female network on which a girl's emotional, spiritual, and intellectual development depended. Although many missionary teachers were well intentioned and some really enjoyed their small charges, all were put off by the unfamiliar habits and values of the girls, and by the physical setting of their new environment. After nine years with the Ojibwa around the La Pointe mission, the ABCFM missionary Sherman Hall told his brother that "it is difficult to reach their hearts, or even their understandings with the truth. They seem almost as stupid as blocks. Yet they are far enough from being destitute of natural endowment. Most of them have superior minds by nature but they are minds in ruins."[44] Hall lasted a long time in the missionary field and was seemingly better able to adjust to his surroundings than many of his peers, yet he described his pupils as "ragged, dirty, lousy and disgusting little objects trying to learn to read their own language."[45] His attitude was more positive than that of one of his coworkers, however, who complained bitterly about "the effects of crowding from 40 to 70 dirty vicious Indian children" into a small schoolhouse.[46]

Not all teachers were so intolerant; most of the women at ABCFM's Dakota missions, for example, expressed real fondness for their students and jobs.[47] However, their commitment to "civilizing" their pupils precluded any real understanding of or concession to those pupils' culture or values. Most tried to treat their charges as they would Anglo-American youngsters.[48] By regarding their students simply as children rather than as *Indian* children, teachers essentially denied their very identities. This lack of cultural awareness or empathy contributed to the gulf between student and teacher and to the children's unhappiness and disorientation. Even well-intentioned but uninformed jollity could be a source of alienation and confusion for the newly (dis)located girl. Zitkala-Sa vividly remembered an incident at the Quaker school that to the staff must surely have seemed an inappropriate response to an innocuous action. On the night she arrived, "a rosy-cheeked paleface woman caught me in her arms. I was both frightened and insulted by such trifling. I stared into her eyes, wishing her to let me stand on my own feet, but she jumped me up and down with increasing enthusiasm. My mother had never made a plaything of her wee daughter: Remembering this I began to cry aloud."[49] Indeed, Native American parents treated their children with respect and reserve. In general, mothers were satisfied to scold a young offender or to threaten that an animal might kidnap her. The rare physical punishment was a light switching with a twig on the hands or knees, and only serious problems warranted it. Mission teachers, however, often were quite free with corporal punishment. Because such punishment was an accepted, even required, part of their own culture, beatings and other methods were frequently used. At ABCFM's Fond-du-Lac mission in Minnesota, Edmund Ely, a contemporary of Sherman Hall, moved Ojibwa parents and children to outrage when he pulled children's hair to discipline them.[50] Both the rough play that Zitkala-Sa was subjected to and the strict discipline and corporal punishment that were standard fare in most schools went against Native American child-rearing methods, frightening and humiliating students.

The difference in educational methods between Anglo-American and Native American cultures exacerbated the disorienting impact of the mission schools on girls. Native peoples did not confine either schooling or pupils to classrooms. Children roamed freely, exploring and learning individually and in groups. "I was a wild little girl of seven," Zitkala-Sa recalled. "Loosely clad in a slip of brown buckskin, and light-footed with a pair of soft moccasins on my feet, I was as free as the wind that blew my hair, and no less spirited than a bounding deer. These were my mother's pride—my wild freedom and overflowing spirits. She taught me no fear save that of intruding myself upon others."[51]

A girl's education took place constantly, through listening to and working with elders or in games with peers. Dakota girls engaged in "small play"—impersonating their mothers, and mimicking marital and domestic roles, conversations, and manners. Little girls worked companionably alongside their mothers, cooking, cleaning, and imitating them in beadwork and preparing medicinal plants. Zitkala-Sa's mother attracted her daughter's interest in beadwork by having her assist in designing and working on her own new moccasins. The woman's guidance made the child feel responsible and secure in her skill: "she treated me as a dignified little individual."[52]

Grandmothers also played a critical role in educating girls, enticing them with stories and reminiscences that illustrated tradition and history, drawing them toward an understanding of tribal philosophy and values. In *Waterlily*, Ella Deloria, a Dakota ethnologist, described a girl's relationship with her grandmother. The older woman's role was to make "well-behaved women" of her young charges. She tutored them in how to move, how to interact with elders, where to sit in the tipi. Only with constant and relentless reminding could she be sure that the girls had absorbed the lessons vital to their success in life. Moreover, the grandmother frequently talked with the girls about the children's early years in the camp, furthering their sense of belonging and place.[53] In the evenings, mothers often sent daughters—proudly bearing presents of tobacco or a favorite food—to invite grandmothers to instruct the girls in the myths and lessons that established their own place within the group and their people's place in the world.[54]

Women also guided their daughters and granddaughters through the ritual activities preparing them for womanhood. For example, Ojibwa girls of four or five understood their first vision quests, heading into the forests with their little faces blackened, hoping to establish a relationship with supernaturals. Over the next few years the length of the quests gradually increased; eventually a girl might spend four or more days fasting, sleeping, and dreaming for power. She was ritually greeted and feasted by her mother or a female relative upon her return home, and all listened attentively as she reported on her guardian spirit dreams.[55]

Mothers and grandmothers also presided over a girl's first menstruation. The Ojibwa built a special small wigwam near the main lodge, to isolate the adolescent's newly expanded spiritual powers from men's hunting powers and infants' weak natures. During these days of seclusion and fasting for dreams, the mother instructed the girl in the responsibilities of adult women and oversaw her beadwork and sewing. When a daughter's first menstrual period had ended, her female kin feasted her upon her return to the household and entry into womanhood. Thereafter, she was chaperoned by a grandmother or aunt until marriage.[56] Dakota girls similarly retired to a new tipi set up beyond the circle of the camp, and female relatives cared for them and instructed them in the duties of a wife and mother. When seclusion had ended, the Buffalo Ceremony took place, and female relatives set up a ceremonial tipi. A medicine man then called upon the spirit of the buffalo to infuse the girl with womanly virtue, and he informed the community that her childhood had ended. The mother now attempted to protect her daughter, insisting that she wear a rawhide chastity belt, and her grandmother took it upon herself to constantly accompany the girl.[57]

Clearly, it was difficult if not impossible for a girl at day or boarding school to engage in vision fasts or menstrual seclusion, both for practical reasons of time and distance from women relatives and because of the missionaries' opposition to such practices.[58] Girls who went to school were inevitably less immersed in their cultures and frequently felt less obligated or able to maintain traditional ways. Otter, daughter of Hidatsa shaman Poor Wolf, was only seven years old in 1881 when Charles Hall sent her to the Santee boarding school, 300 miles from her home near Fort Berthold. When she and her sister returned home, her father felt compelled to move because his daughters no longer fit into the old village life. Moreover, Otter, "having found the Christ-road, told her father how to become a 'child of God'" and convinced him to abandon his lifelong beliefs.[59] Similarly, Zitkala-Sa related that after three years at the mission school she felt that she had no place in the world, that she was caught in between two cultures. Four uncomfortable years as a misfit among her people prompted her to return to school and go on to college—without her mother's approval.[60]

Mission education clearly threatened and sometimes eliminated Native American women's ability to supervise their daughters. Its goal was to alienate girls from the cultural values and practices of their mothers and turn them instead to Christianity and the Anglo-American work ethic and material culture. Although missionaries were not overwhelmingly successful in achieving their goal of shaping a new generation of assimilated citizens, their programs did have a long-term and often devastating impact both on girls and on the daughter-mother-grandmother relationship. For Zitkala-Sa, it was a bitter experience. "Like a slender tree," she remembered, "I had been uprooted from my mother, nature, and God."[61]

NOTES

1. Zitkala-Sa (Gertrude Bonnin), *American Indian Stories* (Washington, D.C.: Hayworth Publishing, 1921; rpt. Glorieta, N.M.: The Rio Grande Press, 1976), pp. 44–45.
2. Ibid., pp. 40–41.
3. The Ojibwa (also known as Chippewa) are Algonquian-speaking peoples in the western Great Lakes region, southern Ontario, and Manitoba. During the nineteenth century most groups still retained a seasonal nomadism based on hunting and gathering, combined with occasional horticul-

ture in the southern groups. For cultural and historical descriptions, see Frances Densmore, *Chippewa Customs*, Smithsonian Institution Bureau of American Ethnology Bulletin 86 (Washington, D.C.: Government Printing Office, 1929); A. Irving Hallowell, *Culture and Experience* (Philadelphia: University of Pennsylvania Press, 1955); Harold Hickerson, "The Chippewa of the Upper Great Lakes: A Study in Sociopolitical Change," in Eleanor Burke Leacock and Nancy Oestreich Lurie, eds., *North American Indians in Historical Perspective* (New York: Random House, 1971), pp. 169–99.

The people generally known to outsiders by the misnomer "Sioux" (a French mispronunciation of a derogatory Algonquian term meaning "little adders") consist of seven linguistic and political subgroups, or "Fireplaces." The eastern groups call themselves "Dakota," while the western dialect pronounces that name "Lakota." Before the reservation era they were seminomadic hunter-gatherers who followed the buffalo. See Roy W. Meyer, *History of the Santee Sioux: United States Indian Policy on Trial* (Lincoln: University of Nebraska Press, 1967); Marla N. Powers, *Oglala Women: Myth, Ritual, and Reality* (Chicago: University of Chicago Press, 1986).

4. The last two decades have seen a significant growth in the written history of mission and government schools and Native American children's experiences in them. See, for example, Robert F. Berkhofer, Jr., *Salvation and the Savage: An Analysis of Protestant Missions and American Indian Response, 1787–1862*, 2d. ed. (New York: Atheneum, 1976); Henry Warner Bowden, *American Indians and Christian Missions: Studies in Conflict* (Chicago: University of Chicago Press, 1981); Mary Lou Hultgren and Paulette Fairbanks Molin, *To Lead and to Serve: American Indian Education at Hampton Institute, 1878–1923* (Virginia Beach: Virginia Foundation for the Humanities and Public Policy, 1989); Elizabeth Muir, "The Bark School House: Methodist Episcopal Missionary Women in Upper Canada, 1827–1833," in John S. Moir and C. T. McIntire, eds., *Canadian Protestant and Catholic Missions, 1820s-1960s: Historical Essays in Honor of John Webster Grant* (New York: Peter Lang, 1988), pp. 23–74; Francis Paul Prucha, *The Churches and the Indian Schools, 1888–1912* (Lincoln: University of Nebraska Press, 1979); Robert A. Trennert, Jr., *The Phoenix Indian School: Forced Assimilation in Arizona, 1891–1936* (Norman: University of Oklahoma Press, 1988). See also James Axtell, *The School upon a Hill: Education and Society in Colonial New England* (New Haven: Yale University Press, 1974).

For contemporary studies, see Estelle Fuchs and Robert J. Havighurst, *To Live on This Earth: American Indian Education* (Garden City, N.Y.: Doubleday, 1972); Margaret Connell Szasz, *Education and the American Indian: The Road to Self-Determination since 1928*, 2d ed. (Albuquerque: University of New Mexico Press, 1977).

Several Native American women have written about their school experiences. In addition to Zitkala-Sa, see Mary Crow Dog and Richard Erdoes, *Lakota Woman* (New York: Grove Weidenfeld, 1990); Polingaysi Qoyawayma (Elizabeth Q. White), *No Turning Back: A Hopi Indian Woman's Struggle to Live in Two Worlds* (Albuquerque: University of New Mexico Press, 1964). Maria Campbell, *Halfbreed* (Lincoln: University of Nebraska Press, 1973), relates her school experiences as a métis woman in Canada.

The following studies address the impact of schooling on Native American women and girls: Robert A. Trennert, "Educating Indian Girls at Nonreservation Boarding Schools, 1878–1920," in Ellen Carol DuBois and Vicki L. Ruiz, eds., *Unequal Sisters: A Multicultural Reader in U.S. Women's History* (New York: Routledge, 1990), pp. 224–37; Ruey-Lin Lin, "A Profile of Reservation Indian High School Girls," *Journal of American Indian Education* 26 (1987): 18–28; Beatrice Medicine, "The Interaction of Culture and Sex Roles in the Schools," in Shirley M. Hufstedler et al., eds., *Conference on the Educational and Occupational Needs of American Indian Women (1976)* (Washington, D.C.: National Institute of Education, 1980), pp. 141–58; Agnes F. Williams, "Transition from the Reservation to an Urban Setting and the Changing Roles of American Indian Women," in Hufstedler et al., eds., *Conference on the Educational and Occupational Needs of American Indian Women*, pp. 251–84.

5. Fuchs and Havighurst, *To Live on This Earth*, pp. 2–3; Charles L. Chaney, *The Birth of Missions in America* (South Pasadena: William Carey Library, 1976), pp. 70–71; Ernest Hawkins, *Historical Notices of the Missions of the Church of England in the North American Colonies, Previous to the Independence of the United States: Chiefly from the M.S. Documents of the Society for the Propagation of*

the Gospel in Foreign Parts (London: B. Stowes, 1845), p. 342. See James Axtell, *The Invasion Within: The Contest of Cultures in Colonial North America* (New York: Oxford University Press, 1985); Cornelius J. Jaenen, *Friend and Foe: Aspects of French-Amerindian Cultural Contact in the Sixteenth and Seventeenth Centuries* (New York: Columbia University Press, 1976); and J. H. Kennedy, *Jesuit and Savage in New France* (New Haven: Yale University Press, 1950), for discussions of French missionary education efforts in the colonial period. For the Spanish efforts to educate Indians in California, see Sherburne F. Cook, *The Conflict Between the California Indians and White Civilization, Ibero-Americana* 21–24 (1943).

6. Berkhofer, *Salvation and the Savage*, pp. 2–3, 12–13; Wade Crawford Barclay, *History of Methodist Missions, Part One: Early American Methodism, 1769–1844* (New York: Board of Missions and Church Extension of the Methodist Church, 1949–50), p. 164; Timothy L. Smith, *Revivalism and Social Reform: American Protestantism on the Eve of the Civil War* (Baltimore: Johns Hopkins University Press, 1980), pp. 58–62. For a detailed examination of the ABCFM, see William R. Hutchinson, *Errand to the World: American Protestant Thought and Foreign Missions* (Chicago: University of Chicago Press, 1987).

7. Sherman Hall to Lydia Hall, 15 June 1833, Sherman Hall Papers, Minnesota Historical Society (hereafter cited as SH), St. Paul.

8. John C. Lowrie, 2 March 1877, *American Indian Correspondence: The Presbyterian Historical Collection of Missionaries' Letters, 1833–1893* (Westport, Conn.: Greenwood Press, 1979), C:310 (hereafter cited as AIC).

9. Rayna Green, "'Kill the Indian and save the Man': Indian Education in the United States," introduction to Hultgren and Molin, *To Lead and to Serve*, p. 9.

10. Szasz, *Education and the American Indian*, pp. 9–10; Zitkala-Sa, *American Indian Stories*, pp. 39–40; Trennert, *The Phoenix Indian School*, pp. 113–14.

11. Charles Hall, "The Story of Fort Berthold," Papers of the American Board of Commissioners for Foreign Missions: Missions to the North American Indians, Houghton Library, Harvard University, Cambridge, Mass., 26: 6.48–49 (hereafter cited as ABC).

12. Ibid., pp. 17–18.

13. See, for example, Carol Devens, *Countering Colonization: Native American Women and Great Lakes Missions, 1630–1900* (Berkeley: University of California Press, 1992), chap. 5.

14. There are many fine works that address nineteenth-century views of women and education. See Polly Weltz Kaufman, *Women Teachers on the Frontier* (New Haven: Yale University Press, 1984); Mary Beth Norton, *Liberty's Daughters: The Revolutionary Experience of American Women, 1750–1800* (Boston: Little, Brown, 1980); Mary Ryan, *Cradle of the Middle Class: The Family in Oneida County, New York, 1790–1865* (Cambridge: Cambridge University Press, 1981); Barbara Leslie Epstein, *The Politics of Domesticity: Women, Evangelism, and Temperance in Nineteenth-Century America* (Middletown, Conn.: Wesleyan University Press, 1981). For discussions of the interactions between Native American women and missionaries, see Kendall Blanchard, "Changing Sex Roles and Protestantism among the Navajo Women in Ramah," *Journal for the Scientific Study of Religion* 14 (1975): 43–50; Devens, *Countering Colonization*; Lillian A. Ackerman, "The Effect of Missionary Ideals on Family Structure and Women's Roles in Plateau Indian Culture," *Idaho Yesterdays* 31 (1987): 64–73; Karen Anderson, "Commodity Exchange and Subordination: Montagnais-Nasakapi and Huron Women, 1600–1650," *Signs: Journal of Women in Culture and Society* II (1985): 49–62; Mary C. Wright, "Economic Development and Native American Women in the Early Nineteenth Century," *American Quarterly* 33 (1981): 525–36.

15. Isaac Baird to John C. Lowrie, 14 July 1883, AIC. G:1:111.

16. *Woonspe Wankantu* (Santee, Nebr.: Santee Normal Training School, 1879), ABC, 18:3.7, V. 5, 85.

17. William Thurston Boutwell, "Diary Kept by the Rev William Thurston Boutwell, Missionary to the Ojibwa Indians, 1832–1837," entry for 11 November 1833, William T. Boutwell Papers, Minnesota Historical Society, St. Paul.

18. Peter Dougherty to Mr. McKean, 25 September 1850, AIC, 7:1:13.

19. Peter Dougherty to Walter Lowrie, 25 December 1848, AIC, 7:3:167; 1 May 1849, AIC, 7:3:166; 4 September 1850, AIC, 7:1:7; 26 September 1853, AIC, 7:1:91; 16 January 1854, AIC, 7:1:108. Dougherty to P. Babcock, superintendent of Indian affairs, Grand Traverse, 14 October 1850, AIC,

7:1:8; J. G. Turner to Walter Lowrie, 5 January 1858, AIC, 7:2:47. For further explanation of these incidents, see Devens, *Countering Colonization*, chap. 5.

20. J. G. Hamilton, U.S. Indian agent, to Mrs. E. W. Blatchford, secretary of Women's Board, Chicago, 7 July 1875, ABC, 183.3.7, v.5, 170.

21. Susan Webb to J. O. Means, 8 February 1881, ABC, 18.3.7, v.4, 274.

22. Hall, "Ford Berthold," p. 46.

23. Isaac Baird to J. C. Lowrie, 30 December 1876, AIC, C:287; Baird to D. C. Mahan, U.S. Indian agent, 30 March 1878, AIC, E:1:3; Zitkala-Sa, *American Indian Stories* (n. 1 above), pp. 42–43. For a detailed discussion of women's responses to mission schools and missionaries in the Great Lakes area, see Devens, *Countering Colonization*, chaps. 3, 5.

24. Susan Webb to J. O. Means, 18 March 1881, ABC, 18.3.7, v.7, 276.

25. The reasons for their enrollment are not often clear. Many appear, like Zitkala-Sa, to have been enticed by the material goods promised them. Polingaysi, a Hopi, recalled that she was fascinated by the cotton dresses and food that the children received at school. See Qoyawayma, *No Turning Back* (n. 4 above), p. 23.

26. Zitkala-Sa, *American Indian Stories* (n. 1 above), p. 51.

27. Ibid., p. 65; Hall, "Fort Berthold," p. 49; J. C. McGillycuddy, *McGillycuddy, Agent* (Stanford: Stanford University Press, 1941), pp. 205–206, quoted in Medicine, "Culture and Sex Roles" (n. 4 above), pp. 149–50.

28. Leonard Wheeler to David Greene, 23 January 1843, ABC, 18.3.7., v. 2, 219. See Berkhofer, *Salvation and the Savage* (n. 4 above); and Michael Coleman, *Presbyterian Missionary Attitudes Toward American Indians, 1837–1893* (Jackson: University Press of Mississippi, 1985), for thorough explications of the workings of a mission classroom. See Barbara Welter's classic piece, "The Cult of True Womanhood, 1820–1860," *American Quarterly* 18 (1966): 151–74, for a perspective on nineteenth-century white female domesticity.

29. Fuchs and Havighurst, *To Live on This Earth* (n. 4 above), p. 19, observe that current pedagogy and curriculum in most schools for Native American children still are intended to alienate them from their own culture.

30. Leonard Wheeler, First Report of Manual Labor Boarding School, 11 January 1869, ABC (n. 11 above), 18.4.1, v. 2, 14.

31. R. David Edmunds, "National Expansion from the Indian Perspective," in Frederick E. Hoxie, ed. *Indians in American History* (Arlington Heights, Ill.: Harlan Davidson), pp. 159–77.

32. Berkhofer, *Salvation and the Savage* (n. 4 above), p. 39.

33. Martha Riggs Morris to J. O. Means, 6 May 1881, ABC (n. 11 above), 18.3.7. v. 6, 165. Boys, of course, did extensive manual labor as well, at most schools.

34. John Sunday to Robert Alder, 7 April 1841, Wesleyan Methodist Missionary Society Archives, London-North American correspondence, microfiche, United Methodist Archives and History Center, Madison, N.J., Box 102, 1841/42, 12C.

35. Martha Riggs Morris to J. O. Means, 6 May 1881, ABC (n. 11 above), 18.3.7, v. 6, 165; Alfred L. Riggs to John O. Means, Report of Santee Agency Station for the Year ending March 31, 1882, ABC, 18.3.7, v. 5, 64; M. A. Shepard to J. O. Means, 17 June 1881, ABC, 18.3.7, v. 7, 241.

36. Zitkala-Sa, *American Indian Stories* (n. 1 above), pp. 65–66. This pattern continued in government boarding schools well into the twentieth century. At the Rice Boarding School in Arizona in the 1920s, children were up at 5 a.m., spent half the day in school and half working, and made their own clothing and shoes. They did this on a diet of bread, coffee, and potatoes, which cost the school nine cents per day per child. (The minimum standard expenditure for healthy growth in those years was set by the government at thirty-five cents per day per child.) See Szasz, *Education and the American Indian* (n. 4 above), p. 19.

37. Susan Webb to J. O. Means, 8 February 1881, ABC (n. 11 above), 18.3.7, v. 7, 274.

38. Zitkala-Sa, *American Indian Stories* (n. 1 above), p. 67.

39. Crow Dog and Erdoes, *Lakota Woman* (n. 4 above), p. 28.

40. Berkhofer, *Salvation and the Savage* (n. 4 above), pp. 17–42; Leonard Wheeler to Selah B. Treat, 21 July 1857, ABC (n. 11 above), 18.4.1, v. 1, 265. Sherman Hall, at the American Board's La Pointe mission in Wisconsin, reported that he was very encouraged when families built and lived in frame

houses, as their closeness and sedentary life made them much easier to teach. See Hall to Laura Hall, 4 February 1835, SH (n. 7 above); Trennert, *The Phoenix Indian School*, (n. 4 above), p. 137.

41. Hall, "Fort Berthold" (n. 11 above), pp. 41, 59; Szasz, *Education and the American Indian* (n. 4 above); Trennert, *The Phoenix Indian School* (n. 4 above); Berkhofer, *Salvation and the Savage* (n. 4 above); and Zitkala-Sa, *American Indian Stories* (n. 1 above), all address the issue of children's deaths at school.

42. Eda Ward to J. O. Means, 13 March 1881, ABC (n. 11 above), 18.3.7, v. 7, 27.

43. Zitkala-Sa, *American Indian Stories* (n. 1 above), pp. 40–41.

44. Sherman Hall to Aaron Hall, 2 February 1842, SH (n. 7 above).

45. Sherman Hall to Laura Hall, 4 February 1835, SH (n. 7 above).

46. A. P. Truesdell, quoted in S. G. Clark to S. L. Pomroy, 11 May 1858, ABC (n. 11 above), 18.4.1, v. 2, 19.

47. Adele Curtis (Sisseton) reported, "I enjoy my work very *much indeed.*" Susan Webb (Santee) claimed that her years at the mission were the happiest of her life, as did Martha Paddock (Santee). Adele M. Curtis to Selah B. Treat, 9 December 1875, ABC (n. 11 above), 18.3.7, v. 6, 29; Susan Webb to J. O. Means, 8 February 1881, ABC, 18.3.7, v. 7, 274; Martha M. Paddock to J. O. Means, 20 June 1881, ABC, 18.3.7, v. 6, 187.

48. Fuchs and Havighurst report that currently "few teachers of Indian children overtly express bigotry, and most have a favorable attitude towards their pupils. But observers of Indian schools were often impressed by a view prevalent among many—that they did not treat their Indian pupils differently than others, that they saw children, not Indians. While this appears as an expression of egalitarianism, it does reflect an absence of sensitivity to the actual differences among pupil populations and a denial of Indian identity" (*To Live on This Earth* [n. 4 above], p. 199). While recognizing Christian missionaries' "need to help," Williams contends that "basic lack of respect for the Indian as a unique Native combined with the urban industrial value of converting others to their own religion also motivated their behavior" (Williams, "Changing Roles of American Indian Women" [n. 4 above], p. 262).

49. Zitkala-Sa, *American Indian Stories* (n. 1 above), p. 50.

50. Sister M. Inez Hilger, *Chippewa Child Life and Its Cultural Background*, Smithsonian Institution, Bureau of American Ethnology Bulletin 146 (Washington, D.C.: Smithsonian Institution, 1951), pp. 58–59; Laurence French, *Psychocultural Change and the American Indian: An Ethnohistorical Analysis* (New York: Garland, 1987), p. 107; Edmund F. Ely, Writing, 1 January 1835, Ely Family Papers, Minnesota Historical Society, St. Paul. For a discussion of Anglo-American child-rearing practices, see Philip Greven, *The Protestant Temperament: Patterns of Child-Rearing, Religious Experience, and the Self in Early America* (New York: Meridian, 1977), pp. 87–99.

51. Zitkala-Sa, *American Indian Stories* (n. 1 above), p. 8.

52. Ibid., pp. 20, 21; French, *Psychocultural Change*, pp. 107–108; Medicine, "Culture and Sex Roles" (n. 4 above), p. 146; Powers, *Oglala Women* (n. 3 above), p. 58.

53. Ella Carla Deloria, *Waterlily* (Lincoln: University of Nebraska Press, 1988), pp. 52–53, 70. The book, based on twenty years of scholarly field work about her people, was written in the form of a novel, with the goal of making it more accessible to a general readership.

54. Hilger, *Chippewa Child Life*, pp. 153–62; Ruth Landes, *Ojibwa Woman* (New York: Columbia University Press, 1938), p. 11; Williams, "Transition from the Reservation" (n. 4 above), p. 254; Medicine, "The Interaction of Culture and Sex Roles" (n. 4 above), p. 146; Zitkala-Sa, *American Indian Stories* (n. 1 above), pp. 13–15.

55. Hilger, *Chippewa Child Life*, pp. 39–50. Mountain Wolf Woman, a Winnebago (a tribe with many cultural similarities to the Ojibwa), described her experience: "My older sister Hinakega and I also used to fast. They used to make us do this. We would blacken our cheeks and would not eat all day. . . . We used coals from the fire to black our cheeks and we did not eat all day. . . . When father returned from hunting in the evening he used to say to us, 'Go cry to the Thunders'. . . . We used to sing and scatter tobacco, standing there and watching the stars and the moon" (Mountain Wolf Woman, *Mountain Wolf Woman, Sister of Crashing Thunder: The Autobiography of a Winnebago Indian*, ed. Nancy Oestreich Lurie [Ann Arbor: University of Michigan Press, 1961], pp. 21–22).

56. Hilger, *Chippewa Childlife*, pp. 50–55.

57. Powers, *Oglala Women* (n. 3 above), pp. 66–70.
58. Medicine, "Culture and Sex Roles" (n. 4 above), p. 153, has pointed out that the matter of learning appropriate gender roles of a child's particular tribe continues to be a problem in contemporary boarding schools.
59. Hall, "Fort Berthold" (n. 11 above), pp. 32, 98, 117 (quote).
60. Zitkala-Sa, *American Indian Stories* (n. 1 above), pp. 69–75. Qoyawayma described a similar experience; she had become "almost a stranger" in her own community. She eventually went to live with local Mennonite missionaries because her home life was too unsettling (Qoyawayma, *No Turning Back* [n. 4 above], p. 76). A Study of Navajo women who had accepted Christianity found that they tended to view themselves as outside traditional structures and did not feel obliged to maintain older social patterns, such as matrilocal residence: Blanchard, "Changing Sex Roles" (n. 14 above), p. 48.
61. Zitkala-Sa, *American Indian Stories* (n. 1 above), p. 97.

9

Margaret D. Jacobs opens her extraordinary exploration of Pueblo dances with a vivid scene: two male clowns, dressed as women and wearing short skirts, parade into an arena where they are subjected to physical humiliations and leers by male clowns dressed as men. In a spectacle that can be read in many ways, the dances involved vigorous action, especially the manipulation of the short skirts and the voyeurism. In some sense, the event as observers described it in the early twentieth century had uncanny parallels to Pueblo ceremonies Spanish colonists described some two or three centuries before, in which women exposed their genitals in an attempt to gain power over dangerous newcomers. In other words, the dances of the 1920s and those of an earlier day shared elements of exhibitionism and voyeurism, and both had profound symbolic significance. Given the overt sexuality of the twentieth-century Pueblo rites, and given what we have learned in the last two chapters about white attitudes and policies in that era, it is hardly surprising that the commissioner of Indian Affairs wanted to ban the dance.

But the saga of the dances involves more than just one official's crackdown on a ceremony that he neither understood nor appreciated. As Jacobs makes clear, many groups became involved in the dispute over the dances. Anglo-American "new feminists" argued that the rites symbolized women's sexual liberation and should therefore be celebrated. More conservative white women considered the dances a form of deviance that threat-ened Pueblo moral purity and therefore must be stopped. And Pueblo men—the only Pueblos to engage in public debate in an age when Pueblo women shared their views within their communities only—considered the dances part of a larger mission to protest and block the further white encroachment (cultural as well as physical). To them, the dances mocked white ways and the white obsession with Indians, a critique all the more powerful when white tourists paid to watch these Pueblo rituals, much to the chagrin of the Bureau of Indian Affairs.

Jacobs's treatment of the controversy reminds us that disputes over what was permissible in Indian Country often had ramifications well beyond the specific topic of discussion. In putting Pueblo clowns onto their reformist agenda, Anglo-American women engaged in debate about the future of their own society as well. The story of the Pueblo dances also reminds us that, for all its rich variety, certain central themes dominated Indian Country during this era. Some of the white women in this tale were part of the field matron program examined by Lisa Emmerich, while some of the Indian girls from boarding schools akin to those discussed by Carol Devens were also part of the controversy. And throughout was the federal campaign to control and to alter Indian life, imbued with white ideas of proper womanhood. Throughout, too, was the no less persistent and no less pervasive assertion by Indians that, as one Pueblo put it in 1926, "we ought to have a voice."

MAKING SAVAGES OF US ALL: WHITE WOMEN, PUEBLO INDIANS, AND THE CONTROVERSY OVER INDIAN DANCES IN THE 1920S

Margaret D. Jacobs

IN 1920, AS PART OF AN EXTENSIVE EFFORT to gather information about the rumored immorality of Pueblo dances, an inspector from the U.S. government took sworn affidavits and written statements from about a dozen Hopi Indians and seven white observers. In one of the statements, witness Evelyn Bentley, a field matron on the Hopi Indian Reservation in Oraibi, Arizona, described the scene:

> Two clowns dressed as women came into the court. Their skirts were very short, not over eleven inches long. The men clowns would go up to them and try to pull the skirts down a little. The clowns who stood behind the women would try to pull the skirts down in the back but while doing so the skirts would slip up in front. Then the clowns who stood in front would stoop down and look up under the skirt as if looking at a woman's private organs. Then the other clowns would come around and have a look, then all would make believe that they were trying to pull the skirts down, then stoop and look under to see how much they could see. All this brought forth much laughter and many yells from the crowd.[1]

Other witnesses testified that the clowns simulated sexual intercourse with Indian women or livestock and enacted skits depicting adultery, prostitution, and divorce. Reformers and Bureau of Indian Affairs (BIA) employees gathered about two hundred pages of this testimony into what became known in Indian reform circles as the Secret Dance File. Because reformers considered the Secret Dance File too obscene to print or to send by mail, they "confidentially passed [it] from hand to hand for two years," and a great chain of gossip developed regarding its contents.[2]

The Secret Dance File proved to be more than a source of shock and fascination to Indian reformers. It served as one of the major factors in 1921 that led Commissioner of Indian Affairs Charles Burke to sign Circular 1665, an order to all BIA superintendents that threatened to ban Indian dances that involved "immoral relations between the sexes" and "any disorderly or plainly excessive performance that promotes superstitious cruelty, licentiousness, idleness, danger to health, and shiftless indifference to family welfare."[3]

In 1923, Burke issued a supplement to the circular that endorsed six recommenda-

SOURCE: *Frontiers: A Journal of Women's Studies*, v. 17, n. 3 (1996), pp. 178–209.

tions made by a 1922 conference of missionaries. Concerned that Indians should adopt white conceptions of thrift and agricultural production, these recommendations prohibited give-aways, banned all dances between March and August, and forbade anyone under fifty from dancing. They also limited dances to one a month in the daylight hours on a day in midweek at one center in each district. Hoping to use moral influence, Burke's supplement called for a year's trial to determine if the Indians would voluntarily give up the "worst features" of their dances and threatened to "take some other course" of action if the Indians did not.[4]

When word of the Secret Dance File and of Burke's circular and supplement reached the newly formed Indian advocacy organizations of the 1920s, they quickly adopted a position in opposition to what writer Mary Austin called the "Bumbletonian Indian Bureau's" circular.[5] Disillusioned by World War I and disheartened by the modernization of America, many members of these new groups had "discovered" the Pueblos as the antidote to the ills of modern America. Together with the All Pueblo Council, they had successfully organized a nationwide campaign to defeat the Bursum Bill, legislation that they believed would have led to the Pueblos losing much of their land to surrounding Anglos, Hispanos, and Mexicans. In the 1920s, their efforts led to the elevation of the Pueblos as the signature Indian in the white imagination, taking the place, temporarily, of Plains Indians. A stormy controversy ensued between defenders of Pueblo dances, both native and white, and a group of reformers, BIA employees, and Pueblo Indians who favored a ban on many Pueblo dances.

Historians who have covered the dance controversy usually treat it just in passing as one of the events in John Collier's reform career before he became Franklin Roosevelt's Commissioner of Indian Affairs. They have generally characterized the public debate over Indian dances as a struggle over whether religious freedom should be extended to Native Americans.[6] To many Native Americans, the threat to ban Indian dances certainly did impinge on their religious practices. Yet, the controversy itself involved more than a constitutional debate on religious freedom. Many of the non-Indian participants in the controversy were white women who, in an era in which gender roles and female sexuality were in flux, used the controversy to voice their anxieties, their hopes, and their visions regarding new roles and sexual standards. In their discourse regarding Indian dances, these white women revealed a greater concern with emerging sexual mores in American society at large than with the traditional religious practices of Native Americans. From 1900 to 1930, a conflict ensued between two groups of feminists over the issue of sexuality. One group— female moral reformers—sought to maintain female purity and exert moral authority, while another group—"new feminists"—argued for women's self-fulfillment and expression of sexual desire.[7] Their debate on changing social and cultural mores did not always take place openly or consciously; often it showed up in arenas in which gender and sex were not explicitly being discussed.[8] In the controversy over Indian dances, female moral reformers tended to view Pueblo dances as symbols of sexual disorder that must be curbed. "New feminists" lauded these same dances as emblems of sexual liberation that should be preserved.

Pueblo men in the debate rejected both of these views of their dances and their culture. Instead, they highlighted a multitude of other interests, centered around land and water rights, deepening economic dependence on non-Indians, and the intrusions of new Protestant missionaries, government bureaucrats, anthropologists, writers, and artists. Their participation in the dance controversy reflected their own quest to come to terms with Mexican and white expansion into both their physical territory and their cultural arenas. To the Pueblos, the perpetuation or elimination of traditional dances represented competing approaches to coping with new economic, social, and cultural forces.

Interestingly, Pueblo women became powerful symbols for all sides in the dance controversy. White women who debated Indian dances, depending on their orientation toward changes occurring in white society, invested Pueblo women with either their greatest fears of sexual degeneration or their greatest hopes for sexual liberation. Pueblo men on both sides of the debate insisted on Pueblo women's modesty. They divided, however, on the role Pueblo women should play in the work of their villages and in the future of their pueblos. Due to the Pueblo custom that only certain men, chosen by the religious hierarchy, should represent their pueblos to outsiders, no evidence of Pueblo women's direct participation in the dance controversy surfaces in the written record. Nevertheless, autobiographies by two Hopi women provide clues as to how Pueblo women viewed themselves in relation to their symbolic roles.[9]

Beginning in the late 1870s, some middle-class Protestant white women had taken an active interest in reforming federal Indian policy. Inspired by a Ponca chief who toured eastern cities to relate the tragedy of Ponca removal, two veteran reformers, Mary Bonney and Amelia Stone Quinton, established the Women's National Indian Association (WNIA) in 1879. In 1881, the publication of Helen Hunt Jackson's *A Century of Dishonor*, which documented atrocities committed against Native Americans, nourished the new reform movement. (Male reformers founded the Indian Rights Association [IRA] in 1882.) These reformers believed that the resolution of the "Indian problem" could be achieved only if Native Americans became fully assimilated into mainstream American society. As one reformer, Mary Dissette, phrased it, "the greatest wrong the Indian has suffered at our hands has been his separation from our own social and national life."[10] Reformers designated a special role for white women to play in the process of assimilating Native Americans: "uplifting" supposedly degraded Indian women and transforming their pagan households into Christian homes.[11]

Taking its cue from this new, vocal, and influential group of reformers, the BIA crafted a policy designed to accelerate the progress of Indians toward "civilization." In the late nineteenth century, Congress passed the Dawes Act, which called for the allotment of communally held Indian lands to individual Indians, and established twenty-five off-reservation boarding schools as well as dozens of on-reservation boarding schools and day schools for Indians around the nation.[12] Institutionalizing the WNIA's notion of "women's work for women," the BIA hired many white women as school-teachers and initiated a field matron program "in order that Indian women may be influenced in their home life and duties, and may have done for them in their sphere what farmers and mechanics are supposed to do for Indian men in their sphere."[13]

Mary Dissette and Clara True, two of the most vociferous opponents of Pueblo Indian dances in the 1920s, had taken up the call for women's work for women among the Indians. In 1888, the Presbyterian Board of Home Missions had sent Dissette to work to convert and civilize the Indians at Zuni Pueblo. She stayed at Zuni for almost twelve years, serving first as the Presbyterian mission schoolteacher, then as superintendent of its Zuni Industrial School, then as a BIA schoolteacher, later as a nurse during the smallpox epidemic of 1898 to 1899, and finally as a field matron.[14] For the next thirty years, Dissette worked in various aspects of Indian education, teaching at Paguate Day School near Laguna Pueblo and at Santo Domingo Pueblo in the 1910s, serving as a librarian at the Santa Fe Indian School in the 1920s, and then working at Chilocco Indian School in Oklahoma before returning to live in Santa Fe.[15] During the course of her career in Indian work, Dissette befriended True, another female reformer. True became involved in Indian reform work in the 1890s when she served six years as principal of the boarding school at the Lower Brule Agency on the Sioux Reservation. From 1902 to 1907, True worked as the school teacher at the Santa Clara Pueblo day school, and in 1908 she became the superintendent of the Mission Indians at the Morongo Reservation near Banning in southern California. Around 1910, she returned to New Mexico to settle in the Espanola Valley, close to Santa Clara Pueblo. Here she owned and operated a series of ranches and managed an apple, hay, and livestock business.[16] From 1910 until the 1940s, although True did not work in an official capacity with the Santa Clara Indians, she involved herself intensely in their affairs.

White women who became interested in Indian reform at this time usually had roots in other women's reform activities. Mary Bonney had founded the Chestnut Street Female Seminary in Philadelphia, had served as an active member of the Woman's Union Missionary Society of Americans for Heathen Lands, and had held the presidency of the Women's Home Mission Circle. Amelia Stone Quinton had equally impressive reform credentials; she had worked in asylums, almshouses, infirmaries, prisons, and women's reformatories and had been a state organizer for the Woman's Christian Temperance Union.[17] Dissette and True also had significant connections to other middle-class female moral reform. For example, in the 1910s, as members of the WCTU, they joined forces to crusade against vice and corruption within the BIA.[18]

Before 1915, Dissette and True and other reformers among the Pueblos seemed to have taken little interest in Pueblo dances. Until that time, reformers' discussions of Indian dances had centered more on the dances of the Plains Indians. The BIA worried that Indian dances promoted "savagery" and warlike behavior and prevented the Indians from becoming more industrious. In 1883, the BIA compiled a "List of Indian Offenses," aimed at eradicating the Ghost Dance, the Sun Dance, give-aways, and other ceremonies that it believed led the Indians to be more warlike and less industrious.[19] The government virtually took no notice of Pueblo dances before 191520 In 1913, a lengthy report on the Pueblos contained nothing about their dances at all.[20]

In 1915, however, P. T. Lonergan, Superintendent of the Pueblo day schools, submitted a report to the BIA entitled "Immoral Dances Among the Pueblo Indians." His report would later be incorporated into the "Secret Dance File." Lonergan asserted that the dances the Pueblos held in secret were "grossly immoral" and that "some of the most disgusting practices are indulged in, the particulars being so bestial as to prohibit their description." To substantiate his claims, Lonergan included six letters from whites and Mexicans "living in the vicinity of the Indians."[21] The complaints regarding Pueblo dances and culture did not emanate only from white observers. Some New Mexico Pueblo Indians contacted BIA officials to alert them to their displeasure at having to perform the dances.[22] Several Hopis contributed their testimony to the Secret Dance File.

Despite these first signs that some whites and Indians found Pueblo dances problematic, it was not until the 1920s that an organized campaign against the dances occurred. In the meantime, female moral reformers focused on the BIA rather than Pueblo Indians as a hotbed of corruption and immorality. Even as Lonergan began his assault on what he deemed "grossly immoral practices among the Pueblo Indians," he and other BIA employees had become the subjects of an attack by True and Dissette. Alleging that several BIA employees under Lonergan's supervision had engaged in extramarital affairs, that Lonergan's assistant had contracted venereal disease, and that Lonergan himself visited houses of prostitution, True and Dissette waged a campaign to have Lonergan and other BIA employees removed from their positions.[23] In the early 1920s, the issue of Pueblo dances suddenly became more pronounced when the BIA sent Inspector E. M. Sweet to gather testimony regarding the alleged sexual immorality of Hopi dances. Dissette and True turned their crusade against sexual immorality toward the Pueblo Indians, finding in their traditional dances gross obscenity and debauchery. A furor built among reformers to condemn and restrict the secret dances of the Pueblo Indians.[24] Reformers saw their efforts come to fruition in 1921 when Commissioner of Indian Affairs Burke issued Circular 1665.

Circular 1665 and its supplement bear the particular mark of female moral reformers. The circular condemned dances that led Indians to neglect their "home interests" and promoted "shiftless indifference to family welfare." It recommended "fixing the standards of individual virtue and social purity that should prevail in all forms of amusement or symbolism" and inculcating "a higher conception of home and family life."[25] As Peggy Pascoe has analyzed, such rhetoric was ubiquitous among female moral reformers of the late nineteenth and early twentieth centuries.[26] The circular also promoted alternatives to dances—"something in the way of wholesome, educational entertainment that will tend to divert interest from objectionable native customs."[27] Urban progressive reformers similarly attempted to provide working-class women with wholesome substitutes for jazz dancing.[28] Indeed, the language of the circular paralleled the rhetoric used by reformers who thought that jazz dancing incited idleness and dissipation among American youth.[29]

Reformers justified their campaign to eradicate Indian dances based on the testimony found in the Secret Dance File. The performances of ritual clowns in the Pueblos' dances elicited particular condemnation from female moral reformers. Although Pueblo dances were solemn occasions in which the participants prayed for rain, a fertile and abundant crop, or a successful hunt, the dances also involved intermittent interruptions by a group of clowns. Moral reformers found the clowns' antics obscene. Field matron Bentley's description of the Hopi clowns' skit, in which they peeked up women's dresses, epitomized the vulgarity of Indian dances to moral reformers. Some Hopi converts to Christianity also testified that the practices of the clowns were sexually immoral. Hopi witness Johnson Tuwaletstiwa described a scene in a dance in which two *katsinas,* male masked impersonators of supernatural beings, pretended to work in their fields in front of the clowns.[30] In this scene, one katsina was dressed as a woman and one as a man:

> The clowns pretended not to see them. These two katsinas at length pretended to grow tired of their work, and went over to a place representing their booth and rested. Then, while the whole crowd of spectators were looking on, men, women and children, the katsina man took hold of the katsina woman and went through the performance of the act of cohabitation. Upon its conclusion the clowns turned and appeared to discover them, and asked what they were doing, to which, feigning shame, they made no reply. Thereupon one of the clowns approached the katsina woman and solicited her to do the same act with him. This led to a quarrel between the katsina husband and wife, ending in the wife discarding her husband, who walked around the street feigning weeping and lamentation because he was thus divorced after the Hopi manner.... Thereupon one and each and all the clowns severally, five in all, went through the act of cohabitation with the katsina woman successively.... The whole scene was a dramatization of the act of Hopi life depicting adultery and prostitution; the crowd meanwhile laughing and apparently approving and enjoying it as a dramatic representation of Hopi life.[31]

As Tuwaletstiwa expressed here, reformers and some Hopi witnesses believed the performances of the clowns to be actual representations of everyday Pueblo life. However, as we shall see, the clowns often performed antics deemed inappropriate by Pueblo Indians.

Reformers also charged that the dances served as occasions for unbridled sexual license, promoting premarital and extramarital sex and encouraging divorce. One Hopi witness, Kuwanwikvaya, asserted that, at Hopi dances, "young unmarried men and women ... commit fornication, and the married ones commit adultery."[32] Another Hopi witness recalled "six women ... who have had five or six husbands, discarding one for another, and nearly always at these dances or growing out of these dances."[33] Reformers and their Hopi informers also expressed alarm that "sex subjects and sex functions are the subjects of common conversation between [Hopi] men and women, boys and girls, in the home, anywhere, without restraint." Again, reformers and their witnesses blamed the dances for cultivating this atmosphere.[34]

Opponents of Pueblo dances also were appalled that Indian women, as they were impersonated by male clowns in the dances, appeared to be active sexual beings. Tuwaletstiwa expressed his disgust at a Hopi dance in which two clowns went through the motions of sexual intercourse. He remarked that "the conclusion of the scene was that the man got up and went leaping and singing happily and thus disappeared, while the woman [clown], more quietly but with expressions indicating happiness, also disappeared."[35] As portrayed by male clowns and as represented in the Secret Dance File, Indian women seemed to be active partners, not passive victims, in adulterous relationships and in fornication. This challenges female reformers' views of Indian women as the innocent victims of Indian male lust and BIA corruption.[36]

In the 1920s, female moral reformers uneasily combined this new view of Indian women with their older notions. In a 1924 letter, Dissette complained that in Pueblo cultures, "the male is supreme and all that contributes to his comfort or pleasure is his by right of his male supremacy."[37] However, in the same letter, Dissette also alleged that Indian women actively engaged in the sexual practices she deplored. She accused older women at Santo Domingo Pueblo of "instructing young girls in sex matters one of which was 'manipulating the penis'" during the ceremony.[38] This conflicted depiction of Indian women mirrored the new conceptions of white womanhood put forward by moral reformers in the 1920s in which, as one historian explains, "the proverbial dark lady and fair maiden were fusing into the same woman."[39]

Though reformers such as Dissette and True had worked with the Pueblos since 1888 and 1902 respectively, neither seemed to express any concern about Pueblo sexual morality until after 1915. As changing sexual mores in white American society became a topic of great controversy in the 1910s and 1920s moral reformers suddenly discovered rampant sexual immorality among Pueblos. Moral reformers' usage and condemnation of concepts current in white debates reveals the extent to which they projected their concerns about white sexual mores onto Pueblo Indians. One Hopi witness claimed that all through the Snake Dance, "men and boys and women and girls mingle freely together—there is 'free love.'"[40] Dissette condemned the supposed ease of divorce among the Zunis as "trial marriage." Notions of "free love" and "trial marriage" gained wide exposure and censure in popular magazines in the first three decades of the twentieth century.[41]

Reformers' concerns about Pueblo dances—that they encouraged promiscuity, adultery, and divorce, and that they led to more open discussions of sexuality and an active sexual role for women—masked their anxiety over these very trends in white society. Between 1867 and 1929, the divorce rate among Americans had escalated 2000 percent, and by the end of the 1920s one in six marriages ended in divorce. Such statistics upset many moral reformers and social critics, who feared that divorce imperiled women.[42] More frequent discussions of sexuality in white American society disturbed moral reformers as well. Ironically, their campaigns against venereal disease and prostitution had actually expanded the public discourse on sexuality.[43] At the same time that moral reformers came to "sexualize" Indian women, they had also begun to allow, with dismay, that white women, too, could be sexual agents. Whereas Victorian female moral reformers blamed male lust for fallen women, 1920s moral reformers raised the specter of "the girl vamp" who corrupted young men.[44] They worried that young white women's newfound expectation for sexual satisfaction was likely to lead to "a pagan attitude toward love itself."[45] In the minds of female reformers, Indian women became, in essence, "new women." Reformers blamed dances in white society as well as in Pueblo cultures for corrupting morals. Some commentators even drew connections between Indian dances and the new jazz dances. As one critic put it, "One touch of jazz makes savages of us all."[46]

Reformers' efforts to enforce Victorian moral codes in white American society seemed to have little effect on preventing what they believed to be rampant social disorder. While ostensibly condemning the supposedly free and easy sexual customs among Pueblo Indians, moral reformers gave voice, in reality, to their anxieties over the social disorder they believed would result from changes in white sexual mores. If this disorder and sexual immorality could be distanced from white culture and located within a "primitive" culture, perhaps it could be properly contained.

Not all white Americans or Pueblo Indians agreed, however, that Pueblo dances were immoral and should be banned. The new group of activists who admired and championed Pueblo culture reacted to the charges of the Secret Dance File in numerous ways. Some activists defended Indian dances based on what might be called an equal rights doctrine. Stella Atwood, founder and chair of the Indian Welfare Committee of the General Federation of Women's Clubs (GFWC), contended that "the Constitution of the United States guarantees religious liberty, [and] the treaty of Guadalupe Hidalgo asserted that none of [the Pueblo Indians'] religious ceremonies or religious life could be interfered with."[47] Another group of dance preservationists argued against the circular on the grounds that it would destroy a valuable part of America's cultural treasure. One of the new 1920s Indian advocacy groups, the American Indian Defense Association (AIDA), characterized the circular as part of the government's efforts to destroy "an incalculable wealth of folklore, of beautiful customs and arts and moral values."[48] Many white women who defended Pueblo dances developed what might be called a "sexually relativist" position in defense of the dances. In the first decades of the twentieth century, these women had begun to shape a new kind of feminism that extolled rather than denied women's "sex expressiveness," called for women's individual self-fulfillment rather than self-sacrifice, and challenged women's quest for moral authority. These new feminists found much to admire, rather than vilify, in Pueblo dances.

To these new feminists, Pueblo ritual clowns did not appear sexually immoral. Writer Erna Fergusson asserted that some of the clowns' sexual acts served as fertility rites, since their "prayers for rain often include appeals for all life, animal and human as well as plant."[49] Writer Mary Austin asserted that "the social function of the [clowns] is to keep the community in order, with whips of laughter. These humorous interludes often take the form of dramatic skits based upon the weakness or the misadventures of the villagers."[50] New feminists had adopted what would become some of the standard anthropological explanations for the clowns' performances. Anthropologist Alfonso Ortiz explains that one function of the clowns' sexual lampoons, particularly those involving phallic jokes, is "intended for . . . cosmic regeneration and renewal." Furthermore, some anthropologists have argued that the clowns could also serve to regulate community behavior by making fun of inappropriate actions. As anthropologist Vera Laski put it, "by discussing, publicly and jokingly, the most recent village gossip, especially that related to sex matters—ridiculing adultery and airing the gossip as to who sleeps with whom—they are the friendliest, gayest, and best liked moral squad any community ever had."[51]

New feminists of the 1920s also added another layer of meaning to the clowns and the dances that extolled Pueblo sexuality as "more natural" than white American sexuality. Austin revered the Hopis as a culture "where procreation is still associated with worship."[52] Fergusson declared that "to an Indian, human generation is no more obscene than is the fertilization and development of a plant."[53] In lauding the "natural" sexuality the clowns supposedly expressed, new feminists seemed to thumb their noses at the moral reformers' standards of acceptable sexuality. They also rejected moral reformers' condemnation of easy divorce. Anthropologist Elsie Clews Parsons (who advocated "trial marriage" in her 1906 book, *The Family*) marveled that Zuni women owned their houses and gardens and that their husbands joined the wife's household. "He stays in it, too, only as long as he is welcome," Parsons wrote. "If he is lazy, if he fails to bring in wood, if he fails to contribute the produce of his fields, or if some one else for some other reason is preferred, his wife expects him to leave her household. He does not wait to be told twice."[44]

Unlike moral reformers, new feminists conceived of Indian women as dignified and strong figures who played prominent roles in Pueblo culture. Fergusson's description of Indian women's part in the Deer-Dance at Taos captures this view of Pueblo women:

> Two women lead. . . . In one hand each woman carries pine twigs, in the other a gourd. At certain points in the dance each woman moves slowly down the line of waiting men, making sharp peremptory motions with the gourd. As she does this, each man drops to his knees. Returning, she makes a reverse gesture and the men rise. This perhaps typifies the call of the universal spirit of fertility, the usual significance of a woman figure in the Indian dances. They are treated with reverence, and during this figure the nonsense and the thieving of the [clowns] are stopped.[55]

New feminists' celebration of Pueblo women challenged reformers' notions that Indian women were either passive victims or active leaders in sexual immorality.

Like moral reformers, however, new feminists used the Pueblos to articulate their views on changing sexual mores in white society. They sometimes even invented a reflection of themselves within Pueblo cultures, as for example when Parsons concluded that a Zuni woman who dressed and acted as a man was a "strong-minded woman, a Zuni 'new woman,' a large part of her male."[56] Much like the moral reformers, in fact, new feminists envisioned Pueblo women as "new women." In their eyes, however, this merited admiration, not contempt.

Much as they often lauded new "sex expressiveness" for women, new feminists also harbored doubts about emerging sexual mores. They often conveyed a sense that women had lost control of their sexuality. For example when writer Mabel Dodge Luhan's lover (and later her third husband), Maurice Sterne, pressured her to have sex, Luhan wrote, "I felt very weary and emancipated. When he argued that it would interfere with his Work if I didn't let him make love to me, that old persuasion convinced me that I might as well be hospitable to him without stint and not be narrow-minded."[57] What Luhan and other new feminists had come up against was an unintended consequence of the new standards they helped to create. As other historians have noted, in the 1920s and beyond, women were not just allowed to be sexually expressive, they were required to be. Women who held back sexually risked being labeled as sexually repressed. As Christina Simmons and Estelle Freedman have argued, Victorian sexual standards had given precedence to women's control of sexual relationships. New sexual standards divested women of this control, "cast women as villains if they refused to respond to" male sexuality, and increased men's power in sexual relationships.[58]

When they set out to defend the Pueblos' dances on sexually relativist grounds, new feminists inevitably confronted their own ambivalence about emerging white sexual standards. This surfaced in some of their portrayals of Pueblo women. For instance, when Luhan acquired a shawl like those Pueblo women wore, she noted, "the Indian women are sheltered in their shawls, seemingly so comfortable and encompassed within them, so that their whole being was contained, not escaping to be wasted in the air, but held close and protected from encroachments. How exposed we live, I thought, so revealed and open! I longed for the insulation of the shawl and wore mine whenever I could."[59] New feminists represented Pueblo women as sexually expressive on the one hand and as modest and protective of their sexuality on the other. The Pueblo woman came to embody new feminists' desires for both a healthy "sex expressiveness" and for women's control over their sexuality.

Ambivalence led many new feminists to retreat from a sexually relativist defense of the dances. Although they often questioned moral reformers' sexual standards, at other times new feminists accepted the terms of moral reformers and merely denied that the Pueblos were sexually immoral. In the most striking illustration of this tendency, Luhan maintained that the Pueblos lead a

> well balanced, natural and usual sex life . . . in their family life. . . . They never *think* sex—or *talk* sex. They all seem to be horrified at bringing it into speech, letter, and discussion as [the moral reformers] are doing here—they are *ashamed* to think "their pueblo" could come under any such consideration. They have a strong natural modesty always. I have never seen a sign of sex exhibitionism in an Indian. They are . . . the purest people I know.[60]

Here Luhan seemed to equate terms describing the new sexuality she championed—"well balanced, natural and usual"—with notions of "modesty" and "purity" that moral reformers had long revered. Increasingly, rather than espousing a "sexually relativist" argument, new feminists came to defend the dances on the moral reformers' terms.

The Indian dance controversy climaxed, as it were, in 1924 at the General Federation of Women's Clubs (GFWC) Biennial Convention in Los Angeles. The GFWC's Indian Welfare Committee and its dynamic chairperson, Stella Atwood, had been instrumental in preventing the passage of the Bursum Bill. In 1924, Atwood hoped to place a resolution before the GFWC that would challenge the BIA's attempt to eliminate Indian dances by upholding the Indians' rights to religious freedom. But other women, led by True, crashed the convention. True organized a delegation of reformers and Pueblo Indians who opposed the dances to go to the "Christian women of the convention with a protest against the program of paganism . . . approved by Atwood." BIA Inspector and prominent Hispana civic leader Adelina "Nina" Otero-Warren accompanied True.[61] When True arrived in Los Angeles, she sized up the crowd of eight thousand women and decided it to be "nearly solidly hostile." She realized "we had to convert them." After much behind-the-scenes organizing, True succeeded in getting ten minutes on the program to make her case. During their allotted time, first Otero-Warren made an appeal to the "Christian women of America." Then Ida May Adams, a member of the Indian Welfare League of California, spoke on behalf of the Pueblo Indians who opposed Indian dances. Adams asked the Indians to stand and they "received vigorous applause." Then, according to True, "everybody knew there was a big fight on right then and there. It was no longer a one-sided game . . . the pagan issue getting all the support. There was a FIGHT on."[62]

In the meantime, hearing of True's planned attack, Atwood and her supporters had organized their own campaign to convince the women delegates of the need to preserve Indian dances. They brought in their own set of Indians to accompany them on stage and to attest to the beauty and dignity of Indian dances and religion. Charles Lummis, a renowned Southwestern writer and magazine editor, had penned a pamphlet in defense of the dances to be distributed at the door of the convention. Interestingly, the new feminists and their view of Pueblo dances as expressions of natural sexuality were all but invisible at this meeting. Lummis's pamphlet in support of the dances appealed to the GFWC women in the terms of the moral reformers. He argued that the GFWC must support Indian religion because "for millenniums" it "has made good husbands and good wives, good fathers and good mothers, obedient and filial children, good neighbors, and good citizens of that tiny Republic. The result of destroying that Faith would be to destroy that home life which no longer has general parallels among ourselves." Lummis further asserted that "no Pueblo dance was ever so provocative, so suggestive or so demoralizing as many—I fear I should say the majority—of the dances which our boys and girls witness and take part in."[63] In this setting, the sexually relativist argument of new feminists would not do. Here, it was necessary to appeal to the GFWC women on the grounds that since "Home" and "Religion" were rapidly disappearing in white culture, that where they still existed, in Indian culture, they must be preserved. In Lummis's pamphlet, the Pueblos became not harbingers of a modern sexuality and a new gender order, but emblems of a pre-modern life where "Home" and "Religion" still mattered. In fact, Lummis and many other defenders of Indian dances extolled Pueblo culture as neither a symbol of sexual degeneracy nor sexual liberation, but as the last bastion of social order.

Despite their differences, both the whites who opposed and the whites who defended Pueblo dances shared many similar assumptions. Each faction believed that one group of Indians represented the "authentic" contingency of the Pueblos. Each side also believed their Indians to be passive victims for whom they could speak. Moral reformers portrayed their Indians both as the victims of a tradition-bound, virtual dictatorship of Pueblo officials and of romantic propagandists who wanted to pre-serve Indians in their "backward" state for the benefit of science and art.[64] The new activists characterized their "authentic" Pueblo Indians as inheritors of an ancient and beautiful religious tradition who were being victimized by over-zealous moral reformers and a misguided Indian Bureau.[65] As at the GFWC meeting in Los Angeles, each faction of white activists often brought their group of representative Indians to white audiences to illustrate their case. On many of these occasions, Indians did not speak but seemed to serve only as props for their white advocates.

But Pueblo Indians did not accept their role as the ventriloquist's dummy and sought to redefine the terms of debate. Both those Indians who opposed and those who defended Indian dances sought to make their voices audible above the din of white debaters. During an All-Pueblo Council meeting in 1926, Pablo Abeita of Isleta Pueblo expressed frustration that whites left Indians out of debates about Indian matters. "They say: 'The Indians want this and the Indians want that,'" he observed of the recent hearings in Washington. "No Indian knows about it. They simply go ahead telling what they think the Indian wants. They ought to call the Indians there and ask what they want. It is not necessary to give him all he wants but it is necessary to listen to him. . . . We ought to have a voice."[66]

If female moral reformers and new feminists had listened to the Pueblos, they would have heard many voices. From those Indians who contested Pueblo dances, reformers would have received different reasons for opposing the dances than they expected. Among the Hopi, opposition to the dances derived from two diverse groups—older members of the tribe who considered themselves "traditional," and *some* younger Hopis who had attended boarding school and converted to Christianity. Many of the older Hopi witnesses explained their decision to testify against the dances as a wish to fulfill a Hopi prophecy. For example, several years before the com-pilation of the Secret Dance File, the Hopi Masawistiwa wrote a letter to the Commissioner of Indian Affairs in which he complained about the immorality of the dances. Masawistiwa explained that "the idea of reporting these matters to the Commissioner did not originate with me. Since the creation of the world, according to the traditions held by the Hopis, a revelation of these things was so ordained."[67]

Although the Hopi witnesses in the Secret Dance File agreed with the moral reformers that Hopi dances were immoral, they often fixed the blame for this alleged immorality on different parties than did the moral reformers. The reformers faulted "traditional Hopis" and vehemently opposed the dances because of their concern that federal boarding school education for Indian children would be a waste of money if the children were then reexposed to traditional dances. However, many Hopi witnesses believed that boarding school students were the cause, not the victims, of the sexual immorality of the dances. Judge Hooker Hongeva contended that "the returned students are the backbone of these immoralities. They have gone off to school and learned enough of the white man's ways to give them a puffed-up mind, or the 'big head,' and they come back and plunge into these ways, with adultery as their bait, and become leaders in these gross wrong things."[68] To at least some Hopis who opposed the dances, boarding school education, not tribal tradition, was to blame for the supposed immorality in Hopi dances.

In New Mexico, opposition to the dances developed mainly among *some* Pueblo Indians who had spent long years in boarding school away from their pueblos. Often their opposition to the dances went hand-in-hand with their rejection of other aspects of Pueblo life. Many chose to wear Western dress and objected to working on their pueblo's communal irrigation ditch. Their refusal to conform to Pueblo norms often elicited beatings and severe punishment from their tribal councils. However, these Pueblos did not seem to disapprove of the dances as sexually immoral. Instead, they had more "practical" reasons for opposing the dances, believing that they interfered with work and impeded the progress of the pueblo. Taos Indian Joe Lujan told reformers who interviewed him that "the only thing is that [the dances] interfere with the progress of the children. I don't know of any immorality connected with them."[69]

Pueblo Indians who defended their dancing also denied any sexual immorality in their dances or in their culture. Turning the tables on moral reformers, many Pueblo Indians contended that it was really white dances that were sexually illicit. As Martin Vigil of Tesuque Pueblo told an interviewer, "our dances are not wicked like you people. . . . You come down to any Pueblo, visit our dances, we don't hug each other when we dance. . . . We dance about five feet apart, not like you people."[70] Ritual clowns in Pueblo dances often used their performances to comically illustrate Vigil's point. Some of the clowns' performances can best be seen, in fact, not as a reflection of either the immorality or liberated quality of everyday Pueblo life, but as a parody of white behavior. Historically, Pueblo clowns had used their performances to "transform what might have been unique and disruptive historical events into a part of the ongoing, internal, cultural dialogue of the people. . . . They make fun of outsiders, thereby reinforcing the community's own sense of self-worth and cultural continuity."[71] Fergusson once observed that the clowns "seem to embody the Indian's real attitude toward whites. The white man is usually the butt of the joke."[72] In some of the clown's skits, what moral reformers (and, to some extent, new feminists) thought they were seeing—reflections of actual Pueblo sexuality—was actually a mirror held up for them to view how the Pueblos represented white sexuality.

The clowns used their acts to parody whites in all their interactions with the Pueblos. At San Ildefonso Pueblo, one of the clowns

> made a specialty of tourists. With parasol and handbag, [he poked] his way around the Indians like a member of the Podunk Woman's Club, gathering material for a lecture on aborigines. He patted the babies, fingered the women's jewelry, asked embarrassingly intimate questions, and made explanatory remarks over his shoulder. "She says she does bathe her baby every day.... Yes, she wears underwear."[73]

The clowns also mocked white sexual behavior, even their dances. Pueblo observations of white dances and loosening sexual mores often became fodder for Pueblo clowns. Writer Elizabeth DeHuff figured out that a group of small Indian boys who were dressed in the "cast-off garments of white neighbors" performed in a "dance closely related to the 'Charleston,'" and DeHuff recognized the popular tune they sang.[74]

The Pueblos even ridiculed the peculiar desire of whites to pry into other people's sexuality. The scene Bentley described in her testimony for the Secret Dance File can be interpreted as the Pueblos' pointed parody of white sexual politics. Two clowns dressed as women in very short skirts entered the dance plaza. Male clowns pretended to try to pull their skirts down, but then stooped and look under their skirts.[75] This skit possibly served both to spoof new sexual mores in white culture (as expressed in dress) and to critique the moral reformers' obsession with finding and rooting out sexual impropriety. Though claiming to be repulsed and shocked by the alleged sexual immorality of Pueblo dances, moral reformers seemed to take a voyeuristic interest in attending the dances and in collecting ever more testimony about them. This phenomenon was not lost upon the Indians.

The clowns' mocking of white behavior served many purposes: to temporarily overturn power relationships between whites and Indians, to critique white culture, and to differentiate Pueblo from white culture. Pueblos had become increasingly dependent on whites for their economic livelihoods in the 1920s, and the government had succeeded in forcing many of their children into schools. Moral reformers repeatedly stressed that Indian cultures were inferior to white civilization. Overpowered by whites in many aspects of their lives, some of the clowns' performances offered the Pueblos a much needed opportunity to symbolically reverse hierarchies, to feel powerful over and superior to whites. Some anthropologists have argued that, in general, the clowns' skits and antics created a carnival-like occasion in which the social order was turned upside down.[76] At the same time, the clowns' parody of white behavior provided another lesson in how good Pueblos should not behave.[77] Given that some Pueblos had become interested in adopting white ways, the clowns may have ridiculed white lifestyles in order to deter young Indians from choosing to abandon Pueblo ways. Presenting whites in the clowns' skits as the virtual opposite of Pueblo Indians served to fortify the boundary between Pueblo and white society.[78]

As they did in white women's debates over the dances, Pueblo women played an important symbolic role in Indian debates. Unlike white women, however, Pueblo men on both sides of the debate insisted on the "modesty" of their women. They often contrasted their women's respectable behavior with that of supposedly immodest white women. Hopi Otto Lomavitu, a contributor to the Secret Dance File, wrote to the editor of the Flagstaff, Arizona, newspaper, "I wish to say that I am proud of my poor benight [*sic*] people that though they lack education, they have enough decency to mark out a woman clothed in nudity, ever admiring herself in a glass, twisting her head like a reptile, ever powdering her nose and painting her lips and eyelids, as absolute shamelessness."[79]

The two Indian sides in the dance controversy, however, presented competing visions of Pueblo women in the realm of the gendered division of labor. As white women had superimposed their view of "new womanhood" on to Pueblo women, Pueblo Indian men also invoked Pueblo women to symbolize their opposing positions regarding Indianness and progress. The dispute in the late 1920s at Santa Clara Pueblo illustrates this point. When representatives from both the "progressive" and "conservative" parties in the pueblo met with Assistant Commissioner of Indian Affairs Edgar Merritt to resolve their differences over who should govern the pueblo, the issue of whether Pueblo women should work only in the home or still participate in the customary cleaning of the entire village proved particularly contentious. Desiderio Naranjo, the governor from the Progressive Party, listed as one of his grievances the way in which the village was cleaned:

> Now according to the regulation of this village, sweeping the village is just once a year. . . . What we don't agree with us is for all to get out, women, children; the men are sweeping the village and the women carrying the dirt out on their backs and that doesn't suit us very well. It may be all right a hundred years ago the time when we didn't have no wagons or teams to throw the trash out. But now we have teams and wagons to haul the trash out of the village. It is not necessary for the women to get out and sweep the village, they have plenty to do at home.

In contrast, Juan Jose Gutierrez, governor for the Conservative Party, insisted that women should still dispose of the trash in the village.[80]

The BIA had also bound Indian women's domesticity in the home to the notion of Indian "progress." Not surprisingly, therefore, Merritt agreed with Naranjo, using the occasion to preach, "We men in America pride ourselves upon our generosity to our women folks. It is said that the American husband is the best husband in the world because he is always generous to his wife and children and he protects them in every way possible. I am sure that you want to be just as good to your women folks as any other man in America." Merritt ruled that on cleaning days, the women be required to work in their homes, but not to haul the trash away.[81]

Since Pueblo custom designated men as their pueblos' representative to the outside world, Pueblo women themselves seem not to have participated in the dance controversy. Nevertheless, autobiographies by two Hopi women—Polingaysi Qoyawayma and Helen Sekaquaptewa—provide some clues as to how some Pueblo women may have reacted to their depictions in the dance controversy. Qoyawayma and Sekaquaptewa reinforced Pueblo men's view of Pueblo women as modest. In her as-told-to autobiography, Qoyawayma, for example, indicted the BIA for their violation of Hopi sexual codes:

> Worst of all [the injustices whites had done to them], she had seen women stripped and marched through a dipping vat like so many cattle, because—so the white man claimed—an epidemic threatened the reservation residents. This was a thing no Hopi woman could forgive. Children may run naked, but grown girls and women are modest. To force the exposure of their bodies in this way had been unthinkable.[82]

Qoyawayma strongly countered white women's images of Pueblo culture and womanhood. Known first as Bessie and then as Elizabeth Ruth by white missionaries, Qoyawayma refused to play the role of victim of Indian male lust assigned to her by some moral reformers (as well as some Hopi witnesses). Inspector Sweet and other moral reformers used Elizabeth Ruth/Qoyawayma as an example to prove their claim that the Hopis were licentious and that Indian women were victims in need of rescue. Sweet wrote:

> Elizabeth Ruth and Minnie Jenkins are fine types of Indian young womanhood ... lifted from an otherwise unspeakable life ... but they must make their home with the missionary and his family, for the reason that their chastity would have utterly no protection in an Indian village where ... promiscuous adulterers ... are allowed to run at large after night.[83]

In her autobiography, however, Elizabeth Ruth/Qoyawayma explained her move to the home of the missionaries in quite different terms. Miserable at home because her parents refused to convert to Christianity and to adopt the American customs she had learned at boarding school, Qoyawayma claimed she had moved to the missionary's home to be in a more hospitable environment in which her views were accepted and in which she could enjoy modern conveniences. Instead of conceiving of herself as the moral reformers did, as an object to be rescued from an "unspeakable life," Qoyawayma framed herself as the active subject who consciously chose to move to the missionary's home.[84] As Qoyawayma represented herself, she did not abandon Hopi ways in her early life because she found her old life "immoral." Rather, she wanted what she believed whites had: "abundant supplies of food, good clothing, and opportunities to travel."[85]

Sekaquaptewa and Qoyawayma also rejected the notion of new feminists that Indian women were victimized by the BIA and moral reformers. New feminists were fond of charging the Indian Bureau with forcing Indian children to go to boarding school. But Sekaquaptewa, after ten years at Keams Canyon Boarding School, wished to continue her schooling. Because she was still a minor, she needed her parents' permission to attend an off-reservation school. She managed to cajole BIA officials into letting her attend Phoenix Indian School for three years without her parents' permission. Qoyawayma ventured down the mesa to the newly opened Keams Canyon School to enroll herself. As described in her autobiography, "No one had forced her to do this thing. She had come down the trail of her own free will." She also hid herself in a wagon bound for Sherman Institute in Riverside, California, an Indian boarding school, and would not get out until her parents signed a paper allowing her to go.[86] Qoyawayma and Sekaquaptewa proved unwilling to accept the role of victim. Although they did not participate directly in the dance controversy, their autobiographies indirectly countered white women's images of Indian women as either sexually immoral or liberated.

Who won the dance controversy? True declared victory at the Los Angeles meeting, believing she had participated "in forming and conducting a small world court in which paganism was tried and found wanting."[87] The GFWC did not pass a resolution calling for the preservation of Indian dances and postponed the election of the Indian Welfare Committee chair.[88] Yet defenders of Indian dances seem to have won the larger dance controversy. After publishing a debate between Austin and reformer Flora Seymour in *Forum,* the editors received many more letters favoring the preservation of Indian dances.[89] Atwood won back her position as chair of the Indian Welfare Committee. In 1925, in a case brought against the governor and council of Taos for allegedly beating two returned Indian students who did not wish to wear Indian costume during a dance, the judge found that the Pueblos should be allowed to regulate their own affairs.[90] Although the BIA continued to use Circular 1665 to suppress native religion among some tribes, by the late 1920s the issue of Indian dances had all but faded from public debate.[91]

At the same time, it is not clear who "won" the subtextual battle over white sexual mores. True believed that "pagan" sexual immorality with all of its parallels to emerging modern sexual mores in America had been convicted and given a death sentence at the GFWC meeting. She may have been right. Though the dance controversy was settled in favor of the Pueblos, those who defended the dances at the GFWC meeting did so on the terms of moral reformers. No one stood up to defend Pueblo dances on the grounds that the Pueblo had more "natural" sexual standards than white Americans. Instead, Lummis's elevation of the Pueblos as the epitome of "Home" and "Religion"—values moral reformers had long upheld—became the major argument in favor of the dances. By the late 1920s, new feminists seem to have adopted Lummis's position. Their uncertainty about emerging sexual mores led them to transform Pueblo women from models for new women to preservers of tradition.

As for the Pueblos, both those who opposed and those who defended the dances actually benefited from the dance controversy. Both sides learned to use white women's interest in their affairs for their own purposes. Pueblo Indians who opposed the dances turned the moral reformers' concern into a vehicle through which they made known their other grievances and through which they also articulated their vision for the future of Indian-white interaction. To some extent, they diverted the moral reformers from their original purposes. What moral reformers initiated as a campaign to eradicate the "immoral" dances of the pueblos evolved instead into a defense of those Indians who did not wish to dance or to clean their pueblo's community irrigation ditch. After the dance controversy died down, the Progressive Pueblo Council and their primary white sponsor, Clara True, sought to challenge the existing leadership structures among the pueblos, calling essentially for a separation of civil from religious affairs by disempowering the religious leader of each pueblo, the *cacique*.[92]

Indians who defended their dances realized that their white allies in the dance controversy could help further their primary interests—the return of land and water rights.[93] During the dance controversy, new white activists had developed images of profoundly religious traditional Pueblo Indians who had kept pure their ancient, nature-based creed against all odds. In their portrayal of the Pueblos, the new activists privileged religion as a defining characteristic of Pueblo life over other cultural, social, and economic traits. In subsequent years the Pueblo Indians, particularly those at Taos Pueblo, turned this white portrayal to work for them in their battles to regain some of their original use-areas. If claims to the land based on pre-contact sovereignty had little impact in courts, perhaps claims based on the sacredness of certain land sites and on religious freedom would resonate among white activists and policymakers. As Sylvia Rodriguez has pointed out, by using the emerging white romantic view of them in the 1920s, Taos Pueblo eventually regained the Blue Lake area in the mountains above the pueblo—land they had once used freely.[94]

Pueblos who defended their dances did not realize all of their goals, however. Although they equated the perpetuation of their dances with the maintenance of autonomy and the prevention of integration into white culture, their dire economic straits forced them to develop some means of earning income. Increasingly, the Pueblos commercialized their public dances as well as their traditional crafts. In essence, they marketed their ethnic identity for tourists in order to cope with the exigencies of dependency. This strategy threatened to corrode the very cultural boundary they sought to strengthen.

The controversy over Indian dances in the 1920s seems in its simplest terms to have been a battle between assimilationists and cultural preservationists over Indian religion. But a deeper reading of the controversy yields insight into a myriad of other issues. The controversy reveals how white women attempted to make sense of rapidly changing sexual mores in their own society. It also illuminates how Pueblo Indians coped with increasing acculturation pressures. Finally, it illustrates how Indian women came to serve as powerful symbols of both tradition and change for all parties in the controversy. These issues all become interwoven in the scene Bentley recounted in the Secret Dance File. Here Bentley expressed her shock that Hopi clowns looked up the skirts of women. Bentley's testimony fueled female moral reformers' attempts to restrict Pueblo Indian dancing, an effort that seemed to become necessary to them only when they sensed that sexual mores were spinning out of control in white society. Other white women—new feminists—opposed efforts to ban Pueblo dancing, discovering in the Pueblos a society that embodied their emerging ideals of women's sexual expressiveness and sexual control. Pueblo men, who enacted this skit, seemed to have actually designed it not to reflect their own society but to comment upon and ridicule white sexual mores. Pueblo women, depicted by male clowns in the dance, became 1920s-style "new women," at once reviled, revered, and ridiculed.

NOTES

1. Statement of Evelyn Bentley, September 30, 1920, E. M. Sweet, Jr., collection, National Anthropological Archives, Smithsonian Institution, Washington, D.C. The Pueblos include both the Hopis of Arizona and all of the Pueblo peoples of New Mexico. Even though all of these groups are considered Pueblos, there are many significant differences of language, religion, social structure, and ceremonial cycle between the Hopi and the Rio Grande Pueblos and among the Rio Grande Pueblos. See Edward Dozier, *The Pueblo Indians of North America* (New York: Holt, Rinehart, and Winston, 1970). The only other historical article I know of that has drawn upon the so-called Secret Dance File (the Sweet collection) is Martin Bauml Duberman, "Documents in Hopi Indian Sexuality: Imperialism, Culture, and Resistance," *Radical History Review* 20 (spring/summer 1979): 99–130. This article reprints some of the affidavits in the Secret Dance File but provides little analysis.

2. John Collier, who became Commissioner of Indian Affairs under Franklin Roosevelt in 1933, railed against the Secret Dance File as "subterranean propaganda." See "For two years, the public has heard," n.t. (1923), and John Collier, letter to the editor, *New York Times,* November 14, 1924, carton 1, "Collier, Pueblos and Religious Persecution," California League of American Indian (CLAI) Papers, Bancroft Library, Berkeley, California.

3. Circular 1665, John Collier papers (Sanford, N.C.: Microfilming Corporation of America, 1980), reel 5.

4. Circular 1665 and supplement, Collier papers, reel 5.

5. Mary Austin, *Land of Journey's Ending* (New York: The Century Company, 1924), 444. These new Indian advocacy organizations included the American Indian Defense Association (AIDA), the New Mexico Association on Indian Affairs (NMAIA), the Eastern Association on Indian Affairs (EAIA), and the Indian Welfare committee of the General Federation of Women's Clubs (GFWC).

6. Lawrence C. Kelly, *The Assault on Assimilation: John Collier and the Origins of Indian Policy Reform* (Albuquerque: University of New Mexico Press, 1983), 298–339; Kenneth Philp, *John Collier's Crusade for Indian Reform* (Tucson: University of Arizona Press, 1977), 57–65; and David M. Strausfield, "Reformers in Conflict: The Pueblo Dance Controversy," in *The Aggressions of Civilization: Federal Indian Policy Since the 1880s,* ed. Sandra Cadwalader and Vine Deloria, Jr. (Philadelphia: Temple University Press, 1984), 19–43.

7. Paula S. Fass, *The Damned and the Beautiful: American Youth in the 1920s* (New York: Oxford University Press, 1977); Paul Robinson, *The Modernization of Sex: Havelock Ellis, Alfred Kinsey, William Masters and Virginia Johnson* (New York: Harper & Row, 1976), 1–41; Elaine Tyler May, *Great Expectations: Marriage and Divorce in Post-Victorian America* (Chicago: University of Chicago Press, 1980); Peter Gabriel Filene, *Him/Her/Self: Sex Roles in Modern America* (New York: Harcourt, Brace, Jovanovich, 1974), 1–168; Ellen K. Rothman, *Hands and Hearts: A History of Courtship in America* (New York: Basic Books, 1984), 179–311; John D'Emilio and Estelle Freedman, *Intimate Matters: A History of Sexuality in America* (New York: Harper & Row, 1988), 171–274; William L. O'Neill, *Divorce in the Progressive Era* (New Haven: Yale University Press, 1967); Kathy Peiss, *Cheap Amusements: Working Women and Leisure in Turn-of-the-Century New York* (Philadelphia: Temple University Press, 1986), especially 163–84; Ruth Rosen, *The Lost Sisterhood: Prostitution in America, 1900–1918* (Baltimore: Johns Hopkins University Press, 1982); and Carroll Smith-Rosenberg, "The New Woman as Androgyne: Social Disorder and Gender Crisis, 1870–1936," in *Disorderly Conduct: Visions of Gender in Victorian America,* ed. Carroll Smith-Rosenberg (New York: Alfred Knopf, 1985), 245–96.

8. While historians Joan Wallach Scott and Carroll Smith-Rosenberg have argued in several essays about ways in which discourses use gender, sexuality, and the body as metaphors for other political and economic conflicts, this article argues that the reverse can be true as well. Discourses about other conflicts can also be used for debating matters of gender and sexuality. See Scott, "Gender: A Useful Category of Historical Analysis," in *Gender and the Politics of History*, ed. Joan Wallach Scott (New York: Columbia University Press, 1988), 28–52; and Smith-Rosenberg, "Hearing Women's Words: A Feminist Reconstruction of History," in *Disorderly Conduct,* 11–52.

9. Many anthropologists have observed that the Pueblos customarily designated certain men as the spokesman for their pueblos to outsiders. See Alice Marriott, *Maria: The Potter of San Ildefonso* (Norman: University of Oklahoma Press, 1948), 119. On the differences between men's and women's roles, see M. Jane Young, "Women, Reproduction, and Religion in Western Puebloan Society," *Journal of American Folklore* 100 (October-December 1987); and Alice Schlegel, "Male and Female in Hopi Thought and Action," in *Sexual Stratification: A Cross-Cultural View,* ed. Alice Schlegel (New York: Columbia University Press, 1977).

10. Mary Dissette to Miss Willard, March 3, 1924, Indian Rights Association (IRA) papers (Glen Rock, N.J.: Microfilming Corporation of America, 1975), reel 40.

11. Amelia Stone Quinton, "Care of the Indian," in *Woman's Work in America,* ed. Annie Nathan Meyer (New York: Henry Holt and Company, 1891), 373–91; Valerie Sherer Mathes, "Nineteenth Century Women and Reform: The Women's National Indian Association," *American Indian Quarterly* 14:1 (1990): 3–18; Helen Wanken, "Woman's Sphere and Indian Reform: The Women's National Indian Association, 1879–1901" (Ph.D. diss., Marquette University, 1981), 7–38; and Peggy Pascoe, *Relations of Rescue: The Search for Female Moral Authority in the American West, 1874–1939* (New York: Oxford University Press, 1990), 7–10.

12. Frederick Hoxie, "The Curious Story of Reformers and the American Indians," in *Indians in American History,* ed. Frederick Hoxie (Arlington Heights, Ill.: Harlan Davidson, 1988), 213; Brian Dippie, *The Vanishing American: White Attitudes and United States Indian Policy* (Middletown, Conn.: Wesleyan University Press, 1982), 108–11, 161–76; Francis Paul Prucha, "Indian Policy Reform and American Protestantism, 1880–1900," in *People of the Plains and Mountains: Essays in the History of the West,* ed. Ray Allen Billington (Westport, Conn.: Greenwood Press, 1973), 126–29, 134–39; Lisa Emmerich, "'To respect and love and seek the ways of white women': Field Matrons, the Office of Indian Affairs, and Civilization Policy, 1890–1938" (Ph.D. diss., University of Maryland 1987), 12–13; and Francis Paul Prucha, *American Indian Policy in Crisis: Christian Reformers and the Indian, 1865–1900* (Norman: University of Oklahoma Press, 1976), 169–401.

13. Quoted in Emmerich, "'To respect and love,'" 24. See also, Helen Bannan, *"True Womanhood" on the Reservation: Field Matrons in the U.S. Indian Service,* Southwest Institute for Research on Women, Working Paper no. 18 (Tucson: Women's Studies, 1984), 5–6; and Emmerich, "'To respect and love,'" 16–36.

14. Dissette to Herbert Welsh, June 18, 1894, Dissette to Mrs. Miller, March 14, 1894, and Dissette to "Friend," April 7, 1894, IRA papers, reel 11; Dissette to Welsh, February 5, 1896, and Dissette to D. R. James, June 4, 1895, IRA papers, reel 12; Dissette to Welsh, April 25, 1898, IRA papers, reel 13; and Dissette to Miss Willard, March 3, 1924, IRA papers, reel 40.

15. See Record Group (RG) 75, Pueblo Records, Superintendent's Correspondence with Day School Employees (entry 40), box 5, Paguate 1914 folder, and box 8, Santo Domingo 1914 folders, National Archives and Records Administration (NARA), Rocky Mountain Branch, Denver; "Dissette Collection of Indian Photographs," *El Palacio* 51 (March 1944): 60; and Fred Kabotie with Bill Belknap, *Fred Kabotie: Hopi Indian Artist* (Flagstaff: Museum of Arizona Press, 1977), 29. Dissette died in 1944.

16. Clara True to Matthew Sniffen, January 29, 1912, IRA papers, reel 25; True to Samuel Brosius, March 22, 1913, IRA papers, reel 27; True to Welsh, April 19, 1922, IRA papers, reel 38; True to Sniffen, June 16, 1919, IRA papers, reel 34; "History of Schools in Santa Clara," Collier papers, reel 29; and True to Superintendent Crandall, August 29, 1902, RG 75, Pueblo Records, entry 38, box 1, NARA, Denver. During her time at Morongo, True oversaw the legendary hunt for "Willie Boy," an Indian man accused of killing his Indian lover and her father. A recent book explores this incident. See James A. Sandos and Larry E. Burgess, *The Hunt for Willie Boy: Indian-Hating and Popular Culture* (Norman: University of Oklahoma Press, 1994). A movie made about the incident, "Tell Them Willie Boy Is Here," made True into a "leggy and handsome" emancipated new woman who had a torrid affair with the character played by Robert Redford (Sandos and Burgess, *Hunt for Willie Boy,* 57, 66). See also Harry Lawton, *Willie Boy: A Desert Manhunt* (Balboa Island, Calif.: Paisano Press, 1960). For more on both Dissette and True, see Margaret Jacobs, "Uplifting Cultures: Encounters Between White Women and Pueblo Indians, 1890–1935" (Ph.D. diss., University of California, Davis, 1996), chap 2.

17. Mathes, "Nineteenth Century Women," 1–3; and Wanken, "Woman's Sphere," 7–12.

18. See Jacobs, "Uplifting Cultures," chap. 2.

19. Robert M. Utley, *The Indian Frontier of the American West, 1846–1890* (Albuquerque: University of New Mexico Press, 1984), 220, 243. The Ghost Dance movement, which started among the Paiutes in Nevada, promised that God would kill off all the whites, bring dead Indians back to life, and return the earth to the Indians. Philip Weeks, *Farewell, My Nation: The American Indian and the United States, 1820–1890* (Arlington Heights, Ill.: Harlan Davison, Inc., 1990), 109–92, 232; and Hazel Hertzberg, *The Search for an American Indian Identity: Modern Pan-Indian Movements* (Syracuse: Syracuse University Press, 1971), 10–14. A circular issued by Commissioner of Indian Affairs W. A. Jones in 1902, entitled "Long Hair Prohibited," mentioned briefly at the end that Indian dances should be prohibited. This circular, however, did not specify which dances it found in need of prohibition, and it did not mention sexual immorality as a justification for banning Indian dances. See Circular 13, January 1920, Special Collections, Knight Library, University of Oregon, Eugene. Thanks to Annette Reed-Crum for bringing this document to my attention.

20. Superintendent, Santa Fe Indian School, "Memorandum for Supervisor Rosenkranz," December 26, 1913, RG 75, Santa Fe Indian School Day School Correspondence, 1913–1914 (entry 42), box 2, folder "S," NARA, Denver; and Commissioner Price to Pedro Sanchez, U.S. Indian Agent, Pueblo Agency, June 27, 1883, RG 75, Northern Pueblos, Misc. Reports and Correspondence, 1868–1934, box 5, folder 103, NARA, Denver. In *The Pueblo Indians of North America,* Dozier writes that up until 1900, Protestant missionaries did not "apparently object to the ceremonies of the pueblos" (105–6). I do not find evidence of concern about Pueblo dances on the part of missionaries until 1915.

21. "Exhibit D," Sweet collection.

22. Rosendo Vargas to Santa Fe Indian School, November 20, 1915, enclosed in Frederic Snyder to Superintendent Lonergan, Pueblo Day Schools, November 23, 1915, RG 75, Southern Pueblos Agency, General Correspondence Files, 1911–1935 (entry 90), box 21, folder 070, NARA, Denver.

23. Dissette to Brosius, April 18, 1913, IRA papers, reel 27; Dissette to Brosius, December 3, 1910, and True to Brosius, December 1, 1910, IRA papers, reel 23; and True to Sniffen, June 2, 1919, and True to Brosius, October 18, 1919, IRA papers, reel 34.

24. For some of the publicity that reformers wrote in condemnation of the dances, see Flora Seymour, "The Delusion of the Sentimentalists," *Forum* 71 (March 1924): 273–80; William E. Johnson, "Those Sacred Indian Ceremonials," *The Native American* 24 (20 September 1924): 173–77; William E. Johnson, "Civilizing Indian Dances and White Writers," typewritten ms., carton 1, "Pueblo Indian Religious Persecution Re. 'Pussyfoot'" folder, CLAI papers; Herbert Welsh, letters to the editor of *The Herald* and *New York Times,* August 22 and October 15, 1924, and "Indian Dances Degrading, Says Y.W.C.A. Leader," *New York Times,* November 25, 1923, clippings in Collier papers, reel 9; Hubert Work, "Our American Indians," *The Saturday Evening Post,* May 31, 1924, p. 92; and letter from Secretary of the Interior Work to San Ildefonso Pueblo, reprinted in *Indian Truth* 1 (March 1924): 4, *Indian Truth* 1 (April 1924): 4, and *Indian Truth* 1 (June 1924): 1–2. *Indian Truth* was an official publication of the Indian Rights Association. See also, G. E. E. Lindquist, *The Red Man in the United States: An Intimate Study of the Social, Economic and Religious Life of the American Indian* (New York: George H. Doran Co., 1923), 68, 267–68, 273, 287. This book published the results of an American Indian Survey begun in 1919 by the Interchurch World Movement.

25. Circular 1665 and supplement, Collier papers, reel 5.

26. Pascoe, *Relations of Rescue,* 32–69.

27. Circular 1665 and supplement, Collier papers, reel 5.

28. Peiss, *Cheap Amusements,* 163–84.

29. Filene, *Him/Her/Self,* 303.

30. Katsinas (more commonly spelled "kachinas") are supernatural beings who live in sacred areas near some of the pueblos. They visit the pueblos at certain times of year for religious ceremonies. According to Frederick J. Dockstader, in *The Kachina and the White Man: The Influences of White Culture on the Hopi Kachina Religion* (Albuquerque: University of New Mexico Press, 1985), "these beings have the power to bring rain, exercise control over the weather, help in many of the everyday

activities of the villages, punish offenders of ceremonial or social laws, and in general act as a link between gods and mortals" (9). What anthropologists have called the "kachina cult" is strongest among the Hopi and Zuni, takes a modified form among the Rio Grande Pueblos, and seems to fade out among the northeasternmost pueblos of Taos and Picuris. Kachinas also refer to the masked impersonators of the supernatural beings who perform at some Pueblo ceremonies. Sometimes the kachinas entertain the crowd alongside the clowns. Dolls representing the masked impersonators of the spirits have become a major tourist item for sale in the Southwest. See also, Alfonso Ortiz, *The Tewa World: Space, Time, Being, and Becoming in a Pueblo Society* (Chicago: University of Chicago Press, 1969), 18; and Fred Eggan, "Pueblos: Introduction," in *Handbook of North American Indians,* vol. 9, ed. Alfonso Ortiz (Washington, D.C.: Smithsonian Institution, 1979), 227–30.

31. Statement of Johnson Tuwaletstiwa, August 14, 1920, Sweet collection.
32. Statement of Kuwanwikvaya, August 26, 1920, Sweet collection.
33. Statement of Tuwaletstiwa, August 14, 1920. See also, Statement of Mango, August 12, 1920, both in the Sweet collection.
34. Statement of Tuwaletstiwa, August 14, 1920. See also Statement of Talasnimtiwa, August 12, 1920, both in the Sweet collection.
35. Statement of Tuwaletstiwa, August 14, 1920, Sweet collection.
36. On female moral reformers' views of Indian women as victims, see Pascoe, *Relations of Rescue;* Bannan, "*True Womanhood*"; and Emmerich, "'To respect and love.'" Kathy Peiss and Christina Simmons argue that before the 1920s, middle-class white women contrasted their own "purity" with other "subordinate groups," whom they "depicted as loose, rowdy, carnal, and debased." See "Passion and Power: An Introduction," in *Passion and Power: Sexuality in History,* ed. Kathy Peiss and Christina Simmons (Philadelphia: Temple University Press, 1989), 3–13. While this may have been true of their depictions of working-class women and black women, interestingly white middle-class women did not seem to "sexualize" Indian women until the 1920s.
37. Dissette to Willard, March 3, 1924, IRA papers, reel 40.
38. Dissette to Willard, March 3, 1924.
39. Filene, *Him/Her/Self,* 165.
40. Statement of Quoyawyma, April 16, 1921, Sweet collection.
41. Dissette to Willard, March 3, 1924, IRA papers, reel 40. In this period, sexologist Havelock Ellis, Judge Ben Lindsey, and anthropologist Elsie Clews Parsons all had advocated the notion of "trial marriage," a "legal marriage with birth control and with the right to divorce by mutual consent for a childless couple." See Robinson, *The Modernization of Sex,* 30; Filene, *Him/Her/Self,* 70, 166; Fass, *The Damned,* 260–90; and Rosemary Lévy Zumwalt, *Wealth and Rebellion: Elsie Clews Parsons, Anthropologist and Folklorist* (Urbana: University of Illinois Press, 1992), 46. Parsons, a "new feminist" and an anthropologist who studied the Pueblos, was also a defender of their dances.
42. May, *Great Expectations,* 2; Filene, *Him/Her/Self,* 42–44; O'Neill, *Divorce in the Progressive Era,* 3, 31, 33–63; and Pascoe, *Relations of Rescue,* 37.
43. D'Emilio and Freedman, *Intimate Matters,* 204–15; 233–34.
44. Filene, *Him/Her/Self,* 149–50. See also, Joanne J. Meyerowitz, *Women Adrift: Independent Wage Earners in Chicago, 1880–1930* (Chicago: University of Chicago Press, 1988); and Regina Kunzel, *Fallen Women, Problem Girls: Unmarried Mothers and the Professionalization of Social Work, 1890–1945* (New Haven: Yale University Press, 1993).
45. Quoted in Fass, *The Damned,* 23.
46. Quoted in Stanley Coben, *The Rebellion Against Victorianism: The Impetus for Cultural Change in 1920s America* (New York: Oxford University Press, 1991), 76. During this time period, social commentators also linked jazz dancing to the spread of black culture, which they deemed another type of "savagery." Thanks to an anonymous reader at *Frontiers* for pointing this out. See also David Levering Lewis, *When Harlem Was in Vogue* (New York: Oxford University Press, 1979, 1981).
47. Stella Atwood speech, June 10, 1924, at 17th Biennial Convention, General Federation of Women's Clubs, Los Angeles, GFWC papers, archives, GFWC International, Washington, D.C. Atwood once wrote to Mabel Dodge Luhan that she was a conservative and was not always comfortable

with the radicalism of those she worked with in Indian affairs. See Atwood to Mabel Dodge Sterne [Luhan], December 21, 1922, Mabel Dodge Luhan papers, Beinecke Rare Book and Manuscript Library, Yale University.

48. Statement of "The American Indian Policies Association" (later the AIDA), February 14, 1923, box 2A, Amelia E. White papers, School of American Research, Santa Fe, New Mexico.

49. Erna Fergusson, *Dancing Gods: Indian Ceremonials of New Mexico and Arizona* (New York: Alfred Knopf, 1931), xiv.

50. Austin, *Land of Journey's Ending,* 258.

51. On explanations of Pueblo clowning as a fertility rite, see Alfonso Ortiz, "Ritual Drama and the Pueblo World View," in *New Perspectives on the Pueblo,* ed. Alfonso Ortiz (Albuquerque: University of New Mexico Press, 1972), 152; Barbara Babcock, "Arrange Me Into Disorder: Fragments and Reflections on Ritual Clowning," in *Rite, Drama Festival, Spectacle: Rehearsals Toward a Theory of Cultural Performance,* ed. John J. MacAloon (Philadelphia: Institute for the Study of Human Issues, 1984), 112; Dozier, *The Pueblo Indians,* 151; Young, "Women, Reproduction, and Religion," 436–38; and Emory Sekaquaptewa, "One More Smile for a Hopi Clown," in *The South Corner of Time: Hopi, Navajo, Papago, Yaqui Tribal Literature,* ed. Larry Evers (Tucson: Sun Tracks, 1980), 14–17. For explanations of clowns as a means of social control, see Vera Laski, *Seeking Life,* Memoirs of the American Folklore Society, vol. 50 (Philadelphia: American Folklore Society, 1958), 13–14; and Dozier, *The Pueblo Indians,* 157–58.

52. Austin, *Land of Journey's Ending,* 255–56.

53. Fergusson, *Dancing Gods,* xv.

54. Elsie Clews Parsons, "Waiyautitsa of Zuni, New Mexico," in *Pueblo Mothers and Children: Essays by Elsie Clews Parsons, 1915–1924,* ed. Barbara Babcock (Santa Fe: Ancient City Press, 1991), 95.

55. Fergusson, *Dancing Gods,* 39. Among the Pueblos, there are many dances in which male clowns impersonate women. There are also some dances—the Deer Dance, Corn Dance, Rainbow Dance—in which women themselves dance. Furthermore, there are a few dances in which female clowns perform burlesques and parodies, particularly of the Navajos. Among the Hopi and at San Ildefonso and Santo Domingo pueblos, there are even dances in which women parody men of their pueblo. See Schlegel, "Male and Female," 257; Charlotte J. Frisbie, "Epilogue," in *Southwestern Indian Ritual Drama,* ed. Charlotte Frisbie (Albuquerque: University of New Mexico Press, 1980), 319–20; and Donald N. Brown, "Dance as Experience: The Deer Dance of Picuris Pueblo," in Frisbie, *Southwestern Indian Ritual Drama,* 71–92.

56. Parsons, "The Zuni La'mana," in *Pueblo Mothers and Children,* 43.

57. Mabel Dodge Luhan, *Movers and Shakers,* vol. 3, *Intimate Memories* (1936; reprint, Albuquerque: University of New Mexico, 1985), 375.

58. Christina Simmons, "Modern Sexuality and the Myth of Victorian Repression," in Peiss and Simmons, *Passion and Power,* 158, 164, 169–70; and Estelle Freedman, "'Uncontrolled Desires': The Responses to the Sexual Psychopath, 1920–1960," in Peiss and Simmons, *Passion and Power,* 199–225. Freedman argues that women paid a high price "for recognition of their sexual desire and the removal of female purity as a restraint on male sexuality" (212). Women who were victims of rape or sexual assault were thereafter portrayed as willing participants. Pamela Haag makes a complementary point, arguing that the so-called sexual liberalization that occurred in the 1920s was still based on older gendered assumptions that associated men with self-mastery and rationality and women with irrationality. In this scenario, women were still not in control of their sexuality. See "In Search of 'The Real Thing': Ideologies of Love, Modern Romance, and Women's Sexual Subjectivity in the United States, 1920–40," *Journal of the History of Sexuality* 2: 4 (1992): 547–77.

59. Luhan to Elizabeth Shepley Sergeant, June 10, [1925], Collier papers, reel 5.

60. Mabel Dodge Luhan, *Edge of Taos Desert: An Escape to Reality* (New York: Harcourt, Brace, and Company, 1937), 179.

61. See *Indian Truth* I (June 1924): 2, 6; telegram and letter from Sniffen to True, May 24, 1924, and Brosius to Sniffen, May 29, 1924, IRA papers, reel 40; and True to Sniffen, July 1 and 23, 1924, IRA papers, reel 41. Of Spanish descent, Nina Otero married Captain Warren of the U.S. Army in 1904. In addition to working as an inspector of the BIA, she was the chair of the New Mexico

Federation of Women's Clubs, the state chair of the women's Republican organization, and from 1917 to 1929 the county superintendent of schools in Santa Fe County. During the 1930s, she directed the literacy project for the Works Progress Administration (WPA). See Women of New Mexico collection, box 2, folder 4, Center for Southwest Research, General Library, University of New Mexico; Ruth Laughlin, *Caballeros*, 2d ed. (Caldwell, Idaho: Caxton Printers, 1945), 393; and Charlotte Whaley, *Nina Otero-Warren of Santa Fe* (Albuquerque: University of New Mexico Press, 1994).

62. True to Sniffen, July 1, 1924, and telegrams from True to Sniffen, June 9 and 10, 1924, IRA papers, reel 41.

63. Charles Lummis, "To the Women of the United States in Biennial Convention Assembled," June 6, 1924, Indian Defense Association of Central and Northern California, private collection of Michael Harrison, Sacramento. Lummis often repeated this sentiment. For just a few examples, see *Mesa, Cañon and Pueblo* (New York: Century Company, 1925), 158; and Lummis's typewritten letter to the editor of the *New York Times*, September 18, 1924, CLAI papers.

64. See, for example, True to Brosius, October 28 and November 27, 1929, IRA papers, reel 45; True to Sniffen, January 12, 1928, IRA papers, reel 44; and Seymour, "Delusion of the Sentimentalists."

65. See, for example, Mary Austin, "The Folly of the Officials," *Forum* 71 (March 1924): 281–88; Elizabeth Shepley Sergeant, "The Principales Speak," *New Republic* 33 (7 February 1923): 273–75; and John Collier, "Do Indians Have Rights to Conscience?" *Christian Century* (12 March 1924): 346–49, clipping in Collier papers, reel 10.

66. "Transcript of Proceedings of All-Pueblo Council," Santo Domingo Pueblo, October 6, 1926, Collier papers, reel 8.

67. Statement of Masawistiwa, December 11, 1920, Sweet collection. See also, statements of Judge Hooker Hongeva, December 9, 1920; Salako, December 9, 1920; Siventiwa, December 10, 1920; and Kuwanwikvaya, August 26, 1920, Sweet collection. In *Religion and Hopi Life in the Twentieth Century* (Bloomington: Indiana University Press, 1991), John Loftin argues similarly that Hopi "Friendlies," who supported cooperation with whites, based their actions on what they believed to be Hopi prophecy (xix–xxi, 78).

68. Statement of Hongeva, December 9, 1920, Sweet collection.

69. Statement of Joe Lujan, May 15, 1924, IRA papers, reel 40. For more on the beatings and punishment meted out to Indians who wore western clothing or refused to dance, see Statement of Don Mondragon, May 14, 1924, IRA papers, reel 40; Rosendo Vargas to Santa Fe Indian School, November 20, 1915, enclosed in Frederic Snyder to Superintendent Longergan, Pueblo Day Schools, November 23, 1915, RG 75, entry 90, box 21, folder 070, NARA, Denver; and Emory Marks to Superintendent Crandall, September 26, 1924, and affidavits from Joe Sandoval, April 1925, and John Gomez, April 9, 1925, RG 75, Northern Pueblos General Correspondence Files, 1912–1938, box 17, folder 070, NARA, Denver.

70. Interview with Martin Vigil, December 10, 1970, Doris Duke American Indian Oral History Project, box 19, folder 754, and January 26, 1971, box 19, folder 764. Center for Southwest Research, General Library, University of New Mexico.

71. Alfonso Ortiz, "Indian/White Relations: A View from the Other Side of the 'Frontier,'" in *Indians in American History*, ed. Hoxie, 12. Alison Freese's "Send in the Clowns: An Ethnohistorical Analysis of the Sacred Clowns' Role in Cultural Boundary Maintenance Among the Pueblo Indians" (Ph.D. diss., University of New Mexico, 1991), also looks at the role of clowns in dealing with Catholicism, the Spanish, and the first white anthropologists. See also Jill Drayson Sweet, "Burlesquing 'the Other' in Pueblo Performances," *Annals of Tourism Research* 16 (1989): 62–75.

72. Erna Fergusson, "Laughing Priests," *Theatre Arts Monthly* 17 (August 1933): 662.

73. Fergusson, "Laughing Priests," 658.

74. Quoted in Mary Roberts Coolidge, *The Rain Makers: Indians of Arizona and New Mexico* (Boston: Houghton Mifflin Company, 1929), 168.

75. Statement of Bentley, September 30, 1920, Sweet collection.

76. Louis Hieb explains that the "ritual clowns turn the world topsy turvy, and their behavior is often described as involving inversion and reversal." See his "Meaning and Mismeaning: Toward an Understanding of the Ritual Clown," in Ortiz, *New Perspectives on the Pueblo*, 164. See also

Dockstader, *The Kachina,* 26. The clown performances often involved sex role and status reversals. See Ortiz, "Ritual Drama," 148–49; Schlegel, "Male and Female," 257; and Dozier, *The Pueblo Indians,* 157, 203. For the ways in which scholars have analyzed European carnivals as occasions for temporarily reversing hierarchies, see M. M. Bakhtin, *Dialogic Imagination: Four Essays by M. M. Bakhtin,* ed. Michael Holquist (Austin: University of Texas Press, 1981); and Terry Castle, *Masquerade and Civilization: The Carnivalesque in Eighteenth-Century English Culture and Fiction* (Palo Alto: Stanford University Press, 1986). For more on the function of "symbolic inversion," see Barbara A. Babcock, ed., *The Reversible World: Symbolic Inversion in Art and Society* (Ithaca: Cornell University Press, 1978). In *Reversible World,* "Arrange Me into Disorder," and "'A Tolerated Margin of Mess': The Trickster and His Tales Reconsidered," *Journal of Folklore Research* 11:3 (1975): 147–86, Babcock argues that symbolic inversion such as that of Pueblo clowns cannot be understood simply as a "steam valve," that is, as an outlet for otherwise inappropriate behavior. She argues instead that the ambiguity and paradox inherent in symbolic inversion serves as a means of promoting creativity. In Babcock's view, clowns do not just promote conformity to social norms but also "prompt speculation about, reflection on, and reconsideration of the order of things" ("Arrange," 122).

77. Sam Gill has noted that one function of the clowns is to "act Kahopi, that is non-Hopi," thereby teaching the distinctions between Hopi and non-Hopi behavior (*Beyond 'The Primitive': The Religions of Nonliterate Peoples* [Englewood Cliffs, N.J.: Prentice-Hall, 1982], 95). See also, Hieb, "Meaning and Mismeaning"; and Ortiz, "Ritual Drama." Joann W. Kealiinohomoku argues that Hopi clowns actually administer a dose of Hopi-style "medicine" to cure inappropriate behavior. Thus kahopi clowning cures kahopi behavior among the Hopi. See her article, "The Drama of the Hopi Ogres," in Frisbie, *Southwestern Indian Ritual Drama,* 58, 64.

78. For more on boundary maintenance as a way of understanding cultural difference, see Fredrik Barth, ed., *Ethnic Groups and Boundaries: The Social Organization of Culture Difference* (Boston: Little, Brown, & Company, 1969); and Sylvia Rodriguez, "Land, Water, and Ethnic Identity in Taos," in *Land, Water, and Culture: New Perspectives on Hispanic Land Grants,* ed. Charles L. Briggs and John R. Van Ness (Albuquerque: University of New Mexico Press, 1987). For a critique of this concept, see Bonnie TuSmith, "Ethnicity and Community," in *All My Relatives: Community in Contemporary Ethnic American Literatures,* ed. Bonnie TuSmith (Ann Arbor: University of Michigan Press, 1993), 6–24.

79. Otto Lomavitu to Editor, *Cococino Sun,* Flagstaff, Ariz., August 29, 1923, clipping in carton 1, "Indian Religious Persecution Correspondence" folder, CLAI papers.

80. Proceedings of Council of Santa Clara Indians with Assistant Commissioner E. B. Merritt, October 22, 1927, Collier papers, reel 29. In 1924, the Progressive Party held its own election. The Conservative Party boycotted the election and chose their own governor so that the pueblo then had two governors. See *Indian Truth* 2 (January 1925): 3; Edward Dozier, "Factionalism at Santa Clara Pueblo," *Ethnology* 5 (April 1966): 172–85, which describes the genesis and development of the conflict in this pueblo between 1894 and 1935; and True to Sniffen and to Edgar Merritt, both letters, January 2, 1928, IRA papers, reel 44; True to Brosius, May 5 and October 28, 1929, IRA papers, reel 45. Factionalism became even more complicated at Santa Clara in the 1930s when both the Progressive and Conservative parties divided into two wings. See Dozier, "Factionalism"; and Elizabeth Shepley Sergeant, "Memorandum on the Santa Clara Situation," Summer 1935, Collier papers, reel 29.

81. Proceedings of Council of Santa Clara Indians with Assistant Commissioners E. B. Merritt, October 22, 1927, Collier papers, reel 29.

82. Polingaysi Qoyawayma [Elizabeth Q. White], *No Turning Back: A True Account of a Hopi Indian Girl's Struggle to Bridge the Gap Between the World of Her People and the World of the White Man,* as told to Vada Carlson (Albuquerque: University of New Mexico Press, 1964), 106; Helen Sekaquaptewa, *Me and Mine: The Life Story of Helen Sekaquaptewa,* as told to Louise Udall (Tucson: University of Arizona Press, 1969).

83. E. M. Sweet to William Layne, February 6, 1921, Sweet collection.

84. Qoyawayma, *No Turning Back,* 74–75, 79–80.

85. Qoyawayma, *No Turning Back,* 49.

86. Sekaquaptewa, *Me and Mine,* 91–92, 132–33; and Qoyawayma, *No Turning Back,* 22–26, 52–54.

87. True to Sniffen, July 1, 1924, IRA papers, reel 41.

88. Telegrams from True to Sniffen, June 13 and June 23, 1924, IRA papers, reel 41.

89. Seymour, "The Delusion of the Sentimentalists"; Austin, "The Folly of the Officials"; and Hertzberg, *The Search for an American Indian Identity,* 205.

90. "Pueblos Have Right to Run Own Affairs, Court Decides," *Santa Fe New Mexican,* August 15, 1925, clipping from Ina Sizer Cassidy papers, Laboratory of Anthropology/Museum of Indian Arts and Culture, Santa Fe, New Mexico.

91. On the BIA's suppression of a northern California tribe in the late 1920s and beyond, see Annette Reed-Crum, "Tolowa 'Hush': Native Response to Circular 1665" (paper presented at 35th annual conference of the Western History Association, Denver, Colo., October 11–14, 1995).

92. True to Brosius, December 16, 1926, and True to Welsh, December 17, 1926, IRA papers, reel 43; True to Sniffen, January 2, 1928, True to Merritt, Assistant Commissioner of Indian Affairs, January 2, 1928, and True to Sniffen, January 12, 1928, IRA papers, reel 44; and True to Brosius, November 27, 1929, IRA papers, reel 45. See also, Sniffen, letter to the editor, *New York Times,* written November 1, 1924, in Collier papers, reel 9; and Kate Leah Cotharin, chair of the Indian Committee for the Women's Auxiliary to the National Council of the Protestant Episcopal Church, letter to the editor, *The Independent* 116 (May 1, 1926): 531–32.

93. The papers of the Southwest Association on Indian Affairs (formerly the New Mexico Association on Indian Affairs, or NMAIA) at the New Mexico State Records Center contain a folder no. 109 of Indian correspondence, 1922–1923. Many Pueblos wrote letters to the NMAIA asking for help in procuring more land or protecting their existing land and water rights. These letters also request assistance in preventing the excavation of burial sites. The minutes of the NMAIA's meetings (folder no. 37) also reveal the way in which Indians made use of the new activists for their own agendas.

94. Sylvia Rodriguez, "Art, Tourism, and Race Relations in Taos: Toward a Sociology of the Art Colony," *Journal of Anthropological Research* 45:1 (1989): 77–99, and "Land, Water, and Ethnic Identity in Taos," 352. For another account of Taos Pueblo's attempt to recover Blue Lake, see R. C. Gordon-McCutchan, *The Taos Indians and the Battle for Blue Lake* (Santa Fe: Red Crane Books, 1991). Sam Gill also points out that Indians put the white view of them as "at one with nature" to work for them in battles to regain land (*Mother Earth: An American Story* [Chicago: University of Chicago Press, 1987], 130, 141, 145). In recent years, by arguing that the land is sacred to them, the Hopi have also tried to stop the expansion of the Snow Bowl ski area on the San Francisco Peaks near Flagstaff, Arizona. Like Taos Pueblo, the Hopis may have found that this argument is more effective than other rationales to prevent development of their prior use-areas. See Loftin, *Religion and Hopi Life,* 91.

IV

RELIGIOUS INNOVATION AND SURVIVAL

While by 1900 or so the federal government could claim to have some control over American Indian bodies—defeating them in war, herding them onto reservations—controlling the Native mind and spirit was another matter. As we have seen already in discussions of the Midewiwin Society on the White Earth Reservation and the deeply spiritual nature of Navajo exchange, religious belief and practice remained powerful antidotes to defeat and despair. Part IV continues this line of inquiry by considering more thoroughly Indian spirituality in the aftermath of conquest. Ranging from New York to Utah to Alaska, these chapters offer portraits of religious leaders who tried to link traditional spiritual values to the modern world. Some forged that connection by defending ancient practices; others did so through spiritual innovations such as the peyote religion; others accomplished it via reinterpretations of Christianity. In each instance, the struggle to find meaning generated new encounters between religious traditions. Here, too, simplistic talk of civilization's triumph and Christianity's dominion cannot capture the complexity of events on the ground—or in the soul.

10

In 1865, as Navajos struggled to settle into their new home at Bosque Redondo, to the north in Utah Territory, the Ute (Nuciu) people faced similar straits. Having surrendered their lands to the United States, they headed for a reservation in eastern Utah. In that same year, a Ute boy named Na-am-quitch was born. As the child grew up, his name changed several times (as custom dictated) until he came to be known as William Wash. Over the course of his long life, Wash became a leading player in Ute affairs as well as a major go-between in his people's tangled relationship with the outside world. He also came to reflect, indeed to personify, the complexities of Ute life in that tumultuous time.

This perceptive biography chronicles how Wash moved with considerable ease through two worlds, Ute and white. Both respected him: Utes measured Wash's importance by his large herd of horses, whites by his 200 head of cattle and forty sheep. Both, too, might praise his beneficence, but as David Rich Lewis points out, Wash's largesse was rooted in customary Ute ways, not white charitable notions. His support of poor neighbors at once acted out customary Ute impulses and redistributed his wealth, which in turn gave him greater influence among his people. Whites who thought Wash "progressive" were confounded time and again when he did not fit that stereotype. When Utes adopted the Sun Dance as a means of coping with wrenching change (like the Pueblo dances Margaret Jacobs described), Wash resisted white efforts to stop the innovation. So, too, with the dispute over peyote, which the government wanted to ban; Wash defended Native use of the hallucinogen to commune with the spirit world, recognizing that its users wanted only to "be good" and avoid the dangers of gambling, fighting, and alcohol. Wash's career illustrates the extent to which the new peyote religion gave Native Americans an ethical way to forge a new community identity in the face of pressure to assimilate. Wash and his fellow peyotists conformed to the expectations of the Indian Office for "civilized" conduct even as they embraced a ritual the government abhorred.

The details about Wash's life and times that Lewis stitches together exemplify the deep insights biography can yield, especially studies of individuals who helped carry on the conversation between Indian and white cultures. Among other things, people like William Wash cast doubt on the validity of the standard dichotomy of "traditional" and "progressive," categories pervasive through Indian Country in this era (and others), as Melissa Meyer and many of the other scholars in this volume suggest. Was Wash traditional? Progressive? Neither? Something else altogether? To what extent does use of such terms obscure more than it clarifies? Whatever the answers to such questions, this chapter demonstrates that, to assess how cultures change, it helps to follow Lewis and other biographers who try to reconstruct the meaning of change in the lives of particular individuals.

Reservation Leadership and the Progressive-Traditional Dichotomy: William Wash and the Northern Utes, 1865–1928

David Rich Lewis

In June 1865 leaders from the Tumpanuwac, San Pitch, and Pahvant bands of Utes (*Nüčiu*) Indians gathered at Spanish Fork to relinquish their lands. In return, O. H. Irish, superintendent of Indian affairs for Utah Territory, promised them a permanent reservation in the isolated Uintah Basin of eastern Utah, where they could hunt and gather until such time as the government saw fit to transform them into settled and self-sufficient agriculturalists. These Ute leaders realized they had few options. They themselves were leaders of recent status—men like Tabby who rallied group consensus away from the Ute war leaders Wakara and Black Hawk. Since the Mormon invasion in 1847, they had watched their people succumb to epidemic disease, starvation, and warfare. In 1865 Ute leaders accepted the Spanish Fork Treaty as a tactical retreat and began moving toward their new homeland.

In that year of change—change in leadership, location, and future—a Uintah Ute child was born. Named Na-am-quitch, he was the eldest son of Zowoff and Nunanumquitch. In later years he became known as Wash's Son and finally as William Wash.[1] Wash was both ordinary and extraordinary. He never became a formal political leader of his people, yet his success as a rancher gained him the recognition and respect of both Utes and whites at the Uintah-Ouray Reservation. Agency officials called him one of the more "progressive" full-blood individuals of the Uintah band, one of three Northern Ute bands to share the four-million-acre reservation. Yet Wash frequently frustrated these same agents by rejecting the progressive and acting in what they considered to be very "traditional" ways. Until his death in April 1928, he moved between two cultural worlds on the reservation. He was what Loretta Fowler calls an "intermediary" or a "middleman," one of the new or transitional types of leader to arise during the early reservation years.[2]

The importance of people like William Wash lies not only in their own unique experiences but in their shared experiences and the larger themes which emerge from study of their lives. Nearly two decades ago Robert Berkhofer, Jr., told ethnohistorians that they must emphasize Indians in their histories, particularly "the uniqueness of the stories of specific individuals."[3] From works on more famous or infamous individuals,[4] the study of Indian biography has begun to focus on "culturally marginal personages," those less-known "bicultural" individuals who spent their lives on the

Source: *Ethnohistory*, v. 38, n. 2 (Spring 1991), pp. 124–140.

borders between ethnic groups, mastering the knowledge of two cultures without being immobilized by the process.[5]

Berkhofer also suggests that this individualized focus will aid scholars in untangling the web of inter- and intragroup factionalism.[6] Existing models of tribal factionalism generalize "group" traits without getting "bogged down" in individual motivation and variation.[7] Without paying close attention over time to individual actors (who are difficult to find and trace in most records), scholars tend to perpetuate the static emic categories of "traditional" and "progressive," an unrealistically neat dichotomy or unilinear continuum created by nineteenth- and twentieth-century observers and frequently used to generalize about the social, economic, and political nature of reservation factionalism. Reliance on these sources, particularly by historians who perhaps have been more susceptible to the generalization, produces a two-dimensional, dichotomous picture of native people, issues, and factionalism.

While anthropologists and ethnohistorians eschew the progressive-traditional dichotomy as ethnocentric and value-laden,[8] the terms and their variants still appear all too frequently.[9] Often qualified with quotation marks, they have become a kind of professional shorthand for describing individuals, factionalism, and the process of acculturation.[10] The unspoken understanding is that we are simplifying a complex, dynamic situation out of necessity, trusting that colleagues will recognize our dilemma and hoping that others will not read overly static meanings into these useful, if somewhat misleading, terms. We deny the dichotomy but we fall back on it, perhaps because in our histories we do not understand or cannot fully untangle the temporal threads of personal motive and behavior which guide individuals and draw them into factions or groups.

The weakness of this progressive-traditional dichotomy becomes most apparent in attempts to categorize complex individuals, particularly the intermediaries, the middlemen, the cultural brokers, the "150% men" who operate on the cultural margins. William Wash became such a figure among the Northern Utes. Not a recognized "headman" yet vocal in councils, Wash represents the substratum of reservation politics, the influential individuals who worked the margins of tribal leadership and white acceptance. His experience mirrors that of perhaps a majority of early twentieth-century Native Americans struggling to come to terms with their own culture and with American society.

William Wash was born into a world of both change and persistence as his people moved toward the Uintah Basin. We know little about his early life other than what we can assume given the history of the Uintah Reservation.[11] There the different Utah Ute bands coalesced into a single band called the Uintah. The federal government encouraged Utes to settle near the agency and begin farming. Most, however, continued their seasonal subsistence pursuits and drew rations in order to avoid starvation on the agency farms. Some, like Zowoff and Wash, tried their hand at farming, braving the ridicule of other Ute males for gathering vegetal material and digging in the earth, the subsistence province of women. Raising cattle or hauling freight for the agency came much more easily for Ute men seeking to reproduce male work and subsistence spheres. Wash and his father received special gratuity payments from the Indian Bureau for their farming efforts. By 1891, Wash owned a number of cattle and worked part-time for the agency as a herder.[12] Agents viewed him as a progressive Indian.

According to Ute agents, the definition of "progressive" revolved around two elements, economic and historical. First, agents identified progressive Utes by their subsistence activities, particularly by their commitment to a settled and self-sufficient agrarian lifestyle. This lifestyle was defined in part by their willingness to dress, act, and speak like whites, live in houses, and send their children to school. Second, this designation devolved to a comparison of Ute bands and their reservation histories, particularly after the 1881 forced removal of White River and Uncompahgre Utes from their Colorado homelands to the Uintah and Ouray reservations. The consolidation of the Uintah, White River, and Uncompahgre bands created a number of problems, including a series of inter- and intraband factional disputes over leadership, past treaty negotiations, and the distribution of natural resources and annuity payments.

Out of these disputes Ute agents identified "progressive" and "traditional" factions. The Uintah Utes, because of their long contact history and exposure to reservation agriculture, were the most progressive of the Northern Ute bands. The Uncompahgre band suffered the most internal divisions between the progressive Indians (led by Shavanaux and Alhandra) who settled on river-bottom farms and those (led by Sowawick) who preferred to maintain a more nomadic, up-country, herding and hunting lifestyle. Finally, there were the White Rivers, whom agents classed as wild and rebellious traditionalists, adamantly opposed to any effort to change their way of life. This growing factionalism, based on what agents perceived as a progressive-traditional dichotomy running along band lines, was in fact individualistic, fluid, and issue- and economics-oriented.[13]

William Wash played some role in these factional divisions by virtue of his Uintah band affiliation and his three marriages, particularly the last, to Lucy Alhandra, daughter of the progressive Uncompahgre leader "Charley" Alhandra.[14] More important factors, however, were his economic activities as a farmer, rancher, and agency herder, as well as his familiar relations with the white agents. As agency herder, Wash came under fire from Tim Johnson, spokesman for the White River traditionalists. Johnson claimed that Wash was in league with agency attempts to lease Ute grazing lands in the Strawberry Valley to white Mormon ranchers. Johnson criticized Wash because "he does all kind of work" and asked that Wash and the agency farmer, men who symbolized progressive agriculture, both be "sent away."[15]

In 1903, the White River and Uintah bands faced a common threat, the prospect of allotment. Despite widespread Ute opposition, 75 Uintah and 7 White River Utes out of 280 eligible males signed the allotment article. These, Special Agent James McLaughlin acknowledged, signed mainly to show their good will in the face of what they understood to be an inevitable process. Yet by signing the allotment agreement, these individuals reaffirmed a perceived division between "progressive" Uintah and "conservative" White River Utes and created a further division within the Uintah band. William Wash, aged thirty-eight, was one of these progressive Uintah signatories. Dissenting White River leaders threatened to leave the reservation if allotment proceeded; indeed, they carried out that threat between 1906 and 1908, leading nearly four hundred Utes to South Dakota.[16]

With this "tribal" division into two apparently distinct factions, Wash began to consolidate his social and economic position as a progressive spokesman. In 1903, he sold 25,530 pounds of loose hay to the troops at Fort Duchesne, and in 1905 he received his eighty-acre allotment on the southeastern end of Indian Bench above Fort Duchesne. That year he raised ten bushels of potatoes, fourteen hundred bushels of oats, and one hundred bushels of wheat and harvested three hundred tons of alfalfa. His 640 rods of fencing and his log cabin attest to his industry but probably more so to substantial assistance from agency personnel. At the same time, Wash ran a sizable cattle herd in the Dry Gulch region southwest of Fort Duchesne.[17]

In a 1907 council with Uintah Utes, Agent C. G. Hall tried to quiet rumors that "Mormons" were going to take over both the opened reservation and allotted lands. In this council, with the absence of so many Utes in South Dakota, William Wash emerged as a Uintah spokesman. He told the assembly:

> I hear about the way Secretary of the Interior talk to us. I always take Washington's advice. About farming, about everything. I never say no any time. This land that is allotted to me is mine. That make my heart [feel good]. I can't wait to go work my land. I have been working the way Washington want me to. I have a fence around eighty acres. I am putting in some crops. I got hands to work with like everybody. I lost a good deal of money in some way by white men renting my farm. This leasing of land to the whites is a swindle. If I work it myself I get the money that comes from the farming. The Indians do not know how to make money off their land. They don't know whether the white man is handling it right or not.

Beneath his own espousal of white economic values, Wash was apparently concerned about the vacant allotments of those White River Utes in South Dakota, fearing the land would be leased or sold—lost in either case from Ute control. He continued: "About the White Rivers. Washington never told them to go to another country. They are getting themselves poor. Losing everything. This is their home. . . . I want everything to be right. Don't want little children starving. It makes me feel sorry when people move around and let little children get hurt. They are pretty hard up I think. Maybe they come back now to raise something."[18]

The White River Utes did return to the allotted reservation in 1908, under military guard, physically defeated, and with little means of support. Many had no idea where their allotments were, had nothing to work their land with if they wanted to, and were reluctant to work for wages on the ongoing Uintah Irrigation Project. Many ultimately leased their lands to white settlers, hoping to earn some money and protect their water rights against usufruct Utah water laws. Wash's hopes seemed dim.

At this juncture we get a glimpse of another side of William Wash, one that casts a different light on his economic activities and social aspirations. Inspector Harwood Hall visited the reservation shortly after the White Rivers returned and reported that all the Northern Utes "are quite poor, and were it not for rations issued by the government and assistance given many of them by an Indian by name of Wash, who is fairly well off, it is difficult to see how they would secure sufficient food to subsist."[19] From this and other evidence, it appears not only that Wash was accumulating wealth in a white-approved manner (ranching and farming) but that he was using the proceeds (particularly his cattle) to help feed needy members of all three Ute bands. Instead of observing market economy values, he reproduced in part the individualistic role of local Ute leaders by distributing goods in return for sociopolitical recognition. Wash used his position as a cultural intermediary in order to help his people, to gain traditional respect, and to attempt to fill a growing vacuum in Northern Ute leadership.[20]

Between 1912 and 1914, Wash's visibility in tribal affairs increased. He was not considered a "chief" in general Ute councils with the federal government, but he was actively involved in reservation politics, particularly over issues of ranching and land use. Once we discern some of the cultural values and motives behind his actions, it becomes clear that Wash's activities are more complex than can be explained with a static model of factionalism based on a simple progressive-traditional dichotomy.

In 1912, Uintah-Ouray agency stockmen expressed concern with the number of "wild ponies" roaming the 250,000-acre Ute Grazing Reserve. The issue of Ute horses had been a constant source of conflict between Utes and agency personnel. Agents argued that horses gave the Utes too much mobility, perpetuated racing and gambling customs, and grazed ranges more profitably reserved for cattle and sheep. Utes, on the other hand, valued horses as prestige items, traditional forms of wealth, status, and security. They felt (and still feel) an attachment to the horse out of proportion to its market value. The destruction of horses in 1879 precipitated the White River attack on the Utes' Colorado agency. Agents in Utah came to realize that horses, not cattle, defined the social and economic status of Ute men.[21]

In 1912, Wash was one of these men, wealthy both by Ute standards (he owned about fifty horses) and by white (two hundred cattle and forty sheep). He headed an affinal and kin-based cattle association which controlled 395 cattle, 115 sheep, and one of the four bands of "wild" horses roaming the grazing reserve. His position gave him a great say in Indian Bureau plans to clear the range. At a gathering of seventeen leading Ute stockmen, Wash initiated a plan to periodically round up unbranded horses and divide them among members of the roundup crew. He offered to supply both mounted men and extra saddle horses for the roundup and agreed to the construction of corrals on his land. Wash may have been interested in rounding up wild horses, but it seems likely that he was interested in doing so not to preserve the range for additional cattle and sheep, as desired by the white officials, but to obtain or retain more horses, thereby adding to his source of traditional wealth and status.[22]

In 1913, Ute livestock owners met in council to oppose leasing the Ute Grazing Reserve to James S. Murdock, a white sheepman. Once again Wash spoke for his people, summarizing Ute opposition to the proposed lease:

> When we used to talk about this reservation a long time ago, way back in Washington, we leased some land. That is past now. . . . Now the way it is about this land, it is different than before we were allotted. All these Indians understand what

you told them to do and now we have talked about it. Now we have some horses, and we know about how to take care of them now and make use of them on this land. The Indian has always held it, they do not want to lease it at all. As we have horses, cattle, and stock there is no place for Murdock to lease, as all the Indians on the grazing land clear up to Lake Fork have stock and we do not want it leased at all. I have the right to depend on that country, I have some cattle of my own.

Superintendent Jewell D. Martin thanked him: "I am glad to hear what Wash has said because he has more stock than any other Indian on the reservation and knows more about the live stock industry here and I am glad he has expressed his judgment."[23]

Two points of interest emerge from this exchange. First, by his words before his assembled peers, Wash indicated his continuing commitment to horses, even his commitment to horses *over* cattle and sheep. He came to this point of view as Ute agents attempted to reduce the number of Ute horses by emphasizing improved livestock and range management. Even progressive Ute stockmen like Wash resisted agency efforts to castrate their "ponie stallions," preferring a culturally derived balance between quantity and quality. Wash emphasized the continuity of the horse, as both symbol and reality, in Northern Ute culture.[24]

Second, Wash opposed leasing the tribally controlled grazing reserve. In council meetings later that year Wash and other progressive ranchers clashed with a group of White River traditionalists over the creation of a tribal herd. The cattlemen argued that a herd would benefit the tribe economically, provide a market for surplus hay, and keep land-grabbing whites from getting a foothold on the reserve through leasing. The White Rivers also feared the threat of white homesteaders, but they desired cash, not cattle—an equitable distribution of benefits from the grazing reserve in the form of lease monies rather than its use by a select few Ute cattlemen.

Although the council approved the proposed tribal herd when the White Rivers walked out, Superintendent Martin killed the plan, which smacked of "tribal interest rather than individual interest." In his haste to stamp out collectivism, Martin missed the point. These progressive cattlemen intended to partition the herd, "allowing each family to take its share of the cattle and take care of them." In effect, these Utes understood better than Martin that the government would spend tribal funds only for tribal (as opposed to individual) economic development plans, that such communalism clashed with their individualistic subsistence traditions, and that in the past, communalistic policies and agency herds had failed. This proposal by Wash and the progressive cattlemen was both a way to get tribal funds over to individuals and a conservative plan to protect the integrity of the Ute Grazing Reserve. Ultimately, it promised to benefit each Ute household in more ways than the simple lease fees desired by the White Rivers—progressive-sounding means securing an essentially conservative outcome.[25]

In 1914, Wash appeared in the middle of another reservation power struggle, between an overly enthusiastic superintendent and commissioner and the Ute Followers of the Sun Dance religion. As early as 1905, Ute agents had complained that the annual Ute Bear Dance and Sun Dance were morally and economically counterproductive, that they destroyed health and morals and took people away from their farms at critical times in the growing season. In 1913, Martin failed to convince Ute leaders to hold the Bear and Sun dances together at midsummer agricultural fairs as a sort of commercial sideshow. Unable to co-opt or halt them, Commissioner Cato Sells officially prohibited both dances, which were "incompatible with industrial development and altogether out of harmony with a higher civilization."[26]

While the Bear Dance was one of the oldest of the Ute rituals, the Sun Dance religion was a recent innovation.[27] Introduced in the 1890s by Grant Bullethead, a Uintah Ute who learned the ceremony at the Wind River Shoshone Reservation, the Sun Dance filled a void for people struggling with the unrest and dislocation associated with allotment. The dance echoed the individualistic tenor of Ute beliefs while offering group strength through communal participation. The Ute people seized the model, reinterpreted it in terms of their own cultural categories, and reproduced their own religious system, with its emphasis on curing, within the framework of that single dance. The Sun Dance religion offered the Northern Utes an active option for binding themselves together and dealing with the directed changes of an allotted agrarian lifestyle.[28]

Despite the Indian Bureau ban, a number of White River and Uintah Utes proceeded with the 1914 Sun Dance. Upset and uncertain what to do, William Wash telegraphed Interior Secretary Franklin K. Lane: "Indians will hold annual harvest dance about June twenty fifth to thirtieth / ancient custom / supervisor objects / wire reply." Cloaking the Sun Dance in harvest imagery to make it more palatable to white officials was an old Ute tactic, but the reply shot back that the Sun Dance, "or dance of a similar nature, such as usually held at this season of year," was prohibited. Superintendent Martin assured the commissioner that after informing a "bunch of the influential ones" who had sent the telegram, the "better class" of Indians agreed not to dance. Still, two Sun Dances went on as scheduled that summer. Martin reported that about 150 "retrogressive White River Indians" insisted on the dance, which was attended by over three hundred Utes—what he dismissed as a "minor fraction." Martin asked for additional assistance to suppress the dance, for, as they often did, his Indian policemen protected their own people by selectively enforcing Indian Bureau orders.[29]

Was William Wash, the leader of the "bunch of the influential ones" who sent the telegram, also one of the "better class" who agreed not to hold the dance? Or did this group concede defeat to Martin and then participate in the dance anyway? After investigating the dance, U.S. Marshall Aquilla Nebeker reported that Martin "believes that the best Indians, and a majority over all, are supporters of his and are in harmony with his ideas; but I am forced to the opinion that in this he is mistaken; and I could recite many circumstances and conversations which I think are withheld from the Agent, but such recitals would burden this communication and probably would not be considered competent." Nebeker heard and saw what Martin and the Indian Bureau ignored, and he probably heard some of it from Martin's own progressive Utes.[30]

Nebeker reported that the dance took place on the grazing reserve around Lake Fork, thirty-five miles northwest of Myton, Utah. Other records indicate that

William Wash "controlled" that particular area of the grazing reserve and thus that he probably knew about and approved of the dance location.[31] It is possible that Wash was there, supporting the dancers and participating in the group event by his very presence. He was a prominent sponsor of other Sun Dances during this period of suppression. In describing the dances in his youth, Conner Chapoose noted that Ute individuals would sponsor dancers or contribute to the feast following the dance: "They'd either donate a beef if they had any cattle, like for instance Mr. Wash. He would make a statement at the time that he would furnish a beef for the food, and that was supporting the program as they was putting it on."[32] In this and in other instances, Wash actively supported a ceremony deemed retrogressive and traditional by the very white officials who dubbed him the leading progressive Ute stockman.

Superintendent Albert Kneale, who replaced Martin in January 1915, was not particularly concerned about the Sun Dance. He considered it to be a fairly benign, rather commercialized celebration put on to attract tourist dollars.[33] Kneale was more concerned about the appearance of peyote at Uintah-Ouray and the threat it posed to the welfare and advancement of the Ute people.

In 1914, Sam Lone Bear, an Oglala Sioux, introduced the peyote Cross Fire ritual to the Northern Utes. Working out of Dragon, Utah, an isolated narrow-gauge railroad terminal seventy-five miles from Fort Duchesne, Lone Bear held services and spread word of the benefits of peyote, particularly its curative properties. By 1916, half of the nearly twelve hundred Northern Utes participated in the peyote religion. Once again, Utes integrated the individualistic, power-seeking, and therapeutic elements of a new ritual into their own belief system. In later years, the Tipi Way became more popular among Northern Ute peyotists, perhaps because Lone Bear's unsavory business dealings and sexual reputation discredited the Cross Fire ritual.[34]

Ute peyotism came under attack between 1916 and 1918 when both Congress and the state of Utah considered bills to outlaw peyote. Witnesses before a House subcommittee testified that peyote roadmen targeted "prosperous" Ute Indians, those with cattle, in order to addict them and "control their funds." They told of once prosperous Ute farms now "neglected" because of peyote addiction and claimed that Lone Bear counselled Ute stockmen to stay at home and pray to Peyote to look after their cattle. Other experts testified to the deaths and other detrimental physical as well as economic effects of the drug on progressive Indian farmers.[35] Superintendent Kneale informed his superiors that "40 to 50 percent of the Indians on this reservation are, or have been, partakers of this drug." Lone Bear, Kneale reported, deliberately set out to interest "some of our very best men, particularly McCook, Witchits, Monk Shavanaux, Captain Jenks, Grant, Corass, and William Wash. These men were all leaders among their people."[36]

As it turned out, Wash, the progressive Uintah Ute farmer, rancher, and emerging leader, was indeed an active and vocal peyotist. In 1917 Kneale called in U.S. Marshals to control the liquor and peyote traffic around Dragon. He advised Utes to abandon peyotism because it would kill them. Once again, Wash took his people's problems to the commissioner of Indian affairs. On 12 May 1917, Wash dictated the following letter, signing it with his thumbprint:

My Dear Commissioner:

We want to know why these United States Marshals come in here and try to get us to stop church. We like Church. We want to meet every Sunday and have Church and pray and be good. We don't want to steal, nor drink whiskey, nor play cards nor gamble nor lie and we want to rest on Sunday and then on Monday we want to work and farm.... Sometimes sick people sometimes die and sometimes we eat Peote and it make us better. Sometimes people die and no eat Peote. They die. Maybe eat Peote, no die. Horses die, cows die, sheep die. They no eat Peote. You can't stop them dieing. Anything die. Long time live maybe so eat Peote. We want to be good and we want you to let us have Church and not send Police from Washington to make us stop. You tell us why you do this. We don't know.

I have been here a long time and all the Indians like me and they ask me to write and ask you what is the matter. Randlett Indians maybe so they eat Peote. Pretty good, I guess. The White Rocks Indians no eat Peote. No like it and they like Whiskey and they play cards and fight, maybe so kill 'em. We don't like that, we want to be good.[37]

Assistant Commissioner E. B. Meritt answered Wash's letter, explaining that he opposed the use of peyote because attending and recovering from peyote meetings took too much time, and because "it is bad medicine making many Indians sick, some crazy and killing others." Meritt noted that Utah state law prohibited the sale and use of peyote. He closed in typically paternal fashion by telling Wash, "If you and your people want to be good you should do what we think is right and best for you and what the laws of the State and the United States require that you should do."[38]

Wash and his friends were not satisfied with his reply or with the suggestion that they talk to Kneale. On 3 July Wash responded to Meritt's objections, stressing the positive aspects of peyote use and pointing out that it was no more disruptive than Christian Sunday services:

You say for me to talk the matter over with my superintendent but he won't talk to me cause I eat peyote. He won't shake hands with me. When I have my Superintendent to write for me I don't get any answer for it.... He don't like to write letters for Indians. The Superintendent's Indians at White Rocks play cards. He lets them play cards and he don't stop them.

I don't drink any more and I don't play cards nor swear. I go to meeting and eat peyote and that made me throw away drinking, playing cards and swearing. Church makes us good people. We are good when we go to Church. We farm all week and just have church on Sunday, just one day. We all work hard all week and go to church on Sunday after week's work is done. I raise all my own garden, all the food to eat myself and have good garden and just go to Church on Sunday. The Bible say that we should go to church on Sunday and rest. The Missionaries say to go to Church on Sunday too.

Meritt answered quickly this time, apparently aware that he was dealing with an influential and persistent individual. He assured Wash that he would write Kneale and have him explain the laws. He applauded Wash's "progress" and admonished him to give up peyotism. "If you are anxious to do what is right I hope you will stop using peyote and advise the other Indians to do likewise. Peyote will not make Indians live longer but instead will shorten their lives."[39] Meritt advised Kneale that "by taking this Indian into your confidence it is possible that he can be induced to give up the peyote habit and use his influence in persuading others to do likewise." Kneale replied that he had held "many conversations with Mr. Wash relative to the peyote situation," and that Wash had discussed it with "many other employees in this jurisdiction," but to no avail.[40]

Wash refused to accept the paternal advice of these two men. His own experiences led him to very different conclusions regarding peyote. He wrote Meritt a final note:

> I received your letter of July 18th and will say that I do not wish to hear from you any more. Do not write to me any more and I will not write to you. Indian no eat peyote, he die anyhow. Sometime he die young and sometime live long time. I will die anyhow. I will die if I eat peyote and I will die if I don't. White people die no eat peyote.
>
> I have a good home and have a good farm. I stay home all the time and watch cattle and sheep. I herd them in the mountain now. I send my boy to white school to learn and be good. I like to have my boy be good and learn to talk and read and write. They don't learn them to be bad and swear and steal, they teach them to be good all the time. I die sometime and my boy will have my house and farm and cattle and sheep. He will stay there and live.[41]

With that, Wash ended his correspondence, but not his involvement with the peyote religion.

Who was Wash defending and why? From the available evidence it appears that Northern Ute peyotists were mostly older full-blood Utes, frequently the people Kneale deemed progressive, the "very best men," the "leaders among their people." Peyote use was centered in the communities of Dragon and Randlett and occurred along the Indian Bench all the way to Myton—areas of predominantly Uintah and Uncompahgre Ute settlement (bands always considered the more progressive and economically self-sufficient among the Utes). Some argue that these progressive full-bloods were seeking a way to maintain particularly "Indian" cultural values in the face of directed culture change, to achieve group solidarity as Utes and as pan-Indians. Contemporaries observed that individuals, particularly young educated Indians, adopted peyotism to gain social prominence and leadership status otherwise denied them under existing tribal structures.[42] Wash's active participation can be seen as an attempt both to revitalize or perpetuate elements he believed valuable in Ute culture and, despite his age, to gain social leadership status in addition to his economic prominence.

While many Northern Utes accepted peyotism, there remained a significant faction adamantly opposed to its use, deeming it dangerous, expensive, or simply an intrusive cultural element. The White River Utes living around Whiterocks, long considered conservative traditionalists, apparently rejected peyotism. Wash exposed them by playing off the "virtues" of peyote against their "vices" of gambling and drinking and thus claimed the moral high ground. Other peyote opponents included mixed-blood and younger boarding school-educated Utes from all three bands. In 1924, forty-six White River Utes petitioned the Interior Department and Congress to "prevent the traffic of peyote and remove it from the Indian reservations of the United States."[43] Indian Bureau suppression and factional opposition within the tribe drove peyotism underground in the 1920s and 1930s. In the 1930s the issue merged with an increasing antagonism between full- and mixed-blood Utes over mixed-blood control of the tribal business committee. The resulting social and political factionalism ultimately contributed to the termination of mixed-blood Utes in 1954.[44]

It is unclear whether William Wash became a peyote leader, yet his open defense of it and his defiance surely increased his influence among segments of the Ute people. Peyote did not physically or financially ruin Wash. Kneale recalled that Wash, "a well-to-do and patriotic Ute," purchased one thousand dollars' worth of coupon bonds during World War I.[45] In 1923, Wash owned six hundred head of sheep, which he leased to the care of white herders, as well as several hundred cattle, which he personally supervised. "He also controls a large acreage of farming land and this is leased to white men," wrote Superintendent Fred A. Gross. "He is one of the most progressive Indians we have and is successful in his various activities."[46] While it is possible that Wash's "lapse" into leasing was a result of his peyote use, it is more probable that, since Wash was getting old and his son was in school, he could not personally manage his considerable estate. Leasing then became a viable short-term option that he could supervise to make sure the land was not lost to white ranchers.

Wash's wealth and political recognition increased dramatically in his later years. He was a leading member of the council which chose R. T. Bonnin as the Ute tribal attorney in 1926, and he represented the Uintah band in council meetings designed to form a tribal business committee in 1927. His age, wealth, peyotism, and outspokenness are probably what kept him off the final business committee, yet they gained him the recognition of both Utes and whites as a spokesman for the full-blood and Uintah Utes.[47]

Wash spoke with particular authority on issues affecting Ute lands and land use. In 1925, Uintah Utes included Wash in a delegation bound for Washington, D.C. While other members focused on "missing" annuity payments, siphoned off to pay for the Uintah Irrigation Project, Wash articulated the fears of his people that whites were scheming to gain control of the grazing reserve. Wash told bureau officials that he ran about 570 cattle, 800 sheep, and 70 horses on the grazing reserve, and that "we do not want any white men to come and take that piece of land away from us again because it is very small." He complained of having trouble with trespassing white ranchers and with forest rangers who restricted his access to former Ute grazing lands within the Uinta National Forest, "so that is makes it pretty hard for me to get along with these fellows." And in particular he complained that white homesteaders and irrigation companies took water properly belonging to Ute allottees.

In the second half of his speech, Wash moved from issues affecting Ute ranchers to the desires of those who were not so economically progressive—those without cattle or allotments. In an apparent ideological flip-flop, he suggested that unused portions of the grazing reserve be leased "so all Indians could get a little benefit of it, those that don't own any stock." He also suggested that arable areas of the grazing reserve be allotted to Ute children. He told the commissioner: "I am making this statement because I am old. I may not live long but I would like to have these children allotted because by and by white men might take it away and the children would be homeless. We would like to have the children allotted so that they will have something when they grow up." Wash, the "progressive" farmer and cattleman, recognized both the needs and rights of those Utes without cattle or land to share in the tribal estate. At the same time he reiterated his desire to preserve the integrity of what was left of the Ute land base, to leave enough land and water to sustain Ute identity and independence against the wave of white homesteaders.[48]

Indian Bureau officials listened to Wash and the other Ute delegates and ultimately acted on Wash's recommendation, but they twisted his intent in the process. In 1927 the bureau levied grazing fees on ranchers running more than one hundred horses or head of cattle or five hundred sheep on the grazing reserve. Ostensibly, the point was to provide a more equitable distribution of tribal assets between those using the range and those without livestock, but in fact the fees promised to open more of the reserve to white stockmen who could afford to pay them. These fees posed a major problem for stock-rich but cash-poor Utes who found few outside markets and low prices for their livestock. The fees and regulations themselves posed a threat to Ute sovereignty. Wash, the premier stockman and cultural middleman, was the one individual most threatened by this fee system.

In January 1928 a number of older full-bloods from all three bands gathered in council to petition the Indian Bureau to lift the fees on livestock. Most owned no stock and had no vested interest in the outcome. Sampannies (Saponeis Cuch), a conservative White River leader, vigorously argued that Wash (and all full-bloods) should be allowed to run his stock on the grazing reserve without paying a fee. "We want his stock to be left alone. They have a right on our grazing land," Sampannies told the council. "We are doing this in order that Mr. Wash can hold our grazing land for us for some day some of us other Indians may have stock and want to run our stock on the grazing land." Sampannies, voicing full-blood Ute resentment toward the growing number and the political and economic influence of mixed-blood Utes, declared that anyone of less than one-half Ute blood had no right to use the tribal grazing reserve. Older full-blood leaders like John Duncan, Cesspooch, and Dick Wash and newer Business Committee leaders like John Yesto agreed. They defended Wash's right to use the grazing reserve, praised him as an example for the younger generation, and denied the mixed-bloods. Yet underpinning their support for Wash was an understanding that the real issue was sovereignty, the ultimate right to control their tribal resources. "Why," asked Cesspooch, "should we pay for our own land?"[49]

Wash spoke at the end of the council, summing up the arguments of sovereignty by recapping his life experiences as a cultural intermediary, as one who tried to play by two sets of changing rules and expectations:

When the agency was first established I was advised that stock raising was very profitable and I took that advice and I have found that it is so. Later our arrangements were made and the grazing land set aside for our use. It was then said that the grazing land was for the Indians['] own use and that they could increase their herds as much as they wanted as long as they had grazing land and were not to be charged any fee whatever. At the present time why should we be charged for our grazing land? I feel that I should be given a little consideration because I am the leading example of the whole tribe. I feel that I have been capable of holding the grazing land as a whole because I have more stock on the grazing land than any other Indian and the other Indians appreciate the fact that I have held the grazing land for them. That is why they have made their statements here today.

Wash played on his dual role, first in holding tribal land against outsiders and secondly in providing a progressive example of the benefits of work and self-sufficiency for Ute schoolchildren. In closing, he reiterated his long-standing objections to the alienation of Ute land and his hopes for an independent future for his people: "We have always been peaceable people and we intend to live here that way always. This is our home and we do not want to be disturbed. . . . We do not like for any white persons or anybody else to try to have our grazing land thrown open. We object to that very much. We feel that our younger people are beginning to realize the benefits derived from our grazing lands. We do not want to be discouraged by such hard regulations."[50] Yet in the end the commissioner ignored the council and reaffirmed the new fee regulation. Shortly after word of the decision reached Uintah-Ouray, William Wash fell ill. Following a month-long struggle Wash, aged sixty-three, died on 30 April 1928 at his home on the Indian Bench near Fort Duchesne.[51]

Wash's life illustrates some of the fundamental problems scholars face in defining individual Indians, or entire factions, for that matter, as progressive or traditional on the basis of narrow social or economic issues. Defining factions is difficult enough. What variables (kinship, residence, economics, religion, etc.) defined factional groups? Were they "floating coalitions of interests rather than of persons," and were the ends always disputed, or just the means to those ends?[52] The activities of William Wash indicate that individuals frequently transcend the bounds of static factional categories; that these coalitions were informal, fluid, and issue-oriented as frequently as not; and that the means were perhaps more divisive than the ends. Wash plotted a course different from the traditionalist White Rivers, clashing with them over certain issues. Each undoubtedly suspected the other's methods and motives. Yet Wash and his White River opponents united on a number of other issues. Factionalism at Uintah-Ouray evolved from preexisting kinship and band differences, bloomed with economic and land use disputes from the 1880s through the 1930s, and played itself out under the guise of mixed-blood–full-blood politics in the 1950s.[53]

The problem with dichotomizing factions into progressive and traditional elements is, as Fred Hoxie points out, that "there were usually more than two sides to most questions, and no single side coincided with the cause of resistance for the survival of tribal culture." Indian communities contained "a variety of interest groups which took a variety of positions on public issues," and accounting for community or cultural survivals by praising one group as traditional against all others "flattens history and distorts the complexity of reservation life."[54] Equating *progressive* with change and *traditional* with resistance sacrifices individually complex behavior, diminishing our understanding of Native Americans' rationales and responses.

Defining traditional and progressive elements or actions is equally difficult because what passes for tradition changes over time. When innovations can be and are interpreted as cultural continuities, the category *traditional* becomes little more than a temporal indicator.[55] Institutions today regarded as conservative among the Northern Utes (the Sun Dance and peyotism, for example) were revitalized or innovative features in Wash's time. The most conservative elements of the Ute society opposed peyote, while so-called progressives embraced the pan-Indian religion. Today at Uintah-Ouray, that group definition would be reversed. Wash's actions, which appeared progressive to agents and other Utes, in time manifested rather conservative intents or results.

Then there is the jockeying for semantic position or advantage. Different sides in a dispute might claim to be traditional in order to gain the moral high ground and discredit the others. Each side usually has some legitimate claims to tradition, and yet each is equally untraditional. The opposite strategy, claiming progressive attitudes and actions for moral or political advantage, is also possible. As Loretta Fowler points out, "Indians have often . . . tried to influence federal policy by presenting themselves and their constituents as 'progressive,'" to preserve or protect certain cultural elements. But this strategy is double-edged.[56] The real problem begins when modern readers see this dichotomy and unwittingly read in a whole set of values and traits which may not be present, allowing no leeway for individual and qualitative distinctions. Given the modern predisposition towards cultural pluralism and the emergence of "pan-traditionalists," progressives have become politically suspect and are not considered particularly "authentic."[57] The result: simplifying or discrediting through semantics alone.

A final problem with the progressive-traditional dichotomy is that it too frequently implies *either* that one is progressive and committed to change *or* that one is traditional and resists attempts to alter cultural features. It also suggests a zero-sum equation, a "cultural replacement" in which one discards Indian ways in proportion to the assimilation of white goods or ways. There appears to be no middle ground in the dichotomy, no ambiguity in individual thought, action, or value, no notion of differential as opposed to unilinear (or unidirectional) change. And yet we acknowledge the presence and importance of certain individuals who embody these ambiguities as cultural middlemen, intermediaries, bicultural brokers in search of balance. As middlemen, they exemplify the coexistence of oppositions. They frequently work both sides (or multiple sides) and run the danger of alienating both reservation officials and various Indian factions.[58] Ambivalence appears more frequently than a progressive-traditional dichotomy among established and emerging leaders and, I would argue, among the more numerous and less visible individuals like William Wash.

These terms are not inherently problematical; indeed, they have some descriptive merit, even if simply as academic shorthand for issue-specific situations. The problem lies in their misuse, in the simplification, the dichotomization, of complex issues, personalities, and relationships. Creating new sets of terms will not solve it. Dividing the progressive-traditional dichotomy into three or four categories—for example, "native-oriented," "transitionals," "lower- and upper-acculturated"—is perhaps better but still suggests overly static organization and a unilinear progression. Describing a group or faction demands a generalization, a search for the "common."[59] But in that search we should never lose sight of individual complexity and variability over time. We must define and redefine circumstances and try to convey the ambiguity of human motive and action within the common. Nowhere are those complexities and ambiguities greater than in the changing nature of nineteenth- and twentieth-century reservation leadership and in the emergence of the intermediaries, the cultural brokers, the William Washes.

NOTES

1. U.S. Bureau of the Census, Indian Census Rolls, 1885–1940, Microcopy 595, Reels 608–12. William Wash's Indian name was recorded variously as Na-am-quitch, Ot-tum-bi-asken, and Witch-chee-wig-up. He was called Wash's Son, William Wash, and William Wash, Jr., to distinguish him from his father, Wash. Little is known of Wash's parents, who disappear from the census records in 1903.

2. Loretta Fowler, "Local-Level Politics and the Struggle for Self-Government," in *Struggle for Political Autonomy*, D'Arcy McNickle Center for the History of the American Indian, Occasional Papers in Curriculum, No. 11 (Chicago, 1989), 125–26; Fowler, "Political Middlemen and the Headman Tradition among the Twentieth-Century Gros Ventres of Fort Belknap Reservation," *Journal of the West* 23 (July 1984): 54–63; Fowler, *Arahapo Politics, 1851–1978: Symbols in Crisis of Authority* (Lincoln, 1982).

3. Robert F. Berkhofer, Jr., "The Political Context of a New Indian History," *Pacific Historical Review* 40 (August 1971): 357, 379–81.

4. Recent collections include Frederick E. Hoxie, "The History of American Indian Leadership: An introduction," *American Indian Quarterly* 10 (Winter 1986): 1–3; Walter Williams, ed., "Indian Leadership," special issue, *Journal of the West* 23 (July 1984); R. David Edmunds, ed., *American Indian Leaders: Studies in Diversity* (Lincoln, 1980); L. G. Moses and Raymond Wilson, eds., *Indian Lives: Essays on Nineteenth- and Twentieth-Century Native American Leaders* (Albuquerque, 1985).

5. See James A. Clifton, ed., *Being and Becoming Indian: Biographical Studies of North American Frontiers* (Chicago, 1989), ix–xii, 29.

6. "Factionalism," Berkhofer wrote, "was a creative response to external white pressures as well as to internal cultural values, and its chronicling provides an Indian view of an Indian way of handling change and persistence." Berkhofer, "Political Context," 379–80. See also Robert F. Berkhofer, Jr., "Native Americans," in *Ethnic Leadership in America*, ed. John Higham (Baltimore, 1978), 119–49.

7. For example, see Berkhofer, "Native Americans," 110–44; Berkhofer, "Political Context," 373–81; Nancy O. Lurie, "The Will-o'-the-Wisp of Indian Unity," in *Currents in Anthropology: Essays in Honor of Sol Tax*, ed. Robert Hinshaw (The Hague, 1979), 323–35; Bernard J. Siegel and Alan R. Beals, "Pervasive Factionalism," *American Anthropologist* 62 (June 1960): 394–417; Siegel and Beals, "Conflict and Factionalist Dispute," *Journal of the Royal Anthropological Institute* 90, pt. 1 (1960): 107–17; David French, "Ambiguity and Irrelevancy in Factional Conflict," in *Intergroup Relations and Leadership*, ed. Muzafer Sherif (New York, 1962), 232–43; James A. Clifton, "Factional Conflict and the Indian Community: The Prairie Potawatomi Case," in *The American Indian Today*, ed. Stuart Levine and Nancy O. Lurie (Baltimore, 1979), 184–211.

8. The following scholars in particular note this problem: Malcolm McFee, "The 150% Man: A Product of Blackfoot Acculturation," *American Anthropologist* 70 (December 1968): 1096–1107; Rebecca Kugel, "Factional Alignment among the Minnesota Ojibwe, 1850–1880," *American Indian Culture and Research Journal* 9, no. 4 (1985): 23–47; Robert A. Brightman, "Toward a History of Indian Religion: Religious Changes in Native Societies," in *New Directions in Indian History*, ed. Colin G. Calloway (Norman, 1988), 223–49.

9. In many cases the terms are used in rendering nineteenth- and early twentieth-century emic norms, yet the problems with those terms are left unexplained for the uninitiated reader. Most notably among the studies of individuals, the terms recur in the commentary and articles in Clifton, *Being and Becoming Indian*, and in Moses and Wilson, *Indian Lives*, particularly in George M. Lubick, "Peterson Zah: A Progressive Outlook and a Traditional Style," 189–216. The dichotomy appears in numerous other recent works, including, but not limited to, Francis Paul Prucha, *The Great Father: The United States Government and the American Indian*, abr. ed. (Lincoln, 1986); Vine Deloria, Jr., and Clifford M. Lytle, *The Nations Within: The Past and Future of American Indian Sovereignty* (New York, 1985); James S. Olson and Raymond Wilson, *Native Americans in the Twentieth Century* (Urbana, 1984), 123; Alvin M. Josephy, Jr., *Now That the Buffalo's Gone: A Study of Today's American Indians* (Norman, 1984); James Axtell, *The Invasion Within: The Contest of Cultures in Colonial North America* (New York, 1985), 78, 117–118, 280–81.

10. The terms setting out this dichotomy include *traditional (traditionalist, conservative, retrogressive, unprogressive, unassimilated, unacculturated, hostiles, pagans, backward, blanket, country, old, old-fashioned, real, full-blood)* and *progressive (progressive, assimilationist, acculturated, Christian, friendlies, town-dweller, young, white-eyes, apples, Uncle Tomahawks, mixed-blood)*, among others. Even the alternatives proposed by anthropologists fared little better: *native, native-modified, American marginal; unacculturated, marginal, acculturated; native-oriented, transitionals, lower- and upper-status acculturated*. See McFee, "150% Man," 1096.

11. See Floyd A. O'Neil, "A History of the Ute Indians of Utah until 1890" (Ph.D. diss., University of Utah, 1973); Fred A. Conetah, *A History of the Northern Ute People* (Salt Lake City, 1982); Joseph G. Jorgensen, *Sun Dance Religion: Power for the Powerless* (Chicago, 1972); David Rich Lewis, "Plowing a Civilized Furrow: Subsistence, Environment, and Social Change among the Northern Ute, Hopi, and Papago Peoples" (Ph.D. diss., University of Wisconsin–Madison, 1988), 89–140.

12. J. B. Kinney, Agent, to Commissioner of Indian Affairs (CIA), 16 January 1886, National Archives, Record Group 75, Records of the Bureau of Indian Affairs, General Records, 1824–1907, Letters Received (hereafter NA, RG 75, LR); William Parsons, U.S. Special Agent, to CIA, 29 May 1886, NA, RG 75, LR; T. A. Byrnes, Agent, to CIA, 24 July 1888, NA, RG 75, LR; Byrnes to CIA, 10 August 1888, NA, RG 75, LR; George W. Parker, Special Agent, to CIA, 18 July 1891, NA, RG 75, LR.

13. Joseph G. Jorgensen, "The Ethnohistory and Acculturation of the Northern Ute" (Ph.D. diss., Indiana University, 1965), 112–35, 257–58, 267; Jorgensen, *Sun Dance Religion*, 48–49, 153; Maj. E. G. Bush, Confidential Report to Assistant Adjutant General, Department of the Platte, 4 June 1886, NA, RG 75, LR; Robert Waugh, Agent, to CIA, 12 August 1892, NA, RG 75, LR; William W. Junkins, Indian Inspector, to Secretary of the Interior (SI), 10 October 1892, NA, RG 75, LR; Waugh to CIA, 24 April 1893, NA, RG 75, LR.

14. Wash lived with three wives during his lifetime and had ten children. The first two marriages, which were exogamous, broadened his kin network throughout the three bands; the final one aligned Wash with the progressive Uncompahgre and Uintah factions. It is also interesting that he named his sons after Ute agents James Randlett, C. G. Hall, and Albert Kneale. See U.S. Bureau of the Census, Indian Census Rolls, 1885–1940, Microcopy 595, Reels 608–12.

15. "Meeting in Washington DC with Delegation of Indians, November 24–26, 1898," CIA to Ute Delegation, 26 November 1898, Federal Archive and Record Center, Denver, CO (hereafter FARC-D), RG 75, Uintah and Ouray Agency (U&O). Conservative White River leaders frequently rejected people or things symbolizing settled agriculture. See Lewis, "Plowing a Civilized Furrow," 180–90.

16. Uintah Reservation Allotment Council Proceedings, 1903, NA, RG 75, LR, U&O, Special Case 147; "Assent of Uintah and White River Utes of the Uintah Reservation, Utah, to the Provisions of

the Acts of Congress ... in Reference to the Opening of the Uintah Reservation," 23 May 1903, NA, RG 75, LR, U&O, Special Case 147; James McLaughlin, Special Agent, to SI, 30 May 1903, NA, RG 75, LR, U&O, Special Case 147. On the Ute outbreak see Floyd A. O'Neil, "An Anguished Odyssey: The Flight of the Utes, 1906–1908," *Utah Historical Quarterly* 36 (Fall 1968): 315–27; Francis E. Leupp, *The Indian and His Problem* (New York, 1910), 170–256.

17. Lieut. Charles A. Hunt, Quartermaster, Ft. Duchesne, to Capt. W. A. Mercer, Agent, 3 December 1903, FARC-D, RG 75, U&O; "Houses for Indians, Built by Government," C. 1905, FARC-D, RG 75, U&O; C. G. Hall, Agent, to Deputy Sheriff Clyde, 15 June 1906, NA, RG 75, General Records, Central Correspondence Files, 1907–1939, Uintah and Ouray Agency (hereafter GR, CCF, U&O), 126. The actual working size of Wash's allotment was 160 acres, his 80 acres and 80 acres belonging to his wife and son.

18. "Report of Proceedings of Council Held with the Indians Held by Capt. C. G. Hall, 5th Cavalry, Acting U.S. Indian Agent, at Whiterocks, Utah," 13 April 1907, FARC-D, RG 75, U&O, Box 6.

19. Harwood Hall, Inspection Report, Uintah and Ouray, Utah, 10 August 1909, NA, RG 75, GR, CCF, 150.

20. Jasper Pike (b. 1885), interviewed in 1969, noted this breakdown in Ute leadership. He mentioned Uintah leaders Tabby, John Duncan, and David Copperfield, then observed, "Well, at that stage of the game, they was about past having chiefs, you know." Jasper Pike, Interview, August 1969, Doris Duke Oral History Project, Mariott Library, University of Utah, MS. 417, No. 267, p. 5. See also Anne Milne Smith, *Ethnography of the Northern Utes*, Papers in Anthropology, No. 17 (Santa Fe, 1974), 124–27.

21. Lewis, "Plowing a Civilized Furrow," 103, 108–10, 156–64; E. W. Davis, Agent, to CIA, 14 August 1883, *Annual Report of the Commissioner of Indian Affairs* (*ARCIA*), 1883, U.S. Serial Set (Ser.) 2191, 198; Jorgensen, "Ethnohistory," 199. For information on the Meeker incident see Marshall Sprague, *Massacre: The Tragedy at White River* (Lincoln, 1980 [1957]); "Testimony in Relation to the Ute Indian Outbreak, Taken by the Committee on Indian Affairs of the House of Representatives, May 1, 1880," 46th Cong., 2d sess., 1880, H. Misc. Doc. 38, Ser. 1931.

22. C. C. Early, Farmer, to CIA, 25 May 1912, NA, RG 75, GR, CCF, U&O, 301; George W. Harmes, Stockman, to Jewell D. Martin, Supt., 15 March 1913, in Martin to CIA, 18 October 1913, FARC-D, RG 75, U&O. For Wash's cattle association see his will of 1911 in Capt. Herbert J. Brees, Agent, to CIA, 12 April 1911, NA, RG 75, GR, CCF, U&O 351.

23. Jewell D. Martin, Supt., to CIA, 25 March 1913, FARC-D, RG 75, U&O.

24. Jewell D. Martin, Supt., to CIA, 19 July 1913, NA, RG 75, GR, CCF, U&O, 916; Martin to CIA, 18 October 1913, FARC-D, RG 75, U&O.

25. Jewell D. Martin, Supt., to CIA, 19 July 1913, NO, RG 75, GR, CCF, U&O, 916; Martin to CIA, 7 October 1913, FARC-D, RG 75, U&O. On the continued push-pull of communalism versus individualism in Indian policy on the Ute reservations, see Jorgensen, *Sun Dance Religion*, 236–20.

26. Oscar M. Waddell, Supt. of Uintah-Ouray Boarding School, to W. A. Mercer, Agent, 17 February 1905, FARC-D, RG 75, U&O; Charles L. Davis, Agency Farmer, to CIA, 14 May 1912, NA, RG 75, GR, CCF, U&O, 63; Jewell D. Martin, Supt., to CIA, 14 August 1912, NA, RG 75, GR, CCF, U&O, 63; Martin to CIA, 24 June 1913, NA, RG 75, GR, CCF, U&O, 63; CIA to Martin, 11 August 1913, NA, RG 75, GR, CCF, U&O, 63.

27. For information on the Bear Dance (*mama'qunikap'*) see Verner Z. Reed, "The Ute Bear Dance," *American Anthropologist* 9 (July 1896): 237–44; Smith, *Ethnography of the Northern Utes*, 220–27.

28. For specific discussions of the Ute San Dance see Smith, *Ethnography of the Northern Utes*, 208; Marvin K. Opler, "The Integration of the Sun Dance in Ute Religion," *American Anthropologist* 43 (October-December 1941): 568–72; Jorgensen, *Sun Dance Religion*, 5–12, 19–20, 207, 216–20, and passim; Lewis, "Plowing a Civilized Furrow," 189–91, 200–202.

29. William Wash to SI, telegram, 23 June 1914, NA, REG 75, GR, CCF, U&O, 63; Cato Sells, CIA, to William Wash, 24 June 1914, NA, RG 75, GR, CCF, U&O, 63;

30. Aquilla Nebeker, U.S. Marshall, to W. W. Ray, U.S. District Attorney, 7 July 1914, NA, RG 75, GR, CCF, U&O, 63.

31. George W. Harmes, Stockman, to Jewell D. Martin, Supt., 15 March 1913, in Martin to CIA, 18 October 1913, FARC-D, RG 75, U&O.

32. Conner Chapoose, Interview, 15 August 1960, Doris Duke Oral History Project, Marriott Library, University of Utah, MS. 417, No. 3, p. 3.

33. Albert H. Kneale, *Indian Agent* (Caldwell, Idaho, 1950), 156–58.

34. For the most thorough treatment of Sam Lone Bear (Aliases Sam Loganberry, Sam Roan Bear, Peter Phelps, Cactus Pete) and Northern Ute peyotism, see Omer C. Stewart, *Peyote Religion: A History* (Norman, 1987), esp. 178–80, 195–201. See also Stewart, *Ute Peyotism: A Study of a Cultural Complex*, University of Colorado Studies, Series in Anthropology, No. 1 (Boulder, 1948); David F. Aberle and Omer C. Stewart, *Navajo and Ute Peyotism: A Chronological and Distributional Study*, University of Colorado Studies, Series in Anthropology, No. 6 (Boulder, 1957), 5–24; Weston LeBarre, *The Peyote Cult*, enl. ed. (New York, 1969); Jorgensen, "Ethnohistory," 161–62; James Monaghan, "Interview with Charlie Wash, Brother of Dick Wash, Uncompahgre, near Randlett, Utah," 1935, Civilian Work Administration Pamphlet, No. 356/6, Colorado Historical Society, Denver.

35. U.S. Congress, *Peyote*, Hearings before a Subcommittee of the Committee on Indian Affairs of the House of Representatives, 65th Cong., 2d sess., 1918, 2 pts., 16–22, 36–37, 59–113, 123–34, 165–66, and passim; U.S. Congress, *Prohibition of the Use of Peyote*, 65th Cong., 2d sess., 1918, H. Rept. 560, Ser. 7308, passim; Stewart, *Peyote Religion*, 197–200.

36. Stewart, *Peyote Religion*, 197.

37. William Wash to CIA, 12 May 1917, NO, RG 75, GR, CCF, U&O, 126.

38. E. B. Meritt, Asst. CIA, to William Wash, 16 June 1917, NA, RG 75, GR, CCF, U&O, 126.

39. E. B. Meritt, Asst. CIA, to William Wash, 18 July 1917, NA, RG 75, GR, CCF, U&O, 126.

40. E. B. Meritt, Asst. CIA, to Albert H. Kneale, Supt., 18 July 1917, NA, RG 75, GR, CCF, U&O, 126; Kneale to CIA, 24 July 1917, NA, RG 75, GR, CCF, U&O, 126.

41. William Wash to E. B. Meritt, Asst. CIA, 7 August 1917, NA, RG 75, GR, CCF, U&O, 126.

42. J. A. Jones, *The Sun Dance of the Northern Ute*, Smithsonian Institution, Bureau of American Ethnology, Bulletin 157, Anthropological Paper No. 47 (Washington, D.C., 1955), 229, 232; Stewart, *Peyote Religion*, xii–xiv, 197–201; Stewart, *Ute Peyotism*, 4–7; Alberle and Stewart, *Navajo and Ute Peyotism*, 1–2, Kneale, *Indian Agent*, 211; F. E. Brandon, Special Supervisor, to CIA, Inspection Report, 11 August 1922, NA, RG 75, GR, CCF, U&O, 150; Robert E. L. Newberne, *Peyote: An Abridged Compilation from the Files of the Bureau of Indian Affairs* (Washington, D.C., 1922), esp. 12–15, 35; U.S. Office of Indian Affairs, *Peyote*, Office of Indian Affairs Bulletin No. 21 (Washington, D.C., 1923), mimeograph, 12–13.

43. Jim Atwine to Cato Sells, CIA, 29 November 1918, NA, RG 75, GR, CCF, U&O, 126; Dick Wanrodes and Sam Robinson to Charles H. Burke, CIA, 27 September 1923, in E. B. Meritt, Asst. CIA, to Fred A. Gross, Supt., 15 October 1923, NA, RG 75, GR, CCF, U&O, 126; F. C. Myers to Congressman Don Colton, U.S. House of Representatives, 13 February 1924, NA, RG 75, GR, CCF, U&O, 126. See also Monaghan, "Interview with Charlie Wash."

44. Conetah, *History*, 150–53; Jorgensen, *Sun Dance Religion*, 151–52; Stewart, *Peyote Religion*, xiii–xiv; Albert H. Kneale, Supt., to CIA, Annual Report, 1925, FARC-D, RG 75, U&O, 37232; Act of August 27, 1954, 68 *United States Statutes at Large (Stats.)*, 868, P.L. 83–671.

45. Kneale, *Indian Agent*, 313–15.

46. Fred A. Gross, Supt., to CIA, 24 September 1923, NA, RG 75, GR, CCF, U&O, 916. See also J. B. Wingfield, Supervisor of Livestock, to CIA, 6 July 1923, NA, RG 75, GR, CCF, U&O, 916; Charles H. Burke, CIA, to Wingfield, 5 November 1923, NA, RG 75, GR, CCF, U&O, 916.

47. F. A. Gross, Supt., to CIA, 28 January 1926, NA, RG 75, GR, CCF, U&O, 174; Council Proceedings, 4 April 1927, 2 May 1927, 7 May 1927, NA, RG 75, GR, CCF, U&O, 54.

48. E. B. Meritt, Asst. CIA, to Fred A. Gross, Supt., 23 January 1926, enclosing "Hearing Held before E. B. Meritt, Assistant Commissioner of Indian Affairs," 3 December 1925, NA, RG 75, GR, CCF, U&O, 56.

49. R. T. Bonnin, Tribal Attorney, to Charles H. Burke, CIA, 10 February 1928, enclosing Council Proceedings, 25 January 1928, NA, RG 75, GR, CCF, U&O, 54, 1–4.

50. Ibid., 4–5.

51. Charles H. Burke, CIA, to H. M. Tidwell, Supt., 29 February 1928, NA, RG 75, GR, CCF, U&O, 56. See the last will and testament of William Wash, along with testimony given to the examiner of

inheritance in the disposition of his estate, all enclosed in "Report on Heirship Case, Gertrude Wash," NA, RG 75, GR, CCF, U&O, 350, File 15816–30.

52. Berkhofer, "Native Americans," 125. See also Berkhofer, "Political Context," 373–80; Kugel, "Factional Alignment," 25–25, 41.

53. For similar examples see Kugel, "Factional Alignment," 28, 41; Melissa Meyer, "Warehouses and Sharks: Chippewa Leadership and Political Factionalism on the White Earth Reservation, 1907–1920," *Journal of the West* 23 (July 1984): 32–45; Ernest L. Schusky, "The Evolution of Indian Leadership on the Great Plains," *American Indian Quarterly* 10 (Winter 1986): 65–82; Fowler, "Political Middlemen," 54–63; Richard White, *The Roots of Dependency: Subsistence, Environment, and Social Change among the Choctaws, Pawnees, and Navajos* (Lincoln, 1983), 64–65, 257–58, 270.

54. Frederick E. Hoxie, "Crow Leadership amidst Reservation Oppression," in *Struggle for Political Autonomy*, D'Arcy McNickle Center for the History of the American Indian, Occasional Papers in Curriculum, No. 11 (Chicago, 1989), 96; Fowler, "Local-Level Politics," 125–33; Clifton, "Factional Conflict," 190, 207–8; White, *Roots of Dependency*, 64–65, 257–58; Robert L. Bee, "The Predicament of the Native American Leader," *Human Organization* 49, no.1 (1990): 56–63.

55. Fowler, "Local-Level Politics," 125–26. See White's comments for the Navajos in *Roots of Dependency*, 257–58.

56. Fowler, "Local-Level Politics," 132. See also White's comments about factionalism for the Choctaws in *Roots of Dependency*, 64–65.

57. Berkhofer, "Native Americans," 142.

58. Examples of this are numerous, but see Clifton, *Being and Becoming Indian*, x–xi, 29–31, and passim; Fowler, "Political Middlemen," 54–63; White, *Roots of Dependency*, passim; McFee, "150% Man," 1097–1101.

59. See McFee, "150% Man," 1096.

11

In the twentieth century the shifting religious life of American Indian communities was evident not only in the rise of new spiritual practices such as the peyote religion, the Ghost Dance, and the Sun Dance. It was also apparent when traditional religious rituals surfaced in unexpected settings and were challenged by shocked non-Indian officials. Sidney Harring explores one such instance in this essay about an Iroquois "witch-craft" trial.

Harring views the case through a legal lens, but like treatment of the murder trial of Xwelas by Coll-Peter Thrush and Robert Keller, Jr., this chapter is also attuned to social context. In March 1930, two Seneca women, Lila Jimerson and Nancy Bowen, were accused of murdering Clothilde Marchand in Buffalo, New York. Jimerson allegedly hired Bowen, a noted herbalist and healer, to kill Marchand so that Jimerson could marry Marchand's husband, Henri. As Harring shows, this sensational murder and the equally sensational trials that followed reveal the persistence of Iroquois ritualism in the modern Seneca communities of western New York. He also demonstrates that because New Yorkers were so horrified that "witchcraft" might survive among this "progressive" nation, they were eager to condemn (and execute) the two women. As it happened, the only party that could stop what would surely have been a legal lynching was the local United States attorney. While not eager to defend traditionalists like Jimerson and Bowen, he had no choice but to insist on his prerogatives as a federal official and demand a fair trial.

Harring's essay argues that beneath the question of guilt or innocence lay a deeper conflict between traditional Seneca beliefs and the expectations of the Indians' white neighbors. In an early display of modern Indian political protest that in some ways presages Native resistance a generation later (see Parts VI and VII) tribal leaders supported the two women and persuaded federal officials to intervene on their behalf out of a desire for fairness and a determination to defend Iroquois lifeways; white accusations of "savagery" would not deflect them from their task. In this sense, the Marchand murder reveals both a persistent indigenous religious tradition and an Indian community unafraid to defend it. "By the end of the trial," Harring writes, "it was clear that the Iroquois constituted a distinct cultural, religious, and politically articulate nation." Like Pueblo dancers and others in this era, the episode demonstrated the assimilation policy's failure. Even as he deftly chronicles the legal ins and outs and the political machinations, Harring sketches a portrait of Iroquois reservation life that merits comparison with White Earth, Pine Ridge, and other reservations in that era visited by authors in this volume.

Red Lilac of the Cayugas: Traditional Indian Law and Culture Conflict in a Witchcraft Trial in Buffalo, New York, 1930

Sidney L. Harring

Native American law is largely the history of government policy toward Indians. Native Americans have struggled, however, to shape that law. While their struggle can be chronicled, it is not reflected in the evolution of legal doctrine: the issues that move people are not necessarily the same issues that move courts.

Assimilation has been the dominant governmental policy in Indian law since the 1880s. But the revival of a strong traditional Indian culture in the late 1960s reflected an undercurrent of traditional Indian life surviving and growing on Indian reservations.[1] The Iroquois of New York State are a good source for a revised history of native American law. The Iroquois were among the first native Americans relegated to reservations and were often distinguished from native Americans in the west. Justice Cuthbert Pound of the New York State Court of Appeals said of them:

> They have in varying degrees adopted the arts and institutions of civilization, and, except in an international sense, they may not fairly be called a "feeble remnant," nor may it be said of them that "their fiery tempers" or "their nomadic habits" show a total want of capacity for self government ranking them with the uncivilized Indians of the west. Farms and orchards abound and dwelling houses and barns are found that compare not unfavorably with those of the neighboring communities. Churches and schools are maintained and modest accumulations of wealth are not unusual. . . . [2]

These images were brought under public scrutiny in Buffalo in 1930 and 1931 when Lila Jimerson, whom the press called the "Red Lilac of the Cayugas," and Nancy Bowen, an old Cayuga traditional healer, from nearby Cattaraugus reservation, were charged with the "witch murder" of a white woman. In this important trial the Iroquois proved themselves articulate strategists for their own interests, at odds with state and federal Indian policy and the image of assimilated natives. The witch murder trial went to the heart of the deep cultural differences between Iroquois and white America, underscoring the fundamental fallacy of the assimilationist model.

The question of individual guilt or innocence is usually the heart of any murder trial. But in the present case, the social context is of particular importance. Briefly, these are the facts: Henri Marchand, Jr., a twelve-year-old, returned from school on March 7, 1930, to a gruesome scene: The body of his mother, Clothilde, was

Source: *New York History,* v. 73 (January 1992), pp. 65–94.
Reprinted courtesy of The New York State Historical Association.

"The Mohawk Warrior Group," depicting the return of Mohawk war party with captives, was one of several groups installed at the New York State Museum in 1915. The figures for this group were cast by Henri Marchand from molds made by him at the Six Nations Reservation at Obsweken, Ontario, in 1908. From Lithgow, *History of the Indian Groups with a Description of the Technic* (1937).

lieing at the foot of the stairs . . . beneath a heavy cabinet containing a radio loud-speaker. . . . The corner of the room was spattered with blood. An electric floor lamp had been overturned. The remnants of a vase which had been standing on the cabinet . . . were scattered about the floor.

Terrified, the boy ran a short distance to the Buffalo Museum of Science to bring back his father and brother Paul. Henri Marchand, Sr., summoned a doctor from nearby Deaconness Hospital who announced that the woman had been dead about two hours.[3]

Three police officers, including two detectives, arrived shortly on the scene. Foul play was suspected because the body was severely lacerated. The autopsy showed that a tightly bound paper wad soaked in chloroform had been stuffed down Clothilde Marchand's throat while she was still alive. There was no other evidence. But a neighbor reported seeing two Indian women walking "up and down the block and every time they passed by the place they would pause, appearing to be examining it." By ten o'clock the police arrested Lila Jimerson at the house of her father, Anson, in a remote area of the Cattaraugus reservation, twenty-five miles from Buffalo. Once in police custody in Buffalo, Lila named Nancy Bowen, whom the police arrested on the reservation and brought back to Buffalo early the next morning.[4]

Within a few hours of their arrests, both women confessed to the murder. Lila Jimerson had known the Marchands for nearly ten years. It must, in fact, have been Henri Marchand who identified Lila as one of the two women and gave police precise directions to her father's house. Henri had often come to the Cattaraugus reservation to vacation and to work on dioramas of Iroquois life that he sculpted for the New York State Museum in Albany and the Buffalo Museum of Science. He had built a life-sized replica of an Indian "cabin," Jimerson's house, and had posed Lila, nude above the waist, in "Iroquois village" scenes. During this interaction, Lila became infatuated with Marchand, and resolved to kill Clothilde Marchand in order to marry Henri.

Lila allegedly recruited Nancy Bowen to this endeavor. Mrs. Bowen, a sixty-six-year-old Cayuga widow—a curer and herbalist—lived on a farm nearby. She was deeply grieving the recent death of her husband, "Sassafras Charlie," who had also practiced traditional medicine. Nancy belonged to a community of Iroquois who shared a strong traditional belief in spirits. According to the confessions, Lila had convinced Nancy that Clothilde Marchand was a "white witch" who used magic to kill off the Cayuga and Seneca people, including Nancy's husband. For six months, Lila and Nancy had resorted to traditional Iroquois witchcraft to kill Clothilde, but had failed.[5]

On March 6, Lila and Nancy walked five miles across the reservation to the trolley line that ran from Dunkirk to Buffalo, and took a streetcar to downtown Buffalo. Nancy carried a bottle of chloroform that Lila had purchased in a village near the reservation, and a tightly wadded paper ball. Then they walked to Jefferson Street, where Lila bought a "ten-cent" hammer. Lila led Nancy to the Marchand house and left her nearby. From a phone booth, she called Henri Marchand at the museum and asked him to take her for a ride in his car. Henri complied, allegedly because "Indians loved to go for automobile rides." They drove around Buffalo from 2:00 to 3:00 p.m., when Henri dropped off Lila to "meet [her] friend."

At virtually the same time, Nancy knocked on Clothilde Marchand's door, was recognized as Lila's friend, and admitted to the house. In poor English, Nancy asked Marchand: "You, witch?" Clothilde laughed and appeared to answer "yes." Nancy hit her on the head with the hammer, which had been concealed in her bag. Clothilde struggled violently and was hit several more times. Nancy then forced the chloroformed wad of paper down her throat and left the house. Lila and Nancy met on Jefferson Avenue at about 3:30 p.m. and returned to Cattaraugus.[6]

District Attorney Guy Moore did everything he could to emphasize the sensational nature of the case. He moved the case with unusual speed to a jury trial. He announced that he would seek the death penalty for both women, and he engaged in deliberate racism, emphasizing the murder as an "Indian" crime. The trial of Jimerson and Bowen became a trial of the Iroquois people in general, and of the traditional Iroquois in particular.

The case against the women was ready in two weeks, faster than any previous capital case in Buffalo. New revelations fell into two categories: first, the nature and extent of witchcraft practices within the Iroquois community, and second, the details of Henri Marchand's relationship with Lila Jimerson. It was the state that decided to delve more deeply into witchcraft. They unearthed the body of Sassafras Charlie Bowen to dispel a rumor that Nancy had shot him accidentally as she shot at "demons," although the connection to Clothilde's murder was at best tangential.[7]

Similarly, the state was obsessed with searching the reservation for evidence, most specifically the hammer used in the murder. According to the confession, Nancy had thrown it into a creek near Jimerson's house. After a week, when the police could not find it, they used its disappearance as an excuse for warrantless and indiscriminate searches. Traditional Seneca and Cayuga societies were exposed to the unrestricted prying of dozens of police agents. Seneca Chief Ray Jimerson protested unsuccessfully this trespassing on Seneca land.[8]

In contrast, it was nine days before District Attorney Moore's attention turned to whites. On March 15, Moore finally arrested Henri Marchand as a material witness. He was compelled to make this move when the Buffalo *Times* printed four love letters Marchand had written to Lila Jimerson, letters that revealed an affair of at least two years' duration.[9] These letters exposed two things about Marchand: he had a motive to kill his wife, and he had repeatedly lied to the police. Furthermore, their anonymous appearance in the newspaper illustrates how alienated the Seneca were from white legal procedure—Lila's family had given the letters to the press, rather than to the police.

Jury selection began on March 19. It proceeded slowly owing to prejudicial pretrial publicity and the fact that many prospective jurors asserted they would not vote to execute a woman.[10] The trial began the following Monday, but was soon interrupted when United States Attorney Richard Templeton entered the courtroom. At the request of the Bureau of Indian Affairs, the United States Attorney General had ordered Templeton to participate in the Indians' defense. State Judge F. Bret Thorne and District Attorney Moore were outraged at this unprecedented federal intervention in New York State affairs, and Thorne delayed the trial only four hours while Templeton familiarized himself with the case. Moore attributed federal intervention to Indian "troublemakers" opposed to the "republican form of government."[11] In truth, the Iroquois community had been working hard to save Jimerson and Bowen from a legalized lynching.

When the trial resumed and Moore put Nancy Bowen on the witness stand, Templeton objected to swearing her in "until he could consult with the Attorney General of the United States to determine her status." Templeton was raising the issue as to whether the State of New York had any right to try an Iroquois. He was overruled and the trial proceeded. Nancy gave five hours of powerful testimony. She spoke in Seneca, the language in which she understood the world. The interpretations into English were at issue, so the defense retained their own interpretation to make sure that what Nancy said was accurately translated for the jury.[12]

When Bowen testified, she introduced new factual information. She had received instructions to kill Mrs. Marchand in three letters sent by an unknown "Mrs. Dooley," postmarked from Buffalo and Cleveland. A quote from one letter indicates their purpose:

> I know something Secret. I decided that I'd better tell you and help you out. What I can. This is what I know Charlie Bowen is killed by a witch in this City of Buffalo. It was from a French woman. . . . She killed Charlie because he have good medicine to sell in the city. Her witchcraft didn't work so good so she decided to kill him. . . .

> She kill many, many that way, indians & whites. But let me tell you more. She said she fixed another doll the same this doll is his wife Nancy.

The letters provided a complete plan for Nancy's murder.[13] District Attorney Moore missed their significance: for if Lila had influenced Nancy so strongly, why did Nancy operate from instructions given in letters?

But Nancy's testimony was sensationally upstaged by that of Henri Marchand. Henri's behavior towards Lila emerged as more complex, manipulative, and sordid. Indian women, he said, were naturally shy, and would not pose for him nude above the waist unless he made love to them. Because he needed accurate representation of their breasts for his dioramas, he made love to them out of "professional necessity." In two days on the stand, Henri claimed so many love affairs that he could not count them. Lila was one of them, but he did not love her. Because Marchand was a free-loving French artist, whose wife knew all about his affairs, he had no motive to kill her.

The case for the defense required less than a day. An expert testified that the handwriting on the "Mrs. Dooley" letters was not Lila Jimerson's, thereby implicating an unknown additional party and undermining Moore's "jealous lover" theory because it is hard to recruit collaborators for such schemes. The defense's major effort was to save Lila from the death penalty. Nancy Bowen did not face such a risk. She was sixty-six years old, and, as the defense portrayed her, the unwilling tool of unknown parties, distraught at the death of her husband, sincerely engaged in Iroquois witchcraft, and lacking a *mens rea* for murder—that is, the required mental element, the specific intent to kill. The defense recalled Henri Marchand to the stand, to discredit him again about lying to and using Lila and to remind the jury what a venal person he was.[14]

On Tuesday, April 1, as both sides were ready to do their summaries, Lila Jimerson collapsed from a lung hemorrhage. At first the reports from the hospital were that her condition was not serious and she would return to trial. But on Wednesday afternoon, Judge Thorne declared a mistrial and discharged the jurors. Immediately there were rumors of a plea bargain, and the next day Lila weakly pleaded guilty to the reduced charge of second degree murder. Although both her family and Iroquois leaders protested, Lila had been worn down and did not want to face another trial.[15]

But the case was not to be disposed of so easily. Within two weeks, the state was ready to retry Nancy Bowen, who had not pleaded guilty. Lila Jimerson soon expressed a desire to withdraw her plea and stand trial again. Sympathizers, including the president of the Seneca Nation, approached the famous attorney Clarence Darrow, who agreed to enter the case if "it would not be too long a trial," but eventually declined because, "no principle of law was involved."[16]

Cattaraugus Reservation Senecas and Cayugas, who had not testified in the trial, agreed to "tell what they know" in the retrial. Lila, strengthened by the support of her people, prevailed in her determination to stand trial again. In the process, she dismissed her original lawyers and hired a new one, John McGovern. District Attorney Moore did not oppose her motion to withdraw her plea, either because he still wanted a capital conviction, or because he did not think a death-bed guilty plea would hold up on appeal.[17]

It was not until March, 1931, that the state retried Lila Jimerson separately from Nancy Bowen. The defense was straightforward: Lila testified that she had had an affair with Henri Marchand, but denied killing Clothilde or inducing Nancy to kill her. She fully implicated Marchand when she stated that he had tried to hire numerous Iroquois to kill his wife because he was "tired of her." Although Henri, who by then had a new, eighteen-year-old, wife, stayed away from the trial and was not called to testify, it is likely that the all-male jury believed he was responsible for the murder. It acquitted Lila in less than an evening of deliberation. One week after Lila's acquittal, Nancy pleaded guilty to second-degree manslaughter and was sentenced to the time that she had already served.[18] The return of the two women to Cattaraugus represented a stunning victory for an Iroquois defense faced with a hostile and racist white court.

What did witchcraft mean to the Iroquois in upstate New York in 1930? What is the significance of the witchcraft issue in the Buffalo trial? Anthropologists have devoted a great deal of effort to understanding the social meaning of witchcraft.[19] Students of comparative law know that when preliterate people are conquered, their legal systems are pushed aside and foreign law imposed on them. Such impositions create resentments as well as injustice. When questions are formulated around what problems conquest creates for the new dominant legal form, the cultural integrity of people as it is embodied in their own law is denied. For example, the forced assimilation of tribal peoples creates problems for Anglo-American law in proving *mens rea*, the required mental element of a crime. Criminal intent can be impossible to demonstrate cross culturally because Western notions of intent do not apply to many of the complex behavior systems existing in other societies.[20] Nancy Bowen's innocence of mind was apparent to all who heard her testify to killing, as a matter of course, a witch who repeatedly killed Iroquois people.

The presence of witchcraft within Iroquois culture after 130 years of reservation life was totally inconsistent with popular views that the Iroquois were assimilated or that New York State's Indians were different from "savages" out west. Because they were deeply rooted in an Iroquois tradition misperceived by whites, Lila Jimerson and Nancy Bowen, who were descended from the most traditional, conservative, and antagonistic Seneca, were beyond the understanding of the dominant alien culture.[21]

Their trial focused a great deal of popular attention on New York Iroquois. For a month, Buffalo's three newspapers were full of stories about their society, religion, education, legal status, and witchcraft. The slant of the Buffalo *Times* suggested that the Iroquois were being rapidly assimilated. The *Courier Express* ran a Sunday magazine feature of photographs of Henri Marchand's Buffalo Museum of Science dioramas under the title "The Iroquois Indian Lives Again in Buffalo." The pictures illustrated strong and handsome Indian figures going about daily chores, and included a half-naked figure of Lila Jimerson.[22] The text was as racist and romanticized as the dioramas.

The Iroquois had indeed returned to Buffalo, but not as museum models. They were living participants in the Jimerson and Bowen trials. Every day the courthouse hallway was filled with Iroquois men and women—Seneca, Cayuga, Tuscarora. They arose by 4:00 a.m., walked many miles, rode trolleys, and waited in the hall to observe, to confer with each other, and to discuss strategy. They were treated rudely by bailiffs and ridiculed in the local papers. The Iroquois were seldom allowed into the courtroom, which was filled with newspaper reporters from all over the country, and also armed security men.[23] This security was unheard of in Buffalo courts of that day. Given that no threats were made during the trial, these security measures reflect an unrealistic racist fear of Iroquois "violence."

Religion, culture, and race were major concerns during the trial. The manner in which Lila and Nancy were portrayed offers insights into the nature of those concerns. Physical descriptions of Lila were unflattering. She "look[ed] like nothing in the world but the happy berry picker who comes to the back door of a hotel." Her coloring was the subject of considerable discussion; Lila's mother was Cayuga, her father was part Seneca and part white. The press tried to explain her involvement in the murder racially: The savagery came from her Indian blood; the careful planning and cunning avoidance of blame, from her white blood.[24]

Lila Jimerson's social background was as ordinary for the Cattaraugus reservation of that time as were her coloring and racial stock. She lived neatly and simply in the more isolated part of the reservation, always with her father and aunt, her mother having died when she was very young. She had never held a regular job, but was a fast and efficient grape picker. Despite her education (she could read and write, and play the piano) and some acceptance of Christianity, in many ways Lila had chosen to participate in customary Iroquois life.

Nancy Bowen was among the most traditional residents of the reservation: short and stocky, she did not speak English very well, dressed only in plain black dresses, and "had never owned a hat." She farmed and gathered herbs and bark in the forests for use during healing rituals. Together with her husband, Charlie, she was at the center of traditional Iroquois medicine on the Cattaraugus reservation and deeply involved in the world of Iroquois religion.[25]

The press was substantially concerned about the extent to which traditional religion was practiced by the Iroquois. Such "paganism" was seen by whites as an impediment to assimilation and a contributing factor in the murder of Clothilde Marchand. The traditional "longhouse" religion of the Iroquois included dances, sacred laws, a system of morality, the tradition of sharing, and belief in the "great spirit," who was "like the Christian god." It did not include witchcraft.[26]

Witchcraft was well established, however, in the original Seneca belief systems. Historical literature on the Seneca describes both witchcraft and the tribally-authorized execution of witches. In the spring of 1799, the Seneca Chief Cornplanter ordered three of his sons to kill a woman who he thought had been responsible for killing his daughter. When they found her working in an open field, they stabbed her to death and buried her. The killing upset the village, so a chief's council was called to deliberate the slaying. The council decided that "justice had been done and in order to put away evil from the people, those of familiar Spirits must be driven out of the land."[27] In an 1822 case, the Seneca Chief Red Jacket personally defended

Tommy Jemmy, who was accused by a white court of carrying out a tribally-ordered witch killing. At issue was Seneca sovereignty as represented by the Seneca Nation's right to apply its own customary laws.[28]

Lewis Henry Morgan wrote in 1851 that the killing of witches was "frequent among the Senecas in the past fifty years." Morgan went on to describe something of the context of the belief system:

> A belief in witches is to this day, and always has been, one of the most deeply-seated notions in the minds of the Iroquois. The popular belief on this subject rose to the most extravagant degree of the marvellous, and the supernatural.... [Witches] were imbued with the power of doing evil, and were wholly bent upon deeds of wickedness.... Such was the universal terror of witches, that their lives were forfeited by the laws of the Iroquois. Any one who discovered the act might not only destroy the witch, but could take to himself the dangerous power of deciding who it was. To this day it is next to impossible, by any process of reasoning, to divest the mind of a Seneca of his deep-seated belief in witches.[29]

Witchcraft was the heart of Lila and Nancy's defense. The witch killing of Marchand was regrettable but nonetheless appropriate. This was testified to by the leading Seneca expert of the day, Arthur J. Parker. Among other activities, he was the author of more than 100 scholarly works on the Iroquois. According to Parker:

> Only confessed witches could be punished for their witchery.... According to the belief a witch is under the control of the Great Spirit, and has an order to tell the truth when questioned. Thus, it is the belief that when a witch is asked the question, 'Are you a witch?', she cannot deny it.... The hammer used in the case was the proper instrument with which to expel the witch supposed to be inhabiting Mrs. Marchand's frail frame. The blows on the forehead and crown were properly struck ... in order to banish the evil spirit.[30]

Another strategy of the defense was to take the press on a walk around the reservation's graveyards and witchcraft sites where all-night vigils had been held to call upon the spirits of dead warriors to kill the witch Clothilde Marchand. The locations contained, among other items, simple paper dolls, cut from Marchand's letters to Lila.[31] This tour was a bold stroke on the part of the attorneys, but it was also controversial. On one hand, it clearly showed that Lila and Nancy's beliefs were well-established, traditional, and genuine; they were not manufactured as a way to escape criminal responsibility. Every means of exorcising the witchcraft had been tried and failed before Clothilde Marchand was killed. On the other hand, the continuing existence of witchcraft embarrassed many Iroquois when those beliefs were equated with the traditional longhouse religion.

It can be seen how deeply rooted in the culture witchcraft practices were from their appearance in many contexts. When a chicken had "gone crazy" on the morning of the murder, Nancy was convinced that "witches were working" and that the "Mrs. Dooley" letters were accurate. A tragic sequence of traditional questions formulated to expose the witch had sealed Clothilde's fate. While Nancy was in jail, Lila's aunt complained that Nancy was "witching" her. Nancy herself asked the jailers for medicine to banish the witches that were giving her headaches.[32]

At this point it is useful to place witchcraft in its social context. Anthropologists have explained the phenomenon as an "adaptive and adjustment" mechanism serving a variety of functions in a society undergoing rapid social change.[33] Kluckhohn's study of witchcraft among the Navajo suggested that it flourished as Indian traditions were increasingly destroyed by white society. To fully encompass witchcraft practices is difficult, however, because of their secretive, specialized nature. Furthermore, in the confusion of conquest, many native populations are divided among themselves. For instance, some Iroquois, embarrassed that the witchcraft issue suggested that they were backward and violent, encouraged their people to renounce Lila and Nancy and leave them to the mercy of white justice.

But the majority of the Iroquois people—even though many were opposed to Lila Jimerson's and Nancy Bowen's behavior, and some even thought them "crazy"— rose to their defense and used the "disgraceful" trial not to hide shame, but to attack racist white justice. Direct Iroquois involvement in the case was completely unexpected, and could not be explained by the prevailing stereotypes. Chief Clinton Rickard of the Tuscaroras reported that some Tuscaroras did not want to defend Lila and Nancy because they were Cayugas, but the majority of the tribe took the position that native Americans must stand together and fight for their rights. Individual Iroquois, stopped in Cattaraugus by newspaper reporters and asked about the trial, criticized white justice.[34]

Visibly moving were the daily demonstrations of support by dozens of Seneca and Cayuga men and women who stood about in the courthouse hallways. The courtroom was full of white officials, reporters, telegraph operators with silent instruments, and security guards unable to comprehend the social context of the event, while the hallway was full of quiet Iroquois.

Though the presence of ordinary Iroquois was significant, the Iroquois leadership also rallied to the cause. As will be shown, Chief Ray Jimerson of the Seneca and Chief Clinton Rickard of the Tuscarora were instrumental in mobilizing Federal intervention. Alice Lee Jimison, a writer and Indian reformer, worked closely with Rickard and Ray Jimerson to combat the racist flow of public opinion surrounding the case.[35]

The growing Iroquois boldness on political matters and the willingness to defend two Iroquois charged with a witch murder were positive developments in the politicization of the Iroquois people. However, some uncertainty was left as to how to deal with the witchcraft issue in Lila and Nancy's defense. Much of the Iroquois nationalism that was beginning to mobilize was deeply rooted in the traditional religion of the longhouse. As the trial progressed, the press confused religion with the Iroquois belief in witchcraft, a side effect regretted by many Iroquois who wanted to protect the integrity of their two traditional belief systems. Apparently the defense chose deliberately to underplay witchcraft at the behest of those Iroquois actively involved in the trial strategy. It is not surprising that the Iroquois should want to protect their traditional belief system and also defend Jimerson and Bowen. They were already facing a strong state drive by New York State to govern the reservation, they lacked control of their educational system, and they confronted continuing pressure from Christian missionaries. In the face of this onslaught, their decision to defend Lila and Nancy was even more remarkable.

Most New Yorkers in the 1930s saw Iroquois reservations as "slums in the wilderness." By taking away their land bases and dividing and recombining tribes, the federal government imposed on the Iroquois a system of social relations incompatible with their traditional structures. Neither family functions, economy, tribal government, language, nor religion continued unchanged on the reservations.[36] The reservation was perceived merely as a transition stage toward full assimilation. As Anthony Wallace described the process, the reservation

> resulted in the creation of slums in the wilderness, where no traditional Indian culture could survive and where only the least useful aspects of white culture could easily penetrate. . . . The Seneca experienced the dilemma that all underdeveloped societies suffer: How to imitate superior alien customs while reasserting the integrity of the ancient way of life.[37]

Consequently, Indian reservation life cannot be viewed as merely social decay and demoralization or as successful assimilation. In the Jimerson/Bowen trial, District Attorney Moore tried to undermine the witchcraft defense by means of questions designed to show that most Iroquois had become whites. Judge Thorne sustained as irrelevant the defense's bitter objections.[38]

Reservation life began for the Seneca in 1797, when, under duress, they sold their lands in western New York to the Holland Land Company in the Treaty of Big Tree. The Seneca retained eleven separate reserves, located around their principal villages. (By 1842, eight of the reserves had been absorbed by whites.) When the Senecas, numbering 1,500 in New York State, took up residence at the Alleghany and Cattaraugus reserves, they had no immediate white neighbors. Their villages were small. The houses too were small and neat, surrounded by fences. Land outside of the village was held in common by the tribe. Descent was traced through the mother's side of the family. Traditional religious and political institutions were outwardly preserved.[39]

The refusal of the Seneca and other Iroquois to become farmers was one of the most visible failures of the policy of assimilation. As whites explained it, either Indians were lazy or Seneca land tenure practices, which held land communally, interfered with individual incentive. Actually, the Iroquois chose not to assimilate, preferring to retain their traditional culture. They achieved this by building their economy within the marginal interstices of the white cash economy.[40] They performed odd jobs for farmers and settlement stores; they did logging and other labor in the woods; road building and railroad track work; and unskilled factory work. Outside of the cash economy, traditional endeavors were sources of subsistence: hunting and trapping, basketry and handcrafts, the gathering and sale of healing herbs, and the small-scale growing of food crops.

While economic issues were highly visible, cultural issues were perhaps more critical to the struggle against assimilation. These struggles occurred primarily over the retention of the Seneca language, religion, and education. By 1930, most Seneca were literate primarily in the Seneca language, most honored the longhouse religion, and few had been to school with any degree of regularity. Traditional Seneca achieved an unrecorded victory over more than 130 years of assimilationist policy; their victory against the attempt to stigmatize Seneca and Cayuga culture as "murderous," "pagan," and full of witchcraft in the Jimerson/Bowen trial was more publicized.

It is clear that the primary language spoken on the Alleghany and Cattaraugus reservations was Seneca, used in almost all interactions by the great majority of the Seneca people. Many of those literate in English were literate only for purposes of engaging in daily commerce. The official 1890 census reported that 1,485 residents of the Alleghany and Cattaraugus reservations could speak English, while 780 could not. Such data, however, did not ask which was the primary language, nor did they set standards for speaking English. Assimilationists assaulted native American languages primarily because they believed "primitive" languages prevented "advanced," "civilized" thought, and handicapped native American people.[41]

Accurate measures of Iroquois "paganism" are even more elusive. A majority of Seneca in 1930 were adherents of traditional Seneca longhouse religion—the messianic revival movement of Handsome Lake. Seneca accommodation of Christianity was, as with English, limited. This was possible because the religions were contradictory neither in content nor in context. Official church membership was low nonetheless: in 1890 only 170 Seneca on the Cattaraugus reservation belonged to three different Protestant denominations out of a population of 1,582. And during traditional Seneca religious holidays, Christian churches were empty.[42]

Education, the final element of acculturation, was an expensive luxury in a society where young people needed to work to contribute to the support of their families. In this sense, the Seneca were similar to poor whites. Many Seneca were able to attend school for at least a few years, and they probably accounted for a good part of the literacy in English among younger people.[43] The six years of schooling that Lila Jimerson had were exceptional. But they did not diminish her adherence to Iroquois traditions.

Another characteristic significant to the Jimerson/Bowen trial was that Indian reservations, like slums in general, were mythologized as centers of crime inhabited by stereotypically "criminal Indians." The prosecution was openly racist when it reflected that the murder could not have been committed by an Indian because it required "too much planning." Crime among Indians is generally categorized as alcoholism, sexual immorality, or inter-Indian violence. The liquor problem is more appropriately linked to violent accidental death than to crime. For instance, in the five years prior to 1890, fifty-one alcohol-impaired Indians had been killed by trains.[44] Still, in the late nineteenth century, as today, the vast majority of Seneca arrests (as for white) were for the common public-order crimes, "drunk" or "drunk and disorderly." Since the Seneca had little money, these minor crimes usually resulted in jail terms; due process consisted of whatever justice reigned in the towns bordering the reservations.

Whites applied a double standard to issues of sexual morality. No one cared about the sexuality of Iroquois men, but there was a fascination with the sexual behavior of the women. The core issue was that Iroquois preferred their own customary marriage laws over white marriage laws, which resulted in their "living in sin." All of the witnesses before the New York Assembly Commission in 1888 stated that Indian women had a reputation for immorality, but they offered no specific evidence. The image was bitterly resented by many Iroquois, whose responses ranged from reverse racism to embarrassment. William Newell of the Cattaraugus reservation, president of the Six Nations Association, an organization of successful Iroquois, responded, "It is well known that Indians are the least emotional and passionate of all races," while Adlai Williams, Clerk of the Seneca Nation, stated, "They come down here with a bottle of whiskey and ask for a woman—you get used to it."[45]

The number of newspaper accounts of murders and serious assaults makes it clear that this kind of crime was a serious problem among Iroquois, although we do not know if the Seneca were more violent than their white neighbors. Still, Seneca murders and assaults received extensive coverage, and the image of violent, murdering Indians was part of the justification for the repression of Seneca culture and traditions, one rationale for assimilation.[46]

Most "criminal" activity involved white/Indian contact. The Cattaraugus reservation had no policemen and no jails. Well-established "peacemaker's" courts—among the first Indian courts in America—were elected by members of the tribe. They handled minor civil and criminal matters, including land disputes, marriages, and divorces. Seneca crime beyond reservation boundaries was prosecuted by local officials under New York State law. Within reservation boundaries, however, the State of New York lacked criminal jurisdiction. Following the passage of the Major Crimes Act in 1885, the few crimes too serious for the peacemaker's courts were prosecuted by the United States Attorney in Buffalo as federal matters.[47]

In spite of over 100 years of being besieged by missionaries, Indian agents, land speculators, corrupt peddlers, and traders of all sorts, the Seneca who confronted the Jimerson/Bowen trial had maintained a substantial portion of their traditional culture. Their success supports the perception that "slum" is a class-biased concept which underrates the complex network of protective social relations that poor people form where they are united by a common culture and tradition.[48] Cultural perseverance has been found to be characteristic of Indian reservations generally, and explains the recent strong resurgence of native American culture.[49]

During the spring of 1930 the United States Congress was considering the Snell Bill, introduced by a New York Congressman, and intended to give the State of New York full sovereignty over the Iroquois. The Snell Bill was the latest attempt in a struggle to gain sovereignty that had been going on since the end of the American

Revolution. Similar bills had been introduced to Congress in 1888, 1906, and 1915. Numerous cases in both federal and state courts had been mounted to challenge Iroquois sovereignty. New York State had repeatedly engaged in schemes to sell Iroquois land and to dissolve the reservations. The state had taken control of Indian education in 1856, and had repeatedly tried to apply state law to the Iroquois on the reservation. Full state control over New York's Native Americans had been asserted a number of times in various legislative acts, and once as an amendment to the state constitution.[50]

Iroquois reservations were under federal authority as provided in the United States Constitution and affirmed by federal court decisions. New York, however, claimed that it had never relinquished its authority over Indian affairs which it held originally under the Articles of Confederation. During the nineteenth century the federal government often did not fully exercise its power in Indian affairs in New York State. The state filled the gap and exercised power in a wide range of matters, including criminal law and the selling and leasing of Seneca and Cayuga lands. In criminal law, for example, the New York State legislature declared that the state had jurisdiction over all crimes committed within the state, including crimes committed on reservations. As late as 1914, in *People ex rel. Cusick v. Daly*, the state resisted both the federal Major Crimes Act of 1885 and the decision in *Ex parte Crow Dog* (1883), which clearly provided that the various tribes had control of their own customary codes of criminal law except for certain enumerated, serious criminal offenses which were under federal authority.[51]

Cusick was a simple case of felony assault between two Tuscaroras committed on the Tuscarora reservation near Niagara Falls. John Lord O'Brien, the attorney for the State of New York, went far beyond presenting a simple challenge to the Major Crimes Act when he argued that the federal government had never held authority over New York State's Indians, and denied the existence of the reservation system. New York's Court of Appeals rejected O'Brien's argument and found New York Sate bound by *Crow Dog*. But O'Brien's reasoning had evolved from a long history in the state. Judge Cuthbert Pound of the Court of Appeals noted casually that *Crow Dog* had sometimes been ignored by state courts which sent Indians to prison for violations of state law on Indian reservations.[52]

New York State had shown the same arrogance toward Indian land issues when it persistently claimed sovereignty, and used that claim to permit repeated incursions onto Indian land. Federal authorities had been slow to protect Indian land from state violations. And, ironically, the most important nineteenth-century court decision backing federal authority was not won at the behest of the federal government. *Buffalo R & PR Co. v. Lavery* (1894) was a dispute between two whites claiming leasehold interest in Seneca land, one interest under a state lease and the other under a federal lease. The state court broadly upheld the lease based on the federal claim.[53]

This ruling did not resolve the question, however, because local courts often ignored it, just as they did decisions in criminal cases. The New York State Assembly showed Indians no more respect when, in 1920, it refused the report of its own commission which had recommended recognition of Indian land claims.[54]

By the time of the Jimerson/Bowen trial, New York State Iroquois were fully alert to further encroachments on their sovereignty. Plans were already in motion to resist the seizure of Onondaga lands for a power plant, and to fight assault charges against two Senecas at Allegheny who chased a police officer off the reservation after he came there to make an arrest.

In retrospect, it is not clear what motivated District Attorney Moore to prosecute Jimerson and Bowen so aggressively. Whether he was moved by political ambition or partisan politics, or racism, he was defeated in the next election.[55] More interesting and more significant is the virtually unprecedented federal intervention in this trial. Rickard argued with U.S. Attorney Templeton about adequate representation:

> He and I argued quite heatedly for a time, and then I produced a law book that contained my proof. It was the 1926 edition of the Code of the Laws of the United Sates, and had been given to me by Congressman Clarence McGregor, Title 25, Chapter 5, Section 175 said: "In all States and Territories where there are reservations or allotted Indians the United States district attorney shall represent them in all suits at law and in equity."[56]

While Chief Rickard was bold in asserting Indian rights, it was from the federal government in Washington that United States Attorney Templeton took direction to intervene. The law that Rickard cited was not particularly appropriate; it provided legal help for Indians in conflict with whites over public lands. Nor was Templeton compelled to mount a federal defense for Lila and Nancy, who had committed their actions outside the Cattaraugus reservation.[57]

Intervention was motivated by a more profound power: native American political action. Alice Lee Jimison, Ray Jimerson, and Rickard had organized a group of activists, Iroquois and white, who were appalled at the "racist" and "lynch mob" quality of the trial. These people spent most of the trial's first week intensively pursuing congressmen, Bureau of Indian Affairs officials, and Vice President Charles Curtis. Their effort began when Chief Jimerson approached Congressman James Mead with an appeal that reflected the special status of the Iroquois in the role of criminal defendants:

> Since . . . their lives are apart from the jurisdiction of the state in all other ways, when one of our women is charged with the most serious of crimes, that it is fitting that the nation take part in their defense. . . .
>
> The life of the Indian on the reserve is not the life of a white man who lives off it. There are many vital differences between the lives of the two. We are fearful that there may be misunderstanding and misinformation that will wreak some unfairness to our people. . . .[58]

Charles J. Rhoades, Commissioner of the Bureau of Indian Affairs, responded negatively to Jimerson's plea:

But we lack jurisdiction in the case. New York Indians are under a different status from Indians in any other state. That condition dates back to the treaty by the New York Indians with the white man. The Indians made their treaty not with the United States government, but with the State of New York. So far as I can see, the appeal for legal aid should be made to the State of New York.[59]

Rhoades's statement reveals his ignorance of basic Indian law. The United States Constitution specifically forbade states to enter into treaties and it made commerce with Indian tribes the exclusive concern of the federal government. Section 71 of the United States Code further provides that "No obligation of any treaty lawfully made and ratified with any Indian nation or tribe prior to March 3, 1871, shall be invalidated or impaired." Rhoades was confusing law with public policy. Because the Bureau of Indian Affairs was committed to a policy of assimilation, it was opposed to recognizing special rights for Indians. But Lila and Nancy's supporters did not let the matter rest. Robert J. Codd, a Buffalo lawyer who occasionally represented the Six Nations, quoted from Section 31 of the United States Code in support of the broad powers granted the Commissioner of Indian Affairs and Indian agents.[60]

While the efforts of the Iroquois and their allies cannot be minimized, it was Vice President Curtis's response to their concerns that produced direct results. Curtis had served as a senator from Kansas before his elevation to the vice presidency. He was one-eighth Kaw Indian and proud of his heritage. On at least two previous occasions he had intervened in criminal actions involving members of Indian nations and racist local officials: one was a murder trial involving a Klamath Indian in Oregon. In Oklahoma, he had induced the United States Attorney to protect Indians owning oil lands who were being cheated by unscrupulous speculators. As an act of protest against the Bureau of Indian Affairs bureaucracy, Curtis held on to family lands in Oklahoma administered for him by the Bureau because, as an Indian, he was incompetent to manage business affairs.[61]

By letter, Curtis asked the Secretary of the Interior and the Director of the Bureau of Indian Affairs to "participate" in the defense of Jimerson and Bowen. United States Attorney Templeton quickly received his orders. Although he intended to involve himself in the defense only on a limited basis, he was spurred to a more active role when District Attorney Moore and Judge Thorne expressed scorn for the authority of the federal government. Templeton was outraged when he had only four hours to familiarize himself with the case. He strongly asserted federal authority over New York's Indians when he objected to putting Nancy Bowen on the stand because she was "a ward of the government." His efforts in jurisdictional matters asserted federal control and Iroquois sovereignty and were bitterly resented by the state.[62]

The core issue for the state was federal mismanagement of Iroquois reservations. For the Iroquois, however, it was state policy toward native Americans that led to frightening mismanagement. The history of the state legislature's attitudes, the criminal prosecution style of Moore, and the legal arguments of people like John Lord

O'Brien demonstrated that Iroquois fear of state dominance was well-grounded. The goal of the Iroquois was to resist assimilation and to retain their cultural and national identity. They were better equipped to achieve that goal through confronting federal authority and mobilizing it to defend Lila and Nancy.

A criminal trial often transcends its status as a legal event because of the popular attention such trials receive and because of the distinct historical data they generate—sometimes in the form of legal documents and transcripts, sometimes from sources outside the courtroom. This allows the historian to see beyond the legal history made by judges and legislators to the legal history made by ordinary people. The Jimerson/Bowen trial contained a number of episodes that reveal the role of native Americans in shaping Indian law. Although Clarence Darrow had not seen it, the Iroquois recognized that the great legal issue at stake in the Jimerson/Bowen trial was their sovereignty. While few Iroquois would have chosen to use a witch murder trial as an occasion to assert basic rights, because of the complex and contradictory messages about Iroquois society that the issues exposed, this was the arena available to them, and they succeeded in using it well. Although the trial early asserted strong anti-Iroquois sentiment, Iroquois action carefully and steadily brought the trial around to a victory for native Americans.

Lila and Nancy were returned to Cattaraugus as free women after their year-long ordeal.[63] But the scope of the victory went further. The Iroquois opposition to New York State control over Indian affairs was strengthened by federal intervention in the case. The Snell Bill became intermeshed with the trial and was defeated. While the state tried to use the trial to show that federal supervision of Indian affairs had not civilized the Iroquois, and that jurisdictional confusion undermined legal authority, the trial actually proved how essential federal intervention was. The trial also provided another opportunity for the Iroquois to develop their political skills and to consolidate political alliances. When representatives of the Iroquois Nation went to Washington to testify against the Snell Bill, they loudly and effectively protested that they had not been consulted on the question of state control over Indian affairs.

Prior to the late 1920s, the Iroquois of New York State were relegated to the margins of social, economic, and political life. They could safely be ignored in policy matters. The roots of change in their status had been laid before the Jimerson/Bowen trial, but in no situation was contemporary reservation life more visible to white society. By the end of the trial, it was clear that the Iroquois constituted a distinct cultural, religious, and politically-articulate nation.

Anthropologists of law who have studied the interaction between witchcraft and social change see witchcraft and witch killings as evidence of the survival of a minority culture in the face of oppressive domination. But a witch murder trial may say as much about the society that holds the trial: first, how much force is the dominant society willing to exert to destroy the integrity of the vanquished? By 1930, the overt genocide of the "Indian Wars" was over, but Indians could still be electrocuted for their crimes. Second, how does the law reflect culturally relativist values? The

Jimerson/Bowen case was a sensation when it concerned "Indian witches," but when it turned to adultery and murder, the case quickly lost momentum. Finally, holding a witch murder trial showed that the dominant culture assumed both assimilation and acquiescence by the Iroquois, when in actuality their traditional belief systems had not been penetrated.

While the traditional practices of Bowen and Jimerson were vestigial and marginal to the reservation, they were sufficiently significant to generate powerful support. An understanding of the witchcraft element is essential to an understanding of the murder, the trial, or Iroquois and white society in western New York in 1930.

The core of this story is a murder trial, so it is not inappropriate to end with the query: Who killed Clothilde Marchand? The Iroquois version never changed: white people did. Chief Rickard accepted the suggestion that Marchand and a friend had done the killing and had paid Lila Jimerson and Nancy Bowen to take the blame.[64] Another scenario that was circulated at the time of the trials is that Nancy and Lila killed Clothilde but that Henri manipulated their belief system into a murder weapon. His knowledge of Iroquois society, his assistant Burmeister's expertise in witchcraft, and his friendship with the most traditional Iroquois people would supposedly have enabled him to set up the tragic chain of events. If this speculation is accurate, then Marchand's reaction upon hearing that Lila had been acquitted is the ultimate insult. He said, "It was a terrible injustice."

NOTES

1. See Rennard Strickland, ed., *Felix S. Cohen's Handbook of Federal Indian Law* (Charlottesville: Michie Bobbs-Merill, 1982), 62–180, which contains a complete list of sources. On the policy of assimilation, see Frederick E. Hoxie, *A Final Promise: The Campaign to Assimilate the Indians, 1880–1920* (Lincoln: University of Nebraska Press, 1984); Francis Paul Prucha, *The Great Father: The United States Government and the American Indians* (Lincoln: University of Nebraska Press, 1984), especially chaps. 24–35; Francis Paul Prucha, *Americanizing the American Indians: Writings of the Friends of the Indian, 1880–1900* (Lincoln: University of Nebraska Press, 1973).

2. The best summary of the unique character of New York State Indian law in historical context is Gerald Gunther, "Governmental Power and New York Indian Lands—a Reassessment of a Persistent Problem of Federal State Relations," *Buffalo Law Review* 8 (1958): 1. A more detailed discussion of the critical period of the late nineteenth and early twentieth centuries is Judge Cuthbert Pound, "Nationals Without a Nation: The New York State Tribal Indians," *Columbia Law Review* 29 (1922): 97. The quotation on modern Iroquois life is at p. 97. A general historical overview of New York State Indian policy is in Helen M. Upton, *The Everett Report in Historical Perspective* (Albany: New York State Bicentennial Commission, 1980), chaps. 2–4.

3. Buffalo *Evening News*, March 7, 1930; Buffalo *Courier Express*, March 7, 1930. No transcript of the trial exists. However, we can study the trial in great detail because it was extensively covered by the news media. More than twenty reporters covered the entire trial, sending "live" Morse Code transmissions from the courtroom, using special silent telegraph instruments. All three of Buffalo's major daily newspapers ran detailed daily accounts, including long segments of transcripts of trial testimony. We are relying on three independent versions, the Buffalo *Courier Express*, the Buffalo *Times*, and the Buffalo *Evening News*.

4. *Courier Express*, March 7–8, 1930; *Evening News*, March 7–8, 1930.

5. This represents the final version of the murder story as it came out at the trial, primarily in the testimony of Nancy Bowen. During the two weeks before the trial, elements of the story were reported as they were "discovered" by the press, through leaks by the police or defense lawyers. *Evening News*, March 26, 1930; *Courier Express*, March 8, 9, 19, 1930.

6. This account is based entirely on the two confessions of Lila and Nancy, taken by the Buffalo police on March 8, the day after the murder. *Courier Express*, March 8–9, 1930; *Evening News*, March 8–9, 1930.

7. *Evening News*, March 14, 1930.

8. *Courier Express*, March 12–14, 1930; *Times*, March 14, 1930.

9. *Times*, March 16, 1930. The publication of the love letters, Marchand's arrest, and a tour of witchcraft rites at Cattaraugus grave sites threw the opening of the trial on March 19 into a state of complete confusion. It also exposed how the state had followed up only on the evidence that supported its own case.

10. *Courier Express*, March 20–21, 24–25, 1930.

11. *Courier Express*, March 20–21, 24–25, 1930.

12. *Evening News*, March 25–26, 1930; *Courier Express*, March 26, 1930.

13. First mention of the Dooley letters appeared in the *Courier* on March 22, 1930.

14. *Courier Express*, March 30–31; April 1, 1930.

15. *Evening News*, April 1–3, 1930.

16. *Courier Express*, April 16–18, 1930.

17. *Courier Express*, April 30, 1930; February 21–March 1, 1931.

18. *Courier Express*, March 13–14, 1930.

19. There is a substantial literature on law and witchcraft that develops these themes. The major article initiating the discussion is Robert B. Seidman, "Witch Murder and Mens Rea: A Problem of Society Under Radical Social Change," *Modern Law Review* 28 (1965): 46. See also Isaac Shapera, "Sorcery and Witchcraft in Bechuanaland," in 51 *African Affairs* 44; T. W. Bennett, "Witchcraft: A Problem in Fault and Causation," *Comparative and International Law Journal of South Africa* 12 (1979): 293; Adrienne van Blerk, "Sorcery and Crime," *Comparative and International Law Journal of South Africa* 11 (1978): 336; Law Reform Commission of Papua New Guinea, "Sorcery among the Sepiks," Occasional paper No. 10 (October 1978); Martin Zelenietz, "The Effects of Sorcery in Kilenge, West New Britain Province," Law Reform Commission of Papua New Guinea, Occasional Paper No. 11 (August 1979); Mathole Motshekge, "The Ideology Behind Witchcraft and the Principle of Fault in Criminal Law," paper presented at a workshop on "Conflict, Accommodation and Conflict Management" in South Africa, Cape Town, August 1984.

   Beyond this legal analysis of the phenomenon of witchcraft, there is literature broader in its historical and sociological coverage that is important in locating witchcraft in its social context. Two examples are John Putnam Demos, *Entertaining Satan: Witchcraft and the Culture of Early New England* (New York: Oxford University Press, 1982), 82; Paul Boyer and Stephen Nissenbaum, *Salem Possessed: The Social Origins of Witchcraft* (Cambridge, Mass.: Harvard University Press, 1974).

   Two general surveys of the range of anthropological explanations of witchcraft are Max Marwick, *Witchcraft and Sorcery* (London: Penguin Books, 1970); John Middleton and E. H. Winter, *Witchcraft and Sorcery in East Africa* (London: Routledge and Kegan Paul, Ltd., 1963); John Middleton, *Magic, Witchcraft, and Curing* (Austin: University of Texas Press, 1976).

20. Sandra Burman and Barbara Harrell-Bond, *The Imposition of Law* (London: Academic Press, 1979); Michael B. Hooker, *Legal Pluralism* (Oxford: Oxford University Press, 1972); Robert Seidman, "Mens Rea and the Reasonable African: The Pre-Scientific World-View and Mistake of Fact," *International and Comparative Law Quarterly* 15 (1966): 1135.

21. Robert Berkhofer, *The White Man's Indian* (New York: Alfred Knopf, 1978), 3. Berkhofer's central thesis is that while the native American is real, the Indian was "invented" by whites. The term "Indian" refers to the white "image" and not to native Americans.

22. *Courier Express*, March 16, 1930; *Times*, March 8, 1930.

23. The daily papers printed numerous accounts of Iroquois spectators in the unfamiliar setting of the trial. See, for example, *Courier Express*, March 16, 21, 23, 25, 29, 30, 1930; April 1, 1930.

24. *Courier Express*, March 13, 20, 1930.

25. *Courier Express*, March 11, 17, 1930; *Evening News*, March 21, 1930.

26. Buffalo *Evening News*, March 27, 1930, from an interview with Wilson Stevens, described in the *Evening News* as a "Seneca Medicine Man" and "one of the [longhouse] cult's leaders."

27. Anthony F. C. Wallace, *The Death and Rebirth of the Seneca* (New York: Alfred Knopf, 1970), 235–236.

28. Arthur C. Parker, "Seneca Belief in Witchcraft," in *Seneca Myths and Legends*, Buffalo and Erie County Historical Society Publications, 23 (1925): 365. Five years before the Marchand murder, Parker had noted that "[t]his belief in witches and sorcerers has not been entirely eliminated."

   The most complete account of the Tommy Jemmy incident is found in William L. Stone, *The Life and Times of Sa-Go-Ye-Wat-Ha or Red Jacket* (Albany: J. Munsell, 1866), 383–387. Another account is Robert W. Bigham, *The Cradle of the Queen City: A History of Buffalo* (Buffalo: Buffalo Historical Society, 1931), 386–388.

29. Lewis Henry Morgan, *The League of the Iroquois* (Secaucus, N.J.: Citadel Press, 1962 [orig. pub. 1851]), 164–166.

30. Although Parker agreed to testify to these conclusions, when he took the stand he was not asked about witchcraft. This may reflect second thoughts about strategy, because the publicity over witchcraft reflected negatively on traditional Iroquois. Parker's testimony went only to Nancy's *mens rea*. She was not facing the same serious threat of death as Lila was. *Courier Express*, March 25, 27, 1930.

31. This story can be found in considerably more detail on the front page of the *Courier Express* for March 17, 1930, under the headline: "Graves Link Witchery, Murder."

32. *Courier Express*, March 20, 22, 27, 1930.

33. See, for example, Donald Parman, "The 'Big Stick' in Indian Affairs: the Bai-a-lil-le Incident in 1909," *Arizona and the West* 20 (Winter 1978): 343–360; J. Lee Correll, "Bai-a-lil-le: Medicine Man—or Witch?" (Window Rock, Arizona: Navajo Parks and Recreation, Research section, 1970); Clyde Kluckhohn, *Navajo Witchcraft*, Papers of the Peabody Museum of American Archaeology and Ethnology, vol. 23 (1944).

34. *Courier Express*, March 10, 24, 1930; Clinton Rickard, *Fighting Tuscarora: The Autobiography of Chief Clinton Rickard*, ed. Barbara Graymont (Syracuse: Syracuse University Press, 1973), 98–100.

35. Rickard, *Fighting Tuscarora*, 69–89.

36. Wallace, *Death and Rebirth*. On the origins of the reservation system see Robert Trennert, *Alternatives to Extinction* (Philadelphia: Temple University Press, 1975). See also the discussion in Stickland, *Cohen's Handbook*, 121–125.

37. Wallace, *Death and Rebirth*, 184.

38. Buffalo *Times*, March 31, 1930.

39. Helen Upton, *Everett Report*, 17–49; Wallace, *Death and Rebirth*, 186–189.

40. New York State Legislature, *Report of the Committee to Investigate the Indian Problem* (1889), pp. 990, 1158, 1166, 1167, 1169–70, 1171, 1189, 1223; Thomas Donaldson, *The Six Nations of New York* (Washington, D.C.: U.S. Census Printing Office, 1892), 49–51. On the contradictions between the destruction of native American economics and perseverance, see Joseph Jorgensen, "A Century of Political Economic Effects on American Indian Society, 1880–1980," *Journal of Ethnic Studies* 6 (Fall 1978): 1; and Rolf Knight, *Indians at Work: An Informal History of Native American Labour in British Columbia, 1858–1930* (Vancouver: New Star Books, 1978). During the Jimerson/Bowen trial, the *Courier Express* (April 1, 1930) noted that Indian men were laid off during the winter months because many worked on roads or railroads.

41. Donaldson, *Six Nations*, 2, 9, 62.

42. Ibid., 8, 9, 42–48. Wallace, *Death and Rebirth*, 239–337; Arthur C. Parker, "The Code of Handsome Lake, the Seneca Prophet," in *Parker on the Iroquois* (Syracuse: Syracuse University Press, 1968).

43. Donaldson, *Six Nations*, 63–70.

44. *Courier Express*, March 25, 1930; *Report of the Special Committee* (1889), pp. 990, 1152. A number of newspaper accounts of these tragedies appear in Andre Lopez, *Pagans in Our Midst* (Roosevelttown, N.Y.: Akwesasne Notes, 1982), 27, 78–79, 96, 103, 107, 114.

45. *Courier Express*, March 10, 23, 30, 1930.

46. Lopez, *Pagans*, 76, 76n., 78–80, 82, 105, 107, 111–114.

47. *Report of the Special Committee*, pp. 979, 981, 984, 997, 1010, 1087, 1125–27, 1154–55, Donaldson, *Six Nations*, note 12, at pp. 3–4.

48. See William F. Whyte, *Street Corner Society: The Social Order of an Italian Slum* (New York: Free Press, 1981). The same point is made in Gerald Suttles, *Social Order in the Slum* (Chicago: University of Chicago Press, 1969). The point here is not only that poor people retain their culture and tradition in the face of economic hardship and social disorganization, but also that cultural ties can actually be strengthened in the face of such adversity.

49. Frederick Hoxie, "From Prison to Homeland: The Cheyenne River Reservation before WWI," *South Dakota History* 10 (Winger 1979): 1–24.

50. The history of New York State efforts to gain jurisdiction over native Americans and their lands within the state can be found in Upton, *Everett Report*, especially chaps. 3, 4, and 5. See also Laurence M. Hauptman, *The Iroquois and the New Deal* (Syracuse: Syracuse University Press, 1981), 7–8. Chapter 1 is an excellent discussion of the whole issue of Iroquois sovereignty.

51. In the Tommy Jemmy case, Laws of New York, chapter CCIV (1822), the New York State legislature pardoned Jemmy for witch murder. It used the opportunity to declare that the state had "sole and exclusive jurisdiction of trying and punishing all and every person, of whatever nation or tribe, for crimes and offenses committed within any part of this state. . . ."

    Ex Parte Crow Dog, 109 U.S. 556 (1883), forced Federal action when the court ruled that native Americans had tribal jurisdiction over crimes committed among them, unless direct federal action removed that power. Congress responded with the Major Crimes Act of 1885, which provided that the federal courts had exclusive jurisdiction over "enumerated" criminal offenses (the most serious ones), while the tribes had jurisdiction over the remainder.

    Tribal authority over non-enumerated offenses was exercised among the Seneca of New York by "peacemaker's" courts. Federal authorities regularly exercised jurisdiction over the "major crimes" committed by New York Iroquois while on their reservations. The New York Court of Appeals in *Cusick v. Daly*, 212 NY 183 (1914), reversed lower state courts and granted a writ of habeas corpus to Cusick, releasing him from state custody to tribal jurisdiction because such an assault was not covered by the Major Crimes Act. The court specifically found that Crow Dog was binding upon New York State.

52. See *Crow Dog* at 185; Pound, "Nationals without a Nation," *Columbia Law Review* 22 (1922): 98–99.

53. *Buffalo R & P R Co. v. Lavery*, 75 Hun, N.Y. 396 (1895), 399–400.

54. See Upton, *Everett Report*. The commission had been appointed in response to *U.S. v. Boylan*, 256 Fed. (1919), at p. 468. In this case an Oneida Indian was returned by a federal court to his family farm on the reservation after having been ejected by a local sheriff when the bank foreclosed on the mortgage.

55. Rickard, *Fighting Tuscarora*, 100.

56. Ibid., 5.

57. 25 U.S. Code Sec. 175 (1893). This analysis is by Donald Bain, former assistant U.S. Attorney, *Evening News*, March 28, 1930.

58. *Courier Express*, March 17, 1930.

59. *Courier Express*, March 18, 1930.

60. 25 U.S. Code Sec. 71, 31.

61. *Courier Express*, March 27, 1930.

62. *Evening News*, March 21, 1930. While federal defense of native Americans accused of criminal charges in state courts was unusual, it was not unheard of. For instance, in 1903, the U.S. Attorney for Wyoming secured the dismissal of state murder charges involving the killing of a county sheriff by a Sioux hunting party in an altercation over hunting rights. Like the Jimerson/Bowen case, the Wyoming case involved both the specter of the death penalty and immense local prejudice. See Barton R. Voigt, "The Lightning Creek Fight," *Annals of Wyoming* 49 (Spring 1977): 12.

63. Sometime after the trial, Lila Jimerson married Wallace Hilliker and lived near Perrysburg, N.Y., in Cattaraugus County, where she died in 1972. Nancy Bowen died many years earlier. Henri

Marchand, who had sculpted several of the figures in the exhibit of Iroquois Indian Groups at the New York State Museum, returned to the Albany area. He died in Troy, N.Y., in 1951. The author is grateful to Lisa Seivert, librarian and archivist at the Buffalo Museum of Science, for her assistance. See also Rickard, *Fighting Tuscarora*, 175 n. 4; David C. Lithgow, "History of the Indian Groups with a Description of the Technic" and Noah T. Clarke, "The Indian Groups of the New York State Museum and a Description of the Technic," in New York State Museum Bulletin 310 (Albany: The University of the State of New York, 1937), 83, 104.

64. Rickard, *Fighting Tuscarora*, 100.

12

The final essay in this section further suggests how Native American religious understandings continued to evolve over time. Sergei Kan's description of Alaskan Tlingit elders' views of shamanism rests on interviews the author conducted with tribal elders between 1979 and 1987. His consultants had undergone an era of intense missionary activity in the first half of the twentieth century, as well as the more ecumenical attitudes of the 1960s and 1970s. Collecting information orally, Kan became intrigued by the way modern Christian Tlingits thought about their "pagan" past. As a cultural anthropologist, Kan was as interested in the contemporary outlook of Tlingit people as he was in the detailed story of the nineteenth-century missions (though his synopsis of that missionary enterprise can be set alongside the accounts elsewhere in this volume). Kan discovered that, in contrast to non-Native Christians who condemn traditional religious leaders, most Tlingits viewed nineteenth-century shamans sympathetically. These Tlingit Christians told of shamans who knew in advance that whites were coming, who cleverly incorporated Christian rites and objects, such as crosses, into their customary practices, and who struggled against evil as energetically as white missionaries did. This more sympathetic view of native ways echoes the attitudes of Native field matrons studied by Lisa Emmerich.

Kan draws two conclusions from this modern Christian sympathy for non-Christian religious leaders. First, he confirms that, as among Iroquois, religious change in Native American communities was not cataclysmic. Indians did not drop their ancestors' faith one day and pick up Christianity the next. Unlike acculturated Cherokees and mixed bloods on the White Earth Reservation who tended to distance themselves from traditional ways and people, Tlingit elders were eager to find continuity between their cultural traditions and their own beliefs. Second, Kan argues that the views of the Tlingits he spoke with demonstrate how the telling of one's history is a dynamic process; it can be a tool, even a weapon, empowering people to mount an effective response to colonization. His essay reminds us that, in every community, but particularly in the ongoing life of a Native American group, memory is malleable; understanding and interpreting historical events is often more important than historical "facts."

Shamanism and Christianity: Modern Tlingit Elders Look at the Past

Sergei Kan

Almost two decades ago Fogelson criticized American ethnohistorians for not paying enough attention to "the native interpretations of critical events and significant historical personages."[1] He contrasted our own Western notion of "objective" "ethnohistory" with that of indigenous history, which he called "ethno-ethnohistory."[2] Even though few ethnohistorians today would quarrel with Fogelson's position, studies that focus on the Native North Americans' own views and interpretations of the past remain rare, with much of our research still concerned exclusively with "what really happened." In the last few years, however, several innovative works on specific North American Indian modes of historical consciousness have finally appeared, notably Harkin's elegant analysis of Heiltsuk narratives of their ancestors' first encounter with the Europeans[3] and Brightman's fascinating paper on the Manitoba Cree traditions of the primitive anthropomorphic "races" chronologically more ancient and culturally less complex than contemporary Cree themselves.[4]

Studies like these show a highly developed sense of historical consciousness[5] and a serious effort to rethink the past in light of more recent experiences. They also demonstrate that the past can be used to make sense of the present, to justify and explain the current predicament of the indigenous people of North America.[6] Finally, they reveal that this changing historical discourse has developed in the context of a dialogue with Euro-American ideologies. In fact the "dialogical" nature of many of the postcontact Native American oral traditions makes them particularly complex and interesting for ethnohistorians.[7] They are, after all, attempts by the colonized people to defend their past against various efforts by Euro-Americans to impose their own, often critical, interpretations on Indian history. To complicate matters even further, some of the key elements of Western ideology, such as Christianity, have been accepted by many Native Americans, so that they now often use Christian concepts to reinterpret their own past. However, while accepting Christianity, they often reject the standard missionary view of traditional Indian religions as "primitive" and "pagan."

In this article I examine one attempt by the elders in a modern-day Native American society to rethink its pre-Christian religion by affirming *its* validity while acknowledging the greater wisdom and power of Christianity. In the course of my

Source: *Ethnohistory*, v. 38, n. 4 (Fall 1991), pp. 363–387.

intermittent work with informants from Sitka, Angoon, Kake, and a number of other mostly northern Tlingit communities from 1979 to 1987, I collected several narratives and heard many statements about the nineteenth-century shamans and their responses to Christianity. These comments ranged from occasional negative characterizations of shamans as "witch doctors" to some very strong endorsements of these religious practitioners as healers, wise men, and prophets. Many comments fell between the two extremes and exhibited some ambiguous feelings about an aspect of indigenous Tlingit culture that once drew heavy fire from missionaries and other zealous agents of Westernization. In 1979–80, when I first heard these stories, I did not pay much attention to them, dismissing them as a recent invention, a rhetorical "use of the past" for ideological purposes by elderly Christian Tlingit.

A more careful look at this ethnographic material has shown that this case is more complex. First, some of the narratives about the shamans predicting the coming of the Europeans and a new and more powerful religion appear to be not recent but rather old. Second, underlying some of these narratives is the historical fact that in the early contact period shamans were curious about the newcomers' spiritual power and were beginning to use Christian paraphernalia and ritual acts. In other words, as in much of the rest of North America,[8] incorporation of Christian ritual acts and objects into indigenous ceremonial activities often preceded intense firsthand contacts with Europeans and conversion to Christianity. Finally, these stories were not simply created for nonnative consumption but played (and continue to play) an important role in my elderly informants' own worldview. At the same time, they are being passed on to subsequent generations of Tlingit as agreed-upon tribal history and will undoubtedly become that in the future. Thus, contemporary Tlingit narratives and comments about shamans are valuable sources of two kinds of information: the more factual history of the nineteenth-century shamans' response to Christianity and the continuously changing native view of these religious practitioners.

NINETEENTH-CENTURY TLINGIT SHAMANISM

Nineteenth-century Tlingit shamanism, as we understand it from the existing historical and ethnhographic sources, was a classical circumpolar type. The centrality of shamanism in Tlingit culture was first pointed out by Swanton, who wrote, "It would appear that, taking the people of the north Pacific coast as a whole, shamanism reached its climax among the Tlingit."[9] The shaman (*íxt'*) was the key intermediary between humans and other-than-human persons and powers of the world. He cured the sick, controlled the weather, brought success in war and in fishing and hunting, foretold the future, communicated with other shamans at a distance, received news about faraway people and places, found and brought hack to their families those who were lost or captured by the anthropomorphic land otter people (sing. *kóoshdaa k̲áa*), revealed and neutralized the evil actions of witches, and made public demonstrations of his[10] power in various awe-inspiring ways. The shaman could do all these things because he was inspired by and controlled one or, more often, several acquired or inherited superhuman spirits (sing. *yéik*). Each of these spirits had a personal name, a special song, and associated regalia. During his initial solitary quest for power and throughout his life, the shaman had to observe a strict regimen of prolonged fasting, thirsting, purging, and sexual abstinence and was forbidden to cut or comb his hair. Every localized clan had at least one íxt', so that larger villages composed of several clans usually had several resident shamans.[11]

CHRISTIANITY AND THE TLINGIT[12]

The first Tlingit encounter with Christianity occurred in Sitka in the mid-1830s when Fr. Ivan Veniaminov began his proselytizing work in the native community bordering on Novo-Arkhangel'sk, a fort established in 1804 as the capital of Russian America. At that time relations between the two settlements were rather strained, with the Russians rarely venturing outside their palisade. In fact, Veniaminov could begin visiting the native homes only after a devastating smallpox epidemic of 1837–38 killed off many elders and shamans, upholders of traditional religion. The epidemic somewhat undermined the natives' trust in their own healers and demonstrated to them the power of the Russians, who seemed invincible to the new and terrifying disease. Gradually, some of the Tlingit began accepting baptism along with vaccination. The first converts included some Tlingit women married to Russian men as well as a few native clan leaders courted by the Russian-American Company and attracted by the splendor of the Orthodox ritual and the possibility of establishing ties with the high-ranking company officials who acted as their godfathers.

From the 1840s to the 1860s the Orthodox church continued its missionizing efforts in southeastern Alaska, focusing mainly on Sitka but also making occasional visits to the surrounding northern villages and to the Stikine area in the south.[13] By 1867, when Russia sold Alaska to the United States, the Orthodox church claimed over four hundred Tlingit converts. This might seem to be an impressive figure, but in fact even in Sitka the baptized natives did not constitute the majority. Moreover, the existing records suggest that most of these converts had only a vague understanding of Orthodoxy, attended services infrequently, and often failed to confess or receive communion. Few church marriages or burials took place; most Tlingit continued to cremate their dead. While for a few Tlingit Christianity might have already become a significant part of their worldview, most converts, in my opinion, saw it simply as an additional source of spiritual power and material benefit. Thus, some of them began adding prayers addressed to the Russian "Great Spirit" to the traditional magical formulas when seeking success in hunting, fishing, or trade.[14]

Of course, one of the major obstacles to Tlingit Christianization was the limited contact they had with the Russians, even in Sitka, not to mention other communities. In order to keep the natives out of Novo-Arkhangel'sk, the Russians built a separate church for them on the border of the two communities, with the Indians having to enter it from their village and the clergy from inside the town. Most importantly, as long as the Tlingit remained politically independent from the Europeans, most of them saw no need to embrace Russian ways as thoroughly as, for example, the Aleuts, whom the Tlingit saw as subservient to the Russians.[15]

The situation changed significantly after the American arrival in 1867 and especially after the establishment of a Presbyterian mission in 1878. The Americans brought numerous trade items of higher quality and jobs in mining, canneries, and lumbering, which many Tlingit were eager to perform to earn money. Much of this new wealth was channeled into the traditional system of potlatching, but some of the younger "nouveaux riches" began accumulating wealth for their own and their nuclear families' use. A more serious blow to the traditional social order was American political domination, which resulted in encroachment on native subsistence resources and interference in their internal affairs. A few attempts at resistance resulted in a show of force by the American men-of-war patrolling the coast, making submission to the newcomers' power and authority inevitable.[16]

Backed by the military and civil authorities, Presbyterians attacked such key aspects of the indigenous culture as communal living in large winter houses, matrilineal descent and inheritance, slavery, blood revenge, accusations of witchcraft, and, of course, shamanism. The Presbyterians also relied on American military might to enforce school attendance among the young in Sitka and several other Tlingit communities. Initially, many native parents were interested in having their children learn the ways of the powerful newcomers (especially reading and writing), but they did not want the youngsters to turn their backs on the traditional values and practices attacked by the zealous American reformers.

The price paid by these Tlingit children for acquiring the new knowledge was high. In the Presbyterian boarding school in Sitka, the center of Protestant education, the use of the native language was forbidden, while the students were indoctrinated in American Protestant values and presented with a bleak picture of their own parents' way of life. Most schoolchildren, even those already baptized in the Orthodox church, were pressured to become Presbyterians. The school graduates were encouraged to intermarry, disregarding the fundamental law of moiety exogamy, and set up nuclear family households in "Boston-style" cottages built near the mission, away from the "evil influence" of their heathen kin. Some of these men and women, who formed the core of the Presbyterian Church of Sitka (officially established in 1884), thoroughly internalized these exogenous beliefs and attitudes, while others seemed to vacillate between the two cultures, taking part in potlatches one day and confessing the next.[17] The heavy-handed tactics of the Presbyterian missionaries discouraged many older natives from joining their church. In fact, by the late 1880s, Tlingit membership in the Presbyterian Church of Sitka had begun to decline.

During the same period, the Russian Orthodox church, which remained in Alaska after 1867, revitalized its missionary efforts and managed to attract most of the more conservative Tlingit in Sitka as well as a significant portion of the Indian population of Killisnoo and neighboring Angoon, Hoonah, and Juneau. By the 1910s all of the Tlingit villages had been Christianized by the Presbyterian and the Russian Orthodox missions. The sudden success of Orthodoxy[18] owed much to the overzealousness of the Presbyterians. At the same time, Orthodoxy, at least in Sitka and Juneau, seemed to appeal to the more conservative segment of the native population, which was less willing to abandon such key aspects of the traditional culture as the solidarity of clan relatives and potlatching.[19] While both churches attacked the "old customs,"[20] the Presbyterians were much more thorough in their efforts to "civilize" the Indians and had much greater control over their parishioners than the understaffed Orthodox church. In addition, Orthodox Christianity, with its emphasis on ritual and the use of sacred objects, was much more susceptible to native reinterpretation and indigenization than the more cerebral Presbyterianism. Finally, the Russian church's greater use of the native language also attracted the more conservative Tlingit.

In the first half of this century a number of other denominations, including the Salvation Army and several fundamentalist and charismatic churches, gained their own converts among the Tlingit. For almost a century now, Christianity has been an important part of Tlingit culture, providing new sources of spiritual power and emotional well-being as well as new social institutions for strengthening intravillage solidarity. It has also become a source of new rhetoric for describing and evaluating traditional culture as well as contemporary life. The degree of commitment of individual Tlingit to Christian principles varies significantly, from the die-hard Presbyterians who reject most of the "old customs" (e.g., refuse to take part in potlatches) to those elderly Orthodox church members who have managed rather successfully to syncretize Christian and indigenous beliefs and practices, especially in mortuary rituals.[21]

Prior to the tolerant era of the 1960s, the Tlingit had to hide their traditional practices from the clergy and other whites and to be defensive when trying to explain the "old customs" to non-Tlingit. Thus, while the potlatch was never outlawed in Alaska, as it had been in Canada, missionaries and civil authorities frequently interfered with this "heathen ceremony" and chastised the Tlingit repeatedly for being "wasteful" and "old-fashioned." Having always been very sensitive to public criticism and wanting very much to be accepted as equals by the dominant society, the Tlingit have tried hard to justify their pre-Christian beliefs and ceremonies, downplaying their "religious" nature and emphasizing their social functions and their important role in maintaining Tlingit identity.[22] Many devout native people have also felt the need to reconcile Christianity and the "old customs" in their own minds to avoid cognitive dissonance.

In the last few decades, the nonnative clergy has eased its acculturative pressure considerably, professing to tolerate indigenous customs as long as they do not directly contradict Christian teachings. Today Tlingit elders feel more free to discuss the old ways with their children and grandchildren as well as with nonnatives. Nevertheless, many of them continue to worry about the contradictions between Christian and pre-Christian beliefs and practices. Those elders nowadays formally referred to as "tradition-bearers" are currently constructing their own version of the "old customs" and passing it on to younger generations through "Indian education" classes and various public occasions.[23] A number of these elders have become my informants, teachers, and friends since 1979. In our conversations, shamanism was often mentioned, since it has been one of the key aspects of the nineteenth-century Tlingit culture that they, in their effort to reconcile the two cultural and religious traditions, have had particular difficulty with.

MISSIONARY ATTITUDES TOWARDS SHAMANISM

To appreciate this difficulty, we have to look at the missionaries' own view of and struggle against the íxt', whom the Orthodox and the Protestant clergymen alike regarded as an archenemy. To begin with, they correctly identified the shaman as the main religious figure in Tlingit society and the only full-time practitioner who enjoyed great authority and respect in his community.[24] In fact, some missionaries of both churches characterized the entire Tlingit religion as "shamanism" and placed it low on the evolutionary ladder.[25] Thus, for example, a Presbyterian minister who served in southeastern Alaska in the late nineteenth and the early twentieth centuries wrote that "the ikt [*sic*] was superstitiously regarded as an all-powerful being. His word was absolute, and he was revered as a god."[26] Bad feelings between the missionaries and the shamans were mutual. The latter saw their position in Tlingit society threatened by the priests and ministers and often discouraged their relatives and neighbors from attending church services. Appalled by the shaman's appearance, his use various material objects ("idols," "fetishes"), and especially the dramatic trance he entered in order to do his job, missionaries often referred to him as "a servant of Satan" and saw him as an epitome of ignorant heathenism. While some of the missionaries admitted being impressed with a certain strange psychic power possessed by the íxt', many believed him to be a fraud and his healing to be quackery, aimed at enriching him at the expense of his gullible patients.[27] In fact, the clergy correctly identified native trust in the shamans as an obstacle in winning them over to Western biomedicine.[28] Finally, missionaries blamed the shamans for the persistence of beliefs in witchcraft and for the persecution of alleged witches, which not only continued after the American arrival but may even have intensified during that era of accelerated social change.

American efforts to free those accused of witchcraft were the main context in which shamans and missionaries confronted each other and in which the latter used force. In addition to preaching constantly against shamanism and witchcraft, Presbyterian missionaries, backed by the navy, the army, and the Alaskan civil authorities, tried to expel the most notorious shamans from their communities and even to arrest them.[29] Among the shamans' secular enemies, one man, Commander Henry Glass of the U.S. Navy, gained special admiration among the Presbyterian missionaries. According to one Russian priest who labored in Sitka in the 1890s,

> hunting shamans was his favorite pastime and sport. A captured shaman was usually invited aboard his boat and received with honor. Glass would talk to him in a friendly manner, inquiring about his life, the number of his *yéik* [spirits], the extent of their strength and power, etc. Then he would announce that he was also a shaman who owned *yéik* and suggested that they compete against each other. Upon his order, a charged electric battery was brought out. The shaman was asked to hold the wires in his hands, while the two poles were being connected. The shaman's body would begin to twist. His own people, witnessing his strange and funny poses and hearing his screams and moans, became frightened. The shaman himself learned a practical les-

son about the power of his white colleague. But the captain did not stop at that. Shamans always left his boat with their heads shaved and covered with oil paint, and having promised not to practice shamanism anymore.[30]

While this Russian missionary found Glass's methods somewhat excessive, he himself demanded that the members of the Archangel Michael Society of Mutual Aid, which he established among the Sitka Tlingit in 1896, "no longer believe in shamanistic spirits."[31]

THE SHAMANS' FATE IN THE POSTCONTACT ERA

What effects did this anti-shamanistic propaganda and these activities have on the shamans? Initially, they resisted missionary pressure, waging their own anti-Christian campaign and later trying to hide from their enemies and conduct their activities underground. Thus, shamans disappeared from Sitka by 1900 or 1910 but continued to practice in more isolated, smaller communities, like Angoon and Klukwaun, until at least the 1930s. The Sitka and Juneau Tlingit occasionally went to these villages to seek help, and, according to my informants, as late as the 1950s there were still some individuals in conservative communities who, while not full-fledged shamans, were reputed to be fortune-tellers and spiritual healers.

At the same time, rather early in their contact with missionaries, Tlingit shamans began taking advantage of the new sources of power introduced by the Russians and Americans. References to the shamans' use of crosses and other sacred objects from Christian worship, as well as instances of their imitation of church services, can be found in several ethnographic accounts[32] and were confirmed by my own informants (see below).[33] As early as the 1830s or 1840s some shamans began to accept baptism; unlike the nineteenth-century priest Veniaminov, however, I am not convinced that by joining the Russian church they were actually renouncing their craft.[34]

Gradually, the shamans surrendered their role as religious practitioners to the missionaries, not simply because of brute force but because of their own inability to combat devastating diseases introduced by the Europeans. While some shamans tried to fight the new diseases, for instance, by adding smallpox spirits to their repertoire of helping agents, many shamans were perceived by their communities as incapable of serving their new needs. Thus, Veniaminov reported that in Sitka the Tlingit were saying that the present-day shamans were much weaker than the old ones and were attributing that decline to the fact that the former were intemperate and weak.[35] The shamans' decline might also be explained by the fact that the Tlingit were losing trust in their power. Humiliated and persecuted, unable to combat new diseases or perform their healing seances without the fear of punishment, shamans increasingly lost their hold on the native community, becoming less and less relevant to its social and religious life. Among the manifestations of this process were the refusal of some of the prominent shamans' descendants to accept the call by inheriting their paraphernalia and by insisting that the shamans' corpses be disposed of, not above ground, in accordance with tradition, but by burial, which prevented their guardian spirits from being inherited.[36] The fact that this began in the 1890s, if not earlier, suggests that some Tlingit began to have strong doubts about the shamans' power soon after their acceptance of Christianity.

MODERN-DAY ELDERS LOOK AT SHAMANISM

Before presenting the ethnographic data I collected from Tlingit informants on the subject of shamanism, I must comment briefly about their background. Most of them ranged in age from sixty to ninety and came mainly from Sitka and Angoon; the rest lived in Kake, Hoonah, Yakutat, and other Tlingit communities. Most of the discussions were conducted in English, with occasional Tlingit words and phrases.[37] The issue of shamanism was discussed in detail with about twenty elders, who belonged to several churches, including Orthodox, Presbyterian, Salvation Army, and Assembly of God. A few of them had seen shamans perform or had at least known the persons allegedly possessing shamanistic power.[38] Others had heard about well-known shamans from their own older relatives. Very few of them dismissed or condemned shamanism totally. Even a very devout sixty-year-old Episcopalian woman who emphatically stated that "God and the íxt' do not go together" and that the shaman "served Satan" mentioned that he did have "a gift from God but turned it into evil." Thus, even the more Americanized older Tlingit who profess not to believe in the power of the íxt' tend to take that power seriously, refusing, for example, to touch or even look at the shamans' regalia and paraphernalia or to come near their graves for fear of being hurt by guardian spirits. Some of my middle-aged informants, who said that today shamanism has no place in Tlingit life, admitted that if they had lived in the old days, they, like everybody else, would have believed in the íxt'.

A few of the oldest and most conservative elders (who tend to be Russian Orthodox) embraced shamanistic beliefs wholeheartedly and claimed that they saw no contradictions between them and Christianity. When asked why all the shamans had disappeared, one of them responded, "When the Tlingit decided to live like the white man, all the medicine men had to go." Another elderly traditionalist commented that shamans could no longer exist because "people do not live right anymore and are not pure."

Most of the informants positioned themselves between these two extreme views, neither totally condemning nor fully accepting shamanism. They tried to divide the shamans into good and bad ones and to differentiate between those shamanistic activities that resembled Christian practices and those that were clearly "heathen." Hence many of the elders spoke about the shamans as "prophets," "healers," "Indian doctors," "spirit men," or "medicine men." They emphasized such positive functions as fighting witches (an activity that they, unlike the missionaries, saw as a useful service to the community), healing, finding missing persons, and upholding morality. One elderly woman from Yakutat, a loyal Presbyterian church member, said: "What the white people call 'witch doctor' was no witch doctor at all. He fought against evil spirits. He fought against witches. The íxt's were real God's people. They taught us about the Ten Commandments. 'Do not kill.' 'Do not steal.' 'Do not commit adultery.'" The notion that the teachings of the old-time shamans contained elements of the Old and/or the New Testament was popular with many of my informants. Some spoke of the shaman having a "gift from the Holy Spirit." Others compared him to Moses, who taught the people about the Ten Commandments, or to John the Baptist, who foretold and facilitated the coming of Christ.

In fact, for these elders the Bible served as a rich source of images in which to couch an "old-fashioned" phenomenon like shamanism and make it more palatable to themselves and their younger native and nonnative audiences. When describing the shaman's trance, several informants compared his imitation of the voices of the different spirits to the Apostles' speaking different languages after they had received the Holy Spirit or to the charismatic church members' speaking in tongues. Shamanistic healing was likened to Christ's miraculous healing by laying hands on the afflicted or to the feats of modern-day faith healers. At least one person drew a parallel between the fasting and other taboos observed by the shaman in training to the restrictions imposed on a man entering the priesthood. "Both of them walk a narrow path," he concluded.

One of my best informants, a very knowledgeable and reflective man in his sixties, a member of a fundamentalist church who claimed not to believe in shamanism but respected the old-time "Indian doctors," offered the following justification for the existence of shamans: "In the absence of Christianity, I am sure that God in Heaven allowed [for the existence of] a bulwark against the rampaging evil. The ultra-evil was held at bay by the presence of these noted practitioners." Another informant of the same age, who claimed to have read about "primitive" shamans in Asia, insisted that the Tlingit íxt' was not like them at all. Yet despite these comparisons between shamanism and biblical religion, none of my informants likened the power of the íxt' to that of God himself. As one man put it: "I do not want to be dogmatic, but I think their [shamans'] power was different from God's power. They were more like the prophets mentioned in the Bible who could foretell the future."

Some people appealed to modern popular science and psychology to explain the íxt's power. Several persons spoke of him as a "great psychiatrist," a "person who practiced telepathy," or the one who possessed "extrasensory perception or the sixth sense." One elderly woman, trying to rationalize the effects of witchcraft on the human body, explained: "The medicine man was a psychiatrist. He told you what was wrong with you. For example, if you hated somebody, that hatred inside of you was making you sick. He could help you deal with that problem."

In their effort to downplay the more "heathen" elements of shamanism, some of the elders were critical of the shaman's use of rattles, masks, and other paraphernalia. The same woman who called the íxt' a psychiatrist pointed out that he "made a mistake when he started wearing crowns, rattles, and bone necklaces and to brag about himself. That is evil!" Another one asserted that "the medicine men were okay until they decided to make themselves big by using rattles, charms, and so forth. Pride is no good!" A third informant compared the use of rattles and other paraphernalia to "a primitive type of voodoo" and contrasted it with the use of "pure" spiritual power by the few "good" shamans.

Many of the people I spoke to separated the good "medicine men" from the bad "witch doctors" (the latter term was popular among the whites in Alaska around the turn of the century). The good "doctors" did not harm anybody and did not ask for payment for their services. The bad ones were greedy and jealous of one another and would use their power to kill or otherwise harm other shamans or ordinary persons. The good ones could cure without using any paraphernalia; the bad ones could not. Thus, these informants have taken many of the actual characteristics and practices of the old-time íxt' that the missionaries condemned (e.g., the spiritual combats between rival shamans) and applied them to the "bad witch doctors," while creating a category of pure "healers" and "prophets." Some insisted that the more recent shamans tended to be bad or at least weaker than the "real old-time Indian doctors." Others echoed the missionaries when they said that many of the more recent shamans were impostors. Thus they accepted some of the criticism leveled by the whites against the shamans, without rejecting their belief in shamanistic power altogether.

According to my informants, the best proof of the power and wisdom of these good old-time shamans was the ability of some of them to predict the coming of the Europeans and especially of Christianity, which they had allegedly recognized and welcomed as a superior religion. A number of people I spoke to knew about specific shamans who had that reputation, remembered their names and the names of their villages, and gave some details about their prophecies. One knowledgeable informant spoke about two shamans from Klukwaan who predicted the European arrival after their spirits had gone out to sea and had seen the European ships. Another told about a powerful íxt' named Shawaan (?) who often spoke about the various technological miracles that the whites would someday bring to southeastern Alaska, including the "four-eyed monster" (automobile) and "a box through which people could talk to each other" (radio and telephone). He also allegedly announced that someday ordinary people, rather than just witches, would be able to fly in the air. A third informant told of a shaman who warned the people to expect trouble from the first Europeans, with their "powerful water" (liquor) and firearms, but encouraged them to trust the next group of newcomers, "with long hair and long beards" (Orthodox missionaries), who were going "to bring a new and more powerful teaching" to the Tlingit.

In several narratives a shaman uses a Russian Orthodox crucifix, holy water, and other sacred objects and substances, speaks "Russian" (actually Church Slavonic), and imitates an Orthodox priest in various other ways. The following narrative was recorded from William Nelson, an elderly Angoon man who was a churchgoer as well as a very knowledgeable traditionalist of noble origin:

> There once lived a man in the Angoon area who was very sick—he had a strong internal bleeding. One night he saw a man coming through the door. He had a long beard and white hair [looked like a Russian priest]. He was coming closer and closer but then disappeared. He went into the shaman's body. It was a power, a healing power spirit. We call it *kugawasu yéik* [good luck spirit]. After that the sick man became a shaman; he would sing shaman's songs at night. He was getting the power. Pretty soon his bleeding stopped—no more blood came out of his mouth.

He felt good and decided to go to the beach to get some fresh water from a stream. When he scooped up some water, on the bottom of his cup he saw a cross. He drank the water with the cross.[39] That night he began making noises like a shaman does when the spirit comes down on him. He was speaking Russian. People knew it was Russian because the Russian boats were already visiting them at that time. He owned a Russian axe and every time he spoke Russian he would pick it up. That is when the Russian spirit came down on him. We call it *Anóoshi yahaayí* [Russian spirit]. He used that axe to chase away the evil spirits that made his patients sick. He told the people that every seventh day this *yéik* would come down on him and that on that day the house had to be cleaned very thoroughly. He was a strong *íxt'* and he had two powers—the healing good luck spirit (*kugawasu yéik*) and the Russian spirit (*Anóoshi yahaayí*). He could tell when somebody was going to be healed or when witches were doing some wicked things. He lived a long time ago but the Russians were already here. He died in a cave near Angoon.

In this story the protagonist still acts as a traditional shaman who simply adds a new guardian spirit to his repertoire. Apparently this is a very powerful spirit (*yéik* or *yahaayí*), since it helps the *íxt'* recover from a life-threatening illness. With the new spirit come new material objects, a secular one (axe) and a sacred one (crucifix), as well as a new language. Of course, any pre-Christian *yéik* manifested itself similarly through its own special song, mask, voice, and language. At the same time, this new Christian ("Russian") spirit uses the shaman as a mouthpiece for a new form of ritual observance, the celebration of the seventh day of the week. The narrator admits that the Russians were already in southeastern Alaska when this happened but insists that the Angoon *íxt'* did not travel to Sitka to visit the Russian church there and had not been baptized.

In other accounts, the shaman is described as having suffered a temporary death when his soul left the body and visited heaven. Upon the soul's return, the shaman comes back to life and begins teaching the people to clean their houses prior to the seventh sacred day and to rest on that day.[40] The most elaborate account of a shaman's prophecy that incorporated elements of Christian teaching comes from the village of Kake and describes the events that took place in the nineteenth century in a community located in Tebenkof Bay on Kuiu Island, the original home of some of the Kake people. I recorded several versions of that story from three Kake informants in 1979, while Billman, an ethnographer from Sheldon Jackson College in Sitka, who worked in the 1960s and the early 1970s, collected similar accounts from informants in several communities outside Kake.[41]

The gist of the story is that a local shaman who goes into the mountains comes back with the warning that, despite the starvation that is coming, the people should not touch the first run of sockeye salmon. In order to avoid a terrible illness they must wait for the next run. In some versions of this story, the people are told to wait until God or spirits purify the fish, kept in a net, and make it edible. The people disobey and soon fall victim to some unknown disease that causes high fever and blisters or sores all over the body, followed by blood coming out of the mouth, and then death. In some versions, afflicted men run around, waving their fists or spears as if trying to kill some unknown spirits. The entire village is destroyed except for one or two survivors who tell the story to the people of Kake. The inhabitants of a neighboring village erect a cross on the spot where the victims' bodies lie. Some of the older informants claimed to have seen the remains of a village on that spot when they were younger. The cross was allegedly still visible a few decades ago. It is unclear what happened to the shaman himself.

According to some versions of this story, the same shaman told the people about observing the Sabbath and especially warned them not to use any sharp objects on that day. He also taught them how to make crosses and spoke in some unknown language, "probably Hebrew." One informant claimed that the shaman wore a "towel" around his neck and lifted his hands up into the air (i.e., dressed and acted like an Orthodox priest). Depending on the storyteller's background, some versions of this narrative place much greater emphasis on the Christian nature of this shaman's prophecies. One man insisted that it was God or "the High Above Spirit," not an ordinary *yéik,* that the Tebenkof Bay shaman was communicating with. Another informant said that God was testing the people and that all they had to do was to wait one more day for him to purify the fish, but they refused to obey God and were punished by him.

Some of my informants denied that the disease that destroyed the people of Tebenkof Bay was an epidemic. However, others insisted that it was in fact smallpox.[42] One of Billman's informants located the event in the early 1830s, when her great-grandmother was a young girl. This, of course, was the time of a terrible smallpox epidemic that swept through many Tlingit communities, possibly including the Tebenkof Bay area. This epidemic, the fact that several informants claimed to be direct descendants of its survivors, and that the location of the unfortunate village is well established suggest that these events may very well have taken place. It is also reasonable to assume that a local shaman was called upon to deal with this terrible affliction. The people's response to the disease was similar to the way Tlingit in other villages dealt with epidemics. For example, as de Laguna was told in Yakutat: "Epidemics were believed to be the work of spirits that came in boats, sometimes paddling in canoes, or riding in a sailing ship or even in a steamboat. They were invisible to any eyes but those of the shaman. In the boat were all those who had previously died of the disease, and in this way they traveled to the Land of the Dead. . . . Some persons received such disease spirits as their *yéik,* and so became shamans."[43]

Even though the Tebenkof Bay story does not mention the spirits of the disease or their origin, the fact that the fish is blamed for it suggests some connection between the water and the illness. The physical manifestations of the illness are also reminiscent of smallpox. The fact that epidemics were terribly frightening and confusing to the Tlingit is confirmed by the Russians who observed some of the sick Sitka Indians in the late 1830s eating snow and desperately jumping into the cold water of the ocean, hoping to relieve their fever. They also mention that the afflicted appealed to the shamans for help and that curing seances were performed, but to no avail.[44]

If this story originated in the mid-nineteenth century, Kuiu area people had already had some contact with the Russians and other Europeans. They might even have heard about the Russian Orthodox church, and it is possible that a few of them had already been to Sitka, had seen its rituals, and had been baptized. It is true that the shaman's interpretation of the disease is very traditional: prohibitions on eating certain foods (*ligaas*) were quite common in the pre-Christian Tlingit religion. The first run of fish or other "first fruits" were often shared with the whole community, given to the poor and the old, or treated in other special ways. Setting aside fish and other edibles and keeping them in a container that is not to be touched by ritually unprepared laypeople is a common theme in Tlingit mythology. In fact, in some versions, the Tebenkof Bay story has nothing to do with the prediction of Christianity, and these versions might actually be the original ones. However, many of them have a strong moralizing flavor. The ultimate cause of the disease is not some unseen evil spirits but the Supreme Spirit or God who punished people for their impatience and the violation of his taboo. Traditionally, illness or death were common forms of punishment for violating a taboo. It is interesting that some storytellers add mistreatment of small birds by children, a typical Tlingit violation (*ligaas*) that brings about death and illness, as another reason for the punishment suffered by the unfortunate village. Finally, the story casts the shaman in the powerful role of a prophet or messenger between mankind and a new spirit that is more powerful than the *yéik*. Even if the original Tebenkof Bay shaman was not the same man who introduced the first elements of Christianity to the people of that area, his ability to interpret the meaning of the new disease might have been seen by subsequent generations as a sign of unusual wisdom. Like other shamans, he could not cure the new disease but could explain why it came, couching his interpretation in traditional cultural idioms while adding new symbols borrowed from a new source of superhuman power.

While stories about the shamans predicting the coming of the whites are rather common, I collected very few narratives about actual encounters between missionaries and shamans. Several informants said that the early missionaries were impressed with the power of the íxt' and allegedly even acknowledged that it was spiritual power. Persons who persecuted shamans harshly are viewed unsympathetically by the Tlingit elders. Thus, the above-mentioned efforts of zealots like Commander Glass were often mentioned, but instead of describing how shamans were humiliated when their hair was cut short, several elders claimed that the whites were afraid to harm those medicine men, who threatened to use their power to kill any person who touched the scissors.

The most interesting account of this kind deals with a Hoonah shaman who was asked by his village to kill a Presbyterian missionary. For several days this powerful íxt' tried to use his spirits to kill the enemy. Finally, he gave up, announcing that there was nothing he could do. "This man's soul is like a big round rock covered with ice. You can't lift it—your hands are too short and it slips away." As the narrator explained: "This was the shaman's way of saying that the man's soul was pure and that he possessed a higher power. The shaman also said that the missionary was bringing them the good news and the beginning of a new life. He came with love and not hate and he was telling them the truth. After that the village accepted Christianity. This story demonstrates the power of the Lord."

INTERPRETATION

What do these narratives tell us about the fate of the Tlingit shamans in the postcontact period and about the modern-day Tlingit elders' interpretation of shamanism? To begin with, it appears that at least some of these stories, like the ones about the events in Tebenkof Bay or the confrontation between an íxt' and a missionary in Hoonah, are not recent inventions but accounts (however modified) of actual events that took place after contact. Thus, for example, the story about an Angoon íxt' who acquired a powerful spirit from a Russian was told to me by an elderly man who claimed to have learned it in his younger days. The nineteenth-century origin of this story, or at least of this type of story, is confirmed by Swanton, who was told in Sitka in 1904 that in the Angoon area there was a shaman who claimed to have acquired his power from "a big Russian."[45]

If such narratives refer to the actual events that took place in the nineteenth century, we are dealing here with the shamans' response to mysterious new phenomena brought about by Europeans and Americans. The shamans, like the rest of the Tlingit, were trying to comprehend not only powerful new diseases but the impressive wealth and military might of the newcomers. Because in the traditional Tlingit culture such things were linked to the possession of spiritual power, the shamans must have concluded that the white man had a lot of it.[46] This idea must have been reinforced by the whites' invincibility to epidemic diseases and their possession of antidotes to them. The fact that the missionaries were involved in administering vaccines undoubtedly contributed to the clergy's high stature in the eyes of the Tlingit religious specialists and laypersons.[47]

However, instead of surrendering to this new power, nineteenth-century shamans tried to harness it for their own purposes, borrowing magical objects, substances, and formulas from their Euro-American rivals. To do so they did not even have to have a face-to-face encounter with a priest but could rely on stories about the mysterious rites conducted in Sitka, stories that had undoubtedly circulated throughout Tlingit country since the beginning of the nineteenth century. It is quite possible that these borrowings appeared to the shamans' tribesmen as independent inventions.

The idea that the shamans could predict the coming of the "People from under the Clouds" made perfect sense in light of the indigenous Tlingit worldview. The shamans, the only persons capable of traveling through time and space, *had* to predict this important event. In fact, it is quite conceivable that a shaman from a village that had not yet experienced white contact would be foretelling the arrival of the Europeans on the basis of the rumors rapidly spreading throughout the Northwest Coast.

All this suggests that my own informants and other twentieth-century Tlingit who have told stories about the old-time shamans predicting the European arrival have been drawing upon earlier accounts with deep roots in the nineteenth century.

Of course, they have tended to rethink and reinterpret these narratives in light of their own historical experience. It is not surprising that such stories have become especially popular since the 1960s, when the Tlingit were no longer subject to heavy-handed missionary control and criticism. These narratives play a very important function in the modern-day Tlingit worldview. They refuse to accept the Euro-Americans' condescending view of shamanism and other aspects of the precontact native religion, though they do concede the ultimate validity of Christianity as the postcontact religion of the Tlingit people. In these narratives the íxt' serves as a powerful and wise mediator between the past and the present, between the old-time religion, which is portrayed as valid but incomplete, and the new one, which is recognized as superior to it. In some sense it is irrelevant whether the narratives I collected go back one hundred years or are more recent. What is essential is that today they play the role of what Fogelson calls "epitomizing events," that is, "narratives that condense, encapsulate, and dramatize long-term historical processes. Such events are inventions but have such compelling qualities and explanatory power that they spread rapidly through the group and soon take on an ethnohistorical reality of their own."[48] In Harkin's terms, such events "mediate between radically different yet consecutive synchronic states, whose conjuncture was ... more subtle and gradual: and yet these epitomizing events provide meaningful cultural symbols and mnemonic devices for the rupture."[49]

The fact that the old-time shamans could predict the coming of Christianity denies the whites their claim of being the givers of truth to the "backward" Indians. As many of my informants insisted: "The white people did not teach us anything new; we had already known about the true religion. We knew about the Great Spirit up in heaven even though we did not worship him the way we do today.[50] The only new thing that the white people brought to us was the Holy Bible." To assert one's equality with the whites by refusing to see them as givers is particularly important to the society where those receiving a gift have traditionally been seen as less powerful than those giving it.

Finally, this view of the old-time shamans as wise prophets and healers relieves some of the modern-day elders of the burden of having to reconcile their devotion to Christianity with their belief in, or at least respect for, the indigenous religion. If the old-time shamans were frauds, why would one still be afraid of touching their paraphernalia, and how would one explain all their miraculous feats, portrayed in numerous stories passed down from generation to generation? In the opinion of contemporary Tlingit elders, their own noble ancestors had to be telling the truth about the powerful medicine men of yesterday.

CONCLUSION

The aim of this article has been to demonstrate the importance of paying attention to indigenous versions of history in reaching a much more thorough understanding of the past and present experience of Native North Americans. For many of them, history is not just some events that happened in the past but a vital force that continues to shape the present. Despite the impact of the written Western culture, oral traditions continue to be passed down from generation to generation, particularly in such societies as the Tlingit, where rank, status, and prestige still depend on one's pedigree and knowledge of it.

At the same time, accounts about and interpretations of the past are constantly being reshaped in response to more recent and current events and experiences. This has always occurred, because few oral traditions remain forever unchanging. However, since the arrival of Europeans and especially since the establishment of American political domination, history has become hotly contested between the colonizers and the colonized. Until recently, the former, particularly those determined to "civilize the natives," tried to denigrate that history and contrast the heathen "old customs" with the new culture of the "competent Christian citizens" (a favorite Presbyterian term). Native Americans, however, while accepting (or being forced to accept) many of the changes introduced by the dominant society, have tried to maintain their own version of the past, which emphasizes the virtues of the ancestors and downplays their vices. Thus the relationship between missionary and native versions of Tlingit history can be seen as a moral dialogue[51] in which the two sides use some of the same language (i.e., Christianity) and describe some of the same events but often disagree on their meaning.

The new rhetoric of Christianity is even used by the Indians to criticize the whites. For example, many of the persons cited in this article said that the Euro-Americans themselves have not lived up to the teachings of Christ, and that it is the Tlingit who are the true Christians and have "always followed the Ten Commandments." Thus the tables have been turned on the colonizers, whose own ideology becomes a weapon in the hands of the colonized.[52]

The material presented here also challenges the notion of the existence of a monolithic "Tlingit culture" equally shared by members of that society. As I have shown recently, there is considerable disagreement among the Tlingit on the role of the potlatch in modern-day society and on the meaning of its specific symbols.[53] Similarly, shamanism is looked upon somewhat differently by individual Tlingit, depending on their religious affiliation, age, education, and other factors. The goal of the ethnographer is to represent these divergent views rather than gloss over them.

Up until now, none of the ethnographers working in southeastern Alaska have paid much attention to these issues. Determined to gain data with which to reconstruct the nineteenth-century ("traditional") Tlingit culture, scholars trained in the Boasian tradition collected numerous narratives, but the latter tended not to deal with Tlingit-white relations. Thus, for example, Swanton—who acknowledged in the introduction to a major collection of Tlingit myths and stories that one of his key informants, Katishan, was a church member who showed a "moralizing tendency"— did not find it important to consider that Christianity might have colored this man's version of the myths of the Raven cycle.[54] Similarly, while de Laguna's remarkably detailed works on the culture and history of two Tlingit villages, Angoon and Yakutat, are aimed at reconstructing their eighteenth- and nineteenth-century histories, native representations of postcontact events involving whites are given short shrift.[55]

It is not my intention here to criticize my predecessors, whose work has been a major inspiration and a source of valuable data. In fact, much of my own ethnographic and ethnohistorical research has also aimed at reconstructing and analyzing the Tlingit culture prior to its dramatic transformation in the 1900s.[56] What I am arguing, however, is that in order to construct a truly comprehensive ethnohistory of Northwest Coast and other Native North American societies, we must incorporate more of Fogelson's ethno-ethnohistory into it. To succeed in this project we, anthropologists and ethnohistorians, will have to enlist the help of archaeologists, linguists, folklorists, and, of course, native historians themselves.[57]

NOTES

1. Raymond D. Fogelson, "On the Varieties of Indian History: Sequoyah and Traveller Bird," *Journal of Ethnic Studies* 2 (1974): 106.
2. Ibid.
3. Michael Harkin, "History, Narrative, and Temporality: Examples from the Northwest Coast," *Ethnohistory* 35 (1988): 99–130.
4. Robert A. Brightman, "Primitivism in Missinippi Cree Historical Consciousness," *Man* 25 (1990): 108–128.
5. Raymond D. Fogelson, "The Ethnohistory of Events and Nonevents," *Ethnohistory* 36 (1989): 139–140.
6. For a fine recent discussion of indigenous South American perspectives on the past (including European contact and colonization), see Jonathan D. Hill, ed., *Rethinking History and Myth: Indigenous South American Perspectives on the Past* (Urbana: University of Illinois Press, 1988). Turner's commentary on these essays is of special interest because it raises general theoretical issues concerning the relationship between "myth" and "history" in non-Western cultures. In his essay Turner uses the term *ethno-ethnohistory*, but (surprisingly) does not credit Fogelson with coining it. Terence Turner, "Ethno-Ethnohistory: Myth and History in Native South American Representations of Contact with Western Society," in Hill, ed., *Rethinking History and Myth*, 235–281.
7. Michael Harkin, "History, Narrative, and Temporality," 102; Michael Harkin, "Dialogues of History: Transformation and Change in Heiltsuk Culture, 1790–1920," Ph.D. diss., Department of Anthropology, University of Chicago, 1988.
8. Leslie Spier, *The Prophet Dance of the Northwest and Its Derivatives*, General Series in Anthropology, No. 1 (Menasha, Wisc.: George Banta, 1935); Wayne Suttles, "The Plateau Prophet Dance among the Coast Salish," *Southwestern Journal of Anthropology* 13 (1957): 352–396.
9. John R. Swanton, "Social Conditions, Beliefs, and Linguistic Relationship of the Tlingit Indians," *Twenty-sixth Annual Report of the Bureau of American Ethnology for the Years 1904–1905* (Washington, D.C.: U.S. Government Printing Office, 1908), 463.
10. Most of the Tlingit shamans were male, even though there were some powerful female ones as well. Throughout this article I refer to shamans with the masculine pronoun.
11. For details on Tlingit shamanism see Ivan Veniaminov, *Notes on the Islands of the Unalashka District*, trans. Lydia T. Black and Richard H. Geoghegan (Kingston, Ont.: Limestone, 1840; rpr. Fairbanks: University of Alaska Press, 1984); Aurel Krause, *The Tlingit Indians*, trans. Erna Gunther (Seattle: University of Washington Press, 1956 [orig. pub. 1885]); Anatolii Kamenskii, *Tlingit Indians of Alaska*, ed. and trans. Sergei Kan, Rasmuson Library Historical Translation Series, vol. 2 (Fairbanks: University of Alaska Press, 1985 [orig. pub. 1906]); Swanton, "Social Conditions, Beliefs, and Linguistic Relationship of the Tlingit Indians"; Frederica de Laguna, *The Story of a*

Tlingit Community: A Problem in the Relationship between Archaeological, Ethnological, and Historical Methods, Bureau of American Ethnology, Bulletin No. 172 (Washington, D.C.: U.S. Government Printing Office, 1972) and "Atna and Tlingit Shamanism: Witchcraft on the Northwest Coast," *Arctic Anthropology* 24 (1987): 84–100.

12. This brief overview is based on Sergei Kan, "Russian Orthodox Brotherhoods among the Tlingit," *Ethnohistory* 32 (1985): 196–223; "Memory Eternal: Russian Orthodoxy and the Tlingit Mortuary Complex," *Arctic Anthropology* 24 (1987): 32–55; "Russian Orthodox Missions," in Wilcomb E. Washburn, ed., *Handbook of North American Indians,* vol. 4, *History of Indian-White Relations* (Washington, D.C.: Smithsonian Institution Press, 1988), 506–521; "Recording Native Culture and Christianizing the Natives: Russian Orthodox Missionaries in Southeastern Alaska," in Richard A. Pierce, ed., *Russia in North America: Proceedings of the Second International Conference on Russian America* (Kingston, Ont.: Limestone, 1990), 298–313; and "Russian Orthodox Missionaries and the Tlingit Indians of Alaska, 1880–1890," in Barry M. Gough and Laird Christie, ed., *New Dimensions in Ethnohistory: Papers of the Second Laurier Conference on Ethnohistory and Ethnology,* Canadian Ethnology Service Mercury Series (Hull, Quebec: Canadian Museum of Civilization, 1991).

13. Petr A. Tikhmenev, *A History of the Russian-American Company,* trans. and eds. Richard A. Pierce and Alton S. Donnelly (Seattle: University of Washington Press, 1978); Veniaminov, *Notes on the Islands of the Unalashka District*; Sergei Kan, "Russian Orthodox Brotherhoods among the Tlingit"; "Russian Orthodox Missions"; "Recording Native Culture and Christianizing the Natives: Russian Orthodox Missionaries in Southeastern Alaska"; and "Russian Orthodox Missionaries and the Tlingit Indians of Alaska, 1880–1890."

14. Kan, "Russian Orthodox Brotherhoods among the Tlingit," 198.

15. Veniaminov, *Notes on the Islands of the Unalashka District,* 434.

16. Ted C. Hinckley, *The Americanization of Alaska, 1867–1897* (Palo Alto: Pacific Books, 1972); Kan, "Russian Orthodox Brotherhoods among the Tlingit."

17. Records of the First Presbyterian Church of Sitka, Billman Collection.

18. Kan, "Russian Orthodox Brotherhoods among the Tlingit"; "Memory Eternal"; "Russian Orthodox Missions"; and "Recording Native Culture."

19. Unlike Sitka and Juneau, which became American towns with substantial native populations, Tlingit villages, especially in the north, were composed almost entirely of conservative people, so that there was not much difference between those who joined the Russian Orthodox church and those who became Presbyterian. In addition, people in the villages were more likely to go back and forth between the different churches, a phenomenon that continues to this day.

20. The term *old customs* was introduced by the Protestants and was frequently used by Euro-Americans and Indians alike to describe the various indigenous practices and beliefs in a somewhat pejorative way. It is still used today by some of the older Tlingit.

21. Kan, "Memory Eternal"; and "Cohorts, Generations, and Their Culture: The Tlingit Potlatch in the 1980s," *Anthropos* 84 (1989): 405–422. For biographical information on modern-day Tlingit elders who comfortably combine indigenous and Christian beliefs and practices, see Nora M. Dauenhauer and Richard Dauenhauer, *Haa Shuká, Our Ancestors: Tlingit Oral Narratives* (Seattle: University of Washington Press,1987), 443–510; and *Haa Tuwunáaga Yís, For Healing Our Spirit: Tlingit Oratory* (Seattle: University of Washington Press, 1990), 521–557.

22. Kan, "Cohorts, Generations, and Their Culture."

23. Kan, "Cohorts, Generations, and Their Culture"; and "The Sacred and the Secular: Tlingit Potlatch Songs Outside the Potlatch," *American Indian Quarterly* 14 (1990): 355–366.

24. Veniaminov, *Notes on the Islands of the Unalashka District,* 400, 435.

25. Kamenskii, *Tlingit Indians of Alaska,* 81–91; Kan, "Recording Native Culture."

26. Livingstone F. Jones, *A Study of the Thlingets of Alaska* (New York: Fleming H. Revell Co., 1914), 158.

27. Carolyn McCoy Willard, *Life in Alaska: Letters of Mrs. Eugene S. Willard,* ed. Eva McClintock (Philadelphia: Presbyterian Board of Education, 1884); S. Hall Young, *Hall Young of Alaska: "The Mushing Parson"* (New York: Fleming H. Revell Co., 1927), 146.

28. Thus Governor John Brady, who started his career in Sitka as a Presbyterian missionary, tried once to dissuade some Sitka Indians from relying on a shaman during the 1898 epidemic of tuberculosis. He invited them to his office and displayed some physiological charts, explaining the cause of the disease and telling them that white people suffered from it as well. Having listened to the lecture, one Tlingit elder replied: "Well, that is what the white men say. We are Indians, and we know that there are witches." Hinckley, *Alaskan John Brady: Missionary, Business, Judge, and Governor, 1878–1918* (Columbus: Ohio State University Press, 1982), 254.

29. See, for example, Victoria Wyatt, *Images from the Inside Passage: An Alaskan Portrait by Winter and Pond* (Seattle: University of Washington Press, 1989), 68–69.

30. Kamenskii, *Tlingit Indians of Alaska,* 85–86; Henry Glass, "Naval Administration in Alaska," *Proceedings of the United Naval Institute* 16:1 (1890): 1–19.

31. Kamenskii, *Tlingit Indians of Alaska,* 111.

32. George T. Emmons, *The Tlingit Indians,* unpublished manuscript, Archives, American Museum of Natural History, New York, 1945; Kalervo Oberg, *The Social Economy of the Tlingit Indians* (Seattle: University of Washington Press, 1973), 19.

33. See Catherine McClellan, *My Old People Say: An Ethnographic Survey of Southern Yukon Territory,* 2 vols., Publications in Ethnology, No. 6 (Ottawa, National Museum of Man, 1957), 2: 529–63, on the Inland Tlingit, Tagish, and Tutchone shamans.

34. See de Laguna, *Under Mount Saint Elias: The History and Culture of the Yakutat Tlingit,* Smithsonian Contributions to Anthropology, No. 7, 3 vols. (Washington, D.C.: Smithsonian Institution Press, 1972), 723, on Yakutat in the early 1900s.

35. Veniaminov, *Notes on the Islands of Unalashka,* 400.

36. De Laguna, *Under Mount Saint Elias,* 671.

37. Because shamanism remains a rather sensitive topic for many of the elders, I do not mention their names in this article.

38. Some informants said that when they, as young children, saw an íxt' perform, they still believed in his power; others claimed that they had already lost that belief. One elderly woman, who had been raised in a devout Christian family in Sitka, told of throwing sand at an Angoon íxt' and thus forcing him to stop a seance when, as a young girl, she saw him perform on her aunt.

39. Compare the Orthodox ritual of consecrating the water by immersing a cross in a full container, performed on the feast of Epiphany. The Tlingit called this ceremony "baptizing the cross."

40. See McClellan, *My Old People Say,* 2: 553–63, on the Inland Tlingit and their Athapaskan neighbors.

41. Transcripts of these accounts are housed in the Billman Collection.

42. Cyrus E. Peck, Sr., *The Tides People* (Juneau: Indian Studies Program, 1975), 5–7.

43. De Laguna, *Under Mount Saint Elias,* 710.

44. Veniaminov, *Notes on the Islands of the Unalashka District,* 434; Tikhmenev, *A History of the Russian-American Company,* 198–199.

45. Swanton, "Social Conditions, Beliefs, and Linguistic Relationship of the Tlingit Indians," 465.

46. Kan, "Russian Orthodox Brotherhoods among the Tlingit"; Harkin, "History, Narrative, and Temporality"; and "Dialogues of History."

47. Veniaminov, *Notes on the Islands of the Unalashka District,* 434.

48. Fogelson, "The Ethnohistory of Events and Nonevents," 143.

49. Harkin, "History, Narrative, and Temporality," 101.

50 While the precontact Tlingit religion might have included a vaguely defined concept of a supreme being or spirit, many of the modern-day elders firmly believe that such a notion existed and that their ancestors prayed to "Our Spirit Above," although only in times of great trouble rather than constantly, as Christians do. For more details see de Laguna, *Under Mount Saint Elias,* 812–16; and Dauenhauer and Dauenhauer, *Ha Tuwunáaga Yís,* 126, 438.

51. Louis M. Burkhart, *The Slippery Earth: Nahua-Christian Moral Dialogue in Sixteenth-Century Mexico* (Tucson: University of Arizona Press, 1989).

52. Jean Comaroff, *Body of Power, Spirit of Resistance: The Culture and History of a South African People* (Chicago: University of Chicago Press, 1985).

53. Kan, "Cohorts, Generations, and Their Culture."

54. Swanton, *Tlingit Myths and Texts,* Bureau of American Ethnology, No. 39 (Washington, D.C.: Government Printing Office, 1909), 1.

55. De Laguna, *The Story of a Tlingit Community* and *Under Mount Elias.* A few references in de Laguna's study of Yakutat support my findings. Her elderly informants, interviewed in the late 1940s and the early 1950s, spoke about a female shaman who predicted the coming of the Russians (*Under Mount Elias,* 713) and compared shamans' guardian spirits to angels or to the Holy Ghost (*Under Mount Elias,* 682).

56. "Symbolic Immortality."

57. One very promising project is being carried out by two linguist-folklorists and speakers of the Tlingit language (one of whom is a Tlingit herself), Richard and Nora Marks Dauenhauer, who since the late 1960s have been collecting, transcribing, translating, and analyzing Tlingit oral traditions. So far they have published two bilingual volumes, *Haa Shuká, Our Ancestors: Tlingit Oral Narratives* and *Haa Tuwunáaga Yís, For Healing Our Spirit: Tlingit Oratory,* in a series that promises to include various other genres of Tlingit folklore.

V

CULTURAL AND POLITICAL TRANSFORMATIONS, 1900-1950

In the popular mind, little of significance happened in Indian Country between the end of the nineteenth-century Indian wars and the advent of modern political activism in the 1960s. The first half of the twentieth century seems, in this view, the Dark Ages of Native history; no bare-chested warriors or gun-toting radicals were around to capture the imagination of white journalists. Those Indians who did attract attention—Olympic champion Jim Thorpe, physician Charles Eastman, dancer and movie star Molly Spotted Elk—hardly fit the stereotype.

But significant developments were indeed taking place in Indian Country. Perhaps the most important was the dramatic rise in population between 1900 and 1950. Disease, dislocation, and warfare had devastated the indigenous population of North America almost from the moment Europeans arrived. The trend had been steadily downward until 1900, when the U.S. Census Bureau reported a Native population of 237,000, the first increase ever recorded. By 1950, that figure had risen to 357,000. (The 2000 census reported more than 2,000,000 Native Americans.) While these numbers represented less than 1 percent of the national total, they belied claims that American Indians were a "vanishing race." Natives and non-Natives alike came to understand that Natives would be a permanent part of the American landscape.

Taking that demographic foundation and historical reality as a given, the essays in Part V explore the many ways Indian peoples organized themselves to cope with (and profit from) the emergence of an industrialized, urban America. Examining legal and policy reforms, cultural revivals, and efforts at political organization, these chapters reveal that Native Americans continued to work with remarkable tenacity to hold their communities together and explore new ways of adapting to altered conditions.

13

At first glance the phrase "Indian explorers" seems as much an oxymoron as "Indian immigrants" did in Melissa Meyer's chapter. And surely by 1900 the "Age of Discovery" was long over. As Frederick Hoxie shows in this wide-ranging and perceptive study, however, Indian explorers were indeed embarking on voyages of discovery to foreign lands in the early twentieth century: in this case, to the white world that had surrounded and (militarily, at least) conquered them. In a process that resembled the immigrant experience, American Indians began to venture abroad—that is, into the United States—and to think about how they might live in the fast-paced, industrialized country that was also their homeland.

Pursuing the metaphor of exploration, Hoxie brings to life the generation of Native Americans who came of age at the turn of the twentieth century, tracing individuals as they gravitated towards academia, literature, art, law, religion, and politics. Each of these pursuits, Hoxie finds, provided an arena where Indians (like William Wash, considered by David Lewis and mentioned again here) could "be heard by whites yet remain recognizable to their kinsmen," a cultural space where Indians and non-Indians could interact "with dignity and mutual respect." This process, Hoxie argues, transformed the people who partic-ipated in it and had a significant impact on the tribal communities from which they came. By World War II, the collective efforts of these pioneers had laid the foundation for a modern version of Native American culture. This essay provides an initial view of the changes that took place within American Indian communities in the early twentieth century, changes that had more to do with the activities of native people themselves than with the doings of white reformers and politicians in Washington.

The tale Hoxie tells is rich in irony. For one thing, many of the people in his story were products of the very boarding schools set up to eradicate "traditional" ways. Far from abandoning their Indian past, these graduates came to celebrate it, to preserve it, to present it to white audiences as a better alternative to urban, industrial America. Their fluency in white ways enabled them to "talk back," to resist and defy and critique the dominant society, in a different fashion. So, too, in politics: these Indians learned what made the surrounding society tick, while forging connections with like-minded Natives beyond tribal boundaries that led to nascent pan-Indian organizations. As on the White Earth Reservation explored by Melissa Meyer, these "modern" Indians discovered opportunities, not just defeat and despair.

Exploring a Cultural Borderland:
Native American Journeys of Discovery in the
Early Twentieth Century

Frederick E. Hoxie

DURING THE EARLY 1930S, A SALISHAN woman from the Colville Indian reservation in eastern Washington State began constructing her autobiography. In its opening sentences, she declared that "there are two things I am most grateful for in my life. The first is that I was born a descendant of the genuine Americans, the Indians; the second, that my birth happened in the year 1888.... I was born long enough ago to have known people who lived in the ancient way before everything started to change."[1]

Mourning Dove's words reach across a great divide in the experience of Native Americans in the United States. She belonged to the first generation of Indian people who saw that Euro-Americans were an inescapable presence on the continent and who had an opportunity to reflect on this fact for a broad audience. Like thousands of her ancestors, she experienced non-Indians, not as visitors on native land, but as a daily, conquering presence. But like few others, Mourning Dove had access to both the English language and modern technology and could therefore communicate her reactions widely. In this sense, Mourning Dove and her contemporaries were the first generation of Native Americans who could explore publicly the meaning of their predicament. Positioned as they were, between a remembered world of relative freedom and the grim realities of industrial society, people like the Colville author attempted to define ways in which their communities and their traditions might be valued in a new setting. They believed they could neither flee from white society nor contemplate an alternative world peopled only by Indians. For Mourning Dove's generation, the future depended on their ability to define and protect areas in American cultural and political life where the "ancient way" might somehow survive. Their efforts in the years between 1900 and 1930, which engaged them in fields as various as literature, anthropology, art, religion, and politics, were Native American journeys of discovery, journeys devoted to the search for a new home in a captured land.

Prior to Mourning Dove's birth, most Indians lived beyond the reach of highways and railroads. Even though tens of thousands of their forebears had died during two centuries of Euro-American invasion, most North American Indians living in the early nineteenth century encountered non-Indians only occasionally. Prior to 1800 relatively little sustained contact or social integration of the two societies took place. Their meetings were often dramatic but were nearly always brief: they crashed into one another on the battlefield or met formally at trading posts or in council. At the

SOURCE: *Journal of American History,* v. 79 (December 1992), pp. 969–995.

turn of the nineteenth century, the 5,000,000 non-Indians living in North America were clustered along the Atlantic seaboard and in the St. Lawrence and Rio Grande valleys, while most of the 600,000 Indians who had survived the colonial era sustained a separate existence in population centers in the Great Lakes region, the Plains, the Northwest Coast, and the Southwest. They lived out their everyday lives in communities that were overwhelmingly Indian in population and character.[2]

As Mourning Dove suggested, it was during the ensuing decades of the nineteenth century that "everything started to change." National expansion obliterated the physical distance separating Native America and areas of United States settlement. The United States population doubled nearly every twenty-five years between 1800 and 1900, while the number of indigenous people declined steadily. By the start of the twentieth century, the United States contained 76,000,000 non-Indians and only 250,000 Indians. These statistics paint only the outlines of a tragic historical narrative; they cannot describe the fervor of Euro-American "settlement" or the national chauvinism it unleashed.[3]

The conqueror's activities are relatively easy to trace, for the nation's continental expansion was supremely self-conscious. Unlike Christopher Columbus, who sailed from Spain in 1492 without soldiers or scientists, the explorers and settlers who enabled the United States to grow were supported by force and accompanied by professional academicians. The Italian admiral had not been prepared to study or even conquer a New World; nineteenth-century citizens of the United States heading into "Indian country" were. For Indians such as Mourning Dove, then, the arrival of the United States at their doorsteps produced a confrontation with a universe of ideas and expectations as well as an encounter with hostile strangers.

The scientific classification of native traditions and material life was a central feature of the dramatic encounter with Indian communities in the nineteenth-century United States. Before 1850 this effort was carried out by individuals who were interested in recording the external appearance and behavior of tribal groups or describing the attributes of the "Indian race." The most famous of these early students were Thomas Jefferson, who excavated a prehistoric earthwork near his home, and Albert Gallatin, the "father of American ethnology," who compiled vocabularies of native languages. Despite their achievements, neither man was concerned with the history of a particular native community or the exploration of an individual tribe's linguistic philosophy. Instead, their concerns were general, and their studies were aimed at uncovering what they believed were characteristically Indian attributes and beliefs.[4]

A similar pattern was evident among the artists of the early nineteenth century. Except for George Catlin, who published his notebooks in 1844, most painters produced accurate renderings of native people and their possessions but paid little attention to tribal traditions and beliefs. Charles Bird King, who painted Indian delegations for the government in his Washington, D.C., studio, and Karl Bodmer, the Swiss illustrator who accompanied Prince Maximilian up the Missouri River in 1833, were typical of this trend. Other students of Indian life recorded physical characteristics (including cranial capacity) and folklore, but prior to midcentury there was little interest in the perspective of living native communities on history or recent events.[5]

At midcentury, however, as the pace of westward migration accelerated, scholars and collectors expanded their efforts to understand native communities. The publication of Lewis Henry Morgan's *League of the Ho De No Sau Nee* in 1851 (the first account of an Indian community's traditions based on extensive interviews with tribal members) marked the beginning of that acceleration of scientific activity, as did the opening of the first Smithsonian Institution exhibits building later in the decade.[6] Although only one of the fifteen display cases inaugurating the Smithsonian's exhibits program contained American Indian materials, the collecting of native artifacts quickly became an institutional priority.

The Smithsonian's ethnological collection grew from 550 items in 1860 to more than 13,000 in 1873. For the remainder of the century, this pattern of enthusiasm spread quickly to other museums; displays of American Indian life became the basis for collection programs at the Peabody Museum of Archaeology and Ethnology at Harvard University (founded in 1866), the American Museum of Natural History in New York (opened in 1869), Chicago's Field Museum of Natural History (launched in the aftermath of the 1893 World's Columbian Exposition). These new institutions organized collecting and scientific expeditions that competed with one another in accumulating Native American artifacts and in laying the foundation for ethnological research in such new topics as language structures, kinship systems, and religious rituals.[7]

By the 1890s research on Native Americans began to occur as well in the graduate programs in anthropology, which had begun to spring up in the nation's new research universities. The rise of graduate programs in anthropology marked the final shift of Indianist scholarship from the realm of dedicated amateurs to that of professional scholars and signaled the transition of thinking about American Indians from generalized speculation to more rigorous, scientific analysis. By 1902 when President Morris K. Jesup of the American Museum of Natural History welcomed the International Congress of Americanists to the United States, America had become, in his words, "a new nation in science."[8]

Johannes Fabian, a modern critic of anthropological scholarship, has written that students of indigenous life have long perceived their subjects as "other men in another time." The engagement of Morris Jesup and his colleagues with Native Americans illustrates the dominance of this perspective among those who studied people like Mourning Dove. Jesup observed that modern technology had caused "even the remotest parts" of the world to be "touched and quickened by the genius and courage of the explorer." Americans, he noted, "have not been idle in the great field of discovery. . . . No more interesting study can occupy the mind of man of the present day than to know for a certainty how this great land was peopled, and the gradual advancement of the human race, from the far back up to the present."[9]

By calling research on Native Americans a "great field of discovery," Jesup was placing this intellectual enterprise within an American experience that coincided with "the advancement of the human race." For Jesup and his audience, the scientific discovery of the continent's indigenous traditions and beliefs provided an opportunity for them to incorporate Indian people into a progressive conception of human history that ran from ancient backwardness to modern achievements, "from the far back up to the present." As historian Curtis M. Hinsley, Jr., has written, "the museum process constructed a meaning of Indian demise within the teleology of manifest destiny." Indian cultures were, in Hinsley's phrase, "dehistoricized," and Indian people transformed into "other men." What Columbus's generation had begun, Jesup and his scientific colleagues were eager to continue.[10]

Because they believed Native Americans represented civilizations from "far back" in history, the new anthropologists also believed that they occupied "another time." Trapped in obscurity, Indians properly should not be thought of as fellow members of the modern world. Like the notion that Indians were historically backward, this sense that their cultures could not have a modern existence was shaped by evolutionary thinking as well as by the relative power scientist-discoverers held over their "discovered" subjects. Jesup's "new nation in science" had conquered a continent. Thus what Fabian observed of European scholars in Africa was no less true of Euro-Americans in "Indian country." Both groups were "under the spell of a . . . mendacious fiction . . . that interpersonal, intergroup, indeed, international Time is 'public time'—there to be occupied, measured, and allotted by the powers that be." Such a perspective allowed anthropologists in the United States to be dispassionate but sympathetic. Once discovered, Indians could become objects for "interesting study," but they should not be confused with human co-residents of the Republic.[11]

Ironically, then, the academic discovery of Indian beliefs and traditions, which Jesup so proudly celebrated before the International Congress of Americanists in 1902, fit neatly within an old tradition that classified native lifeways as both exotic and backward. Like a secret garden, the multiple features of Indian culture that scholars such as Jesup sought to understand in all their richness and complexity were defined from the outset as irrelevant to contemporary concerns.

Even Jesup's professionally trained colleagues shared this view. Franz Boas and his students, who were sympathetic to Indian traditions and assiduous in their scholarship, identified Indian culture with the past and sadly predicted the extinction of tribal traditions. Significantly, in 1924, when Elsie Clews Parsons solicited a series of fictional life stories from her anthropological colleagues, the portraits she received were all set in a world before extensive white contact. The resulting book displayed their collective assumption that the best way to present Native Americans was to isolate them from the continent's recent history. Native American traditions could be admired and examined, but their modern academic discoverers could be confident that indigenous cultures would not contribute to, or even survive in, the twentieth century. People such as Mourning Dove who found themselves discovered by settlers and scientists thus faced intellectual expectations that confined them to the outer margins of both history and society.[12]

The political structures Mourning Dove faced were similarly restrictive. During the years of the Salishan writer's youth, government policies for conquered Indian communities both quarantined and denigrated Native traditions in an effort to promote general social progress. A letter written by an earnest schoolmaster at an eastern Montana Indian agency illustrates this administrative version of anthropological thought. It contained the following advice:

There should be a board fence 12 feet high, enclosing a space 200 by 300 yards around the school buildings. There is now only a wire fence around the school yard, which is not over 50 feet from the front of the school buildings. Every Indian from the camp who wishes to, can converse with the pupils, and it cannot be prevented. The scenes of camp life, which are weekly presented to their view, are very detrimental to the pupils, and the camp gossip, which can not now be shut out, is a serious evil to them. With such a (board) fence they can be separated almost entirely from the demoralizing influences of the camp, and their progress towards civilization will be correspondingly accelerated.[13]

A proposal to wall a group of Indian children off from their parents to accelerate their "progress towards civilization" illustrates vividly the governing conviction that native life and modern life were incompatible. The Montana schoolmaster operated in a context of ideas and institutions that reinforced the separation of discoverer and discovered, thus confining native people to a prescribed place in American thought as well as on the American landscape.

The same year board fences were being recommended to insulate and educate children in Montana, Congress approved the General Allotment Act, which forcibly dismantled communally owned reservations and extended United States citizenship to tribal members. Employing the industrial imagery of the day, Amherst College president Merrill E. Gates (a prominent advocate of "humanitarian" Indian policies) described the new law as "a mighty pulverizing engine for breaking up the tribal mass." Gates and other reformers believed such splintered communities would more readily become "civilized."[14]

Jessup, Gates, and their colleagues thus provided the American public with an image of Indian people and Indian history that conformed to the power relationships of their day. The hegemony of their words and policies in the nineteenth century created the setting within which Native Americans such as Mourning Dove operated in the first decades of the twentieth century. That setting defined indigenous people as objects of a discovery process that stretched back four hundred years. They and their communities were positioned in the background of a national epic of conquest and progress.[15]

It is from that position of confinement that Mourning Dove and her generation spoke. Rejecting the idea of American progress and refusing to identify with her conquerors, Mourning Dove wrote with pride in her ancestry and with nostalgia for a shattered past. Far from welcoming those who taught her the English language she used in her stories, she grieved for what had been lost in the years after "everything started to change." At the same time, however, her use of English and the written word contradicted the idea that she was an artifact of a backward world hopelessly lost in the past. Despite their power, scientific sophistication, and moral rectitude, neither Jesup nor Gates could have explained the insistent tone or the nuanced prose of this outspoken Native American. They could not predict the message contained in her voice once she began to talk back to her discoverers.[16]

Burdened with the weight of scientific and physical domination, Mourning Dove appeared both defiant and willing to engage in an exploration of the non-Indian world. What was the source of this adventuresome pose? How did it alter the formulaic thinking of the curious scientists and bureaucrats who would spend so much time cataloging modern Indian life? And how would her "backtalk" and her explorations affect her contemporaries? The impact of Mourning Dove's generation can be measured by comparing their words with Jesup's and Gates's after one hundred years. Pronounced with confidence, Jesup's and Gates's words now sound hollow; celebrated as discoverers, Jesup and Gates now appear foolish. Mourning Dove's voice, on the other hand, seems to have risen in power and self-assurance. Echoed and repeated by others, her words and ideas helped form the basis for a new Indian identity, an identity that emerged from the Native American discovery of modern America.

Mourning Dove had been born to an interior Salish family whose life was frequently disrupted by American settlement in Idaho and eastern Washington. During the 1890s and afterwards, she was forced to attend missionary and government boarding schools and lived with a variety of relatives across the intermountain West. When she resolved to become a writer, Mourning Dove acted out of her own ambitions and experiences, but her decision echoed the determination of thousands of her contemporaries both to live in and to explore the new world that was rapidly intruding upon their communities. Because Mourning Dove was part of the first generation both to be "discovered" by science and the federal bureaucracy and to communicate to a wide audience, her career and those of her contemporaries sketch the outlines of what that discovery meant to people who could remember those "who lived in the ancient way before everything started to change."

Because nineteenth-century scholars and bureaucrats viewed Indians as people from another time, they did not recognize that even when conquered, Native Americans could still act and make choices. At the end of the nineteenth century, those choices were limited, but individuals continued to shape their own futures. Armed resistance was no longer an option for Indian people. Faced with a choice between accommodating themselves to their discoverers or completely withdrawing from further contact, Native Americans of Mourning Dove's generation selected a middle course. Examples of direct resistance to federal authority were rare, as were examples of complete noncooperation with researchers. Nonetheless, few communities welcomed the missionaries and government schoolteachers or shared Morris Jesup's enthusiasm for the "great field of discovery."

Individuals like Mourning Dove who found that they had been "discovered" confronted an array of people—scholars, politicians, bureaucrats, and businessmen— who represented a combination of coercion and opportunity. The brute power of those outsiders crushed many native traditions. The very process of white settlement, for example, made many traditional subsistence methods impractical. Religious rituals, such as the Plains sun dance or Navajo curing rites, were swiftly outlawed by the government and condemned by missionaries. White authorities discouraged other ceremonial activities, such as vision quests and puberty rites, or rendered them impractical; Indians made still others secret to protect them from the curious.

On the other hand, the discoverers presented Indians with opportunities. Native Americans frequently perceived outsiders as a potential resource. If visiting scholars could violate sacred knowledge by condemning it and exposing it to the outside world, they could also publicize struggles against federal authorities or record local traditions that were in danger of being lost. Similarly, while the teachings of missionaries and schoolmasters could alienate children from their families, they could also provide those children with tools for reforming or combating the institutions that sought to regiment their existence. For example, Reuben Quick Bear, with the support of Catholic missionaries, brought suit against the commissioner of Indian affairs to allow tribal funds to be used for the local Catholic schools so that he could send his children there rather than to government institutions.[17]

Confronted with scientists, governing officials, and the institutions they represented, indigenous people identified limited—but genuine—areas where they could participate in their discoverers' world, areas where whites and Indians could interact. Being discovered provided Native Americans with a limited set of tools for asserting and defining their presence in the modern world. In a sense, they saw avenues open before them for an *Indian* discovery of non-Indian America. Discovery thus presented Indians with interests and public positions from which they could launch their own voyages of exploration. Those voyages, in turn, would help both tribal communities and the larger public define a path leading from the "ancient way" to the twentieth century.

The voyages' starting point was frequently a version of Mourning Dove's statement that modern Indians "had known people who lived in the ancient way." Such an assertion—coupled with the fact that those ways were by definition American—set Native Americans apart from the rest of the population and transformed the native past from a source of shame (the beginning point for the "advancement of the human race") to a badge of distinction. Leaders such as Mourning Dove used the assertion of ancient origins as a rhetorical device to reverse the conventional understanding of discovery and to identify a unique Indian attribute for their audience. Mourning Dove positioned herself as the explorer—emerging from an ancient past no non-Indian could claim, she named objects and people from her distinctive point of view.

Other Indian writers of Mourning Dove's generation chose to present themselves as she did, writing in English both to assert and to celebrate an "ancient way." Best known among them was Charles A. Eastman (Ohiyesa), a Santee Sioux physician who published a partial autobiography, *Indian Boyhood*, in 1902 and followed it with nine other books that presented native life to a general audience. Born in 1858 in western Minnesota, Eastman spent his early childhood outside the orbit of white settlement. He lived a nomadic life, traveling with his relatives as far west as the Yellowstone River until 1872, when he was suddenly taken to a mission school. Eastman later recalled that his grandmother opposed his learning the white man's habits ("I cannot bear to see my boy live a made-up life"), but he recalled her own teachings to justify his decision to accommodate. He remembered that even though her "faith in her people's philosophy and training could not be superseded by any other allegiance," she had also held to the principle that "when you see a new trail, or a footprint that you do not know, follow it to the point of knowing."[18]

According to Eastman, his decision to explore the "new trail" of American education was an extension of his grandmother's ancient principles. He attended the Presbyterian Santee Normal Training School in Nebraska, Beloit College, Knox

College, and Dartmouth College. Following his graduation from Dartmouth in 1887, he entered Boston University Medical School, receiving his M.D. in 1890. Despite his long immersion in white society, Eastman consistently focused on the continuities between his boyhood and his adult values. In his writings he carefully constructed a distinctly modern, yet Indian, point of view.

Eastman frequently cast himself as a modern tribal storyteller, a figure who, like the elders in an oral society, both described the old ways and gave them a contemporary twist. As he wrote in 1911 in *The Soul of an Indian*, "My little book does not pretend to be a scientific treatise. . . . So much has been written by strangers of our ancient faith and worship that treats it chiefly as a matter of curiosity. I should like to emphasize its universal quality, its personal appeal." His books carried out this objective. They included such titles such as *Old Indian Days, Indian Child Life,* and *Indian Scout Talks*.[19]

Significantly, his writing avoided identification with a particular tribal tradition, emphasizing instead a generalized and idyllic past. Not only did Eastman understand that his audience was largely uninterested in or ignorant of differences between tribes, but his principal objective was to counter the public's assumption that Indians were savage and backward. While later generations would detect a Victorian tone in his generalizations, they were offered as an antidote to the stereotypes he so frequently encountered. For example, in *Indian Boyhood*, a record of the physician's "boyish impressions," a chapter on education begins with an attack on the idea that Indians had no system for training their children. "Nothing could be further from the truth," Eastman declared; "all the customs of this primitive people were held to be divinely instituted, and . . . were scrupulously adhered to."[20]

Eastman and the other early Indian writers appeared at an opportune moment. Despite the optimism of Morris Jesup and other museum collectors, the early twentieth century was marked by a current of disenchantment with a society many felt was "overcivilized" and without moral content. As Mourning Dove and Eastman were composing their stories, some white intellectuals were arguing that the size and complexity of industrial society separated individuals from the world around them. They portrayed modern Americans as alone and without purpose. Machines, bureaucracies, and newspapers did their work, organized their cities, and communicated with their neighbors, reducing industrial society to a place devoid of "authentic experience." This sentiment, which historian T. J. Jackson Lears has labeled "antimodernism," was both nostalgic and progressive; it revealed a "vein of deep religious longing, an unfilled yearning to restore infinite meaning to an increasingly finite world." Such feelings surely lay behind the appeal of the early Indian writers, for several of them found that their descriptions of an idyllic ancient life won them an enthusiastic audience of white readers.[21]

By describing ancient traditions and recounting tales of their childhoods, Indian authors could both serve up satisfying, "authentic" experiences and preserve tribal traditions. For example, Zitkala-Sa (Gertrude Bonnin), a Yankton woman who attended Earlham College in Indiana and the Boston Conservatory of Music, published an essay in 1902 that contrasted the coherence of her Indian past with the superficiality of modern Christianity. "Why I Am a Pagan" described a visit the

Charles A. Eastman's search for a way to present himself to his non-Indian audience is reflected in the frontispieces of two of his books. The first (left), from *The Soul of an Indian* (1911), accompanies a description of Native American religious beliefs. The second (right), from *From the Deep Woods to Civilization: Chapters in the Autobiography of an Indian* (1916), reinforces the narrative structure of his life story. Courtesy of The Newberry Library.

author had received from a fellow tribesman who had recently converted to the white man's faith. She wrote that the caller could do nothing but "mouth most strangely the jangling phrases of a bigoted creed," while she—authentically linked to her own past—thought only of "excursions into the natural gardens where the voice of the Great Spirit is heard in the twittering of birds, the rippling of mighty waters, and the sweet breathing of flowers." Aligning herself with this leafy scene, the Quaker-educated author declared, "If this is Paganism, then at present, at least, I am a Pagan."[22]

Zitkala-Sa published two collections of Indian tales celebrating the virtues of native culture, *Old Indian Legends* (1901) and *American Indian Stories* (1921); others of her generation followed a similar path. Mourning Dove published a novel, *Co-ge-we-a, the Half Blood* (1927), that contrasted virtuous Indians with corrupt whites and an anthology of Salish tales, *Coyote Stories* (1933). In 1916, Lucy Thompson, a Klamath woman from Oregon, published a general account of her tribe's history and folklore that emphasized its simplicity and described the ways in which outsiders had corrupted their beliefs. A decade later, Luther Standing Bear (who had attended the government boarding school at Carlisle, Pennsylvania, before embarking on a variety of careers, including a turn as a Hollywood actor) published a memoir, *My People, the Sioux*. His book carried an introduction by silent film star William S. Hart, who wrote of the Sioux, "philosophy was their life." Standing Bear replied to these expectations with a narrative that emphasized his own quiet virtues and the work of Indian people. "The Indian has just as many ounces of brains as his white brother," Standing Bear wrote, and he noted that as a chief of his people, "I will do what is right and proper for them." In each of these collections and memoirs, the authors assumed the role of a storyteller who could assure white readers that the tale was authentic, not because it was scientific, but because it was personal. Mirroring the white craftsmen and nature lovers who stressed the meaning of their new hobbies over their content, the Indian authors posed as bearers of an ancient spirit in the modern age. Agreeing with Thompson that "so much said and written about the American Indians . . . is guessed at and not facts," Zitkala-Sa and the others came forward promising to deliver versions of their culture that could stand as authentic alternatives to the alienation of modern life. "These legends are relics of our country's once virgin soil," Zitkala-Sa wrote in 1901, adding that they provided evidence of the Indians' "near kinship with the rest of humanity and [point] a steady finger toward the great brotherhood of mankind."[23]

Eastman frequently noted the disparity between his inherited, Indian values and the conditions of modern society. According to the Santee writer, a reverence for the natural world and a charitable attitude toward relatives and neighbors were basic to native cultures, but precisely those values, he believed, were undermined by industrialization and organized religion. He argued this case in his books, as well as on the lecture circuit and in popular magazine articles that appeared (among other places) in *Boys' Life*, the magazine of the Boy Scouts of America. Eastman also presented his views at a New Hampshire summer camp he founded in 1915. He called the camp "the School of the Woods" and promised that all who enrolled would receive instruction from "a real Indian." He composed an eloquent summary of his position at the conclusion of his autobiography, *From Deep Woods to Civilization*. "I am an Indian," Eastman wrote, "and while I have learned much from civilization, for which I am grateful, I have never lost my sense of right and justice. I am for development and progress along social and spiritual lines, rather than those of commerce, nationalism, or material efficiency."[24]

As Eastman, Mourning Dove, and their contemporaries grew more comfortable with their roles as conveyors of ancient wisdom to modern audiences, they found that the presentation of traditional Indian culture could identify them as people worthy of respect. Like Thompson, who declared in 1916, "I deem it necessary to first tell you who I am," they employed "Indianness" to gain an audience and to construct a verbal weapon they might employ against "modern" scientists and bureaucrats who threatened native interests or denigrated tribal communities.

Like the Native American writers, Indian men and women contemporary with Mourning Dove who collaborated with anthropologists and museum collectors to record tribal histories and to preserve example of indigenous artistic expression sought to preserve ancient traditions. Frequently those individuals—such as George Hunt, who worked with Franz Boas at the turn of the century among the Kwakiutl of Vancouver Island, British Columbia; Chris (a pseudonym), who told his life story to Morris Opler at the Mescalero Apache reservation (New Mexico) in the 1930s;

and James Carpenter, who assisted Robert H. Lowie in his research among the Crow between 1907 and 1930—were people of mixed ancestry who stood at the border of the local community. For example, Opler's Apache partner, Chris, the child of a Mescalero mother and a Chiricahua father, was born in 1880, "when such marriages were much rarer than they were later to become." Opler's estimation of the consequence of this dual parentage could readily be applied to others in Chris's situation: "Each tribe saw his idiosyncracies as the result of his inheritance from the other group. These allowances and the lack of solid identification may well have encouraged deviation and experimentation."[25]

Other informants (such as the Omaha scholar, Francis La Flesche; the Lakota elder, Black Elk; and the Winnebago leader called Big Winnebago) were more fully centered in their home communities but had traveled widely among non-Indians and had developed an interest in the relationship between Indian traditions and the modern world. They sought both to relate ancient wisdom to contemporary conditions and to interpret their lives for a non-Indian audience. La Flesche spent most of his adult life in Washington, D.C., even though he had grown to adulthood among the Omahas in the decades after the Civil War. (He served as a runner in one of the tribe's last communal buffalo hunts.) In the early 1880s, he met the anthropologist Alice Cunningham Fletcher during her field research in Nebraska and became her partner in an impressive series of monographs. Black Elk traveled to Europe with Buffalo Bill Cody in the 1880s, and Big Winnebago spent a good part of his adult life as an itinerant workman along the rail lines of the upper Midwest. The latter two returned to their reservation homes in midlife and later formed partnerships with white scholars eager to record their memories of traditional culture. Their early experiences exposed them to the scale and technology of modern society, and like La Flesche, they chose to devote themselves to the preservation of indigenous traditions.[26]

Despite their diverse origins, all of these informants understood that by documenting their cultures, they were giving them greater permanence and elevating them in the eyes of the outside world. In 1897 for example, Boas told Kwakiutl chiefs at Fort Rupert (Vancouver Island, British Columbia) that his partner George Hunt "would become the storage box of your laws and your stories." Similarly, Black Elk explained that he worked with John G. Neihardt because he believed that the poet's retelling of his great vision would preserve a part of Lakota culture. "What I know was given to me for men and it is true and it is beautiful," the old man told Neihardt. "You were sent to save it. . . . I can teach you." La Flesche was more direct: "The misconception of Indian life and character so common among the white people has been largely due to an ignorance of the Indian's language, of his mode of thought, his beliefs, his ideas, and his native institutions." The Omaha scholar intended his career to be a response to this fact, for as a recent biographer has noted, La Flesche worked when "old restraints and restrictions upon the divulging of sacred traditions [became]—in the stark awareness of impending cultural loss—pitted against the value of preserving something at least for posterity."[27]

Collaborating with outsiders opened informants up to charges of opportunism, for even the most dedicated anthropologists approached native communities with their professional agendas foremost in their minds. And recorders of stories and histories usually had more than an academic interest in Indians; they were frequently accompanied by artifact collectors who worked closely with local traders and businessmen. Boas's meticulous research, for example, coincided with the ambitious effort of the American Museum of Natural History to bring monumental Northwest Coast carvings to New York City: Boas reminded Hunt in 1901, "under our present arrangement you must continue to collect." The 1937 comment of Boas's student, Robert Lowie, that Boas had "stimulated an enormous amount of high-grade recording by Indians" epitomizes the self-absorption of white researchers in this era. Even after three decades of field research, Lowie could not see that Indian colleagues shared his desire to preserve tribal knowledge. In his mind the influence had run in a single direction, from the scholars to the Indians.[28]

But the risk of being compromised by their involvement with selfish, non-Indian scholars did not prevent dozens of tribal members from participating in anthropological research. Their willingness to explore an intellectual relationship with outsiders made it possible for people like Fletcher, Boas, Lowie, Opler, and Neihardt to grasp the richness and complexity of North America's indigenous traditions. The partnership of native and non-native scholars, however uneven, created a common enterprise, the modern field of cultural anthropology, and provided tribal communities with a cadre of articulate friends who might represent them in the wider world. In the twentieth century, anthropologists would often repeat Boas's pledge to a group of Kwakiutl chiefs at Fort Rupert: "Wherever I can, I speak for you."[29]

Native Americans who found themselves discovered by outsiders in the late nineteenth century also found that their predicament allowed them to create new cultural expressions by combining elements of their own and their discoverers' traditions. This opportunity enabled them to produce new, and possibly more viable, versions of old activities. In the 1990s examples of those combinations are frequently evident in the world of native art. Native Americans explore traditional themes or tribal mythologies employing media as various as acrylic paint, videotape, or metal sculpture. These artists assert that their use of new technologies helps them bring ancient ideas into the present; new materials do not undermine the "Indianness" of their creations. Despite the popularity of this view, students of native culture continue to minimize the extent to which Indian art traditions are the product not only of interaction with non-Indian artists but of Native American artists' ongoing exploration of the commercial art market.

The first Native Americans to explore the world of professional painting were in Oklahoma. Soon after the turn of the century, as white settlers surged into central Oklahoma, a young Arapaho man, Carl Sweezy (1881–1953), began using butcher paper and house paint to record scenes from his own tribal history and to describe the rapidly changing landscape around him. "The way of the white people ... seemed unsociable and lonely," Sweezy later recalled, so he focused on local family life, sacred rituals, and Arapaho social life to create the image of an appealing alternative. In a similar way, Shawnee artist Ernest Spybuck (1883–1949) recorded social and ceremonial scenes taking place in Oklahoma Indian communities near his home. Using watercolors, pencil, and ink, Spybuck created images of costumed dancers, lively tribal gatherings, and solemn religious meetings that are striking for their vivid color and meticulous detail. In their art, Sweezy and Spybuck defined a position much like that of Zitkala-Sa, Eastman, and Black Elk, for they stood between their ancient traditions and their modern white patrons, offering them an appealing version of their Indianness.[30]

In the first decades of the twentieth century, Sweezy and Spybuck's audiences were local, but by the 1920s other groups of Indian artists began to ally themselves with white patrons and to display their work before critics and publics far beyond their homes. In New Mexico and Arizona in the early twentieth century, anthropologists and travelers had occasionally purchased drawings from their informants and hosts, but it was not until 1917 that the archaeologist Edgar L. Hewett began to commission paintings of Pueblo ceremonial life. Hewett began by supporting the work of Crescencio Martinez, who was from San Ildefonso, north of Santa Fe, but following the young man's tragic death in the flu epidemic of 1918, he turned to others. Interest from local Anglo artists, such as Ernest Blumenschein and Bert Phillips in nearby Taos, New Mexico, and the patronage of collectors such as Mabel Dodge Luhan, Mary Austin, and Alice Corbin Henderson encouraged Martinez's followers—Awa Tsireh (Alfonso Roybal) of San Ildefonso, the Hopi Fred Kabotie, and Otis Polelonema of Cochiti, New Mexico—to bring their work before a wider audience. By the early 1920s these artists were exhibiting their work in New York and Chicago.

In western Oklahoma, another combination of white patrons and ambitious young Indians brought a second group of native painters before a national audience. Encouraged by Susan Peters, a young Bureau of Indian Affairs teacher in Anadarko, six Kiowa students began showing their work and winning the attention of the rapidly growing community of Santa Fe collectors. In 1928 the six—Monroe Tsa Toke, Stephen Mopope, Spencer Asah, Jack Hokeah, James Archiah, and Bou-ge-te Smokey—enrolled in the University of Oklahoma to study with O. B. Jacobson. The connection brought them rapid fame. The group exhibited at the International Congress of Folk Arts in Prague, Czechoslovakia, in 1928 and three years later joined their southwestern counterparts and others at the Exposition of Indian Tribal Arts in New York City. The exposition show toured the United States and Europe for two years following its New York appearance.[31]

Exploring the professional art world and using their paintings to display the richness and beauty of tribal life, the Indian painters of the 1920s and 1930s asserted that their art embodied the survival of Native American traditions. Like the other Indian explorers of white America, they presented themselves to the non-Indian public as a bridge connecting an ancient past to the modern era. The enthusiastic public reception of their message set off a chain reaction among young would-be artists. The critic Elizabeth Shepley Sergeant wrote in 1923, for example, that "two writers, four artists, the School of American Research and all the Indian dealers in Santa Fe" claimed to have discovered the San Ildefonso artist, Awa Tsireh. "As a matter of fact," she observed dryly, "he probably discovered himself through his own observation of the work of his immediate precursor [Crescencio Martinez].... [C]ertainly the other boys and girls who are beginning to render the same subject matter in the same general style, have discovered themselves through Awa Tsireh."[32]

The exhibitions of the 1920s were the first to present living native artists whose bold images of ancient ways challenged the public's assumption that Indian people belonged to a backward, vanishing race, but writers unfamiliar with native communities were less insightful than Sergeant. Viewing dramatic paintings of Indian life, most commentators attributed the resurgence of native arts to a previously obscure ethnic genius. The *New York Times*, for example, noted that the 1931 Exposition of Indian Tribal Arts had brought a new generation of racial leaders to the fore. A review of the exhibition concluded, "Lo, the poor Indian . . . begins to emerge before our newly opened eyes, as artist. . . . Our problem child . . . is suddenly seen to be, in his own, a kind of genius passing our full comprehension."[33]

The success of Native American artists thus created an opportunity for tribal perspectives to appear and be appreciated. Indians who took advantage of that opportunity—the Kiowa six, Awa Tsireh, and others—operated within the limits of white expectations, but they persisted in asserting a new identity in which their distinctive traditions might find endorsement. Too often non-Indian patrons continued to view these artists as carriers of a primitive tradition—just as anthropologists overlooked the goals of their informants—but the artists' impact was unmistakable. Their success made it impossible to dismiss Native American traditions as simple curiosities.

Outside the world of art, the most dramatic combination of Indian and non-Indian traditions occurred within a new religious movement that emerged in Oklahoma in the 1890s. This innovation was far less popular with whites than the renaissance in Indian art, yet it won grudging acceptance in many quarters. The modern history of the Native American Church begins in 1881 when the construction of rail lines from Chicago and St. Louis south to the Rio Grande Valley allowed peyote, a hallucinogen that had been used in the valley for centuries in Lipan Apache religious rituals, to be transported to other parts of the country. Reservations occupied by recently relocated Plains Indian tribes lay along this new transportation route, and Lipan teachers apparently brought their ritual to those reservations first.[34]

As it spread across the Southern Plains, the ancient aspects of the peyote ritual were combined with elements of Christianity that had been introduced into Indian communities by missionaries. The result was a new ceremonial complex. Followers of the "peyote way" invoked Jesus in their ceremonies and prayed for hallucinogenic visions that would bring them into contact with Christian as well as native spiritual figures. With steady supplies of the peyote plant coming up from Texas by rail, Lipan, Kiowa, and Comanche religious leaders called "road men" spread their version of the ritual to neighbors and kinsmen across Oklahoma. They quickly generated support for what became a powerful new faith. Modeling their technique on that of the Christian missionaries who now opposed them, they also relied on trains and automobiles to spread their teachings to tribes across the United States and southern Canada. By 1899 groups on at least sixteen different reservations had embraced the new ritual.[35]

Emphasizing the importance of monogamy, sobriety, and hard work, road men won a wide following despite federal authorities' attempts to outlaw ritual use of the peyote plant. Early converts included educated young men such as Fred Lookout of the Osage, who had attended Carlisle Indian School; Albert Hensley, a former chief of tribal police among the Nebraska Winnebagos; and a prosperous Crow farmer named Frank Bethune. In the nineteenth century, Indians met attacks on tribal religions with defiance, but tribal leaders were generally unable to stop government efforts to undermine their priests or to outlaw their ceremonies. In the twentieth century, however, the dynamic was very different, for the peyote road men defended themselves in terms non-Indians would recognize.

When faced with a move to outlaw peyote use in the new Oklahoma Territory, for example, Comanche leader Quanah Parker declared, "I do not think this legislature should interfere with a man's religion." In 1908 a similar proposal came before the new state of Oklahoma's constitutional convention. Sixteen native religious leaders testified in opposition to the prohibition, causing one white legislator to declare, "I have been almost overcome by the talk of these Indians and I do not believe any legislature wants to rob these Indians of their religious rights. . . . It is our duty to protect their rights—religious or otherwise." As a brake on the forces of prohibition, followers of the peyote ritual also incorporated themselves as the Native American Church, an organization formed "to foster and promote the religious belief of the several tribes of Indians in the State of Oklahoma." Groups in Nebraska, South Dakota, Montana, Wisconsin, and Iowa quickly followed suit. All of them argued that the American constitutional guarantee of the right to the free exercise of religion obligated the United States government to protect their worship services from harassment.[36]

Peyote leaders frequently emphasized the compatibility of their beliefs and the expectations of government officials. "We like church," the Ute peyotist William Wash wrote to officials at the Bureau of Indian Affairs, adding, "We want to meet every Sunday and have Church and pray and be good. . . . We want to rest on Sunday and then on Monday we want to work and farm." In 1908 Hensley, by then a Winnebago road man, responded to a government proposal to conduct scientific studies of the peyote plant by declaring that "it is utter folly for scientists to attempt to analyze this medicine." The Carlisle graduate asked rhetorically, "Can science analyze God's body? No."[37]

Like the Indian entrance into the commercial art world, the development of the Native American Church offered Indian people an opportunity to assert their perspectives in an arena sanctioned by whites. The defenders of peyotism discovered the power of political organization and constitutional rhetoric and turned them to the defense of an "ancient" rite; fitting themselves to the language of white piety, they asserted their distinctiveness while presenting themselves as loyal, Bible-reading Americans. Engagement in the new faith propelled the peyotists into a new world of organized religion and seven-day routines of work and worship, even as it allowed them to construct and sustain a ritual complex that stood beyond the reach of science and the Office of Indian Affairs.

In addition to combining elements of their cultural traditions with pieces of the new world surrounding them, Native Americans of Mourning Dove's generation explored ways to use their discoverers' political institutions to defend Indian communities from external threats. These discoveries helped create other elements in twentieth-century native identity: the sense that sharp boundaries separated white outsiders and American Indians and the conviction that interests falling on the *native* side of those boundaries constituted a modern version of ancient traditions.

Among the first generation of native young people educated at boarding schools were hundreds of graduates who used their facility with English, their "civilized" appearance, and their understanding of American institutions to enter political life. They participated in tribal and village councils, circulated petitions attacking the policies of the Office of Indian Affairs, and employed the American legal system to pursue community objectives. Through such actions, the political leaders of a supposedly vanishing race began to define the legal limits of federal and state intrusion into their communities. This effort produced the insight that certain "rights" set Native Americans apart from other residents of the United States. That insight inspired tribal leaders to launch a campaign to defend their rights and to use existing political and legal institutions to reclaim control of community government and communally owned resources.

Examples abound of "returned students" challenging the authority of the Office of Indian Affairs. In northern Wisconsin, Reginald Oshkosh (a graduate of Carlisle and the son of Neopit Oshkosh, who was the Menominee's traditional chief) led the opposition to federal control over the tribe's vast timber reserves. Oshkosh conceded that lumbering on the reservation had brought employment to hundreds of his kinsmen, but he believed federal policy should produce more than wage labor. He declared the Menominee's goal was "to become independent and self-supporting and [to] terminate our relations as wards of the Government."[38]

Another Carlisle student became active in tribal affairs by writing letters to his kinsmen at Fort Yuma, Arizona, from his dormitory in Pennsylvania: Patrick Miguel, son of a Quechan leader whom the government insisted on calling "ex-Chief Miguel," also took on the local agent in 1899, warning him "not to touch the Indians again" or he would be reported to the Office of Indian Affairs. Upon Miguel's return to Yuma a decade later, he continued to advocate tribal self-government. Urging the Commissioner of Indian Affairs to authorize elections at the agency, he struck a conciliatory but insistent tone: "We believe the old Indians should be taught more by members of their own tribe, in a kindly way, to see and adopt the white man's laws and it is to this end the more progressive members of the tribe request that they be allowed to have a council and presiding officer to pilot the ship of state of the Yumas."[39]

In Indian Territory, Delos Lone Wolf, the Carlisle-educated nephew of the Kiowa chief Lone Wolf, returned from boarding school to discover that Congress had unilaterally abrogated its treaty with the tribe in order to open a tract of land for white settlement. Supported by cattlemen who wished to protect their leases on tribal land, Delos persuaded his uncle and other leaders to file suit in United States District Court seeking an injunction against the land sale. Acting on their behalf was a former Illinois congressman, William M. Springer, who had a law practice in Washington, D.C. The result of their efforts was *Lone Wolf v. Hitchcock* (1903), in which the Supreme Court pronounced the congressional abrogation constitutional. This defeat for Lone Wolf and the Kiowas accelerated the rate of federal seizure of tribal land, but it also indicated that Indian explorations of the American legal system had grown remarkably energetic. It sent a warning to federal officials that they should expect future opposition from other close-cropped boarding school graduates.[40]

The United States Court of Claims was the most popular legal forum for tribal leaders in the early twentieth century. Unlike efforts to block congressional decisions (actions that were frequently doomed from the start), using the Court of Claims was relatively safe—losses brought little additional hardship and wins could pay substantial benefits. Indian tribes had been barred from bringing suit in the Court of Claims in 1863, but individual groups frequently lobbied Congress for special legislation exempting them from this restriction. In 1881 Choctaws determined to win compensation for lands lost in Mississippi and Alabama a half-century earlier were the first to gain access to the claims process. Their success inspired others, and by World War I thirty-one claims had been brought to the court.

The steady but unspectacular pace of claims filings suddenly accelerated after 1920. The Teton Sioux opened the decade by winning approval for a resolution enabling them to bring to court their claim for the South Dakota Black Hills. They were quickly followed by dozens of other tribes so that during the next ten years more suits were filed than had been brought in the previous forty years. Responding to the new case load, the Government Accounting Office established an Indian Tribal Claims Section in 1926 to prepare financial data on pending suits. While it remains largely undiscussed by scholars, the history of these claims cases will surely reveal a pattern of political mobilization and the establishment of new ties between tribal leaders and their attorneys.[41]

In addition to the emergence of new leaders and the launching of new lawsuits, the first decades of the twentieth century witnessed the emergence of new Indian political pressure groups. They included the Black Hills Treaty Council, which first met on the Cheyenne River reservation in central South Dakota in 1911 to discuss the filing of a claim to restore the sacred Black Hills to the Sioux. In New Mexico, the All Pueblo Council conducted a widely publicized campaign to resist efforts by squatters and local politicians to reduce Indian landholding. At a meeting in 1922, the All Pueblo Council articulated a position common to many other groups when it declared that the Rio Grande communities had lived "in a civilized condition before the white man came to America" and called on the "American people" to help them preserve "everything we hold dear—our lands, our customs, our traditions." Combining an appeal to public morality with pride in their tribal past, the Pueblo leaders attempted to turn popular interest in their dances and traditions into political clout. By the end of the 1920s, appeals like that one were winning support from sympathetic non-Indians and enabling tribal leaders to carry on campaigns in every region of the United States.[42]

Other regional pressure groups included the Alaska Native Brotherhood and the Alaska Native Sisterhood, founded in 1912 and 1915, respectively. The brotherhood was led during the 1920s by the Tlingit Carlisle graduate William L. Paul, Jr., and together the two groups campaigned against segregation and discrimination in towns across the territory. Similarly, in 1919 the Northwest Federation of Indians launched efforts to protect the fishing rights of Puget Sound tribes; the Wampanoag Nation was founded in 1928 to serve as a representative body for scattered groups of

Cape Cod Indians; and the Four Mothers Society was established by Redbird Smith and other conservative Cherokees to resist the expansion of white influence following Oklahoma statehood.

In the introduction to his memoir of boarding school life, *The Middle Five*, the Omaha scholar Francis La Flesche announced to his readers that the subjects of the stories he was about to tell were Indians who wore "civilized" costumes rather than "boy friends who knew only the aboriginal life. I have made this choice," he continued,

> and not because the influences of the school alter the qualities of the boys, but that they might appear under conditions and in an attire familiar to the reader. The paint, feather, robes and other articles that make up the dress of the Indian, are marks of savagery to the European, and he who wears them however appropriate or significant they might be to himself, finds it difficult to lay claim to a share in common human nature.[43]

Like La Flesche, the leaders and organizers who explored the non-Indian political world in the early twentieth century understood that the assertion of their rights and interests required the simultaneous construction of a new identity. Their discovery of a new place for themselves in American society required them literally to don a new costume even as it enabled them to defend their ancient traditions.

But La Flesche's recognition of the power of costume also suggests that, like the Hollywood producers and labor organizers described elsewhere, native leaders learned from the success of the new Indian identities that discovery could be a flexible process.[44] By removing his feathers to win an audience, La Flesche had conceded that those decorations had become "marks of savagery," tags in a silent cultural conversation. His book, like the work of so many of his Indian contemporaries, contained countless choices, poses, and trade-offs—each selected to link ancient traditions to the world that had engulfed him. The exploration of modern America thus produced both successful adaptations and frequent concessions to Indian and non-Indian audiences.

Like other discoveries, the Indians' twentieth-century explorations in modern America would have remained obscure and insignificant had they not been exploited by successive generations of thinkers, activists, and organizers. In each arena the pioneering efforts of writers, artists, anthropological informants, religious leaders, lawyers, and politicians began a discourse between Native Americans and the wider public and created fragile institutions to nurture further activity. Early Native American artists and writers established a market for their products, and that market alerted publishers and curators to the value of Indian expression in contemporary life. The proliferation of anthropology departments in colleges and universities continued in the 1930s and 1940s, creating both interest in, and a need for, accurate ethnographic presentations. Also in this era, Native Americans began studying in those departments. Pioneers into the world of anthropological scholarship, such as Edward P. Dozier and D'Arcy McNickle, made a more prominent Indian presence in university research programs possible. And while they were regularly embattled and not always successful, the formal institutions of the Native American Church, the growing number of Indian lawyers, the many intertribal organizations, and the emerging tribal governments of the 1930s promised that native voices would continue in these areas as well.[45]

Running parallel to these examples of the continuing Indian exploration of white America was a stunning rise in the native population. Beginning from a low point of 250,000 in 1890, the total number of enumerated Native Americans rose gradually during the first half of this century until in 1960 it exceeded 500,000. By the time Mourning Dove was beginning her autobiography, then, she understood that her life spanned a transition not to obscurity but to survival. Her tribe and her community were greatly outnumbered. They had suffered terribly at the hands of American settlers, but their future existence was no longer in doubt. Efforts like hers would not be preserved by antiquarians as Australians had recorded the dying words of the last Tasmanian but would constitute both testimony abut a vanished time and an example for generations to come. The audience for Indian writers, artists, politicians, and activists could then include other Indians as well as outsiders.[46]

The Indians who explored the non-Indian world in the early twentieth century increasingly spoke to each other and, by the 1930s, considered how their various efforts might combine to form the basis for a modern Native American community. By finding places to be heard and appreciated in an alien world, they created ways of communicating with outsiders and, ultimately, with each other. The growing Indian population in the 1930s and 1940s gave them a sense of confidence and optimism that encouraged greater activism. With that activism came an understanding that artists, politicians, religious leaders, and others shared a common cultural tradition and a set of common interests; and as these insights were communicated among Indian leaders, a national native American community began to take shape. In November 1944, tribal leaders from twenty-seven states gathered in Denver, Colorado, to found the National Congress of American Indians (NCAI). The new group's constitution declared that its purpose would be:

> to enlighten the public toward a better understanding of the Indian race; to preserve Indian cultural values; to seek an equitable adjustment of tribal affairs, to secure and to preserve Indian rights under Indian treaties with the United States; and otherwise to promote the common welfare of the American Indians.[47]

The origins and activities of the NCAI carry us far beyond the limits of this essay, but it is noteworthy that what became the most important Indian political organization of the twentieth century asserted from the outset that the common welfare of Native Americans required the preservation of cultural values, the defense of legal rights, and the education of the general public. One can see reflected in that assertion the efforts of writers, artists, anthropological collaborators, and politicians over the previous forty years. They had been the most successful in exploring areas where their community's vital interests might find recognition in the wider world and had been the most articulate in communicating their findings to others.

In 1933, at about the time when Mourning Dove was beginning to compose her autobiography, Luther Standing Bear, another boarding school graduate, wrote that if he had a child to educate and "was faced with the duty of choosing between the natural way of my forefathers and that of the white man's present civilization," he would "unhesitatingly set that child's feet in the path of my forefathers. I would raise

him to be an Indian!" Standing Bear's statement not only repeats the familiar assertion that native culture can be a corrective to modern civilization, but it calls attention to other Indians—not only his fellow Sioux tribesmen—who share a common
ethnic identity. His position was asserted in an English-language book and couched
in romantic language that would appeal to sympathetic whites; nonetheless the cry, "I
would raise him to be an Indian!" stands in striking contrast to Morris Jesup's self-
confident claim that the discovery of Indian culture would be incorporated into a
tableau of progress. It marks both the discovery of an avenue for the powerless to
participate in a hostile society and an understanding of how that participation could
mark the advent of a new cultural identity.[48]

A recent round table in the *Journal of American History* devoted to the career of
Martin Luther King, Jr., contained this description of the civil rights leader:

> Better than any other American, King embodied and projected the dream of creating
> a world in which people and ideas could travel as far and intermingle as freely as they
> wanted without hindrance from laws and customs erected to keep them apart. . . .
> [King] tried to draw separate worlds together by building borderlands between them
> where people and ideas could mingle instead of collide.[49]

The journeys of discovery launched by Native Americans in the first decades of this
century were similar adventures in the cultural borderlands separating racial communities in the United States. The intellectuals, religious reformers, and political leaders
who emerged in those years all struggled to define and defend areas where their
voices would be heard by whites and yet remain recognizable to their kinsmen. In the
cultural territories they discovered, Indians and non-Indians could interact with dignity and mutual respect. In the aftermath of their struggles, such borderlands have
formed the heartland of a new Native American community.

The results of this process are still uncertain, but clearly American scholars no
longer view Native Americans as "other men of another time." Rather, Indians are
understood by anthropologists, by increasing numbers of their countrymen, and by
each other as heirs to an ancient cultural tradition that was constructed by human
beings and that has been altered by historical circumstance and individual innovation. Students of native life increasingly understand that the history of indigenous
people, like the history of any community, is not locked into a tableau of progress; it
is confined solely by human ambitions, interchange, and discovery. Similarly, there
has been enormous growth in Indian organizations' and tribal governments' power in
using the legal and political system to defend their vital interests. And with that
growth of power, the choices available to individuals have multiplied.

Those who were once themselves the objects of exploration have challenged and
replaced the nineteenth-century notion that the discovery of Native Americans
could be contained by the rhetoric of progress. The Indian people who set off a century ago to explore the new world around them may have led us all away from the
self-serving discoveries described in our textbooks and guided us instead toward a
new conception of what it means to discover the peoples and institutions of this land.

NOTES

1. Mourning Dove, *Mourning Dove: A Salishan Autobiography*, ed. Jay Miller (Lincoln, 1990), 3. For a discussion of the original text for this passage see ibid., xxxv.

2. Russell Thornton, *American Indian Holocaust and Survival: A Population History Since 1492* (Norman, 1987), 90.

3. Crude population figures obscure the fact that the nineteenth century was marked by the intermarriage of Indians and whites and by the rise of a large, non-Anglo-Saxon minority. The 250,000 represented people the U.S. Bureau of the Census classified as Indians, and the 76,000,000 included millions of African Americans, Asian Americans, and European immigrants.

4. Robert E. Bieder, *Science Encounters the Indian, 1820–1880: The Early Years of American Ethnology* (Norman, 1986), 205.

5. See Brian W. Dippie, *Catlin and His Contemporaries: The Politics of Patronage* (Norman, 1990); and Robert F. Berkhofer, Jr., *The White Man's Indian: Images of the American Indian from Columbus to the Present* (New York, 1978), 88–89. Catlin's description of his travels among the Indians was a best seller in England and the United States. George Catlin, *Letters and Notes on the Manners, Customs, and Conditions of the North American Indians* (London, 1844).

6. Lewis Henry Morgan, *League of the Ho De No Sau Nee* (Rochester, 1851).

7. See Douglas Cole, *Captured Heritage: The Scramble for Northwest Coast Artifacts* (Seattle, 1985), 10–12, 50, 165.

8. *Proceedings of the International Congress of Americanists, 13th Session* (Easton, Pa., 1905), xx. See Regna Darnell, ed., *Readings in the History of Anthropology* (New York, 1974), 6–7, 420–21.

9. Johannes Fabian, *Time and the Other: How Anthropology Makes Its Object* (New York, 1983), 143; *Proceedings of the International Congress of Americanists*, xx.

10. Curtis M. Hinsley, Jr., "Zunis and Brahmins," in *Romantic Motives: Essays on Anthropological Sensibility*, ed. George W. Stocking, Jr. (Madison, 1989), 170.

11. Fabian, *Time and Other*, 144.

12. On Franz Boas and his students, see Frederick E. Hoxie, *A Final Promise: The Campaign to Assimilate the Indians, 1880–1920* (Lincoln, 1984), 141–45. Elsie Clews Parsons, ed., *American Indian Life* (1922; reprint, Lincoln, 1991).

13. *Report of the Commissioner of Indian Affairs* (Washington, 1887), 219.

14. For Merrill E. Gates's comments, see Francis Paul Prucha, *The Great Father: The United States Government and the American Indians* (2 vols., Lincoln, 1984), II, 671. See also Hoxie, *A Final Promise*, 41–82.

15. For the term *hegemony*, see Jean Comaroff and John L. Comaroff, *Of Revelation and Revolution*, vol. I: *Christianity, Colonialism, and Consciousness in South Africa* (Chicago, 1991), 19–27.

16. For discussion of "talking back," see Richard White, "Discovering Nature in North America," *Journal of American History*, 79 (Dec. 1992), 874–91.

17. Prucha, *Great Father*, II, 776–79.

18. Charles A. Eastman, *Indian Boyhood* (1902; reprint, New York, 1971). For Eastman's grandmother's comments, see Charles A. Eastman (Ohiyesa), *From the Deep Woods to Civilization: Chapters in the Autobiography of an Indian* (1916; reprint, Lincoln, 1977), 28. Eastman's great-grandfather, Mahpiya Wichasta (Cloud Man), had been an early convert to Christianity, and his mother (who died soon after his birth) had had a white father, but his kinsmen continued to live away from white communities. His father was arrested for having taken part in the 1862 Minnesota Sioux uprising but was pardoned by Abraham Lincoln. (Thirty-eight others were executed.) For a modern biography, see Raymond Wilson, *Ohiyesa: Charles Eastman, Santee Sioux* (Urbana, 1983).

19. For Eastman's comments, see David Reed Miller, "Charles Alexander Eastman, Santee Sioux, 1858–1939," in *American Indian Intellectuals*, ed. Margot Liberty (St. Paul, 1978), 64. Charles A. Eastman, *Old Indian Days* (New York, 1907); Charles A. Eastman, *Indian Child Life* (Boston, 1913); Charles A. Eastman, *Indian Scout Talks* (Boston, 1914).

20. Eastman, *Indian Boyhood*, preface n.p., 73, 87.

21. T. J. Jackson Lears, *No Place of Grace: Antimodernism and the Transformation of American Culture, 1880–1920* (New York, 1981), 57. See also Curtis M. Hinsley, Jr., "Authoring Authenticity," *Journal of the Southwest*, 32 (Winter 1990), 462–78.

22. Zitkala-Sa, "Why I Am a Pagan," *Atlantic Monthly,* 90 (Dec. 1902), 803.

23. Zitkala-Sa, *Old Indian Legends* (1901; reprint, Lincoln, 1985); Gertrude Bonnin (Zitkala-Sa), *American Indian Stories* (1921; reprint, Glorieta, N. Mex., 1976); Hum-ishu-ma (Mourning Dove), *Co-ge-we-a, the Half Blood: A Depiction of the Great Montana Cattle Range* (Boston, 1927); Mourning Dove (Humishuma), *Coyote Stories* (1933; reprint, New York, 1984); Lucy Thompson, *The American Indian* (Eureka, Calif., 1916); Luther Standing Bear, *My People, the Sioux* (1928; reprint, Lincoln, 1975). Standing Bear, *My People, the Sioux,* xiv, 288, 276. See also Luther Standing Bear (Ota K'te [Plenty Kill]), *My Indian Boyhood* (1931; reprint, Lincoln, 1988); Luther Standing Bear, *Land of the Spotted Eagle* (1933; reprint, Lincoln, 1978); Luther Standing Bear, *Stories of the Sioux* (1934; reprint, Lincoln, 1988). For Thompson's comments, see Thompson, *To the American Indian,* 9. For Zitkalal-Sa's comments, see Zitkala-Sa, *Old Indian Legends,* vi.

24. Eastman, *From the Deep Woods to Civilization,* 195. For Eastman's summer camp, see Wilson, *Ohiyesa,* 151.

25. Morris E. Opler, *Apache Odyssey: A Journey between Two Worlds* (New York, 1969), 4.

26. For a collaborative monograph, see Alice C. Fletcher and Francis La Flesche, *The Omaha Tribe* (2 vols., Washington, 1911). For biographical material, see Margot Liberty, "Francis La Flesche, Omaha, 1857–1932," in *American Indian Intellectuals,* ed. Liberty; John G. Neihardt, *Black Elk Speaks: Being the Life Story of a Holy Man of the Oglala Sioux* (New York, 1932); and Paul Radin, ed., *The Autobiography of a Winnebago Indian* (Berkeley, 1920).

27. For Franz Boas's comments, see Cole, *Captured Heritage,* 158; for Black Elk's comments, see Raymond J. DeMallie, ed., *The Sixth Grandfather: Black Elk's Teachings Given to John G. Neihardt* (Lincoln, 1984), 28; Francis La Flesche, *The Middle Five, Indian Boys at School* (Boston, 1900), xiv; Liberty, "Francis La Flesche. Omaha, 1857–1932," 53.

It is difficult to summarize dozens of examples of collaboration across North America. One example is War Eagle's invitation to the anthropologist Frank Speck in 1928 that the two of them write a description of the Delaware Big House ritual, a pivotal tribal event that had last been performed in 1924 and seemed on the verge of disappearing. War Eagle, a tribal leader whose father was Cherokee and whose mother was Munsee, had been born in 1880 and was determined to preserve this aspect of his community's past. See Frank G. Speck, *A Study of the Delaware Indian Big House Ritual: In Native Text Dictated by Witapanoxwe* (Harrisburg, 1931), 7–21. Another notable collaboration is described in James Mooney, *The Swimmer Manuscript: Cherokee Sacred Formulas and Medicinal Prescriptions,* ed. Frans. M. Olbrechts (Washington, 1932). At Pine Ridge Agency, South Dakota, physician James R. Walker compiled a massive description of Lakota life with the assistance of community religious leaders. The religious leaders were convinced in part by the argument of George Sword, a Christian Sioux who, according to Walker, declared that "soon they would go from the world and all their sacred lore would pass with them unless they revealed it so it could be preserved in writing." James R. Walker, *Lakota Belief and Ritual,* ed. Raymond J. DeMallie and Elaine A. Jahner (Lincoln, 1980), 47. The Seneca scholar Arthur C. Parker (1881–1955) followed a career that does not fit neatly with others of his generation. Employed first as a field ethnologist by the Peabody Museum of Archaeology and Ethnology at Harvard University, Parker was named state archaeologist at the New York State Museum in 1906. In 1925 he became director of the Rochester Museum of Arts and Sciences.

28. For Boas's reminder, see Cole, *Captured Heritage,* 159. Robert H. Lowie, *The History of Anthropological Theory* (London, 1937), 133.

29. Cole, *Captured Heritage,* 159.

30. Margaret Archuleta and Rennard Strickland, *Shared Visions: Native American Painters and Sculptors in the Twentieth Century* (Phoenix, 1991), 5; Lee A. Callender and Ruth Slivka, *Shawnee Home Life: The Paintings of Ernest Spybuck* (New York, 1984), 7–10. For a review of Canadian Indian Art in the same period, see Gerald R. McMaster, "Tenuous Lines of Descent: Indian Arts and Crafts of the Reservation Period," *Canadian Journal of Native Studies,* 9 (Winter 1989), 205–36.

31. See Dorothy Dunn, *American Indian Painting of the Plains and Southwest* (Albuquerque, 1968), 188–95, 198–201, 218–40.

32. Elizabeth Shepley Sergeant, "An American Indian Artist," *Freeman,* Aug. 8, 1923, pp. 314–15.

33. *New York Times,* Nov. 29, 1931, sect. 5, pp. 12–13, quoted in Dunn, *American Indian Painting,* 239.

34. See Omer C. Stewart, *Peyote Religion: A History* (Norman, 1987), 62.

35. David F. Aberle, *The Peyote Religion among the Navaho* (New York, 1966), 17.

36. Stewart, *Peyote Religion*, 75, 138, 224, 227–30.

37. David Rich Lewis, "Reservation Leadership and the Progressive-Traditional Dichotomy: William Wash and the Northern Utes, 1865–1928," *Ethnohistory* 38 (Spring 1991): 139, 134; Stewart, *Peyote Religion*, 157.

38. For Reginald Oshkosh's comments, see Brian C. Hosmer, "Creating Indian Entrepreneurs: Menominees, Neopit Mills, and Timber Exploitation, 1890–1915," *American Indian Culture and Research Journal* 15 (Winter 1991): 15.

39. Ironically, Patrick Miguel had been sent to Carlisle Indian School as a punishment for helping burn down some boarding school buildings at the Fort Yuma agency. For Miguel's comments, see Robert L. Bee, *Crosscurrents along the Colorado: The Impact of Government Policy on the Quechan Indians* (Tucson, 1981), 55, 59. Lewis, "Reservation Leadership," 139. For the successful career of another former Carlisle student, see Terry P. Wilson, "Chief Fred Lookout and the Politics of Osage Oil, 1906–1949," in *Indian Leadership*, ed. Walter L. Williams (Manhattan, Kans., 1984), 46–53.

40. William T. Hagan, *United States-Comanche Relations: The Reservation Years* (New Haven, 1976), 263–64, 280.

41. For a broad history of the early claims process, see Harvey D. Rosenthal, "Indian Claims and the American Conscience: A Brief History of the Indian Claims Commission," in *Irredeemable America: The Indians' Estate and Land Claims*, ed. Imre Sutton (Albuquerque, 1985), 35–71. On the number of cases filed, see ibid., 40.

42. *Santa Fe New Mexican*, Nov. 6, 1922, quoted in Willard Rollings, "The Pueblos of New Mexico and the Protection of Their Land and Water Rights," in *Working the Range: Essays on the History of Western Land Management and the Environment*, ed. John R. Wunder (Westport, 1985), 3–24.

43. La Flesche, *Middle Five*, ix.

44. Michael Rogin, "Making America Home: Racial Masquerade and Ethnic Assimilation in the Transition to Talking Pictures," *Journal of American History* 79 (Dec. 1992): 1015–77; James R. Barrett, "Americanization from the Bottom Up: Immigration and the Remaking of the Working Class in the United States, 1880–1930," ibid., 996–1020.

45. Edward P. Dozier (1916–1971) began his anthropological studies at the University of New Mexico in the 1930s, but he completed his Ph.D. in 1952 at the University of California, Los Angeles. D'Arcy McNickle (1904–1977), who had studied at the University of Montana and in Europe, was an adviser to Indian Commissioner John Collier during the New Deal. While he did not earn an academic degree in anthropology, he was active in the field. He was the founding chair of the Department of Anthropology at the University of Regina, Saskatchewan.

46. For a discussion of contemporary Indian attitudes toward the rising population, see Thornton, *American Indian Holocaust and Survival*, 182–85; and Kenneth R. Weber, "Demographic Shifts in Eastern Montana Reservation Counties: An Emerging Native American Political Power Base," *Journal of Ethnic Studies* 16 (no. 4, 1989): 101–16.

47. Hazel Hertzberg, "Indian Rights Movement, 1887–1973," in *Handbook of North American Indians*, vol. IV: *History of Indian-White Relations*, ed. Wilcomb E. Washburn (Washington, 1988), 313. The central role of men and women of mixed ancestry in the exploration process begs to be investigated. For one study of a "mixed blood" who played a central role in the construction of a modern Indian identity, see Dorothy Parker, *Singing an Indian Song: A Biography of D'Arcy McNickle* (Lincoln, 1992).

48. Standing Bear, *Land of the Spotted Eagle*, 258–59.

49. David Thelen, "Becoming Martin Luther King, Jr.: An Introduction," *Journal of American History* 78 (June 1991): 15.

14

Passage of the Indian Reorganization Act in June 1934 was easily the most significant political event affecting Native Americans between Wounded Knee and World War II. The brainchild of Commissioner of Indian Affairs John Collier (who served from 1933 to 1945), the IRA marked a turning point in federal policy. The new law (also called the Wheeler-Howard Act in honor of its congressional sponsors) suspended further allotment of tribal land. It thereby reversed a fifty-year-old policy, inaugurated by the 1887 Dawes Act, aimed at dividing reservations into individual homesteads. In addition, it encouraged tribes to adopt constitutions and corporate charters so that Indian communities could function as independent legal and economic entities. Together these aspects of the new law placed the federal government's Indian Office on the side of supporting Native culture and encouraging communal enterprises.

Naturally, a policy change of this magnitude, particularly one advocated by an appealing and articulate champion of indigenous traditions like John Collier, has attracted significant scholarly attention. In the immediate aftermath of the New Deal, historians wrote glowingly of Collier's achievements and praised his cultural vision. A second generation of scholars, many influenced by the radical critique of IRA-inspired tribal governments that was part of Indian activism in the 1970s, were more critical, pointing out the IRA's shortcomings (for example its requirement that the Secretary of the Interior approve tribal constitutions before they go into effect). Commentators have also found fault with Collier himself, stressing his arbitrary manner, his romantic assumption that Indians represented a lost world, a "Red Atlantis," and his faith that all tribes desired to return to communal ways.

John Savagian's essay offers yet another perspective on John Collier and the Indian Reorganization Act by describing the law's impact on a forgotten Indian community in northern Wisconsin. Several things make the Stockbridge-Munsee story unusual. Descendants of refugees who had come west to Wisconsin during the removal era a century before, the Stockbridge-Munsees were even more poor, and even more landless, than most Native peoples during this period; indeed, the federal government no longer recognized them as an Indian tribe. But despite their intense suffering, and though most seemed culturally indistinguishable from their non-Native neighbors, the Stockbridge-Munsees still considered themselves an Indian community. They elected and supported a tribal leadership, and longed for a way to recover lands lost during the allotment era. The Indian Reorganization Act gave the group a mechanism for becoming a new legal identity, while also providing the tribe with federal assistance. Like the Iroquois Sidney Harring described, the Stockbridge-Munsees, long surrounded by whites, serve as a vivid reminder that Native American cultural persistence and renewal were not limited to isolated western reservations.

Savagian's essay underscores the complexity of the Indian New Deal era, and of the Indian experience more generally. As at other times, the history of native communities during the 1930s was not determined solely by edicts from Washington, D.C. Indian action—such as the Stockbridge-Munsee Business Committee, established three years before the Indians' New Deal—was crucial. On the other hand, the significance of federal reforms should not be too easily dismissed.

The Tribal Reorganization of the Stockbridge-Munsee: Essential Conditions in the Re-Creation of a Native American Community, 1930–1942

John C. Savagian

THE STOCKBRIDGE-MUNSEE COMMUNITY is a small rural village of about 700 people located in Shawano County, Wisconsin. Community members live in contemporary houses, travel in automobiles, dress according to the fashions of the time, attend the same schools, and shop at the same stores as their rural counterparts in nearby Bowler and Gresham. But rather than being formed by the slow accumulation of disparate immigrant groups who chose to settle in the Cutover to escape crowded cities, or to farm as their ancestors did, the Stockbridge-Munsee Community is the end result of a long and at times torturous journey of a band of principally Mahican Indians from the colonial frontiers of western Massachusetts.

In 1734, while living along the Housatonic River, a small band of Mahicans chose to abandon their ancestral ways and settle on a six-acre plot of land in the village of Stockbridge. What lured them was Christianity, as well as their desire to learn and experience at first hand the ways of the Euro-American. Following the American Revolution, though supportive of the Colonies in both blood and spirit, these "Stockbridge" Indians were evicted from their lands. Therein began what they refer to as their own "trail of tears": six migrations over a period of nearly seventy years. Their lands, held in common, and improved with every turn of the plow and stroke of the hammer, were repeatedly lost. Time after time the Stockbridge settled on lands negotiated in good faith, worked hard to improve them, only to be forced out by covetous whites or other bands of Indians. Yet they persevered. New land, it seemed, could always be found. Another migration could always be made. What mattered most was that the small band stayed together and kept its identity intact.[1]

Despite their desire to remain a people and a nation, by the mid-1920s the Stockbridge-Munsee had ceased to exist as a federally recognized tribe. Torn by political factions, exacerbated both by repeated moves and debate over their relationship with the predominant white culture, the people who call themselves Muh-He-Con-Neew more closely resembled their German and Scandinavian neighbors than a tribe of Native Americans. Like their neighbors struggling with the rural depression, the Indians of the Stockbridge-Munsee Community had become a typical mix of poor farmers, unemployed day laborers, and rural indigents.

By all rights, the story should have ended there. As advocates of assimilation theorized, the Stockbridge-Munsee were supposed to melt into the boiling cultural

SOURCE: *Wisconsin Magazine of History* (August 1993), pp. 39–62.

cauldron of America, lose their "Indianness," till the soil, raise families, and assume the same goals and aspirations as their white rural neighbors, becoming one more segment in a population of what one Congressman called "civilized tax-payers."[2]

Instead, in the decade between 1932 and 1942, a small nucleus of Stockbridge-Munsee led a revival of tribal spirit that culminated in the rebirth of the tribe. These new leaders cast a wide net throughout the region, gathering tribal members and settling them on a portion of their old reservation. They wrote a constitution and held elections to form a new tribal government. They built homes, drilled wells, laid out new roads. Perhaps equally important, the Stockbridge-Munsee committed themselves to reconnecting with their Indian heritage through history projects, craft classes, and annual powwows.

In one sense, this Phoenix-like resurrection can be attributed to the political and social genius of John Collier and his able band of anthropologists and lawyers who attempted to reorganize not only Indian life but also the Bureau of Indian Affairs during Collier's tenure as Commissioner of Indian Affairs (1934–1945). Collier, Georgia-born and Columbia-educated, brought high credentials to the job: adviser to the Pueblo Indians in their fight against the Bursum Bill; executive secretary of the American Indian Defense Association; editor of *American Indian Life*. But it was Collier's experience with the massive influx of immigrants into New York City during 1910–1918 that set the pattern for his efforts as Commissioner of Indian Affairs. While at the People's Institute, he had observed a modern industrialized society destroy the social bonds and group controls of the Old World, replacing them with an individualistic and materialistic world-view he found troubling. To John Collier, Native American societies exhibited similar group controls that were destined for extinction by an "Americanization" that in his words "pulverized" tribal bonds.[3]

Collier's appointment as Commissioner of Indian Affairs gave him the opportunity to help Native Americans preserve their culture by utilizing their "latent civic force."[4] The seminal document of Collier's plan was the Indian Reorganization Act of 1934 (the IRA, also known as the Wheeler-Howard Bill), a sweeping piece of legislation that sought to restore tribal lands and governments, and, by so doing, to ensure the continued survival of Native American cultures.[5]

Historians of federal Indian policy during the New Deal era have examined in some detail the apex of the pyramid of power and decision-making over Native American life, scrutinizing John Collier's utopian vision of tribal restoration and his methods for achieving it. The trove of information contained in BIA records and Collier's papers offers excellent material to critically appraise the BIA's success or failure in creating what one scholar has called "cooperative commonwealths" in the rural regions of the nation.[6]

But of course the story goes much deeper than that. What made it possible for the Stockbridge-Munsee to reorganize during the 1930s was the confluence of many interdependent factors, of which Collier and his agents of reform were only one. Therefore, rather than using the Stockbridge-Munsee as a case study for further analysis of Collier's Indian policy, this essay seeks to identify the other main forces which came together to create the Stockbridge-Munsee Community. Its aim is to achieve a better understanding of how fragile a coalition it was, and how unique this decade of reorganization proved to be.

The Stockbridge move into Wisconsin did not begin propitiously. After the white citizens of Stockbridge, Massachusetts, forced them out following the American Revolution, the tribe relocated in New York on lands offered by the Oneida. Within the decade, further encroachments by whites led them to seek a new settlement on lands allegedly owned by the Delaware Indians along the White River in Indiana. But what the Delaware claimed was theirs to give, Congress claimed otherwise and withheld the lands from the Stockbridge.[7] Finally in 1821 the Stockbridge, together with the Oneida and Brotherton, negotiated two treaties with the Menominee and Winnebago for lands east of the Fox River in northeastern Wisconsin (then called the Michigan Territory). Resettled, they once again set about to improve their home, establishing a mission under the guidance of Reverend Jesse Miner, building a school, and farming the land.[8] And just as before, the tranquility they had sought was disturbed. This time factions within the Menominee and Winnebago tribes contested the treaties, causing the federal government to revoke the agreement. A new treaty in 1831 created a reservation for the Stockbridge of two townships east of Lake Winnebago in what is now Calumet County, Wisconsin.[9]

While at this reservation, the Stockbridge merged with the Munsee Indians upon their arrival from New York. As one of the bands of the Delaware (or Lenapi) Indians, the Munsee regarded the Stockbridge as relatives from earlier contact with Mohicans along the Housatanic River valley, from whence the Stockbridge originated. From then on, the tribe was known as the Stockbridge-Munsee Indians.[10]

During the 1830s the Stockbridge-Munsee were beset by an internal conflict that would in time mirror the national debate over the Indian question; namely, would Indians seek a separate existence from white American society or would they opt for assimilation with the prevailing culture? By and large, federal efforts to promote assimilation involved the Indians' removal from their tribal setting through individual allotments of land to the heads of each Indian family. Supporters of allotment assumed that if Native Americans would accept private ownership of the land as the white man had, and adopt all the attendant legalities and cultural notions it implied (such as title and deed, wealth and status), they would be well on the road to civilization. "It is doubtful," wrote the Commissioner of Indian Affairs in 1876, summarizing the popular view, "whether any high degree of civilization is possible without individual ownership."[11]

Although the allotment plan would not see fruition on a large scale until the latter half of the nineteenth century, when the major Indian wars were over and the tribes were restricted to reservations, the controversy over assimilation was as old as the first cultural exchange between Columbus and the Taino on the island of San Salvador. The debate within the Stockbridge-Munsee tribe split the tribe into two camps: the Citizen Party, which sought U.S. citizenship and supported individual allotment of lands; and the Indian Party, which desired to retain both communal ownership of land and federal annuities.[12] To openly display their philosophies, Citizen Party members sought to dress like their white neighbors while Indian Party members continued to cloak themselves in the traditional blanket.[13]

This split proved far more damaging than simply a difference over the tribe's style of clothing. Buoyed by the desires of the Citizen Party, Congress in 1843 ordered the allotment of all Stockbridge-Munsee lands and offered citizenship to the entire tribe.[14] The Citizen Party eagerly accepted these terms and was promised individual tracts of Stockbridge-Munsee land. The Indian Party, led by John W. Quinney, rejected the terms, forcing Congress to repeal it and order a new enrollment to partition lands to better represent the two factions.[15] To foster a solution, Congress passed an amendment to the treaty in 1849 that offered the Indian Party lands west of the Mississippi River and a one-time payment of $25,000 for resettlement and improvement of those lands if the tribe would leave the newly created state of Wisconsin. Unfortunately, no land was forthcoming, although some Stockbridge delegates were sent west to scout for it. As the Stockbridge-Munsee Community tells the story: "Thus matters continued, government neglecting to provide us with lands; and the Stockbridge nation having, on the faith of the treaty, surrendered title to some of the most valuable lands in Wisconsin at a moderate compensation, were unable to move away, simply because they knew not whither to go."[16]

Finally, the Stockbridge-Munsee negotiated a new treaty and abandoned the Calumet area. This Treaty of 1856 ceded all right of tribal ownership to previous land holdings in Wisconsin and Minnesota and allotted individual parcels of land to members of the Citizen Party. The remainder of the tribe moved to a new reservation in Shawano County, Wisconsin, ceded on their behalf by the Menominee Indians.[17] When the passage of the Dawes or General Allotment Act of 1887 made allotment Congress's principal method for breaking up Indian nations, the Stockbridge-Munsee were subjected to a series of federal acts that concluded in 1910 with the final breakup of their communally held lands in Shawano County.[18]

By the 1920s the former Stockbridge-Munsee reservation had become checkerboarded with titles held by non-Indians and lumber companies. Prior to allotment, the Stockbridge-Munsee had managed to subsist on small farming or through employment in logging operations on or near their reservation. Once the lands were allotted and the 160 acres conveyed to each adult Stockbridge-Munsee male, many lost their titles through tax delinquency. Others went into debt and sold their lands to the lumber companies that coveted the Community's large tracts of white pine. A few hung on, only to see inheritance squabbles shrink the land into smaller and smaller sections. Such was a common experience for many Indians whose lands were subjected to individual allotment.[19] Allotment and rapid land sales made moot the past treaties that mandated federal assistance to the Stockbridge-Munsee. The 1910 enrollment, taken for the purposes of final allotment, recorded 582 members of the Stockbridge-Munsee, but in the eyes of the federal government, the Stockbridge-Munsee had ceased to exist. They were on their own to adapt to a predominant and still alien culture that looked with predatory eyes at their forested lands.

The severe economic troubles that gripped rural Wisconsin in the mid-1920s further eroded the ability of individual Stockbridge-Munsee to keep their lands. "During the depression," noted tribal member Bernice Miller Pigeon, "there were only one or two persons who really hung onto their own section of land."[20] Adequate housing was a particular problem. At least three families occupied former chicken coops. A U.S. Indian Service report to Collier noted that "a large number of the Indians who have already lost title to their holdings are reduced to 'squatters' and 'shackers.'" Other families were tenants on former tribal lands. Those Stockbridge-Munsee who had kept their lands usually had mortgaged them for "several times the market value of the land and improvements."[21]

Shawano County whites, as well as Menominee Indians just to the north, were unhappy with their destitute neighbors. According to complaints from the staff of Bureau of Indian Affairs on the Menominee Reservation, the "old Stockbridge Reservation" was a bad influence throughout the area and was known as a place "where intoxicating liquor can be obtained and where the immoral conditions are exceedingly bad."[22] Arvid Miller, who served as Stockbridge-Munsee tribal chairman from 1939 to 1965, painted a more human but even starker image of the conditions for the Stockbridge-Munsee in rural Shawano County during the Depression:

> Picture these people of some 70 families barely subsisting on the one and one-half dollars per week given them in orders on neighbourhood grocery stores. Visualize the frail under nourished human beings who looked into an empty world each day, their spirits broken, their hearts saddened with the anguish of defeat huddled in their little tar paper shacks and small log shanties in which they had not paid their rents for over a year or more, waiting patiently for the turn of fortune, not enough milk for the babies and for the older folk, the dreaded rotation of meals for those hungry families trying to live on this one and one-half dollars per week.[23]

Despite having lost their land base, however, most of the Stockbridge-Munsee remained in the area surrounding their former reservation, particularly the township of Red Springs. In the late 1920s and early 1930s, tribal members experienced a spiritual reawakening of the need to restore their Community. To that end, they became politically active. To the consternation of some area whites who complained that non-taxpayers did not deserve the right to vote, they took control of the Red Springs town board.[24] To the Stockbridge-Munsee, the board acted as the surrogate tribal council, giving Community members a sense of control and a psychological assurance that their tribal government was still intact.[25] During this period, Carl Miller, a strong-willed Mohican educated at an Indian school in Hampton, Virginia, served as town chairman of Red Springs. Among the Stockbridge-Munsee, Miller was the closest of anyone to being their Sachem or principal leader. He had been known in his earlier days as a bit of brawler, one who didn't shy from a drink or a fight. His stubborn character would serve him well as he helped guide the Stockbridge-Munsee Community through a bureaucratic maze of federal and state agencies along the way to tribal rebirth.[26]

* * *

On October 26, 1931, at a meeting in the Red Springs town hall, the Stockbridge-Munsee Business Committee was formed. Its major purpose was to petition the federal government for the reorganization of the Stockbridge-Munsee Community. Carl Miller was elected chairman.[27] The Business Committee's initiative was well in advance of John Collier's call to reorganize. The source of this ideological impulse to create a Business Committee and reinstate contacts with the Indian Service is unknown. It may reflect the policy changes already taking place at the federal level under the leadership of Charles Rhoads, whose ideas for reform Collier enthusiastically adopted.[28] Locally, however, the Business Committee had encountered nothing but resistance from the superintendent at the Keshena Agency who had jurisdiction over the Stockbridge-Munsee. Prior to their reorganization, the annual reports of Keshena Superintendent William Beyer had made little mention of the Stockbridge-Munsee, usually offering the pat answer on reply forms that they were a "non-tribe" for which no information was available.[29] Even as the tribe began to reorganize, initial assistance from Keshena was limited. Eventually Collier would hand tribal jurisdiction over to the Tomah Agency, his assistant complaining that the Menominee Indians had "rigidly excluded the Stockbridge Indians from receiving help and education benefits."[30]

Superintendent Beyer was the most likely source of trouble. He was a holdover from the administration of Herbert Hoover and a firm believer in the need for allotment of the Menominee reservation. Allotment, he repeatedly told his superiors, was "absolutely necessary in order to further the course of industrial advancement among these people." Besides, he concluded, "there has never been a record of any people living successfully a communal life."[31] Clearly, Beyer did not fit in with the new thinking at Collier's Bureau. In 1934 Collier would replace him with Ralph Fredenberg, a Menominee Indian who had begun working for the Indian Service in 1915 and had steadily moved up through the ranks.[32]

The well-organized Business Committee moved ahead despite the lack of assistance at the local level. Their preparations paid off when, early in 1934, according to one tribal member, good news arrived at Red Springs: "Someone (BIA) from Menominee came through and said Government would buy up options. Had a paper with a ribbon tied around. It was authorization to reestablish Indian reservations. So we asked for our old Res. back. Buy up what used to be our land."[33]

Upon receipt of this good news, Carl Miller sent a letter to Commissioner Collier with a modest proposal. He asked for the establishment of a reservation of a few thousand acres, "at least half of which should be good agriculture land so that we could plant and raise good gardens and feed a cow or two." A series of questions followed: "Shall we make a request by petition signed by the whole tribe? Shall we petition our Senators and Congressmen? Just what shall we do to convince the government that we deserve another chance?"[34]

Within four days the Commissioner had responded. Collier assured Miller, "[W]e do want to get land exactly as you indicate and we are going to try." Collier requested from Miller "facts and proof" that the Stockbridge-Munsee people overwhelmingly supported the Business Committee's efforts. Collier did not outline what kind of proof he wanted; he did not mention elections, the formation of a constitution, and the like. But he did make it clear that legislation was being created that would improve their chances for tribal reorganization.[35] For the first time in years, the Stockbridge-Munsee felt someone in charge in Washington was listening.

The Business Committee immediately began to assemble its case for reorganization. It solicited testimonials from important members of Shawano County such as the head of the local chamber of commerce and the postmaster. Invariably these advocates among the white community argued principally that a new reservation and jobs would go far to get the Stockbridge-Munsee off the relief rolls.[36] Miller made himself available for speeches wherever an interest in their plight was shown. Since few tribesmen owned automobiles, he was forced to walk wherever necessary to speak on behalf of the tribe. Weekly he walked the twenty miles to Keshena, on the Menominee Reservation, to discuss the details for tribal reorganization.[37]

To the Stockbridge-Munsee, approval of the IRA by their Indian peers was just as important as approval by the Bureau of Indian Affairs, especially since there was no guarantee that the legislation would pass Congress. A strong show of support was necessary for both Collier and the Stockbridge-Munsee. To that end, on April 24, 1934, Stockbridge-Munsee delegates Carl Miller, Cornelius Aaron, Adrian Yoccum, and Nelson Gardner journeyed northward to Hayward, in Sawyer County, to participate in one of the ten Indian congresses called by the Bureau of Indian Affairs to discuss the Indian Reorganization bill. Delegates from tribes in Wisconsin, Minnesota, and Michigan gathered to hear Assistant Commissioner William Zimmerman, who took Collier's place and read the Commissioner's speech, denouncing the past laws of the nation directed toward the Indians as "wicked and stupid." Like any good politician, Collier had taken care to distance his administration from the failed policies of the past. The previous policy of the federal government, he said, was "to rob the Indians [to] crush Indian life and even to crush the family life of Indians." His speech was laced with good words that most Indians wanted to hear. John Collier promised that things would be different with his Bureau.[38]

At the close of the Hayward congress, each tribe presented its views on the bill. Most deferred to their elders back home, stating that while they saw much good in the bill, they were not empowered to speak for the entire tribe. Not so with the Stockbridge delegation. The Rev. Cornelius Aaron informed the assembly that "the Stockbridge delegation comes here with instructions to accept that bill to the man!" He called the legislation a promise of better relations with the white race: "Ill will, hatred, prejudice have all been laid aside and the silent road of glory leads through enlightenment through enactment of the provisions of the Wheeler-Howard Bill of Indian Rights."[39] Carl Miller was exuberant, calling the event "a great meeting for a great purpose—1,000 Indians, counting visitors, and all with one mind."[40] The following summer, after an equally vigorous debate, Congress passed by a large majority, and President Roosevelt signed into law the Indian Reorganization Act. Though the Act had been reduced to eight pages from an original fifty-two, the principal intent of the bill—to initiate the formation of new reservations and tribal councils—remained intact.[41]

In December 1934, by a near-unanimous vote of 166 to 1, the Stockbridge-Munsee Community voted to accept the Indian Reorganization Act.[42] What had up to that moment been an abstract exercise in hope was now to become the actual reorganization of the Stockbridge-Munsee. Land would have to be located, lengthy negotiations entered into with the owners, and finally, somehow, money would have to be found for financing the purchase.

The land acquisition program the Stockbridge-Munsee counted on was no sure thing; but, judging from tribal files, the Business Committee believed that assurances from Collier were worth their weight in gold. Unfortunately, Collier's prescribed budget for land acquisition was highly speculative, based as it was on the whims of Congress. The final budget for the purchase of land titles (including water and surface rights) under Section 5 of the IRA for the use of Native Americans was $2 million a year.[43] It has been estimated that to purchase land from those who had become hereditary landowners for consolidation of reservations would have taken at least seventeen years at a total expense of $35 million under IRA funding. According to the National Resource Board, the amount of land needed to help the Native Americans maintain simply a "basic subsistence level" was 9,700,000 acres, at a cost of $60 million.[44] For a national policy to purchase lands for the improvement of the Native American condition, the figure of $2 million was grossly inadequate. And John Collier was unable to safeguard even that small amount.

Control over Collier's budget rested in the hands of western Congressmen who had opposed the Indian Reorganization Act from the outset. They were not pleased with the use of federal money to purchase lands for Native Americans, especially when they learned the extent of the land program. Since they dominated the House appropriations subcommittee which reviewed the Interior Department's budget requests, they were able to further reduce the purchasing power of the IRA to $1 million a year. This forced the Commissioner to look elsewhere to secure funds promised to provide to tribes like the Stockbridge-Munsee.[45]

The first program Collier pursued for land acquisition was the Federal Emergency Relief Administration (FERA), administered by Harry Hopkins. Established by Congress on May 12, 1933 (48 Stat. 55), FERA was to work with state emergency relief administrations to assist rural families hurt by drought and unemployment.[46] Besides providing direct relief, FERA was also mandated to buy up farmland which had fallen into disuse. Under the Submarginal Land Retirement Program of Rural Rehabilitation, occupants were to be removed to better farmlands, thus "rehabilitating" them and reducing the relief rolls of the states.[47] On July 17, 1933, as a result of Collier's persistence, Hopkins issued a memorandum expanding the program to include "Indian-wards as well as nonwards."[48] The result was a merging of FERA funding with the land acquisition clause of the Indian Reorganization Act. Lands classified as submarginal were to be used to supply those Native Americans who had accepted the IRA and had shown a need for land.[49] These submarginal lands were privately held lands the government considered economic failures; they could no longer sustain crop yields, were unproductive as grazing or timberland, and had become or were in the process of becoming badly eroded.[50] This of course described much of the land held by Native Americans, and the volume of requests from IRA tribes for land was so great that Collier was forced to restrict them to the "greatest need" reservations. He stressed that submarginal land projects were to be established "where local relief problems are most acute." He was pleased with the use of FERA because it was a program that could directly aid the Indians, who were often on the tax-relief rolls. He also acknowledged that by relieving the state and counties of their burden in providing relief, he was able to gain further "justification of proposed purchases of land for Indian use."[51]

The Stockbridge-Munsee fell under the fourth category of the Bureau's listing of five "demonstration Indian areas," namely, "lands for Homeless Indian Bands or Communities now Forming Acute Relief Problems."[52] This classification helped give the Stockbridge-Munsee early assistance from the Bureau. On May 15, 1934, Collier directed Keshena Superintendent Beyer to provide more information on lands Carl Miller and the Business Committee sought: maps, statistics on the surrounding area, local conditions for both Indian and non-Indian populations, transportation, land usage, etc. Collier stressed the use of local input in the formulation of the project: foresters, farm extension agents, Red Cross, and other welfare workers were to be interviewed.[53] The project was completed on October 8, 1934, under the direction of James W. Balmer.

Balmer's survey revealed that by 1934, of an original reservation of over 40,000 acres, the Stockbridge-Munsee land base had been reduced to less than a hundred acres.[54] As one Community member recalled, many Indians sold out to the lumber companies and then tried to settle on plots of land "far too small to accommodate the rising generation."[55] Once their lands were sold, a number of Stockbridge-Munsee found work with lumber companies, helping to deforest their former home.[56] Ironically, while playing a role in adding denuded lands to the growing blight known as the Wisconsin Cutover, where weak soil made farming tenuous and the practice of clear-cutting spelled eventual economic doom for the lumbermen and their families, the Stockbridge-Munsee created the exact conditions for regaining the lands; for only submarginal lands, cheap and nearly worthless, were to be considered under FERA's program as possible land for homeless Indians.[57]

Balmer's survey team reported that the physical features of the old Stockbridge Reservation land had changed because of the practice of clear-cutting. Once covered by virgin timber of pine and mixed hardwoods, the land was exposed to reveal its rolling slopes with outcroppings of bedrock and glacial boulders. Stumps and a great deal of deadwood littered the area. Brush and poplar saplings covered much of the Cutover, though in a few places decent second-growth timber had begun to take hold. The existing resources would make economic development difficult. A lumber mill would be impossible for at least one generation. Prospects for large-scale farming were just as unlikely. Like much of central Wisconsin, the soils were sandy but generally suitable for grazing and growing timber; but in many areas poor drainage and weak fertility meant cash crops could not be produced without expensive fertilizers and irrigation systems.[58] Three-quarters of the land was listed as "other" than cropland, forest or woodlands, the majority being cutover brush and swamps.[59] It was hardly an ideal spot for locating a new community in the midst of an economic depression.

The purchase of Stockbridge "submarginal" lands was conducted on two levels of the federal government. The regional offices worked out the details and secured the options; the Bureau office in Washington sought the funds necessary to make the purchase. In Wisconsin, both the Keshena Indian Agency and the Tomah Indian Agency were involved in the creation of the new Stockbridge-Munsee Community. The Keshena Agency, because of its proximity on the Menominee Reservation twenty miles northeast of the old Stockbridge Reservation, coordinated the surveying of lands and took out options in the name of the Interior Department. All correspondence from prospective sellers went through the Keshena Agency, and questions and directives from Washington concerning the negotiations were always sent to Keshena. In 1936, the federal government transferred to the Tomah Agency complete jurisdiction over the Stockbridge-Munsee people and their lands.[60]

The two Wisconsin agencies proved adept at working together, sometimes anticipating advice coming from the Washington office. Pushing them at the local level was the Stockbridge-Munsee Business Committee. Even before tribal members had voted to accept the stipulations of the IRA, the Committee had begun to enter into negotiations with the principal owners of their former lands. Collier wrote Tomah Superintendent Frank Christy in August of 1934, advising him: "We have been thinking that the Stockbridge Tribe would probably be the band which could be organized and rehabilitated most effectively and most speedily." By that time, Christy and Fredenberg had already conducted interviews with Carl Miller and gained new data; the major land owners had placed 6,800 acres of land under option to the Keshena Agency, and were in the process of making another 3,608 acres available.[61]

Negotiations had begun as early as June of 1934 (the same month that Congress passed the Indian Reorganization Act) with the principal owners of lands within the boundaries of the 1856 reservation. The Brooks and Ross Lumber Company owned most of the best lands, over 7,000 acres in the Town of Bartelme.[62] Brooks and Ross was a medium-sized lumber company with headquarters at Schofield, in Marathon County. The company was started in the early 1890s by E. Wellington Brooks and his understudy, John D. Ross. Ross and Walter Bissel were responsible for expanding and diversifying the company's operations early in the twentieth century. Besides its holdings in Shawano, the company also held extensive tracts of land in Vilas and Iron counties, and lands in the upper peninsula of Michigan.[63]

Brooks and Ross management's desire to sell the Bartelme land was based on a need to liquidate holdings that had become useless cutover. The company wished to sell its cutover lands because the long distance to markets precluded corporate farming and its short-sighted pursuit of logging ruled out reforestation. It was unlikely that the company pursued negotiations as a way to rescue or to support the New Deal policies of Franklin D. Roosevelt. The managers of Brooks and Ross were directed by the Wausau Group, a conservative operation with no taste for "progressive reforms."[64] In short, the sole reason Brooks and Ross entered into negotiations with the federal government was to dump what to them would soon become worthless lands.[65]

Furthermore, as became clear at the first meeting with representatives of the Stockbridge Business Committee at the Keshena Agency in June of 1934, Brooks

The Brooks and Ross headquarters, about 1936.

and Ross vice-president Mathew McCullough said the company was only willing to sell the lands if it retained rights to all the remaining merchantable timber, approximately 7 million board feet, after the options had been purchased for the benefit of the Stockbridge-Munsee. This point was again stressed as a condition of sale by McCullough in a letter he wrote to Superintendent Ralph Fredenberg in 1935: "We had hoped to take off all of the forest products from these lands the past winter but owing to unfavorable weather this was not done, therefore, we would be obliged to reserve such forest products as we wish to remove, for a period of two years."[66]

On January 8, 1936, President Roosevelt approved six reorganization projects sent from the Bureau of Indian Affairs Regional Office in Minneapolis. The Stockbridge-Munsee Project was included with that of the Twin Lakes, Flat Lake, L'Anse, Bad River, and Lac Court Oreilles reservations. The money budgeted for the Stockbridge-Munsee was $71,980, second-highest of the six. Options had been accepted for 13,134 acres at a cost of $68,552 or 95.2 per cent of their budget.[67] John Collier's local operation under Frank Christy, Ralph Fredenberg, and the Stockbridge-Munsee Business Committee had done their jobs well. Now the question was, where would the money come from to buy the lands? Rural Rehabilitation, FERA's land-purchase program that Collier was banking on to fund the purchase, had recently been placed under the control of the Resettlement Agency (RA), a new appendage to the growing Roosevelt bureaucracy. There was a good deal of uncertainty whether the Resettlement Agency would ever secure lands for poor white farmers, let alone landless Indians.

Creation of the RA was the result of a solution Roosevelt proffered to end an ideological conflict within the Agriculture Department. Agriculture Secretary Henry Wallace was at odds with his assistant, Rexford Tugwell, over the department's focus. Wallace wanted to help large, scientific farms; Tugwell sought to protect the interests of the small farmer and tenant laborer who were hurt hardest by the Depression.[68] Roosevelt solved the problem by wedding small farm programs from other agencies and departments such as Rural Rehabilitation (FERA), Subsistence Homestead (Interior), Land Policy Section (Agricultural Adjustment Administration), and the Farm Debt Adjustment Program (Farm Credit Administration) into one agency which, by Executive Order 7027 (April 30, 1935), became known as the Resettlement Administration.[69] He then appointed Rex Tugwell to administer the new agency.

Although congressional funding restricted him from attempting little more than resettlement experiments such as the development of middle-class "greenbelt communities" outside Washington, Cincinnati, and Milwaukee, Tugwell did show his support for John Collier's efforts to resettle landless Indians.[70] He requested the Commissioner to let him know "whenever the Department of Agriculture can be of any assistance in solving those questions of Indian Development and progress in which we are both so interested."[71] Tugwell's agency may not have been the pot of gold Collier was searching for to settle landless Indians such as the Stockbridge-Munsee, but when revenue allocated under the IRA dried up, his land-acquisition program was able to proceed through funding provided by the Resettlement Administration.

Tugwell's agency was short-lived. In January of 1937 the Resettlement Administration was merged with the Agriculture Department, which had, by an administrative coup, inherited all the former land programs consolidated during the Roosevelt shakeup, plus their staffs and allocations. Under Executive Order 7557, the RA became the Farm Security Administration (FSA), and lands purchased by RA for the Stockbridge-Munsee became known as FSA lands.[72] Thus title to the Stockbridge-Munsee Community lands was now under control of the Agriculture Department.

The Stockbridge-Munsee Business Committee appeared to have trouble keeping up with all this bureaucratic and executive shuffling. Because of drastic cuts in funding, only 2,249.88 acres had been purchased when the IRA money ran out. The Business Committee was informed that if it wanted to protect its options on the remaining lands, it should seek monetary assistance from the newly created FSA. Arvid Miller recalled the Committee's decision: "This plan we agreed to because we saw it as a simple and sure way to close out our land program." Once the Farm Security Administration completed the purchase of lands for the Stockbridge-Munsee, and title to those lands was placed back under the control of the Interior Department, the Community immediately petitioned to have title of the FSA lands transferred to their new tribal government, as had been promised under the IRA.[73] This did not happen, though a simple signature by Secretary Harold Ickes would have consummated the transfer.

This was not a situation unique to the Stockbridge-Munsee. The lands of all the tribes which had accepted the provisions of the IRA remained under the control of the Interior Department.[74] That department in turn refused to move on these lands without the consent of Congress, which had become upset at the extent of Collier's land-acquisition program and was scrutinizing every attempted purchase.[75] Money as well as fear of congressional ire may have motivated the Interior Department to keep title to the land. Harold Gross notes that the Interior Department did not allow Native Americans to use the lands provided under the IRA to cut timber and remove minerals without paying for the privilege. The revenue collected was to be held in "special deposits," but Gross contends they were actually absorbed into the U.S. Treasury. Gross estimates that for the Stockbridge-Munsee purchase alone, $22,732.12 was recovered over and above the actual cost of those lands.[76]

The question of ownership was officially answered by Tomah's new Superintendent, Peru Farver, in a letter to Harry Chicks, the Community's new tribal president: "The title to these lands is taken in the name of the United States and they will not become the property of the Indian tribe, for whose use they were purchased, until Congressional action is obtained specifically transferring such title."[77]

The problems with appropriations for the IRA left the Stockbridge-Munsee with a divided reservation. The title to 2,249 acres was promised to them once they adopted a corporate charter; 13,000 acres called FSA land remained under the control of the Interior Department, and subject to the whim of Congress. Eventually that situation would generate mistrust, since anyone choosing or being assigned to live on FSA lands had to fill out a disclaimer of ownership, stating that they were merely tenants who had no right to the title and would "vacate said premises upon demand for the possession of said lands by the United States of America."[78] This promised future trouble. (Indeed the Stockbridge-Munsee would not gain title to the land until 1972.)

The central occupation of the Stockbridge-Munsee Business Committee in the mid-thirties was collecting the tribe's scattered people. Throughout the duration of the land-purchase program, Stockbridge-Munsee families had begun to gather on the Cutover, taking back land the minute word came that a sale had been secured. Regardless of who had the title—whether it was Resettlement, Farm Security, Interior, or Agriculture—the Stockbridge-Munsee had begun to lay the foundations for the new Stockbridge-Munsee Community. Carl Miller, writing about the universal need for a place to call home, eloquently expressed their driving motivation:

> Each of us needs a home, a bit of land, some growing thing, some treasured bit of beauty. Enough to clothe and feed us with a little margin for gracious hospitality. Each of us needs room for the growth of his spirit, the reason for his presence here on this earth.[79]

In the fall of 1936, five years after forming the Business Committee and two years after passage of the Indian Reorganization Act, the Stockbridge-Munsee began to gather on the cutover lands they were to call Moh-he-con-ock. On September 18,

Nelson Gardner's family, with friends assisting, inaugurated a new era for the Stockbridge-Munsee Community. Their new residence was a log house abandoned during the lumbering days of Brooks and Ross. A few words were spoken to mark the moment. Carl Miller compared their situation to a man who challenges a fast-moving stream. If he dives in without first learning to master its strong currents he will soon be calling for help. If instead he takes his time to learn the stream and gain confidence in his own abilities, he will swim away independent.[80] This analogy of the tribe's struggle to continually adapt to the predominant culture is striking; but, at the time, the excitement of moving "way back in the brush" allowed these IRA pioneers to ignore the currents of American society which swirled about them.[81] Just as he had at the Hayward Conference, Cornelius Aaron looked with optimism to the future, telling those gathered: "Like the sun of a new day, hope is rising over the Moh-he-con-new."[82]

Eleven families were chosen to settle the newly purchased lands that fall. Carl Miller and Superintendent Ralph Fredenberg made the selections. Fredenberg's official report of the selection process listed the criteria for choosing the families: "need—homeless and landless," the size of the family, ambition, and the capacity to "make [a] good showing."[83] One tribal member remembered how the last criterion outweighed the others. Instead of need, which qualified so many, the "men and women who were not afraid of work and could be depended on to make a showing for the Stockbridgers" were the first selections.[84] Among these were the families of Carl Miller, his son Arvid, Adrian Yoccum, Ken Davids, Nelson Gardner, and Bert Miller.[85]

Judging by their first harvest in the fall of 1937, the first eleven families proved their industrious nature and ability to make a "good showing." They gathered 500 bushels of potatoes, 500 bushels of corn, fifty bushels of rutabagas, twenty bushels of beets, fifteen bushels of carrots, and 300 squash and pumpkins. They prepared 500 quarts of fruit preserves, gathered thirty tons of hay and corn fodder, and raised eight cows, nine horses, eight hogs, and 125 chickens. "As I said before," wrote Arvid Miller, "we have all been very busy—and are all very happy. I used to write letters to our commissioner asking him to give us a chance, he gave us this chance and I think that I am justified in saying we are making good."[86]

Once settlement began on their new lands, the Stockbridge-Munsee Community continued to seek government aid. Through the Tomah Indian Agency, the Bureau of Indian Affairs remained their guiding as well as their helping hand during the first decade of tribal reorganization. Assistance came in the form of both direct aid—such as job programs, loans, and grants—and technical and legal advice to the Business Committee (and later the Tribal Council) as they prepared their constitution and corporate charter.

A major success story during their first ten years of reorganization was the Stockbridge-Munsee's utilization of the numerous federal programs implemented during the Depression years to provide aid to rural families. These were not programs created with Native Americans in mind, but rather in response to misery en masse. But without such New Deal programs it is unlikely the tribal leadership would have been as successful in finding both the money and the jobs to keep the Stockbridge-Munsee Community afloat. Without the construction of new homes, loans for subsistence farming, and employment on work crews to turn the Cutover into a productive timber resource, tribal reorganization might have remained a dream.

Through the Indian Reorganization Act, Collier promised the Stockbridge-Munsee loans and grants to resettle their lands if they adopted a corporate charter and became a federal corporation.[87] Collier had warned all Native Americans that if they were to succeed in keeping their reservations intact, they would have to organize themselves to compete in the modern world.[88] Similar to federal regulation of tribal elections, the money administered from a "revolving fund" was under the control of the Secretary of the Interior, who had the power to make rules and regulations regarding their dispersal.[89] The total amount of the fund began at $10 million, but Congress pared this down to $2.5 million.[90] Of the various federal aid programs which the Stockbridge-Munsee took advantage of during their first decade of reorganization, only the revolving trust fund was mandated by stipulations of the IRA.

To gain access to the revolving fund, the Stockbridge-Munsee Community adopted a corporate charter on May 21, 1938, by a vote of 94 to 0. The charter's stated purpose was to "further the economic development of the Stockbridge-Munsee Community by conferring certain corporate rights, powers, privileges and immunities." The Stockbridge-Munsee Community became a "body politic and corporate of the United States of America." Membership was limited to enrollment in the Community. All funds flowed from the Interior Department to the Tribal Council, which was given management powers to disperse the money to individuals.[91] The Council established a Community Credit Committee to issue the loans and seek reimbursement.

The Credit Committee also dispensed monies from various grants given to the Community in its early years of tribal reorganization. The purpose of the grants, according to the order of President Franklin Roosevelt extending Emergency Relief Funds to the Native Americans (January 11, 1936), was to create self-help projects to assist in the rehabilitation of the Indians "in stricken, rural, agricultural areas."[92] These rehabilitation grants were extensive. In a period of two and a half years, a total of $27,515 was given to the Stockbridge-Munsee Community.[93]

Most of the loans and grants issued by the Credit Committee were for agricultural purposes and to maintain existing homes. The Community instituted a pay-as-you-go system, and required individuals to pay for plowing services and such essentials as seeds, onion sets, and berry plants. Loans for agricultural purposes rarely exceeded six dollars, since farming was on small plots and of the subsistence variety.[94] Nor was tribal land very productive. In 1938 alone, seventy-three white-owned farms were foreclosed in Shawano County—and those farms were on land of much higher quality than that of the Stockbridge-Munsee.[95]

Funds for housing were in even greater demand. John Collier recognized new homes as one of the tribe's "crying needs." He expected funds from what he called the "Hopkins Organization" to eventually build new homes; but everyone recognized that in order to affect immediate relocation onto the reservation, the structures that survived from logging days would have to do.[96] While these buildings were far better than the chicken coops that some tribal members had been reduced to living in before reorganization, just a few adequate structures existed, enough for only the first families.[97]

Tomah Superintendent Farver proved his mettle by landing a large Works Project Administration (WPA) project for the new Community. In just four years, WPA expended over $80,000 for the construction of over twenty homes and the refurbishing of existing structures. Farver asserted that WPA funds were crucial, "because of the limited amount of money which the Indian Service has been able to secure."[98]

WPA funds also helped provide paid work for members of the Community, but the major employer during the first decade of reorganization was the Emergency Conservation Work, better known as the Civilian Conservation Corps (CCC). By building roads, cutting brush, laying telephone lines, constructing buildings, and repairing existing facilities, the Stockbridge-Munsee men who worked for the CCC earned much-needed cash. Their work improved the general condition of the reservation and increased its value. Probably it also conferred a sense of pride and accomplishment on those who participated. The impact of the CCC cannot be overemphasized.

Like most of the relief programs that assisted the Stockbridge-Munsee, the Civilian Conservation Corps did not initially specify operations involving Indians; it took the efforts of John Collier, working with Henry Wallace, to expand the Corps to include the first Americans.[99] Besides providing temporary relief, and in keeping with his notion of cooperative communities, Collier envisioned the CCC as a vehicle to test his thesis that reservations were excellent places to conduct experiments on erosion prevention, subsistence farming, and the development of community living.[100] The combined forces of the Agriculture and Interior departments proved successful. Congress authorized the introduction of CCC projects on Indian reservations in April of 1933 and ordered an expenditure of $5,875,000 on seventy-two camps within thirty-three reservations.[101]

Modifications within the CCC were necessary because Native Americans were less willing to roam about the country than were the general enrollees. For Indians, age was not restricted to the eighteen-to-twenty-five-year range, although physical fitness was still mandatory. Nor were Indians required to sign up for a fixed period of time, and they were allowed to return home if necessary. Because many Indians were able to live at home and still work for the CCC-ID, their net earnings were higher. These modifications encouraged the Native Americans to stay at home and develop their reservations.[102]

Carl Miller's initial request through the Tomah Agency for CCC project work was rejected because tribal lands remained under the Agriculture Department's control. Tomah Superintendent Christy explained to Miller that he could not request CCC projects on lands over which the Department had no jurisdiction.[103] When the lands finally passed back to the Interior Department in January of 1937, Christy immediately secured a CCC project for the Stockbridge-Munsee Reservation. About 160 Stockbridge-Munsee men were eligible for work. The actual number of those participating in CCC work force at any one time was about forty-five. The age of the workers ranged anywhere from seventeen to sixty-three, with the majority of men in their thirties.[104]

The CCC-ID proved a mixed blessing to the Stockbridge-Munsee. The work provided food and shelter, some cash for needy families, and general improvement of the land. But organization of CCC-ID work in the Community was not controlled by the Tribal Council. While the intent of the CCC-ID was to allow tribal councils a degree of control over the selection and planning of work projects, in the case of the Stockbridge-Munsee actual control rested with the foreman, Kenneth Abert. Abert, a Menominee and member of the Army Reserve, ran the operation like a military post and treated Council plans and ideas for projects with condescension. His overbearing presence was a constant reminder to the Stockbridge-Munsee Community that they were still subject to rules, regulations, and supervision outside of their tribal council.[105] The CCC-ID was no doubt a great help in settling the reservation, but Abert's strict control and abrasive manner tempered much of the appreciation with the feeling that they were on the public dole. "[T]he Indian men," Carl Miller observed, "were given work with wages barely enough for their families to exist upon and they were always made to understand that they were *Relief* Clients."[106]

The Community recognized that the CCC-ID relief project, controlled as it was by an outsider who had insulted the dignity of the leaders, was almost their sole source of income. Without it, tribal members would have had to seek work elsewhere, possibly jeopardizing the future of a community struggling to find itself. The costs and benefits of such a system—which promoted work, yet guaranteed no future—presented a paradox; for while the Council continued to oppose the operation of the CCC-ID because of its lack of control, it also supported the CCC-ID's continuation when Congress threatened it with termination.

John Collier recognized that the end of the Civilian Conservation Corps would create a vacuum. He asked: "After the depression is over and the emergency grants cease, what will happen to the now-working Indian?"[107] Originally the CCC, which began in April, 1933, was destined to cease operations on June 30, 1940 (50 Stat. 319). On August 7, 1939, President Roosevelt approved congressional requests for an extension of the CCC to July 1, 1943.[108] Despite Roosevelt's three-year reprieve, however, the Corps could not survive competition from the new danger the United States was about to confront in the Pacific. Two months before the Japanese attack on Pearl Harbor, the Stockbridge-Munsee Tribal Council sent a letter to Commissioner Collier expressing their anxiety over the possible loss of CCC funds. "Our community is solely dependent upon CCC-ID employment for an existence," it read, and went on to describe the size of their reservation not in physical terms of acreage, timber, or minerals, but in the human element: "We have 50 families here starting new homes, average age of families past 40 years, average family 5 each. These families trying desperately to get new start in life. Should withdrawal of C.C.C.-I.D. activities be permitted, it would take the life blood from our community, leaving us with unfinished cabins, bare rooms and empty cupboards."[109]

Then came the war. By January of 1942, most young Stockbridge-Munsee men had already left the reservation for the armed forces. Despite the depletion of their most able workers, the Tribal Council had many middle-aged men pulling a monthly salary from CCC-ID work and was adamant that the camp remain. In tune with the times, the Council used patriotic phrases as it tried to drum up allies to keep the work alive.[110] The Community stressed that a vital part of the war effort must be the protection of the nation's valuable timber reserves in Wisconsin. In an address to the

Shawano County board of supervisors, Carl Miller warned that during a time of war—total war—the enemy might start numerous small fires which, if uncontrolled, could develop into a "gigantic, rolling, leaping conflagration such as no man has ever seen and no human power could stop."[111]

Despite these rhetorical flourishes and other efforts, the CCC-ID camp at the Stockbridge-Munsee Community closed on June 30, 1942.[112] Kenneth Albert left for the army and Carl Miller took over as a fire guard. Try as they might, the Tribal Council could not convince the powers that be in Washington that the residents of the Stockbridge-Munsee reservation were an integral part of the national defense. The CCC-ID did succeed in providing many of the young men of the tribe a chance to master a trade, and it improved living standards on the reservation. Yet the security it offered was short-lived, and when it closed down there was again no source of employment. World War II served to reemphasize the lack of jobs in the area. Many young members of the Stockbridge-Munsee Community donned uniforms and took their places on battlefields. Others found work on assembly lines in Sturgeon Bay, Green Bay, Milwaukee, Wausau, or even Seattle—but not on the reservation.[113] The elders remained at home to keep alive the Stockbridge-Munsee Community, which was now a corporation without a work force, a tribal council with few to govern.

The tribal reorganization of the Stockbridge-Munsee was the result of four vital forces working together. John Collier and his agents surely played a large role, overseeing the land and acquisition and filing requests for money to fund the various projects that were vital to the Community's early survival. The evidence also suggests that were it not for the political acumen of the tribal leadership, most notably Carl Miller and members of the Business Committee, the single most propitious moment for reorganization presented by the Indian Reorganization Act would have slipped by. The Stockbridge-Munsee people were not "lucky" that they were given, in Carl Miller's words, "another chance." Luck in this instance was simply experience meeting opportunity.

The third factor was one of supreme irony. Only by having their former forests stripped bare—in some cases contributing to the ecological disaster by hiring themselves out as loggers on their old tribal lands—could the Stockbridge-Munsee have qualified for funds under FERA's submarginal land program. That this was the only acquisition program available after IRA money was depleted made the environmental debacle doubly ironic. Once the Stockbridge-Munsee began to move "way back into the brush," they were able to take advantage of other New Deal relief programs such as the Works Progress Administration, Rural Rehabilitation, and the Civilian Conservation Corps.

The fact that such resources were available as a result of and during one of the most severe economic crises in American history is the fourth and final factor in the creation of the Stockbridge-Munsee Community. It is fair to wonder whether, without the Great Depression acting as impetus for the creation of Roosevelt's alphabet agencies, the Community would have reorganized at all. For good leadership, be it Carl Miller's or John Collier's, could go only so far without adequate resources to fulfill the promises made to the people who call themselves Muh-He-Con-Neew.

NOTES

1. The definitive history of the Stockbridge-Munsee has yet to be written. The best single text of their days in Stockbridge, Massachusetts, is Patrick Frazier, *The Mohicans of Stockbridge* (Lincoln, 1992). The following works offer a general but varied account. E. M. Ruttenber, *History of the Indian Tribes of Hudson's River* (Albany, 1871); Electa F. Jones, *Stockbridge, Past and Present; or Records of an Old Mission Station* (Springfield, Massachusetts, 1854); Jedidiah Morse and Jeremy Belknap, *Report on the Oneida, Stockbridge and Brotherton Indians 1796*, in *Indian Notes and Monographs, A Series of Publications Relating to the American Aborigines*, No. 54 (reprinted, New York, 1955); John N. Davidson, *Muh-He-Ka-Ne-Ok: A History of the Stockbridge Nation* (Milwaukee, 1893); Deirdre Almeida, "The Stockbridge Indian in the American Revolution," *Historical Journal of Western Massachusetts*, 5: (Fall, 1975): 34–39; and Philip S. Colee, "The Housatonic-Stockbridge Indians: 1734–1749" (Ph.D. dissertation, University of New York, 1977).

2. Thomas Skinner (Dem., South Carolina) made this comment during debate on the General Allotment Act of 1887. See Wilcomb E. Washburn, *The American Indian and the United States: A Documentary History*, Vol. 3 (New York, 1973), 1849–1850.

3. Stephen Kunitz, "The Social Philosophy of John Collier," *Ethnohistory*, 18 (Summer, 1971): 216–223; Kenneth R. Philp, *John Collier's Crusade for Indian Reform: 1920–1954* (Tucson, 1977), 24–27.

4. U.S. Department of Interior, Office of Indian Affairs, *Commissioner of Indian Affairs, Annual Report for Fiscal Year Ended 30 June 1935*, p. 114; Philp, *John Collier's Crusade*, 3.

5. Briefly, the final bill sought to establish the Native American prerogative of tribal assembly, association, and government; allow and assist in the creation of new and the restoration of old reservations; overturn the 1887 Dawes Act by forbidding the allotment of lands still held by Native Americans in communal ownership; provide a framework and budget for the purchase of lands opened up under the Allotment Act; prevent the sale, gift, or exchange of any lands without the approval of the Secretary of Interior; reorganize the Indian Service to better place Native Americans in positions of influence; and provide a fund of the issuance of grants and loans for educational purposes. See Washburn, *The American Indian and the United States*, 2210–2217.

6. Works on federal Indian policy during the Collier era include: Graham D. Taylor, *The New Deal and American Indian Tribalism: The Administration of the Indian Reorganization Act, 1934–35* (Lincoln, 1980); and Lawrence C. Kelly, "The Indian Reorganization Act: The Dream and the Reality," *Pacific Historical Review*, 44 (August, 1975): 291–312. One book that offers Indian perspectives on the IRA, generated from a 1983 conference, is Kenneth R. Philp, ed., *Indian Self-Rule: First-Hand Accounts of Indian White Relations from Roosevelt to Reagan* (Salt Lake City, 1986). Two relatively objective accounts of the period from Indian Service personnel are S. Lyman Tyler, *A History of Indian Policy* (Washington, D.C., 1973), and Theodore Haas, "The Indian Reorganization Act in Historical Perspective," in William Kelly, ed., *Indian Affairs and the Indian Reorganization Act: The Twenty-Year Record* (Tucson, 1954), 9–25.

7. Jones, *Stockbridge, Past and Present*, 102.

8. Davidson, *Muh-He-Ka-Ne-Ok*, 23. Upon the death of Rev. Miner in 1829, the famed Rev. Cutting Marsh became director of the Stockbridge Mission. See Marion J. Mochon, "Stockbridge-Munsee Cultural Adaptation: Assimilated Indians," *Proceedings of the American Philosophical Society*, 112 (June, 1968): 201–202.

9. U.S. Congress, House of Representatives, *An Investigation of the Bureau of Indian Affairs*, House Rept., 28 Cong., 2 sess. (1953), 612.

10. Davidson, *Muh-He-Ka-Ne-Ok*, 38–39.

11. Otis S. Delos, *The Dawes Act and the Allotment of Indian Lands* (Norman, 1973), 4.

12. Ibid., 40.

13. Davidson, *Muh-He-Ka-Ne-Ok*, 40.

14. Ibid.

15. U.S. Congress, House, *An Investigation of the Bureau of Indian Affairs* (1953), 989.

16. "To the Hon. the Senate and House of Representative, in Congress convened, the petition of the undersigned, the Chiefs, Head-men and Warriors of the Stockbridge Tribe of Indians, respectfully

showeth" (Calumet City, Wisconsin: Stockbridge, 1865), 2–3, Pamphlet, State Historical Society of Wisconsin.

17. U.S. Congress, House, *An Investigation of the Bureau of Indian Affairs* (1953), 990. As America advanced westward, allotment proved more than simply a method of "helping Indians to assimilate." It was also a tool for opening vast tracts of Indian land to advancing waves of settlers and eastern companies. "Surplus" Indian lands were to be freed for white American consumption, placating the new railroad, timber, and mining consortiums and relieving the overcrowded eastern cities through the gift of Indian territory. The Stockbridge-Munsee labeled the plan "principally an instrument whereby the Stockbridge Indians were deprived of their former holdings of land," a policy which "has wrought great disaster, hardship and suffering upon the Stockbridge Tribe of Indians as a whole and as individuals." See "FSA History," in the Arvid E. Miller, Sr., Papers, p. 1, Stockbridge-Munsee Historical Library, Stockbridge-Munsee Reservation, Shawano County (hereinafter cited as SMHL).

18. Congress actually began to whittle away at the Stockbridge-Munsee's Shawano County lands in 1871 (16 Stat. 404–407). Three more Acts followed: March 2, 1895 (28 Stat. 894, c. 188); April 21, 1904 (33 State. 210, c. 1402); and June 21, 1906 (34 Stat. 356, c.3504). See U.S. Congress, House, *An Investigation of the Bureau of Indian Affairs* (1953), 991. See also Kenneth L. Payton to Leonard Miller, Jr., April 5, 1971, 360. Land Acquisition, General, Stockbridge Reservation, Ashland, Wisconsin, Great Lakes Agency, Bureau of Indian Affairs, Department of Interior (hereinafter cited as BIA, GLA).

19. The problems of the Stockbridge-Munsee typified the troubled policy of the General Allotment Act. Heralded at the 1889 Lake Mohonk conference as a tribe which had made great strides in imitating the western pioneers, the Stockbridge-Munsee nonetheless did not learn fast enough the rudiments of real estate to save their lands from marauding speculators and timber barons. See Lake Mohonk Conference on the Indian Report, *1889 Proceedings of the 7th Annual Meeting of the Lake Mohonk Conference of Friends of the Indian* (Clearwater, [Florida?], 1979), p. 82, card 9. A good scholarly description of the inheritance trap of allotment is provided by Kirke Kickingbird and Karen Ducheneaux in *One Hundred Million Acres* (New York, 1973), 31.

20. Interview with Bernice Miller Pigeon, Stockbridge-Munsee Community, Wisconsin, July 7, 1982.

21. Ibid.; U.S. Department of Interior, United States Indian Service, *Project Proposal for Stockbridge Indian Report* (1934), p. 3, SMHL.

22. 1929 Annual Report, Keshena Agency, R. W. Beyer, Superintendents' Annual Narrative and Statistical Reports from Field Jurisdictions of the Bureau of Indian Affairs, 1907–1938, National Archives, Record Group 75 (hereinafter cited NA, RG 75), M1011, p. 2.

23. "FSA History," Arvid E. Miller, Sr. Papers, p. 1, SMHL.

24. U.S. Department of Interior, United States Indian Service, *Project Proposal* (1934), p. 3.

25. Mochon, "Stockbridge-Munsee Cultural Adaptation," 206.

26. "Chief Carl Miller, A Nostalgic Look at a Leader of His People," *Quin'a Month'a*, 3 (1976): 3, SMHL.

27. "Tribal Reorganization," Arvid E. Miller, Sr., Papers, Book A, SMHL.

28. John Collier, "The Genesis and Philosophy of Indian Reorganization Act Policies," in *Indian Affairs and the Indian Reorganization Act*, 4–5; Tyler, *A History of Indian Policy*, 119–124; Taylor, *The New Deal and American Indian Tribalism*, 15.

29. 1929, 1930, 1931 Annual Reports, Keshena Agency, R. W. Beyer, Superintendents' Annual Narrative and Statistical Reports from Field Jurisdictions of the Bureau of Indian Affairs, 1907–1938, M1011, NA, RG 75.

30. E. J. Skidmore (acting Assistant to the Commissioner) to the Secretary of Interior, December 29, 1936, Tomah Decimal File, 1926–1950, Box 40, NA-GL, RG 75.

31. 1930 Annual Report, Keshena Agency, M1011, NA, RG 75, Section 3, p. 4.

32. Fredenberg obituary, in U.S. Department of Interior, Office of Indian Affairs, "Indians at Work" (June, 1939), 6–8. Fredenberg would prove to be both an excellent representative of Collier's commitment to placing Indians in more important positions in the BIA and a diligent proponent of Stockbridge-Munsee reorganization. He served as Superintendent of Keshena until 1940 when he was transferred to the Grande Ronde-Siletz Agency in Oregon. Fredenberg was forty-six when he died of a heart attack in September, 1944.

33. "On the New Reservation," Elmer L. Davids, Sr., Papers, Bosie's B.S. Book, SMHL.

34. Carl Miller to John Collier, January 2, 1934, Carlton Leo Miller Papers, File H, SMHL.

35. John Collier to Carl Miller, 6 January 1934, Carlton Leo Miller Papers. File H, SMHL.

36. U.S. Indian Service, *Project Proposal* (1934), exhibits 12, 13, and 15.

37. Interview with Bernice Miller Pigeon, July 7, 1982; "A Memorial Honoring Carl L. Miller," *Quin'a Month'a*, 5:2 (March, 1976), SMHL.

38. Speech presented at Hayward, Wisconsin, April 23–24, 1934, in *The John Collier Papers, 1922–1968* (microform, Stanford, North Carolina), reel 30, 0854–55, pp. 2–3.

39. Ibid., 0885, p. 65.

40. Diary, April 24, 1934, Carlton Leo Miller Papers, SMHL.

41. The debate over the merits of the IRA and the final Act which emerged from Congress, however, made it clear that the preservation of a Native American heritage was not a congressional priority. Evidence for this comes from the exclusion of key provisions in the final bill: the statement in Title II that emphasized the desire to promote the preservation and enhancement of Indian culture was deleted and the Indian Claims Commission was eliminated. Collier had hoped to use the Commission to replace the antiquated system operated by the Indian Service. There were no attorneys and no judges, and appeals could only go the Secretary of the Interior. See Kelly, "The Indian Reorganization Act," 297; Philp, *Collier's Crusade*, 143.

42. Tribal Council Minutes File, December 1934, SMHL: Theodore Haas, *Ten Years of Tribal Government Under I.R.A.*, Tribal Relations Pamphlet No. 1 (Chicago: Haskell Institute, 1947), 3.

43. Washburn, *The American Indian and the United States*, 2212.

44. Lawrence C. Kelly, "The Indian Reorganization Act: The Dream and the Reality," *Pacific Historical Review*, 44 (August, 1975): 307–308. The Board further noted (p. 307) that if Native Americans were ever to achieve even a modest living on the level of rural white folk, they would need an additional 15,900,000 acres at a cost of $69 million.

45. Philp, *Collier's Crusade*, 175–176. Ironically, when Collier's actions proved successful, garnering almost $45 million from other agencies, this further raised the ire of the congressmen, who then voted against any additional funds for the IRA, thus forcing Collier to continue his extra-agency activities. See Kelly, "The Indian Reorganization Act," 306.

46. Harold Gross, "Memorandum on Which the National Council of Indians Opportunity Proposal Is Based," p. 1, Farm Security Administration Papers, SMHL.

47. Paul W. Gates, *History of Public Land Law Development* (Washington, D.C.: Public Land Law Review Commission, 1968), 599.

48. Harry Hopkins to State ERA's, memoranda, July 17, 1933, Farm Security Administration Papers, SMHL.

49. Kickingbird and Ducheneaux, *One Hundred Million Acres*, 66.

50. Gross, "Memorandum," 1.

51. John Collier to William Beyer, Circular, May 15, 1934, Submarginal Land, BIA, GLA, pp. 3–4.

52. Gross, "Memorandum," p. 3.

53. John Collier to William Beyer, Circulars, May 15, 1934, Submarginal Land, BIA, GLA, pp. 4–5.

54. William Beyer to John Collier, June 11, 1934, "Project Proposal for Stockbridge Indian Project," ex. no. 6.

55. Elmer L. Davids, Sr., Papers, P. D5–9, SMHL.

56. Interview with Elmer Church, Stockbridge-Munsee Community, Wisconsin, April 25, 1984.

57. Lucile Kane, "Settling the Wisconsin Cutovers," *Wisconsin Magazine of History*, 40 (Winter, 1956–1957): 97.

58. U.S. Department of Agriculture, Soil Conservation Service, *Soil Survey of Shawano County, Wisconsin* (Washington, D.C., 1982), 21–53.

59. "Project Proposal for Stockbridge Indian Project," SMHL, p. 5.

60. E. J. Skidmore (Acting Assistant to the Commissioner) to the Secretary of Interior, December 29, 1936, Tomah Decimal File, 1926–1950, Box 40, NA, GL RG 75.

61. John Collier to Frank Christy, August 2, 1935, Land Acquisition, General, Stockbridge Reservation; J. Stewart to Ralph Fredenberg, February 4, 1935, Tract No. 1–Brooks and Ross; Frank Christy to John Collier, August 8, 1935, Land Acquisition, General, Stockbridge Reservation; Brooks and Ross to Ralph Fredenberg, May 29, 1935, Brooks and Ross (New), BIA, GLA.

62. "Project Proposal for Stockbridge Indian Project," SMHL, p. 4.

63. James J. Lorence and Howard Klueter, *Woodlot and Ballot Box: Marathon County in the Twentieth Century* (Stevens Point, Wisconsin, 1977), 30–31; Louis Marchetti, *History of Marathon County Wisconsin and Representative Citizens* (Chicago, 1913), 522.

64. Lorence and Klueter, *Woodlot and Ballot Box*, 127.

65. The first meeting was held at the office of Keshena Superintendent William Beyer on June 11, 1934. Present were Mathew McCullough, C. W. Cone, and Herman Furhmen of Brooks and Ross; Carl Miller and Adrian Yoccum of the Stockbridge-Munsee Business Committee; and Elrod Putnam, assessor for the Township of Red Springs, but also a Stockbridge Indian. See William Beyer to John Collier, June 11, 1934, "Project Proposal for Stockbridge Indian Project," SMHL, ex. 6, p. 1.

66. Mathew McCullough to Ralph Fredenberg, May 29, 1935, Brooks and Ross (New), BIA, GLA.

67. J. M. Stewart to J. W. Balmer, January 8, 1935, Land Acquisition, General, Stockbridge Reservation, BIA, GLA.

68. James G. Maddox, "Farm Security Administration" (Ph.D. dissertation, Harvard University, 1950), 23.

69. Gross, "Memorandum," p. 3.

70. William E. Leuchtenburg, *Franklin D. Roosevelt and the New Deal* (New York, 1963), 140.

71. Philp, *Collier's Crusade*, 122.

72. Kickingbird and Ducheneaux, *One Hundred Million Acres*, 70; Gross, "Memorandum," ex. 11, p. 3.

73. "Farm Security History," Arvid E. Miller, Sr., Papers, SMHL, p. 2.

74. Gross, "Memorandum," pp. 7–9.

75. Kickingbird and Ducheneaux, *One Hundred Million Acres*, 57.

76. Gross, "Memorandum," pp. 13–15.

77. Peru Farver to Harry Chicks, June 22, 1938, Arvid E. Miller, Sr., Papers, SMHL, Book A.

78. "United States Department of Agriculture; Farm Security Administration Disclaimer," December 14, 1937, Farm Security Administration Papers, SMHL.

79. "Carl Miller," People File, SMHL.

80. "Personal Diary," September 18, 1936, Carlton Leo Miller Papers, File H, SMHL.

81. Interview with Bernice Miller Pigeon, Stockbridge-Munsee Community, Wisconsin, July 7, 1982.

82. "Personal Diary," September 18, 1936, Carlton Leo Miller Papers, SMHL.

83. "Stockbridge-Munsee: Report to I.R.A. and Resettlement Lands," March 6, 1939, 360/Land Acquisition, General, Stockbridge Reservation, BIA, GLA, p. 6.

84. Arvid E. Miller, Sr., Papers, Book A, SMHL.

85. Carlton Leo Miller Papers, File H, SMHL.

86. Arvid E. Miller, Sr., Papers, Book A, SMHL; Washburn, *The American Indian and the United States*, 2216; Philp, *Collier's Crusade*, 145; Donald Parman, "The Indian and the Civilian Conservation Corps," in Norris Hundley, ed., *The American Indian: Essays from the Pacific Historical Review* (Santa Barbara, 1974), 128.

87. Washburn, *The American Indian and the United States*, 2213.

88. Philp, *Collier's Crusade*, 145; Donald Parman, "The Indian and the Civilian Conservation Corps," in Hundley, ed., *The American Indian*, 128.

89. Washburn, *The American Indian and the United States*, 2213.

90. U.S. Department of Interior, Office of Indian Affairs, "Indians at Work" (June, 1939), 6–8.

91. "Corporate Charter," General Files, p. 1, SMHL.

92. Franklin Roosevelt to Federal Emergency Relief Administration, Letter no. 1323, January 11, 1936, Arvid E. Miller, Sr., Papers, 1934–1939, SMHL.

93. Peru Farver to Arvid Miller, March 16, 1940, Arvid E. Miller, Sr., Papers, 1934–1939, SMHL.

94. Loans, General Files, SMHL.

95. "Stockbridge-Munsee: Report on I.R.A. and Resettlement Lands," March 6, 1939, 360/Land Acquisition, General, Stockbridge Reservation, BIA, GLA, p. 3.

96. John Collier to Frank Christy, August 2, 1935, 360, Land Acquisition, General, Stockbridge Reservation, BIA, GLA.

97. *Project Proposal for Stockbridge Indian Project*, p. 3, SMHL; interview with Bernice Miller Pigeon, Stockbridge-Munsee Community, Wisconsin, July 7, 1982.

98. Peru Farver to Mark Muth (District Director of WPA in Green Bay), October 28, 1937, Tomah Agency Decimal File, Box I. Miscellaneous Correspondence, 1937–1938, NA, GL. RG 75: Farver to Xavier Vigeant (Director of Rural Rehabilitation), September 8, 1939, Tomah Agency Decimal File, Box 3. Miscellaneous Correspondence, 1939–1940, NA, GL, RG 75.

99. Philp, *Collier's Crusade*, 187.

100. Perry H. Merrill, *Roosevelt's Forest Army: A History of the Civilian Conservation Corps, 1933–1942* (Montpelier, Vermont, 1984), 12.

101. Calvin W. Gower, "The C. C. C. Indian Division: Aid for Depressed Americans, 1933–1942," *Minnesota History*, 43 (Spring 1972): 6.

102. U.S. Department of Interior, Civilian Conservation Corps, *Annual Report of the Director of the Civilian Conservation Corps for the Fiscal Year Ended 30 June 1939*, pp. 25–26; John A. Almond, *The Civilian Conservation Corps, 1933–1942: A New Deal Case Study* (Durham, 1967), 33.

103. Frank Christy to Carl Miller, May 13, 1936, Land Acquisition, General, Stockbridge Reservation, BIA, GLA.

104. General File, "C.C.C.-I.D.," SMHL; Gower, "The C.C.C. Indian Division," 6.

105. Gower, in "The C.C.C. Indian Division," argues (p. 4) that the CCC-ID did more to encourage Indian self-administration than frustrate it. Salmond, *The Civilian Conservation Corps, 1933–1942*, also lauds the CCC for allowing participation of tribal councils in preparing work plans (p. 33). The Stockbridge-Munsee clash with Kenneth Abert suggests that a reappraisal of the value of CCC-ID projects for encouraging self-rule among participating Indians might be in order.

106. "Our Plan," Carlton Leo Miller Papers, SMHL.

107. S. Lyman Tyler, *Indian Affairs: A Study of the Changes in Policy of the United States toward Indians* (Provo, Utah, 1964), 77.

108. "C.C.C.-I.D. Circular," December 1, 1939, General Files, CCC-ID, SMHL.

109. "Night Letter: Tribal Council to John Collier," September 9, 1941, General Files, CCC-ID, SMHL.

110. Tribal Council to Robert La Follette, Jr., January 8, 1942, General Files, CCC-ID. See also Assistant Secretary William Zimmerman's correspondence with Senator La Follette, September 22, 1941, General Files, CCC-ID, SMHL.

111. Carl Miller to Shawano County Board of Supervisors (no date), General Files, CCC-ID, SMHL.

112. U.S. Department of Agriculture, Forest Service, green notebook, Carlton Leo Miller Papers, SMHL.

113. Interview with Lucille Bowman Miller, Stockbridge-Munsee Community, Wisconsin, August 27, 1983.

15

As John Savagian noted, during the 1930s federal officials publicly supported tribal culture and tribal communities for the first time in modern American history. The Indian Reorganization Act created a mechanism by which Native groups such as the Stockbridge-Munsees could form themselves into legal entities that received federal dollars and exercised a measure of self-government. But federal efforts did not stop there. During John Collier's tenure, the Bureau of Indian Affairs also created education programs that were sensitive to traditional culture, lobbied Congress to create the American Indian Arts and Crafts Board to encourage tribal arts, and supported the compilation of a *Handbook of Federal Indian Law* to assist Native groups wishing to defend their interests in court. After nearly 150 years of opposition to tribal culture, the United States appeared to be changing sides.

Support for tribal cultures conveyed two messages to the American public. First, federal officials declared that Native Americans had a right to their distinct identities. No longer cast as enemies of the state, Indians came to be seen as an ethnic group that, while part of a unique American tradition, was comparable to the other racial and ethnic groups that made up the American mosaic. Second, support for tribal culture suggested that Indian people could find a home in modern America; they were no longer defined as opponents of progress with no claim on national institutions or ideals. Somewhat ironically, then, support for the Indian Reorganization Act often led Native Americans to assert their legal and political claims with renewed enthusiasm. American political leaders now spoke for a legitimate interest group as well as a cultural tradition.

It was in this atmosphere of renewed cultural awareness and political activism that the Alaskan native struggle against segregation and discrimination took place. As Terrence Cole explains, white Alaskans, despite their self-proclaimed identity as members of an egalitarian, frontier community, had systematically discriminated against Native people since the beginning of American occupation in the nineteenth century. Responding to local whites, Congress had created segregated schools in Alaska Territory in 1905. This conformed to Alaskan custom; many stores, theaters, and other public establishments had long refused to admit or serve Natives. Inuits and Indians, led by the Alaskan Native Brotherhood and its partner organization the Native Sisterhood, protested this treatment. But it was not until 1939—when Franklin Roosevelt appointed Ernest Gruening, a liberal Democrat, territorial governor—that Native opposition found official support. Cole's article describes how Gruening and Native leaders worked to change the climate of opinion, and how the influx of new people and new ideas that accompanied the outbreak of World War II brought the issue to center stage. In 1944, a Native woman of mixed ancestry, out on a date with a G.I., refused to move from the "Whites Only" section of the local movie theater and was arrested. The uproar surrounding this incident eventually led to the passage of an anti-discrimination bill in the territorial legislature.

Cole's essay provides a vivid case study of the way Native Americans, acting both as U.S. citizens and as members of an aggrieved group, managed to make their case before a wider public in the 1930s and 1940s. Like the Iroquois leaders treated by Sidney Harring and the Stockbridge-Munsees John Savagian chronicled, Alaskan natives were prepared to take advantage of political changes in the larger American society and to form powerful alliances with sympathetic whites. Yet the Alaska case also illustrates the uphill battle Indians had to wage. While discrimination in public accommodations was outlawed in 1945, the territory's segregated school system remained until after Alaska achieved statehood in 1958.

Jim Crow in Alaska: The Passage of the Alaska Equal Rights Act of 1945

Terrence M. Cole

AMERICANS HAVE LONG BELIEVED THAT the western frontier offered more freedom, justice, and equality than the overcrowded, class-conscious cities of the East. This familiar theme of an egalitarian western society expressed by Frederick Jackson Turner and his followers has been sounded repeatedly in American history and literature. Though the Turner Thesis may no longer be fashionable among professional historians who advocate the "new western history," the significance of the frontier in modern popular culture and politics of Alaska has never dimmed. No matter what political philosophers espouse, most residents of the "Last Frontier" share the conviction that Alaska's geographical isolation has made the northernmost state vastly different from the other forty-nine in the Union. Modern Alaskans prefer to think that their state offers greater freedom and opportunity than the more densely settled "Lower 48," and that Alaska is relatively free from the worst ills of the outside world, including poverty, pollution, racism, and crime. A popular bumper sticker often seen in Alaska claims, "We don't give a damn how they do it Outside."[1]

Modern Alaskans are therefore surprised and shocked to learn that before World War II racial segregation and Jim Crow policies toward Alaska Natives were standard practice throughout much of Alaska. So few blacks lived in the territory, especially before World War II, there was little organized discrimination against them. Natives, however, actually outnumbered the permanent white population of Alaska, and it was not until the late 1930s that whites became the permanent majority. In those pre-war years, pioneer Alaskans often refused Natives the right to vote, prayed every Sunday in segregated churches, and sent their children to segregated schools.[2]

Some Alaskans may have been blind to the inequities of their own society, but the unfair treatment of Natives was plainly evident to outsiders who could afford to be more truthful. During World War II, a visiting war correspondent noted in 1943 that the social position of Indians and Eskimos in Alaska "is equivalent to that of a Negro in Georgia or Mississippi."[3]

The Second World War laid the foundation for the great advances in racial equality that occurred in America during the 1950s and 1960s. As C. Vann Woodward once explained, U.S. pronouncements against the Nazis and Hitler's hated racist doctrines highlighted the "inconsistency" between "American practice at home and propaganda abroad."[4] In Alaska, as elsewhere in the American West,

SOURCE: *Western Historical Quarterly*, v. 23 (November 1992), pp. 429–449.

World War II thoroughly transformed virtually every aspect of life in the territory. Among the sweeping social, economic, and political changes that the war brought to the North, none was perhaps more painful than the successful battle in the 1940s to outlaw racial segregation in Alaska.

Eleven years before Rosa Parks refused to give up her seat on a bus in Montgomery, Alabama, a similar scene took place in Nome, Alaska. Alberta Schenck, a young half-Eskimo woman, was arrested in Nome in 1944 for daring to sit in the "white only" section of the local theater. Schenck's one-woman protest in Nome, and the fight against segregation across Alaska in the 1940s by crusaders such as Governor Ernest Gruening, the Native Rights advocates Roy and Elizabeth Peratrovich, and the other Tlingit leaders of the Alaska Native Brotherhood and Sisterhood, illustrate that Jim Crow was a scourge to Alaska as well as to Alabama. The majority of white residents in pre-war Alaska took public discrimination against Natives for granted. Scars from such discrimination were largely invisible to those who did not have to suffer it. This hidden plague of prejudice was especially hard to cure because so many whites chose to believe it never existed. The early years of American control of Alaska in the late nineteenth century coincided with the peak of the Indian wars in the western states and the gradual legal entrenchment of segregation and white supremacy in the southern states. In 1896, the same year as the Klondike gold strike, the U.S. Supreme Court issued its landmark decision in *Plessy v. Ferguson*, which formally approved segregation as the law of the land with the "separate but equal" rule.

The general American attitude toward Native Alaskans, as with blacks in the South, was reflected in a persistent pattern of discrimination. The Presbyterian missionary, trader, and territorial governor John G. Brady, according to his biographer Ted C. Hinckley, preferred to refer to Alaskan Indians as Natives or "Alaskans," because "for too many whites *Indian* was synonymous with *nigger*."[5] Hinckley explains that Brady ran a general store in Sitka in the 1880s but quit the business when his partner insisted on putting two separate entrances with completely separate departments for Natives and whites "so that tourists would no longer be obliged to rub elbows with smelly, lamp black-smeared Tlingits."[6]

The situation at Brady's store in Sitka was not unique. Numerous bars, restaurants, and hotels in various Alaskan communities posted permanent signs stating "No Natives Allowed," while movie theaters habitually restricted Natives to seats in the balcony with signs such as "For Natives Only."[7] Native residents who migrated to white mining and fishing communities invariably settled in Indian ghettos on the outskirts of town. There were no legal prohibitions against Natives settling wherever they chose in Alaska, but economic, social, and cultural reality dictated that Natives live apart from whites. By both law and custom, however, Alaskan children attended segregated schools. As elsewhere, the deep feelings of parents for their children made the schools in Alaska a flash point for racial strife.

Originally, government officials and missionaries hoped to create a school system in Alaska "without reference to race."[8] In practice, however, whites in Alaska's major communities did not want their youngsters to be educated with Native children, and separate schoolrooms for whites and Natives were the rule. This informal "dual system" of education became law with the passage of the Nelson Act in 1905, which fractured Alaska's educational system into two separate and supposedly equal parts. The Nelson Act gave the responsibility to the territorial governor and local communities to fund fully the education of white children and children of "mixed blood who live a civilized life," while the costs of educating Indian and Eskimo children remained a federal burden.[9]

Some whites opposed the entrance of any "half breeds" into white territorial schools. Furthermore, the courts favored a narrow and highly arbitrary definition of what constituted a civilized person. In a test case brought in Sitka in 1908, the federal district court ruled a mixed-blood child ineligible to attend the Sitka public school because the child's stepfather did not lead a "civilized type of life." Apparently, only those who stopped speaking Native languages, eating Native foods, practicing Native religions, and associating with other Natives, and started speaking English, wearing blue jeans, eating canned food, living in a frame house, and working for wages, could be considered "civilized."[10] And only a Native who had come close to this interpretation of "civilized life" by abandoning his own culture could become an American citizen, since Native Americans throughout the United States were not granted universal citizenship until 1924.

The quest for Native citizenship and equality with whites inspired the establishment in 1912 of the Alaska Native Brotherhood (ANB), an association that evolved into the first significant Native political organization in Alaska. The mission-trained Native leaders of the ANB patterned their goals on the teachings of the missionary schoolteachers, from whom they had learned that Christianity and complete acculturation were the key to both heaven and the American dream. Anything less would doom Native people to certain extinction. The ANB, whose official song was "Onward, Christian Soldiers," and whose official lapel pin was a prospector's gold pan, supported three major initiatives: citizenship for Natives, better education for Native children, and abolition of "uncivilized" Native customs.[11]

In the 1920s, under the leadership of William and Louis Paul, the ANB became a highly effective political machine. William Paul, a skilled Tlingit attorney, successfully battled in the courts for the Natives' right to vote, and he created a Native voting block that held the balance of power in Southeastern Alaska. William Paul himself became the first Native to run for and win a seat in the territorial legislature in 1924, the year that all Native Americans were granted U.S. citizenship. Fear of Paul's political machine and his alleged manipulation of the many Natives who could not read (like a big-city ward boss, he distributed cardboard cutouts to his followers to enable illiterate voters to make their Xs in the right places on the ballot) helped spur passage of the 1925 Alaskan literacy law designed to limit Native voting.[12]

Some white residents responded with anger to the increasing signs of Native political power. A 1926 editorial in the *Fairbanks Daily News-Miner* under the headline "Alaska–A WHITE Man's Country" expressed the fears of many when it charged that Indians were threatening to take control of Alaska. At the time, Alaska's economy was still reeling from the prolonged slump following World War I in its basic industries of mining and fishing, and the exodus of the white population as the economy declined actually left Natives in the majority. "NOT WITHSTANDING THE FACT THAT THE INDIANS OUTNUMBER US," the *News-Miner* claimed, "THIS IS A WHITE MAN'S COUNTRY, and it must remain such." The newspaper described the disaster that had overtaken Sitka when the Indians, whom the paper claimed were people of a "lower order of intelligence," of whom ninety percent could not read, write, or speak English, began to vote with stencils. "The result is that today Sitka has a city council controlled by the Indians," the editorial complained. "It has a half-breed Mayor, an Indian Chief of Police, who can and does put white people in jail—and no one can be so obnoxious as an Indian with a little authority."[13]

High on the ANB's list of political priorities was the reform of the Native educational system. The ANB targeted the dual system of education as a cruel hoax on those who had abandoned their own traditions, only to be rejected by the white culture they had tried to embrace. The Native schools stressed rudimentary education, primarily teaching English and vocational training, while the white schools, in contrast, generally had "a high percentage of high school graduates who continue education in institutions of higher learning."[14] In the larger communities of southeastern Alaska, such as Wrangell, Ketchikan, Juneau, and Sitka, Native children were generally barred from the local public schools and forced to attend the federal Indian schools. Paul nearly succeeded in 1921 in convincing the bureau of education to close the Indian school at Wrangell, in order to forcibly integrate education in the community.[15]

After two Native girls were expelled from the Ketchikan public school in 1929 and ordered to attend the Native school in nearby Saxman, William Paul served as the attorney in a suit against the school board. The case inflamed opinions on both sides of the issue. The tone of one Juneau newspaper editorial headlined "Color Line in Schools" gives an indication of the racial passions that had been stirred. The editorial complained that "breeds" were doomed to remain "social pariahs" because they were clearly inferior and made a "pathetic spectacle" when forced to associate with white children. In the federal schools, the editorial continued, half-breed and Indian children "can grow to manhood and womanhood without that inferiority complex which is bound to be theirs if they are permitted in the white schools."[16]

Despite the newspaper's professed concern for the feelings of Native children, the court reaffirmed the right of youngsters of mixed blood to attend the school of their choice. It was a landmark decision. From that time forward, one authority claims, Indian children began to attend schools regularly throughout Southeast Alaska.[17] But restrictive policies nevertheless remained in force. In 1939, Charles Hawkesworth, a senior official in the Indian service, explained to a U.S. Senate subcommittee in Juneau that some years earlier the local school board had decided that only Indian boys and girls above the fifth grade "would be privileged to come to the city schools." Hawkesworth said he also knew of a case in Valdez where an eighth-grade Native girl "wanted to attend high school, but the school board didn't see fit to take her."[18]

School segregation remained one of the core problems of Alaska's racial dilemma. But race discrimination in other public places, such as restaurants, theaters, playgrounds, and swimming pools, also emerged as a battleground in the 1930s and

1940s. When a grand officer of the ANB was told to sit in the Native-only section in a Juneau movie theater in 1929, he walked out and vowed never again to suffer such an insult. At a meeting of the executive council, the ANB agreed to stage a boycott of the offending theater, not because its policies were any worse than other theaters' in town, but because it had a chain of theaters throughout southeastern Alaska and appeared to be more vulnerable to a boycott. In conjunction with the theater boycott, the ANB also recommended that its members refuse to patronize any establishment that discriminated against Natives. The action proved effective throughout much of southeastern Alaska. Within a month the "No Natives" signs at the theater and other businesses began to come down. As Philip Drucker's history of the ANB explains, "Apparently many white businessmen became aware for the first time of the strength and effectiveness of the Brotherhood."[19]

Though the ANB succeeded in forcing some white businessmen in southeastern Alaska to learn to value Native patronage, there were still glaring examples of blatant discrimination against Natives in the region and throughout Alaska in 1939, when Franklin D. Roosevelt appointed a crusading New Deal Democrat named Ernest Gruening governor of the territory. Gruening was shocked by the signs he saw excluding Natives from public facilities. The new governor met few white Alaskans who seemed to share his sense of outrage. "I found relatively little encouragement . . . from Alaskans with whom I discussed the matter," Gruening later wrote. "It was, they said, 'the custom of the country.' When I proposed to some that these discriminations be forbidden by legislation, I was told that it would stand little chance of enactment by the Territorial Legislature."[20]

On his first visit to Alaska, Gruening said he had been haunted by a sign that hung in Anchorage's leading restaurant, the Anchorage Grill on Fourth Avenue, which said, "We Do Not Cater to Native and Filipino Trade." In 1940, he returned to have a chat with the owner, George Grames, a naturalized American from Greece. In his memoirs, *Many Battles*, Gruening described how he rebuked Grames for the sign and asked him how he would like to see a sign that read "We Do Not Cater to Greeks." Gruening wrote, "I then gave George a pep talk about the meaning of America. He went over and removed the sign. 'It will never be up again,' he said."[21]

In Alaska, as in many other American communities, World War II demonstrated the contradictions between the nation's fight for freedom overseas and its denial of equal opportunities at home. On 30 December 1941, about three weeks after Pearl Harbor, Elizabeth Peratrovich, the grand vice-president of the Alaska Native Sisterhood, and her husband, Roy Peratrovich, the grand president of the Alaska Native Brotherhood, sent an angry letter to Governor Gruening complaining about the "No Natives Allowed" sign over the door of the Douglas Inn, across Gastineau Channel from Juneau. They complained that Natives in Alaska were being treated like Jews in Germany and challenged the hypocrisy of such prejudice. The Peratrovichs wrote that, especially because of "the present emergency, when unity is being stressed," wasn't such a sign "very UnAmerican?" "In the present emergency," their angry letter continued, "our native boys are being called to defend our beloved country, just as the White boys. There is no distinction being made there but yet when we try to patronize some business establishments we are told in most cases that natives are not allowed." The Peratrovichs said they appealed to Gruening because "we know you have the interest of the native people at heart and we are asking that you use your influence to eliminate this discrimination, not only in Juneau or Douglas, but in the whole Territory."[22]

In fact, Gruening had already taken action. He had previously asked both the mayor of Anchorage and the mayor of Douglas to use their influence to have any signs in their communities "indicating discrimination between natives and whites removed."[23] The Governor had also personally asked the owner of the Douglas Inn, John Marin, an immigrant from Italy whose real name was Martini, to remove his offensive sign. Marin claimed he kept the sign up because "I can't have a bunch of dirty, drunken natives in my place." After the war started and the Peratrovichs made their appeal, Gruening went back to talk to Marin again. The governor lectured the hotel owner about the U.S. fight against Nazis and fascists who believed they were a "master race." "The United States is opposed to that idea," Gruening said, "and all that goes with it. So I urge you to paint out that sign."[24]

When Marin still refused to remove the sign from the Douglas Inn, Gruening determined that legislation specifically outlawing such practices was the only answer. In July 1942, the governor informed Guy J. Swope, director of the Division of Territories and Island Possessions, about the situation and asked for the opinion of the solicitor's office on preparing "a suitable bill for introduction into the next Territorial Legislature." The war provided a strong rationale for legislative action. Signs forbidding Natives from entering a public establishment, the governor wrote, were not only offensive, but "are in my judgement distinctly destructive of morale and furnish . . . a psychological impediment to the war effort. They are in effect a replica of Hitlerist policies and cannot be justified." Despite his patriotic appeal, Gruening warned that a fight could be expected. "It should be stated that this prejudice reflects the views of a good many old time Alaskans but that does not alter the fact that such discrimination is inexcusable and disgraceful."[25]

Unfortunately, the most powerful person in Alaska during World War II, General Simon Bolivar Buckner, Jr., the commanding officer of the Alaska Defense Command, demonstrated an intense prejudice against Alaska Natives. Son of the famous Confederate general of the same name, who surrendered to U.S. Grant at Fort Donelson in 1862, General Buckner held racial views in the 1940s that were little different from those of any rabid Southerner during the Civil War.[26] Apparently on Buckner's orders (though he denied it), Alaskan military posts issued regulations prohibiting soldiers from fraternizing with Native women, ostensibly to protect virtue and to stop the spread of venereal disease among the troops. To ensure the separation of whites and Natives, the army encouraged soldiers to patronize restaurants, stores, and hotels that denied access to Natives. Military officials actually placed off limits to military personnel some establishments that welcomed all races, simply because they did not discriminate against Natives.

Roy Peratrovich of the ANB protested bitterly to the congressional delegate, Tony Dimond, and Governor Gruening against the army's discriminatory policies.

"The matter of race discrimination is getting rather out of hand in Alaska," Peratrovich wrote in the spring of 1943. "Before the present war, it was the civilians that discriminated against the Indians. Now it is the civilians and the soldiers." He especially resented the rules that prohibited Indian girls, even those whose brothers were in the army, from becoming members of the USO. "Sometimes I wonder," Peratrovich wrote, "if we really are fighting for democracy."[27]

When Gruening argued against the army's policies of racial segregation in Alaska, Buckner angrily replied: "I can think of no better way to exterminate the native tribes than to encourage their women to associate with unmarried white men, far from home and from white women." If Indians wanted total equality with whites, he charged, then all government programs "giving to the native tribes special hunting, trapping and other privileges denied to white men" should be abolished.[28]

On another occasion, Buckner justified the separation of the races on both moral and practical grounds. He explained that, just as a white oak tree is different from a willow, "Similarly, the Lord in His infinite wisdom has, for reasons beyond our knowledge, created in the Indians a human being differing in many respects from a white man." According to Buckner, the only problem with race relations in Alaska was troublemakers who hoped to exploit the situation, as the general explained in a letter to the assistant secretary of war in July 1943. Buckner claimed that only "shyster lawyers," ambitious politicians, "fifth columnists," and misguided individuals "who see no appreciable differences between the Chinese, the Caucasians, the Japs, the Negroes, and Papuans, the Indians and the Australian Bushmen and who would be happy to intermarry with any of them" were inciting trouble among the Indians in Alaska.[29] When Buckner stubbornly failed to revoke his discriminatory policies, Governor Gruening and Delegate Dimond went over his head, taking their complaints about race discrimination all the way to Secretary of War Henry L. Stimson and to President Roosevelt himself, who ordered a stop to the exclusion of Natives from USOs.[30]

One of the most notorious incidents of racial discrimination in Alaska during World War II was the U.S. government's botched handling of the 1942 forced evacuation of nearly nine hundred Aleuts from their homes in the Aleutian Islands. Unlike the internment at about the same time of 120,000 Japanese Americans in concentration camps, an overtly racist measure born of wartime hysteria, the removal of the Aleuts from a combat zone for their own protection was theoretically a sounder public policy. In fact, the Aleut evacuation was administered so poorly that it caused a horrendous amount of death and hardship among the Native people. Many of the Aleuts died after their evacuation, while those who survived until the end of the war and returned to the Aleutians found entire villages burned to the ground and their personal belongings looted by American military personnel.[31]

The decision to evacuate the Aleuts came after the Japanese bombing of Dutch Harbor on 3 June 1942 and their subsequent occupation of Attu and Kiska islands; the Aleuts were given no notice before U.S. Navy ship arrived to take them away. Though virtually all Natives were required to leave the Aleutian Chain, some whites were permitted to stay. For instance, Charlie Hope, a white man who lived at Unalaska, was allowed to remain in the village, while his native wife was forced to leave.[32]

After the hasty government roundup of the Aleuts, most of the Natives were warehoused in abandoned canneries and camps in Southeastern Alaska for the duration of the war. Sanitary conditions in the camps were deplorable. Small children and the elderly suffered most. About forty of three hundred people died at Funter Bay, where a physician who visited the camp in the fall of 1943 wrote, "As we entered the first bunkhouse the odor of human excreta and waste was so pungent that I could hardly make the grade."[33] Residents of Ketchikan feared that two hundred Aleuts housed in an old CCC camp at Ward Cove eight miles from town would spread an epidemic of venereal disease and tuberculosis among the white population. The city of Ketchikan quarantined the camp, and businessmen urged the Aleuts be moved farther from the city. The proprietor of the Totem Inn said she wanted to keep Aleuts out of her establishment because "they were unsanitary and diseased and thus obnoxious to her regular customers besides requiring an unusual amount of trouble in sterilizing their dishes."[34]

The cavalier attitude of the U.S. government toward the welfare of the Aleut people was due in part to the exigencies of war. But it was also part of a deeper problem: Alaska Natives were second-class citizens in their own land. In an effort to remedy that situation and to outlaw discrimination against Natives, Governor Gruening submitted an anti-discrimination bill to the territorial legislature in early 1943. Passing the bill proved to be difficult, especially because of the complete lack of Native representation among territorial lawmakers. At the time, there was not a single Native member of the Alaska legislature. Though Natives comprised about one-half the population of the territory, only one Alaska Native had ever been elected to the territorial legislature in its history—William Paul, who had served in the mid-1920s.[35]

The anti-discrimination bill failed to pass in the 1943 session by the narrowest margin possible, an 8-8 tie vote in the house. "While I am greatly disappointed in the result," Gruening told Secretary of Interior Harold Ickes in March 1943, "and consider it shocking that in this international crisis the Alaska Legislature should put itself on record before the whole world as in favor of discrimination—an incident which may well be utilized by enemy propagandists—the outcome was a good deal closer than I would have expected." The close vote, Gruening said, would "serve one very useful purpose"; it proved that if only a small number of Native Alaskans became involved in the next election they could make a major difference. "It will awaken the Indians from their political lethargy," Gruening explained to Ickes, "and induce them to take a more active part in politics. This is the first time . . . in which an issue involving an attitude for or against the Indians has been squarely posed and which could not be evaded."[36]

Gruening recognized the Native vote as a potentially powerful constituency in his fight against the Seattle fishing and mining interests that controlled the legislature and blocked his efforts to increase taxes on the huge profits of the canned salmon industry. In addition, the governor hoped that the grip of the "interests" on the territorial government would be loosened by the congressionally authorized 1944 reapportionment of the legislature, doubling the size of the senate to sixteen seats and increasing the house by 50 percent—from sixteen members to twenty-four. He actively campaigned across Alaska to ensure that some of the new lawmakers would be Alaska Natives.

In November 1943, Gruening sent a written message to the annual convention of the Alaska Native Brotherhood, urging the group to find Native leaders willing to serve in the legislature. The proof that Natives were needed in Juneau, he said, was the shameful rejection by the old guard of the anti-discrimination bill. The governor stated that "Native people have both a right and a duty to exert themselves, to assert themselves and, by taking an active part in our political life, to see that such an unfortunate exhibition of prejudice and bigotry is not repeated."[37] When the votes were counted in the 1944 fall elections, two Tlingit Indians had been swept into office with overwhelming support: Frank Peratrovich of Klawock, the older brother of the ANB Grand President Roy Peratrovich, and Andrew Hope of Sitka.[38]

In the spring of 1944, during Governor Gruening's campaign to win support for the anti-discrimination bill in the next legislature, he received an emergency telegram from a seventeen-year-old Nome girl named Alberta Schenck, who had spent the previous night in jail for violating the segregated seating arrangements in the local theater. Her arrest was destined to inspire much debate in the battle for the equal rights bill in the coming legislative session.

Nome, like most other Alaskan towns, had its share of Jim Crow practices. Sadie Brower, daughter of a white father and an Eskimo mother, was a teenager in the early 1930s when she wanted to attend a Nome dance for a planeload of visiting soldiers. "There was a definite line between the natives and the whites," she remembered. "If it was a white man's dance, no one with native blood could go in there." Sadie and another half-Native friend were so eager to go to the dance that they bleached their hair with peroxide. They only began to worry afterwards when the time came for Sadie to return to her home in Barrow. "Well, we started looking for berets to cover our hair, because the roots were starting to come out black as you please, and there was no hair dye available in Nome then, no way to color your hair. So I was like that when I got off the boat in Barrow. Dad took one look at me and said, 'Foolishness. How foolish can you get!'" Sadie said it was a long time before her hair grew out and returned to its normal color, and she never forgot her embarrassment over what she had done for one night of dancing with the white soldiers.[39]

The threat of spreading tuberculosis was a common justification for keeping Eskimos separate from whites, as was the smell given off by Natives' skin boots, which were usually tanned in urine. According to one war correspondent, Eskimos and whites had "complete equality" in Nome in the early 1940s, except at the hotel and the music theater. "They can't live at the hotel," Howard Handleman wrote in 1943, "and they have to sit on their own side of the theater." The balcony, nicknamed "Nigger Heaven," was completely reserved for full-blooded Eskimos.[40]

In the spring of 1944, the forced seating arrangements at the theater particularly bothered Alberta Schenck, a young schoolgirl whose mother was an Eskimo and whose father was a white man. Two of her brothers were on duty with the U.S. Army, and her father was a veteran of World War I. Alberta worked as an usher at the Dream Theater after school and felt ashamed every time she had to tell Eskimos that if they found no seats on the right side of the theater or in the balcony they had to leave, even if there were empty seats on the left side.

She explained her frustration to Major Marvin ("Muktuk") Marston, the head of the Alaska Territorial Guard and a staunch fighter for equal treatment of Alaska Natives. Marston, widely known by his Eskimo nickname Muktuk, had been hired by Governor Gruening to mobilize the Native population during World War II, and he recognized the damage done by race discrimination in Alaska. At every available opportunity he bitterly protested white racism.

Alberta told Marston that she had been fired from her job at the theater for complaining about the management's segregated seating policies. She could not understand why such unfair treatment of those with a different color skin could be allowed in a land that professed such love for freedom and justice. When the major read an essay that Alberta had written at school describing her feelings, he was astounded at the pain and suffering that came through her simple language. "There was no use in evading the issue nor in pretending to this intelligent adolescent that all was well," Marston wrote. "She knew and I knew that here was a festering core of racial prejudice and social injustice wholly incompatible with our loudly proclaimed 'equality and justice for all.'"[41]

Marston suggested that Alberta submit her essay to the editor of the *Nome Nugget* and ask him to publish it. When the next issue came out he was surprised to find her hard-hitting letter to the editor on page three. "I believe we Americans and also our Allies are fighting for the purpose of freedom," Alberta wrote. "I myself am part Eskimo and Irish and so are many others. I only truthfully know that I am one of God's children regardless of race, color or creed. You or I or anyone else is not to blame [for] what we are." She then addressed the situation at the Dream Theater. "What has hurt us constantly is that we are not able to go to a public theater and sit where we wish, but yet we pay the SAME price as anyone else and our money is GLADLY received." Such actions, she said, were not in the spirit of Thomas Jefferson's Declaration of Independence or the U.S. Constitution that she was studying in school, but were instead "following the steps of Hitlerism."[42]

Alberta's letter caused a furor in Nome. The next issue of the paper carried an angry rebuttal from an anonymous reader. "The theater is a private institution, and has the right to make its own house rules and until the native people as a whole live up to public health standards, it would be hard for the management to change their present system even though some of the natives themselves do not like to sit next to 'odoriferous' persons. . . . I, therefore, suggest that those of the native group who are intelligent enough to complain and criticize, start working from within the native population, raise their standards and earn the right for that which they are asking."[43]

Marston said that Alberta wrote a second article in response, but the "newspaper was anxious to drop so hot an issue and the printed discussion came to a sudden close."[44] A few nights after Alberta's letter was published, she went out on a date to see a movie with a white army sergeant stationed at the Nome base. The sergeant escorted her down the aisle and they sat together on the white side of the theater. Suddenly, the manager came down the aisle and ordered her to move to the Native side of the auditorium with the other Eskimos and "half-breeds." When the sergeant told Alberta not to get up, the manager rushed out and returned with the Nome chief of police. When she still refused to get up, Marston said the chief "seized Alberta by the shoulders and literally pulled her into the aisle, pushed her down to the door, and out onto the street."[45]

Alberta Schenck spent that night in the Nome city jail. She was released the next day. Her arrest infuriated the local Native population who threatened legal action but felt helpless to fight the long-established policies of discrimination. As Muktuk Marston later wrote, "When the white called the law in the Arctic, the native was always in the wrong and the white man was always in the right." According to Marston, on the Sunday night following the incident with Alberta, a group of Eskimos purchased tickets and stormed into the theater, sitting wherever they chose. Alberta's father, Albert Schenck, reportedly hired O. D. Cochran, a prominent local attorney and territorial senator, to represent Alberta in a suit against the theater manager and the Nome chief of police.[46]

Marston also helped Alberta compose a telegram to Governor Gruening describing what had happened. When the governor received the news, he immediately wired Nome's Mayor Edward Anderson demanding an explanation. The mayor, ashamed of what the local police had done, wired back a brief response: "A mistake has been made. It won't happen again."[47] In a personal letter to Alberta, Gruening praised her for refusing "very properly" to sit in the Native section. "The discrimination which crops out here and there in Alaska against people of Native blood . . . is very objectionable to me," Gruening wrote. "I consider it un-American. I feel it violates the principles upon which our nation was founded. I deem it contrary to the spirit of our country and directly in conflict with the issues on which this great war is being fought. In this war, American boys of all races and creeds are enlisted. There is no discrimination when they are called upon to lay down their lives for their country and for liberty." Gruening promised Alberta that he would again push for passage of an anti-discrimination bill in the next legislature, and "if it becomes law, you may be certain that the unpleasant experience which has been yours will not happen again to anyone in Alaska. It should never have happened in America."[48]

A sign of how deeply Alberta's arrest angered some member's of the Nome community came only a few weeks later in the annual election of the Queen of Nome. The yearly spring carnival was the highlight of the Nome social scene. In April 1944, only about a month after her experience in the city jail, Alberta Schenck, with massive support from the soldiers of the Nome garrison, was elected the Queen of Nome for 1944. She won the popularity contest by an overwhelming margin, thanks to soldiers who had been angered by the way she had been treated. Individuals could vote as often as they liked at various businesses around the community, and Alberta tallied 63,850 votes, three times the total of her nearest competitor. "The so-called 'Four Hundred' of Nome were dumbfounded," Major Marston wrote in his memoirs published twenty-five years later. "I suspect they have not yet fully recovered from the shock."[49]

Despite obvious resentment among some Nome residents at the way Alberta Schenck had been treated, the Dream Theater continued its notorious segregation practices. On the night of 17 January 1945, Otto Geist observed an incident at the theater. Geist, a pioneer Alaskan archaeologist who served with the Alaska Territorial Guard during World War II, wrote immediately to Major Marston. "I happened to witness this evening," Geist wrote, "to the unpleasant situation when, first one native woman (as I could see a full blood) was removed from the left side of the [aisle], then, a young white man married to what appeared to be a half caste. The full blood woman quietly moved over to the already crowded right side set aside for natives. The white man, however, remonstrated and did not move when the usher girl asked him to move." Eventually, the white man and his wife agreed to change their seats, but only after a woman from the theater office came out and ordered them to sit on the Native side. Geist said that if the man had not backed down, the "local police would have been called upon" to throw them out of the theater.[50]

Five days after Geist's visit to the Dream Theater, the 1945 Alaska legislature convened in Juneau. Near the top of its agenda was the equal rights bill that would abolish segregation as practiced at Nome's only theater. In his message to the legislature, Governor Gruening urged the lawmakers to meet the challenges of the postwar world. "First, let us live up, at home, to the principle for which American boys of every race, creed and color are giving all they have," Gruening said. "Let us get rid of soul-searing race discrimination in our midst to the extent that we can do it by legislative action."[51]

The bill to make segregation a crime was introduced in the house by Representative Edward Anderson of Nome, who as city mayor had apologized to Governor Gruening for Alberta Schenck's arrest. Alberta's lawyer, Senator O. D. Cochran, introduced a senate version. Crowded hearings were held in both bodies to debate the measure, which would guarantee "full and equal accommodations, facilities and privileges to all citizens" throughout Alaska. As one newspaper account of the house proceedings stated, "The ghost of Abraham Lincoln, the Great Emancipator, trod heavily through the halls of the House of Representatives yesterday as that body convened in a committee of the whole before a jammed gallery on the non-discrimination bill introduced by Anderson of Nome."[52] Speaking forcefully from the gallery in favor of the Anderson bill was Roy Peratrovich, the president of the Alaska Native Brotherhood. The ANB president blasted the "unscrupulous white men in our midst" whose actions were "a disgrace to the Democratic form of Government."

During his oration, Peratrovich tied the equal rights measure to the issue of aboriginal land claims for Alaska Natives. At the time, Secretary of Interior Harold Ickes was pushing for the establishment of large Indian reservations in Alaska, as Ickes and prominent Indian rights advocates, such as Felix Cohen, believed that Alaska Natives had a valid potential claim to millions of acres in the territory. White Alaskans were terrified at the prospect that the Interior Department was recommending to return "most of the territory to the Indians on the ground that they have owned it all along." Earlier in 1944, the *Ketchikan Chronicle* had warned that any attempt to give Alaska back to the Indians would only fan the flames of racial warfare.[53]

From the house gallery, Peratrovich told the legislators that the ANB, an organization with a strong assimilationist background, had so far rejected Ickes's "tempting" proposals for reservations. "We have opposed reservations," Peratrovich said. "We are opposed to accepting any kind of special privilege. We want to take our chances with the white man." As the Juneau *Empire* reporter who covered the house hearing pointed out, however, "There was [an] implied threat in Peratrovich's speech when he declared ominously, 'I dare not prophesy what will happen if you folks do not pass this bill—we cannot stand beside you and aid you in your fight against Ickes unless you accept us as one of you.'"[54]

Opponents of the equal rights bill argued that it would not eliminate racial discrimination. An editorial in the conservative Juneau *Empire* admitted the next day that those who said there was no discrimination in Alaska were either "very much mistaken or else not very observant. Racial discrimination certainly does exist in Alaska as it exists not only in every State and Territory of the United States but throughout the world." According to the *Empire,* however, the bill would only make matters worse. "No law can force a business man, who is of one race, to deal pleasantly with a customer who happens to be of another race." The newspaper continued, "We honestly believe that such law which would attempt to force an elimination of racial discrimination, such as this measure now in question, would only serve to heighten racial discrimination." The *Empire* pointed with pride to the fact that it was no longer the custom in southeastern Alaska to have segregated seating in movie theaters. "Many more places of public accommodation are now opened to Indians than was the case 90 years ago. Not because laws were passed, but because this disease of the mind is being cured gradually."[55]

In both the house and senate debates, Senator O. D. Cochran used the Dream Theater as a "prime example" of the injustice of racial discrimination.[56] The notorious case of Alberta Schenck was a lurid reminder of how painful prejudice could be. Several of Cochran's Nome colleagues in the senate, including Tolbert Scott and Frank Whaley, bitterly opposed the equal rights measure. Scott claimed that "mixed breeds" who wished to associate with whites were causing all the problems and that the issue had only been raised to "create political capital for some legislators." Senator Allen Shattuck of Juneau argued that the races, rather than be brought closer together, should be kept farther apart for their own good. The Natives needed time, he said, to adjust to one thousand years of white civilization. "Eskimos are not an inferior race," said Senator Grenold Collins of Anchorage, another opponent of the measure, "but they are an individual race."[57]

After hearing all of the white senators expound on their racial views for nearly two hours, Elizabeth Peratrovich, wife of Roy Peratrovich, took the floor. In her moving testimony she told how it felt to be turned away from a place of business or denied the right to live in a certain neighborhood because of the color of one's skin. She said the opponents of the bill claimed the law would not stop racial discrimination, but that was hardly a reason to vote against it. "Do your laws against larceny and even murder prevent those crimes?" she asked the opponents of the bill. When Mrs. Peratrovich finished, the shrill opposition had been shamed into a "defensive whisper," and she drew "volleying applause from the galleries and Senate floor alike, with a biting condemnation of the 'super race' attitude."[58]

Though the anti-discrimination bill provoked hours of bitter debate in the legislature, in the end it proved to be one of the most popular pieces of legislation during the 1945 session. The legislature passed the equal rights measure by an overwhelming margin: 19-5 in the house and 11-5 in the senate. Governor Gruening signed the equal rights bill into law on 16 February 1945, officially abolishing Jim Crow practices in the Territory of Alaska. Standing behind Ernest Gruening as he put his signature on the bill were the key figures in its passage: Roy and Elizabeth Peratrovich, Senator N. R. Walker of Ketchikan, and the two Nome politicians who had come to Alberta Schenck's defense, Senator O. D. Cochran and Representative Edward Anderson.[59]

With the passage of the 1945 Alaska equal rights bill, the signs in Alaskan businesses prohibiting Natives came down. Discrimination did not end in Alaska, but the 1945 law was nevertheless a significant step forward, for it recognized that no one had the right to post his policies of race discrimination.

Even to this day, however, many Alaskans have blind spots when it comes to the subject of race discrimination toward Alaska Natives. Racism is virtually an invisible topic in Alaska's historical literature, and some old-timers would prefer that it stay that way. As one former white resident of Nome wrote me in 1989, regarding the Alberta Schenck incident: "I am sorry that I have no additional knowledge of the occurrence you are writing about probably because to me there was nothing unusual happening. Whenever two or more groups intermingle, be they of different races or just groups of the same race, there will be friction that will gradually be eradicated if no one keeps poking the embers."[60] With the massive social, political, and economic challenges that still face Alaska Natives today as they struggle for equality and cultural survival, it seems wishful thinking to believe that the problems of the past should be so easily forgotten, or worse yet, to pretend that they never happened at all.

NOTES

1. The best examinations of Alaska in relation to the Turner Thesis are Melody Webb, *The Last Frontier: A History of the Yukon Basin of Canada and Alaska* (Albuquerque, 1985), and Peter Coates, *The Trans-Alaska Pipeline Controversy: Technology, Conservation and the Frontier* (Bethlehem, 1991). See also Orlando Miller, *The Frontier in Alaska and the Matanuska Colony* (New Haven, 1975). For a recent sociological analysis of how Alaska's frontier philosophy shapes the culture and politics of the state, see Lee James Cuba, "A Moveable Frontier: Frontier Images in Contemporary Alaska" (Ph.D. dissertation, Yale University, 1981).

2. Ernest Gruening, *The State of Alaska* (New York, 1954), 306. For a discussion of various examples of segregation and discrimination in Alaska, see: Phillip Drucker, *The Native Brotherhoods on the Northwest Coast* (Washington, D.C., 1958), 45; *Fairbanks News-Miner*, 12 March 1990, p. 10; Stephen W. Haycox, "William Paul, Sr., and the Alaska Voters Literacy Act of 1925," *Alaska History* 2 (Winter 1986/1987): 17–37; Joseph E. Senungetuk, *Give or Take a Century: An Eskimo Chronicle* (San Francisco, 1971); John Tepton, "Between Two Worlds: Growing up Native in Alaska," *We Alaskans* (Sunday magazine of the *Anchorage Daily News*), 24 May 1987, p. 9.

3. Joseph Driscoll, *War Discovers Alaska* (New York, 1943), 302.

4. C. Vann Woodward, *The Strange Career of Jim Crow* (New York, 1974), 131.

5. Ted C. Hinckley, *Alaskan John G. Brady: Missionary, Businessman, Judge, and Governor, 1878–1918* (Columbus, 1982), 62, 136.

6. Ibid., 70.

7. Drucker, *The Native Brotherhoods*, 70.

8. David S. Case, *Alaska Natives and American Laws* (Fairbanks, 1984), 198–199.

9. Charles K. Ray, *A Program of Education for Alaska Natives* (Fairbanks, 1959), 30–57; see also Stephen W. Haycox, "Races of a Questionable Ethnical Type: Origins of the Jurisdiction of the U.S. Bureau of Education in Alaska, 1867–1885," *Pacific Northwest Quarterly* 75 (October 1984): 155–163; Victor William Henningsen, "Reading, Writing and Reindeer: The Development of Federal Education in Alaska, 1877–1920" (Ph.D. dissertation, Harvard University, 1987); Case, *Alaska Natives and American Laws*, 197–207; Richard L. Dauenhauer, *Conflicting Visions in Alaska Education* (Fairbanks, 1980).

10. Drucker, *The Native Brotherhoods*, 59.

11. Ibid., 18, 41; Andrew Hope, *Founders of the Alaska Native Brotherhood* (Sitka, 1975); Rosita Worl, "The Birth of the Civil Rights Movement," *Alaska Native News* 1 (November 1983):10–37.

12. Haycox, "William Paul, Sr., and the Alaska Voter's Literacy Act," 17–37; Drucker, *The Native Brotherhoods*, 37–40.

13. *Fairbanks Daily News-Miner*, 29 October 1926.

14. William K. Keller, "A History of Higher Education in Alaska, 1741–1940" (Ph.D. dissertation, State College of Washington, 1940), 252.

15. Haycox, "William Paul, Sr., and the Alaska Voter's Literacy Act," 19.

16. *Stroller's Weekly* (Juneau), 14 September 1929.

17. Drucker, *The Native Brotherhoods*, 50; Case, *Alaska Natives and American Laws*, 200.

18. U.S. Congress, Senate, Committee on Indian Affairs, *Survey of Conditions of the Indians of the United States*, Part 36, 74th Congress, 2nd Session (Washington, D.C., 1939), 19833–19834. [These hearings were actually held in 1936, ed.]

19. Drucker, *The Native Brotherhoods*, 71.

20. Ernest Gruening, "Ernest Gruening and the Native People of Alaska: A Personal Account of the Record," Gruening Papers, General Correspondence, 1954–57, Box 8, Folder 72, Alaska and Polar Regions Collection, University of Alaska, Fairbanks.

21. Ernest Gruening, *Many Battles: The Autobiography of Ernest Gruening* (New York, 1973), 318–319.

22. Roy and Elizabeth Peratrovich to Ernest Gruening, 30 December 1941, National Archives Microfilm Publication (MF Pub M939), General Correspondence of the Alaska Territorial Governor, 1909–1958 (Washington, D.C., 1973) [hereafter General Correspondence], Microfilm Reel 273, File 40–4b.

23. Gruening to Roy Peratrovich, 2 January 1942, General Correspondence, Reel 273, File 40–4b.

24. Gruening, *Many Battles*, 319.

25. Gruening to Guy J. Swope, 30 July 1942, General Correspondence, Reel 273, File 40–4b.

26. Morgan Sherwood, *Big Game in Alaska: A History of Wildlife and People* (New Haven, 1981), 3–4.

27. Peratrovich to Anthony Dimond, 26 April 1943, General Correspondence, Reel 273, File 40–4b.

28. General S.B. Buckner to Gruening, 7 June 1943, General Correspondence, Reel 273, File 40–4b.

29. Buckner to John J. McCloy, 29 July 1943, Papers of Harold L. Ickes, Secretary of the Interior file, AK-2, Container 93, Manuscript Division, Library of Congress, Washington, D.C.

30. Gruening, *Many Battles*, 321.

31. Committee on Wartime Relocation and Internment of Civilians, *Personal Justice Denied: Report of the Commission on Wartime Relocation and Internment of Civilians* (Washington, D.C., December 1982), 317–359. See also, *Fairbanks Daily News-Miner*, 10 March 1983; 23 April 1985; *Anchorage Daily News*, 1 October 1987.

32. Committee on Wartime Relocation, *Personal Justice Denied*, 334.

33. Ibid., 340.

34. Ibid., 349.

35. Alaska Legislative Affairs Agency, *Alaska Legislature Roster of Members, 1913–1982* (Juneau, 1982).

36. Gruening to Harold L. Ickes, 17 March 1943, General Correspondence, Reel 273, File 40–4b.

37. Ernest Gruening, "Message to the 30th Annual Convention of the Alaska Native Brotherhood at Hoonah, November 8–13, 1943," Gruening Papers, General Correspondence, Box 8, Folder 72.

38. Evangeline Atwood and R.N. DeArmond, comps., *Who's Who in Alaska Politics: A Biographical Dictionary of Alaskan Political Personalities* (Portland, 1977), 47, 77.

39. Margaret B. Blackman, *Sadie Brower Neakok: An Iñupiak Woman* (Seattle, 1989), 96–97.

40. Howard Handleman, *Wartime Alaska, Alaska Life* (December 1943), 46; Bud Richter, phone interview by Terrence M. Cole, 15 February 1989; Loretta Helle, phone interview by Terrence M. Cole, San Diego, California, February, 1989.

41. Marvin "Muktuk" Marston, *Men of the Tundra: Eskimos at War* (New York, 1969), 134.

42. *Nome Nugget,* 3 March 1944.

43. Ibid., 10 March 1944.

44. Marston, *Men of the Tundra,* 134.

45. Ibid., 135.

46. Ibid., 135–137; Bud Richter interview, 13 February 1989.

47. Marston, *Men of the Tundra,* 137.

48. Gruening to Alberta Schenk, 17 March 1944, Nome Correspondence, Box 6, Records of the Alaska Territorial Guard, Geist Collection, Alaska and Polar Regions Collection, University of Alaska Fairbanks.

49. *Nome Nugget,* 17 April 1944; Marston, *Men of the Tundra,* 138.

50. Otto Geist to Marston, 17 January 1945, Marston Correspondence, Box 15, file 11B, Records of the Alaska Territorial Guard, Geist Collection.

51. *Journal of the House of Representatives of the Territory of Alaska,* 17th Session (Juneau, 1945), 71.

52. *Daily Alaska Empire* (Juneau), 31 January 1945.

53. Quoted in *Nome Nugget,* 1 November 1944; see also Stephen W. Haycox, "Economic Development and Indian Land Rights in Modern Alaska: The 1947 Tongass Timber Act," *Western Historical Quarterly,* 21 (February 1990): 20–46; see also Kenneth Philp, "The New Deal and Alaskan Natives, 1936–1945," *Pacific Historical Review* 50 (1981): 309–27.

54. *Daily Alaska Empire* (Juneau), 31 January 1945.

55. Ibid.

56. Ibid., 6 February 1945.

57. Ibid.

58. Ibid.

59. *Nome Nugget,* 11 April 1945; "The Birth of the Civil Rights Movement," 11. In memory of Elizabeth Peratrovich, who died of cancer in 1950, Alaska's Governor Steve Cowper signed a proclamation in 1988 declaring 16 February, the day Gruening singed the equal rights bill, as "Elizabeth Peratrovich Day." See *Anchorage Daily News,* 6 June 1988, p 1.

60. R. B. to Terrence M. Cole, 4 February 1989.

VI

Indian Activism and Cultural Resurgence

Like many aspects of the 1960s and 1970s, it is easy to view the rise of the Red Power movement as simply an artifact of popular culture. Images of gun-toting men wearing their hair in braids and sporting dark glasses threaten to reduce the changes taking place in this era to a series of antiestablishment escapades. In fact, beneath those popular images lies an era of remarkable political activity and cultural renewal. Surveying the lay of the land from several vantage points—ritual, demography, political activism, policymaking—the four essays in this section capture something of the profound changes these years witnessed. The authors show how crosscurrents of social, political, and cultural struggle combined to stimulate new ideas about American Indian identity and the place of Native people in the world at large. Together they suggest the dimensions of change taking place within Indian communities during these tumultuous years. At the same time, however, reading these chapters in light of those earlier in the volume reveals important continuities as well. The Indian cultural renewals Frederick Hoxie discussed, the Pueblo dancers we met before, even the militancy and factional fights in the days of Crazy Horse—all have echoes in the chapters here.

16

Who is an Indian? The question of Indian identity has long troubled scholars, Native peoples, and policymakers alike. Until 1960, federal census takers made up their own minds; hence the same person might be identified as Indian in one census, white in the next, black or mulatto in a third. Calculating "blood quantums," begun in the nineteenth century (see Chapters 4, 6, and 8, for example), and still sometimes practiced today, represents another attempt to solve this conundrum. The very persistence of Indian identity even among acculturated individuals (like Carlos Montezuma, Chapter 13) or groups (like the Stockbridge-Munsee, Chapter 14) only compounds the confusion.

Joane Nagel's study of "American Indian Ethnic Renewal" returns once again to the problem, and to the census (which since 1960 has allowed individuals to identify their own racial or ethnic identity). The essay begins with a startling statistic: the Native American population of the United States tripled in size between 1960 and 1990. Citing studies by demographers and sociologists, Nagel asserts that an increase of this magnitude cannot be explained biologically. Instead, she ventures, this rise in population is a consequence of "ethnic switching," the practice of changing one's identity from one census to the next. If this is true, she wonders, "Why are more and more Americans reporting their race as American Indian?"

Nagel bases her discussion on the assumption that ethnic identity is a social product rather than a biological fact. Membership in a group—indeed, what constitutes an ethnic group—is determined by social attitudes and socially sanctioned traditions, not by birth. What is more, Nagel suggests that Native American identity is largely a product of choice. This is particularly true of pan-Indian identity (identification with the entire group rather than with a particular tribe), something Nagel calls "purely a social construction." By analyzing census data, she develops a series of hypotheses about the kinds of people who would opt to switch identities. She argues that the "new Indians" of the 1970s and 1980s were more likely to be urban, married to non-Indians, and unable to speak a tribal language.

If American Indian ethnic identity has largely been a matter of choice, what forces, Nagel asks, have inspired hundreds of thousands of people, people who previously identified as something else, to opt for the Native American category? She proposes three possibilities: a federal policy that, during the era of tribal "termination" after World War II, pushed Indians to live away from their reservation homelands; the civil rights movement's concern for racial pride; and the immediate impact of protest movements. In general, she notes that Indian people were caught between two conflicting currents. On the one hand, individuals increasingly lived away from their tribal traditions and those who maintained them, but on the other hand they experienced the heightened racial and ethnic sensitivity that accompanied the revivals taking place among African-Americans, Latinos, Asian-Americans, and white women. In this atmosphere of change, many chose to return to their indigenous ancestry.

The appeal of Nagel's essay is its ability to conceptualize an entire era of social and political upheaval. Moreover, like Margaret Jacobs's work, which connected the debate over Pueblo dances to wider currents in American society at large, Nagel ties the changes taking place in the Native American world to trends in other groups. Her work also speaks in interesting and suggestive ways to other studies of renewal in this volume. How persuasive is her argument? Are people only what they say they are?

AMERICAN INDIAN ETHNIC RENEWAL:
POLITICS AND THE RESURGENCE OF IDENTITY

Joane Nagel

THIS ESSAY EXAMINES THE PHENOMENON of ethnic identity change and the role of politics in prompting the reconstruction of individual ethnicity. Specifically, I examine recent demographic trends in the American Indian population to understand the conditions and factors that lead individuals to change their racial identity.[1] Between 1960 and 1990, the number of Americans reporting American Indian as their race in the U.S. Census more than tripled, growing from 523,591 to 1,878,285. This increase cannot by accounted for by the usual explanations of population growth (e.g., increased births, decreased deaths). Researchers have concluded that much of this population growth must have resulted from "ethnic switching," where individuals who identified their race as non-Indian (e.g., White) in an earlier census, switched to "Indian" race in a later census. Why are more and more Americans reporting their race as American Indian?

My research draws on historical analyses and interview data, and combines a social constructionist model of ethnic identity with a social structure approach to ethnic change. I argue that the increase in American Indian ethnic identification reflected in the U.S. Census is an instance of "ethnic renewal." Ethnic renewal refers to both individual and collective processes. *Individual ethnic renewal* occurs when an individual acquires or asserts a new ethnic identity by reclaiming a discarded identity, replacing or amending an identity in an existing ethnic repertoire, or filling a personal ethnic void. Reclaiming a discarded identity might entail resuming religious observations or "retraditionalization" (e.g., the return to orthodoxy by American Jews). Replacing an identity in an existing ethnic repertoire might involve religious conversion (e.g., the conversion to Islam by Christian African Americans); amending an existing ethnic repertoire might involve exploring a new side of one's family tree and including that nationality or ethnicity among one's working ethnic identities (e.g., the taking on of Armenian ethnicity by an Irish Armenian American already involved in Irish American ethnic life). Filling a personal ethnic void might entail adopting a new ethnic identity for the first time (e.g., Americans reconnecting with their ethnic "roots" and joining ethnic social, political, or religious organizations). *Collective ethnic renewal* involves the reconstruction of an ethnic community by current or new community members who build or rebuild institutions, culture, history, and traditions.[2]

SOURCE: *American Sociological Review,* v. 60, n. 6 (December 1995), pp. 974–965.

My thesis is that ethnic renewal among the American Indian population has been brought about by three political forces: (1) federal Indian policy, (2) American ethnic politics, and (3) American Indian political activism. Federal Indian policies have contributed to the creation of an urban, intermarried, bicultural American Indian population that lives outside traditional American Indian geographic and cultural regions. For these individuals, American Indian ethnicity has been more optional than for those living on reservations. Changes in American political culture brought about by the ethnic politics of the civil rights movement created an atmosphere that increased ethnic consciousness, ethnic pride, and ethnic mobilization among all ethnic groups, including American Indians. The resulting "Red Power" Indian political activist movement of the 1960s and 1970s started a tidal wave of ethnic renewal that surged across reservation and urban Indian communities, instilling ethnic pride and encouraging individuals to claim and assert their "Indianness."

Below I provide a constructionist conceptual framework for interpreting ethnic identity generally; review the demographic evidence and explanations for increases in the American Indian population; outline the role of structural factors, such as political policies, ethnic politics, and ethnic political activism in prompting or strengthening Indian ethnic identification; and explore the meaning and consequences of activism for American Indian ethnic renewal.

BACKGROUND

Negotiating and Changing Individual and Collective Identities

In the past 30 years, our understanding of ethnicity has increasingly stressed the socially constructed character of ethnicity. The pioneering work of Fredrik Barth shows ethnicity to be situational and variable.[3] Many studies have followed that have found ethnicity to be more emergent than primordial, ethnic group boundaries to be more fluid than fixed, ethnic conflicts to arise more from clashes of contemporary interests than from ancient animosities, ethnic history and culture to be routinely revised and even invented, and the central essence of ethnicity—ethnic identity—to be multifaceted, negotiable, and changeable.[4]

It is this last assertion—that one ethnic identity can be exchanged for another—that runs most against the grain of common wisdom. Sociologists have long identified forms of ethnic change associated with intergroup contact, such as assimilation, accommodation, and acculturation.[5] These processes have been seen as long-term, often intergenerational, frequently involving the dissolution or blending of immigrant or minority ethnicities into a larger dominant ethnicity or nationality (e.g., from "Indian" to "White" or from "Irish" to "American"). In the case of ethnic renewal, however, individuals adopt a *non*dominant ethnic identity, and thus move from membership in a dominant group to become part of a minority or subnational group (e.g., from "white" to "Indian" or from "American" to "Irish American" or "Jewish American"). This resurgence of nondominant ethnic identity does not fit clearly into traditional models of ethnic change which carry a heavy presumption that ethnic change invariably moves in the direction of assimilation (i.e., from minority to majority).

Opportunities for individual ethnic change vary. Certainly some people, for instance, American Whites, have a wide menu of "ethnic options" from which they are free to choose.[6] It is more difficult for members of other racial or ethnic groups to change their ethnicity, particularly communities of color. This is because in the United States such groups confront a world of "hypodescent," where one drop of particular blood (African, Asian) dictates a specific ethnic group membership, leaving limited options for individual members.[7] European Americans and African Americans represent two ends of an ethnic ascription continuum, in which Whites are always free to remember their ancestry and Blacks are never free to forget theirs. These ethnic boundaries are maintained and policed by both Blacks and Whites, although their content and location can change over time.[8]

Despite such strict racial regimes, and perhaps because of their constructed character, there is constant flux at the edges of individual ethnic identity and ethnic group boundaries. For instance, despite the "one drop rule," Davis describes centuries of defining and redefining "Blackness" in the United States, and discusses divisions among Americans of African descent based on national origin and skin tone.[9] Similarly, many studies describe the shifting and emerging identities of Latinos,[10] Asian Americans,[11] Native Americans,[12] and European Americans.[13]

While historical shifts do indeed occur in ethnic boundaries and definitions, is it really possible to change one's *individual* ethnicity? The answer, of course, is yes. Individuals change their ethnic identity often, singly and *en masse*. Perhaps the most common form of ethnic switching is religious conversion. This sort of ethnic change is most likely to occur when a particular religion-based ethnicity is especially stigmatizing. Schermerhorn reports a common form of ethnic switching in India, where Hindu Untouchables convert to Islam to escape untouchability.[14] Another instance of mass ethnic change occurred in the former Yugoslavia during Ottoman rule, when Christian conversions to Islam created a permanent ethnic boundary; contemporary conflicts between the descendants of these Muslims and the Christian Croat and Serb populations illustrate the resurgent power of ethnicity and nationalism, as these conflicts involve communities marked by varying degrees of intermarriage, residential integration, and religious tolerance.[15] Another type of ethnic change is "passing"—hiding or camouflaging a disadvantageous ethnicity while adopting the dress or behavior of a more advantaged group. Nayar notes that in India many instances of passing were motivated by the British colonial preference for Sikh military recruits: Hindus and others identified themselves as Sikhs to qualify for army posts.[16] Sometimes ethnic switching is pursued bureaucratically. Lelyveld describes how individuals petitioned the South African government to change officially their own or others' racial designations under *apartheid* regulations.[17] Similar challenges to racial designations on birth certificates have been mounted in the United States.[18]

American Indian Ethnicity: Opting for an Indian Identity

American Indians reside at the intersection of two racial regimes: hypodescent and self-identification. In some portions of the United States Indianness is strongly socially ascribed and often mandatory (e.g., in the Southwest or the Northern Plains).

In these settings Indian ethnicity is regulated in two ways. The first is informal and external to Indian communities, and involves ascription mainly, though not exclusively, by non-Indians. In this instance of classic hypodescent, any visible "Indianness" labels an individual as "Indian." The second, more formal way American Indian ethnicity is regulated can be both internal and external to native communities, and involves official membership in Indian tribes. In this case, tribal, state, and/or federal governments recognize an individual as an "enrolled" member or not.

In much of the United States, however, American Indian ethnicity is largely a matter of individual choice; "Indian" ethnicity is an ethnic option that an individual can choose or not. This is *not* to say that *anyone* can choose to be an Indian or that all observers will unanimously confirm the validity of that choice. Indeed, there is enormous controversy among native people about who should be considered an Indian for purposes of receiving tribal services, federal benefits, affirmative action consideration, or rights to participate in tribal governments.[19]

An important point to make here about supratribal "American Indian" ethnicity is that it is purely a social construction. That is, the Native American population is comprised of many linguistic, cultural, and religious groups, more than 300 of which are separately recognized by federal or state governments in the lower 48 states (with many more in Alaska and Hawaii); each group has its own political, legal, and police system, economy, land base, and sovereign authority. Around two-thirds of American Indians identified in the U.S. Censuses are official members of these recognized communities.[20] Thus, when we speak of an "American Indian" race or ethnicity, we are of necessity referring to a group of individuals from various tribal backgrounds, some of whom speak native languages, most of whom converse in English, some of whom live on or regularly visit reservation "homelands," most of whom live off-reservation, some of whom participate in tribal community life, most of whom live in urban areas.

Despite this diversity, researchers assert that, indeed, there are "Indians," and this all-encompassing category can be seen as an "ethnic group."[21] For instance, Deloria argues that as American Indians became increasingly involved in off-reservation political and economic life after World War II, they came to see themselves as minority group members and as part of the larger American ethnic mosaic.[22] In fact, many Native Americans carry within their portfolio of ethnic identities (which may include identities based on kin or clan lineage, tribe, reservation, language, and religion) a supratribal or pan-Indian "Indian" identity, which is often reserved for use when interacting with non-Indians. Finally, as further evidence of the existence of an "American Indian" ethnic group, in recent decades, increasing percentages of Americans who identify their race as "Indian" fail to specify a tribal affiliation, suggesting that their primary ethnic identity is supratribal or "Indian." [23]

Patterns of American Indian Identification, 1960–1990

The U.S. Census provides data for examining both ethnic choice and ethnic ascription in American society. Beginning in 1960, the Census Bureau moved from a system where enumerators assigned each person a race to a system that permitted

TABLE 1. AMERICAN INDIAN POPULATION, 1900–1990

Census Year	Population Size	Percent Change from Previous Year
1900	237,196	—
1910	276,927	17
1920	244,437	-13
1930	343,352	40
1940	345,252	1
1950	357,499	4
1960	523,591	46
1970	792,730	51
1980	1,364,033	72
1990	1,878,285	38

SOURCES: For 1900–1970, Russell Thornton, *American Indian Holocaust and Survival* (Norman: University of Oklahoma Press, 1987), 160; for 1980 and 1990, U.S. Bureau of the Census, "Census Bureau Releases 1990 Census Counts on Specific Racial Groups," Census Bureau Press Release CB91-215, June 12, 1991, table 1.

individual racial self-identification. This move from ascription to racial choice opened the door to individual racial "switching," especially for those ethnic categories not strongly governed by social conventions of hypodescent. Table 1 shows the growth in the American Indian Census population from 1900 to 1990.

Between 1970 and 1980, the American Indian population increased the most: The population grew from 792,730 in 1970 to 1,364,033 in 1980, an increase of 72 percent. Researchers wondered what accounted for this growth. They searched for the usual explanations: increased birthrates, decreased death rates, immigration, changes in census coding procedures.[24] As these explanations were examined one by one and each failed to account for Indian population growth, researchers looked to alternative, more sociological explanations. For instance, Passel and Berman and Deloria argue that the unexplained percentage of Indian population growth is the result of "'recruitment,' i.e., changes in self-definition by individuals from non-Indian in one census to Indian in the next."[25] Thornton suggests that such increases are the result of "'biological migration': the migration of non-Indian genes into the American Indian population," the offspring of whom identify themselves as Indian.[26] Steiner characterizes individuals likely to be included in the ranks of the unaccounted for Indian population as "new Indians"—urban, educated, and multicultural—people whom Snipp describes as "individuals who in an earlier era of American history would have 'passed' unrecognized into white society."[27] Eschbach depicts the Indian population explosion as the result of "new identification" by Americans of varying degrees of Indian ancestry who formerly reported a non-Indian race, but who changed their race to "Indian" in a later census.[28] And, finally, there is the somewhat unkind, informal description of newly identified census Indians as "wannabes," non-Indian individuals who want to be American Indian and thus identify themselves as such.[29]

DESCRIBING THE "NEW" INDIAN POPULATION

Although researchers seem to agree that individual ethnic change is an important factor in the recent growth of the American Indian population, the reasons remain unclear. Phrased as research questions, we might ask: Who are these "new" Indians? And, what motivates them to change their ethnicity?

A survey of U.S. Census data and demographic research on the characteristics of the American Indian population provides some answers to the first question. Demographers calculate "natural increases" in the population by subtracting deaths from births; when population growth exceeds this number, the difference is referred to as the "error of closure."[30] The largest growing segments of the population are those likely to have the highest "errors of closure," and hence the most likely influx of new members. Thus, by examining the fastest growing segments of the Indian population we can infer some of the social characteristics of the "new" Indians.

Table 2 summarizes several social characteristics of the American Indian population for the period from 1960 to 1990. Column 1 of Table 2 shows the percentage of the American Indian population living in cities from 1960 to 1990. The Indian population became increasingly urbanized during these three decades, with the proportion of urban Indians growing from 27.9 percent of the total Indian population in 1960 to 56.2 percent in 1990. As a result, the urban Indian population has grown three times faster than the rural population. During the 1960–1990 period, the urban Indian population increased 720 percent compared to a 218 percent increase in rural areas.[31] Thus, *the "new" Indians are much more likely to live in urban areas than rural areas.*

There are also regional differences in Indian population growth. Passel and Berman compared 1970–1980 population growth rates in "Indian states" with those in "non-Indian states,"[32] and found that the Indian population was growing twice as fast in non-Indian states: A 114 percent increase occurred in non-Indian states compared to only a 56 percent increase in Indian states. Eschbach examined population growth rates in regions of the country with states containing historically small Indian populations similar to Passel and Berman's "non-Indian states."[33] He found that population growth in these regions during the period from 1960 to 1990 was six times greater than in the regions containing states with historical Indian populations. These two studies strongly suggest that *the "new" Indians are much more likely to be from states with historically small Indian populations.*

Researchers have also found that Indian population growth is associated with racial intermarriage. American Indians have very high intermarriage rates compared to other racial groups. For instance, Snipp compared rates of intermarriage of Blacks, Whites, and Indians in the 1980 Census and found that nearly half of Indians were intermarried (48 percent) compared to only 2 percent of Blacks and 1 percent of Whites.[34] Sandefur and McKinnell report that Indian intermarriage has been increasing, rising from approximately 15 percent in 1960 to 33 percent in 1970,[35] and Eschbach reported that in 1990, 59 percent of married Indians had a non-Indian spouse.[36] These findings are summarized in column 2 of Table 2. Indian intermarriage

TABLE 2. SELECTED CHARACTERISTICS OF THE AMERICAN INDIAN
POPULATION, 1960–1990

Year	Percent Living in Urban Areas[a]	Percent Intermarried[b]	Children Given Indian Race[c]	Indian Language at Home[d]
1960	27.9	15.0	—[e]	—[e]
1970	44.5	33.0	—[e]	—[e]
1980	54.6	48.0	47.4	26.1
1990	56.2	59.0	46.7	23.0

[a]For 1960 and 1970, Alan L. Sorkin, *The Urban American Indian* (Lexington, Mass.: Lexington Books, 1978), 10; for 1980, U.S. Bureau of the Census, *Census of Population, Subject Reports, Characteristics of American Indians by Tribes and Selected Areas* (Washington, D.C.: Government Printing Office, 1989), 50; for 1990, U.S. Bureau of the Census, *Census of the Population, General Population Characteristics, American Indian and Alaskan Native Areas, 1990* (Washington, D.C.: Government Printing Office, 1992).

[b]For 1960 and 1970, Gary D. Sandefur and Trudy McKinnell, "American Indian Intermarriage," in *Social Science Research* 15 (1986), 348; for 1980, Snipp, *American Indians*, 157; for 1990, Karl Eschbach, "The Enduring and Vanishing American Indian: American Indian Population Growth and Intermarriage in 1990," in *Ethnic and Racial Studies* 18 (1995), 89–108 , table 1.

[c]For 1980, Eschbach, "Shifting Racial Boundaries," 150; for 1990, Eschbach, "The Enduring and Vanishing American Indian," table 2.

[d]For 1980, U.S. Bureau of the Census, *Census of Population, 1980,* 203; for 1990, U.S. Bureau of the Census, *Census of the Population, 1990,* 66.

[e]Data not available.

is related to region and rates of population growth. Sandefur and McKinnell compared rates of intermarriage in "Indian states" and "non-Indian states" (as defined by Passel and Berman) in the 1980 Census. They found that the intermarriage rate in non-Indian states (nearly 70 percent) was nearly twice that in Indian states (40 percent).[37] Eschbach also found that rates of intermarriage varied by the "Indianness" of a region, with intermarriage ranging from 16 to 64 percent in Indian regions, and from 72 to 82 percent in non-Indian regions.[38] Eschbach also noted that population growth was greatest in those regions with the highest intermarriage rates, increasing from approximately 151,000 in 1960 to 928,000 in 1990—a 500 percent increase.[39] The implication of this research on Indian intermarriage is that *the "new" Indians in the 1970, 1980, and 1990 Censuses are more likely to be intermarried.*

The race assigned to children in mixed marriages provides another important piece of information about the characteristics of the fastest growing segment of the American Indian population. Where hypodescent does not dictate the race of mixed race children, parents may choose their child's race. In 1980 and 1990, mixed Indian-non-Indian couples assigned the race of the Indian parent to only about half of their offspring (see column 3, Table 2). Eschbach reported that in the 1980 Census, 47.4 percent of children from Indian-non-Indian parents were assigned an Indian race; that proportion fell slightly in 1990 to 46.7 percent.[40] Region mattered in such racial decision-making. Eschbach found that in non-Indian regions the proportion of children given an Indian race in 1990 ranged from 33 to 45 percent; in comparison, in historically Indian regions, 36 to 73 percent of mixed race children were assigned an Indian race.[41] Further, those regions with the greatest Indian population growth were areas where children of mixed marriages were *less likely* to be classified by their parents as Indians. These findings suggest that *the "new" Indians are more likely to assign a non-Indian race to their mixed offspring.*

Finally, we come to that major indicator of assimilation—native language loss. Indian language usage has declined dramatically in the past century. As shown in column 4 of Table 2, in 1980, 74 percent of American Indians spoke only English in their homes;[42] by 1990, the percentage had risen to 77 percent.[43] Snipp found, not surprisingly, that native language usage varies by region, with Native Americans from regions with historically large Indian populations much more likely to speak an Indian language than are those from historically non-Indian regions.[44] As Indian population growth is highest in these non-Indian regions, we can conclude that *the "new" Indians are quite likely to speak only English.*

Adding the above data together, a picture emerges of the fastest growing segment of the Native American population: Compared to the total American Indian population, these Indians are more urban, more concentrated in non-Indian states without reservation communities, more often intermarried, less likely to assign their mixed offspring an Indian race, and more likely to speak only English. These characteristics are all descriptive of a population more "blended" into the American demographic and cultural mainstream than their reservation co-ethnics, more likely to have more flexible conceptions of self, residing in parts of the country that permit a wide range of ethnic options. In other words, under the proper conditions, the fastest growing portions of the American Indian population are available for ethnic renewal.

ACCOUNTING FOR AMERICAN INDIAN ETHNIC RENEWAL

What *are* the conditions that promote American Indian ethnic renewal? Restated, what has motivated these new Indians to change their ethnicity? The answers to this question can be found in policy and politics: federal Indian policy, American ethnic politics, and Native American political activism.

Federal Indian Policy

Beginning in the nineteenth century, federal Indian policy was designed to assimilate American Indians into the Euro-American cultural mainstream (e.g., through forced English language acquisition, Anglo-centric education in Indian boarding and day schools, and reservation land reduction programs). Despite a brief pause in federal assimilation programs during the "New Deal" era,[45] the net result of decades of federal Indian policy was the creation of an English-speaking, bicultural, multi-tribal American Indian population living in U.S. cities. World War II also spurred the urbanization and acculturation of the Native American population, as Indians volunteered and were drafted into the military and non-enlisted native workers left reservations for wartime industrial jobs in urban areas. Many of these Indian veterans and workers never returned to the reservation.[46] Post–World War II programs for job training and urban relocation were specifically designed to reduce reservation populations during the "termination" era of federal Indian policy, and provided a further push in the reservation-urban Indian population stream.[47] For instance, Sorkin estimates that from 1952 to 1972, federal programs relocated more than 100,000 American Indians to a number of targeted cities, including Chicago, Cleveland, Dallas, Denver, Los Angeles, Oakland, Oklahoma City, Phoenix, Salt Lake City, San Francisco, San Jose, Seattle, and Tulsa.[48] By 1970, nearly half of American Indians lived in cities as a result of relocation programs and other general urbanization processes. The combined result of decades of these federal Indian policies was the creation of an urbane, educated, English-speaking Indian constituency that was available for mobilization when the civil rights era arrived in the 1960s.

Not only did federal Indian policy help urbanize the Indian population, many programs had a major impact on the organizational fabric of urban Indian life. For instance, relocation programs directly funded the creation and operation of a number of Indian centers in both relocation target cities and cities near large reservation populations.[49] These centers were established to provide services and meeting places for burgeoning urban Indian populations. Further, as an indirect consequence of relocation efforts, other urban Indian organizations blossomed: intertribal clubs, bars, athletic leagues, beauty contests, powwows, and dance groups, as well as Indian newspapers and newsletters, social service agencies, political organizations, and Christian churches.[50]

In a few urban areas, some of these organizations had a specific tribal character and were frequented only by members of a particular tribe.[51] However, the vast majority of urban Indian organizations were intertribal and had names reflecting their inclusionary character: the Cleveland American Indian Center, the *Inter-Tribal Tribune* (newsletter of the Heart of America Indian Center, Kansas City), the Los Angeles American Indian Bowling League, the Many Trails Indian Club, the First Southern Baptist Indian Church.[52] In such intertribal organizations, many urban Indians "sought refuge from the terrible loss of identity that marked modern urban existence."[53] The diverse organizations that populated the urban Indian organizational landscape formed the core of an intertribal network and informal communication system in urban Indian communities. They were important building blocks in the development of a supratribal level of Indian identity and the emergence of a pan-Indian culture, both of which were essential ingredients in the Red Power political mobilization of the 1960s.

American Ethnic Politics

Two forces converged in the 1960s to end the assimilationist thrust of federal Indian policy and to set in motion the contemporary period of American Indian ethnic renewal. One was the civil rights movement and the shifts in American social and political culture that followed in its wake. The other was President Lyndon Johnson's solution to the problem of race in America—the Great Society, the War on Poverty, and the civil rights legislation of the 1960s. The fluctuating currents of cultural change and reform politics that marked the 1960s were responded to by increasingly cosmopolitan and sophisticated American Indians who lobbied successfully to send federal War on Poverty and community development resources into impoverished urban and reservation communities.[54]

This mix of volatile ethnic politics and an explosion of federal resources, many earmarked for minority programs, combined with earlier federal Indian policies, which had concentrated large numbers of tribally diverse, educated, acculturated, and organizationally connected Indians in American cities. The result: a large-scale mobilization of urban Indians marked by a rapid growth of political organizations, newspapers, and community programs. To grasp fully these dynamic changes in many American communities, Indian and non-Indian, it is important to recall the atmosphere of the 1960s. As Hugh Davis Graham writes in the Introduction to *The Civil Rights Era*:

> This is a story about a rare event in America: a radical shift in national social policy. Its pre-condition was a broader social revolution, the black civil rights movement that surged up from the South, followed by the nationwide rebirth of the feminist movement.[55]

The demographic changes that underlay the rise of Black militancy in American cities, namely, the "great Black migration" from the rural south to the urban north,[56] were paralleled by the movement of American Indians off the reservations. The federal response to Black protest—civil rights legislation and the War on Poverty—spilled over into other minority communities, including American Indian communities, which were quickly mobilizing in the wake of Black insurgency. The ethnic militancy of the 1960s redefined mainstream America as "White" and exposed and challenged its racial hegemony. For America's ethnic minorities it was a time to cast off negative stereotypes, to reinvent ethnic and racial social meanings and self-definitions, and to embrace ethnic pride. For American Indians, it marked the emergence of supratribal identification, the rise of Indian activism, and a period of increased Indian ethnic pride. Despite their often brutal treatment by United States' authorities and citizens throughout American history. American Indians have ironically, but consistently, occupied a romanticized niche in the American popular media and imagination.[57] The durable symbolic value of the American Indian as a cultural icon was further enhanced by the increased ethnic pride characterizing the civil rights era. The result increased the appeal of Indian ethnicity for many individuals, and no doubt contributed to the resurgence of Indian self-identification.

In addition to the symbolic allure of Indian ethnicity, there were also material incentives. Castile notes the connection between these ideational and material realms, commenting that American Indians were able "to manipulate their symbolic position [in American history and society] in ways that grant[ed] them a political leverage far greater than their numbers justif[ied]. By keeping a sharp eye on the political waves of ethnicity, which they [could] not raise themselves, shrewd timing ... allow[ed] them to ride those waves and maximize their impact in positive ways."[58] American Indians indeed were able to navigate the changing currents of

American ethnic politics, and their successes resulted in increased federal spending on Indian affairs, making American Indian identification a more attractive ethnic option for many Americans of Indian descent. The settlement of land claims by the Indian Claims Commission and the U.S. federal court system during the 1970s and 1980s was another important source of funds for Indian communities. Churchill reports that more than $128 million in Indian land claims awards were disbursed between 1946 and 1970, and by 1978 the total amount of claims awards exceeded $657 million.[59] In addition, a number of major land claims were settled during the early 1980s, some of which involved large controversial settlements. Most notable are the claims of Maine Passamoquoddy and Penobscot tribes, who in 1980 recovered 300,000 acres of land and received a payment of $27 million.[60]

Increased federal spending in general and land claim awards in particular, along with the inclusion of Indians in many affirmative action and minority set-aside programs, contributed to the American Indian ethnic resurgence in part because they increased both the symbolic and the potential material value of Indian ethnicity. Individuals of Indian ancestry became more willing to identify themselves as Indians, whether or not such identification was a strategy to acquire a share of real or putative land claims awards or other possible ethnically-allocated rewards (such as scholarships, mineral royalties, employment preference). It was in this atmosphere of increased resources, ethnic grievances, ethnic pride, and civil rights activism that Red Power burst on the scene in the late 1960s and galvanized a generation of Native Americans. The rest of the country watched as the media covered such events as the occupation of Alcatraz Island, the takeover of the Bureau of Indian Affairs headquarters in Washington, D.C., and the siege at Wounded Knee.

American Indian Activism: Red Power

The shifting political culture and protest climate of the 1960s and 1970s spawned many Indian activist organizations, such as the American Indian Movement (AIM) and the National Indian Youth Council, and produced a number of Indian protest actions: the 19-month occupation of Alcatraz Island which began in 1969; the 1972 Trail of Broken Treaties which culminated in a week-long occupation of the Bureau of Indian Affairs in Washington, D.C.; the 71-day siege at Wounded Knee, South Dakota in 1973; the 1975 shoot-out on the Pine Ridge Reservation in South Dakota which resulted in the imprisonment of Leonard Peltier; and numerous protest events in cities and on reservations around the United States, concluding with the 1978 Longest Walk to Washington, D.C. These events and this era stand out boldly in the publications and accounts of Native Americans living at that time, particularly native youth.[61] Red Power played an important symbolic role in motivating individual ethnic renewal on the part of Indian participants and observers; this ethnic renewal took two forms, and both forms are relevant to the argument I present here.

The first type of individual ethnic renewal involves individuals who most likely would have identified themselves as Indians in earlier censuses, and thus is best summarized as a resurgence in ethnic pride which did not involve taking on a new ethnic identity (e.g., does not involve racial switching). Instead, this type of individual ethnic renewal involved a reaffirmation, reconstruction, or redefinition of an individual's ethnicity. For example, the slogan, "I'm Black and I'm proud" reflected such a redefinition of "Negro" in the U.S. in the 1960s. These individuals did not change their race, rather they changed the *meaning* of their race. This parallels the resurgence of Native American ethnic pride among individuals who already identified themselves as "Indian."

The second type of individual ethnic renewal involves individuals who would *not* have identified themselves as Indian in earlier censuses, but rather would have "passed" into the non-Indian race categories. For these individuals, a resurgence of ethnic pride meant not only redefining the worth and meaning of their ancestry, but also involved laying a new claim to that ancestry by switching their race on the census form from non-Indian to Indian. This type of individual ethnic renewal is, I believe, reflected in census data; but currently the data do not exist for evaluating directly the influences of federal Indian policy, the ethnic politics of the civil rights era, or the rise of Indian activism on this kind of ethnic renewal. Such an evaluation would require examining the backgrounds and beliefs of those individuals who changed their race from non-Indian to Indian in the 1970, 1980, and 1990 Censuses. As Sandefur and McKinnell state, "it is not possible to know from census data who has changed his or her racial identification since a previous census."[62] Indeed, researchers are awaiting such a definitive study. Snipp notes, while it is plausible that census increases reflect the fact that "more mixed ancestry persons are identifying themselves as American Indians than in the past, . . . [it] is virtually impossible to prove."[63]

PERSONAL PERSPECTIVES ON ETHNIC POLITICS AND RED POWER ACTIVISM

To begin to understand the role of politics and Red Power activism in promoting increased American Indian ethnic pride and awareness, I interviewed and corresponded with 25 Native Americans who participated in or observed the activist events of the 1970s (or, in the case of the 2 youngest respondents, who had heard accounts of the Red Power period from their parents). Of the 25, 11 were women and 14 were men; on average they were in their mid-40s (the youngest was 21, the oldest 79); 5 resided mainly in reservation communities, 9 were urban Indians, and 11 had lived on both settings for significant portions of their lives; 15 were activists during the 1960s and mid-1970s at the height of Red Power, another 5 became activists in the late 1970s and 1980s, and 5 described themselves as nonactivists. I asked each of the 25 whether the movement had any effect on the more their communities, and if so, what its impact was.

In addition to these interviews, I surveyed a large and growing body of oral histories and published personal accounts of recent Indian history. The responses in the archival material, the published literature, and in my interviews were quite similar: The activist period raised individual ethnic consciousness and prompted dialogues about the meaning of Indianness. These various sources also reflected some interesting regional and generational differences in assessments of the meaning and consequences of Red Power. The remainder of this paper provides an interpretive context for these native voices speaking about their ethnic identity and how it was influenced by the decade of American Indian activism that began with the occupation of Alcatraz Island.

Activism and Identity: Reversing the Causal Connection

The traditionally understood relationship between identity and activism is that identity precedes activism, making particular individuals more likely than others to engage in protest activities.[64] Much recent research on social movements questions this assumption, exploring more fully the interrelationships among activism, identity, and culture. Fantasia points out the capacity of both spontaneous and planned protest action to reshape conceptions of personal and collective identity, redefine notions of fairness and justice, and build community consensus and solidarity.[65] Benford and Hunt, Hunt and Benford, and Snow and Anderson document the emergence of collective ideologies and identities in social movement organizations and movements, and the interplay between movement-sited interpretative frames and rhetoric and larger political and cultural themes in the emergence of collective identity.[66] Taylor and Whittier and Groch focus on the importance of group boundaries and collectively negotiated and defined meaning systems in the emergence of oppositional consciousness among movement participants and constituents.[67]

The resurgence of American Indian ethnic identity in the 1970s and 1980s is consistent with these findings and illustrates the power of activism to inspire individual and collective ethnic pride and to raise ethnic consciousness. My interviews most strongly support the notion that activism has its biggest impact on individuals who themselves personally witness or become directly involved in protest action. The narrative accounts of both activists and nonactivists, however, also suggest that social movements exert a wider impact, affecting the attitudes of nonparticipants as well, though to a lesser extent.

Alcatraz, Red Power, and the Resurgence of Indian Ethnic Pride

The 1960s were characterized by increasing levels of American Indian protest activism, much of which tended to be regional and associated with specific tribal groups and grievances (e.g., the "fish-ins" of the mid-1960s in the Pacific Northwest). The national Red Power movement got fully underway in November 1969, when Richard Oakes led a group of fellow Indian students from San Francisco State University and landed on Alcatraz Island in San Francisco Bay. Calling themselves "Indians of All Tribes," they claimed the island by "right of discovery." The takeover caught the attention of a nation already engrossed in the escalating protest and conflict of the civil rights movement, and the rhetoric and demands of the Alcatraz occupiers captured the imagination of many Native Americans. Indians of All Tribes issued the following proclamation which reflected their supratribal roots and agenda:

We, the native Americans, re-claim the land known as Alcatraz Island in the name of all American Indians. . . . Since the San Francisco Indian Center burned down, there is no place for Indians to assemble. . . . Therefore we plan to develop on this island several Indian institutions: 1. A CENTER FOR NATIVE AMERICAN STUDIES. . . . 2. AN AMERICAN INDIAN SPIRITUAL CENTER. . . . 3. AN INDIAN CENTER OF ECOLOGY. . . . 4. A GREAT INDIAN TRAINING SCHOOL . . . [and] and AMERICAN INDIAN MUSEUM. . . . In the name of all Indians, therefore, we reclaim this island for our Indian nations. . . . We feel this claim is just and proper, and that this land should rightfully be granted to us for as long as the rivers shall run and the sun shall shine.

Signed, INDIANS OF ALL TRIBES[68]

During the next nineteen months the Alcatraz occupiers negotiated unsuccessfully with local and federal authorities and eventually were removed from the island in June 1971. Despite the failure to achieve their demands, as Hauptman notes, "the events at Alcatraz were a major turning point in the history of Indian activism . . . [and] became the symbol to many young, disillusioned Indians, . . . stimulating a rash of similar protests."[69] The occupation highlighted Indian grievances and promoted Indian pride. Deloria summarizes its importance: "Alcatraz was the master stroke of Indian activism."[70] Writing at the height of Red Power activism in the early 1970s, he recognized the immediate impact of the movement on American Indian ethnicity:

"Indianness" was judged on whether or not one was present at Alcatraz, Fort Lawson, Mt. Rushmore, Detroit, Sheep Mountain, Plymouth Rock, or Pitt River. . . . The activists controlled the language, the issues, and the attention.[71]

The much publicized Alcatraz takeover and the first months of the occupation constituted a powerful symbolic moment both for those Native Americans involved in the protest and for those who witnessed it from more distant points around the country.[72] Just as the civil rights movement challenged prevailing racial hegemony by reframing Black ethnicity through the assertion of Black pride and Black power, Red Power, in the form of the Alcatraz occupation and the decade of Indian activist events that followed, challenged cultural depictions of Indians as victims of history, as living relics, powerless and subjugated. As a result, the Alcatraz occupation stimulated Indian ethnic pride and prompted a resurgence in American Indian ethnic consciousness. LaNada Means, one of the participants in the occupation, comments:

The protest movement at Alcatraz had positive results. Many individuals were not ashamed to be Indian anymore. People who had relocated in the cities were reidentifying themselves as Indians.[73]

Wilma Mankiller, who went on to become the Principal Chief of the Cherokee Nation of Oklahoma, visited the island many times during the nineteen-month occupation. She describes the personal impact of the event as "an awakening that ultimately changed the course of her life."[74]

> I'd never heard anyone actually tell the world that we needed somebody to pay attention to our treaty rights, that our people had given up an entire continent, and many lives, in return for basic services like health care and education, but nobody was honoring these agreements. For the first time, people were saying things I felt but hadn't known how to articulate. It was very liberating.[75]

My interviews with Native Americans who participated in or observed the events on Alcatraz and later protest events and who were young adults at the time, showed similar reactions. Their reactions affirmed the powerful symbolic meaning of the Alcatraz occupation and its importance in raising ethnic consciousness:

> Alcatraz was a major turning point in my life. For the first time in my life I was proud to be an Indian and an Indian woman. I grew up in an all white area. It was very difficult. You were constantly struggling to maintain any kind of positive feeling, any kind of dignity. Alcatraz changed all that.[76]

> The movement gave me back my dignity and gave Indian people back their dignity. It started with Alcatraz, we got back our worth, our pride, our dignity, our humanity. If you have your dignity and your spirituality and you can pray, then you can wear a tie, carry a briefcase, work a job. If you don't have those things, then you are lost.[77]

> When Alcatraz came, suddenly they bloomed—all the Metis said they were French, now suddenly they said they were Indian. Those with Indian blood hid it, saying they were Turks or Mexicans or Armenians. Now Indians were coming out of the woodwork.[78]

> Every once in a while something happens that can alter the whole shape of a people's history. This only happens once in a generation or lifetime. The big one was Alcatraz.[79]

These quotes communicate a resurgence of ethnic pride and an increased willingness to claim and assert Indian ethnicity. I have argued that assimilation and relocation policies created the population base for a resurgence of Indian ethnicity in cities. Implicit in these policies was also the not-so-subtle subtext of assimilation—that Indianness was something to be discarded, inferior to the larger Anglo culture. While some argue that termination policy was successful in repressing Indian identity in many older native individuals (for instance Baird-Olson refers to those over 30 at the time as the "lost generation"[80]), it seems clearly to have backfired among the younger generation of urban Indians caught up in the youth culture of the 1960s. It was on this mostly younger group that Red Power had its strongest impact.

Mary Crow Dog describes the response of young people on the Rosebud Sioux reservation in South Dakota as AIM swept through on the Trail of Broken Treaties, a nationwide caravan en route to Washington, D.C., in 1972:

> The American Indian Movement hit our reservation like a tornado, like a new wind blowing out of nowhere, a drumbeat from far off getting louder and louder. It was almost like the Ghost Dance fever that had hit the tribes in 1890. . . . I could feel this new thing, almost hear it, smell it, touch it. Meeting up with AIM for the first time loosened a sort of earthquake inside me.[81]

Frances Wise was on the Trail of Broken Treaties:

> Many of the people with us were like me before Alcatraz. They didn't quite understand what was going on, but they were interested. A lot of people joined us [in the auto caravan from Los Angeles to Washington, D.C.]. I remember driving around a freeway cloverleaf outside of Columbus, Ohio. All I could see were cars in front of us and behind us, their lights on, red banners flying from their antennas. It was hard to believe, really. We were that strong. We were fully doing something. It was exciting and fulfilling. It's like someone who's been in bondage. Indian country knew that Indians were on the move.[82]

Despite the power of the times, the actions of Red Power activists were not easily or enthusiastically embraced by all Native Americans. Generational differences were evident in attitudes toward the movement:

> My parents did not want me to get involved [in activism], they weren't active. They were just struggling to live. When they got involved it was out of dire need. Their generation was almost at the point of being beaten into passivity. They would say, "There's nothing we can do; government's too powerful." The defeatism was very strong. One reason things changed then was that the children of those in power were resisting.[83]

> Most of the older generation was forced to assimilate and are still in the mode of assimilation. Their attitude toward activism is "don't rock the boat."[84]

The tendency of the younger generation of Native Americans to recapture a fading or suppressed Indian heritage and to reaffirm Indian identity stood in contrast to the skepticism of their elders. The different reactions to Red Power paralleled the "generation gap" so often used to depict 1960's America, and these differences are consistent with one trend in the 1980 Census data reported by Passel and Berman.[85] They observe that "the 'new' American Indians [those from traditionally non-Indian states] are generally young adults"[86]—precisely the generation that participated in and witnessed Red Power.

Activism as a Crucible for Ethnic Pride and Identity

The occupation of Alcatraz Island was followed by dozens of protest actions around the country throughout most of the 1970s. During this and the following decade, many individuals of native ancestry were motivated to reconnect with their ethnic roots. For Z. G. Standing Bear, the events on Alcatraz and his own participation in protests during the 1970s represented a counterpoint to other aspects of his biography, a tension that took him years to resolve, but one that he settled in favor of his native ancestry:

> I was in Vietnam when I heard about Alcatraz. I thought "Right on! That's great what those guys are doing." . . . It was years later, after hearing Russell Means talk at Florida State University in 1981, that there was a major turning point in my life. I had been on a personal journey to come to terms with my service in the army during the Vietnam War, and Means's talk made me finally decide to go back to my grandfather's culture.[87]

Standing Bear's reference to his "personal journey" is a theme that runs through many oral and written accounts of Red Power and of the individual ethnic renewal that has taken place since that time. The personal journeys described by many Native Americans involve a seeming contradiction: they go forward by going back; or as one native person characterized it to me, "We become what we were." This process of becoming often involves a spiritual component that for many Indians, perhaps for most, represents the symbolic core of Indianness and is a central part of the ethnic renewal process. Deloria acknowledges the cardinal importance of spiritual matters in native life and identifies an underlying spiritual agenda in Indian activism.[88] Indeed, activist Frances Wise noted the direct importance of Red Power activism in changing policies and creating a climate that permitted and supported individual ethnic renewal through traditional dress and spiritual practices. In the early 1970s she was involved in organizing a successful challenge to an Oklahoma school board's restriction on men's hair length. She noted the changes that resulted:

> It had a big impact. People now wear long hair, people who said back then, "Are you sure you know what you're doing with this [protest]?" Now they can wear their hair long—and they do. . . . Another outcome is we have greater numbers of people who have both traditional Indian educations and are also educated in white ways.[89]

During and since the Red Power period, the religious and spiritual dimension of tribal life has become a focal concern among many of the Indian people with whom I spoke. Many reported becoming Sun Dancers for the first time as adults, many spent time with tribal elders seeking instruction in tribal history and traditions, many learned more of their tribal language, many abandoned Christian religions and turned to native spiritual traditions,[90] and some have returned to their home reservations. In recounting his decision to return to the reservation, Horse Capture believes that he is not the only one embarked on such a journey back to what he was:

> Originally I thought I was alone on this quest. But as time has passed, a whole generation and more were influenced by these same forces, and we traveled the same course.[91]

CONCLUSION

The rise in American Indian ethnic identification during the last three decades has resulted from a combination of factors in American politics. Assimilationist federal Indian policies helped to create a bicultural, intermarried, mixed race, urban Indian population living in regions of the country where ethnic options were most numerous; this was a group "poised" for individual ethnic renewal. The ethnic politics of the civil rights era encouraged ethnic identification, the return to ethnic roots, ethnic activism, and provided resources for mobilizing ethnic communities; thus, the climate and policies of civil rights provided individuals of native ancestry (and others as well) symbolic and material incentives to claim or reclaim Indian ethnicity. Red Power activism during the 1960s and 1970s further raised Indian ethnic consciousness by dramatizing long held grievances, communicating an empowered and empowering image of Indianness, and providing Native Americans, particularly native youth, opportunities for action and participation in the larger Indian cause. Together then, federal Indian policies, ethnic politics, and American Indian activism provided the rationale and motivation for individual ethnic renewal.

The overall explanation of the resurgence of American Indian ethnicity I offer here can be seen as part of a general model of ethnic renewal. The impact of federal Indian policies on American Indian ethnic renewal represents an instance of the political construction of ethnicity (i.e., the ways in which political policy, the structure of political opportunity, and patterns of political culture shape ethnic boundaries in society). The impact of events in this larger political arena on Indian ethnic activism and identity illustrates the role of politics and political culture in ethnic mobilization (i.e., the power of political *zeitgeist* and shifting political definitions to open windows of opportunity for ethnic activists and to affirm and render meaningful their grievances and claims). The impact of Red Power on American Indian ethnic consciousness reveals the role of human agency in individual and collective redefinition and empowerment (i.e., the power of activism to challenge prevailing policies, to encourage ethnic awareness, and to foster ethnic community-building). This model of ethnic renewal suggests that, given the capacity of individuals to reinvent themselves and their communities, ethnicity occupies an enduring place in modern societies.

NOTES

1. Consistent with the usage of native and nonnative scholars, I use the terms "American Indian," "Indian," "Native American" and "native" interchangeably to refer to the descendants of the aboriginal inhabitants of North America. I also use the terms "race" and "ethnicity" somewhat interchangeably, although I view ethnicity as the broader concept subsuming race, which generally refers to visible (often skin color) distinctions among populations. Ethnicity can refer not only to somatic or physical differences, but also to differences in language, religion, or culture. I acknowledge the importance, some would say preeminence, of race in historical and contemporary American ethnic relations.

2. Joane Nagel, "Constructing Ethnicity: Creating and Recreating Ethnic Identity and Culture," in *Social Problems* 41 (1994), 1001–26; and Nagel, *American Indian Ethnic Renewal: Red Power and the Resurgence of Identity and Culture* (New York: Oxford University Press, 1997).

3. Fredrik Barth, *Ethnic Groups and Boundaries* (Boston: Little, Brown, 1969).

4. Kathleen N. Conzen et al., "The Invention of Ethnicity: A Perspective from the U.S.A.," in *Journal of American Ethnic History* 12 (1992), 3–41; and Werner Sollors, ed., *The Invention of Ethnicity* (New York: Oxford University Press, 1989).

5. Robert E. Park, *Race and Culture* (Glencoe, Ill.: The Free Press, 1950); Milton Gordon, "Assimilation in America: Theory and Reality," in *Daedalus* 90 (1961), 263–285; and Nathan Glazer and Daniel P. Moynihan, *Beyond the Melting Pot* (Cambridge: Harvard University Press, 1963).

6. Mary C. Waters, *Ethnic Options: Choosing Identities in America* (Berkeley: University of California Press, 1990).

7. Marvin Harris, *Patterns of Race in the Americas* (New York: Norton, 1964); and James F. Davis, *Who Is Black? One Nation's Definition* (University Park, Pa.: Pennsylvania State University Press, 1991).

8. See Sara Collas, "Transgressing Racial Boundaries: The Maintenance of the Racial Order," paper presented at the annual meeting of the American Sociological Association, August 8, 1994, Los Angeles, for a discussion of "transgressing racial boundaries."

9. Davis, *Who Is Black?*; Judith Stein, "Defining the Race, 1890–1930," in Sollors, ed., *The Invention of Ethnicity*, 77–104; Verna M. Keith and Cedric Herring, "Skin Tone and Stratification in the Black Community," in *American Journal of Sociology*, 97 (1991), 760–78; and Mary C. Waters, "Ethnic and Racial Identities of Second Generation Blacks in New York City," in *International Migration Review* 28 (1994), 795–820.

10. Silvia Pedraza, "Ethnic Identity: Developing a Hispanic-American Identity," paper presented at the annual meeting of the American Sociological Association, August 5, 1994; Felix Padilla, *Latino Ethnic Consciousness: The Case of Mexican Americans and Puerto Ricans in Chicago* (Notre Dame, Ind.: University of Notre Dame Press, 1985); Padilla, "Latino Ethnicity in the City of Chicago," in S. Olzak and J. Nagel, eds., *Competitive Ethnic Relations* (New York: Academic Press, 1986); and Marta E. Jimenez et al., *The Politics of Ethnic Construction: Hispanic, Chicano, Latino?* (Beverly Hills: Sage Publications, 1992).

11. Yen Le Espiritu, *Asian American Pan-Ethnicity: Bridging Institutions and Identities* (Philadelphia: Temple University Press, 1992); and William Wei, *The Asian American Movement* (Philadelphia: Temple University Press, 1993).

12. Stephen Cornell, *The Return of the Native: American Indian Political Resurgence* (New York: Oxford University Press, 1988); Sally McBeth, "Layered Identity Systems in Western Oklahoma Indian Communities," paper presented at the annual meeting of the American Anthropological Association, November 17, 1989, Washington, D.C.; and Jack D. Forbes, "Undercounting Native Americans: The 1980 Census and the Manipulation of Racial Identity in the United States," in *Wicazo Sa Review* 6 (1990), 2–26.

13. Richard D. Alba, *Ethnic Identity: The Transformation of White America* (New Haven: Yale University Press, 1990); Waters, *Ethnic Options*; Stanley Lieberson and Mary C. Waters, *From Many Strands: Ethnic and Racial Groups in Contemporary America* (New York: Russell Sage Foundation, 1988); Anny Bakalian, *Armenian-Americans: From Being to Feeling Armenian* (New Brunswick, N.Y.: Transaction Books, 1993); and Mary E. Kelly, "Ethnic Pilgrimages: Lithuanian Americans in Lithuania," paper presented at the annual meeting of the Midwest Sociological Society, St. Louis, March 13, 1994.

14. Richard A. Schermerhorn, *Ethnic Plurality in India* (Tucson: University of Arizona Press, 1978).

15. Randy Hodson et al., "National Tolerance in Yugoslavia," in *American Journal of Sociology* 99 (1994), 1534–58.

16. Baldev Raj Nayar, *Politics in the Punjab* (New Haven: Yale University Press, 1966).

17. Joseph Lelyveld, *Move Your Shadow: South Africa, Black and White* (New York: Penguin, 1985).

18. Davis, *Who Is Black?*

19. Jim Larimore and Rick Waters, "American Indians Speak Out Against Ethnic Fraud in College Admissions," paper presented at a conference sponsored by the American Council on Education: "Educating One-Third of a Nation IV: Making Our Reality Match Our Rhetoric," October 22, 1993, Houston; Jerry Reynolds, "Indian Writers: Real or Imagined," in *Indian Country Today*, September 8, 1993: A1, A3; and C. Matthew Snipp, "Some Observations about the Racial Boundaries and the Experiences of American Indians," paper presented at the University of Washington, April 22, 1993, Seattle.

20. Snipp, "Some Observations."

21. Some native scholars and commentators have taken offense at the notion that Indians are a "mere" ethnic group, arguing that they are instead, sovereign nations. Haunani-Kay Trask, "Politics in the Pacific Islands: Imperialism and Native Self-Determination," in *Amerasia* 16 (1990), 1–19; Trask, "Natives and Anthropologists: The Colonial Struggle," in *The Contemporary Pacific* 3 (1991), 159–67; Glenn T. Morris, "The International Status of Indigenous Nations Within the United States," in W. Churchill, ed., *Critical Issues in Native North America*, Document No. 62 (Copenhagen: International Work Group for Indigenous Affairs, 1989), 1–14; Vine Deloria, Jr., and Clifford Lytle, *The Nations Within: The Past and Future of American Indian Sovereignty* (New York: Pantheon Books, 1984); and Lenore A. Stiffarm and Phil Lane, Jr., "The Demography of Native North America: A Question of American Indian Survival," in M.A. Jaimes, ed., *The State of Native America: Genocide, Colonization, and Resistance* (Boston: South End Press, 1992).

22. Vine Deloria, Jr., "American Indians," in J.D. Buenker and L.A. Ratner, eds., *Multiculturalism in the United States: A Comparative Guide to Acculturation and Ethnicity* (Westport, Conn.: Greenwood Press, 1992).

23. William Masumura and Patricia Berman, "American Indians and the Census," unpublished manuscript. In 1980, about one-fifth of the U.S. Census respondents who identified their race as "American Indian" did not report a tribe. U.S. Bureau of the Census, *American Indian Population Estimates by Tribe*, Unpublished Tables, 1981.

24. Researchers believe that the racial self-reporting introduced by the U.S. Census in 1960 contributed to the 46 percent increase from 1950 to 1960. After 1960, however, census coding procedures were no longer a major explanation for American Indian population growth. See C. Matthew Snipp, *American Indians: The First of This Land* (New York: Russell Sage Foundation, 1989); Russell Thornton, *American Indian Holocaust and Survival*; Thornton, *The Cherokees: A Population History* (Lincoln: University of Nebraska Press, 1990); Stiffarm and Lane, "The Demography of Native North America"; Karl Eschbach, "Shifting Boundaries: Regional Variation in Patterns of Identification as American Indians," Ph.D. diss., Department of Sociology, Harvard University, 1992; Jeffrey S. Passel and Patricia A. Berman, "Quality of the 1980 Census Data for American Indians," in *Social Biology* 33 (1986), 163–82; and U.S. Bureau of the Census, *We, the First Americans* (Washington, D.C.: Government Printing Office, 1988).

25. Passel and Berman, "Quality of the 1980 Census Data for American Indians," 164; and Vine Deloria, Jr., "The New Indian Recruits: The Popularity of Being Indian," in *Americans Before Columbus* 3 (1986), 3, 6–8.

26. Thornton, *American Indian Holocaust and Survival*, 174.

27. Stanley Steiner, *The New Indians* (New York: Harper and Row, 1967); and Snipp, *American Indians*, 57.

28. Eschbach, "Shifting Boundaries."

29. Vine Deloria, Jr., "Native Americans: The American Indian Today," in *The Annals of the American Academy of Political and Social Sciences* 454 (1981), 140; Tim Giago, "Big Increases in 1990 Census not Necessarily Good for Tribes," in *Lakota Times*, March 12, 1991: 3; and Valorie Taliman, "Lakota Declaration of War," *News From Indian Country* 7 (1993), 10.

30. Passel and Berman, "Quality of 1980 Census Data for American Indians," 164; and David Harris, "The 1990 Census Count of American Indians: What Do the Numbers Really Mean?" in *Social Science Quarterly* 75 (1994), 580–593. Errors of closure in the Indian population were estimated to be 9.2 percent for the 1960–1970 decade, 25.2 percent for the 1970–1980 decade, and 9.2 percent for the 1980–1990 decade. In 1980, the year of largest Indian population growth, the error of closure translated into more than 350,000 "new" Indians (See Passel and Berman, "Quality of 1980 Census Data," 164); many of these new identifiers most likely identified their tribe as "Cherokee." Russell Thornton, et al., "Appendix: Cherokees in the 1980 Census," in Thornton, *The Cherokees*, 200.

31. Sorkin, *The Urban American Indian*, 10; U.S. Bureau of the Census, *Census of Population*, 150; and U.S. Bureau of the Census, *Census of the Population, 1990*.

32. Indian states are those states with a native population of 3000 or more in 1950: Alaska, Arizona, Idaho, Michigan, Minnesota, Montana, Nebraska, Nevada, New Mexico, New York, North Carolina, North Dakota, Oklahoma, Oregon, South Dakota, Utah, Washington, Wisconsin, and Wyoming; California was excluded because it "behaved demographically over the last three decades much like a typical 'non-Indian' state." Passel and Berman, "Quality of 1980 Census Data for American Indians, 171.

33. Eschbach, "The Enduring and Vanishing American Indian," 103. The correspondence between Passel and Berman and Eschbach is close, but not perfect. For instance, Passel and Berman's "Indian" states of Michigan, Nebraska, and New York are contained in Eschbach's six non-Indian regions, and unlike Passel and Berman, Eschbach includes California as an Indian region. I follow Passel and Berman in excluding California from Indian regions.

34. Snipp, *American Indians*, 157.

35. Sandefur and McKinnell, "American Indian Intermarriage," 348.

36. Eschbach, "The Enduring and Vanishing American Indian," 93.

37. Sandefur and McKinnell, "American Indian Intermarriage," 348.

38. Eschbach, "The Enduring and Vanishing American Indian," 95.

39. Eschbach, "The Enduring and Vanishing American Indian," 103.

40. Eschbach, "Shifting Racial Boundaries," 150; and Eschbach, "The Enduring and Vanishing American Indian," 97.

41. Eschbach, "The Enduring and Vanishing American Indian," 97.

42. U.S. Bureau of the Census, *Census of Population, 1980*, 203.

43. U.S. Bureau of the Census, *Census of the Population, 1990*, 66.

44. For instance, Snipp (*American Indians*, 175–76) reports that in the Mountain states 62.0 percent of Indians report speaking a native language at home, compared to only 3.6 percent in the South Atlantic states.

45. For instance, the Indian Reorganization Act of 1934 (IRA) reaffirmed tribal rights. Many critics maintain that the IRA was also an acculturation program of sorts, because it created tribal "councils" with "chairmen" linked to the Bureau of Indian Affairs. Deloria and Lytle, *The Nations Within*; and Duane Champagne, "American Indian Values and the Institutionalization of IRA Governments," in J.R. Joe, ed., *American Indian Policy and Cultural Values: Conflict and Accommodation*, Contemporary American Indian Issues Series, No. 6 (Los Angeles: American Indian Studies Center, UCLA Publications Services Department, 1986).

46. Gerald D. Nash, *The American West Transformed: The Impact of the Second World War* (Bloomington: Indiana University Press, 1985); and Alison Ricky Bernstein, "Walking in Two Worlds: American Indians and World War II," Ph.D. diss., Department of History, Columbia University, 1986.

47. The "termination" era in federal Indian policy began in 1946 with the creation of the Indian Claims Commission, which was designed to settle all Indian land claims, and so to begin a process of ending (terminating) the federal-Indian trust relationship. Termination policies were unofficially suspended when the Kennedy administration took office in 1961, although a number of tribes were terminated after that date. A 1970 statement by President Richard M. Nixon that embraced Indian "self-determination" marked the official turning point in federal Indian policy, shifting it from "termination" to "self-determination" (see Felix Cohen, *Felix S. Cohen's Handbook of Federal Indian Law* [Charlottesville, Va., Michie Bobbs-Merrill, 1982] for a summary of federal Indian policy).

48. Sorkin, *The Urban American Indian,* Chapter 3.

49. Joan Ablon, "American Indian Relocation: Problems of Dependency and Management in the City," in *Phylon* 66 (1965), 362–71.

50. Hazel Hertzberg, *The Search for an American Indian Identity: Modern Pan-Indian Movements* (Syracuse: Syracuse University Press, 1971); Jeanne Guillemin, *Urban Renegades: The Cultural Strategy of American Indians* (New York: Columbia University Press, 1975); C. Hoy Steele, "Urban Indian Identity in Kansas: Some Implications for Research," in J.W. Bennett, ed., *The New Ethnicity: Perspectives from Ethnology* (St. Paul: West Publishing Company, 1975), 167–78; Janosz Mucha, "From Prairie to the City: Transformation of Chicago's American Indian Community," in *Urban Anthropology* 12 (1983), 337– 371; and Joan Weibel-Orlando, *Indian Country, L.A.: Maintaining Ethnic Community in Complex Society* (Champaign: University of Illinois Press, 1991).

51. William H. Hodge, "Navajo Urban Migration: An Analysis from the Perspective of the Family," in J.O. Waddell and O.M. Watson, eds., *The American Indian in Urban Society* (Boston: Little, Brown, and Company, 1971), 346–392.

52. Weibel-Orlando, *Indian Country, L.A.*

53. Blue Clark, "Bury My Heart in Smog: Urban Indians," P. Weeks, ed., *The American Indian Experience. A Profile: 1524 to the Present* (Arlington Heights, Ill.: Forum Press, 1988), 289.

54. Shirley Hill Witt, "Nationalistic Trends among American Indians," in S. Levine and N.O. Lurie, eds., *The American Indian Today* (Deland, Fl.: Everett/Edwards, Inc., 1968), 68; and Vine Deloria, Jr., "Legislation and Litigation Concerning American Indians," in *The Annals of the American Academy of Political and Social Science* 436 (1978), 88.

55. Hugh Davis Graham, *The Civil Rights Era: Origins and Development of National Policy, 1960–1972* (New York: Oxford University Press, 1990), 3.

56. Richard A. Cloward and Frances Fox Piven, *The Politics of Turmoil: Poverty, Race, and the Urban Crisis* (New York: Vintage Books, 1975); Thomas B. Edsall and Mary D. Edsall, *Chain Reaction: The Impact of Race, Rights, and Taxes on American Politics* (New York: W.W. Norton, 1991); and Nicholas Lemann, *The Promised Land: The Great Black Migration and How It Changed America* (New York: A.A. Knopf, 1991).

57. Robert F. Berkhofer, Jr., *The White Man's Indian: Images of the American Indian from Columbus to the Present* (New York: A.A. Knopf, 1978).

58. George P. Castile, "Indian Sign: Hegemony and Symbolism in Federal Indian Policy," in G.P. Castile and R.L. Bee, eds., *State and Reservation: New Perspectives on Federal Indian Policy* (Tucson: University of Arizona Press, 1992), 183.

59. Ward Churchill, "The Earth is Our Mother: Struggles for American Indian Land and Liberation in the Contemporary United States," in M.A. Jaimes, ed., *The State of Native America*, 139–188; see also Nancy O. Lurie, "The Indian Claims Commssion," in *Annals of the American Academy of Political and Social Science* 436 (1978), 101.

60. M. Annette Jaimes, "Federal Indian Identification Policy: A Usurpation of Indigenous Sovereignty in North America," in M.A. Jaimes, ed., *The State of Native America*, 123–28.

61. Adam Fortunate Eagle, *Alcatraz! Alcatraz! The Indian Occupation of 1969–71* (San Francisco: Heyday Books, 1992); and Mary Crow Dog and Richard Erdoes, *Lakota Woman* (New York: Grove Weidenfield, 1990).

62. Sandefur and McKinnell, "American Indian Intermarriage," 348.

63. Snipp, "Some Observations," 16; Russell Thornton, et al., "American Indian Fertility Patterns: 1910 and 1940–1980," in *American Indian Quarterly* 15 (1991), 365; and Harris, "The 1990 Census Count of American Indians," 592.

64. For a review of this literature see Doug MacAdam, *Freedom Summer* (New York: Oxford University Press, 1988); and Sidney Tarrow, "Mentalities, Political Cultures, and Collective Action Frames," in A.D. Morris and C.M. Mueller, eds., *Frontiers in Social Movement Theory* (New Haven: Yale University Press, 1992), 174–202.

65. Rick Fantasia, *Cultures of Solidarity* (Berkeley: University of California Press, 1988).

66. Robert D. Benford and Scott A. Hunt, "Dramaturgy and Social Movements: The Social Construction and Communication of Power," in *Sociological Inquiry* 62 (1992), 36–55; Hunt and Benford, "Identity Talk in the Peace and Justice Movement," in *Journal of Contemporary Ethnog-*

raphy 22 (1994), 488–517; and David A. Snow and Leon Anderson, *Down on Their Luck: A Study of Homeless Street People* (Berkeley: University of California Press, 1993).

67. Verta Taylor and Nancy E. Whittier, "Collective Identity in Social Movement Communities: Lesbian Feminist Mobilization," in A.D. Morris and C.M. Mueller, eds., *Frontiers in Social Movement Theory*, 104–120; and Sharon A. Groch, "Oppositional Consciousness: Its Manifestations and Development: A Case Study of People With Disabilities," in *Sociological Inquiry* 64 (1994), 369– 395.

68. Peter Blue Cloud, *Alcatraz Is Not an Island* (Berkeley: Wingbow Press, 1972), 40–42.

69. Laurence M. Hauptman, *The Iroquois Struggle for Survival: World War II to Red Power* (Syracuse: Syracuse University Press), 227.

70. Vine Deloria, Jr., "The Rise of Indian Activism" in R. Gomez et al., eds., *The Social Reality of Ethnic America* (Lexington, Mass.: D.C. Heath, 1974), 184–185.

71. Deloria, "The Rise of Indian Activism," 184–85. In written correspondence with Deloria in the summer of 1993, I asked him about the longer-term impact of the Red Power movement. He wrote: "This era will probably always be dominated by the images and slogans of the AIM people. The real accomplishments in land restoration, however, we made by quiet determined tribal leaders." Deloria, personal communication, 1993.

72. See Troy Johnson, "The Indian Occupation of Alcatraz Island, Indian Self-Determination, and the Rise of Indian Activism," Ph.D. diss., Department of History: University of California at Los Angeles, 1993; also see "Alcatraz Revisited: The 25th Anniversary for the Occupation," a special issue of *American Indian Culture and Research Journal* [vol. 18, no. 4, 1994]).

73. Kenneth R. Philp, *Indian Self-Rule: First-Hand Accounts of Indian-White Relations from Roosevelt to Reagan* (Salt Lake City: Howe Brothers, 1986), 230; also see LaNada Means Boyer, "Reflections on Alcatraz," in *American Indian Culture and Research Journal* 18 (1994), 75–92.

74. Johnson, "The Indian Occupation of Alcatraz Island," 125.

75. Mankiller quoted in Johnson, "The Indian Occupation of Alcatraz Island," 125.

76. Telephone interview with Frances Wise, Oklahoma City, OK, August 24, 1993.

77. Telephone interview with Len Foster, Ft. Defiance, AZ, September 5, 1993.

78. Anonymous interview, summer, 1993.

79. Telephone interview with George Horse Capture, Fort Belknap, MT, May 24, 1993.

80. Karren Baird-Olson, "The Survival Strategies of Plains Indian Women Coping with Structural and Interpersonal Victimization on a Northwest Reservation," Ph.D., diss. Department of Sociology, University of New Mexico, 1994.

81. May Crow Dog and Richard Erdoes, *Lakota Woman*, 73–74.

82. Telephone interview with Frances Wise, Oklahoma City, OK, August 24, 1993.

83. Telephone interview with Leonard Peltier, Leavenworth, KS, June 1, 1993.

84. Interview with Loretta Flores, Lawrence, KS, May 12, 1993.

85. Passel and Berman, "Quality of 1980 Census Data," 173.

86. Passel and Berman, "Quality of 1980 Census Data," 173.

87. Telephone interview with Z. G. Standing Bear, Valdosta, GA, June 25, 1993. To affirm this change, Z. G. reclaimed his family name of Standing Bear. His family's reaction revealed the continuing generation gap: "'What are you trying to prove?' one said, 'all that stuff is over and done with.'" Z.G. Standing Bear, "Questions of Assertion, Diversity, and Spirituality: Simultaneously Becoming a Minority and a Sociologist," in *The American Sociologist* 20 (1988), 363–71.

88. Vine Deloria, Jr., *God is Red: A Native View of Religion*, 2nd ed. (Golden, Col.: North American Press, 1992).

89. Telephone interview with Frances Wise, Oklahoma City, OK, August 25, 1993.

90. This return to traditional spirituality has been particularly evident in prisons, where there has been a legal battle over Native American prisoners' rights to engage in particular spiritual practices (e.g., the building of sweatlodges on prison grounds or the wearing of braids and medicine bundles). These disputes led to the introduction in 1993 of Senate Bill 1021, the Native American Free Exercise of Religion Act (see Little Rock Reed, "Rehabilitation: Contrasting Cultural Perspectives and the Imposition of Church and State," in *Journal of Prisoners on Prisons* 2 [1990], 3–28).

91. George P. Horse Capture, "An American Indian Perspective," in H.J. Viola and C. Margolis, eds., *Seeds of Change* (Washington, D.C.: Smithsonian Institution Press, 1991), 203.

17

As the chapter by Margaret Jacobs has already demonstrated, the dance ground has long been contested ground, with Indians using it as a form of cultural expression while missionaries and federal officials sought to put a stop to what they deemed a pernicious vestige of savagery. In this chapter, Clyde Ellis continues the story. He traces the development of modern community festivals (powwows) in Oklahoma, focusing on the struggle between tribal groups who sustained and reformed the powwow and government authorities who tried to stamp it out.

That struggle produced a variety of innovations. For one thing, as dances came to represent the entire community, women began to participate in large numbers. For another, Wild West Shows (which the government did allow) inspired tribal members to borrow elements from Buffalo Bill's extravaganzas for their own dance spectacles. Ellis further suggests how American Indian participation in modern warfare, a patriotic commitment to the United States, actually accompanied the revival of nineteenth-century warrior societies that many thought had disappeared.

The 1930s, when John Collier's reforms freed Indians from restrictions on their personal behavior, also changed things dramatically. Now ordinary Native Americans eager to demonstrate the vitality of their tribal traditions could more openly use powwows as exciting opportunities to educate their children in group traditions and clarify the boundary between themselves and non-Indians. Ellis's article underscores the popularity and vitality of powwow culture, but its most significant contribution is its historical approach. On the surface, groups of Native Americans donning nineteenth-century costumes and dancing to music sung in the tribal language would appear to be participating in a timeless ritual that bound them to an inherited complex of ancient dance, prayer, and song. Ellis demolishes this assumption, arguing instead that the content of powwow dances, as well as the form of the powwow itself, is a twentieth-century invention. His essay emphasizes the fluidity of modern Native American culture. Influenced by forces originating in many places—government policy, world wars, even the Wild West Show—the powwow emerged not as a pristine artifact of ancient America but as a ragged, shifting, sometimes contentious, always uncertain product of modern history.

"We Don't Want Your Rations, We Want This Dance": The Changing Use of Song and Dance on the Southern Plains

Clyde Ellis

On a Saturday in August 1996, at a dance arbor near Meeker, Oklahoma, the evening session of an annual community powwow was briefly delayed as a local Sac and Fox family brought its teenaged son, dressed in dance clothes, into the arena for the first time. The audience listened patiently as relatives spoke on the boy's behalf and watched as his uncle walked him around the arena. One of his grandfathers roached him, called to the drum for the family song, and asked us to dance with the family to commemorate the boy's decision to pay for his seat. The family then held a giveaway to mark the occasion and urged the audience to bear witness to the fact that this young man had accepted the powwow culture that plays an integral role in the maintenance of cultural identity in many Indian communities on the Southern Plains. "It's your *right* to have this way," said one man on behalf of the boy, "But you have to be careful with it."[1]

The decision of that family to bring its son out in his dance clothes publicly affirmed the importance of the songs and rituals that frame contemporary powwows on the Southern Plains. Song and dance, in turn, are expressions of belief and action that, despite decades of adaptation and change, have remained a forum for expressing values not always adequately or appropriately expressed through other means. Part ceremony and part public show, with roots in Indian and non-Indian worlds, the modern powwow has become an arena for maintaining and reinterpreting cultural practices that might otherwise disappear.

Although they are among the most popular contemporary Indian events, powwows are not well understood outside of the communities in which they play such an important role. Heralded by most observers and outsiders as remnants of a glorious past that resists change, powwows are indeed often compelling expressions of unity and cultural perseverance. Yet, the fabric of Southern Plains powwow culture is considerably more subtle and complicated than might appear at first glance; understanding the place and power of song and dance on the Southern Plains requires a deep understanding of the problematic, even antithetical forces that have shaped the contemporary powwow.

Although widely associated with a kind of unifying force in which disagreements are at best liminal, in fact powwows constitute a complicated encounter with contemporary Indian life. In its evolution from tribally specific, society-centered dance

Source: *Western Historical Quarterly,* v. 30 (Summer 1999), pp. 133–154.

to community-wide, often intertribal, expression, the powwow has become, among other things, an event that mediates the place and meaning of change. Far from being a reflection of cultural stasis, or an example of *communitas*, as one scholar has argued in a recent essay on Kiowa dance, powwows are a component of Southern Plains Indian identity that is continually redefined, contested, and negotiated.[2]

Most accounts about dance are inclined to be narratives that describe and explain a generic powwow culture by relying on descriptions of movement and clothing. Thus, we tend to know a great deal about dance styles but little about how powwow people understand and interpret the history and role of dance. This is unfortunate because dance and song are bound up in the construction of social memory, and so, in relationships that mold and influence ritual, economic, and cultural power. Thus, dance occupies an important and sometimes bitterly contested place in many communities. By sorting out the historic and cultural roots of dance on the Southern Plains, the government's attempts to suppress dance, and the forces that have combined to create contemporary powwow culture, this essay discusses how and why song and dance remain central elements in the construction of identity for many Indian people.[3]

Southern Plains powwow people say that dancing is about more than what can be seen. "We have to take care of it, to pass it on to our children. It's our way of life," says Billy Evans Horse, a Kiowa. "It goes with us all the time, every day." Whether through the acknowledgment of kinship ties, the naming of children, or the appointment of ceremonial leaders, in many communities powwows are the central vehicle by which Indian people negotiate a shared identity and a common cultural fabric. Although hardly the only activity Indians use to address these issues, dance is widely perceived as particularly potent and emotionally satisfying for those who embrace it. "Music and dance are integral parts of the social and cultural life of the native peoples of the Southern Plains," writes Thomas Kavanagh, and constitute "the dynamic and creative expressions of Indian identity and pride, both for individuals and communities."[4]

For Theresa Carter, a Kiowa, powwow music is such a central part of her life that she cannot "imagine being without it.... It's part of our everyday life.... I get *tired* sometimes, and I gripe.... But, I need that music." She is not alone. At the 1996 Kiowa *O-ho-mah* ceremonial, one emotionally overwrought man recounted publicly between sobs how his most precious memories were of his mother, "who sang *O-ho-mah* songs to us kids while she did housework. I'll *always* protect these ways. My mom, my dad, all those old ones from a long time back—I can't ever forget how they loved this dance." Richard West, a Southern Cheyenne, writes that dance is "among the most profound cultural expressions—for me personally—of what it is to be Cheyenne." For Haddon Nauni, a Comanche, powwows reflect a larger sense of Comanche social order: "This arena is our society.... Here you are with all of your people, your family.... If you do it in the right way, it'll be a blessing in your life." Ron Harris, a Sac and Fox, sees powwowing as a vital cultural current: "The simplest way to keep the fires strong," he says "is to keep within the sound of the drums." Harry Tofpi, Sr., a Kiowa, believed that *Daw-K'ee*, or God, had given him this way. He was obligated to protect it, he said, "the best way I know how."[5]

The origins of contemporary dance are found in a variety of sources. It is most clearly linked to pre-reservation military societies in which song and dance were devices to remember and maintain important cultural and social practices. One object of the Omaha *Hethu'shka* society, for example, "was to stimulate an heroic spirit among the people and to keep alive the memory of historic and valorous acts." A martial ethos prevailed across the Southern Plains that, among other things, often dictated social status and privilege relative to one's membership and prominence in military societies. This was not limited to men; the Kiowas had at least two women's societies associated with war power in the pre-reservation era. Because society meetings were often used to announce publicly the accomplishments of members, and because songs, dances, and gift-giving invariably accompanied such occasions, a martial context was an elemental component in societal dances.[6]

Moreover, because members typically accepted obligations that lay outside the immediate context of warfare, dance societies assumed integral roles separate from their immediate martial ethos. The late Sylvester Warrior, a Ponca, commented that the Ponca warrior society known as the *Helushka* was much more than a fraternity of fighting men. *Helushka*, he said, had "several meanings. . . . One of them is charity, love of his fellow men. . . . At various times of the year, when they dance, someone benefitted from these dances. In other words, they were benevolent to the people. That was one way they took care of their indigent people, people who were in need, the orphans and the widows. . . . They practiced generosity. Everything they did was to help someone." Among the Kiowas, military societies supervised the Sun Dance encampment, directed funerary practices, named children, and doctored the ill.[7]

Targeted during the reservation era as vestiges of an uncivilized way of life, the Indian Office vigorously opposed societies and their rituals. Breathlessly denouncing dances as lurid spectacles promoting everything from sexual licentiousness to pagan worship, government officials energetically attempted to suppress them. Particularly concerned about the large number of tribes on the Southern Plains, federal officials believed the region a key to the forced assimilation agenda that dominated post–Civil War policy. Convinced of the efficacy of Protestant Christianity, farming, thrift, and individualism, the Southern Plains seemed the perfect laboratory in which to test the effectiveness of the government's assimilation campaign.

The suppression of dances began in earnest in 1882, when the Indian Office issued its "Rules Governing The Court of Indian Offenses," including provisions against plural or polygamous marriages, intoxication, and, of course, dances. In his annual report for 1882, Secretary of the Interior Henry M. Teller described dances as "a great hindrance to the civilization of the Indians." Such "old heathenish dances," he wrote, "are not social gatherings for the amusement of these people, but, on the contrary, are intended to stimulate the warlike passions of the young warriors of the tribe" (such passions including "theft, murder, and rape"). It would be "extremely difficult to accomplish much towards the civilization of the Indians while these adverse influences are allowed to exist," he continued, and concluded that Indians "must be compelled to desist from the savage and barbarous practices that are calculated to continue them in savagery."[8]

The campaign gained momentum during Thomas F. Morgan's tenure as Commissioner of Indian Affairs from 1889 to 1893. A Methodist minister and educator, Morgan brought a reformer's zeal to the task. In 1890, he issued instructions to agents on the Southern Plains concerning the Sun Dance specifically and all other dances by implication. In July of that year, Morgan rebuked Kiowa-Comanche Agent Charles Adams when word reached Washington that the Kiowas had apparently held a Sun Dance. "I have to say emphatically that your action in permitting such scenes is . . . worthy of censure," Morgan wrote. "You are well aware," he continued, "of the demoralizing influence of such dances." And about the dance that had already been held, Morgan wrote: "you should have taken proper steps to have prevented its occurrence." Adams's failure, Morgan ruefully concluded, had thrown "the weight of white civilization onto the scale of barbarism."

Two weeks later Morgan again wrote Adams when he learned that an army detachment from Ft. Sill had, in fact, forcibly prevented the Kiowa Sun Dance. Morgan was "glad to learn . . . that the 'medicine dance' has not taken place. . . . Other dances, while less debasing, are injurious to the Indians in keeping alive old superstitions . . . [a]nd should be discouraged by all possible means." The edict had some effect; the last attempt to hold a Kiowa Sun Dance occurred in 1890, and it has never been revived. As events proved, however, there was more to suppressing dances than squashing one ceremony.[9]

Six years later the bureau stiffened its regulations when Commissioner Daniel Browning declared that "the 'sun dance,' the 'war dance,' and all other so-called feasts . . . shall be considered 'Indian offenses.'" Those guilty of a first offense would forfeit rations, or be jailed, for up to ten days. Subsequent offenses meant lost rations, or jail, for up to thirty days. Morgan had previously stipulated that dancers would face the forfeiture of their allotments, annuities, and tribal status. That there was no statutory support for such actions went unnoticed by the Indian Office.[10]

To ensure that they could identify offenders, especially Ghost Dance advocates, many agents kept blacklists. Kiowa-Comanche Agent Ernest Stecker energetically compiled a blacklist, required approval from his office before any dance or celebration could be held, and singled out those in the "dance crowd" in 1915 for their pernicious influence and determination "to antagonize every effort made toward their uplift." One year later, his successor, C. V. Stinchecum, informed 109 Indians engaged in dancing that individuals who defied him would not receive per capita payments. He wrote to Commissioner of Indian Affairs Cato Sells that he would withhold payments until the Indians had relegated dances "to the dim past." Sells, in turn, authorized the "use of every practical means" to end such celebrations, especially the Ghost Dance, the practice of which survived well into the twentieth century among the Kiowas.[11]

In their determination to destroy dances, agents found eager accomplices at agency missions. In southwest Oklahoma, Baptist and Mennonite missionaries took a particularly strong stand on the matter. In September 1915, Kiowa-Comanche Agency Field Matron Mary Clouse (a Baptist) sent a stinging indictment of the "dance element" to Agent Stinchecum, charging dancers with corrupting the morals of the young people and tearing down the work of the schools. "These dances are one of the breeding places of the illegitimate children, which is [sic] becoming the shame of the tribe. Lust," she warned the agent, "is on the increase." Her husband, Reverend H. H. Clouse, commended Stinchecum in December 1916 "for the strong and noble stand you have taken against the dance question among the Kiowas. . . . These dances are a financial and moral curse; destructive of all that is noble and upbuilding. The dance element will be down on you and will talk against you . . . but you are right and we Indian missionaries are with you and will pray that you and your force will be strong and go on and break up this question."[12]

At the Mennonite Post Oak Mission near Cache, Magdalena Becker, wife of the missionary and herself a part-time field matron, strenuously objected to Comanche dances. Her husband refused baptism to dancers on the grounds that "they had not been saved from their heathenish ways. What would it profit if their names are put in the church rolls but are not written in heaven?" In August 1919, Magdalena insisted that dances caused violent behavior and noted that "wiping [whipping] wifes [sic] was the fruit" of such occasions. Dances, she continued, were "time and money wasted," and she used her influence in 1920 to break up a large dance, saying that it not only disrupted her work but also encouraged immodest behavior among young Kiowas and Comanches. "These dances and large gatherings," she wrote, "are ruining our Indian boys and girls. . . . [T]hey will be paupers before long and the hospitals filled with boys and girls infected by different decease [sic]."[13]

But not every missionary was so confident of being able to discourage Indians from dancing. After attending a Kiowa Ghost Dance in April 1896 near Saddle Mountain, Baptist missionary Isabel Crawford wrote with obvious distress in her diary of being told that God "had given the Book to the White People and taught them to read it, but He gave to the Indians the dance road and told us to hold on to it tight till He came back to earth with our dead and the buffalo." She repeatedly encountered determined resistance, especially from Ghost Dance advocates who publicly taunted her converts. In December 1898, a Kiowa named Domot told her that "the Ghost Dance chiefs who are making all the trouble do not help anybody for they try to pull us all back to the old bad Kiowa roads." Odlepaugh, one of Crawford's defenders and a deacon in the Saddle Mountain congregation, confided to her that "there is one thing that gives us trouble. The Ghost Dance people are all abusing my brother Lucius very strongly because he is willing to let you build on his land. We do not like this, of course, but we can't help it."[14]

The attempt to forcibly suppress dancing reached its apex in the 1920s when Commissioner of Indian Affairs Charles Burke seized on the issue. Having queried agency superintendents in 1920 about the corrosive effects of the "old Indian dances," and acting with knowledge of "The Secret Dance File," a collection of reports on dance practices considered so obscene that it could not be openly circulated, Burke issued Circular 1665 on 26 April 1921. In it he excoriated dances for their "acts of self-torture, immoral relations between the sexes, the sacrificial destruction of clothing or other useful articles, the reckless giving away of property, the use of injurious drugs or intoxicants, and frequent or prolonged periods of celebration which bring the Indians together from remote points to the neglect of their crops, livestock, and home interest."[15]

Two years later Burke issued a supplement to 1665 in which he assured Indians that while he did not intend to deprive them "of decent amusement or occasional feast days . . . [n]o good comes from your 'give-away' custom and dances and it should be stopped." Burke thought dances should be limited to one a month "in the daylight hours of one day in the midweek," that they be abolished completely in April, June, July, and August, that no one under the age of fifty be allowed to participate, and that "a careful propaganda be undertaken to educate public opinion against the dance." Responding to complaints in 1924 stemming from Burke's policies, Secretary of Interior Hubert Work said he intended no suppression of "any dance that has a religious significance, or those given for pleasure and entertainment which are not degrading," but went on to note that "certain practices . . . are against the laws of nature, or moral laws, and all who wish to perpetuate the integrity of their race must refrain from them." Urging Indians to resist those things "which appeal to lower animal emotions only," Work stood his ground.[16]

Despite concerted attempts to prevent the spectacle of what reformers deemed prurient ritual, the fact of the matter is that government officials failed to eradicate dancing. "Even at the height of the Ghost Dance," notes L. G. Moses, "agents were unable to suppress every performance." Dances, he writes, "continued to be performed on citizen allotments, free from interference by the agents."[17] The immediate problem lay in the very system designed to root out the old ways. The Indian Office, a sink-hole of influence peddling, was captive to bald-faced political intrigue so thinly veiled that even career bureaucrats winced at its practices. Senator James H. Kyle observed in 1894 that federal employees often considered Indian work "a license to filch and rob the Indian." General Henry Heth concluded that the bureau was little more than "the dumping ground for the sweepings of the political party that is in power." Supervised in turn by an Interior Department that one scholar suggests was charged with so many disparate tasks that it ought to have been called "the Department of Miscellany," it is little wonder that talk often turned to despair when the Indian Question arose.[18]

Conditions at many Southern Plains agencies confirm William Hagan's observation that the government's interests lay not in assimilating the tribes but in giving "the stamp of legitimacy to United States efforts to concentrate the Indians and open the region to white exploitation." The reservation system on the Southern Plains was a failure from the beginning.[19] Often staffed by hacks and incompetents, many agencies suffered repeated episodes of fraud and near-collapse. The Kiowa-Comanche Agency, observed one inspector in 1885, was little more than an "asylum for relatives and friends who cannot earn a support elsewhere." Forced to weather five agents in eight years (one of whom described his prior applicable experience as a hotel owner; another had been a grocer; a third, a lumberyard manager), Kiowas, Comanches, and Apaches quickly lost their enthusiasm for listening to, or cooperating with, their agents.[20]

At the same time that government agents were attempting to suppress dances, an interesting series of outside forces began to shape dance by actively encouraging Indians to sing and dance. The various Wild West shows and traveling carnivals popular at the turn of the century are a case in point. "Persons in the Indian service continued to rail against the shows," notes L. G. Moses, "but, when pressed, nevertheless cooperated in the contracting of Indians." Beginning in 1883 with William Cody, by 1890, fifty different shows toured the United States, Canada, and Europe. Hiring hundreds of Indians precisely because they could dance, showmen such as Cody and the Miller Brothers eagerly sought out Indians who would, as Thomas

Morgan dourly admitted, parade "with [their] war dances, paint, and blanket." (Show Indians, he lamented in 1889, were "the lowest type of Indian.") In Oklahoma, the Miller Brothers 101 Ranch Real Wild West employed hundreds of Poncas, Osages, Kiowas, and Comanches between 1908 and 1916.[21]

The arena shows Cody popularized appeared to be little more than Hollywood-style extravaganzas. The Wild West's grand entry parade, for example, complete with galloping Indians and gun-toting cowboys was a crowd pleaser that quickly found its way, in modified form, into powwows. (No powwow worth its salt these days opens without a grand entry, often referred to as "the parade in.") There is also evidence that modern contest powwows have roots in the auditions held by the Wild West shows, in which winners were paid for their performance and rewarded with contracts. Yet, as Moses has observed, the Wild West had deeper significance. Indians need not be dragooned into the shows; many of them eagerly signed on for reasons that included "money, travel, and adventure." Black Elk, notes Moses, enjoyed "the adventure of it all, in performing re-creations of brave deeds, and in getting paid for it." Walter Battice, a Sac and Fox who worked with the Miller Brothers, was more blunt about the attractions of working with a Wild West show. About travel he commented, "[y]ou can bet I saw all the law would allow me."[22]

And it is also quite clear that the chance to perform songs and dances for themselves encouraged many Indians to join. Show Indians knew that performing was neither a culturally moribund act nor a clear-cut case of victimization. One Pine Ridge agent noted in 1899 that "school boys speak longingly of the time when they will no longer be required to attend school, but can let their hair grow, dance the Omaha, and go off with the shows." Moses observes that Show Indians "did more than play supportive roles in the victory tableau of 'pioneer' virtue triumphing over 'savagery.'" Wild West Indians "were spokespersons for the right of Indians to he themselves. They survived the contest . . . they were never destroyed." Joe Rockboy recalled that he joined the Wild West because it gave him a chance "to get back on a horse and act it out again."

As Moses notes, Rockboy and others knew, that "ethnic identity need not be preserved through isolation; it may also be promoted through contact [with whites]." And as Mark Thiel has noted, the shows became a kind of surrogate for older forms of gathering: "Reminiscent of pre-reservation warrior customs," he writes, "the commencement and conclusion of many show seasons became a time of celebration when contenders for employment, performers, and their friends and relatives gathered." Indeed, Cody paid Indians to be Indians, an unwittingly efficient encouragement in the maintenance of traditional institutions. ("The Indians had only to be themselves," writes Moses.) What seemed to be show for eager audiences turned out to be something much more important for the Indians who put them on.[23]

It should also be noted that by the mid-1930s, Commissioner of Indian Affairs John Collier inaugurated what he intended would be a radical departure from previous policy. Committed to reversing the attack on tribal culture, Collier issued Circular 2970 on 3 January 1934 calling for the "fullest constitutional liberty, in all matters affecting religion, conscience, and culture." It further required that the Indian Office show an "affirmative, appreciative attitude toward Indian cultural values. No interference with Indian religious life or ceremonial expression will here-after be tolerated. The cultural liberty of Indians is in all respects to be considered equal to that of any non-Indian group."[24]

But there was more than this going on, and leaving the matter in Cody's hands, or in Collier's, ignores much deeper and important actions in Indian communities. ("They didn't need a white man to tell them they could dance," recalled Harry Tofpi.)[25] At the same time that the reservation system was failing, for example, Indians across the Southern Plains recognized the limits of acceptable behavior; in many places they willingly adapted dances to less confrontational modes, or engaged in clandestine meetings.

Whatever they did, Luke Lassiter observes that across the region, Indian people "continually thwarted the goals of the Indian office." Carol Rachlin has written that "even at the worst period of federal suppression," no ceremony was interrupted for more than two years. "There is no renascence of Indian culture in central and western Oklahoma," she concludes, "because Indian culture there never died in order to be reborn." Aided by isolation, by inept agency officials, and most importantly, by a keen determination to maintain control of their ritual and ceremonial institutions, Indians kept dancing. For the Apaches, writes Clifford Coppersmith, "always there was the Mountain Spirit Dance." In its various forms, says Mark Thiel, dance remained "perhaps the most viable surviving pre-reservation activity."[26]

In some cases there was open and defiant resistance, as in the case of the Kiowa *O-ho-mah* Lodge, a warrior society whose members simply refused to stop dancing. Along with the Kiowa *Ton'konga* (Black Legs) and *Tiah Pah* (Gourd Dance) soci-eties, *O-ho-mah* members continued to meet and dance despite intense pressure. Indeed, the Kiowa calendars record the *revival* of the *Taipego* (an earlier name for the *Tiah Pah* Society) and *Ton'konga* in 1912, following the suppression of the Sun Dance and the issuing of individual allotments where, ironically, advocates found remote locales for dances beyond the immediate reach of agents. *O-ho-mah* members mounted an especially determined resistance to government bans. One Kiowa woman recalls her great-grandfather's testimony: "if you want me to give up my Ohomo ways you'll have to kill me. Death is the only thing that will keep me from Ohomo." An *O-ho-mah* song composed during this time tells *O-ho-mah* dancers, "Do not hesitate to dance; Go ahead and be arrested/jailed."[27]

Because resistance often left dancers and their relatives in harm's way, however, many responses were less confrontational. Typically, Indian people consciously modi-fied the role and use of dancing. Thomas Kavanagh observes that on the Southern Plains, the Omaha Dance (also called Grass Dance or Crow Dance) emerged among the Poncas, Kaws, Omahas, Kiowas, and Pawnees in the late nineteenth century at about the same time as the Ghost Dance, and was closely associated with warrior soci-eties. (*O-ho-mah* is the Kiowa name for their version of the Omaha Dance.) The Ghost Dance waned in most places by the late 1890s, but the Omaha Dance (from whence comes the contemporary term "war dance") became increasingly important among the Southern Plains warrior societies. Originally led by officers who wore feather bustles "symbolizing crows flocking over a battlefield," the dance included "ceremonial and rit-ual acts involving the heroism of war deeds, and an accompanying feast."[28]

When the martial ethos of warrior societies began to fade in the late nineteenth century, the immediate societal purpose of the Omaha Dance eroded and its practice took on meanings that reflected what was happening in tribal cultures all over the West. Among the Pawnees, Omahas, Poncas, and Osages, notes Kavanagh, the dance "dispensed with the crow belt while retaining much of the ritual and many of the officers of the Inloshka societies." Subsequently referred to as "Straight Dance," the new dance showed elements of the *Midewiwin*, also called the Drum or Dream Dance, and was notable for a revitalization ethos similar to that prophesied by the Ghost Dance.

Western Oklahoma Indians were also transforming the Omaha Dance. When government policies prevented young Kiowas and Comanches from earning war honors, and thus denied them the social and ritual prestige associated with such honors, many dances and ceremonies underwent a period of significant change. However, submission was not surrender, and all across the Southern Plains societal dances began to reflect new cultural realities. When dance advocates could not follow the example set by the *O-ho-mah*, other alternatives became more attractive. Among other things, "[t]he exclusive right of the men's societies to participate was abandoned," notes Kavanagh, "and the ceremony was opened to all, including women." Moreover, the Kiowas and Comanches were introducing elaborate new dance clothes and styles with bustles worn not only on the back, but also on the arms and neck. Color coordinated beadwork harnesses, dyed long johns, long strips of bells. and large feather crest headdresses completed the ensemble that shortly came to be called fancy dance.[29]

In a similar example, Morris Foster argues that by the early twentieth century, radically changing conditions in Comanche communities constrained their ability to associate in traditional ways and necessitated new arrangements regarding "the public social occasions used for the purpose of community maintenance." Because public gatherings like dances constitute "a history of the organization and maintenance of the Comanche community," notes Foster, they are crucial in the negotiation of public and private codes of conduct that reflect ongoing change.[30]

In Comanche communities this change took several forms. The use of peyote, the influence of Christian missions, and changing spatial relationships dictated by allotment influenced how, when, and for what purpose Comanches gathered. It is important to remember, however, that whether Comanches were coming together for Christian services, peyote meetings, or powwows, their purpose was to maintain and negotiate different, but nonetheless concrete, visions of Comanche identity. One kind of response began in the summer of 1906, with annual summer encampments that featured traditional dances. Quanah Parker, for example, is known to have hosted a series of such encampments at Cache in the years between 1903 and 1908. Often held at isolated allotments, and characterized by fairly small numbers of participants, "[m]ostly, just the elders took part [that is, danced]. Just a few selected men, maybe five or six," said Tennyson Echawaudah. These encampments shortly became the locus of a revived Comanche dance tradition.[31]

Importantly, although the summer encampments were an attempt to revive pre-reservation rituals, in time they gave way to a new social and cultural order inside the Comanche community that was increasingly based on evolving forms of dance gatherings. As communities began to host annual encampments by the second decade of the century, these events reflected a growing generational and ritual schism in the community. Previously restricted from participating (probably due to the lack of warrior status), once the pre-reservation generation began to decline in numbers and influence, many young Comanches by the 1930s gained prominence in the dance crowd as well as in the Native American Church.

Dancing and the use of peyote, Foster notes, had once been "elements of the same belief system." Rising generations of younger Comanches, however, now assigned powwows a distinctly spiritual power, and thus fostered the rise of "two distinct religions'" in the Comanche community. As a result, "powwows provided these younger Comanches with their first opportunity to participate actively in a Comanche-derived . . . form of gathering. . . . Dance gatherings, which previously had had a carnival atmosphere, became more solemn occasions in the late 1930s."[32]

Two simultaneous events seemed to be occurring. On the one hand, pre-reservation warrior societies and their dance rituals maintained some of the power and utility that had previously made them so important. On the other hand, as dance traditions responded to new realities, the momentum that was helping to revive warrior society dances also produced a new kind of secular, social event increasingly referred to during the post-World War II years as "powwow."[33]

It is important to understand that dance form and content are not static. "Powwows are not unchanging continuations from the depths of time," writes Thomas Kavanagh. For that matter, neither were nineteenth-century dance traditions. Change kept these dances meaningful and relevant, and it was not long before they became the source of new cultural practices responding to new needs. "We don't do dances the same way as a long time ago," a Cheyenne man told me, "but we hold on to the ideas, the thoughts that those old people taught us." When the Kiowas revived the *Tiah Pah* in 1958, for example, it was not as a veterans' society but as a dance open to all Kiowas—men and women, young and old. Dances remained important, but evolved in response to new social, cultural, spatial, and ritual realities. It was the idea, not the object, that remained in force.[34]

Scott Bradshaw, an Osage-Quapaw, notes that even if his great-grandfather could not recognize all of the elements of the contemporary Osage *I'n-Lon-Schka*, he would nevertheless understand its function. "The sense of family, the pride of heritage, the seriousness of the occasion, the humor of the moment," says Bradshaw, "are the same as they have always been when Indians gather." The annual Ponca Powwow, held every year in early August at White Eagle, Oklahoma, is clearly not the same thing as the Ponca *Heluska*, which meets and dances on other occasions. Yet it is clear that Ponca Powwow is a psychologically and culturally vital part of contemporary Ponca life. That it is also "secular" does not in any way lessen its profound role in the Ponca community.[35]

One of the most important influences in the evolution of dance on the Southern Plains is modern warfare. As noted above, warfare was a critical factor during the pre-reservation era in the attainment of status and prestige. The erosion of such contexts rippled through the entire cultural fabric of tribes. Largely denied opportunities for warfare by the end of the nineteenth century, many warrior societies languished. Ironically, modern warfare helped to provide the impetus for the creation of a new yet traditionally inspired warrior ethic.

In the opinion of many powwow people, twentieth-century warfare is the critical link in the recital of many dances and rituals from the preservation period. Indeed, the World Wars dramatically influenced both the form and purpose of dance across the Southern Plains. Drawn to the martial ethos that defined a great deal of their past, Southern Plains people saw participation in the nation's wars as both an obligation to be borne by loyal citizens and a validation of their continued allegiance to specific and honorable traditions. As a result, the utility of dances, songs, and rituals previously associated with warfare reemerged with even greater force.[36]

Presented with an opportunity to celebrate in ways denied them since the late nineteenth century, Indian people used twentieth-century warfare to create a context in which traditional rituals assumed new and useful meaning. Unlike the pre-war years, when many older Indians were ambivalent about the need to pass on knowledge with limited relevance for post-allotment, post-reservation generations, the war years confirmed that traditional martial rituals could be revived to serve the needs of a new generation of warriors. "[M]any aspects of traditional Indian cultures gained renewed importance and vigor during World War I," writes Thomas Britten, "allowing young people to witness, perhaps for the first time, aspects of their cultures about which they had only heard from elders."[37]

Alerted to the appearance of such celebrations, the Bureau of Indian Affairs saw World War I as a turning point in the assimilation campaign and kept up the assault on dances by insisting that they were "acts of disloyalty and an attempt to subvert the will of the government." Kiowa-Comanche Agency officials announced on the eve of the war that "both the Indians and the public should be made to realize that these old customs retard the march of civilization." Once again, agents withheld annuities from dancers, including, with some irony, returning Indian veterans. Unable to prevent homecoming dances, Commissioner of Indian Affairs Cato Sells skeptically commented in 1919 on the Indians' insistence that "by reviving the native costume and some form of old war-time dances they can best express complete approval of those who enlisted under the banner of American freedom."[38]

Undaunted by bureaucratic meddling, Indian communities enthusiastically sponsored dances and celebrations to honor service men. They also inaugurated a flurry of celebrations that became the first wave of a revivified dance culture across the Plains that coalesced, by the 1940s, in the modern intertribal powwow. In Oklahoma, Indian communities sent their young men to Europe with appropriate songs, rituals, and dances widely used in the pre-reservation era. Although not all tribes held military society dances per se, the treatment accorded veterans undoubtedly established a connection between pre-reservation military societies, their dances, and the honor traditionally accorded their members. Between 1917 and 1919, for example, Apaches and Pawnees hosted scalp and victory dances that included the use of German helmets and uniform parts taken from captives and those killed in combat. A 1919 Cheyenne scalp dance in Canton, Oklahoma, reportedly included the use of an actual German scalp. And at a 1919 Pawnee victory dance, dancers wore traditional dance clothes and modern military uniforms.[39]

Other Indian peoples also revived pre-reservation warrior society practices with surprising vigor. A Cannon, North Dakota, 1918 victory dance featured a mock attack on an effigy of Kaiser Wilhelm that became the focal point of the event. "[W]arriors crept forward and shot at the effigy until it fell down. Afterward, four children previously selected for the purpose counted coup on the Kaiser. Next, four men counted coup, the first of whom rode the horse of a Sioux soldier killed in World War I." War songs appeared with the words German and Kaiser prominently featured, the Lakotas going so far as to refer in one song to the Germans as "crying like women." In the Kiowa community, the return of World War I veterans sparked numerous victory and scalp dances at which veterans received new names, engaged in old warrior society practices, and generally enjoyed the same status and prestige as nineteenth-century warriors. Following the war, the Kiowas began to reestablish warrior societies and gave them contemporary names—the Victory Club and the Purple Heart Club, for example, both of which vigorously sponsored dances—to the never-ending irritation of government agents. Indeed, once the commissioner's office informed Kiowa Agent C. V. Stinchecum in 1921 that he could no longer legally withhold annuities and other payments from dancers, Stinchecum fumed that "after more than four years' hard work my entire influence was destroyed."[40]

World War II and Korea proved decisive in the continued use and revival of many society songs and dances. The late George Watchetaker, a Comanche, recalled that "after World War II those veterans were considered warriors, just like a long time ago." Gus Palmer, Sr., a Kiowa who was instrumental in the resurgence of the Kiowa *Ton'konga*, or Black Legs Society, remembered that "the old people said, you younger men are entitled to carry it on. You men today are just like the men in the old days—warriors. You fought for your people." Kracht observes that unlike World War I, when only 14 Kiowas served, World War II "produced numerous veterans who kept alive the Kiowa warrior spirit related to *dwdw,* the 'power' assisting success in warfare." The veterans' service thus necessitated the use of song and ritual previously associated with warrior societies. And Kiowas note that "on battlefields throughout the twentieth century many Kiowas have fought and died without giving ground, as if the Sacred Arrow also held their sashes," a reference to the old *ton'konga* practice of staking a sash to the ground in the face of an attacking enemy, obligating the owner to "remain and die at his post."[41]

During the 1940s and 1950s, dances historically used to honor such service enjoyed renewed importance, and, in several cases, were revived after lengthy periods of dormancy. Leonard Riddles, a Comanche, commented that "with WW II, you got a change with these boys going and coming back from the services. Every week they'd have it [a dance] somewhere, someone's relative coming in on furlough or leaving, and they'd honor him." On the Southern Plains, two especially notable renewals occurred when in the late 1950s, following Korea, the Kiowas brought back the *Tiah Pah,* or Gourd Dance Society, and the *Ton'konga.* When he returned from Korea, Harry Tofpi remembered being welcomed home "just like in the old days—

songs, dances, prayers. They had a big Gourd Dance for me. I talked about what I had done in combat, just like those guys did a long time ago." Scott Tonemah recalled that the revived Gourd Dance reminded Kiowas of the importance of warriors and their obligation to protect and defend their people.[42]

In the Kiowa community this willingness to embrace United States military institutions and values also reveals how women came to take new and active roles in powwow culture. In October 1927, Kiowa women organized a chapter of the American War Mothers, an association of women whose sons and daughters have served in the armed forces and who have been honorably discharged. Formally chartered in February 1944, the Kiowa War Mothers not only embraced the organization's official goals, which included assisting "patriotic works," but also used the chapter to express explicitly Kiowa cultural values through song and dance. "To the Kiowa tribe," notes one account, "this was a unique organization in that 98 percent of its charter members were non-English speaking."[43]

Moreover, the War Mothers honored the service of their children with specific song traditions and dances. "In a sense," according to Luke Lassiter, "they were reviving warrior societies, but did so along gender lines. There were women's organizations prior to this, but this is new, this is not a revival, per se, it's a fashioning of older ideals modified to reflect the twentieth century."[44] A new song tradition called War Mothers' Songs confirmed the deliberate combination of traditional forms of recognition with more contemporary ones. During World War II, for example, numerous War Mother songs appeared with words like these: "Our sons and daughters went overseas. They fought the Germans, they returned safely together."[45]

The War Mothers are one example of a gender specific response to contemporary powwow culture that marks important departures from the past. Indeed, in many Southern Plains communities, women not only influence the form, function, and meaning of powwows, they dominate it. Tina Parker Emhoolah, a Comanche, believes that women are "the most committed participants" in the Comanche Gourd Clan. Florene Whitehorse, a Kiowa, insists that:

> if it wasn't for women . . . there would be no men at this dance. . . . [A]ll of the members know that they are incapacitated if they do not have a woman—a wife, sister, whatever. . . . A woman plays a very integral role in what is going on out there. . . . *That's reality.* Who is the best person that they [the men dancers] would want to back them up. Who stands there behind them in that 104 degrees and gives out the most beautiful tremolos in honor of that man? No one else can do this but a woman. No one else in the world can perform that task.[46]

Unfortunately, scholars know little about the gender aspects of the dances.

By the mid- and late-1940s the modern powwow complex was beginning to take on a clear form. Although revived warrior society dances continued to gain momentum as well, they did so as part of a more diversified dance culture. Encouraged by the burgeoning urban Pan-Indianism of the post-war years, annual intertribal powwows (often located in urban places) appeared with increasing frequency by the early

1950s. Commenting on why intertribal powwows gained popularity in the post-war era, Ralph Kotay, a Kiowa who has been singing at powwows since the 1940s, said "[w]ell, after 1950, powwows began to spread out and it caught on all over. People in town helped to organize it—Oklahoma City, Wichita, Tulsa."[47]

It is important to remember that this phenomenon did not mean the end of society dances; indeed, in some cases, the two were joined. At the July Fourth Kiowa Gourd Clan ceremonial in Carnegie, Oklahoma, for example, as well as at the annual *O-ho-mah* ceremonial, afternoons are taken up with rituals while the evenings are used for powwow. For Ralph Kotay, as for most powwow people, intertribal powwows—even big contest dances—are no less important and meaningful than community dances or even ceremonies. "This was given to us," he says, "it's all the same, even though maybe we don't do it just like we did way back there. All tribes like to dance. These are still our traditional ways," he continued, "our people have been doing this all our lives."[48]

A good example of this occurred among the Comanches, who hosted a homecoming dance for Korean veterans in 1952. Kavanagh writes of the dance, that came to be known as "Comanche Homecoming": "While its immediate origins date to an event held in honor of Korean War veterans, it has antecedents in events held after both World Wars in tribute to returning soldiers." Comanches acknowledged connections between the older practices of military societies and more contemporary forms of dance, but as Foster and Kavanagh note, these post-war dances assumed new and different roles in the Comanche community. Kavanagh writes that Comanche Homecoming, for example, is the "high point of the social year for Comanche powwow people." Indeed, it wasn't until the 1970s that Comanches reformed their veterans' societies; in the interim, powwows became "the consensus form of public gathering Comanches have used to organize their community."[49]

Kiowas, too, witnessed a similar evolution, and the *O-ho-mah* has been cited as a prime example of this adaptation. As early as 1949, John Gamble argued that the appearance of new dance styles at the *O-ho-mah* suggested an important transition marked by "the steady decline of O-ho-mo ceremonialism." After 1900, Lassiter argues that *O-ho-mah* dances became increasingly linked to a new context in which the ceremony "began to develop as a social rather than a warrior society's dance." Attracted to the new and flashy fancy war dance style that had previously spun out of the Omaha complex, the Kiowa *O-ho-mah* took on a new look. And although important vestiges of its original purpose remained in place (the honoring of returning veterans, for example), as the dance's popularity grew it came to be used in new ways, most notably for "community social dances (i.e., community-wide, intertribal dances not framed by society ceremonials), and in Indian shows and fairs." The *O-ho-mah* directly influenced the creation of a new, secular dance in the form of the powwow. While clearly linked to the past, Lassiter observes that the emerging powwow complex "neither followed an unchanging set of rules nor unfolded in a predictably patterned way; instead, it evidenced the unique intersection of individual lives with tradition."[50]

Like the revived society dances, the *O-ho-mah* dance thus assumed a broader social and community purpose during and after World War II by serving as a vehicle to balance convention against context. Its new songs and revived dance continued to serve specific *O-ho-mah* needs, but Lassiter notes that after 1940, the war dance's popular form was distinctly different from the old *O-ho-mah* dance. Yet the relationship between *O-ho-mah* and the emerging powwow complex was clear, and Lassiter concludes that the "O-ho-mah Lodge was a major catalyst for . . . framing the so-called powwow era in southwestern Oklahoma."[51]

Today, dance flourishes on the Southern Plains in a variety of forms. Lassiter describes four dominant expressions of the old Omaha Dance: "first, the original dance ceremony maintained by men's societies like the O-ho-mah Lodge; second, powwows that emerged from the Omaha Dance's popular expression within Plains communities . . . ; third, Plains contest powwows like Oklahoma City's Red Earth; and finally, contest and other powwows outside the Plains." Some dances, like the Kiowa *Tiah Pah*, Ponca *Helushka,* and Osage *I'n-Lon-Schta* remain important as tribally specific men's societies. Adapted to meet contemporary needs, such dances help to maintain cultural boundaries.[52]

On the Southern Plains, few things seem more suited to mediating cultural and community identity than the powwow. Although it is true that powwows reflect complicated and contested interpretations of social memory and action, it is also true that such debates notwithstanding, powwows remain extraordinary for their power to mold and express identity. And as David Lewis reminds us, Indian people "define themselves, their experience and significance every day in hundreds of variations." That was the message conveyed that evening in Meeker: "Being Indian is a hard way," said one man on behalf of his grandchild, "but this arena will help you in life, it will help you find the strength to meet your problems." It is a sentiment expressed often and with great emotion on the Southern Plains. On the last night of the 1996 *O-ho-mah,* an elderly Kiowa man told the story of how as a young boy he had seen his grandfather cornered by the Indian agent at an *O-ho-mah* encampment in the 1910s. The agent denigrated the event, describing it as a heathen ritual, unfit for a people trying to civilize themselves. Determined to cut the Kiowas off from it, the agent announced that if the tribe would stop dancing, rations would be sent to the entire camp. The man telling the story paused. An uncomfortable murmur could be heard in the seats all around me as Indian people reacted to yet another story of how their relatives had been persecuted for believing in traditional ways. Savoring the moment, the man uttered several words in Kiowa and finished his story: "My grandpa looked back at the agent, looked him square in the face and said 'We don't want your rations. We want this dance.'"[53]

NOTES

1. Author's field notes, August 1996. Roaching refers to the act of tying a hair roach (a headdress made of porcupine hair) on a male dancer's head. "Paying for his seat" is a colloquial expression used to describe the act of giving away that signifies one's "payment" for the privilege of dancing. Women, too, pay for their place in much the same fashion as the event recounted above.

General discussions of the contemporary powwow complex may be found in Charlotte Heth, ed., *Native American Dance Ceremonies and Social Traditions* (Washington, DC, 1992); George P. Horse

Capture, *Pow Wow* (Cody, 1989); William K. Powers, *War Dance: Plains Indian Musical Performance* (Tucson, 1990); William K. Powers, "Plains Indian Music and Dance," in *Anthropology on the Great Plains*, ed. W. Raymond Wood and Margot Liberty (Lincoln, 1980), 212–29; Mark Mattern, "The Powwow as a Public Arena for Negotiating Unity and Diversity in American Indian Life," *American Indian Culture and Research Journal* 20, no. 4 (1996): 183–201; Carol K. Rachlin, "Tight Shoe Night," *Midcontinent American Studies Journal* 6 (Spring 1965): 84–100; N. Scott Momaday, "To the Singing, To the Drums," *Natural History* 134, no. 2 (1975): 38–45; James Howard, "Pan-Indianism in Native American Music and Dance," *Ethnomusicology* 27, no. 1 (1983): 71–82.

2. Benjamin Kracht has argued that the contemporary powwow creates and nurtures a feeling of *communitas* that "relates to [Victory Turner's] 'timeless condition' created by rituals bringing together people from different social strata . . . [who] are worshiping in a social environment where the participants are social and cultural equals," Kracht, "Kiowa Powwows: Continuity in Ritual Practice," *American Indian Quarterly* 18, no. 3 (1994): 322. For a reply to Kracht, see Luke E. Lassiter and Clyde Ellis, "Applying Communitas to Kiowa Powwows, Some Methodological and Theoretical Problems," *American Indian Quarterly* 22 (Fall 1998).

3. In this essay, powwow and dance will be used interchangeably. This can be problematic, as some people draw distinctions between dance that occurs at intertribal powwows and dance that occurs at tribal ceremonials. These are indeed two different kinds of dance, but they share common ground in terms of the importance they have as expressions of identity.

For an introduction to Southern Plains dance culture, see Thomas W. Kavanagh, "Southern Plains Dance: Tradition and Dynamism," in *Native American Dance*, ed. Heth, 105–23; Luke E. Lassiter. *The Power of Kiowa Song: A Collaborative Ethnography* (Tucson, 1998); Luke E. Lassiter, "'Charlie Brown': Not Just Another Essay on the Gourd Dance," *American Indian Culture and Research Journal* 21, no. 4 (1997): 75–103; Maurice Boyd, *Kiowa Voices*, 2 vols. (Fort Worth, 1981); Alice Anne Callahan, *The Osage Ceremonial Dance: I'n-Lon-Schka* (Norman, 1990); Willie Smyth, ed., *Songs of Indian Territory: Native American Music Traditions of Oklahoma* (Oklahoma City, 1989); Morris W Foster, *Being Comanche: A Social History of an American Indian Community* (Tucson, 1991), esp. pp. 24–30, 123–53; Clyde Ellis, "'Truly Dancing Their Own Way': Modern Revival and Diffusion of the Gourd Dance," *American Indian Quarterly* 14 (Winter 1990): 19–33; John H. Moore, "How Giveaways and Powwows Redistribute the Means of Subsistence," in *The Political Economy of North American Indians*, ed. John H. Moore (Norman, 1993), 240–69; Kracht, "Kiowa Powwows"; James H. Howard, "Pan-Indian Culture of Oklahoma," *Scientific Monthly* 18, no. 5 (1955): 215–20; James Howard, "The Plains Gourd Dance as a Revitalization Movement," *American Ethnologist* 3, no. 2 (1976): 243–59; John Joseph Beatty, *Kiowa-Apache Music and Dance* (Greeley, 1974); Kenneth Ashworth, "The Contemporary Oklahoma Powwow" (Ph.D. diss., University of Oklahoma, 1986); William C. Meadows, "Remaining Veterans: A Symbolic and Comparative Ethnohistory of Southern Plains Indian Military Societies" (Ph.D. diss., University of Oklahoma, 1995), esp. pp. 136–215.

4. Lassiter, "'Charlie Brown,'" 97; Kavanagh, "Southern Plains Dance," 105. Similar arguments have been made for other regions; commenting on Northern Plains powwows, R. D. Theisz argues that song and dance are crucial for post-World War II Lakota identity. See his "Song Texts and Their Performers: The Centerpiece of Contemporary Lakota Identity Formulation," *Great Plains Quarterly* 7 (Spring 1987) 116–24. Mark Thiel notes that "for generations the Omaha dance has been the most popular social and nationalistic celebration of the Oglala and Sicangu Sioux, thus serving as an obtrusive demonstration of tribal identity and cohesion." See Thiel's article, "The Omaha Dance in Oglala and Sicangu Sioux History. 1883–1923," *Whispering Winds* 23 (Fall-Winter 1990), 4.

5. Lassiter, "'Charlie Brown,'" 75–6; Richard West, Foreword, in *Native American Dance*, Heth ed., ix; Foster, *Being Comanche*, 153; Jeanne M. Devlin, "Oklahoma Tribesmen: Every Picture Tells a Story," *Oklahoma Today* (May-June 1991) 22; author's interview with Harry Tofpi, Shawnee, Oklahoma, 3 May 1997; author's field notes, July 1996.

6. Alice Fletcher and Francis La Flesche, *The Omaha Tribe*, Bureau of American Ethnology, 27th Annual Report (Washington, DC, 1911), 459; Robin Ridington. "Omaha Survival: A Vanishing Indian Tribe That Would Not Vanish," *American Indian Quarterly* II (Winter 1987), 47; James Mooney, *Calendar History of the Kiowa Indians* (1898; reprint, Washington, DC, 1979), 230; Bernard Mishkin, *Rank and Warfare among the Plains Indians* (1940; reprint, Lincoln, 1992); Jane Richardson, *Law and Status Among the Kiowa Indians* (1940; reprint, New York, 1988). Clark

Wissler, *General Discussion of Shamanistic and Dancing Societies*, Anthropological Papers of the American Museum of Natural History, vol. 11 (Washington, DC, 1916).

7. Sylvester Warrior, quoted in Jim Charles, "Songs of the Ponca: Helushka," *Wicazo Sa Review* 5, no. 2 (1989): 2–3; Meadows, "Remaining Veterans," 106–17.

8. Report of the Secretary of Interior, 183, House Exec. Doc. 1, 48th Cong., 1st sess., serial 2190, x–xi; Paul Prucha, *The Great Father: The United States Government and the American Indians* (Lincoln, 1984), 2:646–7; L. G. Moses, *Wild West Shows and the Image of American Indians, 1883–1933* (Albuquerque, 1996), 253.

9. For the quotes in this paragraph, and the paragraph above, see Thomas J. Morgan to Charles E. Adams, 10 July 1890 and 24 July 1890, Indian Celebrations and Dances (1874–1917), microfilm KA 47, Records of the Kiowa Agency, Oklahoma Historical Society, Division of Indian Archives (hereafter KA OHS). For an account of the 1890 Sun Dance, see Mooney, *Calendar History*, 352–9.

10. Daniel Browning to Charles Adams, 4 August 1896, Indian Celebrations and Dances (1874–1917), microfilm KA 47, KA OHS; House Exec. Doc. 1, 52d Cong. 2d sess., serial 3088, pp. 28–9; Moses, *Wild West Shows*, 73.

11. Kracht, "Kiowa Powwows," 329–31, Stecker quote on p. 329; Meadows, "Remaining Veterans," 154–63, Stinchecum quote on p. 159, Sells quote on p. 160.

12. Mary Clouse to C. V. Stinchecum, 15 September 1915, and H. H. Clouse to C. V. Stinchecum, 2 December 1916, both in Field Matron's file, microfilm KA 74, KA OHS.

13. Marvin Kroeker, *Comanches and Mennonites on the Oklahoma Plains: A. J. and Magdalena Becker and the Post Oak Mission* (Hillsboro, KS, 1997), 47, 77–9.

14. Isabel Crawford, *Kiowa: A Woman Missionary in Indian Territory* (1915; reprint, Lincoln, 1998), 26–8; Isabel Crawford Journal for 1898–1899, 8–10, Samuel Colgate Historical Library, American Baptist Historical Society, Rochester, NY.

15. Prucha, *The Great Father*, 2:801; Margaret D. Jacobs, "Making Savages of Us All: White Women, Pueblo Indians, and the Controversy Over Indian Dances in the 1920s," *Frontiers* 17, no. 3 (1996): 178–209.

16. Prucha, *The Great Father*, 2:801–2; Lawrence C. Kelly, *The Assault on Assimilation: John Collier and the Origins of Indian Policy Reform* (Albuquerque, 1983), 304; Hubert Work, *Indian Policies: Comments on the Resolution of the Advisory Council on Indian Affairs* (Washington, DC, 1924), 10–1.

17. Moses, *Wild West Shows*, 253.

18. James H. Kyle, "How Shall the Indian be Educated?" *North American Review* 159 (October 1894): 437; Laurence F. Schmeckebier, *The Office of Indian Affairs: Its History, Activities, and Organization* (Baltimore, 1927): 72; Leonard D. White, *The Republican Era, 1869–1901: A Study in Administrative History* (New York, 1958), 175.

19. William T. Hagan, *United States-Comanche Relations: The Reservation Years* (1976; reprint, Norman, 1990), 42; see also Hagan, "The Reservation Policy: Too Little and Too Late," in *Indian-White Relations: A Persistent Paradox*, ed. Jane F. Smith and Robert M. Kvasnicka (Washington, DC, 1976), 157–69. "Government practice," writes Robert H. Keller, Jr., "depended on white society, promoted white expansion, reflected white values, and protected white frontiersmen." Thus the assimilation agenda of the era rested on three contradictory ends: "protecting Indian rights, promoting westward expansion, and protecting American citizens," Robert H. Keller, Jr., *American Protestantism and United States Indian Policy, 1869–82* (Lincoln, 1983), 11.

20. Quote on agencies as asylums from 7 September 1885 School Inspection Report, in Agents' Reports, microfilm KA 14, KA OHS. Hagan, *U.S.-Comanche Relations*, esp. 166–200; Donald J. Berthrong, *The Cheyenne and Arapaho Ordeal: Reservation and Agency Life in the Indian Territory, 1875–1907* (Norman, 1976); Clyde Ellis, *To Change Them Forever: Indian Education at the Rainy Mountain Boarding School, 1893–1920* (Norman, 1996), 32–4.

21. Moses, *Wild West Shows*, 253, 73; L. G. Moses, "Wild West Shows, Reformers, and the Image of The American Indian, 1887–1914," *South Dakota History* 14 (Fall 1984): 193–221; L. G. Moses, "Indians On the Midway: Wild West Shows and the Indian Bureau at World's Fairs, 1893–1904," *South Dakota History* 21 (Fall 1991): 205–29. On the Miller Brothers, see Fred Gipson, *Fabulous Empire: Colonel Zack Miller's Story* (Boston, 1946); Michael Wallis, "The Miller Brothers and the 101 Ranch," *Gilcrease Journal* 1 (Spring 1993): 6–29; Barbara Roth, "The 101 Ranch Wild West Show, 1904–1932," *Chronicles of Oklahoma* 43 (Winter 1965): 416–31.

22. Battice quoted in Moses, *Wild West Shows*, 180; Moses, "Interpreting the Wild West, 1883–1914," in *Between Indian and White Worlds: The Cultural Brokers*, ed. Margaret Connell-Szasz (Albuquerque, 1994), 161, 172; Thiel, "The Omaha Dance," 5.

23. Moses, *Wild West Shows*, 279; Moses, "Interpreting the Wild West," 177–8; Thiel, "The Omaha Dance," 5–6.

24. Prucha, *The Great Father*, 2:951; Kenneth Philp, *John Collier's Crusade for Indian Reform, 1920–1954* (Tucson, 1977), 55–70.

25. Interview with Harry Tofpi, Shawnee, Oklahoma, 3 May 1997.

26. Lassiter, *The Power of Kiowa Song*, 94; Carol Rachlin, "Tight Shoe Night," 93, 99; Clifford Coppersmith, "Healing and Remembrance: The Chiricahua and Warm Springs Apache Mountain Spirit Dance in Oklahoma," manuscript in author's possession; Thiel, "The Omaha Dance," 5.

27. Lassiter, *The Power of Kiowa Song*, 93–5, 119; Meadows, "Remaining Veterans," 145–53, for quotes see 146, 162. At the 1996 *O-ho-mah* dance, one speaker reminded the crowd that "*O-ho-mah* never stopped dancing," author's field notes, July 1996.

28. Kavanagh, "Southern Plains Dance," 109; James H. Howard, "Notes on the Dakota Grass Dance," *Southwest Journal of Anthropology* 7 (1951): 82. See Alice Fletcher and Francis LaFlesche, "The Omaha Tribe," 441–2, 459–80 for comment on the origin of the Omaha Dance and its diffusion, which led to the development of the *O-ho-mah* (Kiowa), *Iruska* (Pawnee), *Hethu'shka* (Omaha), *Helushka* (Ponca), and *I'n-lon-schka* (Osage) dance societies, among others; Clark Wissler, *General Discussion of Shamanistic and Dancing Societies*, 859–60; Lassiter, *The Power of Kiowa Song*, 80–98.

29. Kavanagh, "Southern Plains Dance," 111; Nancy Lurie, "The Contemporary American Indian Scene," in *North American Indians in Historical Perspective*, ed. Eleanor B. Leacock and Nancy Lurie (New York, 1971), 449–50; James Howard, *The Ponca Tribe*, Bureau of American Ethnology, Bulletin 195 (Washington, DC, 1965), 107–8; James Howard, "Pan-Indianism in Native American Music and Dance," *Ethnomusicology*, 27, no. 1 (1983): 71–82.

30. Foster, *Being Comanche*, 30.

31. Ibid, 123. Foster cites three reasons for the resurgence of Comanche dancing: 1. Concern among older Comanches for reviving traditional rituals; 2. The hiring of Comanches to perform at local civic functions and celebrations; 3. Requests by Comanches for surviving members of military societies to dance at intracommunity events. Reports of Quanah's dances are in Indian Celebrations and Dances (1874–1917), microfilm KA 47, KA OHS; see also William T. Hagan, *Quanah Parker, Comanche Chief* (Norman, 1993), 102–3.

32. Foster, *Being Comanche*, 126–7. Kracht makes a similar argument in a recent essay on Kiowa religion, in which he says that some older people believe that "powwows serve as a religion for the youth." Kracht, "Kiowa Religion in Historical Perspective," *American Indian Quarterly* 21, no. 1 (1997): 28.

33. Lurie, "The Contemporary Indian Scene," 449–50; Powers, *War Dance*, 57–8, 64; Howard, "Pan-Indianism in Native American Music and Dance," 72–3, contend that this emerging form of dance, while rooted in the "ceremonial patterns of the Plains" (Lurie), was highly secular, and imply that it was thus less persuasive as a culturally vital institution. Powers, whose work focused on the Northern Plains, was especially insistent that Oklahoma powwows are merely "secular events."

34. Lassiter, "'Charlie Brown,'" 89; Kavanagh, "Southern Plains Dance," 105; Interview with Scott Tonemah, 8 February 1988, Norman, Oklahoma.

35. Callahan, *The Osage Ceremonial Dance*, 134.

36. The best recent discussions of American Indians and military service are Thomas A. Britten, *American Indians in World War I: At Home and At War* (Albuquerque, 1997); Alison Bernstein, *American Indians and World War II: Toward a New Era in Indian Affairs* (Norman, 1991); Tom Holm, *Strong Hearts, Wounded Souls: Native American Veterans of the Vietnam War* (Austin, 1996), esp. 66–102; Holm, "Fighting a White Man's War: The Extent and Legacy of American Indian Participation in World War II," in *The Plains Indians of the Twentieth Century*, ed. Peter Iverson (Norman, 1985), 149–67; Aaron McGaffey Beede, "The Dakota Indian Victory Dance," *North Dakota Historical Quarterly* 9 (April 1942): 167–78; James Howard, "The Dakota Victory Dance in World War II," *North Dakota History* 18 (1951): 31–40.

37. Britten, *American Indians in World War I*, 149.

38. Britten, *American Indians on World War I*, 149; Foster, *Being Comanche*, 125; *Annual Report of the Commissioner of Indian Affairs*, 1919, 12.

39. Britten, *American Indians in World War I*, 150–1; "Indians Use Human Scalps in Dance," *The American Indian Magazine* 7 (Fall 1919): 184. An essay titled "Lo, The Rich Indian, How He Blows His Coin," *Literary Digest* 67 (November 20, 1920), 62–4, recounted that Bacon Rind, a prominent Osage, had sponsored several dances in honor of his son, a returning World War I veteran; it is difficult to imagine that the *Literary Digest* would have made a similar editorial interpretation of white homecoming celebrations.

40. Britten, *American Indians in World War I*, 149–50; Beede, "The North Dakota Indian Victory Dance," 169–72; Frances Densmore, "The Songs of Indian Soldiers during the World War," *Musical Quarterly* 20 (October 1934): 419–35; R. D. Theisz, "The Bad Speakers and the Long Braids: References to Foreign Enemies in Lakota Song Texts," in *Indians and Europe*, ed. Christian Feest (Aachen, Germany, 1987), 429–30; author's interview with Harry Tofpi, 2 May 1996, Shawnee, Oklahoma; C. V. Stinchecum to Charles Burke, 2 November 1921, Agents and Agency File, 186–1926, KA OHS.

41. Author's interview with Scott Tonemah, 8 February 1988, Norman, Oklahoma; George "Woogie" Watchetaker from "Into The Circle: an Introduction to Oklahoma Powwows and Celebrations" (Tulsa, 1992), videotape; William C. Meadows and Gus Palmer, St. "Tonkonga: The Kiowa Black Legs Military Society," in *Native American Dance*, Heth ed., 117; Boyd, *Kiowa Voices*, 1:71, 73, 112; Kracht, "Kiowa Powwows," 339. Kracht's orthography is unnecessarily obscure: "*dwdw*" is pronounced "dawdaw."

42. Foster, *Being Comanche*, 145; Author's interview with Harry Tofpi, 4 August 1993, Seminole, Oklahoma; Author's interview with Scott Tonemah, 8 February 1988, Norman, Oklahoma; Author's interview with Parker McKenzie, 1 August 1990, Mountain View, Oklahoma.

43. Program for the 59th Annual American Indian Exposition, 20–25 August 1990, Anadarko, Oklahoma, in author's possession.

44. Telephone interview by author with Luke Lassiter, 10 September 1998.

45. Ibid; see also Lassiter, *The Power of Kiowa Song*, 241, n. 4.

46. Ibid., 246, n. 10.

47. Telephone interview by author with Ralph Kotay, 18 July 1998; Howard, "Pan-Indianism in Native American Music and Dance," 71–82. Lassiter notes that "in southwestern Oklahoma's Indian world ... tribal traditions are not necessarily mutually exclusive; they intersect in an intertribal social world. Therefore, we are no longer speaking of *aggregates* of individuals, but different worlds in which *individuals* participate. Powwow, hand-game, church, or peyote people, then, all take part in distinct but interrelated worlds defined by aesthetics, tradition, and history" (Lassiter's emphasis), see his *The Power of Kiowa Song*, 77.

48. Phone interview by author with Ralph Kotay, 18 July 1998. When the Peabody Museum returned the Sacred Pole to the Omaha Tribe in 1989 after an absence of nearly a century, for example, the tribe brought the Pole back into the community with emotional and ritually specific actions at its annual powwow in Macy, where later in the weekend dancers competed for monetary prizes. That this occurred at a contest powwow did not lessen the importance of the moment. As several Omahas later told one interviewer, the powwow grounds in Macy are where matters of importance to the tribe are played out: "The Return of the Sacred Pole," on KUON-TV, Lincoln, 1990.

49. Kavanagh, "Southern Plains Dance," 121, and Foster, *Being Comanche*, 131.

50. Lassiter, *The Power of Kiowa Song*, 81–2; John Gamble, "Changing Patterns in Kiowa Dance," *International Congress of Americanists, Proceedings*, 29, no. 2 (1952), 100–5; Kracht, "Kiowa Powwows," 332–3.

51. Lassiter, *The Power of Kiowa Song*, 90; Lassiter, conversations with the author, 16 July 1998.

52. Lassiter, *The Power of Kiowa Song*, 243.

53. David Rich Lewis, "Still Native: The Significance of Native Americans in the History of the Twentieth-Century American West," *Western Historical Quarterly* 24 (May 1993): 227; author's field notes, July 1996.

Ward Churchill, a Native American activist and scholar, views the American Indian Movement (AIM), founded in Minneapolis in 1968, as the instigator of "a bona fide national liberation movement" that struggled against oppression in a series of dramatic confrontations in the 1970s. In this passionate review of AIM's history, Churchill begins with the assertion that Indian communities in the 1960s were essentially outposts of the third world: politically powerless, economically dependent, and culturally defeated. The fundamental cause of this status was the federal government's refusal in the modern era to deal with Native American communities through treaties. The abandonment of treaty making (which became policy in 1871) was, in Churchill's view, responsible for massive land loss and "an urban diaspora."

According to Churchill, AIM's goal of "decolonizing" native North America spoke to a variety of community needs. Its attacks on media presentations of Indians and its headline-grabbing demonstrations (such as the capture of a replica of the Mayflower on Thanksgiving Day in 1970) instilled pride among dispirited tribal members, as Joane Nagel's essay on Indian identity suggests. Moreover, AIM's willingness to provoke government officials with fundamental questions about the legitimacy of American law and of Indian Bureau policies injected the language of self-determination into political debate. (The Office of Indian Affairs—often referred to during its history as the "Bureau"—was formally renamed the Bureau of Indian Affairs in 1947.) And most significant, AIM's repeated confrontations with federal and state authorities communicated Indians' unwillingness to compromise or await a change in public attitudes. Despite its urban origins, AIM members aligned themselves with reservation elders and invoked the memory of nineteenth-century warriors like Crazy Horse as they forced their agenda to center stage. Readers of Kingsley Bray's article on Crazy Horse should consider how apt the comparison is.

Churchill illustrates his approach to AIM and it history with an overview of events on the Pine Ridge reservation, the scene of the most dramatic confrontations between AIM and both tribal and federal authorities. He describes the arrival of AIM members on the reservation, their role in protests over the murders of Indians by local whites, and their entanglement in an ongoing political struggle between Tribal Chairman Richard Wilson and his traditionalist opponents. Ultimately, he argues, Wilson's efforts to contain AIM led to an alliance between his tribal government and the FBI. Concerned over what they believed was a "terrorist organization," the FBI (which has jurisdiction over major crimes on Indian reservations) became deeply involved in a counterinsurgency campaign to contain and, Churchill argues, destroy AIM. The campaign began with AIM's occupation of the village of Wounded Knee in early 1973 and continued during what Churchill (quoting the U.S. Commission on Civil Rights) calls a federal "reign of terror."

AIM's history remains subject to bitter debate. Then and since, some (Indians as well as whites) have insisted that AIM leaders were more devoted to garnering media attention for themselves than to promoting Indians' interests. Still, Churchill's indictment of federal authorities reminds us that the confrontations of the 1970s, like the Ghost Dance almost a century earlier, were deeply threatening to government officials. It also highlights how far AIM altered the very language of Indian affairs, creating new rhetorical objectives for tribal communities. Churchill's essay says little that is critical of AIM; nor does it explain how a treaty-based Indian policy might actually work. But it does help us understand both how protest leaders came to prominence, and why their legacy continues to inspire many Indian people. AIM's tactics and goals warrant comparison with Native revitalization, "backtalk," and protests by earlier generations chronicled throughout this volume.

THE BLOODY WAKE OF ALCATRAZ: POLITICAL REPRESSION OF THE AMERICAN INDIAN MOVEMENT DURING THE 1970S

Ward Churchill

> *The reality is a continuum which connects Indian flesh sizzling over Puritan fires and Vietnamese flesh roasting under American napalm. The reality is the compulsion of a sick society to rid itself of men like Nat Turner and Crazy Horse, George Jackson and Richard Oakes, whose defiance uncovers the hypocrisy of a declaration affirming everyone's right to liberty and life. The reality is an overwhelming greed which began with the theft of a continent and continues with the merciless looting of every country on the face of the earth which lacks the strength to defend itself.*
>
> —Richard Lundstrom

IN COMBINATION WITH THE FISHING RIGHTS struggles of the Puyallup, Nisqually, Muckleshoot, and other nations in the Pacific Northwest from 1965 to 1970, the 1969–71 occupation of Alcatraz Island by the San Francisco area's Indians of All Tribes coalition ushered in a decade-long period of uncompromising and intensely confrontational American Indian political activism.[1] Unprecedented in modern U.S. history, the phenomenon represented by Alcatraz also marked the inception of a process of official repression of indigenous activists without contemporary North American parallel in its virulence and lethal effects.[2]

The nature of the post-Alcatraz federal response to organized agitation for native rights was such that by 1979 researchers were describing it as a manifestation of the U.S. government's "continuing Indian Wars."[3] For its part (in internal documents intended to be secret), the Federal Bureau of Investigation (FBI)—the primary instrument by which the government's policy of anti-Indian repression was implemented—concurred with such assessments, abandoning its customary counterintelligence vernacular in favor of the terminology of outright counterinsurgency warfare.[4] The result, as the U.S. Commission on Civil Rights officially conceded at the time, was the imposition of a condition of official terrorism upon certain of the less compliant sectors of indigenous society in the United States.[5]

In retrospect, it is apparent that the locus of both activism and repression in Indian County throughout the 1970s centered squarely on one group, the American Indian Movement (AIM). Moreover, the crux of AIM activism during the 1970s, and thus of the FBI's campaign to "neutralize" it,[6] can be found in a single locality: the Pine Ridge (Oglala Lakota) Reservation, in South Dakota. The purpose of this essay, then, is to provide an overview of the federal counterinsurgency program against AIM on and around Pine Ridge, using it as a lens through which to explore the broader motives and outcomes attending it. Finally, conclusions will be drawn as to the program's implications, not only with respect to American Indians, but concerning non-indigenous Americans as well.

BACKGROUND

AIM was founded in 1968 in Minneapolis by a group of urban Anishnaabeg (Chippewa), including Dennis Banks, Mary Jane Wilson, Pat Ballanger, Clyde Bellecourt, Eddie Benton Benai, and George Mitchell. Modeled loosely after the Black Panther Party for Self-Defense established by Huey P. Newton and Bobby Seale in Oakland, California, two years previously, the group took as its first tasks the protection of the city's sizable native community from a pattern of rampant police abuse and the creation of programs for jobs, housing, and education.[7] Within three years, the organization had grown to include chapters in several other cities and had begun to shift its focus from civil rights issues to an agenda more specifically attuned to the conditions afflicting native North America.

What AIM discerned as the basis of these conditions was not so much a matter of socioeconomic discrimination against Indians as it was their internal colonization by the United States.[8] This perception accrued from the fact that, by 1871 when federal treaty-making with native peoples was permanently suspended, the rights of indigenous nations to distinct, self-governing territories had been recognized by the United States more than 370 times through treaties duly ratified by its Senate.[9] Yet, during the intervening century, more than 90 percent of treaty-reserved native land had been expropriated by the federal government, in defiance of both its own constitution and international custom and convention.[10] One consequence of this was creation of the urban diaspora from which AIM itself had emerged; by 1970, about half of all Indians in the United States had been pushed off their land altogether.[11]

Within the residual archipelago of reservations—an aggregation of about fifty million acres, or roughly 2.5 percent of the forty-eight contiguous states—indigenous forms of governance had been thoroughly usurped through the imposition of U.S. jurisdiction under the federal government's self-assigned prerogative of exercising "plenary [full and absolute] power over Indian affairs."[12] Correspondingly, Indian control over what had turned out to be rather vast mineral resources within reservation boundaries—an estimated two-thirds of all U.S. "domestic" uranium deposits, one-quarter of the low sulfur coal, 20 percent of the oil and natural gas, and so on—was essentially nonexistent.[13]

It followed that royalty rates set by the U.S. Bureau of Indian Affairs (BIA), in its exercise of federal "trust" prerogatives vis-à-vis corporate extraction of Indian mineral assets, amounted to only a fraction of what the same corporations would have paid had they undertaken the same mining operations in nonreservation localities.[14] The same principle of underpayment to Indians, with resulting "super-profit" accrual to non-Indian business entities, prevailed with regard to other areas of economic activity handled by the Indian bureau, from the leasing of reservation grazing land to various ranching interests, to the harvesting of reservation timber by corporations such as Weyerhauser and Boise-Cascade.[15] Small wonder that, by the later 1960s, Indian radicals such as Robert K. Thomas had begun to refer to the BIA as "the Colonial Office of the United States."[16]

In human terms, the consequence was that, overall, American Indians—who, on the basis of known resources, comprised what should have been the single wealthiest population group in North America—constituted by far the most impoverished sector of U.S. society. According to the federal government's own data, Indians suffered, by a decisive margin, the highest rate of unemployment in the country, a matter correlated to their receiving by far the lowest annual and lifetime incomes of any group in the nation.[17] It also corresponded well with virtually every other statistical indicator of extreme poverty: a truly catastrophic rate of infant mortality and the highest rates of death from malnutrition, exposure, plague disease, teen suicide, and accidents related to alcohol abuse. The average life expectancy of a reservation-based Indian male in 1970 was less than forty-five years; reservation-based Indian females could expect to live less than three years longer than their male counterparts; urban Indians of either gender were living only about five years longer, on average, than their relatives on the reservations.[18]

AIM's response to its growing apprehension of this squalid panorama was to initiate a campaign consciously intended to bring about the decolonization of native North America: "Only by reestablishing our rights as sovereign nations, including our right to control our own territories and resources, and our right to genuine self-governance," as Dennis Banks put it in 1971, "can we hope to successfully address the conditions currently experienced by our people."[19]

Extrapolating largely from the example of Alcatraz, the movement undertook a multifaceted political strategy combining a variety of tactics. On the one hand, it engaged in activities designed primarily to focus media attention, and thus the attention of the general public, on Indian rights issues, especially those pertaining to treaty rights. On the other hand, it pursued the sort of direct confrontation meant to affirm those rights in practice. It also began systematically to reassert native cultural/spiritual traditions.[20] Eventually, it added a component wherein the full range of indigenous rights to decolonization/self-determination were pursued through the United Nations venue of international law, custom, and convention.[21]

In mounting this comprehensive effort, AIM made of itself a bona fide national liberation movement, at least for a while.[22] Its members consisted of "the shock troops of Indian sovereignty," to quote non-AIM Oglala Lakota activist Birgil Kills Straight.[23] They essentially reframed the paradigm by which U.S.-Indian relations were understood by the late twentieth century.[24] They also suffered the worst physical repression at the hands of the United States of any "domestic" group since the 1890 massacre of Big Foot's Minneconjou by the 7th Cavalry at Wounded Knee.[25]

PRELUDE

AIM's seizure of the public consciousness may in many ways be said to have begun in 1969 when Dennis Banks recruited a young Oglala named Russell Means to join the movement. Instinctively imbued with what one critic described as a "bizarre knack for staging demonstrations that attracted the sort of press coverage Indians had been looking for,"[26] Means was instrumental in AIM's achieving several of its earliest and most important media coups: painting Plymouth Rock red before capturing the Mayflower replica on Thanksgiving Day 1970, for example, and staging a "4th of July Countercelebration" by occupying the Mount Rushmore National Monument in 1971.[27]

Perhaps more important, Means proved to be the bridge that allowed the movement to establish its credibility on a reservation for the first time. In part, this was because when he joined AIM he brought along virtually an entire generation of his family—brothers Ted, Bill, and Dale, cousin Madonna Gilbert, and others—each of whom possessed a web of friends and acquaintances on the Pine Ridge Reservation. It was therefore natural that AIM was called upon to "set things right" concerning the torture-murder of a middle-aged Oglala in the off-reservation town of Gordon, Nebraska, in late February 1972.[28] As Bill Means would later recall, "When Raymond Yellow Thunder was killed, his relatives went first to the BIA, then to the FBI, and to the local police, but they got no response. Severt Young Bear [Yellow Thunder's nephew and a friend of Ted Means] then . . . asked AIM to come help clear up the case."[29] Shortly, Russell Means led a caravan of some thirteen hundred Indians into the small town, announcing from the steps of the courthouse, "We've come here today to put Gordon on the map . . . and if justice is not immediately forthcoming, we're going to take Gordon *off* the map." The killers, brothers named Melvin and Leslie Hare, were quickly arrested, and a police officer who had covered up for them was suspended. The Hares soon became the first whites in Nebraska history sent to prison for killing an Indian, and "AIM's reputation soared among reservation Indians. What tribal leaders had dared not do to protect their people, AIM had done."[30]

By fall, things had progressed to the point that AIM could collaborate with several other native rights organizations to stage the Trail of Broken Treaties caravan, bringing more than two thousand Indians from reservations and urban areas across the country to Washington, D.C., on the eve of the 1972 presidential election. The idea was to present the incumbent chief executive, Richard M. Nixon, with a twenty-point program redefining the nature of U.S.-Indian relations. The publicity attending the critical timing and location of the action, as well as the large number of Indians involved, were calculated to force serious responses from the administration to each point.[31]

Interior Department officials who had earlier pledged logistical support to caravan participants once they arrived in the capitol reneged on their promises, apparently in the belief that this would cause the group to meekly disperse. Instead, angry Indians promptly took over the BIA headquarters building on 2 November, evicted its staff, and held it for several days. Russell Means, in fine form, captured the front page of the nation's newspapers and the six o'clock news by conducting a press conference in front of the building, while adorned with a makeshift "war club," and a "shield" fashioned from a portrait of Nixon himself.[32]

Desperate to end what had become a major media embarrassment, the Nixon administration agreed to reply formally to the twenty-point program within a month and to provide $66,000 in transportation money immediately, in exchange for a peaceful end to the occupation.[33] The AIM members honored their part of the bargain, leaving the BIA building on 9 November. But, explaining that "Indians have every right to know the details of what is being done to us and to our property," they took with them a vast number of "confidential" files concerning BIA leasing practices, operation of the Indian Health Service (IHS), and so forth. The originals were returned as rapidly as they could be photocopied, a process that required nearly two years to complete.[34]

Technically speaking, the government also honored its end of the deal, providing official—and exclusively negative—responses to the twenty points within the specified timeframe.[35] At the same time, however, it initiated a campaign utilizing federally subsidized Indian "leaders" in an effort to discredit AIM members as "irresponsible . . . renegades, terrorists and self-styled revolutionaries."[36] There is also a strong indication that it was at this point that the Federal Bureau of Investigation was instructed to launch a secret program of its own, one in which AIM's capacity to engage in further political activities of the kind and effectiveness displayed in Washington was to be, in the vernacular of FBI counterintelligence specialists, "neutralized."[37]

Even as this was going on, AIM's focus had shifted back to the Pine Ridge area. At issue was the 23 January 1973 murder of a young Oglala named Wesley Bad Heart Bull by a white man, Darld Schmitz, in the off-reservation village of Buffalo Gap, South Dakota. As in the Yellow Thunder case, local authorities had made no move to press appropriate charges against the killer.[38] At the request of the victim's mother, Sarah, Russell Means called for a demonstration at the Custer County Courthouse, in whose jurisdiction the crime lay. Terming western South Dakota "the Mississippi of the North,"[39] Dennis Banks simultaneously announced a longer-term effort to force abandonment "of the anti-Indian attitudes which result in Indian-killing being treated as a sort of local sport."[40]

The Custer demonstration on 6 February followed a very different course from that of the protest in Gordon a year earlier. An anonymous call had been placed to the main regional newspaper, the *Rapid City Journal*, on the evening of 5 February. The caller, saying he was "with AIM," asked that a notice canceling the action "because of bad weather" be prominently displayed in the paper the following morning. Consequently, relatively few Indians turned out for the protest.[41] Those who did were met by an amalgamated force of police, sheriff's deputies, state troopers, and FBI personnel when they arrived in Custer.[42]

For awhile, there was a tense standoff. Then, a sheriff's deputy manhandled Sarah Bad Heart Bull when she attempted to enter the courthouse. In the melee that followed, the courthouse was set ablaze—reportedly, by a police tear gas canister—and the local Chamber of Commerce building was burned to the ground. Banks, Means, and other AIM members, along with Mrs. Bad Heart Bull, were arrested and charged with riot. Banks was eventually convicted and sentenced to three years imprisonment and became a fugitive; Sarah Bad Heart Bull served five months of a one-to-five-year sentence. Her son's killer never spent one day in jail.[43]

WOUNDED KNEE

Meanwhile, on Pine Ridge, tensions were running extraordinarily high. The point of contention was an escalating conflict between the tribal administration headed by Richard "Dickie" Wilson, installed on the reservation with federal support in 1972, and a large body of reservation traditionals who objected to Wilson's nepotism and other abuses of his position.[44] Initially, Wilson's opponents had sought redress of their grievances through the BIA. The BIA responded by providing a $62,000 grant to Wilson for purposes of establishing a Tribal Ranger Group—a paramilitary entity reporting exclusively to Wilson, which soon began calling itself Guardians of the Oglala Nation (GOONs)—with which to physically intimidate the opposition.[45] The reason underlying this federal largess appears to have been the government's desire that Wilson sign an instrument transferring title of a portion of the reservation known as the Sheep Mountain Gunnery Range—secretly known to be rich in uranium and molybdenum—to the U.S. Forest Service.[46]

In any event, forming the Oglala Sioux Civil Rights Organization (OSCRO), the traditionals next attempted to obtain relief through the Justice Department and the FBI. When this, too, failed to bring results, they set out to impeach Wilson, obtaining signatures of more eligible voters on their petitions than had cast ballots for him in the first place. The BIA countered by naming Wilson himself to chair the impeachment proceedings, and the Justice Department dispatched a sixty-five-member Special Operations Group (SOG, a large SWAT unit) of U.S. marshals to ensure that "order" was maintained during the travesty. Then, on the eve of the hearing, Wilson ordered the arrest and jailing of several members of the tribal council he felt might vote for his removal. Predictably, when the impeachment tally was taken on 23 February 1973, the incumbent was retained in office. Immediately thereafter, he announced a reservation-wide ban on political meetings.[47]

Defying the ban, the traditionals convened a round-the-clock emergency meeting at the Calico Hall, near the village of Oglala, in an effort to determine their next move. On 26 February, the Oglala elders sent a messenger to the newly established AIM headquarters in nearby Rapid City to request that Russell Means meet with them. One of the elders, Ellen Moves Camp, later said, "We decided we needed the American Indian Movement in here. . . . All of our older people from the reservation helped make that decision. . . . This is what we needed, a little more push. Most of the reservation believes in AIM, and we're proud to have them with us."[48] Means arrived on the morning of the 27 February, then drove on to the village of Pine Ridge, seat of the reservation government, to try to negotiate some sort of resolution with Wilson. For his trouble, he was physically assaulted by GOONs in the parking lot of the tribal administration building.[49] By then, Dennis Banks and a number of other AIM members had arrived at the Calico Hall. During subsequent meetings, it was decided by the elders that they needed to draw public attention to the situation on the reservation. For this purpose, a two-hundred-person AIM contingent was sent to the symbolic site of Wounded Knee to prepare for an early morning press conference; a much smaller group was sent back to Rapid City to notify the media and to guide reporters to Wounded Knee at the appropriate time.[50]

The intended press conference never occurred because, by dawn, Wilson's GOONs had established roadblocks on all four routes leading into (or out of) the tiny hamlet. During the morning, these positions were reinforced by uniformed BIA police, then by elements of the marshals' SOG unit, and then by FBI "observers." As this was going on, the AIM members in Wounded Knee began the process of arming themselves from the local Gildersleeve Trading Post and building defensive positions.[51] By afternoon, Gen. Alexander Haig, military liaison to the Nixon White House, had dispatched two special warfare experts—Col. Volney Warner of the 82d Airborne Division, and Col. Jack Potter of the 6th Army—to the scene.[52]

> Documents later subpoenaed from the Pentagon revealed Colonel Potter directed the employment of 17 APCs [tanklike armored personnel carriers], 130,000 rounds of M-16 ammunition, 41,000 rounds of M-40 high explosive [for the M-79 grenade launchers he also provided], as well as helicopters, Phantom jets, and personnel. Military officers, supply sergeants, maintenance technicians, chemical officers, and medical teams [were provided on site]. Three hundred miles to the south, at Fort Carson, Colorado, the Army had billeted a fully uniformed assault unit on twenty-four hour alert.[53]

Over the next seventy-one days, the AIM perimeter at Wounded Knee was placed under siege. The ground cover was burned away for roughly a quarter-mile around the AIM position as part of the federal attempt to staunch the flow of supplies—food, medicine, and ammunition—backpacked in to the Wounded Knee defenders at night; at one point, such material was airdropped by a group of supporting pilots.[54] More than 500,000 rounds of military ammunition were fired into AIM's jerry-rigged "bunkers" by federal forces, killing two Indians—an Apache named Frank Clearwater and Buddy Lamont, an Oglala—and wounding several others.[55] As many as thirteen more people may have been killed by roving GOON patrols, their bodies secretly buried in remote locations around the reservation, while they were trying to carry supplies through federal lines.[56]

At first, the authorities sought to justify what was happening by claiming that AIM had "occupied" Wounded Knee and that the movement had taken several hostages in the process.[57] When the latter allegation was proven to be false, a press ban was imposed, and official spokespersons argued that the use of massive force was needed to "quell insurrection." Much was made of two federal casualties who were supposed to have been seriously injured by AIM gunfire.[58] In the end, it was Dickie Wilson who perhaps summarized the situation most candidly when he informed reporters that the purpose of the entire exercise was to see to it that "AIM dies at Wounded Knee."[59]

Despite Wilson's sentiments—and those of FBI senior counterintelligence specialist Richard G. Held, expressed in a secret report prepared at the request of his superiors early in the siege,[60]—an end to the standoff was finally negotiated for 7 May 1973. AIM's major condition, entered in behalf of the Pine Ridge traditionals and agreed to by government representatives, was that a federal commission would meet with the chiefs to review U.S. compliance with the terms of the 1868 Fort Laramie Treaty with the Lakota, Cheyenne, and Arapaho nations.[61] The idea was to generate policy recommendations as to how the United States might bring itself into line with its treaty obligations. A White House delegation did, in fact, meet with the elders at the home of Chief Frank Fools Crow, near the reservation town of Manderson, on 17 May. The delegates' mission, however, was to stonewall all efforts at meaningful discussion.[62] They promised a follow-up meeting on 30 May but never returned.[63]

On other fronts, the authorities were demonstrating a similar vigor. Before the first meeting at Fools Crow's house, the FBI had made 562 arrests of those who had been involved in defending Wounded Knee.[64] Russell Means was in jail awaiting release on $150,000 bond; OSCRO leader Pedro Bissonette was held against $152,000; AIM leaders Stan Holder and Leonard Crow Dog were held against $32,000 and $35,000, respectively. Scores of others were being held pending the posting of lesser sums.[65] By the fall of 1973, agents had amassed some 316,000 separate investigative file classifications on those who had been inside Wounded Knee.[66]

This allowed federal prosecutors to obtain 185 indictments over the next several months (Means alone was charged with thirty-seven felonies and three misdemeanors).[67] In 1974, AIM and the traditionals used the 1868 treaty as a basis on which to challenge in federal court the U.S. government's jurisdiction over Pine Ridge; however, the trials of the "Wounded Knee leadership" went forward.[68] Even after the FBI's and the prosecution's willingness to subvert the judicial process became so blatantly obvious that U.S. District Judge Fred Nichol was compelled to dismiss all charges against Banks and Means, cases were still pressed against Crow Dog, Holder, Carter Camp, Madonna Gilbert, Lorelei DeCora, and Phyllis Young.[69]

The whole charade resulted in a meager fifteen convictions, all of them on such paltry offenses as trespass and "interference with postal inspectors in performance of their lawful duties."[70] Still, in the interim, the virtual entirety of AIM's leadership was tied up in a seemingly endless series of arrests, incarcerations, hearings, and trials. Similarly, the great bulk of the movement's fundraising and organizing capacity was diverted into posting bonds and mounting legal defenses for those indicted.[71]

On balance, the record suggests a distinct probability that the post-Wounded Knee prosecutions were never seriously intended to result in convictions at all. Instead, they were designed mainly to serve the time-honored—and utterly illegal—expedient of "disrupting, misdirecting, destabilizing or otherwise neutralizing" a politically objectionable group.[72] There is official concurrence with this view: As army counterinsurgency specialist Volney Warner framed matters at the time, "AIM's best leaders and most militant members are under indictment, in jail or warrants are out for their arrest.... [Under these conditions] the government can win, even if nobody goes to [prison]."[73]

THE REIGN OF TERROR

While AIM's "notables" were being forced to slog their way through the courts, a very different form of repression was being visited upon the movement's rank-and-file membership and the grassroots traditionals of Pine Ridge. During the three-year period beginning with the siege of Wounded Knee, at least sixty-nine members and supporters of AIM died violently on the reservation.[74] During the same period, nearly 350 others suffered serious physical assault. Overall, the situation on Pine Ridge was such that, by 1976, the U.S. Commission on Civil Rights was led to describe it as a "reign of terror."[75]

> Even if only documented political deaths are counted, the yearly murder rate on the Pine Ridge Reservation between 1 March 1973 and 1 March 1976 was 170 per 100,000. By comparison, Detroit, the reputed "murder capital of the United States," had a rate of 20.2 per 100,000 in 1974. The U.S. average was 9.7 per 100,000. In a nation of two hundred million persons, the national murder rate comparable with that on Pine Ridge between 1973 and 1976 would have left 340,000 persons dead for political reasons alone in one year, 1.32 million in three years. The political murder rate at Pine Ridge was almost equivalent to that in Chile during the three years after a military coup supported by the United States killed President Salvador Allende.[76]

Despite the fact that eyewitnesses identified the assailants in twenty-one of these homicides, the FBI—which maintains preeminent jurisdiction over major crimes on all American Indian reservations—did not manage to get even one of the killers convicted.[77] In many cases, the bureau undertook no active investigation of the murder of an AIM member or supporter.[78] In others, people associated with the victims were falsely arrested as the perpetrators.[79]

When queried by reporters in 1975 as to the reason for his office's abysmal record in investigating murders on Pine Ridge, George O'Clock, agent in charge of the FBI's Rapid City resident agency—under whose operational authority the reservation falls most immediately—replied that he was "too short of manpower" to assign agents to such tasks.[80] O'Clock neglected to mention that, at the time, he had at his disposal the highest sustained ratio of agents to citizens enjoyed by any FBI office in the history of the bureau.[81] He also omitted the fact that the same agents who were too busy to look into the murders of AIM people appear to have had unlimited time to undertake the previously mentioned investigations of the AIM activists. Plainly, O'Clock's pat explanation was and remains implausible.

A far more likely scenario begins to take shape when it is considered that, in each instance where there were eyewitness identifications of the individuals who had killed an AIM member or supporter, those identified were known GOONs.[82] The FBI's conspicuous inability to apprehend murderers on Pine Ridge may thus be explained not by the incompetence of its personnel but by the nature of its relationship to the killers. In effect, the GOONs seem to have functioned under a more-or-less blanket immunity from prosecution provided by the FBI so long as they focused their lethal attentions on targets selected by the bureau. Put another way, it appears that the FBI used the GOONs as a surrogate force against AIM on Pine Ridge in precisely the same manner that Latin American death squads have been utilized by the CIA to destroy the opposition in countries like Guatemala, El Salvador, and Chile.[83]

The roots of the FBI/GOON connection can be traced back at least as far as 28 April 1973, when U.S. Marshals Service Director Wayne Colburn, driving from Pine Ridge village to Wounded Knee, was stopped at what the Wilsonites referred to as "The Residents' Roadblock," One of the GOONs manning the position, vocally disgruntled with what he called the "soft line" taken by the Justice Department in dealing with AIM, leveled a shotgun at the head of Colburn's passenger, Solicitor General Kent Frizzell. Colburn was forced to draw his own weapon before the man would desist. Angered, Colburn drove back to Pine Ridge and dispatched a group of his men to arrest everyone at the roadblock. When the marshals arrived at the Pennington County Jail in Rapid City with those arrested, however, they found an FBI man waiting with instructions to release the GOONs immediately.[84]

By this time, Dickie Wilson himself had reestablished the roadblock, using a fresh crew of GOONs. Thoroughly enraged at this defiance, Colburn assembled another group of marshals and prepared to make arrests. Things had progressed to the point of a "High Noon" style showdown when a helicopter appeared, quickly landing on the blacktop road near the would be combatants. In it was FBI counterintelligence ace Richard G. Held, who informed Colburn that he had received instructions "from the highest level" to ensure that no arrests would be made and that "the roadblock stays where it is."[85]

Humiliated and increasingly concerned for the safety of his own personnel in a situation where the FBI was openly siding with a group hostile to them, Colburn ordered his men to disarm GOONs whenever possible.[86] Strikingly, though, when the marshals impounded the sort of weaponry the Wilsonites had up until then been using—conventional deer rifles, World War II surplus M-1s, shotguns, and other firearms normally found in a rural locality—the same GOONs began to reappear sporting fully automatic military-issue M-16s and well stocked with ammunition.[87]

THE BREWER REVELATIONS

It has always been the supposition of those aligned with AIM that the FBI provided such hardware to Wilson's GOONs. The bureau and its apologists, of course, have pointed to the absence of concrete evidence with which to confirm the allegation and have consistently denied any such connection, charging those referring to it with journalistic or scholarly "irresponsibility."[88]

Not until the early 1990s, with publication of extracts from an interview with former GOON commander Duane Brewer, was AIM's premise borne out.[89] The one-time death squad leader makes it clear that the FBI provided him and his men not only with weaponry but with ample supplies of armor-piercing ammunition, hand grenades, "det cord" and other explosives, communications gear, and additional paraphernalia.[90] Agents would drop by his house, Brewer maintains, to provide key bits of field intelligence that allowed the GOONs to function in a more efficient manner than might otherwise have been the case. And, perhaps most important, agents conveyed the plain message that members of the death squad would enjoy virtual immunity from federal prosecution for anything they did, so long as it fell within the realm of repressing dissidents on the reservation.[91]

Among other murders which Brewer clarifies in his interview is that of Jeanette Bissonette, a young woman shot to death in her car as she sat at a stop sign in Pine Ridge village at about one o'clock on the morning of 27 March 1975. The FBI has insisted all along, for reasons that remain mysterious, that it is "probable" Bissonette was assassinated by AIM members.[92] Brewer, on the other hand, explains, on the basis of firsthand knowledge, that the killing was "a mistake" on the part of his execution team, which mistook Bissonette's vehicle for that of area resistance leader Ellen Moves Camp.[93]

It is important to note that, at the same time that he functioned as a GOON leader, Duane Brewer also was second-in-command of the BIA Police on Pine Ridge. His police boss, Delmar Eastman—primary liaison between the police and the FBI—was simultaneously in charge of all GOON operations on the reservation.[94] In total, it is reliably estimated that somewhere between one-third and one-half of all BIA police personnel on Pine Ridge between 1972 and 1976 moonlighted as GOONs. Those who did not become directly involved covered for their colleagues who did, or at least kept their mouths shut about the situation.[95]

Obviously, whatever small hope AIM and the Oglala traditionals might have held for help from local law enforcement quickly disappeared under such circumstances.[96] In effect, the police were the killers, their crimes not only condoned but, for all practical intents and purposes, commanded and controlled by the FBI. Other federal agencies did no more than issue largely uncirculated reports confirming that the bloodbath was, in fact, occurring.[97] "Due process" on Pine Ridge during the crucial period was effectively nonexistent.

THE OGLALA FIREFIGHT

By the spring of 1975, with more than forty of their number already dead, it had become apparent to the Pine Ridge resisters that they had been handed a choice of either acquiescing to the federal agenda or being annihilated. All other alternatives, including a 1974 electoral effort to replace Dickie Wilson with AIM leader Russell Means, had been met by fraud, force, and unremitting violence.[98] Those who wished to continue the struggle and survive were therefore compelled to adopt a posture of armed self-defense. Given that many of the traditionals were elderly and thus could not reasonably hope to defend themselves alone, they asked AIM to provide physical security for them. Defensive encampments were quickly established at several key locations around the reservation.[99]

For its part, the FBI seems to have become increasingly frustrated at the capacity of the dissidents to absorb punishment and at the consequent failure of its own coun-terinsurgency campaign to force submission. Internal FBI documents suggest that the coordinators of the Pine Ridge operation had come to desire some sensational event that might serve to justify, in the public mind, a sudden introduction of the kind of overwhelming force that would break the back of the resistance once and for all.[100]

Apparently selected for this purpose was a security camp set up by the Northwest AIM group at the request of traditional elders Harry and Cecilia Jumping Bull on their property along Highway 18, a few miles south of the village of Oglala. During the early evening of 25 June 1975, two agents, Ron Williams and Jack Coler, escorted by a BIA policeman (and known GOON) named Robert Eccoffey, entered the Jumping Bull compound. They claimed to be attempting to serve an arrest war-rant on a seventeen-year-old Lakota AIM supporter named Jimmy Eagle on spuri-ous charges of kidnapping and aggravated assault.[101]

Told by residents that Eagle was not there and had not been seen for weeks, the agents and their escort left. On Highway 18, however, the agents accosted three young AIM members—Mike Anderson, Norman Charles, and Wilfred "Wish" Draper—who were walking back to camp after taking showers in Oglala. The agents drove the young men to the police headquarters in Pine Ridge village and interro-gated them for more than two hours. As the men reported when they finally returned to the Jumping Bulls' house, no questions had been asked about Jimmy Eagle. Instead, the agents had wanted to know how many men of fighting age were in the camp, what sort of weapons they possessed, and so on. Thus alerted that something bad was about to happen, the Northwest AIM contingent put out an urgent call for support from the local AIM community.[102]

At about eleven o'clock the following morning, 26 June, Williams and Coler returned to the Jumping Bull property. Driving past the compound of residences, they moved down into a shallow valley, stopped, exited their cars in an open area, and began to fire in the general direction of the AIM encampment in a treeline along White Clay Creek.[103] Shortly, they began to take a steadily growing return fire, not only from the treeline, but from the houses above. At about this point, agent J. Gary Adams and BIA police officer/GOON Glenn Two Birds attempted to come to Williams's and Coler's aid. Unexpectedly taking fire from the direction of the houses, they retreated to the ditch beside Highway 18.[104]

Some 150 SWAT-trained BIA police and FBI personnel were repositioned in the immediate area when the firefight began. This, especially when taken in combination with the fact that more than two hundred additional FBI SWAT personnel were on alert awaiting word to proceed post haste to Pine Ridge from Minneapolis, Milwaukee, and Quantico, Virginia, raises the probability that Williams and Coler were actually assigned to provoke an exchange of gunfire with the AIM members on the Jumping Bull land.[105] The plan seems to have been that they would then be immediately supported by the introduction of overwhelming force, the Northwest AIM group would be destroyed, and the FBI would be afforded the pretext necessary to launch an outright invasion of Pine Ridge.[106]

A number of local AIM members had rallied to the call to come to the Jumping

Bulls' home. Hence, instead of encountering the eight AIM shooters they anticipated, the two agents encountered about thirty, and they were cut off from their erstwhile supporters.[107] While the BIA police, reinforced by GOONs, put up roadblocks to seal off the area, and the FBI agents on hand were deployed as snipers, no one made a serious effort to get to Williams and Coler until 5:50 p.m. By then, they had been dead for some time, along with a young Coeur D'Alene AIM member, Joe Stuntz Killsright, killed by FBI sniper Gerard Waring as he attempted to depart the compound.[108] Except for Killsright, all the AIM participants had escaped across country.

By nightfall, hundreds of agents equipped with everything from APCs to Vietnam-style Huey helicopters had begun arriving on the reservation.[109] The next morning, Tom Coll, an FBI "public information specialist" imported for the purpose, convened a press conference in Oglala—the media was barred from the firefight site itself—in which he reported that the dead agents had been "lured into an ambush" by AIM, attacked with automatic weapons from a "sophisticated bunker complex," dragged wounded from their cars, stripped of their clothing, and then executed in cold blood while one of them pleaded with his killer(s) to spare him because he had a wife and children. Each agent, Coll asserted, had been "riddled with 15–20 bullets."[110]

Every word of this was false, as Coll well knew—the FBI had been in possession of both the agents' bodies and the ground on which they were killed for nearly eighteen hours before he made his statements—and the report was retracted in full by FBI Director Clarence Kelley at a press conference conducted in Los Angeles a week later.[111] By then, however, a barrage of sensational media coverage had "sensitized" the public to the need for a virtually unrestricted application of force against the "mad dogs of AIM." Correspondingly, the bureau was free to run air assaults and massive sweeping operations on Pine Ridge—complete with the wholesale use of no-knock searches and John Doe warrants—for the next three months."[112] By the end of that period, its mission had largely been accomplished."[113] In the interim, on 27 July 1975, given the preoccupation of all concerned parties with the FBI's literal invasion of Pine Ridge, it was finally determined that the time was right for Dickie Wilson to sign a memorandum transferring the Gunnery Range to the federal government. On 2 January 1976, a more formal instrument was signed, and in the spring Congress passed a public law assuming U.S. title over this portion of Oglala territory.[114]

THE CASE OF LEONARD PELTIER

It is unlikely that the FBI intended that its two agents be killed during the Oglala firefight. Once Coler and Williams were dead, however, the bureau capitalized on their fate, not only as the medium through which to pursue its anti-AIM campaign with full ferocity, but as a mechanism with which to block an incipient congressional probe into what the FBI had been doing on Pine Ridge. The latter took the form of a sympathy play: Bureau officials pleaded that the "natural" emotional volatility engendered among their agents by the deaths made it "inopportune" to proceed with the investigation at the present time. Congress responded on 3 July 1975 by postponing the scheduling of preliminary interviews, a delay that has become permanent.[115]

Still, with two agents dead, it was crucial for the bureau's image that someone be brought directly to account. To fill this bill, four names were selected from the list of thirty shooters that field investigators had concluded were participants in the exchange. Targeted were a pair of Anishnaabe/Lakota cousins, Leonard Peltier and Bob Robideau, and Darrelle "Dino" Butler, a Tutuni, all heads of Northwest AIM. Also included was Jimmy Eagle, whose name seems to have appeared out of expediency, since the bureau claimed Williams and Coler were looking for him in the first place (all charges against him were later simply dropped, without investiture of discernible prosecutorial effort).[116]

Butler and Robideau, captured early on, were tried first as codefendants, separate from Peltier.[117] The latter, having managed to avoid a trap set for him in Oregon, had found sanctuary in the remote encampment of Cree leader Robert Smallboy, in northern Alberta.[118] By the time he was apprehended, extradited via a fraudulent proceeding involving the presentation to a Canadian court of an "eyewitness" affidavit from a psychotic Lakota woman named Myrtle Poor Bear, and docketed in the United States, the prosecution of his cohorts was ready to begin.[119] Peltier was thus scheduled to be tried later and alone.

During the Butler/Robideau trial, conducted in Cedar Rapids, Iowa, in the summer of 1976, the government's plan to turn the defendants—and AIM itself—into examples of the price of resistance began to unravel. Despite the calculated ostentation with which the FBI prepared to secure the judge and jurors from "AIM's potential for violence" and another media blitz designed to convince the public that Butler and Robideau were part of a vast "terrorist conspiracy," the carefully selected all-white midwestern panel of jurors was unconvinced.[120] After William Muldrow of the U.S. Commission on Civil Rights testified for the defense regarding the FBI-fostered reign of terror on Pine Ridge and Director Kelley himself admitted under oath that he knew of nothing that might support many of the bureau's harsher characterizations of AIM, the jury voted to acquit on 16 July 1976.[121]

The "not guilty" verdict was based on the jury's assessment that although both defendants acknowledged firing at the agents and Robideau admitted that he had, in fact, hit them both,[122] they had acted in self-defense. Jury foreman Robert Bolin later recounted that, under the conditions described by credible witnesses, "we felt that any reasonable person would have reacted the same way when the agents came in there shooting." Besides, Bolin continued, their personal observations of the behavior of governmental representatives during the trial had convinced most jury members that "it was the government, not the defendants or their movement, which was dangerous."[123]

Although the Cedar Rapids jury had essentially determined that Coler and Williams had not been murdered, the FBI and federal prosecutors opted to proceed against Peltier. In a pretrial conference, they analyzed what had "gone wrong" in the Butler/Robideau case and, in a report dated 20 July 1976, concluded that among the problems encountered was the fact that the defendants had been allowed to present a self-defense argument and their lawyers had been permitted "to call and question witnesses" and subpoena government documents.[124] They then removed the Peltier trial from the docket of Cedar Rapids Judge Edward McManus and reassigned it to another, Paul Benson, whom they felt would be more amenable to their view.[125]

When Peltier was brought to trial in Fargo, North Dakota, on 21 March 1977, Benson ruled inadmissible virtually everything presented by the defense at Cedar Rapids, including the Butler/Robideau trial transcript itself.[126] Prosecutors then presented a case against Peltier that was precisely the opposite of what they—and their FBI witnesses—had presented in the earlier trial.[127] A chain of circumstantial evidence was constructed, often through fabricated physical evidence,[128] perjury,[129] and demonstrably suborned testimony,[130] to create a plausible impression among jurors—again white Midwesterners—that the defendant was guilty.

Following a highly emotional closing presentation by assistant prosecutor Lynn Crooks, in which he waved color photos of the agents' bloody bodies and graphically described the "cold-bloodedness" with which "Leonard Peltier executed these two wounded and helpless human beings," the jury voted on 18 April, after only six hours of deliberation, to convict on both counts of first-degree murder.[131] Bensen then sentenced Peltier to serve two consecutive life terms in prison, and the prisoner was transported straightaway to the federal "super-maximum" facility at Marion, Illinois.[132]

Almost immediately, an appeal was filed on the basis of FBI misconduct and multiple judicial errors on Bensen's part. The matter was considered by a three-member panel of the 8th Circuit Court—composed of Judges William Webster, Donald Ross, and Gerald Heaney—during the spring of 1978. Judge Webster wrote the opinion on behalf of his colleagues, finding that, although the record revealed numerous reversible errors on the part of the trial judge and many "unfortunate misjudgments" by the FBI, the conviction would be allowed to stand.[133] By the time the document was released, Webster was no longer there to answer for it. He had moved on to a new position as director of the FBI. On 12 February 1979, the U.S. Supreme Court declined, without stating a reason, to review the lower court's decision.[134]

Undeterred, Peltier's attorneys had already filed a suit under the Freedom of Information Act (FOIA) to force disclosure of FBI documents withheld from the defense at trial. When the paperwork, more than twelve thousand pages of investigative material, was finally produced in 1981, they began the tedious process of indexing and reviewing it.[135] Finding that the bureau had suppressed ballistics reports that directly contradicted what had been presented at trial, they filed a second appeal in 1982.[136] This led to an evidentiary hearing and oral arguments in 1984, during which the FBI's chief ballistics expert, Evan Hodge, was caught in the act of perjuring himself,[137] and Lynn Crooks was forced to admit that the government "really has no idea who shot those agents."[138]

Crooks then attempted to argue that it did not matter anyway, because Peltier had been convicted of "aiding and abetting in the murders rather than of the murders themselves."[139] This time, the circuit court panel—now composed of Judges Heaney and Ross, as well as John Gibson—took nearly a year to deliberate. On 11 October

1986, they finally delivered an opinion holding that the content of Crooks's own closing argument to the jury, among many other factors, precluded the notion that Peltier had been tried for aiding and abetting. They also concluded that the circumstantial ballistics case presented by the prosecution at trial was hopelessly undermined by evidence even then available to the FBI.[140] Still, they refused to reverse Peltier's conviction, because "[w]e recognize that there is evidence in this record of improper conduct on the part of some FBI agents, but we are reluctant to impute even further improprieties to them" by remanding the matter to trial.[141] On 5 October 1987, the Supreme Court once again refused to review the lower court's decision.[142] Most recently, a third appeal, argued on the basis of habeas corpus (If Peltier was never tried for aiding and abetting, and if the original case against him no longer really exists, then why is he in prison?) was filed. In November 1992, the 8th Circuit, without ever really answering these questions, allowed his "conviction" to stand.

AFTERMATH

The government repression of AIM during the mid-1970s had the intended effect of blunting the movement's cutting edge. After 1977, events occurred in fits and starts rather than within a sustained drive. AIM's core membership, those who were not dead or in prison, scattered to the winds; many, like Wounded Knee security head Stan Holder, sought other avenues into which to channel their activism.[143] Others, exhausted and intimidated by the massive violence directed against them, "retired" altogether from active politics.[144] Among the remainder, personal, political, and intertribal antagonisms—often exacerbated by the rumors spread by federal provocateurs—instilled a deep and lasting factional fragmentation.[145]

In 1978, Dennis Banks, occupying the unique status in California of having been officially granted sanctuary by one state of the union against the extradition demands of another, sought to renew Indian activism by organizing what he called the "Longest Walk."[146] To some extent replicating, on foot, the Trail of Broken Treaties caravan of 1972, the Walk succeeded in its immediate objective: The walkers made it from Alcatraz Island—selected as a point of departure because of the importance of the 1969–71 occupation in the formation of AIM—to Washington, D.C., presenting a powerful manifesto to the Carter administration in July.[147] But there was no follow-up, and the momentum was quickly lost.

Much hope was placed in the formation of the Leonard Peltier Defense Committee (LPDC) the same year, and, for a time, it seemed as though it might serve as a kind of sparkplug re-energizing the movement as a whole.[148] However, with the 12 February 1979 murder of AIM chair John Trudell's entire family on the Duck Valley Reservation in Nevada, apparently as a deterrent to the effectiveness of Trudell's fiery oratory, events took an opposite tack.[149] The result was the abolition of all national officer positions in AIM: "These titles do nothing but provide a ready-made list of priority targets of the feds," as Trudell put it at the time.[150] The gesture completed a trend against centralization which had begun with the dissolution of AIM's national office at the time Banks went underground in 1975, a fugitive from sentencing after his conviction on charges stemming from the Custer Courthouse confrontation.[151]

In 1979 and 1980, large-scale "survival gatherings" were held outside Rapid City in an attempt to bring together Indian and non-Indian activists in collaborative opposition to uranium mining and other corporate "development" of the Black Hills.[152] An ensuing organization, the Black Hills Alliance (BHA), achieved momentary national prominence but petered out after the demise of domestic uranium production in the early 1980s dissolved several of the more pressing issues it confronted.[153]

Meanwhile, Russell Means, fresh out of prison, launched a related effort in 1981, occupying an 880-acre site in the Black Hills to establish a "sustainable, alternative, demonstration community" and "to initiate the physical reoccupation of Paha Sapa by the Lakota people and our allies." The occupation of Wincanyan Zi Tiyospaye (Yellow Thunder Camp), named in memory of Raymond Yellow Thunder, lasted until 1985.[154] By that time, its organizers had obtained what on its face was a landmark judicial opinion from a federal district judge: Not only did the Yellow Thunder occupiers have every right to do what they were doing, the judge decreed, but the Lakota—and other Indians as well—are entitled to view entire geographic areas such as the Black Hills, rather than merely specific sites within them, to be of sacred significance.[155] The emergent victory was gutted, however, by the Supreme Court's controversial "G-O Road decision" in 1988.[156]

Elsewhere, an AIM security camp was established on Navajo land near Big Mountain, Arizona, during the mid-1980s to support the traditional Diné elders of that area in their resistance to forced relocation.[157] Similarly, AIM contingents became involved in the early 1990s in providing physical security to Western Shoshone resisters to forced removal from their land in Nevada.[158] Comparable scenarios have been played out in places as diverse as northern Minnesota and Wisconsin, Oregon, California, Oklahoma, Illinois, Florida, Georgia, Nebraska, Alaska, and upstate New York. The issues involved have been as wide ranging as the localities in which they have been confronted.

Another potential bright spot that ultimately was eclipsed was the International Indian Treaty Council (IITC). Formed at the request of the Lakota elders in 1974 to "carry the message of indigenous people into the community of nations" and to serve more generally as "AIM's international arm," it had, by August 1977, gotten off to a brilliant start, playing a key role in bringing representatives of ninety-eight native groups throughout the Americas together in an unprecedented convocation before the United Nations Commission on Human Rights. This led directly to the establishment of a formal Working Group on Indigenous Populations—mandated to draft a Universal Declaration of the Rights of Indigenous Peoples for incorporation into international law—under the U.N. Economic and Social Council.[159]

Despite this remarkable early success, the 1981 departure of its original director, Cherokee activist Jimmie Durham, caused the IITC to begin to unravel.[160] By 1986, his successors were widely perceived as using the organization's reputation as a vehicle for personal profit and prestige, aligning themselves for a fee with various nation-state governments against indigenous interests. Allegations also abounded that they were using their de facto diplomatic status as a medium through which to engage in drug trafficking. Regardless of whether such suspicions were well founded, IITC today has been reduced to the standard of a small sectarian corporation, completely divorced from AIM and the traditional milieu that legitimated it, subsisting mainly on donations from the very entities it was created to oppose.[161]

With the imminence of the Columbian Quincentenary celebration, the early 1990s presented opportunities for the revitalization of AIM. Indeed, the period witnessed a more-or-less spontaneous regeneration of autonomous AIM chapters in at least sixteen localities around the country.[162] In Colorado, an escalating series of confrontations with Columbus Day celebrants beginning in 1989 and organized by the state AIM chapter led to the galvanizing of a coalition of some fifty progressive organizations, Indian and non-Indian alike, by 1992.[163] In Denver, the city where Columbus Day was first proclaimed an official holiday, quincentenary activities were stopped in their tracks. Much the same process was evident in San Francisco and, to a lesser extent, in other locations.

Perhaps ironically, the most vicious reaction to the prospect of a resurgent movement came not from the government per se but from a small group in Minneapolis professing itself to be AIM's "legitimate leadership." How exactly it imagined it had attained this exalted position was a bit murky, there having been no AIM general membership conference to sanction the exercise of such authority since 1975. Nonetheless, in July 1993 the clique constituted itself under the laws of the state of Minnesota as National-AIM, Inc., announced the formation of a national board and a central committee, and provided the address of what it described as the AIM National Office.[164] Among the very first acts of this interesting amalgam—which proudly reported it was receiving $4 million per year in federal funding and more than $3 million annually from corporations such as Honeywell—was the issuance of letters "expelling" most of the rest of the movement from itself.[165]

A LEGACY

It may be, as John Trudell has said, that "AIM died years ago. It's just that some people don't know it yet."[166] Certainly the evidence indicates that it is no longer a viable organization. And yet there is another level to this reality, one that has more to do with the spirit of resistance than with tangible form. Whatever else may be said about what AIM was (or is), it must be acknowledged that, as Russell Means contends:

> Before AIM, Indians were dispirited, defeated and culturally dissolving. People were ashamed to be Indian. You didn't see the young people wearing braids or chokers or ribbon shirts in those days. Hell, I didn't wear 'em. People didn't Sun Dance, they didn't Sweat, they were losing their languages. Then there was that spark at Alcatraz,

and we took off. Man, we took a *ride* across this country. We put Indians and Indian rights smack dab in the middle of the public consciousness for the first time since the so-called Indian Wars. And, of course, we paid a heavy price for that. Some of us are still paying it. But now you see braids on our young people. There are dozens of Sun Dances every summer. You hear our languages spoken again in places they had almost died out. Most important, you find young Indians all over the place who understand that they don't have to accept whatever sort of bullshit the dominant society wants to hand them, that they have the right to fight, to struggle for their rights, that in fact they have an obligation to stand up on their hind legs and fight for their future generations, the way our ancestors did. Now, I don't know about you, but I call that pride in being Indian. And I think that's a very positive change. And I think—no, I *know*— AIM had a lot to do with bringing that change about. We laid the groundwork for the next stage in regaining our sovereignty and self-determination as nations, and I'm proud to have been a part of that.[167]

To the degree that this is true—and much of it seems very accurate—AIM may be said to have succeeded in fulfilling its original agenda.[168] The impulse of Alcatraz was carried forward into dimensions its participants could not yet envision. That legacy even now is being refashioned and extended by a new generation, as it will be by the next, and the next. The continuity of native North America's traditional resistance to domination was reasserted by AIM in no uncertain terms.

There are other aspects of the AIM legacy, to be sure. Perhaps the most crucial should be placed under the heading of "Lessons Learned." The experience of the American Indian Movement, especially in the mid-1970s, provides what amounts to a textbook exposition of the nature of the society we now inhabit, the lengths to which its government will go to maintain the kinds of domination AIM fought to cast off, and the techniques it uses in doing so. These lessons teach what to expect, and, if properly understood, how to overcome many of the methodologies of repression. The lessons are applicable not simply to American Indians but to anyone whose lot in life is to be oppressed within the American conception of business as usual.[169]

Ultimately, the gift bestowed by AIM is, in part, an apprehension of the fact that the Third World is not something "out there." It is everywhere, including behind the facade of liberal democracy that masks the substance of the United States.[170] It exists on every reservation in the nation, in the teeming ghettos of Brownsville, Detroit, and Compton, in the barrios and migrant fields and sharecropping farms of the Deep South.[171] It persists in the desolation of the Appalachian coal regions. It is there in the burgeoning prison industry of America, warehousing by far the porportionately largest incarcerated population on the planet.[172]

The Third World exists in the nation's ever-proliferating, militarized police apparatus. And it is there in the piles of corpses of those—not just AIM members, but Black Panthers, Brown Berets, Puerto Rican independentistas, labor organizers, civil rights workers, and many others—who tried to say "no" and make it stick.[173] It is there in the fate of Malcolm X and Fred Hampton, Mark Clark and Ché Payne,

Geronimo ji Jaga Pratt and Alejandina Torres, Susan Rosenberg and Martin Luther King, George Jackson and Ray Luc Lavasseur, Tim Blunk and Reyes Tijerina, Mutulu Shakur and Marilyn Buck, and many others.[174]

To win, it is said, one most know one's enemy. Winning the sorts of struggles these people engaged in is unequivocally necessary if we are to effect a constructive change in the conditions they faced and we continue to face. In this, there are still many lessons to be drawn from the crucible of AIM experience. These must be learned by all of us. They must be learned well. And soon.

NOTES

1. On the fishing rights struggles, see American Friends Service Committee, *Uncommon Controversy: Fishing Rights of the Muckleshoot, Puyallup and Nisqually Indians* (Seattle: University of Washington Press, 1970). On the Alcatraz occupation, see Peter Blue Cloud, ed., *Alcatraz Is Not an Island* (Berkeley, Calif.: Wingbow Press, 1972). Also see Adam Fortunate Eagle (Nordwall), *Alcatraz! Alcatraz! The Indian Occupation of 1969–1971* (Berkeley, Calif.: Heyday Books, 1992).

2. This is not to say that others—notably, members of the Black Panther Party—have not suffered severely and often fatally at the hands of official specialists in the techniques of domestic political repression in the United States. The distinction drawn with regard to American Indian activists in this respect is purely proportional. For comprehensive background on the experiences of non-Indians, see Robert Justin Goldstein, *Political Repression in Modern America, 1870 to the Present* (New York; Schenkman Publishing/Two Continents Publishing Group, 1978).

3. Bruce Johansen and Robert Maestas, *Wasi'chu: The Continuing Indian Wars* (New York; Monthly Review Press, 1979).

4. Counterinsurgency is not a part of law enforcement or intelligence-gathering missions. Rather, it is an integral subpart of low-intensity warfare doctrine and methodology, taught at the U.S. Army's Special Warfare School at Fort Bragg, North Carolina; see Maj. John S. Pustay, *Counterinsurgency Warfare* (New York: The Free Press, 1965); also see Michael T. Klare and Peter Kornbluh, eds., *Low Intensity Warfare: Counterinsurgency, Proinsurgency, and Antiterrorism in the Eighties* (New York; Pantheon Books, 1988). For an illustration of the FBI's use of explicit counterinsurgency terminology to define its anti-Indian operations in 1976, see Ward Churchill and Jim Vander Wall, *The COINTELPRO Papers: Documents from the FBI's Secret Wars against Dissent in the United States* (Boston: South End Pres, 1990), 264.

5. U.S. Department of Justice, Commission on Civil Rights, *Events Surrounding Recent Murders on the Pine Ridge Reservation in South Dakota* (Denver: Rocky Mountain Regional Office, 31 March 1976).

6. In his then-definitive study of the bureau, Sanford J. Ungar quotes a senior counterintelligence specialist to the effect that "success in this area is not measured in terms of arrests and prosecutions, but in our ability to neutralize our targets' ability to do what they're doing"; *FBI: An Uncensored Look Behind the Walls* (Boston: Little, Brown, 1975), 311.

7. On the early days of the Black Panther party, see Gene Marine, *The Black Panthers* (New York: New American Library, 1969). On the beginnings of AIM and its obvious reliance on the Panther model, see Peter Matthiessen, *In the Spirit of Crazy Horse* 2d ed. (New York: Viking Press, 1991), 34–37.

8. Although AIM was probably the first to attempt to put together a coherent program to challenge the internal colonization of American Indians, it was by no means the first to perceive the native situation in this light. That distinction probably belonged to the Cherokee anthropologist Robert K. Thomas, with his brief but influential essay "Colonialism: Classic and Internal," first published in the 1966–67 issue of *New University Thought*.

9. The United States is constitutionally prohibited, under Article 1, from entering into treaty relations with any entity other than another fully sovereign nation. Senate ratification of a treaty therefore

confirms formal U.S. recognition of the unequivocal sovereignty of the other party or parties to the instrument. The texts of 371 ratified treaties between the United States and various indigenous nations appear in Charles J. Kappler, *Indian Treaties 1778–1883* (New York: Interland Publishing, 1972). The United States suspended such treaty-making by law in 1871 (ch. 120, 16 Stat. 544, 566, now codified at 25 U.S.C. 71), with the provision that "nothing herein contained shall be construed to invalidate or impair the obligation of any treaty heretofore lawfully made with any Indian nation or tribe."

10. Following the findings of the Indian Claims Commission in its 1979 Final Report, an independent researcher has summarized that "about half the land area of the [United States] was purchased by treaty or agreement . . . ; another third of a [billion] acres, mainly in the West, were confiscated without compensation; another two-thirds of a [billion] acres were claimed by the United States without pretense of a unilateral action extinguishing native title"; see Russel Barsh, "Indian Land Claims Policy in the United States," *North Dakota Law Review* 58 (1982): 1–82. The last category mentioned, to which native title is still plainly applicable, amounts to about 35 percent of the forty-eight contiguous states; it should be contrasted to the approximately 2.5 percent of the "lower forty-eight" currently retaining reservation trust status.

11. U.S. Bureau of the Census, *1970 Census of the Population, Subject Report: American Indians* (Washington, D.C.: U.S. Government Printing Office, 1972).

12. U.S. Plenary Power Doctrine is perhaps best articulated in the Supreme Court's 1903 *Lonewolf v. Hitchcock* opinion (187 U.S. 553). The most relevant statutes are the 1885 Major Crimes Act (ch. 341, 24 Stat. 362, 385, now codified at U.S.C. 1153), the 1887 General Allotment Act (ch. 119, 24 Stat. 388, now codified as amended at 25 U.S.C. 331 et seq.), and the Indian Reorganization Act (ch. 576, 48 Stat. 948, now codified at 25 U.S.C. 461–279).

13. On resource distribution, see Michael Garrity, "The U.S. Colonial Empire Is as Close as the Nearest Indian Reservation," in *Trilateralism: The Trilateral Commission and Elite Planning for World Government*, ed. Holly Sklar (Boston: South End Press, 1980), 238–68.

14. See, generally, Joseph G. Jorgesen, ed., *Native Americans and Energy Development* 2 (Cambridge, Mass.: Anthropology Resource Center/Seventh Generation Fund, 1984).

15. See, generally, Roxanne Dunbar Ortiz, ed., *Economic Development in American Indian Reservations* (Albuquerque: Native American Studies Center, University of New Mexico, 1979).

16. Robert K. Thomas, "Colonialism: Classic and Internal," *New University Thought* 4:4 (Winter 1966–67).

17. U.S. Department of Health, Education, and Welfare (DHEW), *A Study of Selected Socio-Economic Characteristics of Ethnic Minorities Based on the 1970 Census, Vol. 3: American Indians* (Washington, D.C.: U.S. Government Printing Office, 1974). It should be noted that the economic and health data pertaining to certain sectors of other U.S. minority populations—inner city blacks, for example, or Latino migrant workers—are very similar to those bearing on American Indians. Unlike these other examples, however, the data on American Indians encompass the condition of the population as a whole.

18. U.S. Bureau of the Census, Population Division, Racial Statistics Branch, *A Statistical Profile of the American Indian Population* (Washington, D.C.: U.S. Government Printing Office, 1974).

19. Dennis J. Banks, speech before the United Lutheran Board, Minneapolis, Minnesota, March 1971.

20. Notable in this respect was the resuscitation of the Lakota Sun Dance, forbidden by the BIA since 1881. In August 1972, AIM members showed up en masse to participate in the ceremony at Crow Dog's Paradise, on the Rosebud Reservation. As the revered Oglala spiritual leader Frank Fools Crow put it in 1980: "Before that, there were only one, two Sun Dances each year. Just a few came, the real traditionals. And we had to hold 'em in secret. After the AIM boys showed up, now there are [Sun Dances] everywhere, right out in the open, too. Nobody hides anymore. Now, they're all proud to be Indian." The same principle pertains to the resurgence of numerous other ceremonies among a variety of peoples.

21. The U.N. component was developed pursuant to the creation of the International Indian Treaty Council (IITC), "AIM's international diplomatic arm," in 1974. Under the directorship, of Cherokee activist Jimmie Durham, IITC was responsible for convening the first Assembly of Indigenous Nations of the Western Hemisphere at the U.N. Palace of Nations in Geneva, Switzerland, during

the summer of 1977. IITC then became the world's first nongoverning organization (NGO; type-II, consultative) in the U.N. and played a major role in bringing about the establishment of the Working Group on Indigenous Populations—charged with annual review of native grievances and drafting a Universal Declaration of the Rights of Indigenous Peoples—under auspices of the U.N. Economic and Social Council (ECOSOC) in 1981. With Durham's departure from IITC the same year, the organization went into decline. The progressive dynamic it inaugurated, however, is ongoing. See, generally, Glenn T. Morris, "International Law and Politics: Toward a Right to Self-Determination for Indigenous Peoples," in *The State of Native America: Genocide, Colonization and Resistance*, ed. M. Annette Jaimes (Boston: South End Press, 1992), 55–86.

22. The term *National Liberation Movement* is not rhetorical. Rather, it bears a precise meaning under Article I, Paragraph 4 of Additional Protocol I of the 1949 Geneva Convention. Also see United Nations Resolution 3103 (XXVIII), 12 December 1973.

23. Birgil Kills Straight, mimeographed statement circulated by the Oglala Sioux Civil Rights Organization (Manderson, S. Dak.) during the 1973 siege of Wounded Knee.

24. By the mid-1970s, even elements of the federal government had begun to adopt AIM's emphasis on colonialism to explain the relationship between the United States and American Indians. See, for example, U.S. Commission on Civil Rights, *The Navajo Nation: An American Colony* (Washington, D.C.: U.S. Government Printing Office, September 1975).

25. This remained true until the government's 1993 slaughter of eighty-six Branch Davidians in a single hour near Waco, Texas. The standard text on the 1890 massacre is, of course, Dee Brown's *Bury My Heart at Wounded Knee: An Indian History of the American West* (New York: Holt, Rinehart & Winston, 1970).

26. Robert Burnette with John Koster, *The Road to Wounded Knee* (New York: Bantam Books, 1974), 196.

27. Peter Matthiessen, *In the Spirit of Crazy Horse*, 2d ed. (New York: Viking Press, 1991), 38, 110.

28. Yellow Thunder, burned with cigarettes, was forced to dance nude from the waist down for the entertainment of a crowd assembled in the Gordon American Legion Hall. He was then severely beaten and stuffed, unconscious, into the trunk of a car, where he froze to death. See Rex Weyler, *Blood of the Land: The U.S. Government and Corporate War against the American Indian Movement* (New York: Everest House, 1982), 48. Also see Matthiessen, *In the Spirit of Crazy Horse*, 59–80.

29. Quoted in Weyler, *Blood of the Land*, 49.

30. Alvin M. Josephy, Jr., *Now That the Buffalo's Gone: A Study of Today's American Indian* (New York: Alfred A. Knopf, 1982), 237.

31. The best overall handling of these events, including the complete text of the Twenty Point Program, is Vine Deloria, Jr.'s *Behind the Trail of Broken Treaties: An Indian Declaration of Independence* (New York: Delta Books, 1974).

32. See editors, *BIA, I'm Not Your Indian Anymore* (Rooseveltown, N.Y.: *Akwesasne Notes*, 1973).

33. The money, in unmarked twenty-, fifty- and hundred-dollar bills, came from a slush fund administered by Nixon's notorious Committee to Reelect the President (CREEP) and was delivered in brown paper bags. The bagmen were administration aids Leonard Garment and Frank Carlucci (later National Security Council chief and CIA director, respectively, under Ronald Reagan).

34. It was from these files that, among other things, the existence of a secret IHS program to perform involuntary sterilizations on American Indian women was first revealed. See Brint Dillingham, "Indian Women and IHS Sterilization Practices," *American Indian Journal* 3:1 (January 1977).

35. The full text of administration response is included in *BIA, I'm Not Your Indian Anymore*.

36. The language is that of Webster Two Hawk, then president of the Rosebud Sioux tribe and the federally funded National Tribal Chairman's Association. Two Hawk was shortly voted out of both positions by his constituents, replaced as Rosebud president by Robert Burnette, an organizer of the Trail of Broken Treaties. See Ward Churchill, "Renegades, Terrorists and Revolutionaries: The Government's Propaganda War against the American Indian Movement," *Propaganda Review* 4 (April 1989).

37. One firm indication of this was the arrest by the FBI of Assiniboine/Lakota activist Hank Adams and Les Whitten, an associate of columnist Jack Anderson, shortly after the occupation. They were briefly charged with illegally possessing government property. The men, neither of whom was an

AIM member, were merely acting as go-betweens in returning BIA documents to the federal authorities. The point seems to have been to isolate AIM from its more moderate associations. See Deloria, *Behind the Trail of Broken Treaties*, 59.

38. Although he had stabbed Bad Heart Bull repeatedly in the chest with a hunting knife, Schmitz was charged only with second-degree manslaughter and released on his own recognizance.

39. Don and Jan Stevens, *South Dakota: The Mississippi of the North; or, Stories Jack Anderson Never Told You* (Custer, S. Dak.: self-published pamphlet, 1977).

40. More, broadly, AIM's posture was a response to what it perceived as a nationwide wave of murders of Indians by whites. These included not only the murders of Yellow Thunder and Bad Heart Bull but those of a nineteen-year-old Papago named Phillip Celay by a sheriff's deputy in Arizona, an Onondaga Special Forces veteran (and member of the honor guard during the funeral of John F. Kennedy) named Leroy Shenandoah in Philadelphia, and, on 20 September 1972, of Alcatraz leader Richard Oakes near San Francisco. See Ward Churchill and Jim Vander Wall, *Agents of Repression: The FBI's Secret Wars against the Black Panther Party and the American Indian Movement* (Boston: South End Press, 1988), 123.

41. The individual receiving the call was reporter Lynn Gladstone. Such calls are a standard FBI counterintelligence tactic used to disrupt the political organization of targeted groups. See Brian Glick, *War at Home: Covert Action against U.S. Activists and What We Can Do about It* (Boston: South End Press, 1989).

42. A 31 January 1973 FBI teletype delineates the fact that the bureau was already involved in planning the police response to the Custer demonstration. It is reproduced in Churchill and Vander Wall, *The COINTELPRO Papers*, 241.

43. Weyler, *Blood of the Land*, 68–69.

44. The average annual income on Pine Ridge at this time was about $1,000; Cheryl McCall, "Life on Pine Ridge Bleak," *Colorado Daily*, 16 May 1975. Wilson hired his brother Jim to head the tribal planning office at an annual salary of $25,000 plus $15,000 in "consulting fees"; *New York Times*, 22 April 1975. Another brother, George, was hired at a salary of $20,000 to help the Oglala "manage their affairs"; Wilson's wife was named director of the reservation Head Start program at a salary of $18,000; his son "Manny" (Richard Jr.) was placed on the GOON payroll, along with several cousins and nephews; Wilson also upped his own salary from $5,500 per year to $15,500 per year, plus lucrative consulting fees, within his first six months in office; Matthiessen, *In the Spirit of Crazy Horse*, 62. When queried about the propriety of all this, Wilson replied, "There's no law against nepotism"; editors, *Voices from Wounded Knee, 1973* (Rooseveltown, N.Y.: *Akwesasne Notes*, 1974), 34.

45. In addition to this BIA "seed money," Wilson is suspected of having misappropriated some $347,000 in federal highway improvement funds to meet GOON payrolls between 1972 and 1975. A 1975 General Accounting Office report indicates that the funds had been expended without any appreciable road repair having been done and that the Wilsonites had kept no books with which to account for this mysterious situation. Nonetheless, the FBI declined to undertake a further investigation of the matter.

46. The Gunnery Range, comprising the northwestern eighth of Pine Ridge, was an area "borrowed" from the Oglala by the War Department in 1942 as a place to train aerial gunners. It was to be returned at the end of World War II, but it never was. By the early 1970s, the Oglala traditionals had begun to agitate heavily for its recovery. The deposits had been secretly discovered in 1971, however, through a technologically elaborate survey and mapping project undertaken jointly by the National Aeronautics and Space Administration (NASA) and a little-known entity called the National Uranium Resource Evaluation Institute (NURE). At that point, the government set out to obtain permanent title over the property; its quid pro quo with Wilson seems to have been his willingness to provide it. See J. P. Gries, *Status of Mineral Resource Information on the Pine Ridge Indian Reservation, S. D.* (Washington, D.C.: BIA Bulletin No. 12, U.S. Department of Interior, 1976). Also see Jacqueline Huber et al., *The Gunnery Range Report* (Pine Ridge, S. Dak.: Office of the Oglala Sioux Tribal President, 1981).

47. *Voices from Wounded Knee*, 17–26.

48. Quoted in Matthiessen, *In the Spirit of Crazy Horse*, 66.

49. Burnette and Koster, *The Road to Wounded Knee*, 74.

50. The action was proposed by OSCRO leader Pedro Bissonette and endorsed by traditional Oglala chiefs Frank Fools Crow, Pete Catches, Ellis Chips, Edgar Red Cloud, Jake Kills Enemy, Morris Wounded, Severt Young Bear, and Everette Catches. See *Voices from Wounded Knee*, 36.

51. Weyler, *Blood of the Land*, 76–78.

52. One of their first actions was to meet with Colonel Vic Jackson, a subordinate of future FEMA head Louis Giuffrida, brought in from California to "consult." Through an entity called the California Civil Disorder Management School, Jackson and Giuffrida had devised a pair of "multi-agency domestic counterinsurgency scenarios," code-named "Garden Plot" and "Cable Splicer," in which the government was interested. Thus there is more than passing indication that what followed at Wounded Knee was, at least in part, a field test of these plans. See Weyler, *Blood of the Land*, 80–81. Also see Ken Lawrence, *The New State Repression* (Chicago: International Network against the New State Repression, 1985).

53. Weyler, *Blood of the Land*, 83. The quantity of M-16 ammunition should actually read 1.3 million rounds. The military also provided state-of-the art communications gear, M-14 sniper rifles and ammunition, "Starlight" night vision scopes and other optical technology, tear gas rounds and flares for M-79 grenade launchers, and field provisions to feed the assembled federal forces. All of this was in flat violation of the Posse Comitatus Act (18 USCS § 1385), which makes it illegal for the government to deploy its military against "civil disturbances." For this reason, Colonels Warner and Potter and the other military personnel they brought in wore civilian clothes at Wounded Knee in an effort to hide their involvement.

54. Bill Zimmerman, *Airlift to Wounded Knee* (Chicago: Swallow Press, 1976).

55. Clearwater was mortally wounded on 17 April 1973 and died on 25 April; *Voices from Wounded Knee*, 179. Lamont was hit on 27 April, after being driven from his bunker by tear gas. Federal gunfire then prevented others from reaching him until he died from loss of blood; ibid., 220.

56. Robert Burnette later recounted how, once the siege had ended, Justice Department Solicitor General Kent Frizzell asked his assistance in searching for such graves; Burnette and Koster, *The Road to Wounded Knee*, 248. Also see *Voices from Wounded Knee*, 193.

57. The "hostages" were mostly elderly residents of Wounded Knee: Wilbert A. Reigert (age 86), Girlie Clark (75), Clive Gildersleeve (73), Agnes Gildersleeve (68), Bill Cole (82), Mary Pike (72), and Annie Hunts Horse (78). Others included Guy Fritz (age 49), Jeane Fritz (47), Adrienne Fritz (12), and Father Paul Manhart (46). When South Dakota Senators George McGovern and James Abourezk went to Wounded Knee on 2 March to "bring the hostages out," the supposed captives announced they had no intention of leaving. Instead, they stated that they wished to stay to "protect [their] property from federal forces" and that they considered the AIM people to be the "real hostages in this situation." See Burnette and Koster, *The Road to Wounded Knee*, 227–28.

58. The first federal casualty was an FBI agent named Curtis Fitzpatrick, hit in the wrist by a spent round on 11 March 1973. Interestingly, with his *head* swathed in bandages, he was evacuated by helicopter before a crowd of reporters assembled to witness the event; Burnette and Koster, *The Road to Wounded Knee*, 237–38. The second, U.S. Marshal Lloyd Grimm, was struck in the back and permanently paralyzed on 23 March. Grimm was, however, facing the AIM perimeter when he was hit. The probability, then, is that he was shot—perhaps unintentionally—by one of Wilson's GOONs, who, at the time, were firing from positions behind those of the marshals; *Voices from Wounded Knee*, 128.

59. Quoted in *Voices from Wounded Knee*, 47.

60. Held was simultaneously serving as head of the FBI's Internal Security Section and as Special Agent in Charge (SAC) of the bureau's Chicago office. He had been assigned the latter position, in addition to his other duties, in order that he might orchestrate a cover-up of the FBI's involvement in the 1969 murders of Illinois Black Panther leaders Fred Hampton and Mark Clark. At the outset of the Wounded Knee siege he was detached from his SAC position—a very atypical circumstance—and sent to Pine Ridge in order to prepare a study of how the bureau should deal with AIM "insurgents." The result, entitled "FBI Paramilitary Operations in Indian Country"—in which the author argued, among other things, that "shoot to kill" orders should be made standard—

is extremely significant in light of subsequent bureau activities on the reservation and Held's own role in them.

61. The terms of the stand-down agreement are covered in *Voices from Wounded Knee*, 231. The full text of the treaty may be found in Kappler, *Indian Treaties, 1778–1883*, 594–96.

62. Federal representatives purposely evaded the issue, arguing that they were precluded from responding to questions of treaty compliance because of Congress's 1871 suspension of treaty-making with Indians (Title 25 USC § 71). As Lakota elder Matthew King rejoined, however, the Indians were not asking that a *new* treaty be negotiated. Rather, they were demanding that U.S. commitments under an existing treaty be honored, a matter that was not only possible under the 1871 act but required by it. See *Voices from Wounded Knee*, 252–54.

63. Instead, a single marshal was dispatched to Fools Crow's home on the appointed date to deliver to those assembled there a note signed by White House counsel Leonard Garment. The missive stated that "the days of treaty-making with Indians ended in 1871, 102 years ago"; quoted in *Voices from Wounded Knee*, 257–58.

64. U.S. House of Representatives, Committee on the Judiciary, Subcommittee on Civil and Constitutional Rights, *1st Session on FBI Authorization, March 19, 24, 25; April 2 and 8, 1981* (Washington, D.C.: 97th Cong., 2d sees., U.S. Government Printing Office, 1981).

65. Weyler, *Blood of the Land*, 95; Burnette and Koster, *The Road to Wounded Knee*, 253.

66. *1st Session on FBI Authorization.*

67. Ibid. Means was convicted on none of the forty federal charges. Instead, he was finally found guilty in 1977 under South Dakota state law of "criminal syndicalism" and served a year in the maximum security prison at Sioux Falls. Means was, and will remain, the only individual ever convicted under this statute; the South Dakota legislature repealed the law while he was imprisoned. Amnesty International was preparing to adopt him as a "prisoner of conscience" when he was released in 1979; Amnesty International, *Proposal for a Commission of Inquiry into the Effect of Domestic Intelligence Activities on Criminal Trials in the United States of America* (New York: Amnesty International, 1980).

68. For excerpts from the transcripts of the "Sioux sovereignty hearing" conducted in Lincoln, Nebraska, during the fall of 1974, see Roxanne Dunbar Ortiz, ed., *The Great Sioux Nation: Sitting in Judgement on America* (New York/San Francisco: International Indian Treaty Council/Moon Books, 1977).

69. Tried together in the second "leadership trial," Crow Dog, Holder, and Camp were convicted of minor offenses during the spring of 1975. Holder and Camp went underground to avoid sentencing. Crow Dog was granted probation (as were his codefendants when they surfaced) and then placed on charges unrelated to Wounded Knee the following November. Convicted and sentenced to five years, he was imprisoned first in the federal maximum security facility at Lewisburg, Pennsylvania, and then at Leavenworth, Kansas. The National Council of Churches and Amnesty International were preparing to adopt him as a prisoner of conscience when he was released on parole in 1977. See Weyler, *Blood of the Land*, 189; Amnesty International, *Proposal for a Commission of Inquiry.*

70. As a congressional study concluded, this was "a very low rate considering the usual rate of conviction in Federal Courts and a great input of resources in these cases; *1st Session of FBI Authorization.*

71. This is a classic among the counterintelligence methodologies utilized by the FBI. For example, according to a bureau report declassified by a Senate select committee in 1975, agents in Philadelphia, Pennsylvania, offered as an "example of a successful counterintelligence technique" their use of "any excuse for arrest" as a means of "neutralizing" members of a targeted organization, the Revolutionary Action Movement (RAM), during the summer of 1967. "RAM people," the document went on, "were arrested and released on bail, but they were re-arrested several times until they could no longer make bail." The tactic was recommended for use by other FBI offices to "curtail the activities" of objectionable political groups in their areas. The complete text of this document can be found in Churchill and Vander Wall *Agents of Repression*, 45–47. More broadly see U.S. Senate Select Committee to Study Government Operations with Respect to Intelligence Activities, *Final Report: Supplementary Detailed Staff Reports on Intelligence Activities and the Rights of*

Americans, Book 3 (Washington, D.C.: 94th Cong., 2d sess., U.S. Government Printing Office, 1976).

72. This is the standard delineation of objectives attending the FBI's domestic counterintelligence programs (COINTELPROs); see the document reproduced in Churchill and Vander Wall, *The COINTELPRO Papers*, 92–93.

73. Quoted in Martin Garbus, "General Haig of Wounded Knee," *The Nation*, 9 November 1974.

74. A complete list of those killed and their dates of death is contained in Churchill and Vander Wall, *The COINTELPRO Papers*, 393–94.

75. U.S. Department of Justice, *Events Surrounding Recent Murders on the Pine Ridge Reservation in South Dakota*.

76. Johansen and Maestas, *Wasi'chu*, 83–84.

77. FBI jurisdiction on reservations accrues under the 1885 Major Crimes Act (ch. 341, 24 Stat. 362, 385, now codified at 18 USC 1153).

78. For example, Delphine Crow Dog, sister of AIM's spiritual leader, was beaten unconscious and left to freeze to death in a field on 9 November 1974; AIM member Joseph Stuntz Killsright was killed by a bullet to the head and apparently shot repeatedly in the torso after death on 26 June 1975.

79. Consider the case of brothers Vernal and Clarence Cross, both AIM members, who had car trouble and stopped along the road outside Pine Ridge village on 19 June 1973. Individuals firing from a nearby field hit both men, killing Clarence and severely wounding Vernal. Another bullet struck nine-year-old Mary Ann Little Bear, who was riding in a car driven by her father, traveling in the opposite direction. The bullet hit her in the face, blinding her in one eye. Her father identified three individuals to police and FBI agents as the shooters. None of the three was interrogated. Instead, authorities arrested Vernal Cross in the hospital, charging him with murdering Clarence (the charges were later dropped). No charges were ever filed in the shooting of Mary Ann Little Bear. See Weyler, *Blood of the Land*, 106.

80. Quoted in Johansen and Maestas, *Wasi'chu*, 88. Actually, O'Clock's position fits into a broader bureau policy. "When Indians complain about the lack of investigation and prosecution on reservation crime, they are usually told the Federal government does not have the resources to handle the work"; U.S. Department of Justice, *Report of the Task Force on Indian Matters* (Washington, D.C.: U.S. Government Printing Office, 1975), 42–43.

81. In 1972, the Rapid City Resident Agency was staffed by three agents. This was expanded to eleven in March 1973 and augmented by a ten-member SWAT team shortly thereafter. By the spring of 1975, more than thirty agents were assigned to Rapid City on a long-term basis, and as many as two dozen others were steadily coming and going while performing "special tasks." See Johansen and Maestas, *Wasi'chu*, 93; U.S. Department of Justice, *Report of the Task Force on Indian Matters*, 42–43.

82. In the Clarence Cross murder, for example, the killers were identified as John Hussman, Woody Richards, and Francis Randall, all prominent members of the GOONs. Or again, in the 30 January 1976 murder of AIM supporter Byron DeSersa near the reservation hamlet of Wamblee, at least a dozen people identified GOONs Billy Wilson (Dickie Wilson's younger son), Charles David Winters, Dale Janis, and Chuck Richards among the killers. Indeed, the guilty parties were still on the scene when two FBI agents arrived. Yet the only person arrested was a witness, an elderly Cheyenne named Guy Dull Knife, because of the vociferousness with which he complained about the agents' inaction. The BIA police, for their part, simply ordered the GOONs to leave town. See U.S. Commission on Civil Rights, *American Indian Issues in South Dakota: Hearing Held in Rapid City, South Dakota, July 27–28, 1978* (Washington, D.C.: U.S. Government Printing Office, 1978), 33.

83. On the CIA's relationship to Latin American death squads, see Penny Lernoux, *Cry of the People: United States Involvement in the Rise of Fascism, Torture, and Murder, and the Persecution of the Catholic Church in Latin America* (New York: Doubleday, 1980).

84. *Voices from Wounded Knee*, 189. Frizzell himself has confirmed the account.

85. Ibid., 190.

86. The directive was issued on 24 April 1973.

87. *Voices from Wounded Knee*, 213; Weyler, *Blood of the Land*, 92–93.

88. See, for example, Athan Theoharis, "Building a Case against the FBI," *Washington Post*, 30 October 1988.

89. Churchill, "Death Squads in America: Confessions of a Government Terrorist," *Yale Journal of Law and Liberation* 3 (1992). The interview was conducted by independent filmmakers Kevin Barry McKiernan and Michelle DuBois several years earlier but not released in transcript form until 1991.

90. *Det cord* is detonation cord, a rope-like explosive often used by the U.S. military to fashion booby traps. Brewer also makes mention of bureau personnel introducing him and other GOONs to civilian right-wingers who provided additional ordnance.

91. Another example of this sort of thing came in the wake of the 27 February 1975 beating and slashing of AIM defense attorney Roger Finzel, his client, Bernard Escamilla, and several associates at the Pine Ridge Airport by a group of GOONs headed by Duane Brewer and Dickie Wilson himself. The event being too visible to be simply ignored, Wilson was allowed to plead guilty to a petty offense carrying a ten-dollar penalty in his own tribal court. Federal charges were then dropped on advice from the FBI—which had spent its investigative time polygraphing the victims rather than their assailants—because pressing them might constitute "double jeopardy"; Churchill and Vander Wall, *Agents of Repression*, 186, 428.

92. At one point, the bureau attempted to implicate Northwest AIM leader Leonard Peltier in the killing. This ploy was abandoned only when it was conclusively demonstrated that Peltier was in another state when the murder occurred; interview with Peltier defense attorney Bruce Ellison, October 1987 (tape on file).

93. Both Moves Camp and Bissonette drove white over dark blue Chevrolet sedans. It appears the killers simply mistook one for the other in the dark. The victim, who was not herself active in supporting AIM, was the sister of OSCRO leader Pedro Bissonette, shot to death under highly suspicious circumstance by BIA police officer *cum* GOON Joe Clifford on the night of 17 October 1973; Churchill and Vander Wall, *Agents of Repression*, 200–203.

94. Eastman, although a Crow, is directly related to the Dakota family of the same name, made famous by the writer Charles Eastman earlier in the century. Ironically, two of his relatives, sisters Carole Standing Elk and Fern Matthias, purport to be AIM members in California.

95. Churchill, "Death Squads in America," 96.

96. Structurally, the appropriation of the formal apparatus of deploying force possessed by client states for purposes of composing death squads—long a hallmark of CIA covert operations in the Third World—corresponds quite well with the FBI's use of the BIA police on Pine Ridge; see A. J. Languuth, *Hidden Terrors: The Truth about U.S. Police Operations in Latin America* (New York: Pantheon Press, 1978); also see Edward S. Herman, *The Real Terror Network: Terrorism in Fact and Propaganda* (Boston: South End Press, 1982).

97. See, for example, U.S. Department of Justice, *Events Surrounding Recent Murders on the Pine Ridge Reservation in South Dakota*.

98. In late 1973, Means took a majority of all votes cast in the tribal primaries. In the 1974 runoff, however, Wilson retained his presidency by a two-hundred-vote margin. A subsequent investigation by the U.S. Commission on Civil Rights revealed that 154 cases of voter fraud—non-Oglala people being allowed to vote—had occurred. A further undetermined number of invalid votes had been cast by Oglalas who did not meet tribal residency requirements. No record had been kept of the number of ballots printed or how and in what numbers they had been distributed. No poll watchers were present in many locations, and those who were present at the others had been appointed by Wilson rather than an impartial third party. There was also significant evidence that pro-Means voters had been systematically intimidated and, in some cases, roughed up by Wilsonites stationed at each polling place; U.S. Commission on Civil Rights, *Report of Investigation: Oglala Sioux Tribe General Election 1974* (Denver: Rocky Mountain Regional Office, October 1974). Despite these official findings, the FBI performed no substantive investigation, and the BIA allowed the results of the election to stand; Churchill and Vander Wall, *Agents of Repression* 190–92.

99. As the Jumping Bulls' daughter Roselyn later put it, "We asked those AIM boys to come help us . . . [defend ourselves against] Dickie Wilson and his goons"; quoted in an unpublished manuscript by researcher Candy Hamilton (copy on file).

100. See, for example, a memorandum from SAC Minneapolis (Joseph Trimbach) to the FBI director, dated 3 June 1975 and captioned "Law Enforcement on the Pine Ridge Indian Reservation," in which Trimbach recommends that armored personnel carriers be used to assault AIM defensive positions.

101. No such warrant existed. When an arrest order was finally issued for Eagle on 9 July 1975, it was for the petty theft of a pair of used cowboy boots from a white ranch hand. Eagle was acquitted even of this when the case was taken to trial in 1976. Meanwhile, George O'Clock's assignment of two agents to pursue an Indian teenager over so trivial an offense at a time when he professed to be too shorthanded to investigate the murders of AIM members speaks for itself; Matthiessen, *In the Spirit of Crazy Horse,* 173.

102. Ibid., 156.

103. The agents followed a red pickup truck onto the property. Unbeknownst to them, it was full of dynamite. In the valley, the truck stopped and its occupants got out. Williams and Coler also stopped and got out of their cars. They then began firing toward the pickup, a direction that carried their rounds into the AIM camp, where a number of noncombatant women and children were situated. AIM security then began to fire back. It is a certainty that AIM did not initiate the firefight because, as Bob Robideau later put it, "Nobody in their right mind would start a gunfight using a truckload of dynamite for cover." Once the agents were preoccupied, the pickup made its escape. Northwest AIM was toying with the idea of using the explosives to remove George Washington's face from the nearby Mount Rushmore National Monument; interview with Bob Robideau, May 1990 (notes on file).

104. Matthiessen, *In the Spirit of Crazy Horse,* 158.

105. An additional indicator is that the inimitable William Janklow also seems to have been on alert, awaiting a call telling him things were underway. In any event, when called, Janklow was able to assemble a white vigilante force in Hot Springs, S.Dak., and drive about fifty miles to the Jumping Bull property, arriving there at about 1:30 P.M. an elapsed time of approximately two hours.

106. A further indication of preplanning by the bureau is found in a 27 June 1975 memorandum from R. E. Gebhart to Mr. O'Donnell at FBI HQ. It states that Chicago SAC/internal security chief Richard G. Held was contacted by headquarters about the firefight at 12:30 p.m. on 26 June at the Minneapolis field office. It turns out that Held had already been detached from his position in Chicago and was in Minneapolis—under whose authority the Rapid City resident agency, and hence Pine Ridge, falls—awaiting word to temporarily take over from Minneapolis SAC Joseph Trimbach. The only ready explanation for this highly unorthodox circumstance, unprecedented in bureau history, is that it was expected that Held's peculiar expertise in political repression would be needed for a major operation on Pine Ridge in the immediate future; Johansen and Maestes, *Wasi'chu,* 95.

107. Matthiessen, *In the Spirit of Crazy Horse,* 483–85.

108. The FBI sought to "credit" BIA police officer Gerald Hill with the lethal long-range shot to the head fired at Killsright at about 3 p.m., despite the fact that he was plainly running away and therefore presented no threat to law enforcement personnel (it was also not yet known that Coler and Williams were dead). However, Waring, who was with Hill at the time, was the trained sniper of the pair and was equipped accordingly. In any event, several witnesses who viewed Killsright's corpse in situ—including Assistant South Dakota Attorney General William Delaney and reporter Kevin Barry McKiernan—subsequently stated that it appeared to them that someone had fired a burst from an automatic into the torso at close range and then had tried to hide the fact by putting an FBI jacket over the postmortem wounds; ibid., 183.

109. The agents' standard attire was Vietnam-issue "boonie hats," jungle fatigues, and boots. Their weapons were standard army M-16s. The whole affair was deliberately staged to resemble a military operation in Southeast Asia; see the selection of photographs in Churchill and Vander Wall, *Agents of Repression.*

110. Williams and Coler had each been shot three times. The FBI knew, from the sound of the rifles during the firefight, if nothing else, that AIM had used no automatic weapons. Neither agent was stripped. There were no bunkers but rather only a couple of old root cellars and tumbledown corrals, common enough in rural areas and not used as firing positions, in any event. (The bureau

would have known this because of the absence of spent cartridge casings in such locations.) Far from being "lured" to the Jumping Bull property, they had returned after being expressly told to leave (and they were supposed to be serving a warrant). Instructively, no one in the nation's press corps thought to ask how, exactly, Coll might happen to know either agent's last words, since nobody from the FBI was present when they were killed; Joel D. Weisman, "About That 'Ambush' at Wounded Knee." *Columbia Journalism Review* (September-October 1974); also see Churchill, "Renegades, Terrorists and Revolutionaries."

111. This was the director's admission, during a press conference conducted at the Century Plaza Hotel on 1 July 1975, in conjunction with Coler's and Williams's funerals. It was accorded inside coverage by the press, unlike the page one treatment given Coll's original disinformation; Tom Bates, "The Government's Secret War on the Indian," *Oregon Times*, February-March 1976.

112. Examples of the air assault technique include a thirty-five-man raid on the property of AIM spiritual leader Selo Black Crow near the village of Wamblee, on 8 July 1975. Crow Dog's Paradise, on the Rosebud Reservation, just across the line from Pine Ridge, was hit by a hundred heliborne agents on 5 September. Meanwhile, an elderly Oglala named James Brings Yellow had suffered a heart attack and died when agent J. Gary Adams suddenly kicked in his door during a no-knock search on 12 July. By August, such abuse by the FBI was so pervasive that even some of Wilson's GOONs were demanding that the agents withdraw from the reservation; see Churchill and Vander Wall, *The COINTELPRO Papers*, 268–70.

113. By September, it had become obvious to everyone that AIM lacked the military capacity to protect the traditionals from the level of violence being imposed by the FBI by that point. Hence, AIM began a pointed disengagement in order to alleviate pressure on the traditionals. On 16 October 1975, Richard G. Held sent a memo to FBIHQ advising that his work in South Dakota was complete and that he anticipated returning to his position in Chicago by 18 October; a portion of this document is reproduced in *The COINTELPRO Papers*, 273.

114. "Memorandum of Agreement between the Oglala Sioux Tribe of South Dakota and the National Park Service of the Department of Interior to Facilitate Establishment, Development, Administration and Public Use of the Oglala Sioux Tribal Lands, Badlands National Monument" (Washington, D.C.: U.S. Department of Interior, 2 January 1976). The act assuming title is P.L. 90–468 (1976). If there is any doubt as to whether the transfer was about uranium, consider the law as amended in 1978—in the face of considerable protest by the traditionals—to allow the Oglala to recover surface use rights any time they decided by referendum to do so. Subsurface (mineral) rights, however, were permanently retained by the government. Actually, the whole charade was illegal insofar as the still-binding 1868 Fort Laramie Treaty requires three-fourths express consent of all adult male Lakota to validate land transfers, not land recoveries. Such consent, obviously, was never obtained with respect to the Gunnery Range transfer; see Huber et al., The *Gunnery Range Report*.

115. The congressional missive read, "Attached is a letter from the Senate Select Committee (SSC), dated 6–23–75, addressed to [U.S. Attorney General] Edward S. Levi. This letter announces the SSC's intent to conduct interviews relating . . . to, our investigation at 'Wounded Knee' and our investigation of the American Indian Movement. . . . On 6–27–75, Patrick Shae, staff member of the SSC, requested we hold in abeyance any action . . . in view of the killing of the Agents at Pine Ridge, South Dakota."

116. The selection of those charged seems to have served a dual purpose: (1) to "decapitate" one of AIM's best and most cohesive security groups, and (2), in not charging participants from Pine Ridge, to divide the locals from their sources of outside support. The window dressing charges against Jimmy Eagle were explicitly dropped in order to "place the full prosecutorial weight of the government on Leonard Peltier"; quoted in Jim Messerschmidt, *The Trial of Leonard Peltier* (Boston: South End Press, 1984), 47.

117. Butler was apprehended at Crow Dog's Paradise during the FBI's massive air assault there on 5 September 1975. Robideau was arrested in a hospital, where he was being treated for injuries sustained when his car exploded on the Kansas Turnpike on 10 September; Churchill and Vander Wall, *Agents of Repression*, 448–49.

118. Acting on an informant's tip, the Oregon state police stopped a car and a motor home belonging

to actor Marlon Brando near the town of Ontario on the night of 14 November 1975. Arrested in the motor home were Kamook Banks and Anna Mae Pictou Aquash, a fugitive on minor charges in South Dakota; arrested in the automobile were AIM members Russell Redner and Kenneth Loudhawk. Two men—Dennis Banks, a fugitive from sentencing after being convicted of inciting the 1972 Custer Courthouse "riot" in South Dakota, and Leonard Peltier, a fugitive on several warrants, including one for murder in the deaths of Williams and Coler—escaped from the motor home. Peltier was wounded in the process. On 6 February 1976, acting on another informant's tip, the Royal Canadian Mounted Police arrested Peltier, Frank Black Horse (a.k.a. Frank DeLuca), and Ronald Blackman (a.k.a. Ron Janvier) at Smallboy's Camp, about 160 miles east of Edmonton, Alberta; Matthiessen, *In the Spirit of Crazy Horse*, 249–51, 272–78. On the outcome for Dennis Banks and the others, see Ward Churchill, "Due Process Be Damned: The Case of the Portland Four," *Zeta* (January 1988).

119. Poor Bear, a clinically unbalanced Oglala, was picked up for "routine questioning" by agents David Price and Ron Wood in February 1976 and then held incommunicado for nearly two months in the Hacienda Hotel in Gordon, Nebraska. During this time, she was repeatedly threatened with dire consequences by the agents unless she "cooperated", with their "investigation" into the deaths of Coler and Williams. At some point, Price began to type up for her signature affidavits that incriminated Leonard Peltier. Ultimately, she signed three mutually exclusive "accounts"; one of them—in which Peltier is said to have been her boyfriend and to have confessed to her one night in a Nebraska bar that he had killed the agents—was submitted in Canadian court to obtain Peltier's extradition on 18 June 1976. Meanwhile, on 29 March Price caused Poor Bear to be on the stand against Richard Marshall in Rapid City, during the OSCRO/AIM member's state trial for killing Martin Montileaux. She testified that she was Marshall's girlfriend and that he had confessed the murder to her one night in a Nebraska bar. Marshall was then convicted. Federal prosecutors declined to introduce Poor Bear as a witness at either the Butler/Robideau or Peltier trials, observing that her testimony was "worthless" due to her mental condition. She has publicly and repeatedly recanted her testimony against both Peltier and Marshall, saying she never met either of them in her life. For years, members of the Canadian Parliament have been demanding Peltier's return to their jurisdiction due to the deliberate perpetration of fraud by U.S. authorities in his extradition proceeding; in addition, they have threatened to block renewal of the U.S.-Canadian Extradition Treaty in the event the United States fails to comply. The Poor Bear affidavits are reproduced in Churchill and Vander Wall, *The COINTELPRO Papers*, 288–91. On Poor Bear's testimony against Marshall and her recantations, see Churchill and Vander Wall, *Agents of Repression*, 339–42. On the position of the Canadian Parliament, see, for example, "External Affairs: Canada-U.S. Extradition Treaty—Case of Leonard Peltier, Statement of Mr. James Fulton," in *House of Commons Debate, Canada* 128:129 (Ottawa: 1st sess., 33d Par. Official Report, Thurs., 17 April 1986).

120. The disinformation campaign centered in the bureau's "leaks" of the so-called Dog Soldier Teletypes on 21 and 22 June 1976—in the midst of the Butler/Robideau trial—to "friendly media representatives." The documents, which were never in any way substantiated but were nonetheless sensationally reported across the country, asserted that two thousand AIM "dog soldiers," acting in concert with SDS (a long-defunct white radical group) and the Crusade for Justice (a militant Chicano organization), had equipped themselves with illegal weapons and explosives and were preparing to embark on a campaign of terrorism that included "killing a cop a day ... sniping at tourists ... burning out farmers ... assassinating the Governor of South Dakota ... blowing up the Fort Randall Dam," and breaking people out of the maximum security prison at Sioux Falls. The second teletype is reproduced in Churchill and Vander Wall, *The COINTELPRO Papers*, 277–82.

121. Defense attorney William Kunstler queried Kelley as to whether there was "one shred, one scintilla of evidence" to support the allegations made by the FBI in the Dog Soldier Teletypes. Kelley replied, "I know of none." Nonetheless, the FBI continued to feature AIM prominently in its *Domestic Terrorist Digest*, distributed free of charge to state and local police departments nationally; Churchill and Vander Wall, *The COINTELPRO Papers*, 276.

122. The initial round striking both Coler and Williams was a .44 magnum. Bob Robideau testified

that he was the only AIM member using a .44 magnum during the firefight; Robideau interview, November 1993 (tape on file).

123. Videotaped NBC interview with Robert Bolin, 1990 (raw tape on file).

124. FBI personnel in attendance at this confab were director Kelley and Richard G. Held, by then promoted to the rank of assistant director, James B. Adams, Richard J. Gallagher, John C. Gordon, and Herbert H. Hawkins, Jr. Representing the Justice Department were prosecutor Evan Hultman and his boss, William B. Grey; memo from B. H. Cooke to Richard J. Gallagher, 10 August 1976.

125. McManus professes to have been "astonished" when he was removed from the Peltier case; Matthiessen, *In the Spirit of Crazy Horse*, 566.

126. *United States v. Leonard Peltier*, CR-75–5106–1, U.S. District Court for the district of North Dakota, 1977 (hereinafter referred to as Peltier Trial Transcript).

127. Butler and Robideau were tried on the premise that they were part of a conspiracy that led to a group slaying of Williams and Coler. Peltier was tried as the "lone gunman" who had caused their deaths. Similarly, at Cedar Rapids, agent J. Gary Adams had testified that the dead agents followed a red pickup onto the Jumping Bull property; during the Fargo trial, he testified that they had followed a "red and white van" belonging to Peltier. The defense was prevented by the judge's evidentiary ruling at the outset from impeaching such testimony on the basis of its contradiction of sworn testimony already entered against Butler and Robideau; see Peltier Trial Transcript and *United States v. Darrelle E. Butler and Robert E. Robideau*, CR76–11, U.S. District Court for the district of Iowa, 1976, for purposes of comparison; the matter is well analyzed in Messerschmidt, *The Trial of Leonard Peltier*.

128. No slugs were recovered from Williams's and Coler's bodies, and two separate autopsies were inconclusive in determining the exact type of weapon from which the fatal shots were fired. The key piece of evidence in this respect was a .223–caliber shell casing that the FBI said was ejected from the killer's AR-15 rifle into the open trunk of Coler's car at the moment he fired one of the lethal rounds. The bureau also claimed that its ballistics investigation proved only one such weapon was used by AIM during the firefight. Ipso facto, whichever AIM member could be shown to have used an AR-15 on 26 June 1975 would be the guilty party. The problem is that the cartridge casing was not found in Coler's trunk when agents initially went over the car with fine-tooth combs. Instead, it was supposedly found later, on one of two different days, by one of two different agents, and turned over to someone whose identity neither could quite recall, somewhere on the reservation. How the casing got from whoever and wherever that was to the FBI crime lab in Washington, D.C., is, of course, equally mysterious. This is what was used to establish the "murder weapon"; Peltier Trial Transcript, 2114, 3012–13, 3137–38, 3235, 3342, 3388.

129. Agent Frank Coward, who did not testify to this effect against Butler and Robideau, claimed at the Fargo trial that, shortly after the estimated time of Coler's and Williams's deaths, he observed Leonard Peltier, whom he conceded he had never seen before, running away from their cars and carrying an AR-15 rifle. This sighting was supposedly made through a 7x rifle scope at a distance of eight hundred meters (one-half mile) through severe atmospheric heat shimmers, while Peltier was moving at an oblique angle to the observer. Defense tests demonstrated that any such identification was impossible, even among friends standing full-face and under perfect weather conditions. In any event, this is what was used to tie Peltier to the "murder weapon"; ibid., 1305.

130. Seventeen-year-old Wish Draper, for example, was strapped to a chair at the police station at Window Rock, Arizona, while being "interrogated" by FBI agents Charles Stapleton and James Doyle; he thereupon agreed to "cooperate" by testifying against Peltier; ibid., 1087–98. Seventeen-year-old Norman Brown was told by agents J. Gary Adams and O. Victor Harvey during their interrogation of him that he would "never walk this earth again" unless he testified in the manner they desired; ibid., 4799–4804, 4842–3). Fifteen-year-old Mike Anderson was also interrogated by Adams and Harvey. In this case, they offered both the carrot and the stick: to get pending charges dismissed against him if he testified as instructed and to "beat the living shit" out of him if he did not; ibid., 840–42. All three young men acknowledged under defense cross-examination that they had lied under oath at the request of the FBI and federal prosecutors.

131. Crooks' speech is worth quoting in part: "Apparently, Special Agent Williams was killed first. He

was shot in the face and hand by a bullet . . . probably begging for his life, and he was shot. The back of his head was blown off by a high powered rifle. . . . Leonard Peltier then turned, as the evidence indicates, to Jack Coler lying on the ground helpless. He shoots him in the top of the head. Apparently feeling he hadn't done a good enough job, he shoots him again through the jaw, and his face explodes. No shell comes out, just explodes. The whole bottom of his chin is blown out by the force of the concussion. Blood splattered against the side of the car"; ibid., 5011.

132. Peltier's being sent directly to Marion contravenes federal Bureau of Prisons regulations restricting placement in that facility to "incorrigibles" who have "a record of unmanageability in more normal penal settings." Leonard Peltier had no prior convictions and therefore no record, unmanageable or otherwise, of behavior in penal settings.

133. *United States v. Peltier*, 858 F.2d 314, 335 (8th Cir. 1978).

134. *United States v. Peltier;* 440 U.S. 945, cert. denied (1979).

135. Another six thousand-odd pages of FBI file material on Peltier are still being withheld on the basis of "national security."

136. At trial, FBI ballistics expert Evan Hodge testified that the actual AR-15 had been recovered from Bob Robideau's burned-out car along the Wichita turnpike in September 1975. The weapon was so badly damaged by the fire, Hodge said, that it had been impossible to perform a match-comparison of firing pin tool marks by which to link it to the cartridge casing supposedly found in the trunk of Coler's car. However, by removing the bolt mechanism from the damaged weapon and putting it in an undamaged rifle, he claimed, he had been able to perform a rather less conclusive match-comparison of extractor tool marks with which to tie the Wichita AR-15 to the Coler car casing. Among the documents released under provision of the FOIA in 1981 was a 2 October 1975 teletype written by Hodge stating that he had, in fact, performed a firing pin test using the Wichita AR-15 and that it had failed to produce a match to the crucial casing; *United States v. Peltier;* Motion to Vacate Judgment and for a New Trial, Crim. No. CR-3003, U.S. District Court for the district of North Dakota (filed 15 December 1982). The 8th Circuit Court's decision to allow the appeal to proceed, despite Judge Bensen's rejection of the preceding motion, is listed as *United States v. Peltier;* 731 F.2d *550, 555* (8th Cir. 1984).

137. During the evidentiary hearing on Peltier's second appeal, conducted in Bismarck, North Dakota, during late October 1984, it became apparent that AIM members had used—and the FBI had known they had used—not one but several AR-15s during the Oglala firefight. This stood to destroy the "single AR-15" theory used to convict Peltier at trial. Moreover, the evidentiary chain concerning the Coler car casing was brought into question. In an effort to salvage the situation, bureau ballistics chief Evan Hodge took the stand to testify that he, and he alone, had handled ballistics materials related to the Peltier case. Appeal attorney William Kunstler then queried him concerning margin notes on the ballistics reports that were not his own. At that point, he retracted, admitting that a lab assistant, Joseph Twardowski, had also handled the evidence and worked on the reports. Kunstler asked whether Hodge was sure that only he and Twardowski had had access to the materials and conclusions adduced from them. Hodge responded emphatically in the affirmative. Kunstler then pointed to yet another handwriting in the report margins and demanded a formal inquiry by the court. Two hours later, a deflated Hodge was allowed by Judge Bensen to return to the stand and admit he had "missspoken" once again; he really had no idea who had handled the evidence, adding or subtracting pieces at will.

138. *United States v. Peltier;* CR-3003, transcript of Oral Arguments Before the U.S. Eighth Circuit Court of Appeals, St. Louis, Mo., 15 October 1985, 19.

139. Ibid., 18.

140. U.S. 8th Circuit Court of Appeals, "Appeal from the United States District of North Dakota in the Matter of *United States v. Leonard Peltier,*" Crim. No. 85–5192, St. Louis, Mo., 11 October 1986.

141. Ibid., 16.

142. The high court declined review despite the fact that the 8th Circuit decision had created a question—deriving from a Supreme Court opinion rendered in *U.S. v. Bagley* (U.S. 105 S. Ct. 3375 [1985]—as to what standard of doubt must be met before an appeals court is bound to remand a

case to trial. The 8th Circuit had formally concluded that, while the Peltier jury might "possibly" have reached a different verdict had the appeals evidence been presented to it, it was necessary under *Bagley* guidelines that the jury would "probably" have rendered a different verdict before remand was appropriate. Even this ludicrously labored reasoning collapses upon itself when it is considered that, in a slightly earlier case, the 9th Circuit had remanded on the basis that the verdict might possibly have been different. It is in large part to resolve just such questions of equal treatment before the law that the Supreme Court theoretically exists. Yet it flatly refused to do its job when it came to the Peltier case; Ward Churchill, "Leonard Peltier: The Ordeal Continues," *Zeta* (March 1988).

143. Holder moved into secondary education and now works for Indian control of their schools in Kansas and Oklahoma. Others, such as Wilma Mankiller, Ted Means, and Twila Martin, have moved into more mainstream venues of tribal politics. Still others, such as Phyllis Young and Madonna (Gilbert) Thunderhawk, have gone in the direction of environmentalism.

144. Examples include Jimmie Durham and John Arbuckle, both of whom now pursue—in dramatically different ways—careers in the arts.

145. Actually, this began very early on: AIM national president Carter Camp shot founder Clyde Bellecourt in the stomach in 1974 over a factional dispute instigated by Bellecourt's brother Vernon. In the ensuing turmoil, Russell Means openly resigned from AIM but was quickly reinstated; see Matthiessen, *In the Spirit of Crazy Horse*, 85–86.

146. Banks was granted sanctuary by California Governor Jerry Brown in 1977 because of campaign statements by South Dakota Attorney General William Janklow such as, "[T]he way to deal with AIM leaders is a bullet in the head"; he also said that, if elected, he would "put AIM leaders either in our jails or under them." Enraged by Brown's move, Janklow responded by threatening to arrange early parole for a number of South Dakota's worst felons on condition that they accept immediate deportation to California. During his time of "refugee status," Banks served as chancellor of the AIM-initiated D-Q University, near Sacramento; *Rapid City Journal*, 7 April 1981.

147. Rebecca L. Robbins, "American Indian Self-Determination: Comparative Analysis and Rhetorical Criticism," *Issues in Radical Therapy/New Studies on the Left* 13:3–4 (Summer–Fall 1988).

148. An intended offshoot of the Peltier Defense Committee designed to expose the identity of whoever had murdered AIM activist Anna Mae Pictou Aquash in execution style on Pine Ridge sometime in February 1976 (at the onset, it was expected that this would be members of Wilson's GOONs) quickly collapsed when it became apparent that AIM itself might be involved. It turned out that self-proclaimed AIM national officer Vernon Bellecourt had directed security personnel during the 1975 AIM general membership meeting to interrogate Aquash as a possible FBI informant. They were, he said, to "bury her where she stands," if unsatisfied with her answers. The security team, composed of Northwest AIM members, did not act on this instruction, instead incorporating Aquash into their own group. The Northwest AIM group was rapidly decimated after the Oglala firefight, however, and Aquash was left unprotected. It is instructive that, once her body had turned up near Wamblee, Bellecourt was the prime mover in quashing an internal investigation of her death. For general background, see Johanna Brand, *The Life and Death of Anna Mae Aquash* (Toronto: James Lorimer Publishers, 1978).

149. Killed were Trudell's wife, Tina Manning, their three children—Ricarda Star (age five), Sunshine Karma (age three), and Eli Changing Sun (age one)—and Tina's mother, Leah Hicks Manning. They were burned to death as they slept in the Trudells's trailer home; the blaze occurred less than twelve hours after Trudell delivered a speech in front of FBI headquarters during which he burned an American flag. Although there was ample reason to suspect arson, no police or FBI investigation ensued; Churchill and Vander Wall, *Agents of Repression,* 361–64.

150. Personal conversation with the author, 1979.

151. None of this is to say that the LPDC did not continue. It did, even while failing to fulfill many of the wider objectives set forth by its founders. In terms of service to Peltier himself, aside from maintaining an ongoing legal appeals effort, the LPDC is largely responsible for the generation of more than fourteen million petition signatures worldwide, all of them calling for his retrial. It has also been instrumental in bringing about several television documentaries, official inquiries into

his situation by several foreign governments, an investigation by Amnesty International, and Peltier's receipt of a 1986 human rights award from the government of Spain.

152. *Keystone to Survival* (Rapid City, S.Dak.: Black Hills Alliance, 1981).

153. On the U.S. uranium industry and its impact on reservation and reservation-adjacent lands, see Ward Churchill and Winona LaDuke, "Native North America: The Political Economy of Radioactive Colonization," in *The State of Native America: Genocide, Colonization, and Resistance*, ed. M. Annette Jaimes (Boston: South End Press, 1992), 241–66.

154. On the occupation, see Ward Churchill, "Yellow Thunder Tiospaye: Misadventure or Watershed Action?" *Policy Perspectives* 2:2 (Spring 1982).

155. *United States v. Means et al.,* Civ. No. 81 -S 131, U.S. District Court for the district of South Dakota (9 December 1985).

156. *Lyng v. Northwest Indian Cemetery Protection Association,* 485 U.S. 439 (1988).

157. Anita Parlow, *Cry, Sacred Ground: Big Mountain, USA* (Washington, D.C.: Christic Institute, 1988).

158. Ward Churchill, "The Struggle for Newe Segobia: The Western Shoshone Battle for Their Homeland," in Churchill, *Struggle for the Land: Indigenous Resistance to Genocide, Ecocide and Expropriation in Contemporary North America* (Monroe, Maine: Common Courage Press, 1993), 197–216.

159. On the early days of IITC, see chapter 7, "The Fourth World," in Weyler, *Blood of the Land,* 212–50.

160. On Durham's recent activities, see "Nobody's Pet Poodle: Jimmie Durham, an Artist for Native North America," in Ward Churchill, *Indians Are Us? Culture and Genocide in Native North America* (Monroe, Maine: Common Courage Press, 1993), 89–113.

161. See, generally, Rebecca L. Robbins, "Self-Determination and Subordination: The Past, Present and Future of American Indian Governance," in Jaimes, *The State of Native America,* 87–121, esp. 106–7. For further contextualization, see Glenn T. Morris and Ward Churchill, "Between a Rock and a Hard Place: Left-Wing Revolution, Right-Wing Reaction, and the Destruction of Indigenous Peoples," *Cultural Survival Quarterly* 11:3 (Fall 1988).

162. Colorado, Dakota, Eastern Oklahoma, Florida, Illinois, Maryland, Mid-Atlantic (LISN), Northern California, New Mexico (Albuquerque), Northwest Ohio, Southeast (Atlanta), Southern California, Texas, Western Oklahoma, Wraps His Tail (Crow). These organized themselves as the Confederation of Autonomous AIM Chapters at a national conference in Edgewood, New Mexico, on 17 December 1993.

163. M. Annette Jaimes, "Racism and Sexism in the Media: The Trial of the Columbus Day Four," *Lies of Our Times* (September 1992).

164. Incorporation documents and attachments on file. The documents of incorporation are signed by Vernon Bellecourt, who is listed as a central committee member; the address listed for annual membership meetings is Bellecourt's residence. Other officers listed in the documents are Clyde Bellecourt, Dennis Banks, Herb Powless, John Trudell, Bill Means, Carole Standing Elk, and Sam Dry Water. Trudell and Banks maintain that they were not informed of the incorporation and did not agree to be officers.

165. Expulsion letter and associated documents on file. Bill Means states that he was asked but refused to sign the letter.

166. Statement during a talk at the annual Medicine Ways Conference, University of California at Riverside, May 1991.

167. Statement during a talk at the University of Colorado at Denver, February 1988 (tape on file).

168. This assessment, of course, runs entirely counter to those of pro-Wilson publicists such as syndicated columnist Tim Giago—supported as he is by a variety of powerful non-Indian interests— who has made it a mission in life to discredit and degrade the legacy of AIM through repeated doses of disinformation. Consider, as one example, his eulogy to Dickie Wilson—in which he denounced careful chroniclers of the Pine Ridge terror such as Onondaga faithkeeper Oren Lyons and Peter Matthiessen, described the victims of Wilson's GOONs as "violent" and "criminal," and embraced Wilson himself as a "friend"—in the 13 February 1990 edition of *Lakota Times.* In a more recent editorial, Giago announced that his research indicates that "only 10" people were actually killed by Wilson's gun thugs on Pine Ridge during the mid-1970s, although the FBI itself

concedes more than forty such fatalities. Then, rather than professing horror that his "friend" might have been responsible for even ten murders, Giago used this faulty revelation to suggest that the Wilson regime really was not so bad after all, especially when compared to AIM's "violence" and irreverence for "law and order."

169. A good effort to render several of these lessons can be found in Brian Glick, *War at Home* (Boston: South End Press, 1989).

170. For superb analysis of this point, see Isaac Balbus, *The Dialectic of Legal Repression* (New York: Russell Sage Foundation, 1973).

171. A fine survey of the conditions prevailing in each of these sectors can be found in Teresa L. Amott and Julie A. Matthaei, *Race, Gender and Work: A Multicultural Economic History of the United States* (Boston: South End Press, 1991).

172. For details and analysis, see Ward Churchill and J. J. Vander Wall, eds., *Cages of Steel: The Politics of Imprisonment in the United States* (Washington, D.C.: Maisonneuve Press, 1992).

173. For a survey of the repression visited on most of these groups, see Churchill and Vander Wall, *The COINTELPRO Papers*.

174. For biographical information concerning those mentioned who are currently imprisoned by the United States, see *Can't Jail the Spirit: Political Prisoners in the United States* (Chicago: Committee to End the Marion Lockdown, 1989).

19

Robert Bee's assessment of Washington policy-making stands in marked contrast to Ward Churchill's chronicle of the rise and fall of the American Indian Movement. Churchill viewed the 1970s from the perspective of the activist "outsiders"; Bee focuses on the bureaucrats and legislators who operated "inside the beltway," crafting legislation and lobbying for particular tribal interests. Moreover, Bee is less inclined to believe that government institutions acted directly to suppress or defeat new ideas from Indian Country. What he describes is a much less self-conscious process in which bureaucracies and congressional leaders conspire, almost inadvertently, to delay or derail reform. Congress and the Bureau of Indian Affairs (BIA) can thwart Indian interests, he argues, but tribes have been successful when they learn to "ride the paper tiger."

According to Bee, Churchill's notion of Indian tribes as the equivalent of colonial subjects has some appeal, as do other models of policy-making that equate Indians to developing nations or assimilating ethnic minorities. But he argues that the absence of a grand public consensus regarding Indian policy (as there was in the allotment era) and the lack of a dominant personality (such as the New Deal's John Collier) has meant that "policy has become increasingly ad hoc." Bee's research involved extensive anthropological fieldwork, but instead of moving to some remote reservation he set up camp on Capitol Hill, interviewing politicians and bureaucrats while also observing such Native rituals as hearings, press conferences, and floor debates.

Then, drawing on Max Weber's writing on bureaucracy and power, Bee developed a profile of each of the major institutions that create Indian policy "paper": the BIA, the Congress, and the courts. For tribes to advance their interests, they must understand the limits and goals of each. Congress rarely responds to Indian popular opinion because Natives are too scattered to be politically significant. The BIA's authority and credibility have been weakened, but it remains strong enough to resist change, either from Congress or the tribes. Caught between occasional congressional initiatives—most important the Self-Determination and Education Act of 1975—and steady BIA intransigence, Indians have turned to the courts, a new battleground in this guerilla warfare, learning how to threaten legal action that would embarrass or undermine the authority of the other two groups.

As Bee suggests, modern Indian policy rests on two contradictory principles: trust protection established by treaties and self-determination. The first, which grows out of the fact that tribal lands and resources are held under a guarantee of federal protection (i.e., "held in trust" by the United States), implies a strong federal presence. The second, which assumes that local involvement creates the best, most efficient administration, implies the need for strong tribal governments. Indian groups still smarting from the termination era of the mid-twentieth century insist that the government fulfill its trust responsibility. At the same time, Native leaders increasingly view self-determination as an essential antidote to past paternalism. Bee concludes that these twin principles necessitate the continuation of both the BIA (to oversee and protect tribal resources and interests) and an ongoing relationship between Native American communities and Congress (to facilitate self-determination). For better or worse, tribes will need to keep riding the paper tiger.

Riding the Paper Tiger

Robert L. Bee

For years accepted analytical practice has tried to fit reservation-federal relations into a series of general models or types: colonialism throughout the nineteenth century and into the twentieth; assimilation as a fellow traveller after the mid-1800s and extending into today's vocational training and urban relocation programs; "development," both as heavy-handed paternalism and client-centered therapy, for Indians as a special group and as part of the growing underclass; and the metropolitan-satellite model as a distinctive subset of both the colonial and "development" models.

Yet the past three decades, 1960–90, seem the most difficult to portray with a single analytical model or theory. One of the reasons is the increasing complexity of the issues, partly a residue of both intended and unintended effects of past policies. But there is also a lack of policy focus compared with earlier periods. The various components of the Indian policy apparatus leap from issue to issue, and policy has become increasingly ad hoc.[1]

This is not necessarily an unhappy situation for Indian rights. The most disastrous policy periods have featured a single-minded policy cant: removal, termination, assimilation. But although most Indian communities are relatively better off now than in 1960, the 1987 revelations in the *Arizona Republic* and the ensuing congressional investigations underscore two urgent needs: a comprehensive, informed, systematic rearticulation of basic policy; and a major effective effort to implement and enforce it.[2]

Ironically, the period since 1960 has not wanted for informed recommendations for policy overhaul.[3] And basic policy concepts have also been reaffirmed or developed: tribal sovereignty, federal trust protection, the government-to-government relationship, and Indian preferences. But such reaffirmation and development have come mostly from adversarial confrontations before the law, not from innovative, comprehensive, and informed policy overhaul.[4] Policy action caroms off one concept only to bash into another, and then another, keeping the policy play in motion without much apparent refinement of basic concepts or resolution of perennial issues. In fact, the most basic of the policy concepts—tribal sovereignty and the federal trust responsibility—remain logically and operationally contradictory regardless of the semantic gymnastics they are put through.[5] This scarcely helps to dissipate the aura of policy ad-hoccery.

Source: *State and Reservation: New Perspectives on Federal Indian Policy*, edited by George Pierre Castile and Robert L. Bee.

411

I think it is pushing materialist-oriented models too hard to see all this as a product of capitalist economics.[6] Policy ad-hoccery has abetted the exploitation of Indian resources, and Indian economic poverty and the commercial interests of non-Indians are key factors in any analysis of Indian-federal relations. But an analytical model that focuses more specifically on relations of domination between individuals and groups lends another necessary dimension to understanding the recent past of policy dynamics and the structure of Indian-federal relations. The model is based on the work of Max Weber, in particular the ideal types and dynamic relationships he drew from analysis of nineteenth-and early twentieth-century German policies. It proceeds from Weber's declaration that "without exception every sphere of social action is profoundly influenced by structures of dominancy. . . . [T]he structure of dominancy and its unfolding is decisive in determining the form of social action and its orientation toward a 'goal.'"[7]

Superficially, some Weberian notions strike us now as commonsensical: nobody needs to tell folks in Washington that power matters, for example; and everyone knows something—typically unpleasant—about bureaucracy. So the challenge here is to take a well-worn analytical approach and impose it on a situation familiar to most readers in order to offer systematic insight and the possibility of comparison with other cases and other times.

I have assumed that most readers are generally acquainted with the events of the past three decades, and I do not dwell on detailed descriptions except as necessary for illustration or substantiation.[8]

ON DOMINATION

Key to Weber's analytical technique is the careful description of ideal types of social structures and belief systems (*ideal* in this essay meaning "what is expected," not "what is most desirable"). Once developed, these ideal types are then compared with actual structures and belief systems. The discrepancies between the ideal and the real draw attention to important causal variables and provide a means for comparing one case with another.

The concept of domination is a subset of the broader concept of power. Power is simply "the possibility of imposing one's will upon the behavior of other persons."[9] Weber described two basic types of domination: *domination by authority*—that is, the power of command and obedience[10]—and *domination by constellations of interest,* in which parties not bound together by coercion or statute voluntarily agree to follow orders or an agenda because they perceive it is in their best interest or advantage to do so.[11] For our purposes it is more helpful to view the two as referring generally to "official dominance" and "dominance by influence," respectively. Congress, for example, is officially endowed with plenary power over Indian affairs and is capable of issuing "commands" that are binding on other elements in the policy apparatus. Within the executive, the official hierarchy of domination is helpfully drawn out on flowcharts that grace office walls—lest someone forget. Indian tribes, of course, are not in an official position to "command" any federal office to do anything. Instead they, along with (but decidedly not in concert) with private corporations and the various states, attempt domination through influence. Policy analysts have described "power clusters" that subordinate their separate interests to the larger one of influencing the legislative process to some common end.[12]

Both of these pure types of domination are involved in actual policy dynamics, and the distinction between them becomes blurred in the behavior within and between the various groups or components of the policy process. Each component uses both the official structure of power relations and the informal leverage of common interest to obtain the upper hand in making decisions that affect the others.

Weber subdivided domination by authority into three subtypes: *traditional domination, charismatic domination,* and *legal domination.* Each rests on a different principle of justification or legitimation for the exercise of power. The most relevant for considering relations between the tribes and the government is the legal type of domination, whose legitimation is based on written laws, statutes, and regulations.[13] But I will argue later that the traditional basis of authority and legitimacy has had an important effect on those relations as well.[14]

Within the legal type of domination by authority Weber distinguished two basic traditions: the *formal* (or bureaucratic) and the *substantive* (or political).[15] Their relationship is dialectical. Each depends on the other's existence in the complexity of modern state governance; but within the legal system each struggles with the other for ascendancy in the power hierarchy, even though the official relations between them may be spelled out by statute—as is the case between the executive branch and Congress in handling Indian affairs. The interests of each come from different bases and involve distinctive behavior patterns. The best interests of those in the bureaucracy or administration are served by following orders and procedures articulated by those higher in the chain of domination. These orders and procedures, and thus the bases of judgment by the higher-ups, are ideally fixed, unchanging, and routine; innovation is soft-pedaled. The best interests of the politicians, on the other hand, ideally are met by catering to the demands of those outside the formal structure of power: the constituents who put them into office. These demands tend to shift, and meeting them (so as to remain in office) often requires innovative solutions. Ultimately bureaucrats look upward in the chain of power for their support and security; politicians look downward to the voters—or to some of them, at least.[16]

In struggles for dominance with the administration, the politicians of Congress wield the two powerful weapons of legislation and appropriation. As preludes to brandishing either of these, they can also conduct investigations of bureau activities, typically capped with command performances by administrators before congressional committees.[17]

The bureaucracy's greatest weapon in the struggle for domination is its alleged expertise. Weber insisted that there is no other possible structure ideally as rational or efficient at handling the details of running the state. Politicians' interests and expertise must shift to keep pace with changes in their constituents' concerns. Typically they do not have the time to acquire in-depth knowledge of a single area,[18] and thus must rely on the information and procedures supplied by the bureaucrats.

The bureaucracy maintains The Files, the source of the accumulated information and knowledge basic to its power, and stresses the keeping of written records to augment its power base.

But knowledge is merely a prerequisite to the bureaucracy's power. Above all, knowledge must be managed effectively, which means not only retaining and retrieving it, but keeping it away from others who might be competitors in the power struggle. Hence the bureaucracy's emphasis on secrecy and its reluctance to supply information that supports positions contrary to its own.[19] Secrecy can also be used to conceal a lack of expertise or an inability to control certain types of knowledge.

Bureaucratic structures are not only inevitable, they are essentially indestructible because of their role in the governance process. They can be prodded, investigated, publicly chastised, shifted, and renamed, but never obliterated, because of the administrative chaos that would result.

According to Weber's version of the politics-bureaucracy dialectic, the key to effective, enlightened governance lies in keeping a balance of power between the two. Without close supervision and direction the bureaucracy will come to dominate the relationship and create a system throughout government based on its own hierarchical, uninnovative worldview.[20] Weber portrayed politicians as the primary source of enlightened policy innovation juxtaposed to fundamental bureaucratic tendencies.

Still, when focusing on the dynamic of the relationship between bureaucracy and politics, a third element—the courts—is easily overlooked. Congress cannot be sued on Indian issues except for land claims; but officials in the administration can be and have been sued for alleged violations of policy or regulations. This vulnerability acts as a check on bureaucratic domination when and if the legislative branch cannot or will not act as the brake.

This brief ideal-typological prelude shapes the following discussion of relations between the tribes and the federal government over the past three decades. The basic task is to portray the nonprogressive meandering in policy articulation and implementation as a result of dynamics of power relationships within and between the various components of the policy process. The major components in this discussion include Congress, the Bureau of Indian Affairs, the federal courts, and the Indian tribes. States, non-Indian commercial interests, and an assortment of Indian-oriented constellations of interest intrude now and then as relevant components. Of course, there is a discrepancy between the reality as here described and the ideal as drawn by Weber; the point is to understand why the discrepancy exists and what it implies for the future.

CONGRESS

Characteristically, Congress waits for a crisis to erupt in Indian country before flexing its plenary muscle.[21] Constituents and special interest groups (i.e., constellations of interest) either favoring or opposing Indian positions in the crisis bombard members of Congress with grievances and demand redress. The legislators, as politicians, must pay attention to these demands and take action on some of them—ideally, meaningful and innovative action. In their position of power legitimized by statute they can compel executive agencies such as the Bureau of Indian Affairs to change their procedures, restructure, or even to self-destruct in keeping with demands of constituents and the results of congressional investigation. Alternatively they can create significantly new policy directions by passing new laws.

Arguably the most significant legislative measures affecting tribal-federal relations during the last three decades were the Area Redevelopment and Economic Opportunity acts of 1961 and 1964, the Indian Self-Determination and Education Act of 1975, the creation of a *permanent* Senate Select Committee on Indian Affairs in 1984, and an explicit congressional repeal of the termination resolution in 1988. Otherwise, "policy" measures were preoccupied with services to be provided to and by Indian communities and rights or domain to be restored to specific tribes. The contradictory principles of tribal sovereignty and federal trust protection were continually invoked without being systematically articulated or integrated into legislative reform. And major investigations by Congress in 1973–75 and again in 1988–89 showed that while conditions in Indian communities have generally improved since 1960, the dismal poverty, along with flagrant mismanagement and fraud, still prevail. Congress had a hand in redirecting the Bureau of Indian Affairs toward a "technical services" role, but it has repeatedly been unable to coerce the bureau into major restructuring for the sake of efficiency. In both legislation and in oversight on Indian affairs Congress has assumed a minimalist, reactive posture, thereby abdicating much of its potential power for constructive reform. That this posture is in legislators' best political interest is the Weberian point, but it must be substantiated.

Given the need of members of Congress to appeal to the widest (or most powerful) constituency so as to be reelected, being active on issues of Indian policy is considered risky. This is the basic observation from which others related to the wielding of substantive or political power proceed. To come down strongly for or against either Indian sovereignty or federal trust protection is bound to bring on the wrath of some vociferous constituency. In an era when a single-issue mentality dominates much of the voter sensibility, what politician needs another source of polarized pressure?

Add to this risk the fact that one and a half million Indians are scattered widely over the fifty states, with only a few areas having concentrations that could affect election outcomes. The chances are that a representative or senator has a politically insignificant Indian constituency, so why take the time to become active in Indian issues? In a 1988 interview Representative Ben Nighthorse Campbell, a Northern Cheyenne representing a district in Colorado, declared: "I'd like to have a few other Indian people back here [in Congress] to spread the burden, because we get a lot of referrals. An Indian guy will go into some congressman's office from New York and they tell him, 'Oh, go talk to Ben.' Wonderful. I'll help him if I can, but some [members] are taking a hike on Indian problems and pushing them over on us. . . . [T]he thing I obviously have to be worried about is that I can't be perceived in my own district as just being an Indian congressman for Indians and for Indian problems, or I can't get reelected."[22]

Then there is perhaps the major development in tribal-federal relations since

1960: the significant threat of costly court action against the government for failing to adhere to declared Indian policy; that is, to tribal sovereignty or protection of the trust. Given the prevailing obscurity of these concepts, plus the record of past court encounters, precipitous action to meddle more with either issue without intensive and comprehensive preparation would most likely spark a series of protracted court battles that would benefit only the attorneys involved. (Although Congress cannot be sued without its consent, suits can cost constituent taxpayers money and hamstring key administrators with preparations for court appearances.) Best to let sleeping dogs lie, to move only as far and as quickly as is necessary to cope with immediate problems having fairly restricted scope.

In 1978 a legislator from a Western state summarized the situation neatly to one of his staff: "Indian affairs are a no-win issue."[23] An oft-cited manifestation of this conviction: in the mid-1970s no representative could be found to chair the Indian affairs subcommittee of the House Committee on Interior and Insular Affairs. At first the subcommittee was joined—like hens and foxes—with the subcommittee on public lands. Later, the chair of the full committee, Representative Morris Udall of Arizona, placed all Indian issues before the full committee directly, drastically curtailing the staff and committee time they received.[24] The Indian affairs subcommittee on the Senate side was abolished earlier (an indication of the low priority of Indian issues but billed as a "streamlining" move). The fact that the Senate Select Committee on Indian Affairs since has become a permanent fixture to replace it is probably due more to power maneuverings among senators in the late 1970s than to a compelling concern with Indian problems.[25]

The American Indian Policy Review Commission (AIPRC) of the mid-1970s was certainly an involved first step in what was supposed to become a major overhaul of federal policy. But the ensuing scenario unfolded in a familiar pattern: the report was published, the congressional lament of the prevailing conditions was dutifully delivered, the members of the executive branch covering that aspect of federal activities were hauled before congressional committees for grilling and chastisement, and little else has happened since. Again, the inference is that Indian issues do not have high priority and major reform of Indian policy is best avoided.

On the other hand, Congress cannot simply let go of the Indian tribes: the offensive termination resolution is off the books. Various bills to revive it, no matter how deceptively titled,[26] have not been able to marshal the support for passage. Then there is the memory of the termination fiasco itself. Unless they represent Wisconsin or Oregon, legislators might forget; but Indian tribal leaders will always be pleased to remind them.[27] Finally, the financial costs of such a move may well be intimidating, both for predetermination upgrading and for the lawsuits and shifted social program burdens that would surely follow. Accurate estimates of the cost of a termination phoenix are difficult to generate. But compared with what this would likely be, the $3 billion now annually spent on federal Indian programs seems an appropriate budgetary counterpart to the make-no-waves minimalist stance on Indian legislative reform.

So for its own best political interests Congress cannot completely ignore Indian relations, but it has not done much fundamentally to reform them. If "abdication" of policy power seems too harsh a characterization, certainly Congress has put the initiative for systematic reform up for grabs by one of the other components in the policy-making process. According to Weber's view, the administrative bureaucracy is the most likely to seize it.

THE INTRACTABLE, TERMINAL BUREAUCRACY

Perhaps Congress ought to expect major Indian policy initiatives to come from the Bureau of Indian Affairs (BIA), like those launched by Commissioner John Collier and his associates in the mid-1930s. But this expectation assumes the Weberian notion of a rational, efficient bureaucracy, which by virtually all measures the BIA is not. And surely Collier himself stood much closer to the "politician" than to the "bureaucrat" pole of Weber's spectrum.

A disgruntled ex-BIA staffer in the late 1970s declared that the BIA was like "a mindless, spastic zombie" in administering Indian affairs.[28] More recently the BIA's top official dubbed it "an intractable bureaucracy," then resigned in the midst of the 1989 Senate investigation of mismanagement in Indian affairs. For most of the past thirty years the BIA has been incapable of seizing the policy initiative— partly because it is a bureaucracy and partly because it is an ineffective one.

Back to Weber's bureaucracy-politics dialectic: the BIA's power versus Congress comes from its control of important information about Indian life and from its daily involvement in administrative detail. The BIA, or something like it, must exist if Congress is to fulfill its statutory obligations to Indian tribes. But continued dependence on the bureau's administrative effectiveness threatens Congress's ability to meet its statutory obligations.

In the 1960s at least two potentially significant policy initiatives came out of the executive. One was the so-called Indian Omnibus Bill which Secretary of the Interior Stewart Udall sent to Congress in 1967. Indians viewed it as placing too much authority in the hands of the executive, yet paving the way for eventual termination. It expired in committee. The other initiative was the creation of a presidential task force on Indian policy in 1966. To tribal leaders its report also smacked of termination, so it was buried.[29] But for most of the rest of 1960s, and increasingly in the 1970s and 1980s, the bureau was reactive, dodging this way and that to protect its power.

The BIA's direct and largely exclusive control of Indian community development was undermined by the massive antipoverty campaign of the late 1960s. The new programs brought an enthusiastic deluge of new money, new people with new operating styles, and new channels of authority in the relationship between the tribes and Washington.[30] This deluge with its self-help ideology helped to increase congressional and higher-level executive pressure on the bureau to change its administrative role: direct control of reservation programs was out; technical service for tribally run programs was in. Bureau bashing was in by the late 1960s as well.[31] As an apparent response to the criticism there was another flurry of what looked like policy initiative from the administration in President Richard Nixon's policy statement of 1970.[32]

And there was an effort by the executive to reorganize the BIA. In 1969 Louis

Bruce was brought in as commissioner from outside the bureaucracy to clean house at the uppermost BIA levels.[33] This sparked a power struggle between Bruce's reformers and a group of career administrators within the bureau who felt that their power was threatened. The battle raged through 1971, with most of Nixon's suggested reforms being subverted by Interior and BIA people,[34] giving strength to the argument that they were never intended to be effectively implemented.

The reform proposals were further subverted by the Indians themselves: a watershed in power manipulation came in November 1972 when the Trail of Broken Treaties reached Washington. The ensuing occupation and sack of the BIA building were taken as a most public signal that the bureau—already in internal disarray—was at best an administrative and political embarrassment.[35] Whatever the previous doubts about its efficiency, there was now no way the bureau could be trusted to handle its administrative chores effectively. Now more than ever the bureau seemed incapable of effective power manipulation as unfavorable attention from superiors and the public pushed administrators even more deeply into make-no-waves, resist-all-change behavior.

Yet no other agency had the accumulated information necessary to deal with the daily issues of federal-Indian relations. Even though the Indians in the takeover had taken or destroyed some of this all-important lifestuff, the bureau's continued—if very much flawed—access to The Files allowed its survival.

By 1977 Congress had issued explicit and strident demands for BIA reorganization.[36] This was partly the legacy of the angry confrontations with Indians in 1972–73 and the resulting AIPRC recommendations, and partly the continuing effort to transform the bureau into a technical service agency. The AIPRC version of reorganization was more sweeping than that proposed in 1969–70, which is to say even more threatening to the bureau. The new contracting process would put more authority into the hands of the tribes and would cut both personnel and funding for the bureau itself. In particular the control over tribes by the twelve BIA area offices would be cut back.[37]

The bureau behaved accordingly. There was a great deal of planning with a minimum of actual reorganization.[38] Plans called for replacing the twelve area offices with five or six regional service centers, two special programs offices, and three field offices.[39] By 1989—almost fifteen years after they were proposed—these changes still had not been implemented. The area office structure was still intact, although area directors *had* been removed from line authority in BIA education programs in 1978.[40] The charade produced at least one classic example of dialectical symbiosis: when the BIA was finally ready to implement a plan for "realinement" (not reorganization) in 1982, the tribes reversed their earlier position and vehemently opposed elimination of the area offices.[41]

By 1978–79 the contracting system with tribes was hitting one snag after another, threatening to scuttle the process entirely. One of the major problems was the lack of BIA funding for contract support (indirect costs). There was little the bureau could do, it declared, unless it received more resources.[42] Some tribes believed that the contract support controversy was partly an effort to resist the reorganization's perceived threat to bureau power.[43] Nevertheless, some of the BIA's other sources of power have been eroding. Between 1976 and 1988 the bureau lost about 3,500 personnel positions (despite strident objections by civil service lobby groups).[44] In the 1980s BIA funding increased virtually every year, but these increases were wiped out by inflation, leaving a net—if relatively small—funding loss for the decade.[45] Neither of these trends can be traced exclusively or largely to the technical services shift, however. The BIA sustained cuts along with other federal agencies in keeping with the Reagan administration's antipathy to big government.

In the wake of the 1989 Senate hearings into the poor management of Indian and federal mineral resources, members of the special investigating committee issued tough-sounding orders to the secretary of the interior: "Go in there [into the BIA and other resource management agencies] and kick butt."[46] At least two outcomes were predictable: Interior would want more money and people to strengthen its resources administration, and there would be a call for major BIA reorganization.

The bureau for the past three decades, then: no major initiatives for policy reform, inefficiency and credibility crises, but nonetheless surviving, largely because no other agency has as much information and experience and Congress has been unwilling to risk the consequences of starting over with a new administrative structure. Weber emphasized that a bureaucracy is capable of endless adaptive adjustments necessary to sustain its existence. It is thus not only inevitable but indestructible.[47]

Within the Department of the Interior itself the BIA is legendary for its lack of power.[48] Certainly there is a continuing conflict of interest between the agencies that control the entire federal portion of mineral and petroleum wealth and the one that handles the social and material needs of about 600,000 Indians. Not only are the resources a higher priority, but the other agencies in the department are not about to yield any measure of their control (and thus power) to rival bureaucracies.

All administrative departments are subordinate to the Office of Management and Budget (OMB), which screens each executive department's proposals to be certain they are in keeping with the basic politics of the White House and the maintenance of the maximum amount of political power by the executive branch versus that of Congress. Ultimately, then, the major decisions by the administrative agencies, unlike Weber's ideal-typical bureaucracy, are not objective at all but must run a hierarchical gauntlet of political jockeying. To turn Karl Mannheim's comment around, administrative decisions have a way of becoming political decisions.[49]

The dialectic of politics-bureaucracy power relations is manifest not only in the BIA's relations with Congress and executive agencies but within the BIA itself. At this more specific level, too, its dynamics have helped to stifle BIA initiatives for policy reform. As in the case of Louis Bruce, the executive branch's typical reaction to the bureau's administrative lapses is to appoint new BIA leadership to shape things up. Notably, these are *political* appointees who serve only as long as they please those who appointed them; they are without the protection of civil service regulations—a way of ensuring that personal loyalty will prevail over the best interests of BIA longevity. Because these appointees also look upward in the hierarchy rather than downward, they do not fit Weber's "politician" type neatly. They are touted as the "idea people" in charge of developing long-range policy.[50] Both ideally and typically they come from outside the ranks of the BIA; that is, they are not career administrators and owe those beneath them no longstanding favors. Ideally and typically (for the past thirty years, anyway), they also know something about Indian affairs and are themselves of Indian blood. And this sets the stage for conflict between the political newcomers and the career administrators within the bureau; the running battle between Commissioner Bruce and the administrative careerists in the months prior to the BIA takeover is a well-documented example.[51]

Theodore Taylor, a former BIA official, described the impacts of political appointments on bureau operations.[52] Since 1969 there have been at least eighteen appointed or acting assistant secretaries and commissioners, each with a new agenda for shaping up bureau operations. This choppy tenure means that the direction Weber found so crucial to enlightened administration has been missing within the bureau. For the rank-and-file bureaucrats, routines never become established and guidelines and procedures are temporary. For the higher-level career administrators, the frequent changes are demoralizing because there is little incentive to hone their skills and expertise; why bother? A glass wall rises between the career administrators and the top bureau officials. The political appointees move on while a few of the higher-level career bureaucrats move around from job to job in the bureau's operations, showing up at congressional hearings to whisper facts to the commissioner or assistant secretary of the moment, or occasionally filling in as an acting luminary. The two elements of bureau operations never get a chance to know one another and to work together on any long-range program. As a result, the career civil servants' best interests are served by trying to keep a low profile, to be reactive instead of innovative, and all the while to protect the span of control over people and resources.

Thus, while according to Weber's typology bureaucrats are always looking upward in the power hierarchy for direction and commands, thereby in essence linking their professional existence to that hierarchy regardless of who commands it, their obedience to politician superiors is assured only as long as it perpetuates the system. Among Washingtonians, converting administrative positions into political appointments is considered a quick fix for administrative embarrassments.[53] But with their high turnover, the ever-widening networks of political appointments have accomplished exactly the opposite of their anticipated effect: they have actively interfered with policy reform.

Increasing the numbers of political appointments can also lead to a subversion of all administrative objectivity for the sake of personal loyalty. This would be at least as threatening to Weber's version of democracy as the prospect of politicians being dominated by bureaucrats.

If Congress has generally failed to use a greater measure of its available power for policy initiatives, and the BIA has used most of its own power simply to exist, then conceivably Indians' power for seizing the policy initiative has become relatively greater in the past three decades.

INDIAN POWER

The federally recognized Indian tribes' leverage in the system comes ultimately from their unique sovereign status, the ramifications and limitations of which are fleetingly sketched in the Constitution and have been evolving in court findings since the 1790s. From time to time in the history of policy, public appeals to the sad plight of Indian peoples have had some influence (e.g., the late 1920s), but mostly this is an intermittent and unreliable lever. In the past three decades, mass public confrontations between Indians and state and federal authorities have generated some legislative or administrative actions, but the long-term results so far have been mixed and generally disappointing.

Because Indians occupy no formal position in the power structure of Washington, they must wage a kind of guerrilla warfare to exercise what power they have. Their strongest weapon is the threat of court action against administrative officials, states, or corporations for violating the evolved principles of tribal sovereignty, federal trust protection, or both. Several factors have combined to help them wield this threat with increasing effectiveness since 1960. The first is money. Land claims settlements and the proceeds from tribal enterprises and resources have put money into some tribal governments' hands. This allows them to hire lawyers and, in some cases, Washington-based consulting firms whose primary purpose is to influence relevant legislation. The second factor, partly related to the first, is a series of federal court decisions reaffirming the special legal status of tribes, tribal sovereignty, and the federal trust responsibility. Among the most important of these are the reaffirmation of the Boldt decision on Indian treaty fishing rights and the Passamaquoddy-Penobscots' right to sue states for the violation of the 1790 Trade and Intercourse Act. The third factor is sophistication. The antipoverty programs of the 1960s and 1970s promoted firsthand contact between tribal officials and Washington, giving them direct knowledge of how things get done in the capital city. Some tribes have been able to continue this contact despite personnel changes and heavy cuts in so-called social programs spending. And the fourth factor, also related to the other factors, is the availability of effective advocates outside the formal federal network. This includes the influence-for-hire consultants in the city, nonprofit advocacy groups such as the American Friends Service Committee and the Friends Committee on National Legislation, and, most important, the nonprofit legal advocacy groups such as the Native American Rights Fund and various state-level legal services offices.

In power struggles with the BIA, tribes are confronted by the irony that affects all bureaucracies bound to provide services for subordinate clients: the bureau cannot be responsive to Indians' wishes unless ordered to do so by its own superiors in the hierarchy of power. There is also the bureau's inevitable need to present a united front to rivals for power. So the Indians move on to Congress to try to induce it to compel the BIA or some other administrative agency to yield to the Indians' wishes.

Although the tribes and the BIA are rivals for power, they obviously depend on each other. Thus they will operate to limit or reduce each other's power vis-à-vis

Congress, but will join forces against any move to eradicate the bureau or end the special legal status of the tribes. And because of the bureau's statutory administrative power, they will join forces to increase the resources of the bureau for eventual redistribution to the individual tribes. Most fundamentally, the Indians—like Congress—are forced to depend on the bureau because of its administrative apparatus and information. The linkage between many tribal governments and the bureau can be even tighter: the tribal incumbents use the administrative protection and inside information offered by the bureau to bolster their power over rival factions. The situation at Pine Ridge in 1972–73 is an example of this.[54]

Mention of factionalism prompts a crucial caution. In speaking so far of "tribes" or "the Indians" there has been the implication that the Indians are united on basic issues of power relations; that is, that there is not only a constellation but a consensus of interest. This is not the case. While most tribes would agree that there should be a maximum of tribal sovereignty along with maintenance of the federal trust relationship, there are real differences both between and within tribes about the tactics and philosophy involved. There is no universal Indian voice whispering in Congress's ear.

Because tribal leaders of recognized tribes are elected, they fall into the "political" element of Weber's legal authority. This means that the concerns of their constituency (not necessarily the majority of the tribal members) must dominate their strategies. In most cases the constituents' major concerns are localized and immediate: need for money for a continuing agricultural program, more water for the crops, getting more land back for the reservation; more general issues of federal Indian policy are of less concern. It is these local issues that are most likely to bring tribal leaders to the lawyers and to Washington. And this means that localized issues dominate congressional and executive actions. This tends to deflect attention from the issues of general policy articulation and reform. The closest approach to a broader assessment may well come in the appropriations process, which, of course, ignores all important policy issues that cannot be expressed in dollars.

The major national-level Indian organizations that marshal tribal support for or against various moves by Washington reflect some of the fundamental cleavages in the Indian population across the country: the elected tribal leaders versus their opposing factions, the "progressives" versus the "traditionals" (frequently overlapping with the first-named split), urban versus reservation Indians, and federally recognized versus non-federally recognized tribes. At the national level the most persistent cleavage for the past thirty years has been between the National Tribal Chairmen's Association, the National Congress of American Indians, and the American Indian Movement (AIM). The diverse pressures leveled by these groups on Congress and the executive branch have strengthened the tendency to concentrate on localized, immediate issues at the expense of more generalized policy.

The Indians' most effective tactic for instigating broad policy initiatives by Congress or the executive since 1960 has been militant confrontation, in which the legitimacy of the federal power itself is ignored by Indians for the sake of their own bid for influence. The takeover of Alcatraz in 1969, the takeover of the BIA building in 1972, and the second Wounded Knee confrontation four months later are the primary examples. The outcomes, however, were not those intended by the Indians themselves. The crackdown on BIA operations following the takeover was decidedly not an Indian objective; and the AIPRC promised more than it delivered.

By contrast, The Longest Walk of 1978, organized as a broad-based Indian counter to a series of backlash bills introduced in both houses of Congress, was much less effective at instigating action. Once in Washington the marchers kept the peace and created only a minimal stir in the city, which by then was jaded after massive marches on the Capitol by angry farmers, schoolteachers, and antiabortion groups.[55] Congress is more responsive when threatened than when approached.

The government's willingness in the 1960s and early 1970s to see Indian issues as primarily issues of poverty represented a threat to the tribes' power in federal relations.[56] The antipoverty enthusiasm tended to ignore the special legal status of Indian tribes as distinct from all other minorities. (Ironically, for this brief period it was as powerful for tribes to be poor as to be Indian.) For this reason it has not been fruitful for Indians to join forces in a constellation of interest with the poor, or with other ethnic or racial minorities, so as to gain specific rights for Indians only. This is why Vine Deloria has made an effort to distinguish the situation of Indians from that of blacks and Hispanics in this country.[57] Of course, broad-based social programs have helped Indians, as noted earlier. But the tribes dare not allow the impression to surface that these programs alone will meet the full measure of the government's statutory commitment to them.

The Indians have learned how to operate as effectively as possible within the legal power structure, using the same rules and the same bases of legitimation used by policymakers in Washington. AIM members have never operated according to those rules, however, and by the mid-1970s had changed their tactics to emphasize a more "traditional," more "spiritual" approach to power manipulation. This probably helped to create a broader age range among AIM supporters, but it also perpetuated the discontinuity between legal and traditional types of authority.

In some reservation communities, such as Pine Ridge or Taos, this traditional-legal discontinuity has been a long-term issue in tribal political factionalism. Tribal governments have become microcosms of the national government, with burgeoning bureaucracies and political battles over who will control them. Those favoring the traditional authority operate according to a different system, typically not hierarchical but consensual, expressing dissatisfaction by avoidance rather than by angry confrontation. To the extent that it persists as an issue in political conflict on some reservations, and to the extent that the traditional pattern spreads among tribal governments, federal authorities may once again be confronted by a power system much different from their own. The presence of this and other sources of intratribal factional conflict also threatens the constancy and intensity of tribal pressure placed on government, and the high turnover of Indian leaders caused by factionalism affects the directions the pressure favors exactly as high turnover of political appointees has affected the BIA.

But the threat of legal action remains the most effective way for tribes to wield authority. Secretaries of the interior such as the late Rogers Morton have been named personally as defendants in tribes' suits over failed federal trust protection. Lawsuits against the Department of the Interior were filed by 17,000 Navajos and by 7,000 Oklahoma Indians for dereliction of the trust obligation in handling their mineral leasing arrangements with private corporations.[58] States such as Maine and Connecticut agreed to negotiate settlements of tribal land claims once they were convinced that the Indians meant business and had a case that could well hold up in court. That the negotiated settlement procedure has become so pervasive in relations between tribes, states, Congress, and executive agencies since the 1970s clearly means that a good many tribes have the potential power to be even more hurtful to their opponents' best interests should the issue go to court.

In a way, both the negotiated settlement process and the courtroom battles abet the fragmentary, tribe-specific tendencies of policymaking in Congress and the executive branch, and reinforce the tribes' sense that each of them is a special policy case. It is *that* tribe, after all, that goes to the expense and time and endures the anticipatory waiting as the case moves along. To be sure, other tribes or the policy process itself may be affected by any precedent set in the settlement, but the conditions of the exercise of the tribes' legal power contribute to Indians' inability to launch sweeping policy initiatives.

If for diverse reasons the initiative does not come from Congress, or from the executive, or from the tribes themselves, by default it passes to the courts. Charles Wilkinson, an expert on Indian law, wrote in 1987: "Congress has virtually unfettered power over Indian policy and ... has adopted statutes dealing with some aspects of Indian policy. Major issues, however, have not been addressed by Congress. The result is that the task of crafting Indian law has been left in significant measure to the courts."[59]

THE COURTS

On Indian issues the Supreme Court has been neither consistently liberal nor conservative over the last thirty years. Those who in 1978 were distressed at what they saw as a conservative cant in the *Oliphant* decision were cheered only sixteen days later by the Court's ruling in the *Wheeler* case.[60] This is to some extent traceable to a heritage of lower court findings that similarly shifted between conservative and liberal interpretations of the rights of tribes versus the other types of sovereignty (federal, state).[61]

Wilkinson argued that the improvement of Indians' conditions of life since 1960—and even since 1980—is predominantly due to favorable findings in the courts. Despite the apparently contradictory opinions rendered, the overall trend has been in the direction of upholding the concept of Indian sovereignty in its increasingly complex ramifications. And the persistence of those favorable findings is due to a general judicial unwillingness to cave in to realpolitik and a tendency to uphold principles and laws that were entered into in good faith in the past. Thus, he argued, the courts are not apparently or universally responsive—on this issue, at least—to the political-economic interests of the powerful majority. Congress by definition must be;

administrative agencies ideally should not be but are. That is why the existing laws, the precipitate of court decisions, and the resulting threat of court action remain the most effective source of power available to the tribes. Without the law they are virtually powerless against federal, state, and private interests opposed to their own. This is one of the fundamental reasons why the status of Indian communities today cannot be sufficiently explained by their economic subordination and exploitation.

The current fuzziness of the definition and extent of the concepts of sovereignty and federal trust protection has precipitated much of the court action.[62] It is reasonable to expect that the clarification of these concepts will not come from some sweeping action by Congress, or bold policy initiatives from the executive branch, or a protracted, united effort by bribes, but from a step-by-step refinement based on successive court findings in cases launched by local, specific disputes.[63] This is so partly because of the formal structure of power in policy issues and partly because of the way various components of that structure have wielded what power they enjoy, which is in turn the result of each operating according to its own best interest.

GENERAL IMPLICATIONS AND CONCLUSIONS

The past three decades of tribal-federal relations have necessarily centered on the issue of best interests and power manipulations aimed at preserving and enhancing them. It is expedient for Congress to shy away from general policy reform; it is expedient for the Bureau of Indian Affairs and other federal agencies to react passively to orders imposed on them by those above them in the power hierarchy. And it is expedient for Indian tribes to take their most strenuous actions on issues that concern them most directly rather than to band together for the extensive process of hammering out more lofty policy reform goals agreeable to all—assuming such goals could ever be found. The expediency has been traced here as an interplay of several sets of symbiotic yet contradictory factors: political and bureaucratic administrative tendencies, tribal sovereignty and federal trust protection, the tribes and the BIA. And each set is clearly interrelated with the other two.

Weber's politics-bureaucracy dichotomy does not neatly fit the reality of the Indian policy process, of course. The reality is more typically a mixture of typologies and ideal tendencies. Members of Congress must be as concerned with hierarchies of power within their houses as with the sensibilities of their constituents, for example. In particular, political appointees as a type fit neatly into neither tendency. Like their subordinate bureaucrat-administrators, they are looking up, not down the power hierarchy. They are to this extent compromised politicians. They are also compromised as bureaucrats. Whether the bureau would be better able to seize the policy initiative were these appointees to stay in position longer is questionable; it is more probable that the short tenure is not a temporary aberration but rather a manifestation of an inherent bureaucratic nature. From this view, John Collier's decade as commissioner was an aberration.

Weber concluded that any bureaucracy has the power edge over political bodies under ideal conditions. The BIA has used most of its power merely to stay alive. Yet

Weberian comparative analysis directs the analytical focus to the more fundamental issue of why the bureau has been unable to manage its power sources effectively. Although I discussed some of the important power-structural factors bearing on BIA inefficiency, I did not mention inadvertent or deliberate collusion between BIA or other agency employees and non-Indian commercial interests. The Senate investigations and *Arizona Republic* essays described such collusion[64]; it can only flourish under the immortal, organizational, procedural, and personnel status quo. Like angry public confrontations, headlined acts of individual and corporate greed can be effective goads to policy overhaul, even though policy overhaul was manifestly necessary years before the press became involved.

Word of the BIA's demise is always premature. Still, the most recent grand exposé of bureaucratic inefficiency and alleged fraud may finally do it in, because it is both an active perpetrator and a convenient scapegoat.[65] In the Senate's overhaul plan, federally recognized tribes would be allowed to secede from the BIA and Indian Health Service bureaucracies by negotiated agreements with a proposed Office of Federal-Tribal Relations (OFTR).[66] The OFTR would negotiate agreements and oversee their implementation. It would require money, people, offices, and regulations. An administrative department having something like the BIA's present functions is, to be Weberian about it, inevitable. And just as inevitable is the effort of any new department to enhance its own power and growth at the expense of potential rivals, including the BIA.[67] At best it would be another bureaucracy under a different name. By fall 1990 the OFTR's proposal was being ignored in favor of yet another plan for reorganizing the BIA.[68] By spring 1991 the BIA had been coerced into allowing tribes to participate in the planning.[69]

The interplay of political and bureaucratic tendencies is to a degree informed and constrained by the implications of tribal sovereignty and trust protection. Trust protection implies bureaucracy; sovereignty implies political entrepreneurship. Again the extremes overstate the reality. But if there is a search for a reasonable balance between one of the two pairs, it must necessarily involve creation of an optimal balance between the other pair.

NOTES

1. Vine Deloria, Jr., "The Evolution of Federal Indian Policy Making," in *American Indian Policy in the Twentieth Century,* ed. Vine Deloria, Jr. (Norman: University of Oklahoma Press, 1985), 254.
2. A series of investigative articles alleging fraud, waste, and incompetence in the handling of Indian resources and administration appeared in the *Arizona Republic,* October 14–21, 1987. The senate appointed an investigative subcommittee of the Select Committee on Indian Affairs to look into the allegations. After staff investigations, public hearings were held in late January and February and in May and June 1989.
3. For example, President Nixon's 1970 message on executive policy toward Indians is still hailed as a sensitive and realistic statement; the American Indian Policy Review commission's comprehensive report and recommendations in 1976–77 remain unequaled in scale. But for a variety of reasons these hopeful proclamations have not been followed by systematic policy reform. See Francis Paul Prucha, *The Great Father: The United States Government and the American Indians,* vol. 2 (Lincoln: University of Nebraska Press, 1984), 1167, 1170.

4. Russel Barsh and James Y. Henderson, *The Road: Indian Tribes and Political Liberty* (Berkeley: University of California Press, 1980), 256; Charles F. Wilkinson, *American Indians, Time, and the Law* (New Haven: Yale University Press, 1987), 9.

5. Robert Bee, *The Politics of American Indian Policy* (Cambridge, Mass.: Schenkman, 1982), 25; Prucha, 1205–1206.

6. Joseph G. Jorgensen, "Indians and the Metropolis," in *The American Indian in Urban Society*, ed. Jack O. Waddell and O. Michael Watson (Boston: Little, Brown, 1971), 66–113.

7. Max Weber, *Economy and Society: An Outline of Interpretive Sociology*, vol. 3 (Berkeley: University of California Press, 1968), 941. I should emphasize a point often made about Weber: although his work is typically juxtaposed to that of Marx, he took care to stress the material basis for much of the domination he saw in social action.

8. See James E. Officer, "The American Indian and Federal Policy," in Waddell and Watson, eds., 8–65; S. Lymon Tyler, *A History of Indian Policy* (U.S. Department of the Interior, Bureau of Indian Affairs, Washington, D.C.: Government Printing Office, 1973); Barsh and Henderson, *The Road*; Deloria, "The Evolution of Federal Indian Policy Making; Vine Deloria, Jr., and Clifford M. Lytle, *The Nations Within: The Past and Future of American Indian Sovereignty* (New York: Pantheon Books, 1984); Prucha, *The Great Father*; Theodore W. Taylor, *The Bureau of Indian Affairs* (Boulder, Co.: Westview Press, 1984).

9. Weber, *Economy and Society*, vol. 3, 942.

10. Weber's full definition of domination through authority reads: "[T]he situation in which the manifested will (*command*) of the *ruler* or rulers is meant to influence the conduct of one or more others (the ruled) and actually does influence it in such a way that their conduct to a socially relevant degree occurs as if the ruled had made the content of the command the maxim of their conduct for its very own sake. Looked upon from the other end, this situation will be called *obedience*." Weber, *Economy and Society*, vol. 3, 942.

11. Weber, *Economy and Society*, vol. 3, 943.

12. Daniel M. Ogden, "How National Policy Is Made," in *Increasing Understanding of Public Problems and Policies, 1971* (Chicago: Farm Foundation, 1971), 5; Taylor, *The Bureau of Indian Affairs*, 123.

13. Traditional authority is based on the principle that the orders and the obedience are matters of ageless truths, while charismatic authority is based on the conviction that the leader is personally and specially endowed with grade or wisdom that compels obedience. Weber, *Economy and Society*, vol. 3, 954.

14. Robert A. Nelson and Joseph F. Sheley, "Bureau of Indian Affairs Influence of Indian Self-Determination," in Deloria, ed., *American Indian Policy in the Twentieth Century*, 182, 187.

15. Weber, *Economy and Society*, vol. 3, 960.

16. Weber, *Economy and Society*, vol. 3, 960.

17. In Weber's view, similar inquiry was not possible in the German parliament of 1917, a condition strengthening the control of the bureaucracy in the governance process at that time. Weber, *Economy and Society*, vol. 3, 1418.

18. *In-depth* here is a relative term; many members of Congress develop real (as distinct from publicly proclaimed) expertise in issues of special interest to them, and it would be inappropriate to refer to them as "dilettantes" without this qualification.

19. Weber, *Economy and Society*, vol. 3, 992.

20. A case in point, he caustically observed in 1917, was the German government of his time. "Since the resignation of Prince Bismarck Germany has been governed by 'bureaucrats,' a result of his elimination of all political talent." What was needed, Weber declared, was direction by a politician, "not by a political genius, to be expected only once every few centuries, not even by a great political talent, but simply as politician." Weber, *Economy and Society*, vol. 3, 1404–1405.

21. Taylor, *The Bureau of Indian Affairs*, 107.

22. Cindy Darcy, "Interview with Representative Ben Nighthorse Campbell, 13 October," Friends Committee on National Legislation Background Paper G-841 (Washington D.C., 1988).

23. Robert L. Bee, Unpublished field notes, January-July 1978, in the author's possession.

24. Bee, *The Politics of American Indian Policy*, 74; Taylor, *The Bureau of Indian Affairs*, 120.

25. Bee, *The Politics of American Indian Policy*, 153–162. It could be argued that much—if not all—of the then-hopeful movement toward Indian policy reform of the mid-1970s was due to the efforts of Senator James Abourezk of South Dakota. Significantly he was effective because he understood how to wield power and apparently didn't give a damn bout his political best interests. This political kamikaze, a vegetarian in a beef-growing state, did not run for reelection. See Kandy Stroud, "James Abourezk Calls It Quits (But Won't Go Away)" in *Politicks and Other Human Interests* 1:13 (1978): 17–18, for a lively account.

26. One of the most sweeping of these "backlash" measures (HR 9054) was the Native Americans Equal Opportunity Act.

27. Prucha, *The Great Father*, vol. 2, 1099.

28. Bee, Unpublished field notes, 1978.

29. Prucha, *The Great Father*, vol. 2, 1097–98.

30. James E. Officer, "The American Indian and Federal Policy," 51–53; Robert L. Bee, *Crosscurrents Along the Colorado: The Impact of Government Policy on the Quechan Indians* (Tucson, University of Arizona Press, 1981), 122–59; George P. Castile, "Federal Indian Policy and the Sustained Enclave: An Anthropological Perspective" in *Human Organization* 33:3, 219–28; Castile, "Mau Mau in the Mechanism: The Adaptations of Urban Hunters and Gatherers" in *Human Organizations* 35:4, 394–97.

31. Senator Edward Kennedy told the National Congress of American Indians convention in late 1969 that the bureau was "incapable of reforming itself. It presently has the authority to contract out almost all its functions to Indian tribes." Jack D. Forbes, *Native Americans and Nixon: Presidential Politics and Minority Self-Determination*, Native American Politics Series, no. 2 (Los Angeles: UCLA American Indian Studies Center, 1981), 35. See also Edgar S. Cahn, ed., *Our Brother's Keeper: The Indian in White America* (New York: New Community Press), 1969.

32. Among other things, the message called for an explicit renunciation of the termination policy, a procedure to enable tribes to take over federally funded programs when they wished to do so, tribal control of their local schools, more funding for Indian health, creation of an Indian Trust Council Authority to represent Indian resource rights without the inherent conflict of interest in the Interior and Justice departments, and creation of a new position of assistant secretary of Indian affairs to improve the clout of the BIA versus other agencies in the Department of the Interior. Bills that would accomplish some of these changes were sent to Congress by the interior secretary but congress waffled on passing them. Some were later revived by Congress itself and eventually passed; others were forgotten (Prucha, *The Great Father*, vol. 3, 1113–15). Analysts have since wondered why an essentially conservative administration promulgated such a liberal-sounding program. A former BIA official involved in the drafting declared in 1978 that it was cynically conceived, playing up the administration's civil rights record with a small, relatively "safe" minority to offset the generally dismal executive efforts on behalf of the much larger black and Hispanic minorities. Others have suggested that the real aim was to influence white voters in an election year (Roxanne Dunbar Ortiz, foreword to *Native Americans and Nixon*, 10; Forbes, *Native Americans and Nixon*, 39).

33. Forbes, *Native Americans and Nixon*, 33.

34. Forbes, *Native Americans and Nixon*, 55.

35. Robert Burnette and John Koster, *The Road to Wounded Knee* (New York: Bantam Books, 1974); Vine Deloria, Jr., *Behind the Trail of Broken Treaties* (New York: Dell, 1974); Forbes, *Native Americans and Nixon*.

36. Senate Select Committee on Indian Affairs (hereafter SSCIA), *Oversight on the Reorganization of the Bureau of Indian Affairs*, Hearings April 10 and 12, 1978 (Washington, D.C.: Government Printing Office, 1978), 127–28.

37. AIPRC, *Bureau of Indian Affairs Management Study, Section 2 Study Provision: Report on BIA Management Practices to the AIPRC* (Washington, D.C.: Government Printing Office, 1976), 8.

38. SSCIA, *Oversight on the Reorganization of the Bureau of Indian Affairs*, Hearings April 10 and 12, 1978, 127–28.; SSCIA, *Realinement of the Bureau of Indian Affairs*, Hearings June 11, 1982 (Washington, D.C.: Government Printing Office, 1984).

39. The American Indian Policy Review Commission's final report included a management study of

the BIA by a private firm (AIPRC, *Bureau of Indian Affairs Management Study*). The study recommended replacing the twelve BIA area offices with six regional service centers; the local BIA agencies would become local service centers. This would save about $11 million annually in 1976 dollars. Ultimately, the report went on, the regional service centers would be eliminated and the local service centers would be merged with local tribal council operations in the spirit of tribal self-determination (AIPRC, *Bureau of Indian Affairs Management Study*, 52, 53). The report reiterated the special need for enforcing implementation of the recommendations, suggesting that the OMB fund and staff a special Management Improvement Implementation Review Office to see that the BIA complied. Furthermore, the report declared, "something more than problem identification and proposed resolutions is necessary" (AIPRC, *Bureau of Indian Affairs Management Study*, 9, 55). Late in 1977 the secretary of the interior appointed a departmental task force to determine how the reorganization would proceed. At about that time a series of reports by the General Accounting Office pinpointed major BIA management problems. In April 1978 a frustrated Senator Abourezk convened a hearing of top Interior Department officials to determine why the reorganization was proceeding so slowly (SSCIA, *Oversight on the Reorganization of the Bureau of Indian Affairs*, 127). He was not satisfied with their testimony, including Under Secretary James A. Joseph's expressed hope that "in the next 3 to 4 years we will have a totally different organization, one that is efficient, effective, and humane" (SSCIA, *Oversight on the Reorganization of the Bureau of Indian Affairs*, 129). Four years later, after more study (including another area office review in 1979), the BIA's 1982 "realinement" plan called for a consolidation of the twelve area offices into five regional service centers, two special program offices, and three field offices. In the plan there was no call for eventual withering away of this structure in favor of tribal self-determination.

40. SSCIA, *Realinement of the Bureau of Indian Affairs*, 40.

41. The Senate Select Committee on Indian Affairs reported "overwhelming" tribal approval for changing the area office system in 1978 (SSCIA, *Oversight on the Reorganization of the Bureau of Indian Affairs*, 130). By 1982 the tribes were concerned that the BIA's plan for doing so would end up costing them more money and provide a lower level of service. They also were angered at what they considered a lack of adequate consultation between them and the BIA before the "realinement" plan was floated. The tribes and members of the civil service employees' union charged that the BIA's 1982 scheme was in no way the culmination of a long, careful planning and consultation process, but was instead prompted by OMB demands that the bureau cut its operating costs by $16 million per year (SSCIA, *Realinement of the Bureau of Indian Affairs*, 60, 65). In fact, the tribes' reversal may not have been inconsistent; whether they would turn down a more reasoned plan for elimination of the area offices remains moot.

42. General Accounting Office (hereafter GAO), *The Indian Self-Determination Act: Many Obstacles Remain*, Report to the Congress HRD-78–59, March 1, 1978 (Washington, D.C.: General Accounting Office, 1978); Bee, *The Politics of American Indian Identity*, 95–110, 232.

43. GAO, *The Indian Self-Determination Act*, 16; Prucha, *The Great Father*, vol. 2, 1161.

44. SSCIA, *Realinement of the Bureau of Indian Affairs*, 59–63.

45. Friends Committee on National Legislation (hereafter FCNL), "Here We Come Again," in *FCNL Washington Newsletter* 489 (March 1986), 7.

46. Bill McAllister, "Lujan Vows to Correct Abuses in Indian Programs," *Washington Post* 9 June 1989: A22.

47. Weber, *Economy and Society*, vol. 1, 224.

48. Cahn, *Our Brother's Keeper*, Chapter 2.

49. Karl Mannheim, *Ideology and Utopia: An Introduction to the Sociology of Knowledge* (New York: Harcourt, Brace, and World: 1936), 118.

50. In an interview with the author and others on February 17, 1978, Assistant Secretary Forrest Gerard portrayed his ideal role in those terms but lamented the fact that he had thus far been unable to get beyond the day-to-day issues of administrative detail. Thirteen years later this problem had still not been resolved. Joint Tribal/BIA/Interior Advisory on Bureau of Indian Affairs Reorganization, "Report to the Secretary of the Interior and Appropriations Committees of the Congress on the Status of Activities," unpublished typescript dated April 30, 1991, 5.

51. Forbes, *Native Americans and Nixon*, 49.

52. Taylor, *The Bureau of Indian Affairs,* 127–29.

53. Taylor, *The Bureau of Indian Affairs,* 129. In the midst of a crisis over the unseemly authority being assumed by some BIA area directors in 1978, Indian Affairs Assistant Secretary Forrest Gerard suggested converting all area directorships from civil service positions to political appointments (Bee, unpublished notes, February 1978).

54. Forbes, *Native Americans and Nixon,* 116–18; Burnette and Koster, *The Road to Wounded Knee,* 239, 242. As long as he remained the elected tribal chairman, the BIA steadfastly supported the incumbent, Richard Wilson, against the challenges of Russell Means and others. Excessive treatment of political rivals by Wilson's armed supporters helped spark the angry confrontation at Wounded Knee in 1973 and subsequent events on the Pine Ridge reservation.

55. Bee, *The Politics of American Indian Policy,* 148. The backlash bills died, but they may well have expired even if the Walk had not been organized. However, this is not to minimize the positive fallout of the Walk on communities where it paused in its way across the country, or the real—if temporary—political and strategic alliances formed among Indian groups and between them and the government.

56. Vine Deloria, Jr., *Custer Died For Your Sins; An Indian Manifesto* (New York: Macmillan, 1969), 168–196; Deloria, "The Evolution of Federal Indian Policy Making," 251; Bee, *The Politics of American Indian Policy,* 210–11.

57. Deloria, *Custer Died For Your Sins,* 168–196.

58. *Arizona Republic* 4 October 1987: A20.

59. Charles Wilkinson, *American Indians, Time, and the Law,* 9.

60. Wilkinson, *American Indians, Time, and the Law,* 61–62. *Oliphant* v. *Suquamish Indian Tribe* declared that the tribe lacked jurisdiction over crimes committed on its reservation by non-Indians. The wording of the justices' opinion was viewed as a very narrow interpretation of the concept of tribal sovereignty. *United States* v. *Wheeler* found that an Indian could be tried by both tribal and federal courts for crimes committed on an Indian reservation. The wording of the decision this time featured a strong endorsement of tribal sovereignty, declaring it to be an inherent right of tribal governments (Wilkinson 63). In 1991 Court watchers were dismayed by further apparent loss of tribal sovereignty in the *Duro* v. *Reina* decision.

61. Wilkinson, *American Indians, Time, and the Law,* 29.

62. Barsh and Henderson, *The Road,* 255–56.

63. Deloria, "The Evolution of Federal-Indian Policy Making," 254–56.

64. SSCIA, *Report of the Special Committee on Investigations,* Report 101–216, November 20, 1989 (Washington, D.C.: Government Printing Office, 1989).

65. SSCIA, *Report of the Special Committee on Investigations.*

66. SSCIA, *Report of the Special Committee on Investigations,* 213.

67. The OFTR would coexist with the BIA and Indian Service conceivably for as long as a significant number of tribes chose to remain under the old system. The Senate recommendations did not mention non-federally recognized tribes, nor did they address programs for Indians in urban areas.

68. Joint Tribal/BIA/Interior Advisory on Bureau of Indian Affairs Reorganization, "Report to the Secretary of the Interior and Appropriations Committees of the Congress on the Status of Activities,"

69. Tribal leaders were outraged that the bureau had drafted a plan without meaningful consultation with them, so they went to Congress to protest. As a result, the Fiscal Year 1991 Appropriations Act stipulated that the BIA could allocate none of its money for reorganization planning until the plans had been reviewed by a task force including tribal representatives. Joint Tribal/BIA/Interior Advisory on Bureau of Indian Affairs Reorganization, "Report to the Secretary of the Interior and Appropriations Committees of the Congress on the Status of Activities," 7.

VII

Perspectives on Native America, 2000

The 500th anniversary of the Columbian landfall and the passing of the second Christian millennium eight years later have offered a golden opportunity to reflect on the past, present, and future of American Indian peoples. This historical moment is a time of relative calm. Even though poverty, ill health, social dislocation, and official indifference continue to plague Indian Country, Natives' prospects seem brighter than they have at any time in the past 150 years. The Indian population appears to be returning to its pre-1492 level. Tribal leaders have unprecedented access to government officials and policymakers. The paternalism that characterized white attitudes and practices towards the continent's indigenous peoples seems to be in retreat. And tribal groups in the United States are able to engage in their own rituals with less interference than previous generations. In this final section, several observers pause, step back from the rush and roar of daily events, and assess the current state of Indian America. The authors treat a wide variety of subjects, from Indian sovereignty and Indian women to casinos and scholars' ties with tribes. Together, they leave us with enduring portraits of a Native America with both serious problems and striking possibilities. The essays also agree, and remind us, that the Indian present and future cannot be understood without a better sense of the Indian past.

20

Journalist Fergus Bordewich offers a tour of contemporary Native American communities as background to a discussion of tribal sovereignty. Taking us first to the Mississippi Choctaw reservation where an industrial park has made the tribe one of the largest employers in the state, Bordewich demonstrates how sovereignty can be the instrument of rebirth. But while Choctaw Chief Philip Martin was building a workforce to assemble circuit boards for Xerox machines, the author notes, Navajo Chairman Peter MacDonald was shaking down contractors and lining the pockets of his political cronies. Ironically, MacDonald attacked his critics as enemies of tribal sovereignty and declared that accepting gifts from business associates was consistent with Navajo tradition. Other examples stress Bordewich's fear—a fear that, as Ward Churchill argued, AIM leaders confronting Richard Wilson at Pine Ridge in the 1970s shared—that strong tribal governments can become dictatorial if allowed to function without federal restrictions or internal restraints. "The drive towards sovereign autonomy," Bordewich declares, "is freighted with the seeds of potential disaster."

Bordewich's essay challenges readers to think beyond the simple formulation that sees tribal sovereignty as the solution to problems afflicting Indians. Besides raising the question of how best to police corrupt tribal leaders, he asks what obligations those leaders have toward both Indians and non-Indians within their jurisdiction. Must tribes encourage a free press? Should they police and jail non-Indian people who cannot participate in their governments? Should tribes require more oversight than county or village governments in other parts of the country? Finally, Bordewich asks us to speculate about the direction of change within Native American governments. As they become more powerful, do they become more distinctively Indian? Or do they become more like their local and regional counterparts? The examples here could support several different answers to these pressing questions.

"Our Lives Have Been Transmuted, Changed Forever"

Fergus M. Bordewich

PHILADELPHIA, MISSISSIPPI, IS THE kind of place that seemed to survive more from habit than reason after the timber economy that was its mainstay petered out in the 1950s. Mills closed, people drifted away, but the town somehow hung on. There is a scruffy, frayed-at-the-edges look to the empty shopfronts and the discount stores where more vibrant businesses used to be, but by the standards of rural Mississippi, Philadelphia counts itself lucky. The mayor, an amiable former postman by the name of Harlan Majors, is not above boasting. "Kosciusko and Louisville, they have to wait to buy a tractor or, sometimes, even to meet their payrolls. And they don't have a fire department worth a hoot. I have sixteen full-time firemen." Philadelphia's trump, the thing that other towns will never have, is Indians. "Our best industry by far is the Choctaw Nation," Majors says. "They're our expansion and upkeep. They employ not only their own people but ours, too. It has never been as good as it is now for the last forty years. Our economy depends on them. If the tribe went bankrupt, we'd go into a depression."

Until a generation ago, the Choctaws virtually defined the futility of reservation life. Over the last quarter century, however, they have defied even their own modest expectations by transforming themselves from a welfare culture into one of the largest employers in the state. Today, Choctaw factories assemble wire harnesses for Xerox and Navistar, telephones for AT&T, and audio speakers for Chrysler, Harley-Davidson, and Boeing. The tribal greeting card plant hand-finishes 83 million cards each year. Since 1992, the tribe has operated the largest printing plant for direct-mail advertising east of the Mississippi River. By 1995, sales from the tribe's industries as a whole had increased to more than $100 million annually from less than $1 million in 1979.[1] As recently as fifteen years ago, 80 percent of the tribe was unemployed; now, having achieved full employment for its own members, nearly half the tribe's employees are white and black Mississippians. Says William Richardson, the tribe's director of economic development, "We're running out of Indians."

The quality of life for the great majority of Choctaws has measurably improved. The average income of a family of four is now about $22,000 per year, a sevenfold increase since 1980. Brick ranch houses have largely supplanted the wood-frame huts and sagging government-built bungalows amid the jungle of kudzu-shrouded

SOURCE: *Killing the White Man's Indian,* by Fergus Bordewich.
Used by permission of Doubleday, a division of Random House, Inc.

oaks and pines that forms the heart of the seventeen-thousand-acre reservation in east-central Mississippi. The new Choctaw Health Center is among the best hospitals in Mississippi, while teachers' salaries at the new tribal elementary school are 25 percent higher than at public schools in neighboring, non-Indian towns. "They're willing to buy the best," says a non-Indian teacher who formerly taught in Philadelphia. "I never heard of anyone being fired in the public schools. Here, they fire Indians and non-Indians alike in a heartbeat, if they don't do their job."[2] The tribal television station, the primary local channel for the region, broadcasts an eclectic daily menu of shows that includes thrice-daily newscasts, Choctaw-language public service shows on home financing and microwave cooking, and, on one recent day, reruns of *The Cisco Kid,* a British film with Dirk Bogarde, and Choctaw-produced commercials for local clothing and food stores and for a quilting display sponsored by the Daughters of the American Revolution.

The Choctaws are also a national leader in transferring the administration of federal programs from the Bureau of Indian Affairs to the tribes. Virtually everything once carried out by the bureau—law enforcement, schooling, health care, social services, forestry, credit, and finance—is now performed by Choctaw tribal bureaucrats. "We're pretty well gone," says Robert Benn, a courtly Choctaw who is the BIA's local superintendent and whose sepulchral office is one of the last still occupied in the bureau's red-brick headquarters in Philadelphia. "We've seen our heyday. The tribe is doing an exemplary job. They're a more professional outfit than we ever were."

Some Choctaws hold that their forebears arose pristine from the earth at Nanih Waiya, in present-day Winston County.[3] "After coming forth from the mound, the freshly made Choctaws were very wet and moist, and the Great Spirit stacked them along the rampart, as on a clothesline, so that the sun could dry them," as one story has it. Others say that they came from the West, carrying huge sacks filled with their ancestors' bones. Throughout historical times, the Choctaws were mainly an agricultural people, raising corn, beans, pumpkins, and melons in little plots by their cabins. However, exhibiting an instinct for business that was probably far more prevalent among Native Americans than those who think of Indians only as innocent children of nature wish to believe, they raised more corn and beans than they needed for their own use and sold the surplus to their neighbors.[4] During most of the eighteenth century, the Choctaws were prominent allies of the French in their wars for influence over the tribes of the Southeast. Although they, like their neighbors the Cherokees, were adapting rapidly to a modern way of life, the relentless pressure of settlement steadily whittled away at their lands until, in 1830, in the rather poignantly named Treaty of Dancing Rabbit Creek, they relinquished what remained of their land in the East and agreed to remove themselves to the Indian Territory, where their descendants still inhabit the Choctaw Nation of eastern Oklahoma.

There were, however, a few Choctaws who remained behind, scattered through the familiar forests of oak and pine.[5] Many more eventually drifted back from the West, disillusioned by the anarchy of tribal politics and the difficulties of life on the distant frontier. Ironically, the tripartite racial segregation that deepened as the century progressed only strengthened the Choctaws in their traditions, language, and determination to be Indian in a part of America where, for all intents and purposes, Indians had simply ceased to exist. Rather than send their children to schools with blacks, the Choctaws refused to send them to school at all. By the time the federal government winkled enough land from private owners to establish the present-day Choctaw reservation in the 1920s, nearly 90 percent of the tribe were still full-bloods and most spoke no English at all.

Today it would be difficult to find a community anywhere in the United States that makes the case for tribal self-determination better than the Mississippi Band of Choctaws. There is, in their story, no underlying irony, no tragic catch, no corrosive seed of failure. It is a success story, pure and simple, not by any means the only one in Indian Country, or even the most dramatic, but nonetheless one of the most important of all just because it was so improbable, so much against the odds. It is a story that also suggests that tribal sovereignty, far from being a universal threat to neighboring non-Indian communities, has the capacity to become an engine for rural revitalization. Says Mayor Harlan Majors, "All the little towns up and down the state look at me and say, 'How do you do it?' I say, 'Get yourself an Indian chief like Phillip Martin.'"

The story of the Choctaw revival is inseparable from that of Phillip Martin, the remarkable chief who has guided the tribe's development for most of the past thirty years. Martin is a physically unimposing man, short and thick-bodied, with small opaque eyes and thinning hair that he likes to wear slick and combed over his forehead. Beneath the grits-and-eggs plainness, he combines acute political instincts with unflagging tenacity of purpose and a devotion to the destiny of his people that is capable of disarming even his enemies. "He's like a bulldog at the postman, he just won't go away," says Lester Dalme, a former General Motors executive who has managed the tribe's flagship plant since 1979. "At the same time, he'll give you the shirt off his back whether you appreciate it or not. He truly loves his people. He can't stand even one of his enemies to be without a job." At 9:30 p.m., Martin is still at work in his office, reading and signing documents from the alp of folders stacked on his desk. "Folks elected me," he says, "and they expect me to do my job."

By all rights, Martin's fate should have been as gloomy as that of any Choctaw born in the Mississippi of 1926. "Everybody was poor in those days. The Choctaws were a bit worse," he recalls. As a boy, he cut pulpwood, herded cows, and chopped cotton for fifty cents per hundred pounds. In those days, Choctaw homes had no windows, electricity, or running water. Alcoholism and tuberculosis were endemic. The Choctaws' cultural isolation was intense. Few had traveled outside Neshoba County, and many had never even been to Philadelphia, only seven miles away. The etiquette of racial segregation was finely modulated. Although Choctaws were not expected to address whites as "sir" or to step off the sidewalk when whites passed, they were required to sit with blacks in movie houses and restaurants. "But we never had enough money to eat in a restaurant anyway," Martin says in his porridge-thick drawl.

Martin, rare among Choctaws of that time, earned a high school diploma at the BIA boarding school in Cherokee, North Carolina. His first experience of the larger world came in the Air Force at the end of World War II. Arriving in Europe in

1946, he was stunned by the sight of starving French and Germans foraging in garbage cans for food. White people, he realized for the first time, could be as helpless as Indians. At the same time, he was profoundly impressed by their refusal to behave like defeated people and by their determination to rebuild their lives and nations from the wreckage of war. He wondered, if Europeans could lift themselves back up out of poverty, why couldn't the Choctaws? After the war, he returned to Mississippi, but he soon learned that no one was willing to hire an Indian. Even on the reservation, the only jobs open to Indians were as maintenance workers for the BIA, and they were already filled. Martin recalls, "I saw that whoever had the jobs had the control, and I thought, if we want jobs here we're going to have to create them ourselves."

He eventually found work as a clerk at the Naval Air Station in Meridian. He began to take an interest in tribal affairs, and in 1962 he became chairman at a salary of $2.50 per hour. Although the tribe had elected its own nominal government since 1934, the tribal council had no offices, no budget, and little authority over anything. In keeping with the paternalistic style of the era, the BIA superintendent presided over the council's meetings. He also decided when tribal officials would travel to Washington and chaperoned their visits there, as Indian agents had since the early nineteenth century. Says Martin, "I finally said to myself, 'I've been all over the world. I guess I know how to go to Washington and back. From now on, we don't need the superintendent.' So after that we just up and went." Martin became a fixture in the Interior Department and the Halls of Congress, buttonholing agency heads and begging for money to replace obsolescent schools and decrepit homes and to pave the reservation's corrugated, red-dirt roads.

The tribe's first experience managing money came during the War on Poverty in the late 1960s, when the Office of Economic Opportunity allowed the Choctaws to supervise a unit of the Neighborhood Youth Corps that was assigned to build new homes on the reservation; soon afterward, the tribe obtained one of the first Community Action grants in Mississippi, for $15,000. "That $15,000 was the key to all the changes that came afterward," says Martin. "We used it to plan a management structure so that we could go after other federal agency programs. I felt that if we were going to handle money, we had to have a system of accountability and control, so we developed a finance office, and property and supply. Then we won another grant that enabled us to hire accountants, bookkeepers, personnel managers, and planners."

The Choctaws remained calculatedly aloof from both the Civil Rights Movement of the 1960s and the Indian radicalism of the 1970s. Martin says, "We didn't want to shake things up. Where does it get you to attack the system? It don't get the dollars rolling—it just gets you on welfare. Instead, I thought, we've got to find out how this system works." Eighty percent of the tribe's members were then on public assistance and receiving their food from government commodity lines. "It was just pathetic. By now we had all these federal programs, but that wasn't going to hold us together forever. I knew that we had better start looking for a more permanent source of income." It would have to be conjured from thin air: the reservation was devoid of valuable natural resources, and casino gambling was an option that lay far in the future.

In key respects, Martin's plan resembled the approach to East Asian states that recognized, at a time when most of the third world was embracing socialism as the wave of the future, that corporate investment could serve as the driving force of economic development. Martin understood that corporations wanted cheap and reliable labor, low taxes, and honest and cooperative government. He was convinced that if the tribe constructed a modern industrial park, the Choctaws could join the international competition for low-skill manufacturing work. Says Martin, "We know who our competitors are: Taipei, Seoul, Singapore, Ciudad Juárez." In 1973, the tribe obtained $150,000 from the federal Economic Development Agency to install water, electricity, and sewer lines in a twenty-acre plot cut from the scrub just off Route 7. "It will attract somebody," Martin promised. For once he was dead wrong. The site sat vacant for five years.

With his characteristic tenacity, Martin began writing to manufacturers from one end of the United States to the other. He kept on writing, to 150 companies in all, until one, Packard Electric, a division of General Motors, offered to train Choctaws to assemble wired parts for its cars and trucks; Packard would sell the materials to Chahta Enterprises, as the tribe called its new company, and buy them back once they had been assembled. On the basis of Packard's commitment, the tribe obtained a $346,000 grant from the Economic Development Administration, and then used a Bureau of Indian Affairs loan guarantee to obtain $1 million from the Bank of Philadelphia.

It seemed, briefly, as if the Choctaws' problems had been solved. Within a year, however, Chahta Enterprises had a debt of $1 million and was near bankruptcy. Production was plagued by the kinds of problems that undermine tribal enterprises almost everywhere. Many of them were rooted in the basic fact that for most of the tribe, employment was an alien concept. Workers would abruptly take a day off for a family function, and not show up for a week. Some spoke no English. Others drank on the job. Many were unmarried women with small children, no one else to take care of them, and no reliable way to get to work. The tribe's accountants had already recommended selling everything off for ten cents on the dollar. But Martin knew that if the plant was sold, the tribe would never get a loan again.

The man to whom Martin turned was Lester Dalme, who was then a plant manager for GM and who had been raised in rural Louisiana with a virtually evangelical attitude toward work. "My mom taught us that God gave you life and that what you're supposed to do is give Him back your success," says Dalme, now a trim man of about fifty, whose office at Chahta Enterprises is as plain as his ethics. "If you don't, He's going to be very unhappy with you." Martin promised Dalme freedom from political interference and full control in the plant; there would be no pressure to hire relatives or to keep people who wouldn't work, problems that were well known to be common on other reservations. Dalme remembers facing the plant's demoralized workers. "They had no idea how a business was run, that loans had to be paid. None of them, none of their fathers, and none of their grandfathers had ever worked in a factory before. They had no idea what quality control or on-time delivery meant. They thought there was a big funnel up there somewhere that money came down. They thought profit meant some kind of plunder, something someone was stealing."

Dalme told them, "Profit isn't a dirty word. The only way you stay in business and create jobs is to make a profit. Profit is what will finance your future."

Dalme cut back on waste, abolished the manager's golf club fee, and put supervisors to work on the assembly line. Baby-sitters were hired for workers with small children, and a pair of old diesel buses organized to pick up those without cars. Dalme told employees that he would tolerate no alcohol or hangovers in the plant. Anyone late or absent two times in the first ninety days would receive a warning; the third time would mean probation, the fourth extended probation, and the fifth immediate dismissal. He kept an average of three of every ten people he hired, but those who survived were dependable workers. Thirty days after Dalme took over, Chahta Enterprises turned its first profit.

Dalme saw people who had been totally destitute begin to show up in new shoes and clothes without holes, and then in a car. After six or seven months, he saw them begin to become hopeful and then self-confident. Workers speak with an almost redemptive thrill of meeting deadlines for the first time. Wayne Gibson, a Choctaw in his mid-thirties who worked the assembly line for several years and is now in management training, recalls, "Factory work taught us the meaning of dependability and punctuality. You clock in, you clock out. It also instilled a consciousness of quality in people. You're proud of what you do. When I was on the production line and I had rejects, it really bothered me. I had to explain it the next day. We're proud of coming in here and getting that '100 percent zero defects' rating."

Chahta Enterprises grew steadily from fifty-seven employees in 1979 to more than nine hundred in the mid-1990s. Once the tribe had established a track record with lenders, financing for several more assembly plants and for a modern shopping center followed. In 1994, the Choctaws inaugurated Mississippi's first inland casino as part of a resort complex that also included a golf course, conference center, and 314-room hotel. "Now we're more into profit centers," says William Richardson, a former oilman from Jackson who was hired by Martin to function as a sort of resident deal-maker for the tribe. "Our philosophy is, if it's good business, if it's legitimate, if it makes a profit, there ain't nothing wrong with it. That's what we're about. We're as aggressive as hell and we take risks." By the mid-1990s, the jobs that the tribe had to offer its members were increasingly technical and intellectual, as engineers, business managers, teachers, and statisticians: it was, in short ready to create a middle class.

In the 1980s, the Reagan administration hailed the Choctaws as a model of entrepreneurship and self-reliance. It was a mantle that Martin accepted with considerable unease. "Some of the current administration's representatives are now touting us as an example of the kind of success that all tribal governments should be able to achieve, which is fine," he said in a speech to the Association on American Indian Affairs. "But it begs the question of how we got to the point of even being able to think of success in the first place. Though we are proud we have received considerable attention from the administration, we are somewhat uncomfortable with it."[6] He criticized what he called the administration's "Horatio Alger view" of reservation development and went on to emphasize that the foundation of the tribe's economic progress—"a stable tribal government, efficiently managed and with centralized administration systems"—lay upon federal programs that originated during the Great Society era of the 1960s. "Without the Office of Economic Opportunity and the philosophy of local control of policy by low-income people, we would never have had the chance to develop tribal governmental institutions to a point of sophistication at which the representatives of some of America's largest corporations would think of speaking with us." He might have added that the tribe's willingness to hire professional managers unencumbered by ties to tribal politics was also a contributing factor to its success.

Martin continues to call for unflagging federal investment in Indian tribes, the kind of commitment that is today increasingly out of fashion among Americans embittered at the perceived ineffectiveness of government and swollen budgets, not to mention the seemingly inexhaustible demands of aggrieved minorities. "We don't want anything more than what the U.S. gives the state governments," he says. "But you cannot bring people out of poverty with minimum wages and minimum budgets. When people control their own lives, you'll see better results. We are able to manage our own programs. Control by others kills initiative. Give tribes the responsibility for development and management and how they live their lives. If we screw up, let us deal with it."

The onus of history is inescapable wherever Indians have conspicuously disappeared from the American landscape. It is no great wonder that many Americans have for so long been reluctant to face the magnitude, or the moral implications, of the catastrophe that befell Indians during the settlement of the nation. The mind shrinks from the full impact of the deaths of so many men, women, and children from centuries of rampant disease, the damage done to so many cultures, the acts of deliberate genocide, the repeated removals, and the revolving-door policies that attempted, no matter what the human cost, to reinvent the Indian with each succeeding generation. Collectively, by anyone's measure, it is a history that constitutes one of the great long-lasting tragedies in human existence. It is as impossible to deny, should anyone wish to, the effects that such a history continues to exert on the hearts, minds, and politics of modern Indians, as it is painful to contemplate history's many missed opportunities, the many New Echotas that a more farsighted nation might have encouraged to rise on the American landscape.

Nevertheless, historical guilt, like romanticism or mindless pity, is a narrow and cloudy lens through which to view present-day realities, including that of Native Americans. It makes no more sense to hold white Americans forever guilty for the settling of the continent than it does to blame Muslims for conquering the Middle East, the Mongols for spreading the Black Plague to Europe, the British for colonizing Ireland, or, for that matter, the Sioux for overrunning the Great Plains. "If the Sioux keep demanding an apology from the U.S. government for what it did to them, we're going to demand one from the Sioux for what they did to us," the Omaha historian Dennis Hastings says with palpable bitterness.

It is also important to realize, without minimizing the degree of trauma that was suffered by virtually every Indian tribe in North America, that American history cannot be measured solely, or even mainly, by the plunder and cruelty that was committed against native peoples. More consistently than any other in the nation's history, Indian policy has embodied the nation's unending struggle to apply moral standards to the conduct of public policy. Whatever the limitations of federal Indian schools, they represented a genuine commitment on the part of Americans to open up isolated and vulnerable native communities to a larger world. Allotment was originally conceived as a plan to make Indians free and independent participants in American society. And while many Indian land cessions were negotiated under pressure, and to Indians' disadvantage, it is also true that, by the estimate of Felix Cohen, a profoundly sympathetic advocate for Indian interests as solicitor of the Bureau of Indian Affairs in the 1930s and 1940s, the United States paid more than $800 million for the lands it purchased from tribes since 1790.[7] Asked if that was an honest price, Cohen replied: "The only fair answer to that question is that except in a very few cases where military duress was present, the price paid was one that satisfied the Indians. Whether the Indians should have been satisfied and what the land would be worth now if it had never been sold are questions that lead us to ethereal realms of speculation."[8] Since the establishment of the Indian Claims Commission in 1946, an additional $818 million has been awarded to a number of tribes as reparation for "grossly inadequate and unconscionable" payment for lands that were ceded in the nineteenth century.[9] The federal government has continued to provide substantial sums to ensure the survival of Indian communities; in the last twenty-five years alone it has appropriated roughly $50 billion for the nation's tribes, quite apart from land claims settlements.[10] It is a record that, though flawed, is unequaled by any other nation in its dealings with aboriginal peoples.

Charles Wilkinson, whose writings on Indian law are among the most trenchant since those of Cohen a half century ago, has pointed out that the recurring theme during the modern era is whether and to what extent old promises should be honored today. The essential promise made to tribes primarily in the nineteenth-century treaties was that they would be guaranteed a measured separatism on their reservation homelands, free to rule their affairs outside of state compulsion but subject to an overriding federal power and duty of protection. Although that promise has often been honored more in the breach than in the observance, it has never been abandoned. "For all its many flaws, the policy of the United States toward its native people is one of the most progressive of any nation," writes Wilkinson. He adds:

> The United States never disavowed its relationship with native tribes, has never abrogated its treaty commitments, nor withdrawn its recognition of Indians as distinct peoples with cultures, lands of their own. From even the earliest colonial times, settlers felt obliged to purchase Indian lands, and to make some kind of provision for displaced tribes. These facts set the United States above other nations in its treatment of native people, and provide a moral and legal setting from which a forward-looking policy of Federal-Indian relations must progress.[11]

Seen in its most positive light, the deepening national commitment to tribal sovereignty thus reflects the latest phase in an ongoing, and today largely unchallenged, effort to accommodate what are perceived to be unique Indian rights and cultural values. "There is no reason for me or for any of you not to support the permanency of tribal sovereignty any more than we would be reluctant to support the permanency of federal or state sovereignty," Ada Deer, a veteran Menominee activist from Wisconsin, and the first woman to head the Bureau of Indian Affairs, told the Senate Select Committee on Indian Affairs at her confirmation hearing in 1993, adding, "The role of the federal government should be to support and to implement tribally inspired solutions to tribally defined problems. The days of federal paternalism are over."[12]

On one plane, tribal sovereignty is simply a form of government decentralization, a pragmatic alternative to the federal micromanagement and failed social engineering of earlier generations. When Indian leaders speak of "sovereignty," they are sometimes only claiming rights and powers that other American communities have always taken for granted. Even as many tribes seem to struggle to set themselves apart from the rest of the United States in the name of sovereign autonomy, in practice they do not usually behave much differently from ordinary county or state governments. Beleaguered in her café on the South Dakota prairie, Micki Hutchinson plaintively wonders aloud, "Why can't they just be more like us?" In fact, for the most part, they are. What the Cherokees began at New Echota a century and a half ago has largely become the Native American norm. Indeed, when Indians speak of "national sovereignty," they are, after all, espousing a European concept of the nation-state that never existed in pre-Columbian America and a modern government whose practical authority is expressed mainly by means of zoning, tax codes, and the American legal system. It is hard to refute Ivan Makil, the chairman of the Salt River Pima-Maricopa Tribe, when he says, "Washington tells us that we can develop our land, establish businesses, govern our community, and make laws, but that we can't enforce them on one group of people. Why is it that when we go to Phoenix or Scottsdale, we're subject to their laws, but when they come here, they're not subject to ours? It is basically a racist point of view."

But the sovereignty movement also has other, more disturbing implications. While it is giving much-needed flexibility to tribes, it is also creating a hodgepodge of economically, and perhaps politically, unviable states whose role in the United States is glaringly undefined in the U.S. Constitution. Even more troubling, the ideology of separatism is partly rooted in the questionable premise that Indians will be better off if they are protected from contact with mainstream America. While it is probably true that tribal governments funded by federal tax dollars will serve the self-interest of their bureaucracies quite well indeed when they are protected from accountability by the principle of "sovereign immunity," there is little evidence at all that sovereignty serves the rights of Indians as individuals. Tribal sovereignty, unfortunately, is not synonymous with democracy. Indeed, the continuing expansion of tribal powers has the potential to create governments that are, in effect, impervious to federal oversight, and where it may be possible to institutionalize discrimination and the abuse of civil rights against both Indians and others and to elevate racial separatism into an ideology of government.

"'Sovereignty' is often just a mask for individuals who rob people of their rights as U.S. citizens," says Ramon Roubideaux, a member of the Rosebud Sioux Tribe, who has probably litigated more civil rights cases than any other lawyer in South Dakota over the last half century. Round-faced and owl-eyed, he speaks with ferocious intensity. "Tribes are able to deny fundamental rights in tribal court and then hide behind the principle of sovereignty. They have the power to do anything they want to do. Many tribal court decisions have nothing to do with fairness. Without the separation of executive, legislative, and judicial powers that exists everywhere else in the United States, we have no way to enforce justice on the reservation if the tribal council says no, irrespective of the lip service that may be paid to tribal and appellate courts. Otherwise, you will see a worsening of every aspect of life on the reservation, because there is no place we can go to get an appeal on a decision. We've got to live within the legal framework of the U.S. whether we like it or not. We've got to develop along those lines because at least it has the goal of honesty and fair dealing."

No single event more vividly revealed the inherent weakness that characterizes many tribal governments than the crisis which led, in 1989, to the downfall of Peter MacDonald, the chairman of the Navajo Nation. The story of what some have called the "Navajo Watergate" is preserved on rolls of microfilm that may be found in the archives of the tribal government at Window Rock, its capital, in the ruddy desert of eastern Arizona. In contrast to most reservation towns, Window Rock truly feels like a seat of government, With signs pointing officiously to the "Supreme Court," "Tribal Computer Center," "Legal Aid," and the like, and the stolid field-stone office buildings clumped beneath the dramatic, punctured sandstone scarp that gives the place its name. Thanks to the policy of open government instituted by MacDonald's successor, Peterson Zah, the microfilmed transcripts are available to anyone who asks for them and will be handed over by young women whose cheerful efficiency typifies the professionalism of Navajo administration. Within the whirring spools lies a tale of revolution.

Now picture the scene.[13] It is a frigid day in February of 1989. MacDonald sits on the chairman's raised dais, facing the epic murals of the sacred sandpainters and women grinding the maize that was the traditional Navajo staff of life. His craggy, thickening features are inscrutable. He wears the mantle of authority as naturally as his expensive Italian suits. As chairman of the Navajo Nation, MacDonald is the most powerful leader in Indian Country, presiding over a reservation larger than West Virginia, with a population of 125,000 and a budget of nearly $100 million per year. He surveys the tribal council that he has dominated for nearly a quarter of a century. What does he feel? Calm self-assurance? Imperious disdain? Well-concealed terror? Perhaps a little of each. Scores of councilmen are clamoring to be recognized. MacDonald knows by now that his fate hangs on the impending vote.

There is a tragic dimension to what is about to happen. There has always been something larger than life about MacDonald.[14] He was born on the open range in the midst of a sheep drive; he enlisted in the Marines at the age of fifteen; having earned a degree in electrical engineering after World War II, he served on the team that designed the guidance system for the Polaris nuclear submarine for Hughes Aircraft. He had, in many ways, been a brilliant tribal chairman. He had successfully renegotiated mineral leases worth millions of dollars annually to the tribe. He founded the first tribal college in the United States as well as one of the first tribal forestry programs and was among the first chairmen in the country to assert the sovereign rights of tribes.

As time went on, however, MacDonald's style of governing had become increasingly imperial. He told a local journalist, Bill Donovan, in 1982, "As long as you allow committees to run government, you'll have five different opinions, and nothing will happen. You need someone to be very strong to be in power, to accomplish what he believes needs to be accomplished."[15] Navajo government, like that of many other tribes, was a mostly ad hoc arrangement in which political power went to the most aggressive bidder. There was a structural vagueness, an identification of powers that fairly invited strong-arm rule. There was no tribal constitution and no statutory separation of powers. The chairman controlled who was allowed to speak from the council floor, what items could be listed for debate, and the length of time members were allowed to speak. Critics increasingly compared MacDonald to Manuel Noriega and Ferdinand Marcos.

There had been rumors for years of bribes and payoffs. Finally, in 1988, a U.S. Senate investigation prompted by revelations in the *Arizona Republic* (based mainly upon the work of a young Shoshone-Bannock reporter named Mark Trahant) revealed an appalling pattern of corruption.[16] MacDonald had accepted hundreds of thousands of dollars in kickbacks from contractors, along with Christmas shopping expenses, money for his wife's birthday party, all-expenses-paid trips to Hawaii and Las Vegas, and more than $20,000 for a private jet trip to the Orange Bowl.[17] He had also managed to spend $650,000 to renovate his private office; Navajos called it "the palace." MacDonald maintained power in the tribal council by spreading around the largesse, often in the form of loans that wound up as gifts, and by awarding "consulting" contracts to his supporters on the council. In the process, he had virtually bankrupted the tribal treasury.

"Big Bo" was the last straw. In the autumn of 1988, MacDonald had used his power as chairman to suppress debate over the purchase of the half-million-acre Big Boquillas ranch from an oil and gas company for $33.4 million. Earlier the same day, the oil company had bought the same property from a cattle company for only $26.2 million. Both the president of the gas company and the broker for the sale were longtime friends of MacDonald. In essence, MacDonald had helped them flip the ranch for an instant profit of $7.2 million. According to the Senate investigators, his share was to be $850,000 and a BMW.[18]

MacDonald admitted taking the money but asserted, astonishingly enough, that his various benefactors were simply "showing appreciation" for his friendship and assistance.[19] Accepting such gifts was a Navajo "tradition," he cynically claimed, a form of politeness. He hadn't wanted to insult anyone by saying no. But with "Big Bo" he had finally overstepped the bounds that even the traditionally passive Navajo electorate could accept. Fewer and fewer Navajos believed him. Now, in February, the reservation was in political chaos, fueling fears that the tribe was headed for collapse. A petition drive calling for MacDonald's removal had obtained more than forty thousand signatures. For the first time ever, Navajo demonstrators had taken to the streets. Protesters crowded outside the council chamber, demanding the chairman's resignation. MacDonald's supporters retorted with shouted warnings that his defeat would lead to a takeover of the tribe by the BIA.

Inside, MacDonald repeatedly accused his opponents of trying to destroy tribal government, of overthrowing sovereignty, of playing into the hands of their "enemies."[20] He blamed his troubles on the Senate, the FBI, and the Bureau of Indian Affairs. The tribal government would come to a standstill, he warned. "No one will want to do business with this tribe ever again without having weekly reports on the chairman's popularity."[21]

You can still hear, in the transcripts of the debate, the sour Nixonian blend of self-flattery and pain, the disbelief of a man who had accustomed himself to imperial power, who amazingly believed that it was he who was the real victim. He told the council, "Ronald Reagan had the Iran-Contra Affair, Jimmy Carter the hostage crisis, Lyndon Johnson the Vietnam situation."[22]

Never before had a Navajo council attempted to remove a sitting official. Many wondered whether they even had the right to try. Councilman Gilbert Roger, speaking in Navajo, said, "It hurts my heart very deeply. Are we in fact doing the right thing? Are we going in the right direction? Are we just throwing out our laws? What will the Navajo people say now? Will they say that we change the laws as we go along?"[23]

Councilman Leo Begay turned to James Stevens, the area director of the BIA, whom he humbly referred to as "our trustee," a revealing locution that suggested how difficult it is to break ingrained habits of paternalism and deference. Begay asked plaintively, "Are we doing right? Are we having this meeting legally?"[24]

Stevens replied, "The Supreme Court has pretty well ruled that the Bureau of Indian Affairs has no part in these types of deliberations. In the Martinez case, they very carefully told us that we have no business there. I appreciate your consideration of my expertise, but there you are."

Eloquently expressing the sentiment of the majority, Councilman Morris Johnson said:

> Our government is like a young, new concept that is developing, is struggling to grow, and I think that we should all be aware that it is a growing nation, and that there are still a lot of things that need to be changed about our government, making it so it's more responsive and receptive to the people in this nation of ours. I see this only as one stage of growth, maybe what one might refer to as a growing pain, because that's what we're going through. But I think it's essential, because we all talk about the need to develop a government that will be standing for the future of our kids, and I think this is only one step in that direction.[25]

In the end, the council voted to strip MacDonald of all executive and legislative power and to place him on leave. It did not end the crisis, however. Just days after MacDonald grudgingly stepped down, his supporters forcibly reoccupied the tribal offices. MacDonald, emboldened, then signed an executive order creating his own judges, one of whom immediately reinstated him as tribal chairman. Soon there were two courts, two chiefs of police, and two governments. At one point, there were even two different chairmen, one representing MacDonald and the other the tribal council, who sat side by side on the dais, each with his own gavel.

The three-member Navajo supreme court was faced with the most difficult decision in its history. Without a constitution or laws to guide it, the court had to determine whether the tribal council in fact had the authority to remove the tribal chairman. Intense political pressure was brought upon the members of the court to find in favor of MacDonald. MacDonald argued demogogically that his power came directly from the people and that since there was no established balance of powers, the legislature had no authority to remove him or to appoint a successor. In the end, seeking precedent, the court ruled that ultimate power must lie with the tribal council, because it had appointed the tribe's first modern chairman in the 1930s.[26]

In 1990, MacDonald was found guilty on forty-two counts of accepting fraud, bribes, conspiracy, and the violation of Navajo ethics. Two years later, he was convicted on sixteen federal charges of taking bribes and kickbacks. In February 1993, he was sentenced in federal court to fourteen and a half years in prison for conspiracy and burglary, stemming from a riot in 1989, along with a concurrent sentence of seven years for extortion, bribery, and fraud.

In subsequent months, profound structural reforms were undertaken. The tribal chairman was stripped of the power to preside over the council and to appoint committees, and legislative and executive powers were formally separated. The position of tribal chairman was replaced by that of a president with the authority to veto legislation, which the council could override by a two-thirds vote. Peterson Zah, a prominent reformer, was elected to fill the new office. In the course of the campaign to unseat MacDonald, a different, equally encouraging kind of transformation had also taken place: Navajos had discovered their own political voice. "It was a political awakening for a vast number of Navajos," says John Chapela, a Navajo civil rights lawyer who organized the petition drive for MacDonald's recall. "There was a real change in the way that Navajo people looked at their government. The recall drive, for the first time, gave them the idea that they didn't have to be servile to an individual or to a group of politicians any more. They realized that they had a right to be told why a politician had acted the way he did. They began to feel that government was answerable to them."

The "Navajo Watergate" demonstrated that with political will tribal institutions can be made to work successfully and democratically, and, perhaps most important, that even tribes with a legacy of corruption and passive voter involvement are capable of reforming their governments without federal help. It presented a new model for the expression of popular democracy as well as setting a new standard for judicial activism and probity; for the first time ever, tribal courts had resolved a constitutional crisis without resorting to the power of the BIA. However, the far-reaching influence that, in a more perfect world, MacDonald's ouster might have had was hampered by the isolation and diversity of the nation's tribes, for many of whom the Navajo revolution seemed as remote as if it had occurred on the other side of the world.

Even as Navajo democrats were struggling to reform the organs of their own government, all-too-typical reports of official corruption continued to seep out of Indian

Country.[27] In 1990, the former casino manager of the White Earth Band of Chippewas, in Minnesota, was found to have forged enough absentee ballots to throw the tribal election. In 1992, the chairman of the Rosebud Sioux Tribe was forced to resign when it was proved that he had pocketed reimbursements for his trips to Washington, D.C. The same year, a BIA investigation revealed the looting of expense accounts by the chairman of the Crow Creek Sioux Tribe. In 1993, the police chief of the Pyramid Lake Paiute Tribe was fired for arresting two powerful members of the tribal council for drunken driving. When Tribal Chairman Elwood Lowery resigned in protest, one of the arrested councilmen was elected chairman in his place and appointed an unemployed mechanic as police chief; within days, the new chief himself was arrested for drunken driving and violation of probation. To be fair, a certain amount of official wrongdoing only reflected the sort of petty graft to which underpaid officials are vulnerable anyplace where public money lies easily to hand and where the power of the investigative press is weak or nonexistent. Elsewhere, however, it bore troublingly on rights that other Americans take for granted.

"On the reservation, you don't have any rights at all," says Robin Powell, who attempted to bring modern journalism to the reservation of the Turtle Mountain Band of Chippewas in North Dakota. "They can just be violated at any time. It's in the atmosphere. How can you fight it?"

In 1993, Powell was working on a master's degree in journalism at the University of North Dakota when she received an offer from the tribal chairman, Richard L. "Jiggers" LaFramboise, to become the editor of a new tribal newspaper. "It was my dream," she recalls. In numerous ways, Powell was the epitome of the new Indian that educators like Janine Pease-Windy Boy have struggled to shape. She was independent and ambitious, well schooled in her tribal culture and language in classes at Turtle Mountain Community College, experienced in the ways of the outer world, and committed to her own community. "I felt lucky," she says. "I thought, 'Things are really changing.'"

There were warnings. Friends told her, "You won't last long. You don't think that you're going to be able to report the news, do you?" Nevertheless, Powell was filled with anticipation as she put out the first issue of the *Turtle Mountain Times*. "It was like going into a no-man's-land," she says. "We were brand-new. No one knew the rules." Typical stories reported on the appointment of a new manager for the tribal casino, the tribe's effort to obtain payments from the federal government under an old treaty, and a sixth-grade class's collection of pennies for a leukemia fund; there were traditional animal stories for small children and regular installments of Norwegian folk tales for the descendants of immigrants who had settled in the area.

Some difficulties were ones she had anticipated, in a community where work styles reflected the habits of the ranch more than those of a newsroom. Sometimes reporters simply failed to show up for work; when they failed to get a story, they were often too shy to call in. The real problems began when Powell ventured to publish a story about several local murders. She learned that one of the victims, a housewife, had gone to the tribal court and told the judge that her husband had threatened to kill her. "The judge laughed at her and sent her home," Powell recalls. Soon afterward, the husband murdered not only the wife but her sister and an uncle, as well. When she tried to dig deeper, she discovered an impenetrable layer of fear. "Everyone knew who did it, but no one was ever prosecuted for it. People were afraid to stand up and speak out. There was so much fear—fear of the authorities, fear of speaking the truth. I began to realize that's just the way people live there."

Increasingly, she began to feel that the tribal government itself was part of the problem. "Reservation politics was very corrupt. It's dog eat dog. It was outrageous." There were allegations that one councilman had built a commercial gym for himself with tribal funds so that he would have something to fall back on if he was defeated for reelection and that certain officials were able to walk into the tribal casino at any time and demand money. "There was no accountability. Everyone got money. It was a way of life."

Like many tribal governments, the government of the Turtle Mountain Band had operated in virtual secrecy for as long as anyone could remember. When Powell sought statistics on drunken driving, both the police and courts simply refused. "I was told 'Where is it written that you have a right to anything?'" Then she began requesting, and eventually demanding, copies of the minutes of council meetings. The council refused, without explanation. In an effort to force the council's hand, Powell began printing a blank gray box in each issue of the paper: "Day 126," it read, for instance, on March 21, 1994. "This space is still reserved for the tribal minutes."

After only eight months on the job, Powell was fired, in April 1994, allegedly because of personality differences with members of her staff. "It's not really a firing," a spokesman for the tribe declared. "It's a reduction in force."[28] In a letter to Powell confirming her dismissal, Chairman LaFramboise stated, "It is very disturbing to find people who are thinking they are professional and only have hidden agendas including manifestations of political grandeur."[29]

"The issue here is not the fact that the Turtle Mountain tribal council fired Ms. Powell; they have that right as an employer, in accordance with established personnel policies," Elmer Savilla, a former director of the National Tribal Chairman's Association, wrote in *Indian Country Today*. "The overriding issue is the responsibility of any tribal government to its people to inform them of its activities. Otherwise the democratic government perishes and is replaced by an autocracy, or worse, a dictatorship."[30]

"In a city, they wouldn't have been allowed to get away with this," says Powell, who returned, if anything emboldened by her experiences at Turtle Mountain, to her graduate studies at the state university. "Too many people there are aware of their rights. A paper is supposed to contain news, to find out what people want to know and give them a voice, give them a sense of empowerment But the council didn't understand that. They thought it would just write good news about them." Somewhat facilely perhaps, she blames the failure of tribal government on the way in which Indians "were taught to copy white government, in all its corrupt, devious systems." But in her determination there lies a kind of hope whose power cannot be underestimated. "People have been hurt so many times, they can't trust any more. Every time a promise was made, it wasn't kept. We live not as our ancestors had planned, but as their worst nightmare, a nation of bureaucrats of the worst kind. We have become so imbalanced in our world that the chances of getting punished for doing a good job are higher than for doing a bad job. If each one should speak out, we could begin to trust each other once again and respect each other for having the courage to try and change."

Superficially, the May 1994 Albuquerque "Listening Conference," as it was rather self-consciously billed by its sponsors, the Departments of Justice and the Interior, provided a spectacle of enlightened official concern.[31] Three members of the President's cabinet—Attorney General Janet Reno, Secretary of the Interior Bruce Babbitt, and Secretary of Housing and Urban Development Henry Cisneros—along with Commissioner of Indian Affairs Ada Deer sat side by side in a stylishly appointed meeting room at the Albuquerque Conference Center, cocking the ear of government both literally and symbolically to the oratory of a hundred or so assembled tribal leaders who had been invited to express their concerns. The conference differed from similar periodic gatherings that take place mostly in Washington only in the lofty credentials of the satraps on the dais, who were determined to show the depth of the new Democratic administration's interest in Indian problems.

For two days, the procession of tribal leaders recited the incantatory formulas of the sovereignty movement. "Sovereignty is a nonnegotiable item," Wendell Chino of the Mescalero Apaches, the longest-serving tribal chairman in the country, declared. He then demanded that President Clinton issue an executive order "so that the whole U.S. knows that we are governments." A spokesman for the Sisseton-Wahpeton Sioux called for Indian affairs to be transferred to the State Department because "the Department of the Interior deals with wildlife, and State deals with governments." Appropriations to tribes, it was asserted by others, should be treated as foreign aid. State and federal courts were called upon to recognize Indian "national" courts for the "extradition" of convicted criminals. The establishment of gambling casinos was described repeatedly as "a fundamental sovereign right," while several speakers called upon the federal government to create an official Indians-only game of chance that would give tribes a permanent competitive edge in the gambling industry. Others demanded the complete ouster of state governments from regulatory oversight and all other aspects of tribal affairs. "Since tribes are governments," Joanne Jones of the Wisconsin Winnebago Tribe said with breathtaking logic, "their activities are thus self-regulating."

There was a monotony to all this after a while, as the dialogue took on the strange, stylized quality that it always does at such affairs, as if Indians and officials had been forever frozen like figures in a Babylonian frieze, facing each other in postures of complaint and defensiveness, rage and guilt, as if it were impossible to consider Indians as anything but beleaguered victims and government as anything but the culpable heir to an unbroken history of deceit and repression. Not a soul spoke about the need to protect the civil rights of individual Indians from their own governments or those of non-Indian residents of "sovereign" reservations No one spoke of the need to ensure a free press, free speech, and separation of powers. No one spoke of the futility of attracting investment to remote reservations without resources, trained workers, transportation, or nearby markets, or asked how Indian tribes might fit into the larger national and world economies. No one spoke of the bloated and expanding tribal bureaucracies or the inherent contradiction in proclaiming "national sovereignty" while relying on federal and state appropriations or about the urgency of finding common cause between tribes and their non-Indian neighbors. No one mentioned the catastrophic effects of alcoholism on Indian economies, governments, and families, or showed even the slightest grasp of the social consequences that may ensue from widespread tribally run gambling. Nor did anyone even hint at the long-term political implications that may one day result from the fact that, by any traditional measurement of ethnicity, Native Americans are rapidly becoming less "Indian" by the decade.

Behind the boilerplate rhetoric of tribal sovereignty, modern Indians are still as difficult to see clearly as the Wiyots of Indian Island were for the nervous townsfolk of Eureka. (The Wiyots were a California tribe who were attacked by their white neighbors.) For the most part, their concerns still come to us like distant voices distorted by the lingering effects of guilt, arrogance, and wishful thinking. For much of American history, the national discourse about Indians has seemed like a kind of intellectual solipsism, a closed dialogue among popular fantasies about a people who are simultaneously "savage," "noble," and "pathetic" and who are forever said to be on the brink of vanishing from the earth. As a result, even the best intentioned efforts to create a place for Indians in American society have sometimes proved disastrous to the very people they were intended to help.

In an age when guilt and romantic fantasy masquerade as politics, tribal sovereignty seems like a panacea for the wounds of the past. However, like so many other hopeful policies that have gone before, along with the obvious benefits it brings tribes, the drive toward sovereign autonomy is freighted with the seeds of potential disaster. Profound questions that bear upon the very nature of the United States itself hovered glaringly unasked in the mauve conference room at Albuquerque: What are the limits of federal powers? How can tribalism be squared with the legal and moral dictates of equal protection under the law? What is the role of the states in Indian Country and of the tribes in the constitutional democracy? What is the scope of tribal regulatory powers? What is the civil jurisdiction of tribal courts? How can the United States support tribal regimes that reject fundamental aspects of American democracy? What does it mean to be a citizen of a state and yet to be immune from its laws? What is the basis for asserting that reservation Indians shall have representation in state government but without taxation? On the other hand, what is the basis for asserting that non-Indian residents of Indian Country shall not be represented in tribal government yet be subject to tribal law, courts, and taxation. How can we, as Americans, tolerate double standards?

There is nothing abstract about such concerns in Glencross, South Dakota. Once, 150 people lived there. There was a railroad station, two schools, three lumberyards, two feed companies. Trucks used to line up twenty deep alongside the grain elevators. "The elevators were right over here, but they're gone now," Steve Aberle is saying in his softly modulated, lawyerly voice. His compact frame and pale, finely boned features accentuate the impression of a man who values efficiency and control; in his business suit and tie, he seems almost spectral amid the desolation. "There was a real nice Catholic church. It's abandoned now. All around here there were dozens of houses. Over there"—pointing to a squat peak-roofed building—"that was a school. And here was the café. They sold up and moved to Texas." Aberle's clapboard house is one of the last three still occupied in Glencross. He likes the emptiness; in his spare time, he plants trees. "It's a good place for my kids. They can raise their own livestock. They get to see how things grow."

It is also an eerie place. Buffalo grass has reconquered the un paved streets. Perfectly aligned tree belts mark the boundaries of farms that no longer exist. The decaying buildings seem too recent, too familiar to be ruins; there is an unsettling sense of witnessing the end of one's own world. How fast it all happened! In the span of a single lifetime a town was born, flourished, shriveled, and died, a monument to the demise, or at least to the ambiguous transformation, of the American West. Nothing breaks the silence, not even the B-1 bomber that streaks soundlessly high over the coppery green prairie toward some destination in another world.

Glencross suffered no special, violent fate. The Great Plains are filled with failed communities like this, which seem to drift like derelict ships upon the rolling hills, sinking before your eyes. Trail City has shrunk from a population of 350 to 30, Firesteel to a single general store; Landeau has disappeared completely. The entire region is hemorrhaging jobs and people.[32] In Dewey County, the only labor market that is expanding is the bureaucracy of the Cheyenne River Sioux Tribe. Six of the neighboring counties have lost half their population since 1930. Fifty of Nebraska's fifty-two Plains counties have lost population, thirty-eight of North Dakota's forty-one, twenty-two of Oklahoma's twenty-three. Entire towns have lost their doctors, banks, and schools. Dreamers speak seriously of returning vast tracts to the buffalo. From a certain angle of vision, Sioux demands for the restoration of the reservation to its original nineteenth-century limits are simply an anticlimax.

Every morning, Aberle drives to the storefront office that he shares with his father across the street from Pepsi's Cafe in Timber Lake, nine miles west of Glencross. The glory days when Indians pledged their allegiance here, as if Timber Lake were some capital city of the prairie, are long past. But there is nonetheless a certain suggestion of steadiness in the cottonwood-lined streets of frame cottages, Quonset huts, and trailers. Timber Lake is one of the lucky places: the presence of the Dewey County offices will keep it alive, along with the jobs at the rural electric co-op, the central school, the cheese factory. Even so, one hundred of the six hundred people who lived here a decade ago have moved away to places with better prospects and more hope.

The people of Timber Lake—the mechanics, the teachers, the co-op clerks, the men who work at the grain elevator, the retired farmers—are the human fruit of allotment, the flesh-and-blood culmination of the cultural blending that Senator Henry L. Dawes so idealistically envisioned a century ago. "Everyone here has got some relatives who are Indian, or a brother or a sister married to an Indian," says Aberle. There is the white nurse who just married a Sioux, and a few houses down from her the quarter-Indian school aide who married a white man; down the block lives Timber Lake's former mayor, who is married to a one-eighth Indian, and beyond him a farmer married to another one-eighth Indian.

Aberle is one of the offspring of the Senator's dream, too. His paternal grandparents were ethnic Germans who fled Russia eighty years ago, family tradition holds, to escape some kind of now only vaguely remembered persecution. His father married a Ducheneaux, the descendant of a prominent clan of French trappers and traders who had intermarried with the Sioux and become powers in the tribe. Steve Aberle, who was born in 1960, is thus one-eighth Sioux; he is a voting member of the tribe and served for two and a half years as chairman of the tribal police commission. "Probably I associate myself more with the Indian quantum because people make more of it. But I don't deny that I'm Russian-German or that I'm part French."

There is little support in Timber Lake for the kind of blanket sovereignty that the tribal leaders in Eagle Butte now claim. Although Aberle is himself a tribe member, he shares the resentment of non-Indians who feel themselves slipping toward a kind of second-class citizenship within reservation boundaries. "It would be better to be in a situation where everybody works together and deals with people as people, but it's hard to do that when people know they pay taxes but are excluded from benefits and services. My grandparents were outcasts in Russia. The United States government told them that they would be full citizens if they moved out here. Now I see people being told that they can't even take part in a government that wants to regulate them. Something is inherently wrong when you can't be a citizen where you live because of your race. It just doesn't fit with the traditional notion of being a U.S. citizen. At some point, there has to be a collision between the notion of tribal sovereignty and the notion of being United States citizens. The people who settled here never had any idea that they would be living on an Indian reservation. The land was given to them fair and square by the government. These people have been here almost one hundred years themselves now. Then the rules were changed in midstream. Anytime you have a group not represented in the political process, they will be discriminated against. It's going to hurt these communities. People start looking for jobs elsewhere. You lose a business here, a business there. There's going to be more and more friction. People don't want to see their kids growing up feeling victimized by the Indians."

In 1994, the Supreme Court rejected the bar owners' last appeal against the Cheyenne River Sioux Tribe. By the following summer the tribe was earning between $15,000 and $17,000 a month in taxes on the sale of alcohol. "Every penny goes to our halfway house and our alcoholism treatment centers," says Gregg Bourland.[33] There were vague though unsubstantiated rumors of Ku Klux Klan activity among disgruntled whites. "The rednecks haven't backed off completely, but they have to follow the law," Bourland says. "Basically, they don't have much choice. They're fully under our regulation."

The Lakotas were the victims of nineteenth-century social engineering that decimated their reservation. But the adventurous emigrants from Oslo and Odessa were also the victims of a terrible historical prank, the trick of the disappearing and now magically reappearing reservation. Their grandchildren are today discovering themselves in a strange new political world that was not of their making, hungry for protection and obliged to learn the new and difficult language of tribal power. It is a rhetoric that, reasonably enough, demands for tribes a degree of self-government that is taken for granted by other Americans; it also asks non-Indians to live under tribal taxation, police, and courts of sometimes dubious reliability. Moreover, the achievement of a sovereignty that drives away taxpayers, consumers, and enterprise may be at best but a pyrrhic victory over withered communities that beg for cooperation and innovation if they are to survive at all.

On a deeper plane, the ideology of sovereignty seems to presume that racial separateness is a positive good, as if Indian bloodlines, economies, and histories were not already inextricably enmeshed with those of white, Hispanic, black, and Asian Americans; it seems to presuppose that cultural purity ought to, or even can, be preserved. With little debate outside the parochial circles of Indian affairs, a generation of policymaking has jettisoned the long-standing American ideal of racial unity as a positive good and replaced it with a doctrine that, seen from a more critical angle, seems disturbingly like an idealized form of segregation, a fact apparently invisible in an era that has made a secular religion of passionate ethnicity. As Arthur Schlesinger has written in *The Disuniting of America:*

> Instead of a transformative nation with an identity all its own, America increasingly sees itself in this new light as a preservative of diverse alien identities. Instead of a nation composed of individuals making their own unhampered choices, America increasingly sees itself as composed of groups more or less ineradicable in their ethnic character.[34]

The belief that Indians are somehow fundamentally different from other Americans, however romantically the idea may be expressed in terms of native "tradition" or magical notions of affinity for the earth, implies a failure of basic American values, for it leads inexorably toward moral acceptance of political entities defined on the basis of racial exclusion. Although the concept of tribal sovereignty has parallels in other ideologies of racial and ethnic separatism, it is potentially far more subversive, for Indian tribes, unlike the nation's other minorities, possess both land and governments of their own and have at least the potential to transform not only their hopes and creativity but also their biases into political power in a way that others never can. It should, moreover, be obvious to anyone that legitimizing segregation for Indians will set a precedent for its potential imposition upon black, Asian, and Hispanic Americans.

Such critical concerns will surely be further exacerbated in the years to come as Indian identity becomes increasingly ambiguous. Virtually all Indians, whether they acknowledge it or not, are moving along a continuum of biological fusion with other American populations. "A point will be reached—perhaps not too far in the future—when it will no longer make sense to define American Indians in generic terms, only as tribal members or as people of Indian ancestry or ethnicity," Russell Thornton, a Cherokee anthropologist based at the University of California at Berkeley and a specialist in native demographics, has written.[35] Statistically, according to Thornton, Indians are marrying outside their ethnic group at a faster rate than any other Americans. Most Indians are already married to non-Indians, and by the late twenty-first century only a minuscule percentage of Native Americans will have one-half or more Indian blood. It is plain that the principle, or the pretense, that blood should be a central defining fact of being Indian will soon become untenable.

How much blending can occur before Indians finally cease to be Indians? Unfortunately, the implications of this dramatic demographic trend remain virtually unexamined. The question is sure to loom ever larger in the coming generations, as the United States increasingly finds itself in "government-to-government" relation ships with "Indian tribes" that are, in fact, becoming less ethnically Indian by the decade. Within two or three generations, the nation will possess hundreds of semi-independent "tribes" whose native heritage consists mainly of autonomous governments and special privileges that are denied to other Americans.

In the meantime, relations between Indian tribes and both the federal and state governments are likely to become more complicated. Increasing control over their sources of revenue will enable more and more tribes—primarily those with marketable natural resources, well-run tribal industries, and proximity to big cities—to achieve some degree of practical autonomy. However, without enlightened leadership and an educated and self-confident electorate, not to mention the collaboration of the federal government, political sovereignty is only a pipe dream. "There's no such thing as being half sovereign any more than there is being half pregnant," says Ramon Roubideaux. "We are only sovereign insofar as the U.S. allows us to be. Sovereignty can only be preserved as long as you have the force to protect it, not just brute force, but political force, too. So unless you have an army, you'd better get used to that. Indians who think differently are just kidding themselves."

The scene on the factory floor of the Choctaw Manufacturing Enterprise, just outside Carthage, Mississippi, is prosaic enough at first glance. Although the building itself is architecturally undistinguished, just a low, white-painted rectangle hard against the cow pastures and pine woods, it is modern and spacious, and well ventilated against the withering summer heat. Inside, workers perch at long worktables, weaving wires onto color-coded boards that will become part of Xerox photocopiers. It is slow work; as many as three hundred wires must go into some of the harnesses and be attached to up to fifty-seven different terminals. Painstakingly, in deft and efficient hands, the brown and green wires are made to join and bifurcate, recombine and intertwine again in runic combinations that to the untutored eye seem as intricate and mysterious as the interwoven clans of the Lumbees. As they work, the long rows, mostly of women, listen like factory hands in similar plants most anywhere in America to the thumping beat of piped-in radio, and swap gossip, and news of children, and of planned trips to Jackson, and menus for dinner. Across the floor, at other similar tables, more women and men are weaving harnesses, assembling telephones, putting together circuit boards for computers, audio speakers, and motors for windshield wipers.

In another sense entirely, the factory floor is remarkable and profound. The faces bent over the wires and phones and speakers record a transformation that no one in Mississippi could have envisioned forty years ago, when Phillip Martin came home from Europe looking for some kind of job. The faces are mostly Choctaw, but among them are white and black faces, too, scores of them, all side by side in what was once one of the poorest backwaters of a state that was second to none in its determination to keep races and classes apart.

In 1989, there were four Choctaws in the plant's management; now there are twenty-five. "The next generation will be able to manage their own businesses," says Sam Schisler, the plant manager, a freckled Ohioan in mauve trousers and a navy-blue polo shirt who joined the Choctaws after running plants for Packard Electric. "I'm happy to manage myself out of a job." There is also something more. The audio speakers whose parts have been imported from Thailand and the circuit boards that have came from Shreveport are not glamorous, but they are symbolic: the children of the sharecroppers for whom a visit to Philadelphia, Mississippi, was a major undertaking have begun to become part of the larger world. "We'll be building these ourselves at some point," Schisler says.

The plant, the humid pastures, and the pine woods lack the drama of the rolling prairie and the sagebrush desert that are the more familiar landscape of Indian Country. But the red clay of Neshoba County has endured the same trials as the soil of Pine Ridge, the Truckee basin, and the Little Big Horn. It has been equally warred over, and equally as stained with racism, ineradicably one might have said, until less than a generation ago. It is also a land of redemption; not the exotic redemption of evangelical traditionalists who would lead Indians in search of an ephemeral Golden Age that never was, but a more prosaic and sustainable redemption of a particularly American kind, which comes with the opportunity to work a decent job and know that one's children will be educated and that the future will, all things being equal, probably be better than the past. It is one culmination of a natural and perhaps inevitable human process of adaptation that Indians have been choosing to undertake ever since the arrival of Columbus.

History was, after all, not only a story of wars, removals, and death but also one of calculated compromises and deliberately chosen risks and of both Indian communities and individuals continually remaking themselves in order to survive. To see change as failure, as some kind of cultural corruption, is to condemn Indians to solitary confinement in a prison of myth that whites invented for them in the first place. In the course of the past five centuries, Indian life has been utterly transformed by the impact of European horses and firearms, by imported diseases and modern medicine, by missionary zeal and Christian morality, by iron cookware, sheepherding, pickup trucks, rodeos and schools, by rum and welfare offices, and by elections, alphabets, and Jeffersonian idealism as well as by MTV, *Dallas*, and *The Simpsons* and by the rich mingling of native bloodlines with those of Europe, Africa, and the Hispanic Southwest. In many ways, the Indian revolution of the 1990s is itself a form of adaptation, as Indians, freed from the lockstep stewardship of Washington, search out new ways to live in the modern world.

"Our lives have been transmuted, changed forever," Rayna Green, who is of mixed Cherokee extraction and director of the Native American Program at the Museum of American History, said in a speech at the New York Public Library in 1993.[36] "We live in a world where everything is mutable and fragile. But we are here, and we are not going to go away. Indians look around at the malls and stores of

America, and say, 'None of this is ever going to be ours.' But none of it is going to go away either. This is still our home. We are all here willy-nilly together. Somehow we must face the consequences of history and live with it. We don't need only to remember the tragedy, but to also remember the gift, to live in this place, to know it gave us birth, to feel the responsibility we have for it. We have to sit down and figure out how to not hurt each other any more."

Self-determination gives Indian tribes the ability to manage the speed and style of integration, but not the power to stop it, at least for long. Integration may well mean the eventual diminishing of conventional notions of "tribal identity," but it must also bring many new individual opportunities along with membership in the larger human community. Those tribes that succumb to the impulse to exclude and to segregate, to build walls against the outside world, are likely to pay a high price. "People and their cultures perish in isolation, but they are born or reborn in contact with other men and women, with man and woman of another culture, another creed, another race," the Mexican author Carlos Fuentes has written. Indians will continue to survive as people, although they will surely be much less recognizable as the white man's idea of "Indians" as time goes on. Tribes, too, will survive, if anything as stronger and more problematic entities than they have been for many generations. The question is whether they will attempt to survive as islands isolated from the American mainstream or as vital communities that recognize a commonality of interest and destiny with other Americans.

"I don't like what this country did to the Indians: it was all ignorance based on more ignorance based on greed," Phillip Martin is saying in his meditative drawl. It is now past 11:00 p.m. The night shift has begun at the plants down the hill from the tribal offices. Outside, in the humid moonlight of east Mississippi, the red earth is a landscape of shadows and the kudzu an eerie shroud over the pines. "But I don't believe that you have to do what others did to you. Ignorance is what kept us apart. But we'd never have accomplished what we did if we'd taken the same attitude. We only have a short time to live on this earth. Everybody has got to get along somehow. We live here surrounded by non-Indians. We have to live with our neighbors and with our community. I don't condemn anyone by race. What kept us down was our own lack of education, economy, health care—we had no way of making a living. At first, I never thought that Choctaws could fit into the larger society and remain Choctaw. But, in fact, we don't have to give up our language, our culture, or our traditions. I believe that if we're going to fit in this country, we'd better try our best to do it on our own terms. If we can help local non-Indian communities in the process, we do it. And when we do it, we build up a lot of political and social support. We all have a common cause here: the lack of jobs and opportunities has kept everyone poor and ignorant. The future is going to bring a lot of change for everyone. It's going to be very difficult for a tribe to isolate itself and develop its own economy. We all depend on one another, whether we realize it or not."

NOTES

N.B.: This article was based in part on interviews with the following individuals: Phillip Martin, Harlan Majors, Robert Benn, Lester Dalme, Sam Schisler, William Richardson, Choctaw reservation, Mississippi, June 1999; Dennis Hastings, Macy, Nebraska, May 1991; Vicki Hutchinson, Isabel, South Dakota, July 1999; Ivan Makil, Salt River Pima-Maricopa reservation, Arizona, November 1991; Ramon Roubideux, Rapid City, South Dakota, July 1999; Steve Aberle, Glencross, South Dakota, July 1999; John Chapela, Gallup, New Mexico, November 1991; Robin Powell and Elmer Savilla, by telephone, November 1994.

1. Telephone interview with William Richardson, June 1995.

2. Interview with the author.

3. Carolyn K. Reeves, ed., *The Choctaw Before Removal*, 6–19.

4. Ibid., 34, 40.

5. Interview with Bob Ferguson, tribal historian, June 1992.

6. Speech by Phillip Martin to the annual meeting of the Association on American Indian Affairs, May 12, 1986.

7. Francis Prucha, *American Indian Treaties*, 230–31.

8. Quoted in ibid., 230.

9. Ibid., 939.

10. Mark N. Trahant et al., "Fraud in Indian Country," *Arizona Republic*, October 4, 1987; also, "Indian Country," *Arizona Republic*, January 21,1990. Of the $3 billion in direct federal spending on Indians each year, approximately $1 billion each is spent by the Bureau of Indian Affairs and the Indian Health Service. The remainder is spread among many federal agencies, with the largest amounts being appropriated by the departments of Education, Housing and Urban Development, and Agriculture. An additional $3 billion in profits from the management of properties held in trust by the federal government is also transferred to Indians each year.

11. Charles Wilkinson, *American Indians, Time, and the Law*, (New Haven: Yale University Press, 1987), 4–5.

12. Quoted in "Standing Ovation for Deer," *Indian Country Today*, July 21, 1993.

13. The narrative of events is based partly on interviews with tribal councilmen Duane "Chili" Yazzie and Daniel Tso, local journalists Mark Trahant and Betty Reid, and BIA counsel Tom O'Hara, in Window Rock, Arizona, 1991, and with journalist Bill Donovan and John Chapela, a prominent Navajo lawyer, in Gallup, New Mexico, November 1991.

14. MacDonald's remarkable life story is recounted in detail in his autobiography, *The Last Warrior* (New York: Crown, 1993).

15. As quoted by Bill Donovan to the author.

16. Trahant, op. cit.; "Extravagance, Hint of Scandal in Mark MacDonald's Leadership," *Arizona Republic*, January 15, 1989.

17. *Final Report of the Special Committee on Investigations of the Select Committee on Indian Affairs of the United States Senate*, 1989, 183–91.

18. Ibid., 191–97.

19. Tribal council minutes, February 14, 1989.

20. Ibid.

21. Quoted in Ibid.

22. Ibid.

23. Ibid., February 17, 1989.

24. Ibid.

25. Ibid.

26. *The Navajo Nation v. Peter MacDonald*, April 13, 1989; also interview with Tom Tso, chief justice of the Navajo Supreme Court, November 1991.

27. "White Earth Woman Says She Forged Election Ballots," *News from Indian Country*, October 1990; "Alex Lunderman Out at Rosebud," *Lakota Times*, May 20, 1992; "Crow Creek Chairman Welcomes Investigation," *Lakota Times*, April 15, 1992; "Normalcy Slowly Returning" (to Pyramid Lake), *Nevada Appeal*, May 25, 1993; also *Final Report of the Special Committee on Investigations*, op. cit., 198–202.

28. Quoted in "Newspaper Editor Canned by Council," *Indian Country Today*, April 6, 1994.

29. Letter from Richard LaFramboise to Robin Powell, April 8, 1994.

30. "It's the People's Right to Know," *Indian Country Today*, May 18, 1994.

31. The description of the conference is based on the author's notes.

32. Data are from Frank J. Popper and Deborah E. Popper, "The Future of the Great Plains" (draft paper); and Frank J. Popper, "The Strange Case of the Contemporary American Frontier," *Yale Review*, Autumn 1986. The changing rural culture of the Great Plains is vividly chronicled by Richard Critchfield in *Trees, Why Do You Wait?*

33. Telephone interview with Gregg J. Bourland, July 1995.

34. Arthur M. Schlesinger, Jr., *The Disuniting of America: Reflections on a Multicultural Society* (1988), 16.

35. Thornton, *American Indian Holocaust and Survival: A Population History Since 1492* (Norman, 1987), 236–37.

36. Quote by Rayna Green from author's notes.

21

Ever since Christopher Columbus, Europeans in America have been collecting information about Indians in order to write, as "Indian experts," the reports, books, and articles that disseminate this information. A little over century ago, as Frederick Hoxie's essay mentioned, this sort of gathering became more formal with the development of anthropology as a discipline. Few scholars then, and few enough since, have paused to consider the ethical implications of their endeavors, the wider consequences—especially for their Native "subjects"—of such research and writing. In this chapter Vine Deloria, Jr., the most prolific Native American nonfiction writer during the last generation and a lifelong advocate of Indian rights, reflects on the tangled, troubled relationship between Indians and scholars.

Deloria's principal concern is how research and writing can benefit tribal communities. He points out the need for accuracy, of course, but more important, he asserts, scholars must establish a mutually beneficial relationship with the tribes they study. In addition, Deloria suggests how tribes might guide future research through the establishment of committees that would select "Master Scholars" and by developing better access to sources of research funds. Even in academe, the federal government looms large; Deloria insists that Indians should be the "constituents" of foundations and government grant agencies, not their "clients."

Deloria's essay appeared when discussion of such issues was prominent. Just one year earlier, in 1990, Congress passed the Native American Graves Protection and Repatriation Act (NAGPRA), which mandated that each museum inform tribes about artifacts in its collections and that it return ("repatriate") to these groups the human remains and other specified objects are in its care. NAGPRA also established the National Museum of the American Indian (NMAI) as part of the Smithsonian Institution. Together these actions help establish the context for Deloria's words. Tribes had succeeded in gaining the attention of museums, and a new institution had been created that would constitute an ideal locus for collaborative intellectual exchange. The moment had come for another look at the relationship between Native Americans and those who study them. Whether one agrees with all of Deloria's arguments—Who would decide when a particular tribe or custom had been sufficiently studied? Could Indians, or scholars, agree on a list of Master Scholars?—none can deny that better communication between Indians and scholars would benefit both.

Vine Deloria, Jr.

Discussion of the ethics of social research has increased significantly in recent years. We have fine taxonomies of the field and, most important, Indians are beginning to make clear some of their interests and concerns in arenas where they are being heard. It would be hazardous for me to wade into this thicket now without a complete knowledge of the arguments and findings that compose the subject matter of the field. However, since a chapter in *Custer Died For Your Sins* dealing with the attitude of Indians toward anthropologists was at least partially responsible in identifying some of the themes now under discussion, I find it impossible to avoid offering some additional comments lest it appear that I have abandoned the argument. My comments in this essay will be restricted to observations and reflections of a personal nature, however, and I will not try to provide a comprehensive analysis of the present state of Indian-scholar/researcher relations.

Ackerman, Burkhalter, and Echo Hawk[1] offer a reasonably comprehensive survey of the literature in the field, and some of their points are not only well taken but cry out for additional commentary and expansion. Scientists must not only keep abreast of the developments in the area of ethical and professional behavior but, I believe, must be prepared to take certain additional steps to protect themselves from unjustified and unwarranted attacks and, more important, from the necessity of bearing burdens that are not rightfully their own. It is almost commonplace today in many Indian communities to identify the intrusive researcher as an "anthro," and to allow the cumulative resentments against these intruders to be lodged against anthropologists alone while letting freelance writers, bureaucratic educators, economists, and religious groupies go scot free.

My original complaint against researchers was that they seem to derive all the benefits and bear no responsibilities for the way in which their findings are used. In making this accusation I said that scholars should be required to put something back into the Indian community, preferably some form of financial support so the community can do a few things it wants to do. In the past two decades all manner of researchers have arrived in Indian country, and they have written some terrible stuff. Their excuse when entering a reservation is that they are not "anthros" but have arrived to find out the "real truth" about Indian life. By distinguishing themselves from anthropologists, these characters find they have a free hand, and so they gather material, often stories that even the worst-trained social scientists would recognize as

Source: *American Indian Quarterly*, v. 15, n. 4, pp. 457–468.

gossip, and write their version of Indian life. They even advertise on their book jackets that their version is true and has avoided the pitfalls and mistakes of the trained social scientist. Through carefully orchestrated publicity campaigns their books are touted as the "first real" look behind the buckskin curtain—and these writings in some cases push out the scholarly work.

Two popular writers come to mind in this respect: Ruth Beebe Hill and Peter Matthiessen. Mrs. Hill made extravagant claims about her book *Hanta Yo*, and as a result it was purchased for thousands of school libraries. She alleged to have written it in the "original" Sioux language extant before the missionaries put the sounds and symbols together to form vocabularies and dictionaries. Hill deliberately interpreted Sioux customs as an extreme form of individualism and spiced the book with exotic sexual practices that horrified traditional people on the Sioux reservations. She utterly gutted all substance in the kinship tradition and reduced the Sioux religion to a bizarre mysticism that few people of any existing human culture would recognize. The book was advertised as a new and corrective version of Sioux culture that undid the wrongs done by scholars. Even Mrs. Hill's Indian informant turned out to have an exotic checkered past that bore no relationship to the actual and factual events of his own life.

Matthiessen seemed to have a point of view long before he visited Indian country, and his travels through the reservations appear to be only for the purpose of verifying his suspicions and obtaining some factual items for inclusion in his book. He seemed completely incapable of knowing when he was being given facts and when he was hearing gossip. He nearly involved his Indian friends in a costly and prolonged lawsuit over some statements he made about a prominent western politician. When describing existing tribal government and their elected officials, Matthiessen had an ingrained hostility and seemed to be saying that an immediate reversion to traditional forms of government would solve all contemporary Indian problems. Indian history under Matthiessen became a monstrous conspiracy with few respectable motives and not the slightest recognition that times had changed since the people went onto the reservations. Indeed, few people of genuine good will are to be found in any of Matthiessen's rendering of government, church, school, or corporate relationships with Indians. How all of these people could have formed a century-long conspiracy and carried it out with such efficiency remains a mystery that he does not answer.

In the short term, it can be argued that these books did a great deal to bring needed public attention to Indian affairs. But a popular potboiler is carried along on its own momentum, and people get its message as much from word-of-mouth as from actual reading. After the commotion had subsided, the book remains in the library where naive and uninformed people will read it for a decade to come. These people know only that the book was once popular and assume that it has withstood all the challenges to its veracity that can be made. So they take the content of the book as proven and derive their knowledge of Indians from it. Over the long term, therefore, these books are extremely harmful to Indians because they perpetuate a mass of misinformation and improper interpretations for another generation of readers. Additionally, popular writers rarely return anything to the Indian community. Ruth Beebe Hill in fact spent much of her time attacking contemporary Indians and telling them that they were but pale imitations of their ancestors.

Scholarly writings, on the other hand, withstand the test of time very well. They do phrase their explanations in the terms and styles of the scholarship of their times, and in some instances this format makes it difficult for modern readers to understand. But on the whole they provide us with the best information on subjects that would otherwise remain obscure. Walker, for example, places the Sioux experiences of power and divinity in a rigid history-of-religions framework and creates a hierarchy where there is no need to do so. But his efforts to describe the various manifestations of sacred power have considerably more substance than much of what passes for explanations of the same subject matter today. Additionally, there exists within the scholarly community a continuing dialogue, so that a scholar who steps too far beyond the line of credibility faces a challenge from within the scholarly community that is understood as a necessary corrective to protect the integrity of the discipline.

Indians are not allowed this luxury of complaining about the misrepresentations of their culture. When *Hanta Yo* was being well received by the reading public, many Indians, including the Rosebud Sioux Medicine Men's Association, lodged major complaints against it, citing numerous mistakes of fact and interpretation and deploring the misuse of language in explaining the major ideas of the Sioux. The author promptly accused the Sioux of both not knowing their own culture and of being insanely jealous of her success. These accusations, although entirely fictional, carried the day against the Sioux, making it evident that popularity, not accuracy, was the standard by which the content of the book should be judged.

Today there are numerous popular writers either claiming to be Indian or alleging that the last medicine man or woman in the tribe has designated them, rather than a tribal member, to be the final authority on culture and religion. One imposter even alleges, when caught plagiarizing, that he did not have final editing privileges on his manuscript, implying that after he had submitted the final draft of his book, his editor took down one of the existing classics of the field and promptly inserted several pages of material.

Scholars may complain that becoming involved in the criticism of popular writing has no ethical implications, and certainly no one would want a committee of scholars to function as a censorship board. But there is a necessity for scholars to find a way to distinguish themselves from others who purport to have knowledge of Indians and who generally intrude upon the province of scholarship by insisting that their work contains the same degree of care and accuracy as does social science research. Much of the value of the cumulative production of social scientists is the standard of scholarship it represents. American Indians are rapidly losing their languages, and the oral tradition is fading very vast in this generation. Instead of gathering around the elders in the evening to hear stories of the tribal past, children today rent a videotape and watch *Star Wars* or horror films. With few exceptions, scattered in obscure parts of the reservations, the best place to get accurate information about tribal beliefs and practices today is the library or archives. Whether we will admit it or not, American Indians have become a literate people. Consequently scholars must work ever closer to Indians in order to help us distinguish between accurate and approved information about the tribe and the popular drivel that increasingly comes to represent Indians.

Here Indians and scholars find themselves as close working partners. Each group has a duty to the generations to come to make certain that they have a culture, way of life, and set of beliefs that correctly reflect the generations that have gone before. No one is suggesting that Indians "revert" to the old days or old ways. Rather we must be able to understand what those old days and ways really were and model our present actions and beliefs within that tradition. Scholars have an equal responsibility here because the essence of scholarship is its cumulative effect on a subject of investigation. It is the cooperative effort of generations of good scholars that we must protect, not the individual efforts of a few scholars in authority or positions of prestige.

Somehow a new vehicle for Indian/scholar communication must be established, and this vehicle must lead to some nationally recognized committee, board, or council that can speak out on matters of importance to Indians and scholars alike. Credentials in Indian matters must depend upon more than a sincere interest, a tube of ManTan and a wig, or a lucrative book contract. It seems to me that the ethical issue is clear: We must protect the corpus of work that has been done and ensure that work contemplated or presently being conducted is recognized for its quality and accuracy. Apart from this kind of protection, I can see no useful purpose for any additional research or writing on Indians, other than as a form of entertainment. The justification for research is that it provides us with information that did not previously exist or that existed but in unusable form. If research is indistinguishable from the fiction and fantasy that pervade Indian affairs, there is no good reason to do much more than statistical abstracts and demographic studies.

Protection of the corpus of knowledge raises the question of whether we need to continue research in Indian communities at all. After several centuries of investigation and publication of an immense body of information, what further needs to be done? We can, I would suppose, synthesize existing studies and offer a corrective in the emphasis placed on certain kinds of interpretations previously given to Indian materials. But the need for any profound or prolonged study of an Indian community by people from the outside seems to be artificial and fruitless. For some tribes we do not know a whole lot about past cultural practices, and for other tribes we seem to know so much that our studies bump into each other. How many additional studies are going to be needed, or wanted, on the Oglala Sun Dance? Enthusiasts for these kinds of repetitive studies are often people who have recently entered the field and have the energy and zeal of a newcomer. For those who are acquainted with the subject and the literature of the field, each new study that plows old ground is boring and stirs up considerable resentment.

If we are going to bring some kind of order out of this chaos, we certainly need a prestigious panel of scholars to survey what has been done and to identify subjects and tribes that might benefit from additional research. A survey would enable both scholars and tribal leaders to gain some sense of perspective on what information exists about the group so that certain kinds of projects could be fruitfully undertaken. Publication of the survey could be made widely available to tribal leadership and Indian scholars, and they should be encouraged to respond to the survey in the most constructive manner possible. Now that we have many tribal museums and a national organization of Indian museums, there is no reason not to use this generation of Indian curators as the cultural voice of tribal concerns. They need not allege any expertise in traditionalism, since they represent the historic concern of the rank and file of the tribe in portraying everything that the tribe has experienced.

Apart from restoring and renewing the old practices through systematic and concentrated research, there is a great and pressing need for research on the contemporary affairs and conditions of Indians. Using science to assist in solving contemporary problems is a major Indian concern, but finding the proper vehicle for doing so presents many seemingly insuperable barriers. Tribal concerns and scholarly concerns do not always match when we look at present research. The expansion of professional fields to produce many related subfields makes it virtually impossible for Indians to find the proper scholar to assist them. And many scholars find it necessary to retool themselves in order to keep pace with the demands of their field. Thus an anthropologist as such is a very rare bird. Rather we have ethnologists, ethnohistorians, ethnomusicologists, and so forth. The academic arena is often as bewildering to the people in it as it is to Indians, and there do not seem to be any good guidelines for locating good scholars and using them for tribal purposes.

We need to have some method of identifying capable scholars and avoiding people whose only expertise seems to be grantsmanship. A good deal of the research done today that is distasteful to Indian people is not done by good scholars but by academic hustlers who have access to funds. I have reviewed many grant proposals that dealt with Indians, and the claims of expertise made by grant applicants is appalling. People allege that they have books under contract that do not exist; they cite a collection of essays as an original work when their only contribution may be an eight-page essay; they inflate the importance of an administrative job completely out of proportion. Indians do not have the background to realize that scholarly vitas and proposals must be taken with a very critical eye. The academic community does very little to disrupt this condition. Professional reputations may suffer in the little conversations at annual meetings but there is a solid conspiracy of silence when it is necessary to identify poor or bad scholarship for public consumption and understanding.

No one is asking the scholarly professions to attack the poor scholars by name or hold courts of inquisition to prevent certain academic fringe personalities from raising money or establishing institutes. However, the public does need to be protected from the waste and misuse of research resources by academic hustlers. We can accomplish this task by creating a new prestigious ranking within the various disciplines and thereby identify and elevate the capable scholars from the rank and file who are also in the game. I would suggest a designation of "Master Scholar" for a certain number of people whose academic accomplishments are impeccable.

It would not be difficult, for example, for a committee of social scientists to designate a dozen scholars as "Master Scholars" on the Sioux, Navajo, Hopi, Pueblos, and so forth. This designation would help Indian people learn to identify scholars who have made and are making a significant contribution to our understanding. It would create a prestige status within the discipline and encourage quality work by all scholars. Personally, I am infuriated when I am asked to review a research proposal and find a third-rate person on the verge of getting a half-million-dollar grant to study the Sioux when I can name at least twenty scholars of greater competence who have not been considered or consulted on the project.

Master Scholar designation could be a status conferred by a joint committee of recognized authorities in the field and Indian tribes and communities who can testify as to the scholar's status and contributions to the community. The list of Master Scholars can be made available to Indian communities who wish to undertake research that is needed by their people. Use of the list would resolve one of the present problems of tribes. Many tribal officials simply go to the nearest state college or university and take whatever scholar is willing to listen to them. Some of the worst studies done on reservations were the product of less-than-willing scholars at local colleges who had neither the resources nor the supporting libraries to do an adequate job but who felt an obligation to do something to assist the tribes.

The listing of Master Scholars might assist both Indians and scholars in breaking the funding bottleneck that presently hampers significant research. It is an open secret that the different federal agencies have their own list of favorite grantees and that, regardless of how objective their screening and review process may seem, the same people and institutions generally get grants over and over while more competent scholars are never funded. Federal agencies seem to have an "old boy" network that strives to find inadequate and incompetent scholars and floods them with funds. One comes to suspect that the Roman Hruska admonition, "Mediocre people need representation also," has now become the watchword for many federal agencies. With a list of Master Scholars the selection process for grants would have to become more objective, since an agency would have to give some good reason for "wiring" a grant around the best people in the field in order to give it to some incompetent friend.

Private funding sources, particularly the large foundations, have a sporadic record of successes. A foundation will give several good grants and then change its policy and direction, and for the next several years its funding pattern will reflect complete confusion and an ignorance of the field in which it alleges to be working. There is not nearly the "old boy" network in research that there is in community development or civil and constitutional rights among the larger foundations, but anyone who looks at the funding grants of private foundations over a ten- or twenty-year period will see little evidence of the rational mind at work. Somehow private foundations find little comfort in funding basic research and prefer pilot projects that they wistfully expect federal agencies to pick and support permanently. So designation of Master Scholars may not have much impact on their funding habits. But it could, on the other hand, encourage some foundations to take the first step in this area.

No professional society or academic discipline can make any fundamental changes in the ethics of funding sources because of the intense pressure on scholars to raise funds for colleges and universities. Two decades ago a scholar was valuable to a university because he or she was regarded as an expert in his or her discipline. Today academic status is largely determined by the amount of dollars that the scholar hustles. The more dollars, the more overhead university administrators have to squander. Competition between scholars for scarce research dollars will certainly inhibit any efforts by disciplines and professional societies to exercise a measure of self-restraint and ethical behavior. Yet much of the ethical question in research originates in the funding source and not in the scholar. Something must be done about this situation, because funding sources largely determine *who* is going to be the subject or research and *what* is going to be investigated. Until both scholars and Indians have clearly in mind the role and influence of the funding source, determining a code of ethics for the scholarly researcher is a little extraneous.

With federal agencies representing the single greatest source of research funding, the power equation has shifted from both the scholars and Indians to government bureaucrats. Not only is this group of people singularly incapable of making intelligent decisions on research in Indian communities, but for the most part these people are unable to decide what the relationship between Indians and their agencies should be. Most federal agencies hold their grant funds until quite late in the fiscal year before they announce their awards. Some agencies hold funds until almost the last minute and then quickly shove grants out the back door to their friends and clients. Consequently many research projects are not even well-considered efforts; they are designed primarily to spend the federal funds, not to learn anything that would be helpful to the Indian community. Indians are left with the choice of cooperating with the project or trying to frustrate it. The famous Havinghurst education study is an example of this kind of grant making. Indians were called to Penn State for an education conference to determine the feasibility of doing something in the field of Indian education. During the conference they learned, entirely by accident, that a study had already been authorized and that the conference was only designed to make it appear that Indians had been consulted on it.

Federal agencies presumably have some constituency that they represent but which is never clearly identified. It may be the law under which they are authorized to spend money, or the congressional committees that supervise their operations, or the administration's policy conceived in very broad terms. Indians, for some reason, never appear as a federal constituency but always as federal clients. The difference should be clear: constituents receive benefits, while clients are recipients of largesse depending upon their eligibility for the program. Clients are always viewed at a subsistence level, while constituents are expected to build their own interests and investments with each grant. One need only survey the multitude of so-called "Indian education" centers at various state universities to understand how federal funding agencies have distinguished between their clients and their constituents.

The corollary of the federal funding problem is the audience of the report. Many times the reports are designed to show that the agency is not doing as much as it could because of inadequate funding, or that the problem that it is commissioned to address is much greater than suspected. With some few and notable exceptions, research done for federal agencies is designed to enhance the image and expand the task of the agency. Congress and its appropriations committees are presumably the audience to be addressed by much of the current research. Indian communities, therefore, almost always find themselves described in derogatory terms regardless of the progress they believe they have made and seen around them. The reports inevitably become a matter of internal tribal politics because they demonstrate the lack of progress that the tribe had made under its current leadership. Additionally, Indians are taught to view themselves as the lowest group on the scale of social indicators. It seems as if they have been condemned to be deprived, and this feeling, coupled with the sense of historical betrayal by the government, generates a constant attitude of complaints and focuses the source of the solution on federal and foundation funding rather than the community's innate strengths and resources. People often become overwhelmed by the description of their problem and look helplessly to Washington for answers. In time people believe that only by formal programming of their problems can anything be solved.

One of the questions raised by Ackerman and colleagues is whether the scientist should help the community in ways totally independent of the project. Initially I argued that the researchers should be required to raise a sum of money equal to the project budget to be given to the community. This measure was drastic and is today completely unworkable, but when I described the plan there was sufficient flexibility in funding sources that it was not a completely unrealistic suggestion. Today, as we purchase $800 toilet seats for the military and $7,000 coffee pots for airlines, it is unrealistic to expect the scientist to be able to raise any more than his or her budget, and sometimes even the original budget must be drastically reduced in order to do research. Yet there must be some way that scientists can make a contribution to the communities they study that will go beyond the impact of their research.

Many tribes today have their own museums and archives and a number have their own community colleges. These new institutions need resources of an entirely different kind than tribes have ever needed. Most of all, they need to be connected to the proper networks in the larger society that grant status and recognition. One way that scientists can materially assist Indian institutions is to offer to participate in some of their programs. Several anthropologists have recently taught an evening course at a reservation community college as their effort to contribute something to the community that they have been researching. Adjunct and cooperating professorships can be worked out that will prove useful to the Indian institution and place the scholar on a better footing if he or she wants to continue working with the community. Scientists should not appear to be unduly influencing the Indian institution, since there is a great tendency among Indians to view with suspicion overtures made with too much enthusiasm. People will feel that the scholar is "taking over" and will become at first inhibited in their actions and then resentful, so some discretion must be used in offering assistance. Nevertheless, if a reservation institution is accorded some recognition by representatives of the scholarly community it gains immeasurably in the esteem of the tribe, the surrounding white population, and the funding agencies.

We have reached the subject of the researcher's personality and the community's perception of the scholar. A good deal of the negative view of researchers originates in the scholar's sincere effort to relate to the community. Naturally nervous and wondering if he or she will be accepted by the Indians, the researcher often makes special effort to show how well prepared or knowledgeable he or she is about the tribe's history, culture, and present conditions. Sometimes, although not frequently, the researcher will mention a subject that cannot or should not be discussed profanely. More often, however, demonstration of an intimate knowledge of the community will be perceived as the researcher setting him- or herself up as an authority on the community, as seeking to gain some leverage by appearing to be one of the community elders. Young people in particular seem to resent this kind of behavior. It only reminds them that the researcher has the luxury of studying the community as an object of science, whereas the young Indian, who knows the nuances of tribal life, receives nothing in the way of compensation or recognition for his knowledge, and instead must continue to do jobs, often manual labor, that have considerably less prestige. If knowledge of the Indian community is so valuable, how can non-Indians receive so much compensation for their small knowledge and Indians receive so little for their extensive knowledge?

The nuisance threshold for researchers is not high and seems to be getting lower and lower as Indian communities reflect on their lot. A fundamental questions exists in this respect. Does the researcher really know enough about the subject of investigation, or are his or her questions simply a means of self-orientation to the community? Often questions are embarrassingly naive and harmless, but they indicate an absence of understanding so profound that the scholar is no longer taken seriously and the information he or she seeks is not forthcoming. Better preparation would help to resolve this question, but the simple fact remains that social scientists often have a disagreeable personality and a built-in sense of arrogance about what they do know. Just as professional athletes seem to glory in physical strength and skills, so social scientists seem unable to resist demonstrating their knowledge of the human animal and its communities. Perhaps it is an occupational hazard, the fact remains that the researcher, *because he or she appears as a scientist*, bears the burden of past mistakes of the species, and consequently special care must be taken when showing knowledge of the community to avoid being perceived as a person insensitive to the community's own sense of identity.

We can sum up the various ethical concerns with a few general observations. First, serious researchers need to begin to establish a more precise identity with respect to Indian communities in order to accomplish several goals: (1) to distinguish serious research from popular writing, (2) to minimize bad science and bad or useless research, and (3) to provide some way that Indians and scholars can gain a little more leverage over funding sources and their agendas. Second, we need to eliminate useless or repetitive research and focus on actual community needs; it is both unethical and wasteful to plow familiar ground continually. Third, research should have some definite relationship to the community and its growing institutions, and here scholars can help Indians link themselves with the larger academic and scientific world. Finally, researchers should establish reasonably clear guidelines so that their existing knowledge about communities is not perceived as establishing themselves as authorities in defiance of the community wishes and identity.

The major problem today, at least as I see it, is the inability of funding sources to establish clear agendas so that research is useful to both scholars and Indian communities. This problem will require a new sense of ethical behavior by funding sources and perhaps even a new sense of identity among grant makers. Only a coalition between Indians and scholars can bring this ethical dimension into being by establishing their own higher standards of behavior and cooperative endeavor. Indians and scholars must now perceive themselves to be members of a higher moral order that is truly seeking knowledge in order to succeed.

NOTE

1. Alan Ackerman, Barton R. Burkhalter, and Marlene Echo Hawk, "Suggestions to Tribal Leaders and Scientists to Improve the Utility and Acceptance of Research." Paper presented at the Annual Meeting of the Society for Applied Anthropology, Reno, Nevada, March 28, 1986.

22

Future historians might someday conclude that passage of the American Indian Gaming Regulatory Act in 1988 was the most significant event in Native American history during the late twentieth century. Largely overlooked or downplayed by experts, this law confirmed a 1987 decision by the U.S. Supreme Court that recognized a tribal right to operate gaming establishments. The new law also established procedures to govern these establishments; the most significant of these is the requirement that reservation governments intending to establish casinos must enter into a regulatory compact with the states where they are located. Tribal gaming operations began gradually, but, as Joseph Jorgenson here explains, they grew dramatically in the 1990s. In 1997, the last year for which reliable figures are available, 235 tribal casinos generated gross revenues above $6 billion, more than double the total federal appropriations for Indian affairs.

Jorgensen writes candidly about his early belief that casinos would not be significant sources of economic growth for Indian communities. As late as 1994, he thought that these enterprises would saturate the limited market for gambling and be quickly undermined by self-serving non-Indian managers or by rivals who would tie them up in court. Moreover, Jorgensen confesses, he could not imagine how casinos could overcome problems he had previously identified in his studies of Indian economic activity: geographical isolation and lack of access to capital. His previous work had convinced him that reservation communities had no assets other than their land, water, and mineral resources, and that private lenders would not use these as collateral since they are formally held in trust by the federal government.

Jorgensen's brief overview of the recent history of Indian gaming provides powerful evidence that his doubts were misplaced. The Indian Gaming Act's requirement that joint ventures with non-Indian enterprises could last only five years seems to have prevented outsiders from taking over tribal casinos. Public scrutiny and pressure from tribal members seem to have prevented widespread corruption. Most important, casino gambling proved so popular that private lenders have been willing to lend money to tribes with little collateral other than the Indian Gaming Act. Problems have arisen with gambling addiction, crime, and struggles with state governments over the details of gaming pacts, but none of these have slowed the growth of casino revenues.

Jorgensen's candor and his tardy enthusiasm for Indian gaming leave us with some serious questions. Does gaming constitute an exception to the failures that have dogged reservation economic development schemes over the last century? Can this new industry overcome the political weakness and geographical isolation of many tribes? Can Indian gaming continue to attract customers? Can the uneven nature of the industry—with several small tribes earning far more than larger, more isolated tribes—be overcome so that Indians themselves might remain united in support of gaming? And can tribes reinvest their profits in more sustainable enterprises? In short, was Jorgensen really wrong to predict the ultimate demise of gaming? It is also worth noting that some Indians bitterly oppose their tribe's establishment of casinos, fearing that this new feature of Indian Country will warp Indian values and destroy Native traditions.

Gaming and Recent American Indian Economic Development

Joseph G. Jorgenson

A MERE FOUR YEARS AGO IN TULSA, Oklahoma a knowledgeable group of American Indians and scholars of American Indian topics gathered to forecast the future of American Indian sovereignty, economics, relations with governments, and general well-being.[1] With far too much temerity I stood in front of the gathering to forecast American Indian economic development. As was my wont after nearly forty years of observation and analysis of Indian economic ventures, particularly agriculture, but also recreation, industrial park, mining, energy, and sundry smaller business activities, I assumed that the future of economic developments among America's Indian tribes would be similar to past attempts to develop Indian economies. Indeed, I argued that it was wise to accept David Hume's proposition that the past is the best predictor of the future for social phenomena.[2] Hence, I foresaw nothing but failures, the exception being the *maquiladora*-like assembly operations owned and managed by the Mississippi Choctaw.[3]

I argued that reservation subjugation brought with it not domination alone, but expropriation of resources from which Indians gained their livelihoods, in some instances and in some places exploitation of Indian labor, and everywhere the dole. Tribal domination was made complete by the plenary powers over Indian affairs invested in Congress. Expropriation was made complete by the Cherokee decisions in regard to the impaired title to Indian land. The dole is not complete, but when it is forthcoming its source is the federal government.

Agriculture has not been a successful avenue for economic development for any North American Indian tribe. Nearly a full decade before the great stock market crash of 1929, the United States experienced its first agriculture market glut. Indian agricultural production was not a significant factor in causing that glut, and it has only lost ground in agricultural production since that time as centralization of crops and livestock, transformation from intensive labor to intensive capital, lack of access to capital, lack of political influence, long distances from market, generally arid and unproductive land, and modest educations and technical skills have coalesced to eliminate agriculture as a viable means for Indian economic development.

In 1994 I argued that a spate of legislation enacted since 1887 so as to rectify Indian economic problems as defined by Congress, or its lobbies, or both, had been unsuccessful in rectifying those problems. My list, well known to Indian scholars,

SOURCE: *American Indian Culture and Research Journal*, v. 22, n. 3 (1998), pp. 157–172.

includes the pieces in the history that define the swings back and forth between policies that prompted individual, competitive behavior in the market and those that made some provisions for collective, tribal economic affairs.[4] The General Allotment Act of 1887 (individual), Indian Reorganization Act of 1934 (collective), Indian Claims Commission Act of 1946 and subsequent specific termination acts (individual), and the Indian Self-Determination and Education Act (collective) marked the swings in my view. In retrospect, the last mentioned is especially interesting because I recognized it as the most significant piece of legislation that offered some possibility to assist Indian economic development. I think I was half right. Whereas the Self-Determination Act laid the groundwork, I completely missed the significance of the Indian Gaming Regulatory Act (IGRA), although it had been enacted in 1988, six years prior to the occasion of the Tulsa symposium. As a matter of fact, when asked by one participant why I was so pessimistic about Indian development when Indian gaming operations were opening and, apparently, succeeding, my response was, in short, ignorant.

I responded that Foxwood, the Pequot casino in Connecticut, was a success, as was Mystic Lake, the Chippewa casino in Minnesota. Yet off the top of my head I foresaw a host of financial, management, ownership, location, seasonal, governmental, and legal problems that would sink most Indian gaming operations—operations that Indians would seldom own or control. The more obvious problems were saturation (several casinos within modest proximity would compete for a limited patron pool, as in San Diego and Riverside counties, California); long distances from population centers and from major highways (poor marketing and bad locations would operate against most Indian casinos in the mountain and Plains states); seasonal fluctuation (casinos in the mountain and Plains states and others within proximity of vacation destinations would wither from fall through spring); non-Indian capital and control, often from organized crime, would deny Indians anything beyond employment (non-Indians, as in many bingo operations of the 1970s, would build and operate the casinos and maintain the books); paucity of acumen about gaming and the gaming business; lack of access to capital; and legal problems with state and federal governments.

Although each of the foregoing factors, often in combinations of three or four, have caused some problems, the more remarkable outcome at this stage is that Indian gaming operations have been so successful. Since passage of the IGRA of 1988, legalized gambling on Indian lands has provided revenues for tribes that I forecast to be impossible. Access to capital and control of the casino I considered to be insurmountable problems. Yet one of the features of the act is intended to deny the control of casinos by non-Indian corporations, the mob, and outside firms in general. Outside firms can invest in casinos, even manage casinos, but they cannot gain more than 30 percent of profits, and they can do so for only the first five years of operations. After that, the IGRA requires that operations be turned back totally to the tribe. Hence, the tribe must learn to manage its own casino, or if it chooses to hire outside management, the tribe retains full control over that management.

A symposium at the California Indian Conference for 1995 (held at the University of California, Los Angeles) brought together participants from several tribes that have gaming operations within California. These representatives discussed the poignant issues of the day, including the obstacles they were encountering in seeking a compact with the state of California to operate their casinos within the legal parameters established by IGRA; the inability to purchase electronic gambling machines (one-armed bandits and the like) because of pressures put on suppliers by Nevada hoteliers and gaming operators; and the threat of raids by state police intended to close casinos because of illegal (machine) gambling on the premises.

Discussions also turned toward the economic successes, if marginal, of some of the smallest and most disadvantageously located casinos; the managerial help contracted by tribes of leading casino operators, such as Caesar's Palace and Full House (contracts that had explicit termination dates, which required merit review and so forth); the employment provided for all local Indians willing to work and for many non-Indian locals as well; and the distribution of revenues as benefits to elders, and to health, education, recreation, and culture-historical projects, including tribal museums.

The early evidence from the testimony of the participants was that gaming was an economic development in and of itself and, as a multiplier, a source for further economic developments in areas surrounding the tribe which owned the casino. The revenues were being used to enrich Indian lives and to nourish Indian culture.

Research on Indian gaming operations is extremely meager, but analyses of the IGRA; a major suit spawned by that act, *Seminole Tribe v. Florida*;[5] and the questions of taxation, termination, and social consequences that are anticipated as consequences of the IGRA were presented at a symposium hosted by the Arizona State University College of Law's Indian Legal Program in Tempe, October 11–12, 1996. In the publication of symposium papers, Eric Henderson—a Ph.D. in anthropology as well as a J.D.—provides a magisterial treatment of what is known and what is not known about the social and cultural consequences of Indian gaming.[6] There are more learned questions than answers about Indian gaming and its consequences for families and individuals, problem gambling for Indians and non-Indians, intratribal social and political arrangements, economic benefits, factionalism, and other pressing topics, undoubtedly because of the recency of Indian gaming. There is much to learn and much to study. We are looking at Indian gaming through a very dark glass.

SELF-DETERMINATION

So let us recall the Self-Determination Act and related legislation enacted a quarter of a century ago which, collectively, sought to provide Indian tribal governments with some controls over various aspects of their private and public economic affairs. Forty years prior to the Self-Determination Act, the Indian Reorganization Act of 1934 was envisaged as self-determination legislation for tribes. Yet in this 1930s form of self-determination, Congress vested the secretary of Interior with veto authority over tribal decisions. A bit later, realizing that the reorganized tribes had no money to drive their new corporations, Congress provided a minuscule revolving credit fund for which tribes could compete to fund development projects—such as livestock or farm operations. The Self-Determination Act of 1975 enabled tribes to exert control over public sector services and to compete for public sector grants and programs. In a replay of the 1930s, a separate act created another minuscule revolving credit fund for economic development available to the nation's federally recognized tribes (more than 275 in 1975) on a competitive basis.[7]

The Reagan Administration did not add one penny to the revolving credit fund, yet it managed to decrease the federal budget for Indian programs in each of the administration's eight years. Reagan's administration replaced dollars with encouragement to Indians to nourish their entrepreneurial activities and to seek independence from the federal dole.

Indian economic development is closely tied to self-determination, while Indian economic *un*development is tied to the structure of the nation's political economy and to the unique niche that tribes occupy by law and by context in that economy (see note 4). The extinguishing of Eskimo, Aleut, and Indian claims to aboriginal hunting, fishing, and land rights in Alaska in 1971, the Arab oil embargo of 1973, and actions of Congress and of successive administrations over the past three decades have regularly turned scholarly attention to the political economic structure of dependency. Impartial observers can no more easily deny that structure than can tribes, through some formula, generate sustainable and growing economies in which they do *not* exercise ownership and control of production.

About fifty years ago the nation's total agricultural products were produced by about 25 percent of the work force. The nation's manufactured goods were produced by about 50 percent of the work force. In 1998, the nation's total agricultural products, including exports, are produced by less than 2 percent of the work force, while the nation's manufactured goods are produced by about 15 percent of the work force. Given the incentives for capitalists to reduce costs while seeking maximum profits, coupled with the technological advances which increase production while displacing labor, fewer jobs and fewer manufacturing sites in the United States appear to be in the offing. If the future is to be like the past, it is a reasonable bet that total production of goods in the United States will be manufactured by 2 percent of the population in the not too distant future.

The structure of contemporary capitalism, nested in worldwide competition, is recognizable. Businesses seek government assistance through tax incentives and through the development and maintenance of roads, sewers, airports, docks, communication systems, and security, while eschewing the burdens of environmental, safety, health, minimum wage, and equal employment laws and of the regulatory compliance red tape that has grown from those laws.

GAMING: ECONOMIC DEVELOPMENT AND SOVEREIGNTY

Indian sovereignty was limited with the ratification of the First Article of the Constitution which gave Congress plenary powers over tribes. With several important exceptions in which the Supreme Court has stepped up to define and restrict tribal sovereignty, Congress has defined what Indians own and control. Lenders have been more willing to offer advice than to lend capital. Title to trust land, after all, is impaired, so it doesn't provide good collateral for loans from, say, a megabank such as NationsBank-BankAmerica for deals that must be approved by Congress to proceed.

The obstacles to Indian economic development are structural: Tribes are domestic dependent nations whose decisions can be vetoed, whose title to land and resources are impaired. Until the advent of Indian gaming operations, recognized tribes in the United States have had extremely limited access to capital, and have suffered disadvantages in access to and control of information pertinent to their own resources as well as to the market. Most recognized tribes are located long distances from markets of all kinds, and because the interests and obligations of most tribal governments focus on the nourishment of the well-being of tribal members—whose needs are endless—decisions to use scarce resources to benefit many as soon as possible have dominated decisions to allocate tribal funds. When engaged in business ventures—whether joint with non-Indian corporations or whether as renters to lessees of land and resources—almost all tribal corporations have watched profits generated from reservation resources drain from reservations to the coffers of corporations in distant metropolises. And members of almost all reservation societies suffer from discriminatory words and acts from their nearest non-Indian neighbors, themselves situated in struggling rural areas.

With such a tiny proportion of the nation's population producing all of the nation's agricultural and manufactured goods, what, possibly, is the future of the economic development of Indian tribes? While it is the case that most reservations are located in marginal areas long distances from manufacturing and agricultural markets and suffer unique political constraints, their access to capital and to information has been dramatically altered in the past five years. Indian tribes have some options not available heretofore. It is no longer the case that non-tribal-owned companies and corporations whose offices are located long distances from reservations own or control all of the businesses operating on reservations, draining the profits from the reservation to their corporate headquarters, keeping the books, and dribbling back to Indian tribes some crumbs in the form of royalties, a few jobs, or lease income.

The Pequot of southern Connecticut have been uniquely successful in the gaming business. The Pequot, whose capital to build Foxwood casino came from a federal judgment, have not required infusions of federal capital to maintain the casino and its work force. Rather, the casino has flourished, causing alarm to casino operators in Atlantic City who claim that the proximity of the Pequot operation to the densely populated region from Boston to New York City has throttled their own operations.

The successes of the Pequot's Foxwood Casino and the Chippewa's Mystic Lake Casino have not been lost on the nation's recognized and unrecognized tribes. In mid-1997 there were 273 Indian-owned casinos. Among these, 145 tribes located in twenty-four states had entered into compacts (161 in all) with the governments of the states in which their casinos are located.[8] The gross revenues of all Indian gaming operations in mid-1997 have been estimated at $6 billion annually. The 128 tribal casino owners who have not arrived at agreements with the states in which they operate are seeking to do so, often against considerable obstacles.

For example, tribes operating forty-one limited gaming facilities in California—in which 13,000 video slot machines are the principal source of revenues[9]—had been thwarted for more than four years in their attempts to agree to a compact with the state. On March 7, 1995, Governor Pete Wilson's administration signed a compact with one of those forty-one tribes, the Pala Band of Mission Indians in northern San Diego County, allowing video lottery games in *all* California Indian casinos. Wilson's administration envisaged the compact as comprehensive, the formula for all compacts with California's tribes. Those compacts would restrict each tribe currently operating casinos to 199 video lottery machines[10] and all other federally recognized tribes in California to that same number of video machines, if and when they open casinos. There are 106 federally recognized tribes in California and dozens more unacknowledged tribes that are seeking federal recognition. Governor Wilson's comprehensive formula would reduce the number of machines now in use by about 5,000 (38 percent). The government-to-government agreement did not proceed in "good faith" according to thirty-nine California tribal governments currently operating casinos.

California's casino operating tribes responded quickly to the Pala compact. They gained sufficient signatures to place an initiative on the November 1998 statewide ballot in California: the Tribal Government Gaming and Economic Self-Sufficiency Act. The initiative ensures that California tribal gaming operations can continue to operate on tribal lands to support Indian economic self-sufficiency.[11] They estimated that their forty-one casinos directly provide 15,000 jobs in the state, and they provided evidence that Indian gaming operations will not impact California's $2.3 billion non-Indian gaming industry (bingo, card rooms, horse racing, lottery).

The stakes are high. The claims that casinos are crucial to the development of self-sufficient tribal economies, although not without some negative effects and some business failures, appear to be measured. Because of a paucity of research on Indian gaming nationwide, I must rely on anecdotal evidence in the following assessment of the successes of and the problems associated with Indian gaming.

Let us begin with Oregon's Grande Ronde Confederated Tribes, in part because they had so little and so few prospects when they opened a casino, and in part because the consequences to the tribe and to the local area from their casino's short history is similar to so many tribal casinos from Connecticut to California. Oregon's Grande Ronde Confederated Tribes were terminated from federal services and stripped of federal recognition. Twenty-three years later the Confederated Tribes successfully sought Congress to restore federal recognition to them, and the Grande Ronde were awarded a reservation of about 10,000 acres located about sixty miles from Portland. When the timber industry in which they were engaged for more than a decade faltered, the tribe voted to avail itself of the IGRA. According to Michael Killeen, the tribe sought to create jobs for Natives and non-Natives while building an income base that would allow them to invest in education, the environment, and the arts, while also becoming a multiplier for the local area.[12] They intended as well to implement measures to avert gambling addiction and crime, and to create treatment centers for gamblers with problems.

In 1996, Grande Ronde established the Spirit Mountain Casino, hired a tribal member and attorney as CEO, and in its first year of operation generated a profit of

$30 million.[13] Killeen points out that the tribe hired 1,200 people, only 200 of whom were Indians. And of the new hires, 46 percent had been out of work, 35 percent had been on welfare, and 42 percent lacked health insurance. In the first year alone, $8 million in gambling profits were used to build and improve highways, the water and sewer system, and a new medical facility (for Natives and non-Natives), while $335,000 was invested in studies on the negative impacts of gaming, rescue helicopters for Portland hospitals, and to an exhibition of Native American Art at the Portland Art Museum.[14] The $335,000 represents 6 percent of net revenues. This proportion is committed to a community fund for non-tribal causes.

The San Manuel Serrano Indians, located near San Bernardino, California, opened a bingo parlor in 1986, expanding their types of games following passage of the federal gaming act. The tribe encountered opposition from the city and county of San Bernardino which they overcame by agreeing to finance road and traffic improvements for seven years (through 1993). They also overcame opposition from home owners in the area adjacent to the casino by agreeing in federal court to compensate them up to $300,000 total for devaluation of property.[15] In 1988 about 75 percent of the tribe's work-eligible population was unemployed and about the same proportion of tribal members received welfare benefits. In 1993, according to Mark Henry,[16] the casino embarked on an energetic advertising program and soon began drawing 100,000 gamblers per month. In short order the casino eliminated tribal unemployment and welfare. Any member who seeks work obtains it so long as he or she passes the background check and drug test required of all applicants. In 1996 the casino had a $26-million payroll, providing jobs for 25 percent of the tribe's total population and 1,400 jobs total. Employees come from a five-county area; most are non-Natives. As is the case for Grande Ronde, the San Manuel Serranos used casino profits to donate about $600,000 to charities in 1996; build a new water system, roads, and homes for tribal members; and provide per-capita distributions among tribal members. The tribe offers to pay the cost of college educations for any member who wishes to attend. In 1997 one person had accepted the offer.

Three bands in San Diego County, California—Barona, Viejas, Sycuan—totaling about 700 members, were mired in poverty a decade ago. Each opened casinos on their reservations following passage of the federal gaming act. "Barona closed three times between 1988 and 1991 when management companies failed to make it profitable."[17] Troubles were frequent: Video games were confiscated by San Diego County law enforcement officers at the direction of the state attorney general (only to have them returned by a federal court judge). By 1994, following Barona's lead, Viejas and Sycuan had become successful running high-stakes bingo games, off-track betting, Indian blackjack (cards), and video poker. By 1995 high-stakes bingo gave way to high-jackpot video poker (up to $100,000 payoffs).[18] Video machines account for 70 percent or more of profits. Currently, the three casinos have about 2,500 video games (total) and draw about 15,000 gamblers daily (5.5 million per year), mostly from within San Diego County. The aggregate revenues for the three casinos are estimated at well over $1 billion annually. The San Diego casinos have restaurants, snack bars, and stores, but no alcohol.

All tribal members who desire employment are employed by the casinos. But of the 1,600 employees at one casino, only sixteen are tribal members. If but one person per household is employed, about 30 percent of the households have a casino employee. Inasmuch as all tribal members receive per-capita distributions from profits (about $4,500 per month for Barona tribal members), the modest number of casino employees per Indian household is not surprising. Per capitas are distributed each month only after basic services, improvements, and investments are determined by the tribal governments. Within the bands, improvements and public investments include gymnasiums, college funds, trust funds for all persons eighteen years of age with high school diplomas, libraries, computer centers, Head Start programs, homes. Outside the bands, contributions totaling over $2.4 million in 1995 and 1996 were made to San Diego area charities, symphonies, community centers, and the like. And as for investments in the area economy, Viejas purchased a controlling interest in a local bank, and is building a discount outlet shopping center-entertainment complex. Barona operates a gas station that cost the band $600,000 to build and that employs sixteen people. Sycuan runs a regional health clinic.[19]

Many of the personal problems associated with Indian gaming are similar to problems associated with non-Indian gaming, namely, gambling addiction, the setting and occasions for crime, and the stresses that can occur within families because of gambling habits. Tribes have sought to counter these problems through the ways in which they advertise (some downplay enormous payoffs), prohibiting the sale and use of alcohol, prohibiting the use of checks or credit cards, prohibiting the development of tabs (credit) for regular customers, and educating persons against gambling addiction.

Problems of other kinds emerge as well. Former non-Indian managers and investors in Indian casinos have been convicted of operating illegal gambling operations and sentenced to prison terms and fines (while having charges dropped for skimming millions of dollars from one tribe).[20] Small casinos located in close proximity to large and successful casinos, such as the Cahuilla Creek casino in the little town of Anza near the profitable Indian casinos of the Palm Springs area, struggle to maintain a work force of seventy-five people, down from 150 in 1992. It draws no more than two hundred customers on a good night. The casino is unable to donate money to the community or to tribal services, nor is it able to invest in other businesses.[21] The National Indian Gaming Commission, established by the IGRA, requires all Indian casinos to submit annual audits and background investigations of key employees. In 1997 the commission found that nearly half of the 273 tribal casinos failed to submit either audits or background investigations of their key employees.[22]

And finally I call to attention problems that have been created within and between tribes as a direct consequence of the Indian Gaming Regulatory Act. The Juaneño Band of Mission Indians in Orange County, California, are not recognized by the federal government. In 1978 the Juaneño Band sought to be recognized through provisions of the Federal Acknowledgment Process. A list of tribal membership was prepared and a petition responding to the requirements of the acknowledgment process were submitted. The Federal Acknowledgment Process, administered by the Bureau of Indian Affairs (BIA) has had a hoary history. Not until 1994 was the Juaneño Band's petition close to being decided by the BIA. Between 1990 and 1994, however, the tribal leaders responsible for filing the petition were approached by Nevada gaming investors who offered to invest in a casino when the tribe gained recognition, established a sovereign government, and received land on which the casino could be placed. Soon an anti-gambling faction formed and filed a second petition with a different, but overlapping, list of tribal members, and new responses to the questions posed in the BIA petition guidelines. By 1998 the person who had been the chairman when the original petition was prepared, but who did not stand for reelection, returned to represent the original petition, bringing with him several persons. Yet the faction that had stuck with the original petition had elected a new chairman. Thus, the original petition was claimed by two factions, while the second petition retained a faction and chair of its own. The confusion of petitions and petitioners has not been resolved by the BIA's Branch of Acknowledgment Research, but if and when they recognize the Juaneño Band, it will be only one of the petitions, hence only one of the tribal membership lists will be approved as enrolled members.[23]

A second problem pitted the Torrez-Martinez tribe against several casino-operating tribes in the Palm Springs area of California. Half of the Torrez-Martinez reservation was flooded in 1905 by a famous accident in which a Colorado River canal burst, causing the formation of the Salton Sea. The Salton Sea has inundated Torrez-Martinez land ever since. Recently the Torrez-Martinez received 14 million dollars from Congress to purchase new land farther north in the Palm Springs-Palm Desert-Coachella Valley area (approved by the Department of Interior), and sought the assistance of Full House Resorts to help them establish and manage a casino. The casino has not gone forward because of intense lobbying by established Indian-owned casinos in the area that do not want to see their own revenues reduced by another casino in their vicinity.[24]

The problems in starting and maintaining successful gaming operations are many. Gaming offers, however, the most likely source of sustained economic successes for impoverished tribes, and is a remarkable employer and multiplier for moribund rural areas.

In conjunction with successful gaming operations made possible by the IGRA and agreed to in good faith compacts struck with state governments, the Self-Determination Act can be used by tribes to gain (and in some instances, regain) control over the federal services they now receive. If they are careful, obtain good advice, and are situated within good transportation networks, they may be able to create assembly firms similar to those of the Mississippi Choctaw as well, further lifting local economies. The obstacles to the smallest tribes located the longest distances from markets and population centers are, as in the past, structural and many. Yet the initiative placed on the ballot by California gaming tribes goes a long way to sharing wealth among tribes that do not have gaming operations and would not enjoy success if they had them.

NOTES

1. "Native America: Faces of the Future," Conference held at the University of Tulsa, Tulsa, Oklahoma (April 15–16, 1994).
2. For a full development of Hume's position, which is much richer and much more cautious than my claim about it, see Frederick L. Will, "Will the Future Be Like the Past," *Mind* (1956) for the most widely accepted critique of Hume's position.
3. About twenty years ago the Choctaw of Philadelphia, Mississippi successfully penetrated the automobile industry in the United States by installing cassette decks into the baskets which were hung in Ford, General Motors, and Chrysler cars and trucks for a lower price than any of those corporations could match should they install the cassettes in-house. Choctaw labor was eager and the price was right. Hours for employees were flexible, health benefits for Indians were covered by the Indian Health Service, and jobs were provided for non-Indians in the community as well. The Mississippi Choctaw recognized the niche and the competition posed by businesses that fled across the border to Mexico. Manufacturers sought lower costs and higher profits. For more than twenty years the Choctaw have been successful in acquiring new contracts to assemble a wide variety of products; hiring more local whites, blacks, and Indians; and building more buildings to assemble the items that come to them. The future of the Choctaw enterprise is surely bound to the future of manufacturing and to their ability to provide high-quality assembly at low cost to the manufacturers. Their competition is *maquilladore* operations along the U.S.-Mexico border.
4. These issues have been addressed in detail from various perspectives in the past. My view has undergone only modest change in the past thirty-five years. See Joseph G. Jorgensen, *The Ethnohistory and Acculturation of the Northern Ute*, Ph.D. Dissertation in Anthropology (Indiana University, 1964); "Indians and the Metropolis," in Jack O. Waddell and O. Michael Watson, eds., *The American Indian in Urban Society* (Boston: Little Brown, 1971), 67–113; *The Sun Dance Religion. Power for the Powerless* (Chicago: University of Chicago Press, 1972); "A Century of Political Economic Effects on American Indian Society," *Journal of Ethnic Studies* 6:3 (1978a): 1–82; "Energy, Agriculture, and Social Science in the American West," in Joseph G. Jorgensen, et al., *Native Americans and Energy Development* (Cambridge: Anthropology Resource Center, 1978b), 3–16; "Energy Development in the Arid West: Consequences for Native Americans," in Cyrus McKell, ed., *Paradoxes in Western Energy Development*, American Association for the Advancement of Sciences (Boulder: Westview Press, 1984), 297–322; "The Political Economy of the Native American Energy Business," in Joseph G. Jorgensen, ed., *Native Americans and Energy Developments II* (Boston: Anthropology Resource Center, 1984b), 10–51; "Federal Policies, American Indian Polities and the 'New Federalism,'" *American Indian Culture and Research Journal* 10:2 (1986a): 1–13; "Sovereignty and the Structure of Dependency at Northern Ute," *American Indian Culture and Research Journal* 10:2 (1986): 75–94; *Oil Age Eskimos* (Berkeley: University of California Press, 1990). Differences are rather slight between my view and those expressed by several recent contributors to the analysis of American Indian economic development, including David F. Aberle, "Navajo Economic Development," in Alfonso Ortiz, ed., *Southwest*, Vol. 10, gen. ed., William Sturtevant, *Handbook of North American Indians* (Washington, DC: Smithsonian Institution, 1983), 641–658; Matthew C. Snipp, "The Changing Political and Economic Status of the American Indians: From Captive Nations to Internal Colonies," *American Journal of Economics and Sociology* 45:2 (1986): 145–158; Irene Castle McLaughlin, *Colonialism, Cattle, and Class: A Century of Ranching on the Fort Berthold Indian Reservation*, Ph.D. Dissertation (Columbia University, 1993); Sandra Faiman-Silva, "Multinational Corporate Development in the American Hinterland: The Case of the Oklahoma Choctaws," in John H. Moore, ed., *The Political Economy of North American Indians* (Norman: University of Oklahoma Press, 1993), 214–239; Thomas D. Hall, "Northwest New Spain," in Matthew C. Snipp, ed., *American Indians and Economic Dependency* (Norman: University of Oklahoma Press, 1998); and Shepard Krech, "Dependency Among the Northern Cree," in Matthew C. Snipp, ed., *American Indians and Economic Dependency* (Norman: University of Oklahoma Press, 1998).
5. "Symposium, Indian Gaming," *Arizona State Law Journal* 29:1 (Spring 1997).
6. Eric Henderson, "Indian Gaming: Social Consequences," *Arizona State Law Journal* 29:1 (1997): 205–50.

7. If every tribe had equal access to the $10 million at the same time, each would receive about $36,000—an amount that may not have been sufficient to buy a McDonald's franchise in 1980. Another contrast of rich and poor will give perspective to that $10–million revolving credit fund in 1995: The CEO of the Walt Disney Corporation received about twenty-three times the amount of the total revolving credit fund as his annual compensation in 1995.

8. I skirt the details of tribal-state compacts here except to point out that under federal law the regulation of certain types of games—called Class III gaming—must be governed by an agreement between the tribe that establishes a casino and the state in which it is located. The state must negotiate these agreements with tribes in good faith (see Henderson, "Indian Gaming: Social Consequences," 1997).

9. Eleven tribes from northern Santa Barbara County to southern Riverside County gain more than 75 percent of their revenues from video games.

10. The Pala compact allows a tribe to operate a maximum of 975 video machines if they buy allocations from other tribes. Several Indian casinos in the Palm Springs-Indio area (southern California desert) currently operate more than 1,000 electronic games.

11. The measure seeks to extend the benefits of tribal gaming to tribes that do not have gaming facilities by dedicating part of the net revenues from Indian gaming to non-gaming tribes for health care, education, economic development, and cultural preservation programs. It will direct part of the net winnings to supplement emergency medical resources in each county in California and to a local benefits grant fund for cities and counties where Indian gaming facilities are located. It also puts into law strict gaming limitations, regulations, and public health, safety, and environmental standards.

12. Michael Killeen, "Prosperity in the Cards," *Hemisphere* (1997): 41–45.

13. Killeen, "Prosperity in the Cards" (1997): 42.

14. Killeen, "Prosperity in the Cards" (1997): 44.

15. Mark Henry, "Gamble Pays Off," *The Press-Enterprise*, reprinted in *Indian Times* (Spring 1997), 6.

16. Henry, "Gamble Pays Off," 1, 5.

17. Henry Garfield, "Casinos Deal County Indians a Winning Hand," *City Magazine* (San Diego, February 1997), reprinted in *Indian Times* (Spring 1997), 4–6.

18. Garfield, "Casinos Deal County Indians a Winning Hand," 4.

19. Garfield, "Casinos Deal County Indians a Winning Hand," 4.

20. George Ramos, "4 Plead Guilty to Running Illegal Reservation Casino," *Los Angeles Times* (November 7, 1996), A32.

21. Stephanie Simon, "Legal Dispute Simmers in Remote Casino," *Los Angeles Times* (Saturday, May 27, 1997), A24–5.

22. "N.M. Tribe Casinos Fail Fed Standards," *The Albuquerque Tribune* (Wednesday, April 9, 1997).

23. Yoriko Ogawa, "Honors Paper in Social Science" (School of Social Sciences, University of California, Irvine, June 1998).

24. Tom Gorman, "Dispute Stalls Land Deal for Impoverished Tribe," *Los Angeles Times* (Monday, September 23, 1996), A3, A15.

23

This last essay returns to themes introduced at the beginning of the volume, raising questions that were passionately debated in the mid-nineteenth century: What is the nature of the American nation? How sovereign are tribal governments? Can there be multiple nations within the borders of the United States? Peter d'Errico puts these questions in a contemporary context by reviewing the political relationship between Native Americans and the national government over the past two centuries—and indeed, into even more remote reaches of the past. He argues that "the same conflicts" have endured. For d'Errico these contests—over "land and water rights, hunting and fishing, religious freedom, and criminal and civil jurisdiction"—signal the persistence of a fundamental divide in how the two groups understand their place on the continent.

The issue dividing Indians and non-Indians, d'Errico believes, is Native American sovereignty, the fact that Indians have survived as *peoples* rather than as individuals. If *peoples* survive, then they can trace their heritage back to a time before the arrival of Europeans. If they exist in the present and take their identity from an ancient past, d'Errico asks, how can they be considered part of the United States? American law defines Indian communities as subservient to the power of Congress and the greater sovereignty of the United States, but d'Errico rejects this construction as a "legal scheme ... useful to the United States because it denies indigenous self-determination." The only justification for American national sovereignty over Indians, he claims, is the heritage of Christian colonialism first articulated by Pope Alexander VI in 1493. The idea that Christians were destined to rule over infidels, he

argues, is "the conceptual core of colonization of the New World."

Presenting the historical record as he does, d'Errico views modern tribal leaders as "puppet" governors who accept the domination of the United States. Contemporary conflicts between tribes and federal authorities merely argue about concepts—trust, wardship, tribal rights—that are inventions of the conquerors and do little besides "legitimize federal power." It is worth asking what d'Errico might have to say about the Mississippi Choctaws Fergus Bordewich visited, or those Indian pioneers Frederick Hoxie examined. It is no less worth pondering what those Indians might have to say about his argument.

This essay ends with a challenge to both students of history and believers in democracy: "[can] conventional sovereignty ... be an instrument of liberation from policies rooted in colonialism?" If the sovereignty of the United States government (in theory the protector of our freedoms as citizens) is an instrument of conquest and colonialism, how can American institutions liberate Native Americans from colonial domination? With such questions the conversation truly comes full circle. In the nineteenth century whites could not see a place for Native Americans within the American state, while Indians (such as the Cherokees) struggled to find a way to accomplish that goal. Now, at the dawn of the twenty-first century, these roles seem reversed: tribal leaders doubt the ability of American law to satisfy their demands, while policymakers in Washington, D.C., struggle to craft programs that will bridge the gap between Native aspirations on the one hand and a desire for national unity on the other.

Native Americans in America:
A Theoretical and Historical Overview

Peter d'Errico

LATE-TWENTIETH-CENTURY NATIVE AMERICA presents the same conflicts as the late eighteenth century: land and water rights, hunting and fishing, religious freedom, criminal and civil jurisdiction. In fact, these conflicts are typical of relations between indigenous peoples and colonizers on the American continent as a whole beginning more than five centuries ago.

Occasional "hot spots" receive wide attention—Anishinaabe fishing in Wisconsin, Puyallup fishing in Washington, the Black Hills in the Dakotas, Yucca Mountain in Western Shoshone territory, Big Mountain in Navajo and Hopi territory, Venetie Village in Alaska, Mohawk communities on the New York-Canadian border. These are heightened examples of continual and widespread political conflict involving Native Americans in America.

It is likely there is no region of America at any given time not facing at least one Native issue in more than one venue, including subsistence rights, grave desecration and repatriation, child and family custody matters, and sports mascot and other commercial uses of Native names and images. It may appear that the last issue is wholly "modern," with no precedent in early history, but sports mascots are contemporary manifestations of what appeared in colonial fund-raising: the Puritans of the Massachusetts Bay Company circulated in English churches cartoon images of a Native American holding out his hands and saying, "Come over and help us."[1] This was the official seal of the company between 1629 and 1684. Native Americans have had no end of "help" since then and no end of exploitation for the financial benefit of others.

The persistence of fundamental issues over a period of five hundred years demonstrates the ongoing existence of Native Americans as distinct peoples, despite repeated attempts to make them disappear. America was not a virgin land when boat people from across the Atlantic arrived. From the earliest days to the present, Native peoples have been a presence in America. The existence of Native Americans as *peoples*—as self-governing groups, rather than simply as individuals sharing personal and cultural traits—is what sets them apart from other "minorities" in America. This difference warrants theoretical and historical overview so that the variety of particular issues and controversies active at any given time or place can be understood in an overall perspective. As Barry O'Connell wrote,

SOURCE: *Wizaco Sa Review* (Spring 1999), pp. 7–29.

Neither the indigenous histories and concerns of native peoples nor the complex relations between them and the Euro-Americans can be comprehended by the providential history that has generally passed for the actual history of the United States. To include these would undermine the construction of the particular ideological history that has shaped "America" as a virgin land settled by God's chosen people.[2]

MINORITIES AND PEOPLES

A "minority" is conventionally defined as a group whose shared cultural and personal characteristics distinguish them from the rest of the population, which both outnumbers them and discriminates against them on the basis of these characteristics. An ameliorative response to this kind of discrimination in American politics is "civil rights"— legal measures to assure toleration of, if not actual advancement for, minority groups.

Civil rights struggles have been a more or less constant feature of American politics, perhaps since adoption of the U.S. Constitution, when a "Bill of Rights" was politically necessary to ratification. The focal point of civil rights politics has varied over time, but its basic ideas have remained relatively constant: that the state should propound limits to its own power; that state power should apply to all persons equally; and that a proper focus of politics is the use of state power to address, if not redress, social discrimination.

Native political struggles differ markedly from civil rights, although the surface aspects may not reveal this. Controversies about the use of Native American images for sports mascots, for example, appear as a conventional dispute about respect for ethnic difference. But the deepest, most pervasive, and persistent issues involve land and group rights. In a word, Native American issues involve questions of "sovereignty"—challenges to state and federal jurisdiction to protect territorial integrity and self-determination as separate peoples.

Native Americans asserting sovereignty are not seeking a "fair share" in American society but are declaring the existence of a separate domain. Sovereignty demands of the American Indian Movement (AIM) in the 1970s departed radically from the concerns of the African American civil rights movement, which was sometimes cited as an inspiration for AIM. The only other group to come close to raising a sovereignty issue is the separatist wing of African American politics, which has from time to time called for the creation of a separate African American homeland in North America. In that context the demand is clearly revolutionary, whereas in Native American terms sovereignty is not revolutionary but traditional.

Self-government is thus the primary factor that distinguishes Native American from other "minority" struggles. This crucial difference has generated envy from some twentieth-century "militias" who seek independence from state and federal controls, and hostility from others who see the special position of Native Americans as a form of inequality that violates everyone else's rights.

Native American independence as a model to emulate or criticize is itself a recurring phenomenon in American history. Benjamin Franklin's observation is one of the most oft-quoted early examples:

> It would be a very strange Thing, if six Nations of ignorant Savages should be capable of forming a Scheme for such a Union, and be able to execute it in such a Manner, as that it has subsisted Ages, and appears indissoluble, and yet that a like Union should be impracticable for ten or a Dozen English Colonies.[3]

Native American self-determination does not fit neatly within a "multicultural" perspective of American society. Multiculturalism is a view of America as a conglomerate society of individuals belonging to different ethnic groups. In this view, ethnic difference is a matter for pride but not a basis for independence. The uniqueness of Native American ethnicity is that it may be expressed through independent political structures. This situation is defined in the phrase "government-to-government relationship," which is used to explain that the United States relates to Native Americans as sovereign groups rather than as individuals.

One must immediately add qualifiers to the assertion that self-determination is the fulcrum of Native American politics. Native American sovereignty is not as complete as the government-to-government phrase suggests. Indeed, the first time the United States dealt with Native Americans through the State Department—the normal vehicle for government-to-government relationships—was in May 1996. This was a "consultation" meeting preparatory to the United States taking a position on the United Nations Draft Declaration of the Rights of Indigenous Peoples. Prior to that meeting, and continuing since, the government-to-government relationship consisted primarily of Native American governments dealing with the United States through various domestic agencies, especially the Department of the Interior. From a historical perspective, there was more real government-to-government relationship when the United States dealt with Native Americans through the War Department, where the first Bureau of Indian Affairs was created (1824), than in subsequent years, when "Indian affairs" became institutionalized as a "domestic" rather than an international concern.

Native American sovereignty has been the object of a legal shell game—"now you see it, now you don't"—since the beginning of federal Indian law. An especially revealing explanation was provided in 1973 by the federal District Court for the District of Montana in the case of *United States v. Blackfeet Tribe*. The facts of the case were simple: the Blackfeet Business Council had passed a resolution authorizing gambling on the reservation and licensing of slot machines. An FBI agent seized four machines. The Blackfeet Tribal Court issued an order restraining all persons from removing the seized articles from the reservation. The FBI agent, after consultation with the U.S. Attorney, removed the machines from the reservation. A tribal judge then ordered the U.S. Attorney to show cause why he should not be cited for contempt of the tribal court. The U.S. Attorney applied to federal court for an injunction to block the contempt citations. The Blackfeet Tribe argued that it was sovereign and that the jurisdiction of the tribal court flows directly from this sovereignty. The federal court said:

> No doubt the Indian tribes were at one time sovereign and even now the tribes are sometimes described as being sovereign. The blunt fact, however, is that an Indian tribe is sovereign to the extent that the United States permits it to be sovereign—neither more nor less.[4]

The court explained the basis for this "blunt fact":

> While for many years the United States recognized some elements of sovereignty in the Indian tribes and dealt with them by treaty, Congress by Act of March 3, 1871, ... prohibited the further recognition of Indian tribes as independent nations. Thereafter the Indians and the Indian tribes were regulated by acts of Congress. The power of Congress to govern by statute rather than treaty has been sustained. *United States v. Kagama*, 118 U.S. 375, 6 S. Ct. 1109, 30 L.Ed. 228 (1886). That power is a plenary power ... and in its exercise Congress is supreme. ... It follows that any tribal ordinance permitting or purporting to permit what Congress forbids is void. ... It is beyond the power of the tribe to in any way regulate, limit, or restrict a federal law officer in the performance of his duties, and the tribe having no such power the tribal court can have none.[5]

In other words, "tribal" peoples have a diminutive form of sovereignty, which is not self-determination, but dependence. This legal framework was articulated by Supreme Court Chief Justice John Marshall, one of the most celebrated figures in the pantheon of the Court. In *Cherokee Nation v. Georgia*, Marshall wrote that Native peoples, though they are "nations" in the general sense of the word, are not fully sovereign.[6] He suggested they are "domestic, dependent nations," a phrase implying that they are "wards" of the United States. Marshall's suggestion almost immediately passed from dictum to dogma.

Over the years since Marshall coined his phrase, the federal government has truncated and parceled "tribal sovereignty" in myriad ways, developing a vast system of overlapping and contradictory rules premised on the notion that the United States has "plenary power" to act as "trustee" for tribal "wards." The fact that *plenary power, trustee,* and *ward* are not in the U.S. Constitution is only a small nuisance to the judges who have promulgated these concepts. In fact, the Constitution mentions "Indians" only twice: once to exclude "Indians not taxed" from calculations to apportion representatives and direct taxes, and again to declare that Congress shall have power "To regulate Commerce ... with the Indian Tribes."[7]

"American Indian sovereignty" under federal "plenary power" is a legal scheme especially useful to the United States because it denies indigenous self-determination in the name of indigenous sovereignty. At the same time, it justifies federal control over lands and economic resources that might otherwise be viewed as subject to state and local jurisdictions. On the basis of this judicially created nonsovereign "tribal sovereignty," the United States has built an entire apparatus for dispossessing indigenous peoples of their lands, social organizations, and original powers of self-determination. George Orwell's Big Brother would have been proud of such doublethink.

One of the most visible of Native American issues at the close of the twentieth century is gaming—high-stakes casinos on "Indian reservations," out of reach of state tax and regulatory powers. Similar tax and regulatory issues are presented in controversies over "smoke-shop" and other "reservation" business operations. Some states—New York in the case of Mohawk businesses—have fought for control over revenue from Native economic ventures; others—Connecticut in the case of the monumentally profitable Pequot casino—have accommodated themselves to a negotiated share of the proceeds. Still others—Maine in the case of Penobscot and Passamaquoddy investments—have simply accepted benefits that overflow from businesses based outside their powers but inside their borders.

Economic success has not immunized Native Americans from discrimination. Before the era of reservation casinos, Native Americans were accused of welfare dependency, as if federal services provided to them were largesse and not the result of treaty agreements in which land sufficient for self-subsistence was exchanged for promises of government economic support. After the success of high-stakes gaming, Native Americans were criticized as recipients of undeserved wealth, benefitting from an "inequality" of rights in their favor.

Not all casinos are productive, let alone of great wealth. Not all reservation businesses succeed, let alone produce overflowing revenue streams. For the majority of Native communities, poverty and welfare dependence are the norm, as they have been for decades. Many enduring issues of Native Americans in America are occasioned by widespread, endemic economic depression. Despite such circumstances, Native communities have retained their identities as separate peoples and persisted in asserting rights as organized societies separate from the American "mainstream." Despite centuries of overt and covert aggression against them as peoples, despite every attempt to convert Native political conflicts from sovereignty struggles to civil rights issues, Native Americans endure as independent societies with the goal, if not the guarantee, of independent political existence.

THE LARGER CONTEXT

Native peoples entered American politics well before the American Revolution. One might fairly say that Native Americans have been part of American politics during the entire period from initial colonial settlements to the present. One might stretch the matter only a little to say that the real beginning was in 1492, since the entire hemisphere is "America," not only that portion of territory between present-day Mexico and Canada.

This larger context is more than an academic matter. Native American issues are common to indigenous peoples in all the Americas. A full understanding of these issues depends on a grasp of the hemispheric picture of American colonialism.

The (in)famous story of Christopher Columbus is known around the world: his adventure and daring as he set sail into uncharted waters, his great mistake in thinking he had reached the Indies, his lust for gold, his passion for the spread of Christianity; all these are part of the public imagination. What is less widely known is that his adventure was not sponsored by Spain but by the kingdoms of Castile and Leon, which were only in the process of becoming "Spain"—a process that included the conquest of the Iberian Peninsula from the Moors, which would be fueled by wealth extracted from the New World.[8]

The significance of this point is that it contradicts a conventional view of American civilization as something transplanted more or less whole from across the Atlantic—"the providential history" of the United States. What moved across the ocean was not "European civilization" but something much more fragmentary and undefined, something in the making, and the "making" that followed was intertwined with events unfolding on the "new" side of the Atlantic. In other words, the colonization of "America" was an integral part of the creation of "Europe."

The dominance of the United States over Native peoples was achieved not only through warfare but through cooperation. Prior Native rights to land, as well as their prior ability to organize workable economies, were factors that worked toward the perpetuation of some form of Native independence, circumscribed as it may have become. Francis Jennings wrote:

> Thus, in examining the American past, an ethnohistorian finds not the triumph of civilization over savagery, but an acculturation of Europeans and Indians that was marked by the interchange or diffusion of cultural traits and the emergence of social and cultural dominance by the Europeans in a large society marked by a submerged Indian subculture.[9]

Felix Cohen, the architect of federal legal policy concerning Native Americans in the important years of the New Deal, went even further, declaring that "what is distinctive about America is Indian, through and through."[10]

It is crucial to understand that the "new world" was not new but already ancient when it was "discovered" by Columbus. Multiform civilizations existed across the length and breadth of the land, literally from the Arctic to Amazonia. As Jennings said, America was not "virgin" when the colonists arrived but became "widowed" by disease and genocide.[11] In the process, something new was created from the interactions of what was already present and what was imported. That something is what became America. The colonizers and natives made use of each other's economies and social structures. Even after the colonizers felt strong enough to attempt to ignore or remove the natives, something of the original inhabitants remained, either separate from the colonizing society or incorporated within it, as a determining factor in the shape and extent of what was possible in America.

ANCIENT ROOTS: CHRISTIAN COLONIZATION

Detailed reassessment of early history may seem unnecessary to a present understanding of Native Americans. Some may think it enough to acknowledge the fallaciousness of the notion of "discovery," with all it implies in the way of colonial arrogance. But the fact that "discovery" became part of the institutional structure of America means that America consists of a continual reaffirmation of colonialism. The nature of this colonialism explains much of the present scene.

The Western response to the "discovery" of the peoples of the Americas was "an effort to . . . [make] everything speak . . . with one voice":[12]

> [T]he discovery of the American Indians . . . [t]he confrontation with something radically different from the Christian way of life raised the question of what kind of relations it is possible to entertain with this Other. First, to what extent is it possible to know the Indian except as something inferior . . . ? Second, . . . to what extent is it possible to bring him into the framework of universal law by giving him the status of a legal subject?[13]

In this confrontation, native peoples were given a "choice": to assimilate to the colonial system and give up their independent self-definitions, or to maintain their self-definitions and be denied a place in the world's legal and political order. The underlying assumption was that there is only one reality and it is Western.

It is best to be specific about the conceptual core of colonization of the "new world"—to emphasize that it was "Christian" as opposed to "European." Columbus's voyage was the occasion for Pope Alexander VI to issue a bull dividing the world between Spain and Portugal, laying down the doctrine of Christian discovery and conquest:

> *INTER CAETERA*, MAY 3, 1493—Among other works well pleasing to the Divine Majesty and cherished of our heart, this assuredly ranks highest, that in our times especially the Catholic faith and the Christian religion be exalted and everywhere increased and spread, that the health of souls be cared for and that barbarous nations be overthrown and brought to the faith itself. . . . [O]ur beloved son Christopher Columbus, . . . sailing . . . toward the Indians, discovered certain very remote islands and even mainlands . . . [W]e, . . . by the authority of Almighty God . . . do . . . give, grant, and assign forever to you and your heirs and successors, kings of Castile and Leon, all and singular the aforesaid countries and islands.

An earlier papal bull issued by Nicholas V had already declared the legitimacy of Christian domination over "pagans," sanctifying their enslavement and expropriation of their property:

> ROMANUS PONTIFEX, JANUARY 8, 1455— . . . [W]e bestow suitable favors and special graces on those Catholic kings and princes, . . . athletes and intrepid

champions of the Christian faith . . . to invade, search out, capture, vanquish, and sub-
due all Saracens and pagans whatsoever, and other enemies of Christ wheresoever
placed, and . . . to reduce their persons to perpetual slavery, and to apply and appropriate . . . possessions, and goods, and to convert them to . . . their use and profit.

Leaping four centuries ahead, we find that Chief Justice John Marshall borrowed
from these papal bulls the essential legalisms needed to affirm American power over
indigenous peoples. He encased Christian religious premises within the rhetoric of
"European" expansion in deciding *Johnson v. McIntosh*:

On the discovery of this immense continent, the great nations of Europe were eager
to appropriate to themselves so much of it as they could respectively acquire. Its
vast extent offered an ample field to the ambition and enterprise of all; and the character and religion of its inhabitants afforded an apology for considering them as a
people over whom the superior genius of Europe might claim an ascendancy. The
potentates of the old world found no difficulty in convincing themselves that they
made ample compensation to the inhabitants of the new, by bestowing on them civilization and Christianity.[14]

Henry Wheaton, reporter for the *Johnson* Court, later elaborated on the concept
of Christian nationalism:

[T]he heathen nations of the other quarters of the globe were the lawful spoil and
prey of their civilized conquerors, and as between the Christian powers themselves,
the Sovereign Pontiff was the supreme arbiter of conflicting claims. . . . It thus became
a maxim of policy and of law, that the right of the native Indians was subordinate to
that of the first Christian discoverer.[15]

Supreme Court Justice Joseph Story also independently discussed the laws of Christendom as the basis for the Court's opinion in *Johnson*: "[I]nfidels, heathens, and savages . . . were not allowed to possess the prerogatives belonging to absolute, sovereign
and independent nations."[16]

Later cases tended to omit explicit reference to Christian doctrines, in keeping
with a general understanding that the government of the United States was separate
from any establishment of religion. Some explicit references and acknowledgments
did occur. For example, regarding federal interference with "occupancy of the
Indians": "[I]t is to be presumed that in this matter the United States would be governed by such considerations of justice as would control a Christian people in their
treatment of an ignorant and dependent race."[17] As recently as 1946, Supreme Court
Justice Reed argued against monetary compensation for a federal taking of Native
American lands on the ground that "discovery by Christian nations gave them sovereignty over and title to the lands discovered."[18]

The fact that papal authority is at the core of American law affecting Native
Americans is not generally understood, even by lawyers. The essential jurisprudential
point has been summarized succinctly by Steve Newcomb:

Indian nations have been denied their most basic rights … simply because, at the time of Christendom's arrival in the Americas, they did not believe in the God of the Bible, and did not believe that Jesus Christ was the true Messiah. This basis for the denial of Indian rights in federal Indian law remains as true today as it was in 1823.[19]

The Supreme Court's decision in *Johnson v. McIntosh* has never been overruled. "Christian discovery" remains the legal foundation for U.S. sovereignty over Native Americans and their lands. But it is concealed, as most foundations are. *Johnson v. McIntosh* acts as a Laundromat for religious concepts: after Marshall's opinion, no lawyer or court would need to acknowledge that land title in U.S. law is based on a doctrine of Christian supremacy. From that time on, in law and history books, "European" would be substituted for "Christian," so that schoolchild and lawyer alike could speak of the "age of discovery" as the age of "European expansion."

Marshall knew what he was doing. After writing that "Christian princes" could take lands "unknown to all Christian peoples," he admitted that the doctrine was an "extravagant … pretension" that "may be opposed to natural right" and may only "perhaps, be supported by reason." Nonetheless, he concluded that it "cannot be rejected by courts of justice."

The "discovery doctrine" was not self-effectuating. It required force. As Marshall wrote, "These claims have been maintained and established … by the sword." The infamous "Spanish Requirement" of 1513 is perhaps the most straightforward example. It was called the "requirement" because royal law required it to be read before hostilities could be undertaken against a native people. In Latin and/or Spanish, witnessed by a notary, the conquistadors read:

> On the part of the king, Don Fernando, and of Doña Juana, his daughter, queen of Castile and Leon, subduers of the barbarous nations, we their servants notify and make known to you, as best we can, that the Lord our God, living and eternal, created the heaven and the earth, and one man and one woman, of whom you and we, and all the men of the world, were and are descendants, and all those who come after us….
>
> Of all these nations God our Lord gave charge to one man, called St. Peter, that he should be lord and superior of all the men in the world, that all should obey him, and that he should be the head of the whole human race, wherever men should live, and under whatever law, sect, or belief they should be; and he gave him the world for his kingdom and jurisdiction….
>
> One of these pontiffs, who succeeded that St. Peter as lord of the world in the dignity and seat which I have before mentioned, made donation of these isles and Terrafirma to the aforesaid king and queen and to their successors, our lords, with all that there are in these territories….
>
> … Wherefore, as best we can, we ask and require you that you consider what we have said to you, and that you take the time that shall be necessary to understand and deliberate upon it, and that you acknowledge the Church as the ruler and superior of the whole world….

But if you do not do this, and maliciously make delay on it, I certify to you that with the help of God, we shall powerfully enter into your country, and shall make war against you in all ways and manners that we can, and shall subject you to the yoke and obedience of the Church and of their highnesses; we shall take you, and your wives and your children, and shall make slaves of them, and as such shall sell and dispose of them as their highnesses may command; and we shall take away your goods, and shall do you all the mischief and damage that we can, as to vassals who do not obey, and refuse to receive their lord, and resist and contradict him: and we protest that the deaths and losses which shall accrue from this are your fault, and not that of their highnesses, or ours, nor of these cavaliers who come with us.[20]

This document and the precision of its jurisprudentially ordained violence are generally not studied in current legal education, even in courses on federal Indian law. It is fashionable, especially around Columbus Day, to speak about the "encounter" of the "old" and "new" worlds, as a way of trying to forget exactly how bloody this event was. Michael Shapiro challenged this soft terminology with the comment, "National societies that . . . have thought of themselves as a fulfillment of a historical destiny, could not be open to encounters."[21]

The Puritans are a good example of violent Christianity. Skillful Puritan propaganda has secured them a historical niche as champions of religious freedom. The image of Puritan godliness survives as one of the great American myths. Their self-proclaimed mission to "save the souls of the natives" was a formula for success in garnering financial support from English churches. Nevertheless, these "lords" of "New England" were ruthless in their attacks on "heathen" natives whose economic and military aid they outgrew.

The American holiday of Thanksgiving, accurately understood, is a day of mourning for the Native peoples who met Pilgrim thievery with generosity. One of the first things the Pilgrims did was to rob Wampanoag storehouses for food and graves for tools. The Wampanoag, seeing all this and realizing how unfortunate these boat people were, extended the hand of friendship and offered help instead of retribution. Probably the Wampanoag also realized that it is better to feed your neighbors than to have them desperate with hunger at your door.

The Wampanoag understood that these newcomers from across the water must have been fleeing terrible conditions to endure the hardship and privation of such a journey. Who would willingly leave the land of their birth, home of their ancestors? The colonists claimed to be seeking freedom for their faith, and told stories of corruption and oppression in the lands they left behind. When the Wampanoag showed themselves open to spiritual teachings, but not necessarily to conversion, the Puritans reacted with anger.

Massacres of Pequot (1637) and Narrangansett (1675) communities are the most horrific large-scale incidents of Puritan violence against Natives. Lesser-known incidents include the establishment of groups of "praying Indians," the first "Indian reservations"—or, as they were called well into the nineteenth century, "concentrations"—where natives were forcibly subjected to the missionary work of such icons of Puritan purity as John Eliot. The only path for natives to relative security from Puritan violence was to move to those villages established under Puritan command and to attend to missionary preaching. "Freedom" in Puritan terms as the freedom to impose an orthodoxy of Bible worship, and to eradicate the diversity of indigenous spiritual practices, which were seen as ignorance, "devil-worship," and idolatry.

Christianity was affirmed as an essential part of "civilizing" native peoples under British colonial policy well into the nineteenth century. A House of Commons Select Committee on Aborigines (1837) declared: "True civilization and Christianity are inseparable: the former has never been found, but as a fruit of the latter."[22]

As Michael Dorris wrote, encompassing the whole history of American politics from colonial era to the present:

> The pre-existent variety of Native American societies ... has been consistently obscured and disallowed. Every effort has been made to almost existentially enclose the non-Western world into a European schema, and then to blame unwilling elements for being backward, ignorant, or without vision.
>
> Federal Indian policy was ... shaped from the beginning at least as much toward deculturation as acculturation.[23]

It has often been noted that the work of missionaries was intertwined with the work of soldiers. For their part, Native Americans frequently point out that their original forms of self-government are spiritually based, given to them as part of their "original instructions" from the Creator. The eradication of Native American spirituality—through forcible induction of individuals into missionary churches and through political subversion of the power and respect accorded to traditional spiritual leaders—was a key element in colonial policy that continues in twentieth-century U.S. policy.

Formal renunciation of Bureau of Indian Affairs prohibitions of Native spiritual practices occurred in conjunction with the Indian Reorganization Act (1934). Explicit recognition was withheld until 1978, when Congress passed the American Indian Religious Freedom Act (AIRFA). As to the latter, the Supreme Court ruled in 1988: "Nowhere in the law is there so much as a hint of any intent to create a cause of action or any judicially enforceable individual rights."[24] AIRFA survives as a general statement of unenforceable federal policy. In 1990, Congress passed the Native American Graves Protection and Repatriation Act to require federally funded institutions to return skeletons and burial goods to Native American communities who can prove ancestral connections to these items. Disturbance of Native American graves continues to be an issue, however, since many state laws protecting graves have been held inapplicable to traditional Native burials, where there is no headstone or other conventional cemetery paraphernalia.

"TRIBAL COUNCILS" AND "TRUSTEESHIP"

The colonies and later the United States did not have sufficient resources to maintain direct military rule over peoples and territories they wanted to control. They resorted to "indirect rule" by puppet governments through the mechanism of appointed (and often bribed) "chiefs." But they found that despite every attempt to make indigenous social structures disappear—including "allotment" of communal lands and prohibition of spiritual practices—Native Americans survived as peoples.

By the first quarter of the twentieth century, conditions of Native American life were an embarrassment to the United States. Franklin Roosevelt's New Deal administration set out in 1934 to "reorganize" Native American societies into elected corporate political structures—a formalized system of "tribal councils." The concept of "American Indian sovereignty" was used to justify sufficient authority in the tribal councils to maintain order within the "tribe" while denying these councils any authority beyond the territory that was "reserved" for them.

The Indian Reorganization Act was presented as a restoration of Native American self-government. It halted some of the most destructive government policies—especially forced land cessions authorized by the 1887 General Allotment Act (Dawes Act)—but, as its title states, its primary purpose was to "reorganize" the Indians, overthrowing traditional organizations and promoting a "democratic" tribal council system structured along the lines of a corporate business. Not all Native peoples formally adopted the council system, but its major features became the typical form of "tribal self-government."

In 1971, the Alaska Native Claims Settlement Act—designed as a "final settlement" of all Native land rights (and hunting and fishing rights) in Alaska—took the corporate model approach much further. The Settlement Act displaced traditional political structures and created regional and village for-profit corporations to manage land and business activities for "stockholders," who were the Native peoples themselves.

The complexities of Native American "self-government" under the federal "plenary power," "trustee," and "tribal council" system can be illustrated by the case of the Western Shoshone. In 1863, the Western Shoshone and the United States signed a Treaty of Peace and Friendship at Ruby Valley in the heart of Western Shoshone country. The treaty acknowledged the Western Shoshone's control over their homelands and provided for easements across their land and some mining and related activities. One hundred years later, massive strip mines were tearing up Western Shoshone lands, polluting and destroying the waters. The United States added to this destruction by designating Yucca Mountain in Shoshone territory as a disposal site for high-level radioactive waste.

Although the Western Shoshone's land title was never proven to have been ceded or lost, the Supreme Court ruled that they are precluded from litigating their title. Western Shoshone people who oppose the destruction of their lands as violations of their title and treaty are depicted by the government as outlaws.

This situation came about in accordance with federal Indian law principles. The federal government "recognized" various Western Shoshone "tribal councils" as the agents of Western Shoshone "sovereignty." The Temoak Band, one of the councils empowered to "reorganize" the Western Shoshone people and to "represent" them in dealing with the outside world, filed a claim in 1951 under the Indian Claims

Commission Act (1946). That act was passed ostensibly to compensate for previous land takings that had violated Native American ownership. More fundamentally, the act was intended to wipe out all Native title for non-reservation lands by providing money compensation for such lands. The act did not require that a claim filed under it represent all or even a majority of the people in whose name it was filed. As a result of the Temoak claim—which the traditional, "non-recognized" Western Shoshone opposed (1974) and the Temoak council subsequently tried to withdraw (1976)—the Indian Claims Commission held (1979) that Western Shoshone lands had been "taken" and that they would receive compensation.

The Western Shoshone refused to accept the compensation. One family (the Danns), charged by the United States with trespassing on "public lands," defended themselves by asserting the Western Shoshone's title. The Ninth Circuit Court of Appeals ruled (1983) that the Western Shoshone's title had never actually been litigated, that none of the claims made against it were sufficient to take it away, and that since the Western Shoshone had refused the Claims Commission compensation, they still held title. The Supreme Court reversed the Ninth Circuit (1985), declaring that the Western Shoshone could not argue about their title because the compensation *had* been accepted on their behalf by the United States, acting as their "trustee"!

> [T]he Court held a "payment" had been effected, although the Indians received no money and opposed the conversion of their land. The trust doctrine was the device the Court struck upon for executing this maneuver. The United States was not only the judgment debtor to Indians, the Court said, but was also trustee to the Indians. Therefore the United States as debtor can pay itself as trustee, say this change in bookkeeping constitutes payment to Indians, and the Court will certify the fiction as a reality.[25]

The Western Shoshone case is not unusual. "American Indian sovereignty" in federal law—defined as the powers of federally sponsored tribal councils—is a tool for separating Native American lands from state and local control and for subordinating the original powers of indigenous self-determination to U.S. jurisdiction. "American Indian sovereignty" operates in conjunction with "trust," "wardship," and "plenary power" doctrines, concepts proclaimed unilaterally by the Supreme Court to legitimize federal power over Native Americans and to determine the scope and structure of Native American self-government.

The Western Shoshone case demonstrates that the United States is intent on maintaining powers it has asserted for almost two centuries on the basis of fifteenth-century theological decrees:

> To argue that the Indian people may not challenge the theoretical framework set forth by Marshall in the Johnson ruling is to say that they must simply acquiesce in a one hundred-and-seventy-year-old precedent predicated on the belief that the first Christian discoverer (or its legal successor) has a divine right to subjugate the heathens who were discovered. It is to contend that Indian nations ought to learn

to accept a judicial pretention based on religious and cultural prejudice that asserts that their rights to complete sovereignty and to territorial integrity may be impaired, diminished, denied, or displaced simply because they were not Christian people at the time of European arrival to the Americas. It is to accept the preposterous idea that federal Indian law will forever rest on the foundation of a subjugating Christian ideology.[26]

"TERMINATION" AND "SELF-DETERMINATION"

The legal position of Native Americans in America appears as a crazy-quilt pattern in decisions of the Supreme Court. In 1831, the Cherokee Nation sued the state of Georgia in the Supreme Court to protect Cherokee lands. The Court denied the Cherokee Nation's suit on the ground that an Indian nation is not a "foreign nation" entitled to sue a state in the Supreme Court.[27] That decision has never been overruled and is cited frequently today. In 1997, the Supreme Court decided that the Coeur d'Alene Tribe could litigate its land claims against the state of Idaho only in Idaho's courts. The Coeur d'Alene were claiming "aboriginal title," a subsidiary title subject to the "trusteeship" of the United States. They were trying to work within the limited concept of "American Indian sovereignty." In throwing the Coeur d'Alene Tribe's suit out of federal court, the Supreme Court stated that the basis of its decision is that "Indian tribes . . . should be accorded the same status as foreign sovereigns, against whom States enjoy Eleventh Amendment immunity."[28] The Cherokee were barred from suing in the Supreme Court because an Indian nation is *not* a foreign nation. The Coeur d'Alene were barred from suing a district court because an Indian nation *is* a foreign nation!

In the 1950s, as political support for New Deal programs waned, a concerted effort was mounted in Congress to "terminate" all federal relations with Native Americans as separate peoples. House Concurrent Resolution 108 (1953) declared the "policy of Congress . . . to make the Indians within the United States subject to the same laws and entitled to the same privileges . . . as are applicable to other citizens." Two weeks later Public Law 280 was passed, authorizing state governments to exercise civil and criminal jurisdiction on "Indian reservations" without Native American consent.

The premise of the "termination" policy was that elimination of federal "trusteeship" over Native American "wards" would result in assimilation of individual Native Americans into the general population and divest Native communities of all "reservation" lands. It is one of the great anomalies of "federal Indian law" that termination of the trust would result in the assets of the trust going to the former trustee rather than the former beneficiary. Such a result is contrary to the ordinary law of trusts and is a further example of the bizarre in federal Indian law.

Termination remained official U.S. policy through the 1960s though it was pursued with less vigor as its economic unworkability and moral and political unpalatability became clear. In 1968 President Lyndon Johnson declared that Native American "self-determination" should be the basis of federal policy and Congress passed an Indian Bill of Rights that limited the application of Public Law 280 but also subjected "tribal" governments to federally defined "civil rights" standards.

In 1970, President Richard Nixon formally recommended that Congress "renounce, repudiate and repeal the termination policy," because it is "morally and legally unacceptable, . . . [and] produces bad practical results."[29] The 1975 Indian Self-Determination and Education Act was Congress's response and continues to be official policy. Under this act, "tribal councils" may subcontract to perform services previously provided by federal agencies. As Vine Deloria Jr. has noted, this policy is not real self-determination:

> Indian-controlled education was not actually self-determination because Indians did not determine what kind of education their children would receive; they only replaced non-Indian bureaucrats and educators in institutions that changed very little with the shifting of personnel. Nevertheless, Indians believed that they were directing their own fortunes because they were at least visibly in charge.[30]

In an overall sense, self-determination policy puts tribal councils on the same footing as state and municipal governments with regard to acquiring federal funds, thus undermining the unique treaty-based position of Native Americans in American politics.

Self-determination policy has not eradicated federal termination concepts. In 1997, the U.S. Senate appropriations bill for the Department of the Interior became the focus of an attempt to eliminate Native American sovereignty as a condition for receipt of federal funds. Although the provision was rejected after substantial outcry, the very attempt shows several important things. First, the struggle over Native American sovereignty—however it is defined and limited—is far from over. Second, even the congressional defenders of Native American sovereignty argued that the United States could eliminate it if Congress wished to do so. Third, the notion that federal funding to Native American governments is rooted in treaty obligations, not in discretionary programs, was almost wholly suppressed in favor of a welfare definition of the status of Native Americans. Fourth, the attack on Native American sovereignty was packaged in a discourse of "helping the poor Indians." Puritan rhetoric survives in the U.S. Senate.

NATIVE AMERICANS AS INDIGENOUS PEOPLES

Native Americans are increasingly turning toward a global international perspective. In light of the history of treaty making and with an eye toward restoring the sense of equality between nations that justified the treaty process to begin with, Native Americans—in concert with indigenous peoples worldwide—are asserting their own sense of sovereignty. The United Nations Draft Declaration of the Rights of

Indigenous Peoples is at the center of this global struggle. The declaration was the product of twenty years of negotiating among indigenous peoples and U.N. bodies. Its very title draws the line of battle—rights of indigenous peoples.

The term *peoples* in international law implies rights of self-determination, which the United States has challenged as not applicable to indigenous peoples. The United States argues that self-determination exists only through states, and that people not organized in nation-state form are merely groups of individuals with shared cultural, linguistic, and social features without any legal status as peoples. This argument contradicts the U.S. claim that it deals with Native Americans on a "government-to-government" basis, a fact that has been noticed by those whose critique of limited sovereignty under federal law has been increasingly strong.

The classical attributes of nation-state sovereignty—absolute, unlimited power held permanently in a single person or source, inalienable, indivisible, and original (not derivative or dependent)—foreshadow the problem of applying this concept to Native Americans. These are characteristics associated with divine-right monarchy and the Papacy. They were the brainchildren of Western political theorists of the sixteenth and seventeenth centuries (especially Jean Bodin and Thomas Hobbes) put forth as a solution to the problem of religious civil wars. They are not characteristics of power among traditional indigenous peoples.

Contemporary Native American political theory confronts the question whether conventional sovereignty can be an instrument of liberation from policies rooted in colonialism. If *state* and *sovereignty* refer to a framework of "supreme coercive power," and such power is absent in "tribes," is this a justification for "domestic dependent nation," or is it rather a sign of the inadequacy of state sovereignty as the organizing principle of global politics? Is the resurgence of Native American self-determination—defined within a global indigenous peoples' movement—the threshold of a new way of organizing politics that will, like the state before it, rearrange everything from villages to the world?

As one observer noted, the Native American challenge to federal power raises questions about the nature of that power in general:

> [W]e hold our government to be limited and to have no unlimited power. If the federal government nevertheless exercises unrestrained power over Indian nations, then what we say is not true, and we have a different kind of government than we think we have. And if our government is different in fact in relation to Native Americans, perhaps it is not what we believe it is in relation to other Americans, including ourselves. The Court is regarded as the institution of restraint and a protector of rights. If the Court restrains neither Congress nor itself in taking away tribal rights, then we are confronted by a fundamental contradiction between our political rhetoric and our political realities.[31]

Nation-state sovereignty is today a theory under siege. Indigenous peoples are only one of the besiegers, but their presence is felt worldwide. Who would have thought that Canada would enter the twenty-first century in deep conflict with indigenous peoples within its borders, or that the Australian high court would find it necessary in 1992 to abandon the doctrine of *terra nullius*—the legal fiction that the land was empty before colonization?

Colonial powers have achieved worldwide hegemony but have not been able to end their conflicts with those they regard as "aboriginal," here before the beginning. The prior inhabitants of colonized lands have survived and continue to assert prior ownership of lands. Colonialism continues internationally in the guise of multinational corporatism and in welfare-state "social service" programs. The twin political problems of domination and resistance persist. The world is not yet "safe" for the juggernaut of Western (Christian) "civilization." Nor is it comfortable for humans whose societies persist around ancient and sustainable relations with the earth.

From indigenous peoples' perspectives, state sovereignty is a claim that violates their own preexisting self-determination. Western jurisprudence has done a great deal to exclude "non-state societies" from the domain of law because they lack hierarchical authority structures. This Western thinking itself is grounded in theological-political concepts of "Christian nationalism." The notion of "absolute, unlimited power held permanently in a single person or source, inalienable, indivisible, and original" is a definition of the Judeo-Christian-Islamic God. This "God died around the time of Machiavelli. . . . Sovereignty was . . . His earthly replacement."[32]

State sovereignty "is a 'religion' and a faith":

> The skillfully drawn borders that cartographers have provided for us are . . . spiritual and philosophical abstractions representative of a form of quasi-belief. They are . . . not detached maps of reality as proponents would have us believe. These geographies reflect an ardent desire to make (or impose) sovereignty as a physical reality as natural as the mountains, rivers and lakes.[33]

What does this mean for Native Americans, with a multitude of non-sovereign Creators and an entire Creation of sovereign beings? Native Americans at the close of the twentieth century are reassessing political discourse, working toward a terminology and perspective that will link postmodern world politics and premodern indigenous roots.

The most pressing problem for indigenous self-determination is the problem of "the people." Indigenous peoples who have been subjected to centuries of state violence in the name of state sovereignty face "a profound crisis of the meaning of community, a crisis of political identity."[34]

Ultimately, it is land—and a people's relationship to land—that is at issue. Understanding *sovereignty* as a legal-theological concept allows us to view self-determination struggles as spiritual projects. Self-determination arises from within a people as a unique expression of themselves among other peoples. It is produced by the ability of a people to sustain themselves in a place.

It as been said that Native American self-determination will be attained "through means other than those provided by a conqueror's rule of law and its discourses of conquest." The "anachronistic premises" of the current system of international law— "discovery" and "state sovereignty"—are being challenged by Native Americans in order to understand self-determination clearly and see a way to manifest it. This is the struggle: "to redefine radically the conceptions of their rights and status ... to articulat[e] and defin[e] [their] own vision within the global community."[35]

NOTES

1. Francis Jennings, *The Invasion of America: Indians, Colonialism, and the Cant of Conquest* (New York: W. W. Norton, 1976), 229.
2. Barry O'Connell, ed., *On Our Own Ground: The Complete Writings of William Apess, a Pequot* (Amherst: University of Massachusetts Press, 1992), xvii.
3. As quoted in Wilcomb E. Washburn, *Red Man's Land, White Man's Law: The Past and Present Status of the American Indian*, 2nd ed. (Norman: University of Oklahoma, 1995), 49.
4. *United States v. Blackfeet Tribe*, 364 F. Supp. 192, 194 (1973).
5. Ibid.
6. *Cherokee Nation v. Georgia*, 5 Pet. 1 (1831).
7. U.S. Constitution, art. 1, secs. 2, 8.
8. Jack Weatherford, *Indian Givers* (New York: Crown Publishers, 1988).
9. Jennings, *The Invasion of America*, 13.
10. Felix S. Cohen, "Americanizing the White Man," in *The Legal Conscience* (Hamden, Conn.: Archon Books, 1970), 316.
11. Jennings, ch. 2.
12. Jens Bartelson, *A Genealogy of Sovereignty* (Cambridge: Cambridge University Press, 1995), 108.
13. Ibid., 128, 131.
14. *Johnson v. McIntosh*, 8 Wheat. 543, 572–573 (1823).
15. Henry Wheaton, *Elements of International Law* (Boston: Little, Brown, 1855), 220.
16. Joseph Story, *Commentaries on the Constitution of the United States* (Boston: Hilliard, Gray, and Co., 1833), 134.
17. *Beecher v. Weatherby*, 95 U.S. 517, 525 (1877).
18. *United States v. Alcea Band of Tillamooks*, 329 U.S. 40, 58 (1946).
19. Steve Newcomb, "The Evidence of Christian Nationalism in Federal Indian Law: The Doctrine of Discovery, *Johnson v. McIntosh*, and Plenary Power," *N.Y.U. Review of Law and Social Change*, 20, 2 (1993): 303–41, 309.
20. Wilcomb E. Washburn, ed., *The Indian and the White Man* (New York: New York University Press, 1964), 306–9.
21. Michael Shapiro, "Moral Geographies and the Ethics of Post-Sovereignty," in Mark E. Denham and Mark Owen Lombardi, eds., *Perspectives on Third-World Sovereignty* (Basingstoke: Macmillan Press, 1996), 56.
22. Andrew Armitage, *Comparing the Policy of Aboriginal Assimilation: Australia, Canada, and New Zealand* (Vancouver: University of British Columbia Press, 1995), 76.
23. Michael Dorris, "Twentieth Century Indians: The Return of the Natives," in Raymond L. Hall, ed., *Ethnic Autonomy: Comparative Dynamics, the Americas, Europe, and the Developing World* (New York: Pergamon Press, 1979), 66–84, 75, 76.
24. *Lyng v. Northwest Indian Cemetery Protective Association*, 485 U.S. 439, 452 (1988).
25. Milner S. Ball, "Constitution, Court, Indian Tribes," *American Bar Foundation Research Journal* 1 (1987): 65.
26. Newcomb, "The Evidence of Christian Nationalism in Federal Indian Law," 336.
27. *Cherokee Nation v. Georgia*, 5 Pet. 1 (1831).
28. *Idaho v. Coeur d'Alene Tribe*, No. 94–1474 (June 23, 1997).

29. John R. Wunder, *"Retained by the People": A History of American Indians and the Bill of Rights* (New York: Oxford University Press, 1994), 160–61.

30. Vine Deloria Jr. and Clifford Lytle, *The Nations Within: The Past and Future of American Indian Sovereignty* (New York: Pantheon Books, 1984), 223.

31. Ball, "Constitution, Court, Indian Tribes," 61.

32. R. B. J. Walker, "Space/Time/Sovereignty," in Mark E. Denham and Mark Owen Lombardi, eds., *Perspectives on Third-World Sovereignty* (Basingstoke: Macmillan Press, 1996), 22.

33. Mark Owen Lombardi, "Third-World Problem-Solving and the 'Religion' of Sovereignty: Trends and Prospects," in Mark E. Denham and Mark Owen Lombardi, eds., *Perspectives on Third-World Sovereignty* (Basingstoke: Macmillan Press, 1996), 154.

34. Lester Edwin J. Ruiz, "Sovereignty as Transformative Practice," in R. B. J. Walker and Saul H. Mendlovitz, eds., *Contending Sovereignties: Redefining Political Community* (Boulder, Colo.: Lynn Rienner Publishers, 1990), 79–96, 86.

35. Robert A. Williams, Jr., *The American Indian in Western Legal Thought: The Discourses of Conquest* (New York: Oxford University Press, 1990), 327–28.

Further Reading

GENERAL WORKS

Berkhofer, Robert F. *The White Man's Indian: Images of the American Indian from Columbus to the Present.* New York: Alfred A. Knopf, 1978.

Cornell, Stephen. *The Return of the Native: American Indian Political Resurgence.* New York: Oxford University Press, 1988.

Edmunds, R. David, ed. *Twentieth Century Warriors: Native American Leadership, 1900–2000.* Lincoln: University of Nebraska Press, 2001.

Hoxie, Frederick E. *A Final Promise: The Campaign to Assimilate the Indians.* Lincoln: University of Nebraska Press, 1984.

————, ed. *Encyclopedia of North American Indians.* Boston: Houghton Mifflin Co., 1996.

Moore, John H. *The Political Economy of North American Indians.* Norman: University of Oklahoma Press, 1993.

Nabokov, Peter, ed. *Native American Testimony: A Chronicle of Indian-White Relations from Prophecy to the Present, 1492–2000.* Rev. ed. New York: Penguin Putnam, 1999.

Prucha, Francis Paul. *The Great Father: The United States Government and the Indians.* Lincoln: University of Nebraska Press, 1984.

Shoemaker, Nancy. *American Indian Population Recovery in the Twentieth Century.* Albuquerque: University of New Mexico Press, 1999.

Snipp, Mattew C., ed. *American Indians and Economic Dependency.* Norman: University of Oklahoma Press, 1998.

Sturtevant, William C., ed. *Handbook of North American Indians.* Washington, D.C.: Smithsonian Institution, 1978– .

Szasz, Margaret Connell. *Education and the American Indian: The Road to Self-Determination Since 1928.* 3rd ed. Albuquerque, University of New Mexico Press, 1999.

Trigger, Bruce, and Wilcomb Washburn, eds. *The Cambridge History of the Native Peoples of the Americas.* New York: Cambridge University Press, 1996.

White, Richard. *The Roots of Dependency: Subsistence, Environment, and Social Change Among the Choctaws, Pawnees, and Navajos.* Lincoln: University of Nebraska Press, 1984.

PART I   AGENCY AMID CONQUEST, 1850–1900

Adams, David Wallace. *Education for Extinction: American Indians and the Boarding School Experience, 1875–1928.* Lawrence: University Press of Kansas, 1995.

Bailey, Garrick, and Roberta Bailey. *A History of the Navajos: The Reservation Years.* Santa Fe: School of American Research Press, 1986.

Child, Brenda. *Boarding School Seasons: American Indian Families, 1900–1940.* Lincoln: University of Nebraska Press, 1998.

Greene, Jerome A. *Yellowstone Command: Colonel Nelson A. Miles and the Great Sioux War, 1876–1877.* Lincoln: University of Nebraska Press, 1991.

Iverson, Peter. *The Navajo Nation.* Albuquerque: University of New Mexico Press, 1981.

Kugel, Rebecca. *To Be the Main Leaders of Our People: A History of Minnesota Ojibway Politics, 1825–1898.* East Lansing: Michigan State University Press, 1998.

Lomawaima, K. Tsianina. *They Called It Prairie Light: The Story of Chilocco Indian School.* Lincoln: University of Nebraska Press, 1994.

Utley, Robert M. *The Indian Frontier of the American West, 1846–1890.* Albuquerque: University of New Mexico Press, 1984.

Walker, James R. *Lakota Society.* Raymond J. DeMallie, ed. Lincoln: University of Nebraska Press, 1982.

Welch, James, with Paul Steckler. *Killing Custer: The Battle of the Little Bighorn and the Fate of the Plains Indians.* New York: W.W. Norton, 1994.

PART II   RESERVATION CULTURES, 1880–1930

Blu, Karen. *The Lumbee Problem: The Making of an American Indian People.* New York: Cambridge University Press, 1980.

Boxberger, Daniel L. *To Fish in Common: The Ethnohistory of Lummi Indian Salmon Fishing.* Lincoln: University of Nebraska Press, 1989.

Debo, Angie. *And Still The Waters Run.* Princeton: Princeton University Press, 1940.

Fowler, Loretta. *Shared Symbols, Contested Meanings: Gros Ventre Culture and History, 1784–1984.* Ithaca: Cornell University Press, 1987.

Harmon, Alexandra. *Indians in the Making: Ethnic Relations and Indian Identities around Puget Sound.* Berkeley: University of California Press, 1998.

Hoxie, Frederick E. *Parading through History: The Making of the Crow Nation in America, 1805–1935.* New York: Cambridge University Press, 1995.

Meyer, Melissa L. *The White Earth Tragedy: Ethnicity and Dispossession at a Minnesota Anishinaabe Reservation, 1889–1920.* Lincoln: University of Nebraska Press, 1994.

Wilson, Terry. *The Underground Reservation: Osage Oil.* Lincoln: University of Nebraska Press, 1985.

PART III   GENDER AND CULTURE CHANGE

Albers, Patricia, and Beatrice Medicine. *The Hidden Half: Studies of Plains Indian Women.* Washington, D.C.: University Press of America, 1983.

Devens, Carol. *Countering Colonization: Native American Women and Great Lakes Missions, 1630–1900.* Berkeley: University of California Press, 1992.

Harjo, Joy, and Gloria Bird. *Reinventing the Enemy's Language: Contemporary Native American Women's Writing of North America.* New York: W.W. Norton, 1997.

Jacobs, Margaret. *Engendered Encounters: Feminism and Pueblo Cultures, 1879–1934.* Lincoln: University of Nebraska Press, 1999.

Osburn, Katherine. *Southern Ute Women: Autonomy and Assimilation on the Reservation, 1887–1934.* Albuquerque: University of New Mexico Press, 1998.

Shoemaker, Nancy, ed. *Negotiators of Change: Historical Perspectives on Native American Women.* New York: Routledge, 1995.

Williams, Walter L. *The Spirit and the Flesh: Sexual Diversity in American Indian Cultures.* Boston: Beacon Press, 1986.

PART IV   RELIGIOUS INNOVATION AND SURVIVAL

Fitzgerald, Michael Oren. *Yellowtail: Crow Medicine Man and Sun Dance Chief: An Autobiography.* Norman: University of Oklahoma Press, 1991.

Harrod, Howard. *Becoming and Remaining a People: Native American Religions on the Northern Plains.* Tucson: University of Arizona Press, 1995.

Jorgensen, Joseph G. *The Sun Dance Religion: Power for the Powerless.* Chicago: University of Chicago Press, 1972.

Kehoe, Alice Beck. *The Ghost Dance: Ethnohistory and Revitalization.* New York: Holt, Rinehart and Winston, 1989.

Mooney, James. *The Ghost Dance Religion and the Sioux Outbreak of 1890. Fourteenth Annual Report of the Bureau of American Ethnology, 1892–1893, Part Two.* Washington, D.C.: Government Printing Office, 1896. (Modern edition: Chicago: University of Chicago Press, 1965.)

Neihardt, John Gneisenau. *Sixth Grandfather: Black Elk's Teachings Given to John G. Neihardt.* Raymond J. DeMallie, ed. Lincoln: University of Nebraska Press, 1984.

Ruby, Robert H., and John A. Brown. *Dreamer Prophets of the Columbia Plateau: Smoholla and Skolaskin.* Norman: University of Oklahoma Press, 1989.

Steltenkamp, Michael F. *Black Elk: Holy Man of the Oglalas.* Norman: University of Oklahoma Press, 1993.

Stewart, Omer C. *The Peyote Religion: A History.* Norman: University of Oklahoma Press, 1987.

PART V   CULTURAL AND POLITICAL TRANSFORMATIONS, 1900–1950

Bernstein, Alison R. *American Indians in World War II: Toward a New Era in Indian Affairs.* Norman: University of Oklahoma Press, 1991.

Biolsi, Thomas. *Organizing the Lakota: The Political Economy of the New Deal on Pine Ridge and Rosebud Reservations.* Tucson: University of Arizona Press, 1992.

Britten, Thomas A. *American Indians in World War I: At War and At Home.* Albuquerque: University of New Mexico Press, 1997.

Deloria, Vine. *Nations Within: The Past and Future of American Indian Sovereignty.* New York: Pantheon, 1984.

Hauptman, Laurence W. *The Iroquois and the New Deal.* Syracuse: Syracuse University Press, 1981.

Hertzberg, Hazel. *The Search for an American Indian Identity: Modern Pan-Indian Movements.* Syracuse: Syracuse University Press, 1971.

Hosmer, Brian. *American Indians in the Marketplace: Persistence and Innovation Among the Menominees and Metlakatlans, 1870–1920.* Lawrence: University Press of Kansas, 1999.

Iverson, Peter. *Carlos Montezuma and the Changing World of American Indians.* Albuquerque: University of New Mexico Press, 1982.

———. *When Indians Became Cowboys: Native Peoples and Cattle Ranching in the American West.* Norman: University of Oklahoma Press, 1994.

Kelly, Lawrence C. *The Assault on Assimilation: John Collier and the Origins of Indian Policy Reform.* Albuquerque: University of New Mexico Press, 1983.

Liberty, Margot, ed. *American Indian Intellectuals.* St. Paul: West Publishing, 1978.

Parman, Donald. *The Navajos and the New Deal.* New Haven: Yale University Press, 1976.

Philp, Kenneth, ed. *Indian Self Rule: First-Hand Accounts of Indian-White Relations from Roosevelt to Reagan.* Salt Lake City: Howe Brothers, 1986.

———. *Termination Revisited: American Indians on the Trail to Self-Determination, 1933–1953.* Lincoln: University of Nebraska Press, 1999.

PART VI   INDIAN ACTIVISM AND CULTURAL RESURGENCE

Ambler, Marjane. *Breaking the Iron Bonds: Indian Control of Energy Development.* Lawrence: University Press of Kansas, 1990.

Castille, George Pierre. *To Show Heart: Native American Self-Determination and Federal Indian Policy, 1960–1975.* Tucson: University of Arizona Press, 1998.

Cowger, Thomas W. *The National Congress of American Indians: The Founding Years.* Lincoln: University of Nebraska Press, 1999.

Deloria, Vine, ed. *American Indian Policy in the Twentieth Century.* Norman: University of Oklahoma Press, 1985.

———. *Behind the Trail of Broken Treaties: An Indian Declaration of Independence.* New York: Delacorte Press, 1974.

———. *God Is Red.* New York: Grosset and Dunlap, 1973.

Fixico, Donald L. *Termination and Relocation: Federal Indian Policy, 1945–1960.* Albuquerque: University of New Mexico Press, 1986.

Johnson, Troy, Joane Nagel, and Duane Champagne, eds. *American Indian Activism: Alcatraz to the Longest Walk.* Urbana: University of Illinois Press, 1997.

Josephy, Alvin M., Jr., Joane Nagel, and Troy Johnson, eds. *Red Power: The American Indian's Fight For Freedom.* 2nd ed. Lincoln: University of Nebraska Press, 1999.

Lazarus, Edward. *Black Hills, White Justice: The Sioux Nation versus the United States, 1775 to the Present.* New York: HarperCollins Publishers, 1991.

Means, Russell with Marvin J. Wolf. *Where White Men Fear to Tread: The Autobiography of Russell Means.* New York: General Publishing Group, 1995.

Peroff, Nicholas. *Menominee Drums: Tribal Termination and Restoration, 1954–1974.* Norman: University of Oklahoma Press, 1982.

Smith, Paul Chaat, and Robert Allen Warrior. *Like A Hurricane: The Indian Movement From Alcatraz to Wounded Knee.* New York: New Press, 1996.

Steiner, Stan. *The New Indians.* New York: Dell Publishing, 1968.

Whaley, Rick, with Walter Bresette. *Walleye Warriors: An Effective Alliance Against Racism and for the Earth.* Philadelphia: New Society Publishers, 1994.

PART VII   PERSPECTIVES ON NATIVE AMERICA, 2000

Barsh, Russell, and James Youngblood Henderson. *The Road: Indian Tribes and Political Liberty.* Berkeley: University of California Press, 1980.

Cornell, Stephen, and Joseph P. Kalt, eds. *What Can Tribes Do? Strategies and Institutions in American Indian Economic Development.* Los Angeles: American Indian Studies Center, American Indian Manual and Handbook Series No. 4, 1992.

Hill, Ruth Beebe. *Hanta Yo.* New York: Warner Books, 1981.

Mason, W. Dale. *Indian Gaming: Tribal Sovereignty and American Politics.* Norman: University of Oklahoma Press, 2000.

Matthiessen, Peter. *In the Spirit.* New York: Viking, 1993.

Ortiz, Simon. *Speaking for the Generations: Native Writers on Writing.* Tucson: University of Arizona Press, 1998.

Paredes, J. Anthony. *Indians of the Southeastern United States in the Late Twentieth Century.* Tuscaloosa: University of Alabama Press, 1992.

Walker, James R. *Lakota Belief and Ritual.* Lincoln: University of Nebraska Press, 1991.

Wilkins, David E. *American Indian Sovereignty and the U.S. Supreme Court: The Making of Justice.* Austin: University of Texas Press, 1997.

Wilkinson, Charles. *American Indians, Time, and the Law: Native Societies in a Modern Constitutional Democracy.* New Haven: Yale University Press, 1987.

Notes on Contributors

Robert L. Bee is professor of anthropology at the University of Connecticut and the author of *Crosscurrents along the Colorado: The Impact of Government Policy on the Quechan Indians* and *State and Reservation: New Perspectives on Federal Indian Policy*.

Thomas Biolsi, associate professor of anthropology at Portland State University, is the author of *Organizing the Lakota: The Political Economy of the New Deal on the Pine Ridge and Rosebud Reservations* and *Indians and Anthropologists: Vine Deloria, Jr., and the Critique of Anthropology*.

Fergus M. Bordewich is a journalist whose articles have appeared in Reader's Digest, The Atlantic Monthly, The New Yorker, the New York Times Magazine, and other publications. He is also the author of Killing the White Man's Indian: Reinventing Native Americans at the end of the Twentieth Century.

Kingsley M. Bray writes extensively on the history of the Plains Indians.

Ward Churchill is professor of American Indian studies at the University of Colorado, Boulder, and the author of numerous books, including *Fantasies of the Master Race, Struggle for the Land, Indians Are Us?, Since the Predator Came,* and *Draconian Measures: History of FBI Political Repression.* He is a Creek/Cherokee Indian, the recognized national spokesperson for the Leonard Peltier Defense Committee, and an organizer with the Colorado American Indian Movement.

Terrence M. Cole is professor of history at the University of Alaska, Fairbanks.

Vine Deloria, Jr. is professor of history at the University of Colorado, Boulder. A member of the Standing Rock Sioux Tribe of North Dakota and former director of the National Congress of American Indians, he is also the author of *God is Red, Black Elk Speaks, Custer Died for Your Sins,* and *American Indian Policy in the Twentieth Century*.

Peter d'Errico is professor of legal studies at the University of Massachusetts at Amherst.

Carol Devens, is assistant professor of history at Central Michigan University and author of *Countering Colonization: Native American Women and Great Lakes Mission, 1630–1900*.

Clyde Ellis, associate professor of history at Elon College, is currently at work on a collection of oral traditions from Texas tribes, an ethnography of Christian missions at the Kiowa-Comanche Reservation in the late 19th and early 20th centuries, and an ethnography of Southern Plains powwow culture.

Lisa E. Emmerich teaches history at California State University, Chico.

Sidney L. Harring, professor of law at the City University of New York School of Law, has held numerous teaching positions abroad. He has written *Policing a Class Society, Crow Dog's Case, White Man's Law: Native People in Nineteenth Century Canadian Jurisprudence,* and numerous articles on American and British colonial history, Native American law, indigenous rights, and criminal law.

Frederick E. Hoxie (editor), professor of history at the University of Illinois, Urbana-Champaign, is the author of *A Final Promise: The Campaign to Assimilate the Indians, 1880–1920* and *Parading Through History: The Making of the Crow Nation in America, 1805–1935*, editor of *The Encyclopedia of North American Indians*, and series editor for Time-Life Books American Indians series. He has served as director of the Newberry Library's D'Arcy Center for the History of the American Indian and president of the American Society for Ethnohistory; currently, he is on the Executive Board of the Organization of American Historians.

Margaret D. Jacobs is assistant professor of history at New Mexico State University and the author of *Engendered Encounters: Feminism and Pueblo Cultures, 1879–1934*.

Joseph G. Jorgensen is professor emeritus of anthropology at the University of California, Irvine.

Sergei Kan is professor of anthropology and Native American studies at Dartmouth College and author of numerous publications on the Tlingit Indians of Alaska.

Robert H. Keller, Jr. teaches history at Western Washington University and is the author of *In Honor of Justice Douglas*, *American Protestantism and U.S. Policy*, *Whatcom Places*, and *American Indians and National Parks*.

David Rich Lewis is associate professor of history at Utah State University, coeditor of the *Western Historical Quarterly*, and the author of *Neither Wolf nor Dog: American Indians, Environment, and Agrarian Change*.

Peter C. Mancall (editor) is professor of history at the University of Southern California and author of *Valley of Opportunity: Economic Culture along the Upper Susquehanna, 1700–1800* and *Deadly Medicine: Indians and Alcohol in Early America*. He also serves on the editorial board of *Reviews in American History*.

Robert S. McPherson teaches history at the College of Eastern Utah and has published numerous books and articles on Indian history in Utah.

James H. Merrell (editor) is professor of history at Vassar College and the author of *The Indians' New World: Catawbas and Their Neighbors from European Contact through the Era of Removal* and *Into the American Woods: Negotiators on the Pennsylvania Frontier*.

Melissa L. Meyer is associate professor of history at the University of California, Los Angeles, and the author of *The White Earth Tragedy: Ethnicity and Dispossession at a Minnesota Anishinaabe Reservations, 1889–1920*.

Joane Nagel, professor of sociology at the University of Kansas, is the author of *Race, Ethnicity, & Sexuality: Intimate Intersections and Forbidden Frontiers*, *Red Power: The American Indians' Fight for Freedom*, *American Indian Activism: Alcatraz to the Longest Walk*, and *American Indian Ethnic Renewal*.

Katherine M. B. Osburn is an assistant professor of history at Tennessee Technological University and author of *Autonomy and Assimilation: Southern Ute Women on the Reservation, 1887–1934*.

John C. Savagian is an assistant professor of history at Alverno College.

Coll-Peter Thrush is a graduate student in history at the University of Washington, Seattle.

Permissions Acknowledgments

Robert L. Bee, "Riding the Paper Tiger," in *State and Reservation: New Perspectives on Federal Indian Policy*, ed. George Pierre Castile and Robert L. Bee. Copyright © 1992 The Arizona Board of Regents. Reprinted by permission of the University of Arizona Press.

Thomas Biolsi, "The Birth of the Reservation: Making the Modern Individual among the Lakota," *American Ethnologist*, v. 22, n. 1 (1995), pp. 28–53. Reproduced by permission of the American Anthropological Asssociation from *American Ethnologist* 22(1). Not for sale or further reproduction.

Fergus M. Bordewich, "'Our Lives Have Been Transmuted, Changed Forever,'" in *Killing the White Man's Indian*. Copyright © 1996 Fergus Bordewich. Used by permission of Doubleday, a division of Random House, Inc.

Kingsley M. Bray, "Crazy Horse and the End of the Great Sioux War," *Nebraska History* 79 (Fall 1998), pp. 94–115.

Ward Churchill, "The Bloody Wake of Alcatraz: Political Repression of the American Indian Movement during the 1970s." Reprinted by permission of the author.

Terrence M. Cole, "Jim Crow in Alaska: The Passage of the Equal Rights Act of 1945," *Western Historical Quarterly* 23 (November 1992), pp. 429–449.

Peter d'Errico, "Native Americans in America: A Theoretical and Historical Overview," *Wizaco Sa Review* (Spring 1999), pp. 7–29.

Vine Deloria, Jr., "Research, Redskins, and Reality," *American Indian Quarterly*, v. 15, n. 4, pp. 457–468. Reprinted by permission of the University of Nebraska Press. Copyright © 1991 by the University of Nebraska Press.

Carol Devens, "'If We Get the Girls, We Get the Race': Missionary Education of Native American Girls," *Journal of World History*, v. 3, n. 2 (1992): pp. 219–237. Copyright © 1991 by the University of Hawai'i Press.

Clyde Ellis, "'We Don't Want Your Rations, We Want This Dance': The Changing Use of Song and Dance on the Southern Plains," *Western Historical Quarterly* 30 (Summer 1999), pp. 133–154.

Lisa E. Emmerich, "'Right in the Midst of My Own People': Native American Women and the Field Matron Program," *American Indian Quarterly*, v. 15 (Spring 1991), pp. 201–216.

Sidney L. Harring, "Red Lilac of the Cayugas: Traditional Indian Law and Culture in Conflict in a Witchcraft Trial in Buffalo, New York, 1930," *New York History* 73 (January 1992), pp. 65–94. Reprinted courtesy of The New York State Historical Association.

Frederick E. Hoxie, "Exploring a Cultural Borderland: Native American Journeys of Discovery in the Early Twentieth Century," *Journal of American History*, v. 79 (December 1992), pp. 969–995.

Margaret D. Jacobs, "Making Savages of Us All: White Women, Pueblo Indians, and the Controversy over Indian Dances in the 1920s," *Frontiers*, v. 17, n. 3 (1996), pp. 178–209.

Joseph G. Jorgensen, "Gaming and Recent American Indian Economic Development," *American Indian Culture and Research Journal*, v. 22, n. 3 (1998), pp. 157-172.

507

Index

Italicized numbers denote pages where figures/tables appear